Lecture Notes in Computer Science 14320

Founding Editors

Gerhard Goos
Juris Hartmanis

Editorial Board Members

The series Lecture Notes in Computer Science (LNCS), including its subseries Lecture Notes in Artificial Intelligence (LNAI) and Lecture Notes in Bioinformatics (LNBI), has established itself as a medium for the publication of new developments in computer science and information technology research, teaching, and education.

LNCS enjoys close cooperation with the computer science R & D community, the series counts many renowned academics among its volume editors and paper authors, and collaborates with prestigious societies. Its mission is to serve this international community by providing an invaluable service, mainly focused on the publication of conference and workshop proceedings and postproceedings. LNCS commenced publication in 1973.

João Paulo A. Almeida · José Borbinha ·
Giancarlo Guizzardi · Sebastian Link ·
Jelena Zdravkovic
Editors

Conceptual Modeling

42nd International Conference, ER 2023
Lisbon, Portugal, November 6–9, 2023
Proceedings

 Springer

Editors
João Paulo A. Almeida 🔾
Federal University of Espírito Santo
Vitória, Brazil

Giancarlo Guizzardi 🔾
University of Twente
Enschede, The Netherlands

Jelena Zdravkovic 🔾
Stockholm University
Stockholm, Sweden

José Borbinha 🔾
Universidade de Lisboa
Lisbon, Portugal

Sebastian Link 🔾
University of Auckland
Auckland, New Zealand

ISSN 0302-9743   ISSN 1611-3349 (electronic)
Lecture Notes in Computer Science
ISBN 978-3-031-47261-9   ISBN 978-3-031-47262-6 (eBook)
https://doi.org/10.1007/978-3-031-47262-6

This Springer imprint is published by the registered company Springer Nature Switzerland AG
The registered company address is: Gewerbestrasse 11, 6330 Cham, Switzerland

Paper in this product is recyclable.

Preface

This volume of the *Lecture Notes in Computer Science* series contains the proceedings of the 42nd International Conference on Conceptual Modeling – ER 2023, held in Lisbon, during November 6–9. Throughout history, Lisbon has been a key hub for maritime endeavors, and is famous for its beautiful coastal location and delightful architecture. As the cultural, economic, educational, and political center of Portugal, the city is a magnificent example of how rich past and modern energy should be blended.

Very much likewise, the ER conference is the world-leading forum for discussing the state of the art, emerging issues, and future challenges of *conceptual modeling*. The first ER conference was held in 1979 in Los Angeles, and then took place every two years until 1985, when the conference evolved into an annual event. Over this time, the conference has been held in 20 countries on five continents, establishing a globally connected, scientifically rigorous community of academics and practitioners.

Conceptual modeling is becoming even more critical in this age of extreme dynamics and huge proliferation of data. Indeed, conceptual modeling research enables our community to not only understand but describe and analyze these complex phenomena, to facilitate the development of effective software and information systems at any scale and level of detail required and bring forward their implementation in industry and the public sector.

ER 2023 attracted a broad spectrum of classical and modern topics on conceptual modeling, including research and practice in the theories of concepts and ontologies, techniques for transforming conceptual models into effective implementations, and methods and tools for developing and communicating conceptual models. These topics followed a call for original research on subjects as diverse as new foundations, links, applications, and extensions to current boundaries of the discipline, but also industry reports and vision papers.

In total, ER 2023 received 120 paper submissions. For the first time in the history of ER, the review process was double-blind. Out of all submissions, three were desk rejected as the program co-chairs unanimously found them to be outside the scope of the conference, and all the remaining submissions were reviewed independently by at least three Program Committee (PC) members. That was followed by an extensive discussion period moderated by senior PC members, who also summarized and explained the recommendations for each submission in a meta-review to the authors. Finally, all recommendations were discussed by the co-chairs, revisions of reviews and meta-reviews were sought, and final decisions made. Following this process, 21 submissions were accepted based on the novelty of the work and the depth of contributions to the advancement of the state of the art. In fact, eleven of these 21 submissions were accepted directly, while the remaining ten were accepted conditionally, subject to specific improvements the authors were able to address in a minor revision checked by the PC chairs. The outcome is presented in this volume, comprising 21 innovative and high-quality papers, with an acceptance rate of 18 percent. In addition, we recommended six submissions for consideration by the ER Forum, and another three submissions for consideration at one of the ER workshops.

As a tradition at ER, the conference program started with the Workshops and the Symposium on Conceptual Modeling Education. The main conference included sessions on Research papers, Keynotes, Tutorials, Panels, the Forum for short visionary papers, Doctoral Consortium, Posters and Demos, Project Exhibitions, as well as a Journal-First session.

The accepted papers were grouped into the following seven topical sessions: The Conceptual Modeling Task, The Meta Level, Model-Based Analysis and Implementation, Process Mining and Abstraction, Modeling Events and Processes, Conceptual Modeling in Context, and Applications of Conceptual Modeling.

The four invited keynote presentations were "Software Design, Concepts and AI" by Daniel Jackson, Massachusetts Institute of Technology; "Conceptual Modeling and Knowledge Representation: A journey from Data Modeling to Knowledge Graphs" by Maurizio Lenzerini, Sapienza University of Rome, the Peter Chen Award recipient of 2022; "Reverse Engineering of Language at Scale: Towards Symbolic and Explainable Large Language Models" by Walid S. Saba, Northeastern University; and "True or False? The Impact of Negative Knowledge in Biomedical Artificial Intelligence", by Catia Pesquita, University of Lisbon. Speaking on behalf of our community, we are grateful to the keynote speakers for showcasing the significant impact of conceptual modeling research on our society yesterday, today, and tomorrow. The three tutorials, accepted after an open call, addressed relevant and timely topics at the core interest of our community.

As the editors of this volume, we want to express heartfelt thanks to all authors submitting their novel research results to the conference; also to the members of the Program Committee and Senior Program Committee for their dedication and expertise in reviewing and discussing paper submissions. We are indebted to the Organizing Committee for carefully arranging all aspects of running the conference, including its promotion, attracting submissions, administering conference information, designing the portal, communicating, and actioning any progress towards and throughout the conference. Finally, we warmly thank the INESC-ID, the Instituto Superior Técnico - University of Lisbon, and their local teams for hosting ER 2023. While this volume presents the work that has brought our community together in Lisbon, it cannot show any memories, discussion, or new lines of thought resulting from the in-person experience at the ER conference.

September 2023

João Paulo A. Almeida
José Borbinha
Sebastian Link
Giancarlo Guizzardi
Jelena Zdravkovic

Organization

General Chairs

José Borbinha   INESC-ID, IST, Universidade de Lisboa, Portugal
Giancarlo Guizzardi   University of Twente, The Netherlands

Program Chairs

João Paulo A. Almeida   Federal University of Espírito Santo, Brazil
Sebastian Link   University of Auckland, New Zealand
Jelena Zdravkovic   Stockholm University, Sweden

Industrial Track Chairs

Wolfgang Maass   Saarland University, Germany
Pedro Sousa   INESC-ID, IST, Universidade de Lisboa, Portugal

Forum Chairs

Sotirios Liaskos   York University, Canada
David Aveiro   Universidade da Madeira, Portugal

Symposium on Conceptual Modeling Education Chairs

Maria Keet   University of Cape Town, South Africa
Fernanda Baião   Pontifical Catholic Univ. of Rio de Janeiro, Brazil
Estefania Serral   KU Leuven, Belgium

Panels Chairs

Veda Storey   Georgia State University, USA
Oscar Pastor   Universidad Politecnica di Valencia, Spain

Posters and Demos Chairs

Sergio de Cesare University of Westminster, UK
Miguel Mira da Silva INOV, IST, University of Lisbon, Portugal

Project Exhibitions Chairs

João Araújo Universidade Nova de Lisboa, Portugal
Tiago Prince Sales University of Twente, The Netherlands

Tutorials Chairs

Pnina Soffer University of Haifa, Israel
Maribel Yasmina Santos University of Minho, Portugal

Workshops Chairs

João Araújo Universidade Nova de Lisboa, Portugal
Tiago Prince Sales University of Twente, The Netherlands

Doctoral Consortium Chairs

Helena Sofia Pinto INESC-ID, IST, Universidade de Lisboa, Portugal
Ladjel Bellatreche LIAS/ENSMA, France
Simon Hacks Stockholm University, Sweden

Publicity Chairs

Anna Bernasconi Politecnico di Milano, Italy
Claudenir M. Fonseca University of Twente, The Netherlands

Sponsorship Chairs

Luiz Olavo Bonino da Silva Santos University of Twente, The Netherlands
Sérgio Guerreiro INESC-ID, IST, Universidade de Lisboa, Portugal

Local Committee

Volunteers Chair

André Vasconcelos   INESC-ID, IST, Universidade de Lisboa, Portugal

Treasurer

Daniel Faria   INESC-ID, IST, Universidade de Lisboa, Portugal

Web Master

António Higgs   INESC-ID, Portugal

Senior Program Committee

Jacky Akoka	CEDRIC-CNAM & IMT-TEM, France
Paolo Atzeni	Università Roma Tre, Italy
Stefano Ceri	Politecnico di Milano, Italy
Karen Davis	Miami University, USA
Gill Dobbie	University of Auckland, New Zealand
Xavier Franch	Universitat Politècnica de Catalunya, Spain
Ulrich Frank	Universität Duisburg-Essen, Germany
Aldo Gangemi	Università di Bologna, Italy
Nicola Guarino	ISTC-CNR, Italy
Jennifer Horkoff	Chalmers University of Technology, Sweden
Matthias Jarke	RWTH Aachen University, Germany
Manfred Jeusfeld	University of Skövde, Sweden
Paul Johannesson	Royal Institute of Technology, Sweden
Alberto Laender	Federal University of Minas Gerais, Brazil
Steve Liddle	BYU, USA
Heinrich C. Mayr	Alpen-Adria-Universität Klagenfurt, Austria
John Mylopoulos	University of Ottawa, Canada
José Palazzo M. de Oliveira	Federal University of Rio Grande do Sul, Brazil
Jeffrey Parsons	Memorial University of Newfoundland, Canada
Oscar Pastor	Universidad Politécnica de Valencia, Spain
Henderik A. Proper	TU Wien, Austria
Jolita Ralyté	University of Geneva, Switzerland

Colette Rolland	Université Paris 1 Panthéon-Sorbonne, France
Motoshi Saeki	Nanzan University, Japan
Peretz Shoval	Ben-Gurion University, Israel
Pnina Soffer	University of Haifa, Israel
Veda Storey	GSU, USA
Bernhard Thalheim	Christian-Albrechts-Universität zu Kiel, Germany
Juan Carlos Trujillo	Universidad de Alicante, Spain
Gerd Wagner	Brandenburg Univ. of Tech. at Cottbus, Germany
Isabelle Comyn-Wattiau	ESSEC Business School, France
Carson Woo	University of British Columbia, Canada
Eric Yu	University of Toronto, Canada

Program Committee

Mara Abel	Federal University of Rio Grande do Sul, Brazil
João Araújo	Universidade NOVA de Lisboa, Portugal
Alessandro Artale	Free University of Bozen-Bolzano, Italy
Wolf-Tilo Balke	TU Braunschweig, Germany
Monalessa Barcellos	Federal University of Espírito Santo, Brazil
Anna Bernasconi	Politecnico di Milano, Italy
Devis Bianchini	University of Brescia, Italy
Sandro Bimonte	INRAE, France
Luiz O. B. S. Santos	University of Twente, The Netherlands
Dominik Bork	TU Wien, Austria
Shawn Bowers	Gonzaga University, USA
Robert Andrei Buchmann	Babeș-Bolyai University of Cluj Napoca, Romania
Jordi Cabot	ICREA – UOC, Spain
Diego Calvanese	Free University of Bozen-Bolzano, Italy
Maria Luiza M. Campos	Federal University of Rio de Janeiro, Brazil
Cinzia Cappiello	Politecnico di Milano, Italy
Luca Cernuzzi	Universidad Católica "Nuestra Señora de la Asunción", Paraguay
Sharma Chakravarthy	University of Texas at Arlington, USA
Suphamit Chittayasothorn	King Mongkut's Institute of Technology Ladkrabang, Thailand
Tony Clark	Aston University, UK
Dolors Costal	Universitat Politècnica de Catalunya, Spain
Fabiano Dalpiaz	Utrecht University, The Netherlands
Johann Eder	Alpen-Adria-Universität Klagenfurt, Austria
Vadim Ermolayev	Ukrainian Catholic University, Ukraine

Steering Committee

Chair

Jeffrey Parsons   Memorial University of Newfoundland, Canada

Vice Chair

Giancarlo Guizzardi   University of Twente, The Netherlands

Treasurer

Stephen W. Liddle   BYU, USA

Emeritus

Peter P. Chen   Louisiana State University, USA

Steering Committee Members

Peter P. Chen
Isabelle Comyn-Wattiau
Karen Davis
Ulrich Frank
Giancarlo Guizzardi
Jennifer Horkoff
Matthias Jarke
Paul Johannesson
Gerti Kappel
Kamal Karlapalem
Alberto Laender
Stephen W. Liddle
Tok Wang Ling
Hui Ma
Heinrich Mayr

Antoni Olivé
José Palazzo Moreira de Oliveira
Jeffrey Parsons
Oscar Pastor
Jolita Ralyte
Sudha Ram
Motoshi Saeki
Peretz Shoval
Vítor Estêvão Silva Souza
Il-Yeol Song
Veda Storey
Juan Carlos Trujillo
Yair Wand
Carson Woo
Eric Yu

Additional Reviewers

Ali, Syed Juned
Barat, Souvik
Benzin, Janik-Vasily
Calhau, Rodrigo
Castellanos, Arturo
Christ, Sven
Cremerius, Jonas
Curty, Simon
Fernandes, André
França, Juliana
Fumagalli, Mattia
Gavric, Aleksandar
Gemeinhardt, Felix
Invernici, Francesco
Jabbari Sabegh, Mohammad Ali
Kaczmarek-Heß, Monika

Kaur, Karamjit
Kunkler, Michel
Köpke, Julius
Molina de Armas, Elvismary
Muff, Fabian
Reddy, Sreedhar
Roca Antunes, Cauã
Scheibel, Beate
Segundo, Washington
Selway, Matt
Shekhovtsov, Volodymyr A.
Sint, Sabine
Sunkle, Sagar
Barros, Claudio D. T.
Välja, Margus
Winkler, Philip

Keynote Speeches

Software Design, Concepts and AI

Daniel Jackson

Computer Science and Artificial Intelligence Lab (CSAIL),
Massachusetts Institute of Technology (MIT), USA
dnj@mit.edu

We've known since the 1970s how important conceptual models are in the design of software. If a system's conceptual model is too complex to grasp, or isn't faithfully projected in the user interface, usability suffers. Despite lots of progress in conceptual modeling, two central aspects have not been addressed. First, we've often assumed that the conceptual model is given—defined by the problem domain or by an existing mechanism—when in fact it is usually explicitly designed. Second, although many representations have been proposed, none of them separated out the individual concepts, allowing them to be analyzed and reused in a modular way.

In this talk, I'll explain a new approach to software design that centers on the design of individual concepts, which are composed together to form a system. I'll show how this allows usability problems to be diagnosed more effectively, stimulates new designs that work more effectively, and allows apps to be constructed with a more modular structure that has better separation of concerns and less coupling. I'll also explain how LLMs can be used synergistically in design by concept.

Conceptual Modeling and Knowledge Representation: A Journey from Data Modeling to Knowledge Graphs

Maurizio Lenzerini

Department of Computer, Control, and Management Engineering of Sapienza,
University of Rome, Italy
lenzerini@diag.uniroma1.it

While data constitute one of the most important components of an information system, many research efforts today focus on Machine Learning models and algorithms, with the properties of data feeding such algorithms playing a secondary role. Thus, shifting the attention to data has been recently proposed as one of the most timely topics in Data Analytics and Artificial Intelligence (AI) research, under the name of Data-Centric AI. Arguably, the field of Conceptual Modeling (CM), and in particular its connection to the area of Knowledge Representation and Reasoning (KRR), can provide important contributions towards shaping the research on Data-Centric AI. In this talk I will try to summarize the most important steps of the research done at the crossing between CM and KKR in the last decades, from the early work on Data Modeling and Semantic Networks to the investigation on ontologies and Knowledge Graphs.

True or False? The Impact of Negative Knowledge in Biomedical Artificial Intelligence

Catia Pesquita

LASIGE, Faculdade de Ciências da Universidade de Lisboa, Portugal
clpesquita@fc.ul.pt

Most of our data is about positive facts: a patient has hypertension, the BRCA2 gene is related to breast cancer, Lisbon is the capital of Portugal.

In many applications, the assumption is made that everything that is not stated is false (the closed-world assumption), but for real-world and critical domains, such as those in biomedical research and healthcare, conflating what we don't know with what is false carries a high risk: patients with unreported symptoms can be given the wrong diagnosis, drugs with unknown interactions can be prescribed in tandem.

Knowledge graph-based machine learning applications are a prime example of this mismatch between algorithms that operate under the closed-world assumption and real datasets that are open-world.

In this talk, I will discuss the challenges faced by machine learning and artificial intelligence applications over knowledge graphs when the difference between a negative fact and an unknown fact is crucial. We will further explore what negative knowledge is, why it is important, how it can be harnessed, and what we are missing when we ignore it. The discussion will be supported by real use cases in biomedical research and healthcare.

Reverse Engineering of Language at Scale: Towards Symbolic and Explainable Large Language Models

Walid S. Saba

Institute for Experiential AI, Northeastern University, USA
w.saba@northeastern.edu

Scientific explanation proceeds in one of two directions: by following a top-down strategy or a bottom-up strategy. For a top-down strategy to work, however, one must have access to a set of general principles to start with and this is certainly not the case when it comes to thought and how our minds externalize our thoughts in language. Lacking any general principles to start with, a bottom-up approach must be preferred in the process of discovering how language works. As such, we believe that the relative success of large language models (LLMs), that are essentially a bottom-up reverse engineering of language at scale, is not a reflection on the symbolic vs. subsymbolic debate but is a reflection on (appropriately), adopting a bottom-up strategy. However, due to their subsymbolic nature, LLMs are not really models of language, but statistical models of regularities found in language and thus whatever knowledge these models acquire about how language works will always be buried in billions of microfeatures (weights), none of which is meaningful on its own. Because they are incapable of maintaining the compositional structure of language, LLMs can never provide an explainable theory of how language works. To arrive at an explainable model of how language works, we argue in this talk that a bottom-up reverse engineering of language at scale must be done in a symbolic setting. Hints of how this should be done can be traced back to Frege, although it was subsequently and more explicitly argued for by Sommers (1963), Hobbs (1985) and Saba (2007).

An invited companion paper for this keynote speech is included in these proceedings.

Tutorials

Combining BPMN with Artefact-Centric Business Process Modeling

Monique Snoeck[1,2] and Charlotte Verbruggen[1]

[1] KU Leuven, Belgium
{monique.snoeck,charlotte.verbruggen}@kuleuven.be
[2] University of Namur, Belgium

Conceptual data modelling and process modelling have evolved as two separate domains with little cross-overs. The tutorial addresses the need for a cross-over between the two domains and will present a way to combine artefact-centric modelling and process modelling in a consistent way. The tutorial thus addresses data-aware process modelling, combining object-oriented domain modelling with BPMN and offers valuable insights for developing object-centric process mining.

The goals of the tutorial are:

- To provide an overview of the state of the art in combining process modelling with domain modelling and pinpointing the gap to be addressed in future research.
- To illustrate how domain modelling and process modelling can be combined in a genuine multi-modelling approach that makes use of existing standard modelling languages to ensure its usability.

The specific objectives of the tutorial are:

- To provide attendees with an overview of the state of the art in data-aware and artefact-centric business process modelling.
- To make attendees aware of the open problems with existing approaches.
- To identify rules on how to combine several modelling languages, each addressing a particular viewpoint consistently and harmoniously.

Accounting as Knowledge Graphs – Ontological Lessons for Your Teaching and Research

William McCarthy

Michigan State University, USA
mccarthy@broad.msu.edu

This tutorial covers material from a recently released American Accounting Association Research Monograph entitled "The Resource-Event-Agent (REA) Accounting Model as an Accounting and Economic Ontology" by William McCarthy, Guido Geerts, and Graham Gal. REA is a semantic enterprise model whose origin dates back to a seminal 1982 paper in The Accounting Review, the top research journal in the accounting field. Material related to REA was presented at the Entity-Relationship Research Conferences in 1979, 1981, and 1997, and its basic tenets have been incorporated in ISO standards (15944-4 in 2015 and 15944-21 in 2023) and in the Workday ERP system.

I assume no prerequisites except for a familiarity with data modeling and simple accounting ideas. The overall goal for this tutorial is to familiarize MIS and CS professionals with the Resource-Event-Agent accounting and economic ontology in a very general fashion. Members of the ER modeling community should be aware of semantic modeling concepts from accounting and economics. REA is a long-established knowledge representation scheme whose most recent projects have incorporated advanced ideas from economics and information technology. However, the presentation of REA ideas has not occurred recently at the ER conferences. Publication of the AAA research monograph on REA represents an opportunity for conference attendees to immerse themselves in this body of research and to see how its concepts can be used in both undergraduate and graduate teaching. Slides will be distributed as well an REA modeling tool written in EXCEL.

Semantic Enrichment and Digital Twins Based on Conceptual Modeling: The Bee-Up Tool

Robert Andrei Buchmann[1], Patrik Burzynski[2] and Wilfrid Utz[2]

[1] Faculty of Economics and Business Administration, Babes,-Bolyai University, Romania
robert.buchmann@econ.ubbcluj.ro
[2] OMiLAB NPO, Germany
{patrik.burzynski,wilfrid.utz}@omilab.org

This tutorial presents an approach to semantic enrichment and digital twins based on conceptual modeling, demonstrated through specific features of the Bee-Up multi-language modeling tool which expands the value of conceptual models beyond their traditional functions. Bee-Up supports modeling with several established languages – e.g. BPMN, EPC, ER, UML, Petri Nets. The goal of the tutorial is to highlight how Bee-Up facilitates knowledge externalization and mediation for the "digital-first era" – firstly, in RDF format as it enables several layers of semantic enrichment towards a specific flavor of model-driven Knowledge Graphs; secondly, by interoperating with cyber-physical devices towards a specific-flavor of Digital-Physical Twin binding. Such features are show- cased during the tutorial, while also discussing the metamodeling approach that is under the hood of Bee-Up's model processing capabilities.

The tutorial provides insight about innovative possibilities of processing models, advocating that they should be treated as knowledge structures and abstraction mediators. The attendees learn about the capabilities provided by the chosen environment – Bee-Up – through showcases that focus on the design-time semantic enrichment of visual models and on their run-time treatment in a Digital Twin context.

Contents

Applications of Conceptual Modeling

Invited Paper

Stochastic LLMs *do not* Understand Language: Towards Symbolic, Explainable and Ontologically Based LLMs

Walid S. Saba[✉]

Institute for Experiential AI, Northeastern University, Portland, ME 08544, USA
w.saba@northeastern.edu

Abstract. In our opinion the exuberance surrounding the relative success of data-driven large language models (LLMs) is slightly misguided and for several reasons (i) LLMs cannot be relied upon for factual information since for LLMs all ingested text (factual or non-factual) was created equal; (ii) due to their subsymbolic nature, whatever 'knowledge' these models acquire about language will always be buried in billions of microfeatures (weights), none of which is meaningful on its own; and (iii) LLMs will often fail to make the correct inferences in several linguistic contexts (e.g., nominal compounds, copredication, quantifier scope ambiguities, intensional contexts). Since we believe the relative success of data-driven large language models (LLMs) is not a reflection on the symbolic vs. subsymbolic debate but a reflection on applying the successful strategy of a bottom-up reverse engineering of language at scale, we suggest in this paper applying the effective bottom-up strategy in a symbolic setting resulting in symbolic, explainable, and ontologically grounded language models.

Keywords: Bottom-up reverse engineering of language · Symbolic large language models · Language Agnostic Ontology

1 Introduction

The recent successes of so-called large language models (LLMs) have taken the world of artificial intelligence (AI) and natural language processing (NLP) by storm. Indeed, with the release of GPT-4 it has become apparent that large language models (LLMs), that are essentially a massive experiment in a bottom-up reverse engineering of language, have crossed some threshold of scale at which point there was an obvious qualitative improvement in their capabilities[1]. In our opinion, however, the spectacular exuberance towards these advances is slightly misguided. For one thing, these large 'language models' are not exactly models of language but are statistical models of regularities found in language. In fact, and due to their subsymbolic nature, whatever 'knowledge' these

---

[1] GPT stands for 'Generative Pre-trained Transformer', an architecture that OpenAI built on top of the transformer architecture introduced in (Vaswani et al., 2017).

J. P. A. Almeida et al. (Eds.): ER 2023, LNCS 14320, pp. 3–19, 2023.
https://doi.org/10.1007/978-3-031-47262-6_1

models acquire about how language works will always be buried in billions of micro-features (weights) none of which is meaningful on its own. This is also the reason why *explainability* can never be attained in such models since explainability is 'inference in reverse' and this can only happen in one of two ways: (i) either the computation is invertible, or (ii) symbolic structures must be employed to preserve a *semantic map* of the computation, and neither of this is true in deep neural networks (DNNs). As shown in Fig. 1(a) computation in DNNs proceeds by performing a linear combination (a weighted sum) of the inputs followed by the application of some activation function. But this computation is not invertible, since the number of decompositions of a tensor (vector, or scalar) are infinite. Thus, once a computation is performed in the forward path of a DNN the constituents of the compositional computation are not anymore available, unlike computations in symbolic systems where structures such as abstract syntax trees are used to preserve a semantic map of the computation. Note that the inputs x_1 and x_2 (left leaf nodes) and weights w_1 and w_2 (right leaf nodes) in Fig. 1(b) are just one combination of infinitely many inputs that produce 0.87 as an output.[2]

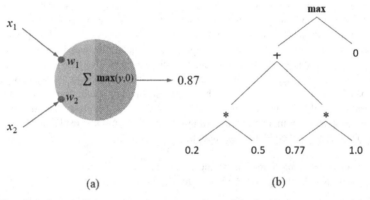

(a)   (b)

Fig. 1. Neural (subsymbolic) computations are not invertible: in (a) we cannot explain how we arrived at 0.87; in symbolic systems, on the other hand, a semantic map of the computation is maintained, for example using an abstract syntax tree as shown in (b).

In addition to the issue of *explainability*, (i) LLMs will always be susceptible to bias and toxicity in their training data; (ii) LLMs can never differentiate factual information from non-factual information since for LLMs all text was created equal; and (iii) LLMs will fail to capture the inferential aspects of linguistic communication in many contexts. It is the last point that we would like to focus on here since this is what will hinder the use of these stochastic models in the enterprise, and in particular in critical applications such as finance, the judiciary system, healthcare, etc.

In the rest of the paper we will first examine some linguistic contexts where, regardless of scale and the specific details of the neural model, LLMs will always fail to make

---

[2] See (Saba, 2022) for a more detailed discussion on the relationship between compositionality, structured semantics and explainability, and (Fodor and Pylyshyn, 1988) for a more detailed critic of subsymbolic systems and their inadequacy in preserving semantic systematicity.

the correct inferences. Subsequently, we will briefly discuss why LLMs made more progress than symbolic approaches and how the bottom-up reverse engineering strategy could be done in a *symbolic* setting. We will then briefly discuss how a symbolic bottom-up reverse engineering process also allows us to 'discover' the nature of the ontology that seems to underlie our ordinary spoken language. Finally, we will show how discovering the symbolic dimensions of meaning along with the underlying ontology can help us deal with well-known challenges in the semantics of natural language.

2 Language 'Understanding' and the Limitations of LLMs

Claims about the linguistic competency of natural language understanding (NLU) systems are often exaggerated (positively or negatively), ranging from claims of human-like performance to systemic inadequacy (Sugawara and Tsugita, 2023). In our opinion this is due to overlooking the difference between subjective and objective evaluations of NLU systems. For example, it is difficult to come up with an objective measure by which one can evaluate an NLU system's *text summarization*. The same is true of the results of a *search* query, or of an extracted set of *key topics* (see Fig. 2a).

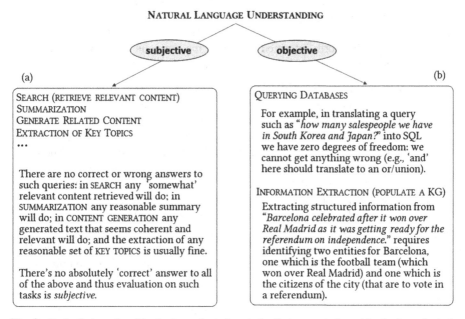

Fig. 2. Tasks that can be objectively evaluated vs. tasks that can only be subjectively evaluated.

While most of what are referred to as 'downstream NLP tasks' can in fact only be subjectively evaluated, objective measures do exist for some other NLP tasks; for example the translation of a natural language query into a formal SQL query to be executed against some enterprise database. In translating a query such as '*how many salespeople in the Chicago branch do we have now on vacation*' into SQL we have zero degrees of freedom since getting anything wrong will mean getting the wrong answer. The reverse operation, namely translating free-from text into structured information also has zero degrees of freedom (see Fig. 2b). Successful translation of a natural language question to the correct SQL query or extracting the right entities and relations from free-form text to some relational structure are therefore the right objective tests for language understanding. It is in these situations that an NLU system must *get everything right*, and that means handling a number of linguistic phenomena such as compound nominals, copredication, quantifier scope ambiguities, prepositional phrase attachments, and so on. As discussed below, and notwithstanding their relative success in subjective tasks, LLMs often fail in making the correct inference in these contexts.

2.1 Compound Nominals

One linguistic phenomenon that seems to be beyond LLMs is that of nominal compounds in utterances of the form [*Noun₁ R* [*Adj Noun₂*]] where the LLM always picks out *Noun₂* as the object of modification by *Adj*, although the object of modification could, in general, be *Noun₁*, *Noun₂*, both (where the utterance is considered ambiguous), or neither (where the utterance is simply not sensible)[3]. Here's a simple example:

PROMPT What is 'informed' modifying here? Mary gave a very informed talk to the Cognitive Science Group.

LLM   In the sentence "Mary gave a very informed talk to the Cognitive Science Group," the word 'informed' is modifying the noun 'talk.' This means it's describing the type of talk that Mary gave as being an informed talk.

The LLM answer is clearly wrong since it is Mary who was very informed and not the 'talk' itself (which is an abstract event that has a time, a place, and a duration). The same failure occurs when the LLM inferred that the gift (an artifact) is what is 'thoughtful' in "Mary appreciated the thoughtful gift she received from David", while clearly the correct interpretation is that "it was thoughtful of David" to give Mary a gift. There are two other combinations to be tested: (i) tests where the *Adj* in [*Noun₁ R* [*Adj Noun₂*]] could apply to both *Noun₁* and *Noun₂*, and (ii) tests where *Adj* does not apply to any of the two nouns. In the former case we have an ambiguous utterance (e.g., "Everyone thinks Olga is a beautiful dancer" where 'beautiful' could be modifying Olga as a person, or Olga's dancing). In the second case we have a situation where modifying any of the nouns should be rejected, rendering the whole utterance as not being sensible, as in "The room needs an articulate corner table". Again, the LLMs failed all these combinations, by always deciding that the modified noun is the one that is preceded syntactically by the adjective, even when it was nonsensical. What these tests show is that LLMs do not exhibit the kind of understanding that requires commonsense knowledge, but that they simply make inferences based on statistically significant syntactic patterns.

2.2 Intension

LLMs are based on a purely extensional paradigm, namely that of neural networks that can only deal with numerical values (or vectors and matrices of those). But quite a bit

---

[3] For more on nominal compounds see (McShane et al., 2014) and (Larson, 1998).

of reasoning in language (and cognition, in general) does not happen at the data level but at the conceptual and intensional levels (see von Fintel and Heim, 2002 for a good tutorial on intension in semantics). This might seem like a trivial stumbling block, but far from it. To appreciate this point let me start by showing an example where, regardless of what our high school teachers taught us, we cannot assume that SQRT(256) and 16 are replaceable in all contexts. Consider the following:

PROMPT   Since SQRT(256) = 16, can I replace one for the other in "I saw Mary teaching her little brother that $7 + 9 = 16$"?

LLM   Yes, you can replace the square root of 256 with its actual value 16 in "I saw Mary teaching her little brother that $7 + 9 = 16$." The statement would still be accurate: "I saw Mary teaching her little brother that $7 + 9 = $ SQRT(256)"

Clearly the answer of the LLM is wrong: from a sentence that reflects reality (it is a fact that "I saw Mary teaching her little brother that $7 + 9 = 16$") we cannot alter or create a new reality and infer something that is not true, namely that "I saw Mary teaching her little brother that $7 + 9$ is SQRT(256)". What's at issue here is that 16 and SQRT(256) are only extensionally equal (i.e., equal by value only) but otherwise they are two different objects. This failure applies not only to mathematical expressions, but to all objects of cognition (anything that we can refer to in language). Consider the following:

PROMPT   Since 'Madrid' = 'the capital of Spain' can I replace one for the other in "John thinks Madrid was not always the capital of Spain"

LLM   Yes, you can replace 'Madrid' by 'the capital of Spain' in "John thinks Madrid was not always the capital of Spain." The new sentence will be "John thinks Madrid was not always Madrid."

Again, while it is true that Madrid *is* the capital of Spain, the expressions "Madrid" and "the capital of Spain" have different cognitive content and thus the replacement of one by the other in some contexts will lead to wrong (and absurd) conclusions. DNNs (and thus LLMs) cannot account for or model the intension of objects of cognition and thus will always fail in making the right inferences in these contexts.

2.3 Copredication

Copredication refers to the situation where a single entity is (implicitly) assigned two different categories (or types) in the same linguistic context (see Asher, 2011; Asher & Pustejovsky, 2011; Viebahn, 2020). For example, in the sentence "That massive red book on the top shelf is written by Tolstoy" we are using a 'book' to refer to two different types of entities, simultaneously: 'book' the **physical** object that is massive and red; and 'book' the **information content** that was authored by Tolstoy. Failure to recognize these copredications results in absurd conclusions as the following illustrates:

PROMPT   Suppose this is true: The wet newspaper that fell down off the table is my favorite newspaper. But now that my favorite newspaper fired the editor I might not like reading it anymore. Can I replace 'my favorite newspaper' by 'the wet newspaper that fell down off the table' in the second sentence?

LLM   Yes, you can replace "my favorite newspaper" with "the wet newspaper that fell down off the table" in the second sentence to maintain the same meaning. So the revised sentence would be: "But now that the wet newspaper that fell down off the table fired the editor, I might not like reading it anymore."

The answer the LLM provided is clearly wrong since the **physical object** that is the 'wet newspaper that fall off the table' is not the one that fired 'my favorite columnist' but the organization – or, more accurately, it is a group of people in that organization. The LLM failed here because it failed to detect a *copredication*, namely referring to two types of objects using a single entity. The above example can also be restated so that the erroneous inference is translated into making the wrong reference resolution. Consider a slight change in the above test:

PROMPT   What does 'it' refer to here? The newspaper on the table in front of me used to be my favorite. However, since it fired my favorite columnist, I do not read it anymore.

LLM   In the sentence, "it" refers to "the newspaper on the table in front of me." The speaker is talking about a specific newspaper that was their favorite but is no longer because it fired their favorite columnist."

Here the wrong understanding is more explicit by resolving "it" with "the newspaper on the table in front of me" which is clearly wrong since the (physical) newspaper on the table is not the entity that fired 'my favorite columnist'. The failure of LLMs in detecting copredication can even be shown more explicitly. Consider the following test where we explicitly ask GPT to identify and list all entities in some linguistic context, along with their category/type:

PROMPT   List all entities mentioned in this sentence, along with their category, or type: The city of Barcelona celebrated on Sunday after it won over Real Madrid as it was getting ready to vote for independence the next day.

LLM   Entities mentioned in the sentence:
1.   The city of Barcelona (Category: Geographic Location)
2.   Sunday (Category: Day of the Week)
3.   Real Madrid (Category: Sports Team or Organization)
4.   Independence (Category: Political Action or Event) These entities encompass a geographical location, days of the week, sports teams, and a political event".

Besides missing "the vote" as the main event, the LLM failed to detect reference to two types of entities that are also implied by 'Barcelona': the Barcelona Football Club (that won over Real Madrid), and *the citizens* of Barcelona (that celebrated the victory and are getting ready to vote for independence).

2.4 Quantifier Scope Ambiguity

For decades, the problem of resolving quantifier scope ambiguities has been one of the most challenging problems in computational linguistics (see Kiss and Pafel, 2017). While quantifier scope is not very important when generating a summary for a piece of text (a subjective NLP task), when translating a question posed in natural language into an unambiguous SQL query deciding on the right scope of quantifiers makes all the difference in getting the correct answer to the query. Since resolving quantifier scope ambiguities often requires making inferences that require some commonsense knowledge (Saba, 2001), LLMs also failed most of these tests. Consider the following:

PROMPT How many states are we referring to here? Every senator in a key electoral state voted for the amendment.

LLM   In the sentence, "Every senator on a key electoral state voted for the amendment," it implies that there is one key electoral state being referred to. The use of "a key electoral state" suggests a singular state rather than multiple states.

The LLM interpreted the sentence incorrectly as "in some key electoral state, every senator voted for the amendment" which is clearly not the intended meaning. Basically, it would seem that the indefinite "a" triggered a single state, although the scope ordering most speakers would choose is ∀senator∃state, implying several electoral states. The wrong inference is also made here, although the situation is reversed:

PROMPT How many journalists are we referring to here? A journalist from the BBC is always present in every civil war.

LLM   In the sentence, "A journalist from the BBC is always present in every civil war," it refers to one journalist from the BBC. The use of "a" indicates a singular journalist, not multiple journalists.

The LLM also failed here, although most readers would reverse the scope of quantifiers from ∃j∀w to ∀w∃j thus interpreting the sentence as saying "in every civil war, a journalist from BBC is always present". These failures can be even more acute in situations where some subtle social background knowledge is required, as in the following:

PROMPT In the following, are we talking about a specific cowboy or some indefinite cowboy? Next week Susan is going to be married to some cowboy from Arizona.

LLM   In the sentence, "Susan is going to be married to some cowboy from Arizona," it appears that we are talking about an indefinite cowboy. The use of "some cowboy" suggests that the cowboy is not a specific individual but rather any cowboy from Arizona.

Although it is plausible to assume an indefinite cowboy in "*Someday* Susan is going to be married to some cowboy from Arizona", but in the world we live in it is unlikely for Susan to be planning on getting married *next week* to someone yet to be identified, but that she has *someone specific* in mind. This kind of background knowledge is not available to LLMs, and thus such inferences are clearly beyond these statistical models.

2.5 Prepositional Phrase Attachments

Resolving the ambiguity in prepositional phrase attachments is also a very challenging task. Basically, the issue here is what do various prepositional phrases (PPs) attach to (or modify)? While in many situations the attachment is very clear, there are certain situations that require some subtle reasoning that involves access to some background knowledge. Consider for example the following:

PROMPT What does the phrase "in the briefcase" modify here? Put the book on the table in the briefcase.

LLM   In the sentence, "Put the book on the table in the briefcase," the phrase "in the briefcase" modifies "the table." It specifies the location of the table, indicating that the table is inside the briefcase.

The LLM incorrectly read the sentence as [Put the book on [the table in the briefcase]]. Clearly, what is meant here is [Put [the book on the table] in the briefcase] – that is, the book (that is on the table) is to be put in the briefcase and thus the correct attachment of the PP "in the briefcase" is to the verb 'put'. The LLM made the wrong inference here since it has no knowledge of the relation that might exist in the world we live in between books, tables, and briefcases. The LLM also failed in the example below but in this case by incorrectly attaching the PP to the verb[4]:

PROMPT What does "in the U-Haul truck" modify here? The gangsters decided to sell the shotguns in the U-Haul truck.

LLM   "In the U-Haul truck" modifies the verb "sell." It specifies where the gangsters have decided to sell the shotguns, indicating that they plan to conduct the sale from or within the U-Haul truck.

Again, the LLM made the wrong inference since it does not have the relevant background knowledge that it is much more likely for the shotguns to be in the U-Haul truck than for the 'selling of the guns' to occur inside the U-Haul truck.

2.6   Metonymy

We conclude examining the linguistic competency of LLMs with another phenomenon in the semantics of natural language, namely metonymy, which is the use of one entity to make an indirect reference to another *related* entity[5]. Consider the following:

PROMPT The waiter told Rita that the loud omelet wants another beer. Who is it that wants another beer?

LLM   In the sentence, "The waiter told Rita that the loud omelet wants another beer," it seems there might be an error or confusion in the wording. Typically, omelets don't have desires or drink beer, so this sentence appears to be constructed in a way that doesn't make logical sense. Please provide additional context or clarification if there's an intended meaning you'd like to convey.

While all competent speakers would immediately infer that "the loud omelet" is a reference to some "loud person eating the omelet", the LLM cannot "uncover" this missing information since it does not 'know' that *eating* is the most salient relationship between people and food (e.g. omelet), although there are many other plausible relations.

2.7   Summary of Tests

So where do we stand now? On one hand, LLMs have clearly proven that one can get a handle on syntax and quite a bit of semantics by executing a bottom-up reverse

---

[4] Example taken from (Peckenpaugh, 2019), with some modification.

[5] See (Shelestiuk, 2005) and (Piñango et al., 2017) for a good discussion of metonymy.

engineering strategy; yet on the other hand what we have are stochastic LLMs that fail to make the correct inferences in many linguistic contexts, and in particular in contexts where some background knowledge might be required. As we believe that the relative success of LLMs is not a reflection on the symbolic vs. subsymbolic debate but is a reflection on (appropriately) adopting a bottom-up reverse engineering strategy, we think that combining the advantages of symbolic representations with a bottom-up reverse engineering strategy is a worthwhile effort. The idea here is that discovering the syntax and semantics of language by analyzing how we actually communicate in language is not exclusive to linguistic work in the empirical tradition but can in fact be done in a symbolic setting. We discuss this next.

3 Concerning 'the Company a Word Keeps'

The idea that the meaning of words are acquired by children by observing their syntactic distribution in language is not new (Lidz, 2022). In fact, the genesis of modern LLMs is the *distributional semantics hypothesis* which states that the more semantically similar words are, the more they tend to occur in similar contexts – or similarity in meaning is similarity in linguistic distribution (Harris, 1954). Summarized by "you shall know a word by the company it keeps", a saying attributed to the linguist John R. Firth, the basic idea was to approximate word meanings by embeddings (vectors) that are essentially points in a multidimensional space. While these vectors were initially constructed to approximate word meanings, it was not until the transformer model (Vaswani et al., 2017), however, that embeddings started the encoding of *syntactic patterns* and even quite a bit of compositional semantics. At the root of this encoding scheme is a bottom-up approach that "reverse engineers the process and induces semantic representations from contexts of use" (Boleda, 2020). Below we suggest applying this successful bottom-up reverse engineering strategy in a symbolic setting where 'the company a word keeps' is not determined statistically but semantically and ontologically.

3.1 Symbolic Reverse Engineering of Language

In discussing possible models (or theories) of the world that can be employed in computational linguistics Jerry Hobbs (1985) once suggested that there are two alternatives: on one extreme we could attempt building a "correct" theory that would entail a full description of the world, something that would involve quantum physics and all the sciences; on the other hand, we could have a promiscuous model of the world that is isomorphic to the way we talk it about in natural language. What Hobbs is suggesting here is a reverse engineering of language to discover how we actually use language to talk about the world. In essence, this is similar to Frege's Context Principal to "never ask for the meaning of words in isolation" (Dummett, 1981) but that a word gets its meanings from analyzing all the contexts in which the word can appear (Milne, 1986). Again, what this suggests is that the meaning of words can be *discovered* by analyzing all the ways we use these words in everyday discourse. While Hobbs' and Frege's observations might be a bit vague, the proposal put forth by Fred Sommers (1963) is very specific. For Sommers, the process of understanding the meaning of some word *w* starts by enumerating all the properties *P* that can sensibly be said of *w*. For example, while [*delicious apple*] is sensible, [*delicious Thursday*] is not. Moreover, since [*delicious cake*] and [*delicious soup*] are also sensible, there must be a common type (perhaps **food**?) that subsumes *apple*, *soup* and *cake*. Similarly, while [*imminent sugar*] is not sensible, [*imminent trip*], [*imminent conference*] and [*imminent election*] are, again suggesting that *trip*, *conference*, and *election* must have a common supertype (**event**?). Thus, as argued in (Saba, 2007), this type of analysis can also be used to 'discover' the ontology that seems to be implicit in all natural languages.

Let us now consider the following naïve procedure for some initial reverse engineering of language, where **app**(*p*, *c*) means the property *p* can sensibly be said of the concept *c*:

1. Consider concepts $C = \{c_1,..., c_m\}$ and properties $P = \{p_1,..., p_n\}$.
2. Assume a predicate **app**(*p*, *c*) that is true iff the property *p* applies to (or can
3. sensible be said of) objects of type *c*, where $c \in C$ and $p \in P$.
4. A set $Cp = \{c \mid \textbf{app}(p, c)\}$ is generated for all $c \in C$ and all property $p \in P$
5. such that the property *p* is applicable to (or can sensibly be said of) *c*.
6. A concept hierarchy is then systematically discovered by analyzing the subset
7. relationship between the various sets generated.

Applying the above procedure on a fragment of natural language and taking, initially, *C* to be a set of nouns and *P* a set of adjectives and relations that can sensibly be applied to (or can be said of) nouns in *C*, would result in something like the following:

R_1: **app**(OLD, entity)   in ordinary language we can say OLD of any entity
R_2: **app**(HEAVY, physical)   we say HEAVY of objects that are of type physical
R_3: **app**(HUNGRY, living)   HUNGRY is said of objects that are of type living
R_4: **app**(ARTICULATE, human)   ARTICULATE is said of objects that are of type human
R_5: **app**(MAKE(human, artifact)) MAKE holds between a human and an artifact

R_6: **app**(MANUFACTURE(human, tool)) MANUFACTURE relates a human and a tool

R_7: **app**(RIDE(human, vehicle)) RIDE holds between a human and a vehicle
R_8: **app**(DRIVE(human, car))   DRIVE holds between a human and a car

Note that since **app**(HEAVY, car) – that is, since it is sensible to say 'heavy car' it would seem that car must be a subtype of physical since HEAVY can sensibly be said of all physical things. Similarly, since it makes sense to say MAKE and MANUFACTURE of a tool, a tool must be a subtype of artifact. The fragment hierarchy that is implicit in R_1 through R_8 is shown in Fig. 3 below.

3.2 Discovering the Language Agnostic Primitive Relations

The fact that **app**(ARTICULATE, human) – namely that it is sensible to say 'articulate human' in ordinary discourse, can be restated as **hasProp**(articulation, human), to say that in ordinary discourse it is sensible to attribute the property of articulation to a human. What we have done here is a reification (nominalization) of ARTICULATE to get the abstract object (or trope) articulation (see Moltmann, 2013). The same can be done with **app**(HUNGRY, living) which states that it is sensible to say 'hungry' of any living thing, by restating this as **inState**(hunger, living), which says that is sensible to say that any living thing can be in a state of hunger.

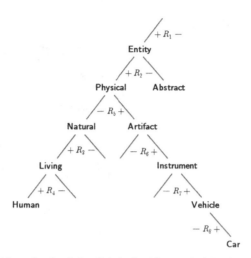

Fig. 3. The hierarchy that is implicit in the 'discoveries' R_1 through R_8 above.

It should be noted here that these transformations add quite a bit of information. While **app**(ARTICULATE, human) and **app**(HUNGRY, living) simply state that it is sensible to say 'articulate' of any human and 'hungry' of any living thing, **hasProp**(articulation, human) and **inState**(hunger, living) are saying that a human can have the *property* of articulation, and that a living thing can be in a *state* of hunger. Other universals can also be obtained. For example, **app**(MANUFACTURE(human, tool)) is saying more than "it is sensible to speak of a human manufacturing a tool" – it is also saying **agentOf**(manufacturing, human) and **objectOf**(manufacturing, tool); i.e., that a human can be the *agent* of a manufacturing (activity) and that tool can be the *object* of such an activity.

These primitive relations (**hasProp**, **inState**, **agentOf**, **objectOf**, etc.) can actually be discovered by analyzing all the ways we describe objects in everyday discourse. In general, when describing an object or an entity x by some property P we are, indirectly, making a statement such as 'x is P'. If we analyze the various ways these descriptions can be made (using the copular 'is'), it will lead us to different types of primitive relations, as shown in Table 1. For example, in saying *Mary is wise*, we are essentially saying that *Mary has the property of wisdom*. Similarly, in saying *Carlos is ill*, we are essentially saying that *Carlos is in the* (physiological) *state of illness*. Analyzing all the ways different types of entities can be described leads us to discover the language agnostic primitive relations summarized in Table 2 below.

Here's a summary of the overall process we discussed so far: (*i*) analyze a large corpus to discover facts such as R_3: **app**(HUNGRY, living) and R_4: **app**(ARTICULATE, human); (*ii*) construct the ontology implicit in all the discovered relations; and (*iii*) via a nominalization process convert all **app**(p, c) to two entities related by a primitive, language agnostic relation: **inState**(human, illness) and **hasProp**(human, articulation).

Table 1. Discovering primitive relations by analyzing all the ways we can say '*x* **is** *P*'.

LINGUISTIC CONTEXT	IMPLICIT PRIMITIVE RELATION
Frido *is* a dog	Frido *instanceOf* dog
Billy the Kid *is* William H. Boney	Billy the Kid *eq* William H. Boney
JFK *is* John Fitzgerald Kennedy	JFK *eq* John Fitzgerald Kennedy
Mary *is* wise	Mary *hasProp* wisdom
Julie *is* articulate	Julie *hasProp* articulation
Jim *is* sad	Jim *inState* sadness
Carlos *is* ill	Carlos *inState* illness
Sara *is* running	Sara *agentOf* running
Olga *is* dancing	John *agentOf* dancing
Sara *is* greeted	Sara *objectOf* greeting
Sara *is* acknowledged	Sara *objectOf* acknowledgment
John *is* 5'10" tall	John's *height* *hasValue* 5'10"
Dan *is* 69 years old	Dan's *age* *hasValue* 69 yrs
Sheba *is* running	Sheba *participantIn* running (event)
Olga *is* dancing	Olga *agentOf* dancing (activity)

Table 2. Some of the language-agnostic primitive relations.

PRIMITIVE RELATIONS	DESCRIPTION
$Eq(x, y)$	**individual** x is identical to **individual** y
$Part(x, y)$	individual x is part of individual y
$Inst(x, y)$	individual x instantiates **universal** y
$Inhere(x, y)$	individual x inheres in individual y
$Exemp(x, y)$	individual x exemplifies property y
$Dep(x, y)$	individual x depends for its existence on individual y
$IsA(x, y)$	universal x is a sub-kind of universal y
$Precedes(x, y)$	individual process x precedes individual process y
$HasParticipant(x, y)$	individual y participates in individual occurrent x
$HasAgent(x, y)$	individual y is agent of individual occurrent x
$Realizes(x, y)$	individual process x realizes individual function y
$TypeOf(x, t) = (x :: t)$	individual x is an object of type t

Unlike in data-driven and statistical approaches where meaning is approximated by vectors in a multidimensional space, it is these primitive relations that for us form what we call 'dimensions of meaning'. In Fig. 4 we show how these relations are used to represent one meaning for the word 'book', namely "a written work or composition that has been published". Note that as an entity a 'book' (i) can be the agent of a changing event (as in 'Das Kapital **changed** many opinions over the years'); (ii) can have the popularity property (as in 'The Prince is a very **popular** book'); and (iii) can be the object of a writing event (as in 'William Shakespear **wrote** Hamlet').

Ironically, we can use GPT-4 to generate some of these vectors along the various dimensions since these systems are good at *predicting* a masked word. The data in Fig. 5

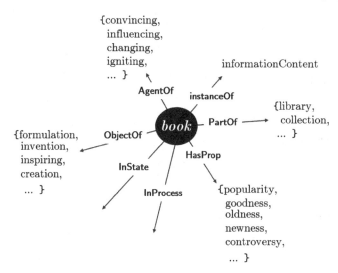

Fig. 4. Primitive and linguistically agnostic relations as the dimensions of word meaning.

is obtained by asking GPT-4 to provide 25 "plausible" (or "sensible") replacements for the [**MASK**]. The three syntactic variations in the sentences are intended to recover entities along three dimensions, namely **agentOf**, **objectOf** and **hasProp**. As we stated earlier this strategy can also be used to 'discover' the underlying ontology that seems to be implicit underneath our ordinary language. In Fig. 5 below we apply masking to generate the most plausible actions that a computer, a car, and a couch can be the object of. Note that while the three types of objects can be the objects of ASSEMBLE, we can sensibly say a computer or a car is RUNNING (or that a computer or a car is ON/OFF) but the same is not true of a couch. This tells us that while a computer and a car must have some common supertype (**machine**?), these two types seem to eventually belong to a different branch from couch although they all have a common supertype at some level of abstraction since they can all be 'assembled' (see Fig. 6).

Incidentally, defining meanings along these dimensions should also shed a new light on Wittgenstein's notion of 'family resemblance' (see Aitchison, 2012). That is, while it might be difficult to think of a set of common features that define all kinds of *games*, *how we speak about all games* should not be different (see Fig. 7).

4   Concept Similarity

In Fig. 4 above we saw that a book can be described by the properties *influential* and *profound*, among others. That is, using the nominalized form we can say:

$$influence \in book.\textbf{HasProp}$$
$$profoundness \in book.\textbf{HasProp}$$

The book has [MASK] millions of people		Jon has [MASK] the book		Das Kapital was a very [MASK] book	
1.	influenced	1.	wrote	1.	influential
2.	inspired	2.	criticized	2.	impactful
3.	educated	3.	endorsed	3.	controversial
4.	affected	4.	debated	4.	challenging
5.	engaged	5.	read	5.	analytical
6.	perplexed	6.	quoted	6.	detailed
7.	challenged	7.	discussed	7.	scholarly
8.	reached	8.	interpreted	8.	complex
9.	enlightened	9.	appreciated	9.	profound
10.	motivated	10.	translated	10.	radical
11.	stirred	11.	reviewed	11.	enlightening
12.	provoked	12.	studied	12.	dense
13.	intrigued	13.	analyzed	13.	thought-provoking
14.	alarmed	14.	examined	14.	significant
15.	shaped	15.	dismissed	15.	rigorous
16.	guided	16.	understood	16.	comprehensive
17.	fascinated	17.	refuted	17.	polemical
18.	informed	18.	praised	18.	controversial
19.	captivated	19.	digested	19.	transformative
20.	provoked	20.	researched	20.	critical
21.	challenged	21.	referenced	21.	pivotal
22.	transformed	22.	challenged	22.	historical
23.	touched	23.	summarized	23.	theoretical
24.	awakened	24.	defended	24.	intricate
25.	stimulated	25.	bought	25.	philosophical

Fig. 5. Querying GPT-4 to complete contexts with plausible actions/relations and properties that can plausibly (sensibly) be said of (or apply to) a book: as an agent of some action or activity, a book can influence, inspire, motivate, educate, etc. people; as the object of some activity, a book can be translated, interpreted, examined, refuted, etc. and finally, a book can have the property (or can be described as being) significant, critical, historical, influential, controversial, etc.

Note that it might be the case that in our ordinary language use we speak of *influential* books more so than we speak of *profound* books. Thus, in general we might have

$$(w_1, \text{influence}) \in \text{book.}\textbf{HasProp}$$
$$(w_2, \text{profoundness}) \in \text{book.}\textbf{HasProp}$$

where $w_1 > w_2$ indicates that influence is used when describing books more than profoundness. The sets along some dimension $\mathbf{D}_1$ therefore look like this:

$$C_1.\mathbf{D}_1 = \{(w_{11}, p_{11}), (w_{12}, p_{12}), \ldots\}$$
$$C_2.\mathbf{D}_1 = \{(w_{21}, p_{21}), (w_{22}, p_{22}), \ldots\}$$

The join for C_1 and C_2 along the dimension $\mathbf{D}_1$ is then computed as follows:

DimensionJoin($C_1, C_2, \mathbf{D}_1$)
$= \{\langle(w_1, p_1), (w_2, p_2)\rangle \mid (p_1 = p_2) \wedge (w_1, p_1) \in C_1 . \mathbf{D}_1 \wedge (w_2, p_2) \in C_2 . \mathbf{D}_1\}$

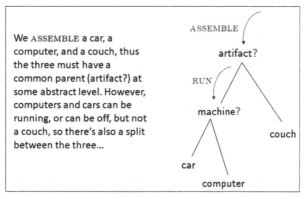

We ASSEMBLE a car, a computer, and a couch, thus the three must have a common parent (artifact?) at some abstract level. However, computers and cars can be running, or can be off, but not a couch, so there's also a split between the three...

Fig. 6. A computer, a car, and a couch can be assembled, so at some level of abstraction they must have a common parent (artifact?). However, cars and computers, although not couches, RUN and can be described by being ON/OFF so they eventually must be in different branches.

ObjectOf	AgentOf	HasProp
John has [MASK] *the* **game**.	*The* **game** [MASK] *everyone*.	*The* **game** *was very* [MASK].
Won	Amazed	Exciting
Enjoyed	Thrilled	Difficult
Lost	Challenged	Enjoyable
Played	Engaged	Frustrating
Started	Entertained	Amazing
Finished	Frustrated	Innovative
Played	Bored	Disappointing
Abandoned	Exhausted	Entertaining
Dominated	Amused	Intriguing
Continued	Relaxed	Boring
Observed	Intrigued	Thrilling
Completed	Captivated	Challenging
Quit	Delighted	Easy
Dominated	Confused	Outstanding
Mastered	Bored	Complicated

Fig. 7. While it is difficult to come up with features that are common to all *games*, we can uncover the descriptions we use in how we talk about games in everyday discourse.

As an example, we might have the following join along the **hasProp** dimension for one meaning of 'book' and one meaning for 'publication':

$$\text{DIMENSIONJOIN}(book_1, publication_3, \textbf{hasProp})$$
$$= \{\langle(0.75, \text{popularity}), (0.72, \text{popularity})\rangle,$$
$$\langle(0.73, \text{controversy}), (0.71, \text{controversy})\rangle, \ldots \}$$

The similarity along the **hasProp** dimension can now be computed as follows:

DIMENSIONJOIN($book_1$, $publication_3$, **hasProp**)
= **sum**([FEATURESIM(p) for p in fs]) / $|fs|$
    where
    fs = FEATURESET($book_1$, $publication_3$, **hasProp**)
    FEATURESIM$\langle(w_1, p_1), (w_2, p_2)\rangle$ = **if** $p_1 = p_2$ **then** $1 - $ **abs**$(w_1 - w_2)$ **else** 0

The final similarity between $book_1$ and $publication_3$ is then a weighted average of the similarity across all dimensions, where, for simplicity, the weights are all equal here:

CSIMILARITY($book_1$, $publication_3$)
= **sum**([DSIMILARITY($book_1$, $publication_3$, **D**) for **D** in $dims$]) / $|dims|$
    where
    $dims$ = {**hasProp, agentOf, objectOf, inState, partOf, …** }

One final note regarding concept similarity is that the above similarity is based on linguistic dimensions – that is, it is a similarity based on how we sensibly speak about concepts in our ordinary language. Thus, it will be expected that a *book* and a *publication*, for example, are quite similar, and not because their vectors are in close proximity in a multidimensional space, but (crucially) because almost anything that can sensibly be said of a book can also be said of a publication, and vice versa. The implications of this change of perspective are substantial. While current LLMs can only account for proximity and similarity, they do not account for concept 'identity' which makes their concept representation circular as has been eloquently pointed out by (Lopes, 2023).

5   Concluding Remarks

While LLMs have shown impressive capabilities in producing coherent and human-like text, these models do not truly 'understand' language and they do not differentiate between factual and nonfactual information. LLMs will also fail in making correct inferences in intensional contexts or in contexts where syntactic patterns with high probabilities must be overruled by semantics and background knowledge. Since it is our firm belief that the relative success of LLMs is due to a successful bottom-up reverse engineering strategy, we suggested in this paper applying this method in a symbolic setting. The reverse-engineering method we proposed allows us also to 'discover' the ontology that seems to be implicit underneath language. The reader is referred to (Saba, 2020) for a detailed discussion on how the system described here can be used to handle most challenges in the semantics of natural language.

References

Aitchison, J.: Words in the Mind – An Introduction to the Mental Lexicon, Wiley (2012)
Asher, N.: Lexical Meaning in Context, a Web of Words. Cambridge University Press (2011)
Asher, N., Pustejovsky, J.: A type composition logic for generative lexicon. Journal of Cognitive Science **6**, 1–38 (2011)

Boleda, G.: Distributional Semantics and Linguistic Theory. Annual Review of Linguistics **6**, 213–234 (2020)

Dummett, M.: Frege: Philosophy of Language. Harvard University Press (1981)

Fodor, J. A. and Pylyshyn, Zenon W.: Connectionism and cognitive architecture: A critical analysis, Cognition, 28 (1), pp. 3–71 (1988)

Hobbs, J.: Ontological promiscuity. In Proc. of the 23rd Annual Meeting of the Assoc. for Computational Linguistics, Chicago, Illinois, 1985, pp. 61–69 (1985)

Harris, Z.S.: Distributional Structure. Word **10**, 146–162 (1954)

Kiss, K. E. and Pafel, J.: Quantifier Scope Ambiguities, In Martin Everaert and Henk C. van Riemsdijk (Eds.), The Wiley Blackwell Companion to Syntax (2017)

Larson, R.: Events and Modification in Nominals, In Devon Strolovitch and Aaron Lawson (eds), SALT VIII, 145- 168, Ithaca, NY (1998)

Lidz, J.: Children's Use of Syntax in Word Learning, In Anna Papafragou, John C. Trueswell & Lila R. Gleitman (eds.), The Oxford Handbook of the Mental Lexicon, Oxford University Press (2022)

Lopes, J.: Can Deep CNNs Avoid Infinte Regress/Circularity in Content Constitution?, Minds and Machines, https://doi.org/10.1007/s11023-023-09642-0 (2023)

McShane, M., Beale, S. and Babkin, P.: Nominal Compound Interpretation by Intelligent Agents, Linguistic Issues in Language Technology (LiLT), vol. 10, No 1 (2014)

Milne, P.: Frege's Context Principle. Mind **95**(380), 491–495 (1986)

Moltmann, F.: Abstract Objects and the Semantics of Natural Language, Oxford University Press (2013)

Peckenpaugh, T.: Prepositional phrase attachment ambiguities in declarative and interrogative contexts: Oral reading data, PhD Thesis, The City University of New York (2019)

Piñango, M.M., Zhang, M., et al.: Metonymy as Referential Dependency: Psycholinguistic and Neurolinguistic Arguments for a Unified Linguistic Treatment. Cogn. Sci.. Sci. **41**(S2), 351–378 (2017)

Saba, W.: New Research Vindicates Fodor and Pylyshyn: No Explainable AI Without 'Structured Semantics, Blog of the Communications of the ACM, September 14 (2022)

Saba, W.: Language, Knowledge and Ontology: Where Formal Semantics Went Wrong, and How to Go Forward, Again. Journal of Knowledge Structures and Systems (JKSS) **1**(1), 40–62 (2020)

Saba, W., Corriveau, J.-P.: Plausible Reasoning and the Resolution of Quantifier Scope Ambiguities, Studia Logica – Int. J. Symb. Log.Symb. Log. **67**, 271–289 (2001)

Saba, W.: Language, logic and ontology: Uncovering the structure of commonsense knowledge. Int. J. of Human Computer Studies **7**(65), 610–623 (2007)

Shelestiuk, H. V.: Metonymy as a tool of cognition and representation: A natural language analysis, Semiotica, pp. 1–20 (2005)

Sommers, F.: Types and ontology. Philos. Rev. **72**(3), 327–363 (1963)

Sugawara, S. and Tsugita. S.: On Degrees of Freedom in Defining and Testing Natural Language Understanding, In Findings of the Association for Computational Linguistics: ACL, pp. 13625–13649 (2023)

Vaswani, A., Shazeer, N., et. al.: Attention is All You Need, In NIPS'17: Proceedings of the 31st Int. Conference on Neural Information Processing Systems. pp. 6000–6010, (2017)

Viebahn, E.: Copredication, polysemy and context-sensitivity, Inquiry, Volume 65 (2020)

von Fintel, K. and Heim, I. Lecture Notes on Intensional Semantics, available online here https://www.phil-fak.uni-duesseldorf.de/summerschool2002/fintel.pdf, (2002)

The Conceptual Modeling Task

A Survey of Ethical Reasoning Methods, Their Metamodels, and a Discussion on Their Application to Conceptual Modelling

Sergio España[1,2(✉)] [ID], Chris van der Maaten[2], Jens Gulden[2] [ID], and Óscar Pastor[1] [ID]

[1] Valencian Research Institute for Artificial Intelligence,
Universitat Politècnica de València, València, Spain
[2] Utrecht University, Utrecht, The Netherlands
{s.espana,j.gulden}@uu.nl

Abstract. There is wide acknowledgement of the benefits we reap from information and communication technology (ICT) in many facets of our lives. But there is also an increasing concern over the negative ethical, social and environmental impacts it sometimes has. This leads many stakeholders, such as conceptual modellers, programmers, users and policy makers, to situations where they need to reason about the ethical implications raised by ICT engineering or usage. This paper offers a survey of ten ethical reasoning methods suitable for the ICT domain. We present the method metamodels we have authored and then validated through expert interviews. We also reflect about the application of such methods within conceptual modelling. We expect to pave the way for further research on reasoning about the ethical implications of ICT, in general, and conceptual models, in particular.

Keywords: Conceptual modelling · Ethics · Ethical reasoning · Sustainability assessment · Method engineering

1 Introduction

Nowadays, there is awareness of the range of positive and negative impacts of information and communication technology (ICT) in business, society and the environment [40]. It is increasingly common to reason ethically about the implications of a specific ICT [10], to incorporate value management during ICT design (e.g, Value Sensitive Design -VSD- [31]), or to compare two or more designs as part of a trade-off analysis of their impacts (e.g. [43,99]), motivated by intrinsic (e.g. engineers' moral values) and extrinsic (societal pressure) factors. In the last decade, several methods have been proposed to perform such ethical reasoning, some specifically targeted at the ICT domain and others adapted

Sergio España is supported by a María Zambrano grant of the Spanish Ministry of Universities, co-funded by the Next Generation EU European Recovery Plan.

J. P. A. Almeida et al. (Eds.): ER 2023, LNCS 14320, pp. 23–44, 2023.
https://doi.org/10.1007/978-3-031-47262-6_2

for or demonstrated to be applicable to the ICT domain (e.g. we have been using these in higher education [44,50,70]). For many ICT engineers, conceptual models play a pivotal role in the analysis and design of ICT, given their potential to be subjected to quality assessments [16,49], different sorts of analyses [68], simulations [75], and transformations or code generation [36,65]. In this paper, we claim that conceptual models can be the subject of ethical assessments. However, to date, there has been no comprehensive survey of existing *ethical reasoning methods for ICT* (that is, methods that aid in ethical reasoning, aimed at the ICT domain), nor a discussion on how they can be applied to conceptual models to discover the ethical implications of ICT conceptualisations and designs.

This paper applies a multivocal literature review to collect a set of such methods, and makes the following contributions:

– A description of each ethical reasoning method, including the method meta-models using Process Deliverable Diagrams (PDDs) [94].
– A discussion on how ethical reasoning methods can be applied to assess conceptual models, along with an example.

We first explain the research method in Sect. 2. We review the literature in Sect. 3. Section 4 presents the ethical reasoning methods we have found so far, and their metamodels. Then, in Sect. 5, we discuss the application of ethical reasoning methods to assess conceptual models. After a discussion of the results (Sect. 6), we conclude the paper and anticipate some future work (Sect. 7).

2   Research Method

Multivocal Literature Review (MLR). We opt for an MLR [32] because grey literature can report valuable methods. We have searched IEEE Xplore, ACM Digital Library, Web of Science, Scopus, and Google Scholar for scientific literature, and Google for grey literature. The search string is constructed from Table 1. We retrieved the first 100 results from each engine. After removing duplicates, we applied inclusion criteria that checks whether it indeed presents an ethical reasoning method for ICT (C1-C3) that is up to date (C4):

– **C1.** As a method, it prescribes a specific way of thinking, consisting of directions and rules, structured in a systematic way in activities with corresponding products [13].
– **C2.** It aids in ethical reasoning, that is the ability to identify, assess, and develop ethical arguments from a variety of ethical positions [88].
– **C3.** Regarding the ICT domain, either of these subconditions holds true:
  • **C3a.** It is specifically aimed for use in ICT-related situations.
  • **C3b.** It comes from a different discipline, but earlier research projects have empirically proven its applicability to the ICT domain.
– **C4.** In the case of method versions, we kept the most recent one.

Table 1. Concepts defining our unit of analysis, along with related terms

Concept	Related terms
Ethical reasoning	Moral reasoning, ethical decision making, moral decision making, moral dilemma, ethical dilemma, ethical impact, ethical evaluation, ethical assessment, incorporating ethics
Method	Methodology, modelling, framework, tool, approach, guideline
ICT	Information and communication technology, IT, ICT ethics, digital ethics, computer ethics, information ethics, cyber ethics, technology ethics

This resulted in 10 studies with their corresponding methods to be analysed. For each study, we performed forward snowballing [97] to collect additional method manuals and studies reporting extensions or validations.

Method Analysis and Metamodelling. For each of the methods, we have performed a perspective-based reading [4] of all sources in order to identify the method background, purpose, process and product descriptions, and applications or validations. We then have metamodelled the methods with Process Deliverable Diagrams (PDD), consisting of a UML Activity Diagram (representing the flow of activities prescribed by the method) and a UML Class Diagram (representing the information structure of the input, intermediate and final products of the method), interlinked with output relationships [94].

Validation of Method Metamodels. The resulting PDDs were first subjected to peer reviewing. Then we conducted expert assessment semi-structured interviews [96, p. 63] with the method creators (i.e. authors of the studies) where we verified the completeness of our method documentation, we validated our understanding of the background and purpose of the method, and we guided the method expert through the PDD, asking whether it represented the method well. We elicited improvement points, asking for explicit changes they would suggest and the rationale behind those changes. Find the detailed protocol in the technical report [24]. We then updated the PDD accordingly, keeping track of the changes in a PDD validation matrix, inspired by [19].

Reflection on the Application to Conceptual Modelling. Some of the reviewed studies discuss assessments of ICT-related products and research. These, along with the analysis of the methods, and our own first-hand experience in teaching and applying the methods, have allowed us to hold a few discussion sessions about the role of ethical reasoning methods within conceptual modelling. Herein, we elaborate on our thoughts, illustrate the application of one method, and include conceptual model sketches and rich pictures [6].

3   Review Results

The review has yielded ten ethical reasoning methods for ICT, summarised in Tables 2 and 3. The *Method* column shows its name and main reference;

Background lists disciplines or theories the method builds upon; we express the method *Purpose*; we summarise its *Process*; *Empiricism* indicates reported endeavours to test or validate the method. For the sake of brevity, we select a couple of methods which have a graphical notation to elaborate on them and offer an example; the technical report provides longer descriptions and examples of each [24].

Architecture Decision Maps [50] are part of the Sustainability Assessment Framework Toolkit [51], and allow framing ICT architecture design concerns around four sustainability dimensions (technical, economic, social and environmental), ascribing these concerns to impact levels (immediate, enabling and systemic, which are equivalent to those in the LES model [40]). The map also expresses positive (+), negative (-), and undecided (unlabelled) cause-effect relationships from the ICT towards the concerns and among concerns, in the fashion of Causal Loop Diagrams [37]. To create the maps, the engineers should engage the stakeholder, ideally in a participatory modelling workshop. Figure 1 shows a decision map depicting the trade-off analysis among the impacts that a mobility as a service (MaaS) system might have, from the perspective of the system users. On the one hand, the `MaaS system` offers a `Flexibility of mobility means` that enables citizens to shift from the `Possession of personal cars`, to relying on other means to ensure their mobility (e.g. public transportation, shared cars and bikes). This is likely to produce the beneficial effect of having less `Cars on road`. On the other hand, since a greater number of people will have access to cars owned by others through the car-sharing feature of the system, they will likely be used more often (meaning more `Cars on road`); but it is unlikely that this would cancel out the overall beneficial effect. During system design, the model represents the stakeholder concerns and agreements elicited during the workshops, but the model assumptions should be supported by earlier empirical evidence or be validated by the engineers.

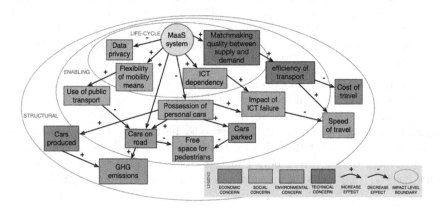

Fig. 1. Example of an Architecture Decision Map of a mobility-as-a-service (MaaS) ICT (own re-creation of model from [50])

Table 2. Summary of ethical reasoning methods (part 1)

Method	Background	Purpose	Process	Empiricism
Architecture Decision Maps [50]	• Sustainability as a software quality [52] • Impact levels of ICT [7,40]	Make sustaina-bility-driven ICT design decisions, despite trade-offs	**1.** Determine sustainability concerns **2.** Determine impact levels of concerns **3.** Relate effects.	• Expert assessment [23] • Action research [50,61]
Design Solution Matrix [44]	• VSD [31] • Virtue Sensitive Design [89] • Regulative ideas as the best possible solutions [45]	Structuredly comparing different ICT designs decisions, from an ethical point of view	**1.** Identify norms ICT should abide by **2.** Identify design fragment affected by each norm. **3.** Define regulative idea **4.** Agree on best feasible solution	• Action research [44]
Square of Values for Business Informatics [70]	• Values as guiding principles [39,86] • Aristotelian virtues [76] • Value synthesis framework [38]	Modelling ethical dilemmas and alternative designs using a quadrant	**1.** Model initial and sister values **2.** Model exaggeration values **3.** Describe current, alternative and negative designs **4.** Discuss options and agree on design	• Action research [70] • Expert assessment in participatory workshop [71]
Ethics Canvas [73]	• Business Model Canvas [64] • Science and Technology Studies [2, 27,42,67,78,91] • VSD [31]	Identify and discuss ethical impacts of technologies and come up with countermeasures.	**1.** Identify stakeholder groups **2.** Consider potential ethical impacts on them **3.** Consider non-stakeholder-specific impacts **4.** Discuss actions to overcome impacts	• Student testing [57] • Action research [41,57,62].
Ethical Dilemma Scenarios [98]	• Scenarios in strategic management [34] and policy making [17]	Collaborate in describing plausible futures where emerging technologies raise ethical issues requiring discussion among stakeholders.	**1.** Create matrix ICT applications⊥ ethical values/issues **2.** Fill in cells **3.** List *sunny, dark, popular push-back* and *unintended consequences* scenarios. **4.** Agree on story line, write scenarios.	• Participatory workshop [98]

The **Square of Values** guides analysts and engineers in visualising, discussing and resolving interests between conflicting values. Each corner of a rectangle represents a different value. Values in the upper corners represent positive intentions and are desirable. However, because they are conflicting, they cannot be achieved at the same time. Values in the lower corners should be avoided and are undesirable. This defines a space where system design options can be geometrically positioned and compared with respect to their proximity to the four values. Figure 2 shows the example of a healthcare management system (HMS). The HMS should allow the healthcare provider `Control` over the patient records,

Table 3. Summary of ethical reasoning methods (part 2)

Method	Background	Purpose	Process	Empiricism
MEESTAR [56]	• Developed during industrial project	Identify ethical issues caused by a socio-technical arrangement (i.e. an ICT in its context of use)	1. Interdisciplinary groups reflect from social, individual, organisational perspectives 2. Identify ethical issues in 7 ethical dimensions 3. Assign stage 1–4 to each dimension	• Action research [48,83,99]
Techno-Ethical Scenarios [11]	• Moral principle of *prudence* [84] • NEST-ethics [85]	Enhance techno-moral imagination to anticipate coevolution of technology and morality	1. Analyse current moral landscape 2. Envision controversies by ICT introduction 3. Determine plausible resolutions 4. Write scenarios	• Method demonstration by authors [11]
Strategy Mapping for ICT [92]	• Strategy maps in Organisational Management [46]	Give stakeholders common understanding of human value tensions in project, and how to estimate, measure and validate. [26,92]	1. Model elements and relationships: (i) ICT owner goals, (ii) customer values, (iii) intended ICT effects, (iv) existing/alternative processes/ICT designs 2. Specify indicators for each element 3. Design monitoring cycle 4. Validate empirically causal relationships	• Action research [18,63,92,93]
Ethical Framework in Information System Decision Making [12]	• Stockholder theory [30] • Stakeholder theory [25] • Social contract theory [20]	Provide framework to examine the ethical dimensions of ICT professionals decisions	1. Define dilemma 2. Adopt the ethical lens of each theory consecutively 3. Combine results.	• Method demonstration [12,54]
Ethical Matrix in Digital Innovation [80]	• Ethical Matrix for biotechnology [59] • Value-Sensitive Design [29]	Provide structural framework to examine the ethical dimensions of ICT professionals decisions	1. Value investigation (e.g. literature review, interviews, workshops) 2. Create matrix of stakeholders⊥values 3. Workshops to identify positive, neutral, and negative impacts of existing, alternative or final ICT designs	• Action research [80,82]

while respecting the `Privacy` according to legal and social standards. Both are considered desirable, but cannot be fully achieved at the same time. Without the balancing tension between both values, the values can easily degenerate into exaggerations; that is, when taken to the extreme, the system could run into `Heteronymy` due to over-control, or `Negligence` due to not storing any data to avoid privacy concerns. The engineers have generated four design scenarios in yellow boxes and placed them close to the values they realise. Two negative scenarios are associated with undesirable values, shown in red boxes. And the main scenario is deemed to find a balance between the two positive values

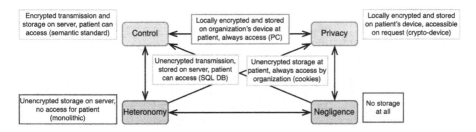

Fig. 2. Example of a an application of the Square of Values method to a healthcare management system (own creation, adapting a model from [70]).

(i.e. locally encrypting and storing while allowing the organisation to access the information), shown in a green box located between the two desirable values.

4 Metamodelling the Ethical Reasoning Methods

4.1 Process Deliverable Diagrams

We decided to create rigorous metamodels that provide a unified view on the examined methods. Process Deliverable Diagrams (PDD) [94] allow us to describe each method in detail and make them comparable among each other, as shown in Fig. 3 and Fig. 4. While metamodelling the process dimension we had to make some assumptions, such as the (total or partial) ordering of activities. With respect to the deliverable dimension, we had to find a balance to the following trade-off: accurately describing the information infrastructure of the method while keeping the elements in the diagram recognisable to method creators. At this point of our long-term research project, we are not yet attempting to develop tool support for the methods, so we made some concessions (e.g. specifying the Ethics Canvas as an aggregation of specialised blocks, rather than modelling it as a single class). To offer a complete method specification, PDDs need to be accompanied by tables that explain each activity and deliverable. For the sake of space, we include these in the technical report [24].

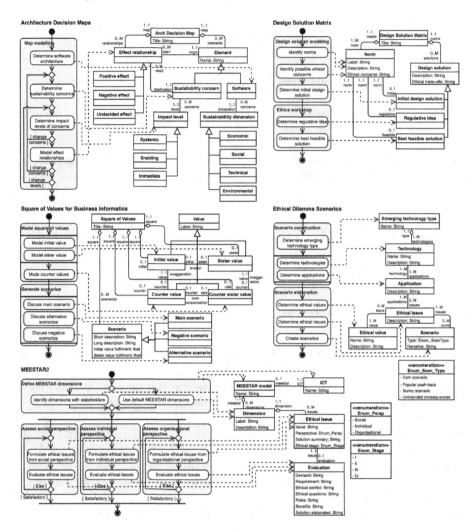

Fig. 3. Process deliverable diagrams of the following methods (left-right and top-down): Architecture Decision Maps, Design Solution Matrix, Square of Values for Business Informatics, Ethical Dilemma Scenarios and MEESTAR. Final versions after validation (own creation).

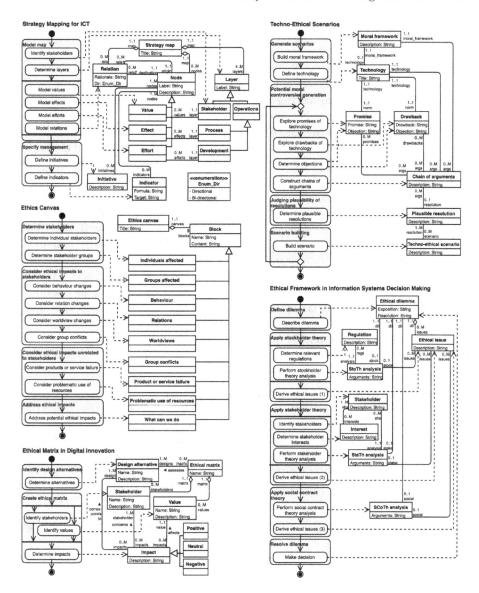

Fig. 4. Process deliverable diagrams of the following methods (left-right and top-down): Strategy Mapping for ICT, Techno-Ethical Scenarios, Ethics Canvas, Ethical Framework in Information Systems Decision Making, and Ethical Matrix in Digital Innovation. Final versions after validation (own creation). We expressed *many* cardinalities with M because earlier experience interviewing non-ICT professionals showed us that they understand it better than *. We keep this notation consistent throughout the paper.

4.2 Validation

We peer-reviewed the PDDs several times within the research team, improving the layout and structure by following good practices for process [58] and information modelling [22], changing the names of some activities, classes and relationships, revising cardinalities and adding role names. Then, we conducted eight interviews with method creators, to validate the PDDs of eight methods, along with their tables. In the case of MEESTAR, we interviewed an experienced method user. Overall, method experts stated that the PDDs reflect the methods well. Some pointed towards slight inaccuracies or proposed concrete changes, such as adding process loopbacks, or improving activity and deliverable descriptions. We revised the diagrams and tables accordingly. The changes are summarised in Table 4. For instance, the PDD of Architecture Decision Maps was not revised after the interview, since the creator deemed it accurate. In turn, the validation of the PDD of Strategy Mapping for ICT led to adding three activities to the process (to reflect the specialisation of a deliverable), changing two flows to make sequential activities unordered, changing tha name of one activity, creating three specialised classes, along with their three specialisation relationships, adding three relationships, changing the name of two classes to more appropriate ones (i.e. Perspective to Layer and Objective to Node), and changing two cardinalities. Overall, the number and nature of the changes make us confident of the accuracy of the metamodels.

5   Application to Conceptual Modelling

Earlier research has demonstrated the utility of conceptual (general-purpose of domain-specific) modelling languages to analyse or design ICT for ethics-related purposes, such as environmental management [47], corporate social responsibility [15], sustainable building design [33], ethical machine learning [100], social-ecological systems [1], and social impact [9]. During our MLR we have not found

Table 4. Matrix indicating how many elements were created (C), updated (U) or deleted (D) in each method metamodel artefact, after the expert validations.

Method	Process			Deliverables			Tables		
	C	U	D	C	U	D	C	U	D
Architecture Decision Maps									
Design Solution Matrix							1		
Square of Values for Business Inform.					4				
Ethics Canvas									
Ethical Dilemma Scenarios		2	2	2			1	2	
MEESTAR2	1	2	1						
Strategy Mapping for ICT	3	3			4				
Ethical Matrix in Digital Innovation			1	1				7	

any evidence of an application of ethical reasoning methods within conceptual modelling. Nonetheless, it is plausible that modellers do sometimes reason about the ethical consequences of their models. Perhaps such reasoning takes place indeliberately or in an unstructured way, triggered by situations where a conceptual model fragment elicits feelings of dissonance or ambivalence in the modeller, when the human values instantiated in the model are incongruent with the human values important to the modeller. Social and experimental psychology has explained the mechanisms by which value incongruence produces feelings of ambivalence [90] or dissonance [81]. Ethical reasoning methods give modellers the opportunity to plan the assessment of the models they are responsible for, or assess them contingently upon a feeling of discomfort. Herein, we further reflect on the role of ethical reasoning methods within conceptual modelling.

Let us define a fictional, illustrative case. A Dutch research institute is developing a software named Cancer Research Management Information System (CaRMISy), to support a research project investigating genetic and contextual factors that increase the probability of developing several types of cancer, using patient samples and clinical data from hospitals. Part of the project studies the prevalence of certain cancers in families. As a result, one fragment of the conceptual model underlying CaRMISy represents a family tree (see Fig. 5). Karin has joined the project recently and is extending the conceptual model with classes devoted to genetic mutations based on the current state of the art [8], when she feels that there is something 'wrong' in the way families are modelled. Apart from finding that the minimum cardinalities of the roles **father** and **mother** do not account for situations where the biological parents are unknown, Karin feels that the model does not match well with some of the families around her. Two of her best friends are a gay couple who have two children: one that was born from one of the fathers with a previous woman partner, and one that the couple have adopted recently. Also, a niece of hers does not feel represented by neither the man nor the woman labels.

Karin decides to apply the Square of Values method (see Fig. 6). Since her husband has recently conducted research on the Theory of Basic Human Values [79], she decides to frame the ethical dilemma in terms of this theory. She selects **Self-direction** as the initial value, representing that CaRMISy should perhaps accommodate to the gender expressions of the research subjects, and **Conformity** as the sister value, since most database designs she has seen in the healthcare domain conformed with binary genders. As an exaggeration value, she opted for **Anarchy**, representing that data would be impossible to analyse properly if

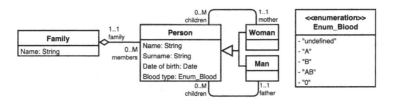

Fig. 5. Controversial fragment of a conceptual model of the illustrative case.

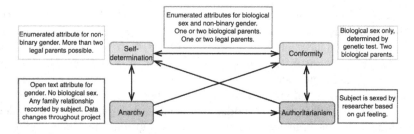

Fig. 6. Application of the Square of Values method in the illustrative case.

subjects were given the chance to describe their perceived gender in an unconstrained open text field. For the other one, she chose `Authoritarianism`, and she entertained the idea that the researchers themselves would sex the subjects based on gut feeling. She did not spend much more thought on negative scenarios, and instead concentrated on alternative scenarios, in search for some balance among the positive values. After considering what scenarios would embody the `Self-direction` and `Conformity` values and even drafting some conceptual model fragments realising such designs, she came up with a solution that felt like a reasonable trade-off: (i) including attributes for biological sex and non-binary gender, which would have enumerated data types, (ii) the model would include relationships to express both the biological and legal parents. She considered whether to open the model to the possibility of more than two legal parents, given that the Dutch government had been recommended to reform the law to recognise plus-two-parent families [14]. But she left that for an alternative scenario; she also did not want to push too far before getting to know her project colleagues better. Afterwards, Karin revised the conceptual model (see Fig. 7) and presented it to the CaRMISy project manager, who agreed to the changes. It became clear that the research team was not willing to do genetic tests to determine the biological sex during the intake process, but rather rely on the subjects self-reporting; only in the case when phenotypic traits did not match the reported sex, they would politely inquire the subject further. They agreed that including gender information would make subjects more comfortable than merely asking about sex, since it would offer some chance for gender expression. The conversation with her manager went on for one hour and they ended up agreeing to further revise the model and (later) the user interface designs, to account respectfully for transgender situations [3].

The example shows a conceptual modeller resorting to an ethical reasoning method for ICT, when confronted with an ethical dilemma, during conceptual modelling activities. We propose to distinguish the moments, relative to conceptual modelling, when the methods are applied, adopting categories from [74]:

– **Ex ante.** Before starting the conceptual modelling (e.g. when just a vision for the ICT is available), as a way to detect potential value conflicts, impacts, or ethical dilemmas of the envisioned ICT, then informing the conceptual modelling activities in the form of requirements, constraints or just warnings.

- **Intra.** During or right after conceptual modelling or right after producing the pre-final version, as a one-time or recurrent reflection where versions or fragments of the conceptual model are assessed. It likely results in changes to the conceptual model and in rationale for some modelling decisions.
- **Ex post.** Assessing the system already in use. If relevant impacts or ethical concerns are detected, a feedback loop towards conceptual modelling allows correcting the issues and reengineering the ICT implementation.

The example above relates a case of an *intra* application. Figure 8 provides an overview of these different contexts of use. Stakeholder groups and other elements in the domain provide knowledge that is key to the processes depicted below. Ethical reasoning methods enable a cycle safeguarding the ethical integrity of the conceptual model.

Figure 9 shows a draft of the conceptual model that underlies Fig. 8. As research in this area progresses, the community will propose or discover more concepts, details and relationships. For instance, it is likely that the results of applying a method in a (fragment of a) conceptual model will point directly to specific elements of the model, either highlighting them as ethically problematic or expressing a sustainability or ethical trade-off among two or more elements (or fragments). Some methods are clearly judging designs (e.g. the Design Solution Matrix); in such cases it is probably easy to assign (fragments of) a conceptual model to cells of the matrix. Some methods assess the ICT as a black box

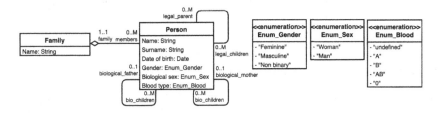

Fig. 7. Conceptual model fragment, after the main scenario of the Square of Values.

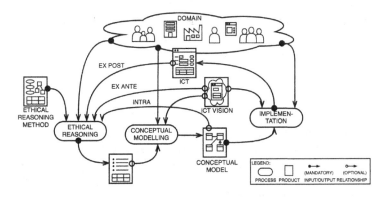

Fig. 8. Contexts of use of ethical reasoning methods within conceptual modelling.

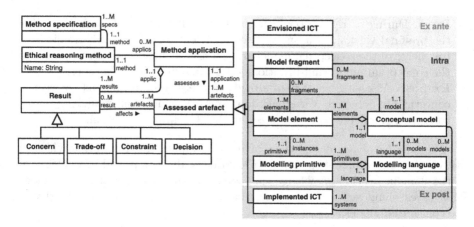

Fig. 9. Conceptual model of ethical reasoning methods within conceptual modelling.

(e.g. Techno-Ethical Scenarios); then it might be necessary to build a bridge between the results of the method and the conceptual model. This will perhaps require an extension of the method in the form of an activity that elicits and documents the requirements or constraints that will affect the conceptual model (in *ex ante* situations), or that performs a change impact analysis identifying the elements of the model that are affected (in *intra* or *ex post* situations). We expect traceability and model evolution analysis to play a role here [77].

6   Discussion

6.1   Interpretation of the Results

This research is located at the cross-point of ICT ethics and conceptual modelling, involving a method engineering approach. The foundation for reasoning about ethical consequences of ICT was laid by Wiener in the book "The human use of human beings" [95]. In 1978, Maner [55] defined the field of Computer Ethics and developed curriculum materials and pedagogical advice for university lecturers. The information revolution sparked interest on this field (e.g. [60]) and there has been an increase in such research during the last decade [10]. Reasoning about the ethical consequences of ICT is a subdiscipline of applied ethics, the application of ethical principles in practical situations [10,66]. When defining the scope of our method survey, we opened it to sustainability reasoning methods, such as Architecture Decision Maps, based on the widespread regard of sustainability either being a field within applied ethics [5, p. 18] or being linked by important conceptual and operational relationships to ethics [87].

Most of the studies we collected during the MLR present methods that have been specifically engineered to assess ICT, with the exception of the Square of Values and Strategy Mapping, which were nonetheless included thanks to condition C3b (Sect. 2). The studies described the methods textually, with some diagrams representing aspects of the method (e.g. MEESTAR is often represented as a cube). We only found a metamodel for Architecture Decision Maps [51], which covers just the deliverable dimension. During the expert interview, the method creator expressed that our metamodel is equally valid.

Different methods refer as *value* to different things. In the context of Value-Sensitive Design, human values refer to "what is important to people in their lives, with a focus on ethics and morality" [28, 4]; Design Solution Matrix focuses on norms used to refer to ICT behaviours ought to be considered valid by project stakeholders; within Strategy Mapping for ICT, values also encompass stakeholder goals such as "Quicker response" of the ICT [92]. Similarly, the focus of the ethical issues and values differs across methods, some embracing sustainability more explicitly (e.g. Architecture Decision Maps) than others (e.g. MEESTAR2). However, all methods fall within the realm of ethical reasoning by offering guidelines to elicit such concerns from the affected stakeholders or by putting the method user in the skin of the stakeholders, guiding a reflection on the effects of the ICT, and spotting where there is a need or a space for improvement. Some methods also offer means to propose design solutions.

6.2 Limitations and Threats to Validity

As in any structured literature review, we can claim that we have followed a rigorous procedure but we are careful not to make strong claims concerning the completeness of our results. In fact, we are aware that some methods have fallen out of our radar. We discovered a couple while writing this article. For instance, the Ethical OS toolkit, which intends to help ICT practitioners to reflect on the possible unintended consequences of their work [53], especially regarding dark user experience patterns [35]. In future iterations of this research, they shall be considered in order to provide a more comprehensive method repository. There are also methods which allow for ethical reasoning which, even when they are not specifically designed for the ICT domain, they could in principle be applied. This of course, requires validating such assumption. Among them we find Consequence Scanning [21] and the RRI Roadmap [69].

To validate the method information and PDDs, we approached method creators because we expect them to have the most detailed and accurate knowledge about the method, including the goals and method design rationale, which may not be described in the paper. The creators of two methods declined or ignored our interview invitation. Finally, when determining the extent to which the methods have been investigated empirically, we have considered that an application of a method by researchers in the context of a real project is action research, without judging the quality of the protocol they applied.

7   Conclusions

This paper presents a survey of ethical reasoning methods for the ICT domain, that we collected through a multi-vocal literature review. Their metamodelling offers opportunities to incorporate them within conceptual modelling practices and research.

We have placed a foundation stone upon which other projects can be defined. We now outline a few. The method base can be extended with additional ones that have escaped our review or might arise in the future. Some authors might be interested in modifying our definition of ethical reasoning methods for ICT to expand or shift the scope. Also, studying the characteristics of the methods might help discover which are more suitable to *ex ante*, *intra* or *ex post* situations, which are scalable in terms of participants, which facilitate trade-off analysis among the concerns of several stakeholder groups or which focus on ethical dilemmas confronting just two concerns. We plan to adopt a situational method engineering approach to investigate the situational factors that make one method preferable over another one when confronted with a given ICT engineering or ethical assessment, so as to guide engineers, analysts and other stakeholders in selecting the method that better suits their context.

It will be insightful to empirically evaluate ethical reasoning methods for ICT under controlled circumstances or in actual practice, with a single or multiple users, applying them to different ICT artefacts (e.g. visions, requirements, conceptual models, beta versions, deployed systems). Comparing the performance will allow discovering their strengths, weaknesses, trade-offs and sensitivities. It is also relevant to investigate the loopback cycle that conceptual modellers enact in cases where the model is subject to ethical reasoning while being created. Similarly, we find it relevant to investigate situations in which more than one method is applied simultaneously or sequentially over the same or different versions of a conceptual model, how to do this efficiently, and study the strengths and weaknesses of such method combinations. This can be addressed by applying situational method construction approaches [19, 72]. Lastly, the development of tools that support these methods might facilitate their integration with conceptual modelling. We are interested in investigating whether engineering domain-specific language editors and other supporting technologies influences the applicability of the methods and the performance of the method users.

Such empirical research will eventually lead to developing a theory on the application of ethical reasoning methods within conceptual modelling, which should probably be grounded on complementary disciplines (e.g. Philosophy, Cognitive Psychology, Ontology). We are hopeful that these research avenues will contribute to assisting conceptual modellers in conducting their professions with greater commitment to ethics and sustainability.

Acknowledgements. We are thankful to the interviewees, for their time and for sharing their method knowledge with us. Also to the students of Responsible ICT (Master in Business Informatics, Utrecht University), for their insightful comments on some of the methods.

References

1. Adamo, G., Willis, M.: Conceptual integration for social-ecological systems. In: Guizzardi, R., Ralyté, J., Franch, X. (eds.) RCIS 2022. LNBIP, pp. 321–337. Springer, Cham (2022). https://doi.org/10.1007/978-3-031-05760-1_19
2. Akrich, M.: The de-scription of technical objects (1992)
3. Barnes, H., Morris, E., Austin, J.: Trans-inclusive genetic counseling services: recommendations from members of the transgender and non-binary community. J. Genet. Couns. **29**(3), 423–434 (2020)
4. Basili, V.R., et al.: The empirical investigation of perspective-based reading. Empir. Softw. Eng. **1**, 133–164 (1996)
5. Becker, C.: Sustainability Ethics and Sustainability Research. Springer, Cham (2011). https://doi.org/10.1007/978-94-007-2285-9
6. Bell, S., Morse, S.: How people use rich pictures to help them think and act. Systemic Pract. Action Res. **26**, 331–348 (2013)
7. Berkhout, F., Hertin, J.: Impacts of information and communication technologies on environmental sustainability: speculations and evidence. Report to the OECD, Brighton 21 (2001)
8. Bernasconi, A., García, S.A., Ceri, S., Pastor, O.: A comprehensive approach for the conceptual modeling of genomic data. In: Ralyté, J., Chakravarthy, S., Mohania, M., Jeusfeld, M.A., Karlapalem, K. (eds.) ER 2022. LNCS, vol. 13607, pp. 194–208. Springer, Cham (2022). https://doi.org/10.1007/978-3-031-17995-2_14
9. Betz, S., Fritsch, A., Oberweis, A.: TracyML-a modeling language for social impacts of product life cycles. In: ER 2017 Forum/Demos, pp. 179–192 (2017)
10. Bock, A.C., España, S., Gulden, J., Jahn, K., Nweke, L.O., Richter, A.: The ethics of information systems: the present state of the discussion and avenues for future work. In: 21st European Conference on Information Systems (ECIS 2021). Association for Information Systems (2021)
11. Boenink, M., Swierstra, T., Stemerding, D.: Anticipating the interaction between technology and morality: a scenario study of experimenting with humans in bionanotechnology. Stud. Ethics Law Technol. **4**(2) (2010)
12. Bose, U.: An ethical framework in information systems decision making using normative theories of business ethics. Ethics Inf. Technol. **14**, 17–26 (2012)
13. Brinkkemper, S.: Method engineering: engineering of information systems development methods and tools. Inf. Softw. Technol. **38**(4), 275–280 (1996)
14. Cammu, N.: 'Legal multi-parenthood' in context: experiences of parents in light of the Dutch proposed family law reforms. Family & Law **07** (2019)
15. Campos, C., Grangel, R.: A domain-specific modelling language for corporate social responsibility (CSR). Comput. Ind. **97**, 97–110 (2018)
16. Cherfi, S.S.-S., Akoka, J., Comyn-Wattiau, I.: Conceptual modeling quality - from EER to UML schemas evaluation. In: Spaccapietra, S., March, S.T., Kambayashi, Y. (eds.) ER 2002. LNCS, vol. 2503, pp. 414–428. Springer, Heidelberg (2002). https://doi.org/10.1007/3-540-45816-6_38
17. Costa, O.D., Boden, M., Friedewald, M.: Science and technology roadmapping for policy intelligence: lessons for future projects. In: The Second Prague Workshop on Futures Studies Methodology, pp. 146–161 (2005)
18. Cöster, M., Olve, N.G., Walldius, Å.: Usability and strategic logic in information systems: supporting insight and action in IT-enabled change. In: Nordisk Workshop 17 i Ekonomi-och Verksamhetsstyrning, Uppsala 2012 (2012)

19. Deneckère, R., Hug, C., Onderstal, J., Brinkkemper, S.: Method association app-roach: situational construction and evaluation of an implementation method for software products. In: IEEE 9th International Conference on Research Challenges in Information Science (RCIS 2015), pp. 274–285 (2015). https://doi.org/10.1109/RCIS.2015.7128888

20. Donaldson, T.: Corporations and Morality. Prentice-Hall (1982)

21. doteveryone: Consequence Scanning: an agile event for responsible innovators v1. Technical report, TechTransformed (2019)

22. Eichelberger, H., Schmid, K.: Guidelines on the aesthetic quality of UML class diagrams. Inf. Softw. Technol. **51**(12), 1686–1698 (2009)

23. España, S., Lago, P.: Software Sustainability Assessment (SoSA) exercise report. Technical report, Vrije Universiteit Amsterdam (2016)

24. España, S., van der Maaten, C., Gulden, J., Pastor, Ó.: Ethical reasoning methods for ICT: the technical report. Technical report, OSF Preprints (2023). https://doi.org/10.31219/osf.io/ebmtp

25. Evan, W.M., Freeman, R.E.: A stakeholder theory of the modern corporation: Kantian capitalism. In: Beauchamp, T.L., Bowie, N. (eds.) Ethical Theory and Business, 3rd edn., pp. 97–106. Prentice-Hall (1988)

26. Falk, T., Petri, C.-J., Roy, J., Walldius, Å.: Illustrating an organisation's strategy as a map. In: Nilsson, F., Petri, C.-J., Westelius, A. (eds.) Strategic Management Control. MP, pp. 9–30. Springer, Cham (2020). https://doi.org/10.1007/978-3-030-38640-5_2

27. Feenberg, A.: Questioning Technology. Routledge (2012)

28. Friedman, B., Hendry, D.G.: Value Sensitive Design: Shaping Technology with Moral Imagination. MIT Press, Cambridge (2019)

29. Friedman, B., Kahn Jr., P.H., Borning, A.: Value Sensitive Design and Informa-tion Systems, chap. 4, pp. 69–101. Wiley (2008)

30. Friedman, M.: Capitalism and Freedom. University of Chicago press (2020)

31. Friedman, P.B., Kahn, H., Borning, A.: Value sensitive design and information systems. In: The Ethics of Information Technologies, pp. 289–313. Routledge (2020)

32. Garousi, V., Felderer, M., Mäntylä, M.V.: The need for multivocal literature reviews in software engineering: complementing systematic literature reviews with grey literature. In: 20th International Conference on Evaluation and Assessment in Software Engineerin (EASE 2016). ACM (2016)

33. Geyer, P.: Systems modelling for sustainable building design. Adv. Eng. Inform. **26**(4), 656–668 (2012)

34. Godet, M.: The art of scenarios and strategic planning: tools and pitfalls. Technol. Forecast. Soc. Chang. **65**(1), 3–22 (2000)

35. Gray, C.M., Kou, Y., Battles, B., Hoggatt, J., Toombs, A.L.: The dark (patterns) side of UX design. In: Proceedings of the 2018 CHI Conference on Human Factors in Computing Systems, pp. 1–14 (2018)

36. Gulden, J.: Methodical support for model-driven software engineering with enter-prise models. Ph.D. thesis, Universität Duisburg-Essen, Berlin (2013)

37. Haraldsson, H.V.: Introduction to system thinking and causal loop diagrams. Department of Chemical Engineering, Lund University Lund, Sweden (2004)

38. Hartmann, N.: Ethik. W. de Gruyter (1926)

39. Helwig, P.: Charakterologie. Herder-Bücherei, Freiburg, Basel, Wien (1967)

40. Hilty, L.M., Aebischer, B.: ICT for sustainability: an emerging research field. In: Hilty, L.M., Aebischer, B. (eds.) ICT Innovations for Sustainability. AISC, vol.

310, pp. 3–36. Springer, Cham (2015). https://doi.org/10.1007/978-3-319-09228-7_1

41. Hogan, G., et al.: Can a blockchain-based MaaS create business value? Multidisc. Digit. Publ. Inst. Proc. **28**(1), 8001 (2019)

42. Ihde, D.: Postphenomenology and Technoscience: The Peking University Lectures. SUNY Press (2009)

43. Jagroep, E.A., et al.: Software energy profiling: comparing releases of a software product. In: 38th International Conference on Software Engineering (ICSE 2016), pp. 523–532. Association for Computing Machinery (2016)

44. Jahn, K., et al.: More than ticking off a checklist? Towards an approach for quantifying the effectiveness of responsible innovation in the design process. In: Second International Workshop on Ethics and Morality in Business Informatics (EMoWI 2020), 15th International Conference on Wirtschaftsinformatik, pp. 311–320 (2020)

45. Kant, I.: Critique of Pure Reason: Unified Edition (with all Variants from the 1781 and 1787 Editions). Hackett Publishing Company, Inc. (1996). Translated by Werner S. Pluhar

46. Kaplan, R.S., Norton, D.P., et al.: Having trouble with your strategy? Then map it. Harv. Bus. Rev. **78**(5), 167–176 (2000)

47. Khaiter, P., Erechtchoukova, M.: Conceptualizing an environmental software modeling framework for sustainable management using UML. J. Environ. Inform. **34**(2) (2019)

48. Klein, B., Schlömer, I.: A robotic shower system: acceptance and ethical issues. Zeitschrift Gerontol. Geriatrie **51**, 25–31 (2018)

49. Krogstie, J., Sindre, G., Jørgensen, H.: Process models representing knowledge for action: a revised quality framework. Eur. J. Inf. Syst. **15**, 91–102 (2006)

50. Lago, P.: Architecture design decision maps for software sustainability. In: IEEE/ACM 41st International Conference on Software Engineering: Software Engineering in Society (ICSE-SEIS 2019), pp. 61–64 (2019). https://doi.org/10.1109/ICSE-SEIS.2019.00015

51. Lago, P., Condori-Fernandez, N.: The sustainability assessment framework (SAF) toolkit: instruments to help sustainability-driven software architecture design decision making (2022). https://github.com/S2-group/SAF-Toolkit

52. Lago, P., Koçak, S.A., Crnkovic, I., Penzenstadler, B.: Framing sustainability as a property of software quality. Commun. ACM **58**(10), 70–78 (2015)

53. Lilley, M., Currie, A., Pyper, A., Attwood, S.: Using the ethical OS toolkit to mitigate the risk of unintended consequences. In: Stephanidis, C., Antona, M., Ntoa, S. (eds.) HCII 2020. CCIS, vol. 1293, pp. 77–82. Springer, Cham (2020). https://doi.org/10.1007/978-3-030-60700-5_10

54. Manaf, P.A., Suryadi, S.: Stakeholder marketing deficiency: a practical synthesis on ethical issue during Indonesian banking industry agency era. J. Bus. Strategy Execut. **10**(1), 1–15 (2018)

55. Maner, W.: Starter kit in computer ethics. Helvetia Press and the National Information and Resource Center for Teaching Philosophy (1980)

56. Manzeschke, A., Weber, K., Rother, E., Fangerau, H.: Ethical questions in the area of age appropriate assisting systems. VDI/VDE Innovation + Technik GmbH (2015)

57. McGinn, C.: Informing the design of HRI systems through use of the Ethics Canvas. In: Proceedings of the Workshop Dangerous HRI: Testing Real-World Robots has Real-World Consequences ACM/IEEE International Conference on Human-Robot Interaction (2019)

58. Mendling, J., Reijers, H., van der Aalst, W.: Seven process modeling guidelines (7PMG). Inf. Softw. Technol. **52**(2), 127–136 (2010)
59. Mepham, B.: A framework for the ethical analysis of novel foods: the ethical matrix. J. Agric. Environ. Ethics **12**(2), 165 (2000)
60. Moor, J.H.: What is computer ethics? Metaphilosophy **16**(4), 266–275 (1985)
61. Niggebrugge, T., Vos, S., Lago, P.: The sustainability of mobility as a service solutions evaluated through the software sustainability assessment method. Technical report, Vrije Universiteit Amsterdam (2018)
62. O'Brien, C., O'Mara, M., Issartel, J., McGinn, C.: Exploring the design space of therapeutic robot companions for children. In: Proceedings of the 2021 ACM/IEEE International Conference on Human-Robot Interaction, HRI 2021, pp. 243–251. Association for Computing Machinery, New York (2021)
63. Öhrwall Rönnbäck, A., Demir, R., Walldius, Å.: A reflection on openness in collaborative product development. In: The 4th ISPIM Innovation Symposium: Managing Innovation for Sustained Productivity: Creating Advantage and Resilience, Wellington (2011)
64. Osterwalder, A., Pigneur, Y.: Business Model Generation: A Handbook for Visionaries, Game Changers, and Challengers, vol. 1. Wiley, Hoboken (2010)
65. Panach, J.I., et al.: Evaluating model-driven development claims with respect to quality: a family of experiments. IEEE Trans. Softw. Eng. **47**(1), 130–145 (2018)
66. Petersen, T.S., Ryberg, J.: Applied ethics. In: Oxford Bibliographies. Oxford University Press (2019)
67. Pinch, T.J., Bijker, W.E.: The social construction of facts and artefacts: or how the sociology of science and the sociology of technology might benefit each other. Soc. Stud. Sci. **14**(3), 399–441 (1984)
68. Polyvyanyy, A., van der Werf, J.M.E.M., Overbeek, S., Brouwers, R.: Information systems modeling: language, verification, and tool support. In: Giorgini, P., Weber, B. (eds.) CAiSE 2019. LNCS, vol. 11483, pp. 194–212. Springer, Cham (2019). https://doi.org/10.1007/978-3-030-21290-2_13
69. Porcari, A., Pimponi, D., Borsella, E., Mantovani, E.: RRI-CSR roadmap (PRISMA project deliverable 5.2). Technical report, PRISMA (2019)
70. Rachmann, A.: Das wertequadrat als werkzeug der wirtschaftsinformatik. In: First International Workshop on Ethics and Morality in Business Informatics (EMoWI 2019), 14th International Conference on Wirtschaftsinformatik, pp. 42–48 (2019)
71. Rachmann, A., Gulden, J.: Preface: ViVaRE!'23-workshop on virtues and values in requirements engineering. In: Joint Proceedings of REFSQ-2023 Workshops, Doctoral Symposium, Posters & Tools Track and Journal Early Feedback, vol. 3378. CEUR (2023)
72. Ralyté, J., Rolland, C.: An assembly process model for method engineering. In: Dittrich, K.R., Geppert, A., Norrie, M.C. (eds.) CAiSE 2001. LNCS, vol. 2068, pp. 267–283. Springer, Heidelberg (2001). https://doi.org/10.1007/3-540-45341-5_18
73. Reijers, W., Koidl, K., Lewis, D., Pandit, H.J., Gordijn, B.: Discussing ethical impacts in research and innovation: the ethics canvas. In: Kreps, D., Ess, C., Leenen, L., Kimppa, K. (eds.) HCC13 2018. IAICT, vol. 537, pp. 299–313. Springer, Cham (2018). https://doi.org/10.1007/978-3-319-99605-9_23
74. Reijers, W., et al.: Methods for practising ethics in research and innovation: a literature review, critical analysis and recommendations. Sci. Eng. Ethics **24**, 1437–1481 (2018)
75. Robinson, S.: Conceptual modelling for simulation part II: a framework for conceptual modelling. J. Oper. Res. Soc. **59**(3), 291–304 (2008)

76. Ross, W., Aristotle, Brown, L.: Nicomachean Ethics (Oxford World's Classics). Oxford University Press, Oxford (2009)
77. Ruiz, M., España, S., Pastor, Ó., Gonz, A., et al.: Supporting organisational evolution by means of model-driven reengineering frameworks. In: IEEE 7th International Conference on Research Challenges in Information Science (RCIS), pp. 1–10. IEEE (2013)
78. Schot, J., Rip, A.: The past and future of constructive technology assessment. Technol. Forecast. Soc. Chang. **54**(2–3), 251–268 (1997)
79. Schwartz, S.H., et al.: An overview of the Schwartz theory of basic values. Online Read. Psychol. Cult. **2**(1), 2307–0919 (2012)
80. van der Stappen, E., van Steenbergen, M.: The ethical matrix in digital innovation projects in higher education. In: BLED 2020 Proceedings, p. 20 (2020)
81. Steele, C.M., Liu, T.J.: Dissonance processes as self-affirmation. J. Pers. Soc. Psychol. **45**(1), 5 (1983)
82. van Steenbergen, M., van der Spoel, I.: Online proctoring: Adding human values to the equation. In: BLED 2021 Proceedings, p. 44 (2021)
83. Strenge, B., Schack, T.: AWOSE-a process model for incorporating ethical analyses in agile systems engineering. Sci. Eng. Ethics **26**, 851–870 (2020)
84. Swierstra, T., Rip, A.: Nano-ethics as nest-ethics: patterns of moral argumentation about new and emerging science and technology. NanoEthics **1**, 3–20 (2007)
85. Swierstra, T., Rip, A. Nano-ethics as NEST-ethics: patterns of moral argumentation about new and emerging science and technology. Nanoethics **1**, 3–20 (2007). https://doi.org/10.1007/s11569-007-0005-8
86. von Thun, F.S.: Miteinander reden 2: Stile, Werte und Persönlichkeitsentwicklung: Differentielle Psychologie der Kommunikation, vol. 2. Rowohlt Verlag GmbH (2013)
87. Torelli, R.: Sustainability, responsibility and ethics: Different concepts for a single path. Soc. Responsib. J. **17**(5), 719–739 (2020)
88. Wesleyan University: Ethics in society. https://www.wesleyan.edu/ethics/reason.html. Accessed 05 May 2023
89. Vallor, S.: Technology and the Virtues: A Philosophical Guide to a Future Worth Wanting. Oxford University Press, Oxford (2016)
90. Van Harreveld, F., Van der Pligt, J., De Liver, Y.N.: The agony of ambivalence and ways to resolve it: introducing the maid model. Pers. Soc. Psychol. Rev. **13**(1), 45–61 (2009)
91. Verbeek, P.P.: What Things Do: Philosophical Reflections on Technology, Agency, and Design. Penn State Press (2005)
92. Walldius, Å.: Strategy mapping: a method for making value tensions explicit in design and deployment of IT systems. Ethics Inf. Technol. **23**, 45–48 (2021)
93. Walldius, C.Å., Lantz, A.: Exploring the use of design pattern maps for aligning new technical support to new clinical team meeting routines. Behav. Inf. Technol. **32**(1), 68–79 (2013)
94. van de Weerd, I., Brinkkemper, S.: Meta-modeling for situational analysis and design methods. In: Handbook of Research on Modern Systems Analysis and Design Technologies and Applications, pp. 35–54. IGI Global (2009)
95. Wiener, N.: The Human Use of Human Beings. Houghton-Mifflin (1950)
96. Wieringa, R.J.: Design Science Methodology for Information Systems and Software Engineering. Springer, Cham (2014). https://doi.org/10.1007/978-3-662-43839-8

97. Wohlin, C.: Guidelines for snowballing in systematic literature studies and a replication in software engineering. In: 18th International Conference on Evaluation and Assessment in Software Engineering, pp. 1–10 (2014)
98. Wright, D., et al.: Ethical dilemma scenarios and emerging technologies. Technol. Forecast. Soc. Chang. **87**, 325–336 (2014)
99. Wutzkowsky, J., Böckmann, B.: Using MEESTAR to identify ethical and social issues implementing a digital patient-centered care platform. In: 12th eHealth, pp. 278–285 (2018)
100. Zucker, J., d'Leeuwen, M.: Arbiter: a domain-specific language for ethical machine learning. In: Proceedings of the AAAI/ACM Conference on AI, Ethics, and Society, pp. 421–425. Association for Computing Machinery (2020)

Use of Competency Questions in Ontology Engineering: A Survey

Glaice Kelly Q. Monfardini[1,2](✉) , Jordana S. Salamon[1] ,
and Monalessa P. Barcellos[1]

[1] Ontology and Conceptual Modeling Research Group (NEMO), Computer Science
Department, Federal University of Espírito Santo, Vitoria, Brazil
{jssalamon,monalessa}@inf.ufes.br
[2] Federal Institute of Espírito Santo, Vitoria, Brazil
glaice.monfardini@ifes.edu.br

Abstract. The interest in the ontology subject has grown in recent decades. Ontologies can be used to assign semantics to information items and solve interoperability and knowledge-related problems. Many methods have been proposed to improve the ontology engineering process. The use of competence questions (CQs) is suggested by several of them as a means to define the ontology requirements and help identify the necessary concepts, properties, and relations. CQs are questions that the ontology should be able to answer. Thus, they provide a mechanism to verify if the ontology is in accordance with the established requirements and properly represents the desired knowledge. Despite the important role of CQs, there is a lack of deeper investigation to provide evidence about their use. Therefore, aiming to investigate how CQs have been used in ontology engineering practice, we performed a survey with 63 ontology engineers. The results indicate that CQs have helped mainly to define the ontology scope and evaluate the ontology conceptualization. However, ontology engineers still face difficulties when writing, using, and managing CQs. Although there is a range of methods and tools that support ontology development, guidance regarding CQs is still limited. This paper presents our study and discusses its main findings.

Keywords: Competency Questions · Ontology · Survey

1 Introduction

An ontology is a formal representation of a common conceptualization of a universe of discourse [17]. Ontologies have been a useful instrument for reducing conceptual ambiguities, making knowledge structures transparent, supporting knowledge sharing and interoperability between systems [49]. They have been successfully used in several domains, such as IT Service Management [30], Health [38], Education [52], and Software Engineering [4]. Nowadays, ontology engineers are supported by a wide range of ontology engineering (OE) methods and tools. However, building ontologies is still a complex task even for experts [27].

J. P. A. Almeida et al. (Eds.): ER 2023, LNCS 14320, pp. 45–64, 2023.
https://doi.org/10.1007/978-3-031-47262-6_3

To assist ontology engineers in the ontology development process, ontology engineering methods break it into other processes and recommend activities for each one [20]. Although methods differ in many aspects, they often include a process or activity addressing requirements specification, when the ontology scope, intended uses, users, and competence are established [50]. Some methods suggest defining the ontology requirements by means of competency questions (CQs) specified in natural language (e.g., [9, 28, 31, 43]). CQs encompass the purpose of the knowledge base and suggest the concepts and relationships to be included in the ontology [2]. They can also be used in later stages of ontology development to verify and validate the knowledge represented by the ontology aiming to ensure that the ontology correctly reflects the real world [15].

Despite the important role CQs play in ontology engineering, there is a lack of consensual and detailed guidance on how to identify, write, and use them [1, 50]. Even works that address how to specify ontology requirements (e.g., [1, 11, 33, 44, 50]), point out that it is still necessary to deepen studies about CQs. This can lead to doubts, contradictions, oversights, and ambiguities when defining CQs. Not discovering and properly defining CQs early in ontology development may result in a poorly specified ontology, increasing the time and effort spent in the development process [1, 10] and hampering ontology quality [10, 11].

Exploring CQs in ontology development is not a new idea itself. However, a broader spectrum of CQs and their utility in ontology engineering has not been investigated in depth [36]. To take a step in this direction, we decided to investigate the use of CQs in ontology engineering practice. For that, we performed a survey with 63 ontology engineers aiming to understand how they have used CQs when developing ontologies, the perceived benefits, and faced difficulties. The results provide a preliminary panoramic picture of the state of practice of the use of CQs in ontology engineering. With this panorama, we intend to share practices and perceptions with other ontology engineers and shine a light on research opportunities to provide advances in the research topic.

In summary, the results corroborate statements from the literature (e.g., [9, 12, 15, 28, 33, 43]) by showing that CQs have been used mainly in requirements specification and ontology evaluation and, thus, help define the ontology scope and evaluate the ontology conceptualization. Moreover, most of the time they have been defined iteratively and refined along the ontology development process. Time constraints have been the main reason for not using CQs and there is a lack of supporting tools. Furthermore, guidance on how to define and use CQs is still limited, which causes ontology engineers to face difficulties when writing, using, and managing CQs.

In this paper, we provide an overview of our study, summarize the main findings, and discuss the results. It is organized as follows: Sect. 2 presents the theoretical background for the paper; Sect. 3 presents the study protocol; Sect. 4 synthesizes the results; Sect. 5 discusses the results; Sect. 6 addresses the study limitations; and Sect. 7 presents our final considerations.

2   Ontologies and Competency Questions

An ontology is a formal and explicit specification of a shared conceptualization [41]. The conceptualization is an abstract and simplified view of the world which is intended to be represented for some reason. Every knowledge base, knowledge-based system, or knowledge level agent is committed, either explicitly or implicitly, with one conceptualization [45].

Ontologies have been widely used in several domains in applications related to knowledge management, natural language processing, intelligent integration information, information retrieval, database design, among others [6], and have become the predominant way to deal with semantic aspects in semantic integration initiatives [23]. They can solve or minimize problems related to communication between people, organizations, and systems by eliminating or reducing the lack of knowledge of the concepts involved in communication processes [48].

An important distinction sets apart ontologies as conceptual models, called *reference ontologies*, from ontologies as computational artifacts, called *operational ontologies* [18]. A reference ontology is constructed with the goal of making the best possible description of the domain in reality, representing a model of consensus within a community, regardless of its computational properties. Operational ontologies, in turn, are machine-readable ontologies designed with the focus on guaranteeing desirable computational properties [9].

The literature presents several OE methods (e.g., [3,9,12,28,31,43,48]). In general, developing ontologies involves management, development, and support activities. The first covers the organizational setup of the overall process (e.g., managing resources, controlling the project schedule, and the quality of the produced artifacts). The second refers to ontology development itself and includes activities such as ontology specification, conceptualization, formalization, and implementation. The third involves activities related to knowledge acquisition, documentation, and configuration management, among others, which are carried out in parallel with development activities to support them [7].

When designing an ontology, requirements can be captured through CQs. They play a key role, consisting of a set of questions that the ontology to be built should be able to answer [13]. By establishing CQs, we reach an effective way to determine what is relevant to the ontology and what is not. They define the ontology scope and provide a way for evaluating the ontology [9]. Therefore, CQs can be used to support both, ontology specification and ontology evaluation. In the former, CQs help model the domain, i.e., through questions that the ontology should be able to answer, it is possible to have a notion of which are the relevant concepts of the domain and the relationships between them. In the latter, CQs can be used to identify ontology flaws in domain modeling, and thus contribute to the ontology quality assessment [48].

CQs can be informal or formal [16]. Informal CQs are expressed in natural language and do not require knowledge of Descriptive Logic, facilitating its use by people unfamiliar with it. They connect the proposed ontology to its application scenarios, thus providing an informal justification for the ontology. Formal CQs, in turn, are expressed in formal language and are created from informal questions by using axioms and the ontology terminology [16].

CQs can be identified from different sources, using different strategies, and can be written in different granularity levels. When defining CQs, the ontology engineer can start with complex questions that are decomposed into simpler ones (top-down approach) or with simple questions that are composed to create complex ones (bottom-up approach). The ontology engineer can also start just writing down important questions that are composed or decomposed later on to form abstract and simple questions, respectively (middle-out approach) [42]. Simple CQs are important for deriving test cases, while complex and more abstract CQs are important to guide ontology modularization [9].

3   Study Design

A survey aims at identifying the characteristics of a broad population by generalizing on the data collected from a representative sample of individuals [8]. It is conducted to produce a snapshot of the situation to capture the current status [51]. We chose this method because, as we aimed at a panoramic view, we needed to reach several ontology engineers and ask about many practices. We followed the process defined in [51], which comprises five activities: *scoping*, when we scope the study problem and establish its goals; *planning*, when the study design is determined; *operation*, which consists in collecting data; *analysis and interpretation*, which involves analyzing data to get conclusions about the research topic; and *presentation and package*, when the results are communicated.

The study **goal** was to investigate the use of CQs in OE practice. Aligned with the study goal, we defined the following two main **research questions**: (RQ1) How have CQs been defined, used, and supported in OE? (RQ2) Which benefits and difficulties have been perceived?

The **instrument** used in the study was a form created by using Google Forms. It contains a consent term for participation in the study and two sections of questions. The first has five closed questions to characterize the participants. The second has 16 closed questions related to the study research questions. Three of them allow the participant to complement the answer by providing further information in text format. There is also an open question for collecting comments and suggestions. In some questions referring to the frequency in which the participants perform some practices, we used a scale based on the Likert scale but excluded the neutral option in order to obtain meaningful information. The form used in the study is available in the study package [25].

The **participants** must be a sample of the target population. Thus, we aimed at ontology engineers with knowledge of and experience in OE and CQs.

The **procedure** followed in the study consisted of three steps. In the first, we ran a small pilot to evaluate the form and the study protocol. We asked two ontology engineers with experience in OE and CQs to answer the questionnaire and report problems, suggestions, and response time. Based on their feedback, we made minor adjustments in the form. In the second step, we sent messages inviting people to participate in the study. The messages were sent to research groups that work with ontologies, mailing lists involving OE researchers and practitioners, contact networks in universities, public, and private organizations, and authors of the papers selected in an ongoing systematic literature mapping about CQs we are conducting. We also asked the invitees to forward the invitation to other people they thought could participate in the study. The final step consisted of gathering data from the answered questionnaires, representing data in tables and graphs, and analyzing them.

4   Study Execution and Data Synthesis

The invitation was sent in late March and early April 2023. We contacted 115 people and received 65 answers until May 1st, 2023, which amounts to a response rate of 56%. Two respondents declared in the questionnaire that they have never used CQs when developing ontologies. As they did not have a suitable profile for participating in the study, we removed their answers from the sample, resulting in 63 participants. In this section, we summarize data collected in the study. For questions in which the participants could choose more than one answer, the sum of the absolute values is higher than 63 and, thus, the sum of the rates exceeds 100%. For simplification reasons, we rounded the percentage values to the first decimal place. The complete set of collected data plus tables and graphs representing them is available in the study package [25].

Most of the participants are Brazilians (32; 50.8%). Other participants are from Spain (9; 14.3%), Germany (5; 7.9%), Netherlands (4; 6.3%), Malaysia (3; 4.8%), Italy (2; 3.2%), United States (1; 1.6%), Mexico (1; 1.6%), Argentina (1; 1.6%), Belgium (1; 1.6%), South Africa (1; 1.6%), Uganda (1; 1.6%). Two participants did not inform where they were from. The participants' profile was identified through questions regarding the context in which they have worked with ontologies, how long they have worked with OE, how they have acquired knowledge of the subject, and their experience level with CQs. Figure 1 summarizes data about the participants. As can be noticed, most participants have worked in the academic context (85.7% in total, 63.5% exclusively in this context), have worked with ontology development for five or more years (68.3%), and have high or very high experience in CQs (58.7%). Knowledge of the subject has been acquired in several ways and most of the participants have learned from different sources – mainly masters/PhD courses (71.4%), scientific events (60.3%), and searching by themselves (60.3%).

In the following, we synthesize collected data by grouping questions into six topics: Ontology development, Use of CQs in OE, Ways of developing CQs, CQs supporting tools, CQs management, and Benefits and difficulties of using CQs. Questions related to the five first topics aimed to get data to answer the research question RQ1. Questions related to the last topic are aimed to answer RQ2.

Ontology Development: The way ontology engineers develop ontologies can influence the use of CQs. Thus, to identify how ontology engineers have developed ontologies, we asked them about the ontology types they have developed, how

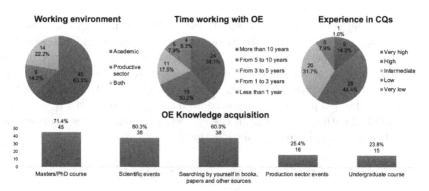

Fig. 1. Participants profile

often they have used OE methods, and which ones they have used (Uschold and King [47], TOVE [16], METHONTOLOGY [12], Ontology 101 [28], NeOn [43], SaBiO [9], XD [3], LOT [33], or others). Figure 2 shows the results. Most participants (54%) have developed both, reference and operational ontologies. Only 6.3% of the participants have developed operational ontologies exclusively, while 39.7% have focused on reference ontologies. Most of the participants (90.5%) have often used OE methods when developing ontologies (always or most of the time). The used methods are diverse, with a predominance of SABiO [9] (47.6%), METHONTOLOGY [12] (25.4%), and NeOn [43] (23.8%). Some participants (17.5%) have adapted existing methods and a few (3.2%) have combined different methods. Moreover, three participants (4.8%) chose the option "Other" and declared the use of Ontokem [46], OBO Foundry [40], and Modular Ontology Modeling (MOMo) [39](each one cited by one participant).

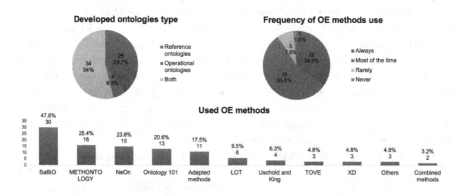

Fig. 2. Ontology development

Use of CQs in OE: To understand how the participants have used CQs when developing ontologies, we asked how often and in which phase of the OE process they have used them. Figure 3 shows the results. Most participants (32;

50.8%) declared that they have always used CQs when developing ontologies. For those who answered that have not always used CQs (34.9% indicated that have used them most of the time and 14.3% rarely), we asked what has caused them not to use CQs. Most of them (27%) pointed out time constraints. Some participants indicated that do not always use CQs because do not think they are necessary (12.7%) or because they find them difficult (11.1%). Reasons informed by participants who selected the "Others" option (9.5%) were a lack of under- standing of how the CQs aid in the OE process, the type or purpose of the ontology, difficulties in writing CQs, and keeping track of them while discussing the domain with domain experts. Concerning when the participants have used CQs, we asked them to indicate the ontology development phases and provide information about how they have used CQs in each phase they selected. Most of the participants (90.5%) have used CQs in Requirements Specification, to repre- sent functional requirements, define the ontology scope, and capture knowledge the ontology needs to represent. 68.3% have used CQs in Verification, Validation & Testing, to guide these activities by checking how the ontology model answers the CQs, testing the completeness of the ontology, and the ontology implemen- tation. 56.6% have used CQs in Conceptualization, to help identify concepts and relationships, guide on what needs to be addressed in the ontology model, doc- ument the ontology, and guide and deepen the scope. 23.8% have used CQs in Design, to define axiom rules and aid the design of the ontological model. 12.7% of the participants have used CQs to support Implementation decisions.

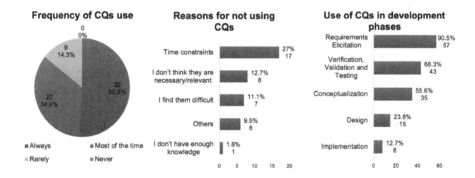

Fig. 3. Use of CQs in OE

Ways of Developing CQs: To capture how CQs have been developed, we asked the participants about the procedure they have followed to develop CQs, the terminology used in CQs, the types of CQs, and the sources used to define CQs. Table 1 summarizes the results. Regarding the procedure adopted to define the CQs, we asked if CQs have been defined iteratively or at once and if they are adjusted/refined along the ontology development. Most of the participants (63.5%) have defined CQs iteratively and refined them during the ontology devel- opment. 34.9% of the participants have defined all CQs at the beginning of the ontology development but have also adjusted them during the ontology development. As for the terminology adopted in the CQs, we investigated if the terms used in the CQs are closer to the ontology terminology or to the users terminology. Most of the participants (88.9%) indicated that they have used terms closer to the user. We also asked the participants to provide information about the type of CQs they have defined. In this question, we consider that *CQs in the universe of concepts* are those whose answer is given directly by the ontology concepts/terms, while *CQs in the universe of instances* are those whose answer is obtained from instances of the ontology concepts [1]. In the questionnaire [25], we provided a brief explanation and examples regarding the types of CQs considered in the question. Most participants (65.1%) have used both types of CQs, while 25.4% have preferred the use of CQs in the universe of concepts. Only one participant (1.6%) declared that have preferred the use of CQs in the universe of instances. To investigate the sources of CQs, we asked the participants to indicate which ones they have used. The predominant sources have been domain experts (92.1%), papers, books, standards, and other documents about the domain (87.3%), and existing ontologies or ontology patterns (76.2%).

Use of guidelines to write CQs

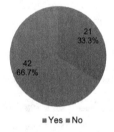

Use of CQs supporting tools

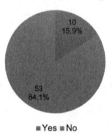

Fig. 4. CQs supporting tools

CQs Supporting Tools: To investigate if ontology engineers have been supported by tools or guidelines when defining or using CQs, we asked the participants about methods, frameworks or approaches that have provided them with guidelines on how to write CQs. Most of the participants (66.7%) declared that have not had the support of any guideline. Two declared that have used CLaRO [24] and the others informed that they have followed guidelines given by the OE methods they use or basic guidelines defined by themselves (e.g., general knowledge of lexico-syntactic patterns used to express CQs). We also asked the participants about the tools they have used. The majority of them (84.1%) declared that have not used any tool. The others indicated that have used some tools and cited text editors, electronic spreadsheets, Protegé [26], CLaRO (and associated tools) [24], OntoKEM Tool [46], and Freemind [34]. Figure 4 shows the results related to CQs supporting tools.

CQs Management: Depending on the ontology scope, many CQs may be necessary. Organizing them in groups or modules can help divide the problem, better

Table 1. Procedure, terminology, types and knowledge sources

Procedure to define CQs	Quantity	%
I identify the CQs iteratively and I adjust/refine them in the course of the ontology development if necessary	40	63.5%
I identify all needed CQs in the beginning of ontology development and I adjust/refine them in the course of the ontology development if necessary	22	34.9%
I identify the CQs iteratively	1	1.6%
I identify all needed CQs in the beginning of ontology development	0	0%
Terminology used in CQs	Quantity	%
Initially, I define questions with terminology closer to that used by users. In the course of the ontology development, I review the questions to bring them closer to the ontology concepts	45	71.4%
They are questions that use the terminology used by users	11	17.5%
They are questions that use the terminology used in the ontology	7	11.1%
Types of CQs	Quantity	%
I use both CQs in the universe of concepts and CQs in the universe of instances	41	65.1%
They are usually CQs in the universe of concepts (e.g., CQ1 above)	16	25.4%
I don't use CQs in the requirements elicitation phase	5	7.9%
They are usually CQs in the universe of instances (e.g., CQ2 above)	1	1.6%
Knowledge sources used to define CQs	Quantity	%
Interaction with domain experts (interviews, surveys, etc.)	58	92.1%
Papers, books, standards, and other documents about the domain	55	87.3%
Existing ontologies or ontology patterns	48	76.2%
Information systems developed for the domain	26	41.3%
Others	4	6.3%

understand the addressed domain and contribute to establishing the ontology modularization [9,39]. To investigate if CQs grouping has been a concern, we asked whether and how the participants have grouped CQs. Most participants (86.9%) declared that have grouped CQs at some degree – 19.7% always, 49.2% most of the time, and 18% rarely. The others (13.1%) informed that have never grouped CQs. The participants who have grouped CQs informed that the CQs groups have been based on the ontology modules, subontologies, or subdomains, or considering the proximity of concepts. We also investigated if ontology engi-

Grouping

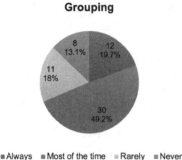

■ Always ■ Most of the time ■ Rarely ■ Never

Design Rationale

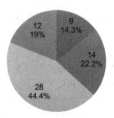

■ Always ■ Most of the time ■ Rarely ■ Never

Fig. 5. CQs management

neers have defined the CQs design rationale. A design rationale is the explicit listing of decisions and the reasons why those decisions were made [22]. Its primary goal is to provide a means to record and communicate the argumentation and reasoning behind the design process [19]. Therefore, the design rationale makes explicit the reasons that led someone to define a CQ, i.e., the intentions behind the CQ. Most of the participants have not been concerned with describing the design rationale of the CQs (19% have never defined and 44.4% have rarely defined). Around one third of the participants declared that have defined the design rationale of the CQs (14.3% have always done that and 22.2% have done that most of the time). Figure 5 illustrates these results.

Benefits and Difficulties of Using CQs: Aiming at identifying the benefits and difficulties of using CQs, we asked the participants to indicate which ones they have perceived. We provided a list of options and the participants were allowed to indicate others. Figure 6 shows the results. The most cited benefits were: CQs help define the ontology scope (92.1%) and CQs aid in ontology evaluation (82.5%). On the other hand, the main difficulties reported were: ensuring that the defined CQs are the ones necessary and sufficient for the ontology (77.8%), identifying CQs truly capable of representing the ontology scope (63.5%), and writing the CQs properly (49.2%). Difficulties reported by the participants that selected the "Others" option were: identifying CQs when the ontology engineer is still learning about the domain; extracting CQs from the interaction with domain experts; making domain experts understand the value of CQs and how they help the ontology development; and work with CQs in a systematic way from the beginning to the end of ontology development.

5 Discussion

In this section, we discuss the collected data and results by considering the topics identified in the previous session.

Concerning **ontology development**, most of the participants (54%) have developed both, reference and operational ontologies, which indicates that attention has been given to ontologies as conceptual models and also as computational

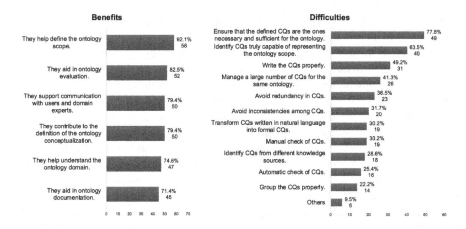

Fig. 6. Benefits and difficulties of using CQs

artifacts. This can also suggest that there has been a concern with modeling the knowledge addressed in the ontology before building the machine-readable version to handle data related to that knowledge. However, when we look at each ontology type, we notice a predominance of reference ontologies (93.7% in total) when compared to operational ontologies (60.3% in total). This indicates that in many cases, ontologies have been developed to be used at the conceptual level (e.g., in ontology-driven software development [29]), not requiring operational ontologies to be applied at run-time (e.g., to support reasoning). More than 90% of the participants have used OE methods to guide ontology development. This is aligned with the OE literature (e.g., [9,11,14]), which points out that developing ontologies is not an easy task and, thus, guidance is needed. This also indicates that the community has some maturity regarding the use of standardized practices. We must observe that this result may have been influenced by the fact that most participants work in the academic environment, where many OE methods have been proposed and their use is encouraged.

Regarding the **use of CQs in OE**, as the study focused on ontology engineers with experience in CQs, it was expected that CQs would be used to some degree. Around 85% of the participants declared that have systematically used CQs, which suggests that the key role of CQs has been recognized. It must be noted that this result is probably related to the fact that most participants have used OE methods such as SABiO [9], METHONTOLOGY [12], and NeOn [43], which recommend the use of CQs. The predominance of the use of CQs in Requirements Elicitation, Conceptualization, and Verification, Validation and Testing phases corroborates the literature, which states that CQs should be used mainly to support specifying the requirements the ontology should fulfill [16], identifying the ontology concepts, properties and relationships [9], and verifying if the ontology properly represents the intended knowledge and meets the established requirements [15]. The results also highlight time constraints as the main reason for not using CQs. On one hand, time and effort are indeed necessary to understand the domain, identify the stakeholders needs and describe the requirements in the form of CQs. On the other hand, CQs help define the ontology scope and establish a kind of "contract" about what the ontology must address, supporting communication among stakeholders and providing the basis for the next ontology development activities [44]. Therefore, the time spent on defining the CQs is rewarded when rework decreases, the ontology is documented, and the CQs aid in other development steps [44]. Despite that, 13% of the participants declare that, in some cases, they do not consider CQs necessary. Moreover, 11% find them difficult. This suggests a need for guidelines and ways to facilitate the use of CQs for ontology engineers to make the most of them. Furthermore, this also raises attention to the need for investigating CQs limitations in depth and comparing the use of CQs to other methods that address ontology requirements.

As for the **ways of developing CQs**, there has been a predominance of iterative approaches (63.5%), in which the ontology engineer defines CQs in a development process performed in multiple cycles and refines the CQs as the knowledge of the domain grows and gets more mature. The use of iterative approaches is particularly important when developing large ontologies, when requirements are not clear at the beginning, or when there are many stakeholders or many conflicts between stakeholders' needs. The uncertainty about the ontology requirements or the need to focus on a domain portion each time lead to a gradual definition of CQs. Around one third of the participants have defined all needed CQs at the beginning of the ontology development and refined them later, if necessary. This approach is suitable when the ontology scope is well-known and the ontology is not large or complex. Although the two aforementioned approaches differ mainly in when CQs are defined (at each iteration or at the beginning of the OE process), both consider the need to refine CQs along the ontology development. This fact is a recognition of the dynamism of CQs, which is itself a consequence of the dynamic and knowledge-intensive character of the OE process. In both cases, top-down, bottom-up, or middle-out strategies (see Sect. 2) can be used to refine the CQs. The predominance of the iterative approach also suggests that OE methods should address ontology development as an iterative process. This is aligned with some perceptions from the literature, which points out that some ontology applications require OE methods that help ontology engineers continuously gather and prioritize requirements from several stakeholders, keep domain experts engaged, deliver ontology modules according to time demands, respond to changing knowledge, and evolving the ontology, in an agile [5] and continuous [37] approach.

When asked about the types of CQs, most of the participants (65.1%) indicated that have used CQs expressed in an interrogative form that works over both concepts and instances [1]. CQs focusing on the ontology concepts concern the ontology conceptualization itself and, thus, usually help identify the ontology concepts and relationships. CQs focusing on instances, in turn, are usually concerned with data handled by the ontology and, thus, are particularly valuable for evaluating the ontology. This result is consistent with the OE phases where CQs have been used more often (Requirements Elicitation, Conceptualization, and Verification, Validation and Testing).

As for the terminology used in the CQs, around 70% of the participants declared that they initially define CQs closer to the users and later review the CQs to bring them closer to the ontology concepts terminology. These results once again emphasize the dynamic and evolutive character of CQs. The growing understanding of the domain promotes a better understanding of the ontology purpose and scope, which can lead to changes in CQs already captured [9]. A terminology closer to users adopts a vocabulary easily understood by domain experts. This terminology may be changed along the ontology development process to be more consistent with naming conventions used to represent the ontology concepts. However, this change requires careful attention because if, on one hand, it can be beneficial to ontology engineers involved in the development process, it can prevent users from properly understanding the ontology. Moreover, it can also affect ontology reuse because if the scope of an ontology candidate to reuse is represented by CQs and the person interested in reusing that ontology is not able to understand them, the opportunity to reuse it can be lost.

Ontology engineers have used multiple sources of knowledge to define CQs and interaction with domain experts (92.1%), documents (87.3%), and existing ontologies or ontology patterns (76.2%) have been the main ones. They can be used together to elucidate knowledge. For example, brainstorming techniques, informal interviews with experts, and inspecting similar ontologies allow elaborating a first glossary with terms potentially relevant. Formal and informal analysis of text (documents) might be used to refine the terms. Interviews with experts might help build concept classification trees [12]. Reusing ontologies or design patterns[1] provides knowledge about ontology requirements and also helps speed up the ontology development process. By containing concepts and relationships relevant to the domain of interest, ontology and ontology patterns helps identify CQs. Moreover, if the ontology/ontology pattern also provides the respective CQs, they can be reused in the new ontology.

With respect to **CQs supporting tools**, the results show a lack of tools to support defining and using CQs (84.1% of the participants declared not having had the support of any tool) and also a lack of guidelines on how to write CQs (66.1% have not followed any guideline). Concerning guidelines, some participants informed that have used the ones provided by the OE methods they use. However, the existing guidelines on how to define, write and use have not been enough. As for supporting tools, the participants cited generic tools such as text editors and electronic spreadsheets. Protégé [26] was also cited, but it is a tool for ontology implementation, thus support for requirements elicitation is limited. Automation is a key factor to build, release, and maintain ontologies effectively [21]. Collaborative editing tools and communication systems are necessary to support requirements elicitation activities. Providing support for writing CQs and automating tasks such as grouping CQs, retrieving terms candidates from the CQs for the ontology, generating documentation, and tracing requirements could help decrease development time and improve the ontology quality [33].

---

[1] An ontology design pattern is a generic solution to a recurring ontology modeling problem [39].

Regarding **CQs management**, grouping CQs has been a common practice (around 70% of the participants have grouped CQs always or most of the time). Grouping CQs help manage the ontology complexity by dividing the problem into smaller ones and organizing knowledge. CQs grouping can serve as a basis to the ontology modularization (or vice-versa), providing a way to structure the ontology as an interconnected collection of modules, each of which resonating with the corresponding part of the domain conceptualization [9,39,43]. Grouping CQs is especially important when managing large ontologies, which require many CQs. In these cases, it is hard to keep track of CQs and prioritize them if we do not know which part of the ontology they impact.

The results also show that describing the design rationale behind the CQs has not been usual. More than 60% of the respondents declared that have never or rarely made the design rationale explicit. Clarifying the design rationale is important to enable a better understanding of the ontology scope and requirements. It contributes to the ontology development and also to its reuse. The lack of concern with declaring the design rationale has been highlighted in ontology reuse literature. One of the challenges of ontology reuse is the obscurity of the design rationale of the available ontologies [22]. Unknown design rationale makes it difficult to select the ontologies to be reused as well as to understand them, which is crucial to integrate them properly [35]. We hypothesize that the lack of design rationale is related to the time constraints indicated by the participants as a drawback when using CQs. Identifying and writing CQs demand time, which is certainly increased if one describes the reasons for defining each of them.

Finally, with regard to the **benefits and difficulties of using CQs**, most of the participants declared to have perceived all the benefits presented in the questionnaire. The most cited ones (CQs help define the ontology scope (92.1%) and CQs aid in ontology evaluation (82.5%)) are consistent with the OE phases where the participants have used CQs the most (Requirements Elicitation, and Verification, Validation and Testing). These results are also consistent with the literature (e.g., [9,15,33,43]) and provide evidence of CQs usefulness.

On the other hand, the reported difficulties demonstrate that identifying CQs is not trivial. Although ontology engineers have used several OE methods that suggest the use of CQs, they have still faced difficulties mainly to ensure that the defined CQs are the ones necessary and sufficient for the ontology, identify CQs truly capable of representing the ontology scope, and write the CQs properly. We believe that these difficulties (particularly the first and second ones) are due to the fact that defining CQs involves a lot of tacit knowledge and, even though general guidelines as the ones provided by some OE methods are helpful, they have not been enough to address the gap between theory and practice. As a knowledge-intensive activity, defining CQs relies on the ontology engineer's knowledge and experience. Thus, there is bias and subjectivity [32] because it depends on the way the ontology engineer thinks to follow in one direction or another (e.g., to use one type of CQ or another, to choose one or other terminology). Concerning difficulty of writing CQs correctly, some initiatives in the literature have tried to mitigate this issue through some controlled natural language or lexico-syntactic patterns [1,11,32,36,50]. However, it seems that, in general, the proposed guidelines have not reached the ontology engineers or have not been enough. Anyway, there is a need to better support ontology engineers to define CQs either by providing detailed and practical guidelines and tools, or by improving the access and use of the existing ones.

6   Threats to Validity and Limitations of the Study

In this section, we discuss some threats involved in the survey and that should be considered together with the results. We use the classification presented in [51].

The main threat refers to the study sample, which might not reflect experiences from the entire OE community. Ideally, the sample should be larger and the geographic distribution of the people more diverse. Thus, the number of participants and the fact that the sample was selected by convenience is a limitation that affects *External Validity* (i.e., to what extent it is possible to generalize the study results). To minimize this threat, we invited people from different countries and organizations and also the authors of papers selected in an ongoing systematic literature mapping we are carrying out. Moreover, we asked people to freely invite other people.

The decisions and data interpretations made by the researchers affect *Reliability Validity*, which refers to what extent data and analysis depend on specific researchers. To minimize this threat, analysis was initially carried out by two of the authors and, thus, reviewed by the other. Discussions were performed to refine the conclusions and reach a consensus.

There are also threats to *Construct Validity*, which refers to the constructs involved in the study and how they can affect the results. The main threat is the possibility of the participants misunderstand the questions. To address this threat, we performed a pilot that allowed us to improve and clarify questions. Moreover, we provided examples and definitions for the used terms, so that the participants could better understand how to answer the questions. Another threat is related to the scale used in some questions. Since we did not provide any common grounds, different participants may have interpreted terms (e.g., rarely) subjectively. The alternatives of answer provided in each question can also represent a threat, since they may not represent all the relevant alternatives. To address this threat, when defining the questions and the respective alternatives of answer, we considered results from the systematic literature mapping about CQs we are carrying out and, in addition, we included "Others" as an alternative the participants could choose and provide further information. Still regarding the questionnaire, it is important to be aware that the results reflect the participants' personal experience, interpretation and beliefs. Hence, the answers can embed subjectivity that could not be captured through the questionnaire.

Finally, concerning *Internal Validity*, which refers to the ability of a new study to repeat the behavior with the same participants and objects, the main threat refers to the participants providing inaccurate answers for thinking that they could be evaluated. To mitigate this threat, we informed the participants that data would not be evaluated individually. In addition, the participants were free to inform or not their identification (email) when filling in the form.

7   Final Considerations

This paper presented a survey that provides a panoramic picture of how CQs have been used in OE. In summary, the results show that CQs have been considered useful and have helped mainly define ontology scope and evaluate ontology conceptualization. Most of the time they have been defined iteratively and refined along the ontology development process. Different knowledge sources and types of CQs have been considered. Grouping CQs has been frequent while making the design rationale explicit has not been a common concern. Time constraints have been the main reason for not using CQs and there is a lack of supporting tools. Although there are OE methods that provide guidelines to define CQs, they are still limited, which causes ontology engineers to face difficulties when writing, using, and managing CQs.

These results provide a panorama of the use of CQs in OE and also raise some issues that can be addressed in future research. The lack of practical and detailed guidelines and supporting tools certainly contributes to the difficulties faced by ontology engineers and to increasing the time needed to use CQs. There are opportunities to go deeper into existing guidelines or provide new ones and enrich examples of using CQs along the OE process. The study reported in this paper gives a step towards better understand the use of CQs in OE. However, further investigation is needed to address CQs limitations and improve CQs use. Moreover, as there are other techniques to support requirements elicitation (e.g., natural language statements, tabular information [33]), comparing their use and also studying the combination of them may provide further evidence and help ontology engineers to use the ones more suitable for their needs.

Currently, we are carrying out a systematic mapping of the literature to provide a panorama of the state of the art about the use of CQs in OE. We intend to analyze the results of both studies to reach an overview of the state of the art and the state of practice in CQs use and shine a light on the road ahead. Moreover, we envision repeating the survey with a larger and wider geographically distributed sample. We also intend to investigate aspects related to the CQs content. We expect that, based on the studies results, we can establish recommendations to help ontology engineers use CQs. Aiming at supporting reuse, efforts towards the creation of a knowledge base containing domain-related CQs can also be addressed in future work.

Acknowledgments. We thank all the study participants and also all the people who helped spread the study call for participation. This research is supported by FAPES (Process 2023-5L1FC and T.O. 1022/2022).

References

1. Bezerra, C., Santana, F., Freitas, F.L.G.: CQChecker: a tool to check ontologies in OWL-DL using competency questions written in controlled natural language. Learn. Nonlinear Models **12**, 115–129 (2014)
2. Bharti, P., Yang, Q., Forbes, A., Romanchikova, M., Hippolyte, J.L.: Ontology development for measurement process and uncertainty of results. Meas. Sens. **18**, 100325 (2021)
3. Blomqvist, E., Hammar, K., Presutti, V.: Engineering ontologies with patterns-the extreme design methodology. Ontol. Eng. Ontol. Design Patterns **25**, 23–50 (2016). https://doi.org/10.3233/978-1-61499-676-7-23
4. Borges Ruy, F., de Almeida Falbo, R., Perini Barcellos, M., Dornelas Costa, S., Guizzardi, G.: SEON: a software engineering ontology network. In: Blomqvist, E., Ciancarini, P., Poggi, F., Vitali, F. (eds.) EKAW 2016. LNCS (LNAI), vol. 10024, pp. 527–542. Springer, Cham (2016). https://doi.org/10.1007/978-3-319-49004-5_34
5. Copeland, M., Brown, A., Parkinson, H.E., Stevens, R., Malone, J.: The SWO project: a case study for applying agile ontology engineering methods for community driven ontologies. ICBO **7**, 2012 (2012)
6. Corcho, O., Fernández-López, M., Gómez-Pérez, A.: Ontological engineering: principles, methods, tools and languages. In: Calero, C., Ruiz, F., Piattini, M. (eds.) Ontologies for Software Engineering and Software Technology, pp. 1–48. Springer, Heidelberg (2006). https://doi.org/10.1007/3-540-34518-3_1
7. Corcho, O., Fernandez-Lopez, M., Gomez-Perez, A.: Ontological engineering: what are ontologies and how can we build them? In: Semantic Web Services: Theory, Tools and Applications, pp. 44–70. IGI Global (2007)
8. Easterbrook, S., Singer, J., Storey, M.A., Damian, D.: Selecting empirical methods for software engineering research. Guide Adv. Empir. Softw. Eng. 285–311 (2008)
9. Falbo, R.D.A.: SABiO: systematic approach for building ontologies. In: 1st Joint Workshop ONTO.COM/ODISE on Ontologies in Conceptual Modeling and Information Systems Engineering. Fois (2014)
10. Fernandes, P.C.B., Guizzardi, R.S., Guizzardi, G.: Using goal modeling to capture competency questions in ontology-based systems. J. Inf. Data Manag. **2**(3), 527 (2011)
11. Fernández-Izquierdo, A., Poveda-Villalón, M., García-Castro, R.: CORAL: a corpus of ontological requirements annotated with Lexico-syntactic patterns. In: Hitzler, P., et al. (eds.) ESWC 2019. LNCS, vol. 11503, pp. 443–458. Springer, Cham (2019). https://doi.org/10.1007/978-3-030-21348-0_29
12. Fernández-López, M., Gómez-Pérez, A., Juristo, N.: Methontology: from ontological art towards ontological engineering. American Association for Artificial Intelligence (1997)
13. Fox, M.S., Grüninger, M.: Ontologies for enterprise integration. In: CoopIS, pp. 82–89. Citeseer (1994)
14. Gašević, D., Djurić, D., Devedžić, V.: Model driven Architecture and Ontology Development, vol. 10. Springer, Cham (2006). https://doi.org/10.1007/3-540-32182-9
15. Gómez-Pérez, A.: Evaluation of ontologies. Int. J. Intell. Syst. **16**(3), 391–409 (2001)
16. Grüninger, M., Fox, M.S.: The role of competency questions in enterprise engineering. In: Rolstadås, A. (ed.) Benchmarking—Theory and Practice. IAICT, pp. 22–31. Springer, Boston, MA (1995). https://doi.org/10.1007/978-0-387-34847-6_3

17. Guarino, N.: Formal ontology in information systems. In: Proceedings of the First International Conference (FOIS 1998), 6–8 June 1998, Trento, Italy, vol. 46. IOS press (1998)
18. Guizzardi, G.: Conceptualizations, modeling languages, and (meta) models. In: Databases and Information Systems IV: Selected Papers from the Seventh International Baltic Conference, DB&IS 2006, vol. 155, p. 18. IOS Press (2007)
19. Horner, J., Atwood, M.E.: Effective design rationale: understanding the barriers. In: Dutoit, A.H., McCall, R., Mistrík, I., Paech, B. (eds.) Rationale Management in Software Engineering, pp. 73–90. Springer, Heidelberg (2006). https://doi.org/10.1007/978-3-540-30998-7_3
20. Iqbal, R., Murad, M.A.A., Mustapha, A., Sharef, N.M., et al.: An analysis of ontology engineering methodologies: a literature review. Res. J. Appl. Sci. Eng. Technol. 6(16), 2993–3000 (2013)
21. Jackson, R.C., Balhoff, J.P., Douglass, E., Harris, N.L., Mungall, C.J., Overton, J.A.: ROBOT: a tool for automating ontology workflows. BMC Bioinform. 20, 1–10 (2019)
22. Jarczyk, A.P., Löffler, P., Shipman, F.M.: Design rationale for software engineering: a survey. In: Proceedings of the Hawaii International Conference on System Sciences, vol. 25, p. 577. IEEE Institute of Electrical and Electronics (1992)
23. Júnior, P.S.S., Barcellos, M.P., de Almeida Falbo, R., Almeida, J.P.A.: From a scrum reference ontology to the integration of applications for data-driven software development. Inf. Softw. Technol. 136, 106570 (2021)
24. Keet, C.M., Mahlaza, Z., Antia, M.-J.: CLaRO: a controlled language for authoring competency questions. In: Garoufallou, E., Fallucchi, F., William De Luca, E. (eds.) MTSR 2019. CCIS, vol. 1057, pp. 3–15. Springer, Cham (2019). https://doi.org/10.1007/978-3-030-36599-8_1
25. Monfardini, G.K.Q., Salamon, J.S., Barcellos, M.P.: Survey about the use of competency questions in ontology engineering - protocol & data extraction (2022). https://doi.org/10.6084/m9.figshare.23280698
26. Musen, M.: The protégé project: a look back and a look forward. AI Matt. 1(4), 4–12 (2015). https://doi.org/10.1145/2557001.25757003
27. Noppens, O., Liebig, T.: Ontology patterns and beyond: towards a universal pattern language. In: Proceedings of the 2009 International Conference on Ontology Patterns, vol. 516, pp. 179–186 (2009)
28. Noy, N.F., McGuinness, D.L., et al.: Ontology development 101: a guide to creating your first ontology (2001)
29. Pan, J.Z., Staab, S., Aßmann, U., Ebert, J., Zhao, Y.: Ontology-Driven Software Development. Springer, Heidelberg (2012). https://doi.org/10.1007/978-3-642-31226-7
30. Pardo, C., Pino, F.J., Garcia, F., Baldassarre, M.T., Piattini, M.: From chaos to the systematic harmonization of multiple reference models: a harmonization framework applied in two case studies. J. Syst. Softw. 86(1), 125–143 (2013)
31. Peroni, S.: A simplified agile methodology for ontology development. In: Dragoni, M., Poveda-Villalón, M., Jimenez-Ruiz, E. (eds.) OWLED/ORE -2016. LNCS, vol. 10161, pp. 55–69. Springer, Cham (2017). https://doi.org/10.1007/978-3-319-54627-8_5
32. Potoniec, J., Wiśniewski, D., Ławrynowicz, A., Keet, C.M.: Dataset of ontology competency questions to SPARQL-OWL queries translations. Data Brief 29, 105098 (2020)

33. Poveda-Villalón, M., Fernández-Izquierdo, A., Fernández-López, M., García-Castro, R.: LOT: an industrial oriented ontology engineering framework. Eng. Appl. Artif. Intell. **111**, 104755 (2022)
34. Freemind Project: Freemind (2023). http://freemind.sourceforge.net/wiki/index.php/Documentation. Accessed 31 May 2023
35. Reginato, C., et al.: A goal-oriented framework for ontology reuse. Appl. Ontol. **17**(3), 365–399 (2022). https://doi.org/10.3233/AO-220269
36. Ren, Y., Parvizi, A., Mellish, C., Pan, J.Z., van Deemter, K., Stevens, R.: Towards competency question-driven ontology authoring. In: Presutti, V., d'Amato, C., Gandon, F., d'Aquin, M., Staab, S., Tordai, A. (eds.) ESWC 2014. LNCS, vol. 8465, pp. 752–767. Springer, Cham (2014). https://doi.org/10.1007/978-3-319-07443-6_50
37. Salamon, J.S., Barcellos, M.P.: Towards a framework for continuous ontology engineering. In: XV Seminar on Ontology Research in Brazil (ONTOBRAS 2022), pp. 158–165 (2022)
38. Sene, A., Kamsu-Foguem, B., Rumeau, P.: Data mining for decision support with uncertainty on the airplane. Data Knowl. Eng. **117**, 18–36 (2018)
39. Shimizu, C., Hammar, K., Hitzler, P.: Modular ontology modeling. Semant. Web **14**(3), 459–489 (2023)
40. Smith, B., et al.: The obo foundry: coordinated evolution of ontologies to support biomedical data integration. Nat. Biotechnol. **25**(11), 1251–1255 (2007)
41. Studer, R., Benjamins, V.R., Fensel, D.: Knowledge engineering: principles and methods. Data Knowl. Eng. **25**(1–2), 161–197 (1998)
42. Suárez-Figueroa, M.C., Gómez-Pérez, A.: Ontology requirements specification. In: Suárez-Figueroa, M.C., Gómez-Pérez, A., Motta, E., Gangemi, A. (eds.) Ontology Engineering in a Networked World, pp. 93–106. Springer, Heidelberg (2012). https://doi.org/10.1007/978-3-642-24794-1_5
43. Suárez-Figueroa, M.C., Gómez-Pérez, A., Fernández-López, M.: The NeOn methodology for ontology engineering. In: Suárez-Figueroa, M.C., Gómez-Pérez, A., Motta, E., Gangemi, A. (eds.) Ontology Engineering in a Networked World, pp. 9–34. Springer, Heidelberg (2012). https://doi.org/10.1007/978-3-642-24794-1_2
44. Suárez-Figueroa, M.C., Gómez-Pérez, A., Villazón-Terrazas, B.: How to write and use the ontology requirements specification document. In: Meersman, R., Dillon, T., Herrero, P. (eds.) OTM 2009, Part II. LNCS, vol. 5871, pp. 966–982. Springer, Heidelberg (2009). https://doi.org/10.1007/978-3-642-05151-7_16
45. Sure, Y., Staab, S., Studer, R.: On-to-knowledge methodology (OTKM). In: Staab, S., Studer, R. (eds.) Handbook on Ontologies. International Handbooks on Information Systems, pp. 117–132. Springer, Heidelberg (2004). https://doi.org/10.1007/978-3-540-24750-0_6
46. Todesco, J.L., Rautenberg, S., Speroni, R., Guembarovski, R., Gauthier, F.O.: ontoKEM: a web tool for ontologies' construction and documentation. In: IKE, pp. 86–92 (2009)
47. Uschold, M., King, M.: Towards a methodology for building ontologies (1995)
48. Uschold, M., Gruninger, M.: Ontologies: principles, methods and applications. Knowl. Eng. Rev. **11**(2), 93–136 (1996)
49. Uschold, M., Jasper, R.: A framework for understanding and classifying ontology applications. In: Proceedings of the IJCAI-99 Workshop on Ontologies and Problem-Solving Methods (KRR5), Stockholm, Sweden, vol. 2 (1999)

50. Wiśniewski, D., Potoniec, J., Ławrynowicz, A., Keet, C.M.: Analysis of ontology competency questions and their formalizations in SPARQL-OWL. J. Web Semant. **59**, 100534 (2019)

51. Wohlin, C., Runeson, P., Höst, M., Ohlsson, M.C., Regnell, B., Wesslén, A.: Experimentation in Software Engineering. Springer, Heidelberg (2012). https://doi.org/10.1007/978-3-642-29044-2

52. Yago, H., Clemente, J., Rodriguez, D.: ON-SMMILE: ontology network-based student model for multiple learning environments. Data Knowl. Eng. **115**, 48–67 (2018)

How Inclusive Is Conceptual Modeling? A Systematic Review of Literature and Tools for Disability-Aware Conceptual Modeling

Aylin Sarioğlu, Haydar Metin, and Dominik Bork[(✉)]

TU Wien, Business Informatics Group, Favoritenstrasse 9-11, 1040 Vienna, Austria
dominik.bork@tuwien.ac.at

Abstract. The reports on Disability by the World Health Organization show that the number of people with disabilities is increasing. Consequently, accessibility should play an essential role in information systems engineering research. While software and web engineering research acknowledge this need by providing, e.g., web accessibility guidelines and testing frameworks, we show in this paper, based on a systematic review of the literature and current modeling tools, that accessibility is, so far, a blind spot in conceptual modeling research. With the paper at hand, we aim to identify current research gaps and delineate a vision toward more inclusive, i.e., disability-aware conceptual modeling. One key finding relates to a gap in research and tool support concerning physical disabilities. Based on these results, we further present the first modeling tool that can be used keyboard-only, thereby including users with physical disabilities to engage in conceptual modeling.

Keywords: Conceptual Modeling · Accessibility · Disability · Modeling tools · Systematic Literature Review · Tool Review

1 Disability in Information Systems Engineering

As the world's population continuously grows, the number of people with disabilities also increases. Over the years, the World Health Organization (WHO) has published different reports on disability, the latest article [44] states, that about 16% of the world's population live with some form of disability. Each disability is as unique as the person who is affected by it. Some are minor and temporary, while others are more severe and long-lasting. Disabilities can be grouped into five categories (see Table 1), while it is not always possible to assign disabilities to one of them, as multiple disabilities, changing abilities, and situational limitations also exist. People with disabilities often face obstacles in different aspects of their everyday lives - and using information systems is one of them.

Recently, information systems moved from heavy-weight desktop applications to lightweight Web-based applications that run in the browser or browser-like client applications. The Web is widely used for sharing and exchanging information. It is a constantly expanding and evolving system, so creating websites

J. P. A. Almeida et al. (Eds.): ER 2023, LNCS 14320, pp. 65–83, 2023.
https://doi.org/10.1007/978-3-031-47262-6_4

and web applications that everyone can access is essential. The Web is designed to work for all people, and that must include those people with disabilities, as stated by Tim Berners Lee in 1997 [36]: *"The power of the Web is in its universality. Access by everyone regardless of disability is an essential aspect. "* Consequently, the term Accessibility is used in many diverse contexts and areas. In this paper, Web Accessibility is the main topic of discussion. The term Web Accessibility is defined by the Web Accessibility Initiative (WAI), a field of the World Wide Web Consortium (W3C), as follows [38]: *"Web accessibility means that websites, tools, and technologies are designed and developed so that people with disabilities can use them. "* According to WebAIMs accessibility report of 2023 [42], about 96.3% of the top 1.000.000 home pages examined include Web Content Accessibility Guidelines (WCAG) 2 faults [40]. Further developments in web engineering are increasing the complexity of online pages, making the attainment of accessible websites all the more difficult [28,42].

The software and web engineering communities have already acknowledged the importance of accessible applications and started to use, e.g., the aforementioned web accessibility guidelines or test frameworks to make their applications accessible to a broader audience. One example is the WCAG standard [37] which aims to guide designers, software and web programmers to achieve digital accessibility for their applications. Additionally, it is possible to evaluate the state of digital accessibility for existing software products. The WCAG system classifies how well an application conforms to the standard. However, it would also be possible to integrate accessibility aspects during the software development process to pursue a disability-aware approach from the beginning [26]. Furthermore, literature about accessibility exists in software and web engineering (see Paiva et al. [28] for a recent systematic literature review). Moreover, several publications focus on the fundamentals of accessibility and disability (cf. [2,5,15,26]) and point out gaps and problems in the software & web engineering field. Others try to reach awareness for diversity by discussing or presenting ideas and solutions. There are publications that focus in particular on visual disabilities (cf. [18,21,23]), while others speak about disabilities in general (cf. [19,31,43]). Other disability categories were not well represented.

Contrary to the field of software & web accessibility, the accessibility situation is different in conceptual modeling, where accessibility—as we will show throughout this paper—is so far a blind spot. This not only hampers modeling to be an inclusive discipline that accounts for the diversity and heterogeneity of modelers, it even excludes many people having disabilities from engaging in conceptual modeling. State of the art in disability research in conceptual modeling literature and the accessibility of current web modeling tools are systematically surveyed and analyzed in Sects. 2 and 3, respectively. Based on the identified research gaps, a research agenda toward disability-aware conceptual modeling is sketched in Sect. 4. In Sect. 5, we make a first contribution toward mitigating one of the identified research gaps by presenting the realization of the first keyboard-only web modeling tool that enables humans with physical disabilities to engage in conceptual modeling. Finally, we conclude this paper in Sect. 6.

Table 1. Classification of disability types

Disability	Description
Auditory	A person experiencing different extents of hearing loss.
Cognitive, Learning, & Neurological	A person experiencing neurodiversity, neurological disorders, behavioral, or mental changes. This may affect any part of the nervous system, such as speaking or hearing ability, or problems in comprehending information.
Physical	A person experiencing impeded movement, sensation, or control caused by muscular weakness, pain, limitation or lack of coordination, joint disorders such as arthritis, or missing limbs.
Speech	A person with a disability to speak clearly and be comprehended by others (e.g., difficulties in loudness or clarity of speech).
Visual	A person experiencing different extents of vision loss in one or both eyes (i.e., "low vision"), severe and uncorrectable vision loss in both eyes (i.e., "blindness"), or lack of sensitivity to brightness or (specific) color (i.e., "color blindness")

2   Disability Research in Conceptual Modeling

This section reports the structure and the findings of a systematic literature review (SLR) [17,29] that explores the current state of research on (web) accessibility in conceptual modeling. A detailed version of the SLR steps and results can be observed in this submission's supplementary material[1]. The SLR shall respond to these research questions:

– **RQ-1: What is the state of research and its evolution regarding web accessibility in the field of conceptual modeling?**
– **RQ-2: Which disabilities are covered in existing literature?**
– **RQ-3: Which solutions are proposed to improve accessibility?**
– **RQ-4: What is the current state of web modeling tools in terms of their support for individuals with disabilities?**

To respond to these research questions, a search string was defined that combines keywords about disability and web accessibility (D) with conceptual modeling keywords (CM). The query was not constrained to specific years, was focused to find matches in any or all of the *Title*, *Abstract*, and *Keywords* of the publications, and was run on 15.05.2023 in the scientific databases Scopus, IEEE, and ACM. We further used two seminal works (cf. [19,45]) to conduct an additional search for relevant papers using ConnectedPapers [7].

$$\text{Query} = (\textstyle\bigvee CM_i) \wedge (\textstyle\bigvee D_j) \ \textbf{\textit{where}}$$
$CM_i \in \{$ *"Modeling Method"* $\vee$ *"Modelling Method"* $\vee$ *"Modelling Tool"* $\vee$
"Modeling Tool" $\vee$ *"Diagram Tool"* $\vee$ *"Modeling Editor"* $\vee$ *"Modelling Editor"*
$\vee$ *"Diagram Editor"* $\vee$ *"Web Modeling"* $\vee$ *"Web Modelling"* $\vee$ *"Editor"*$\}$
and
$D_j \in \{$ *"Accessibility"* $\vee$ *"Disabilit*"* $\vee$ *"Impairment*"* $\vee$ *"Accessible Internet"*
$\vee$ *"WCAG"* $\vee$ *"Web Content Accessibility Guideline"*$\}$

---

[1] https://drive.google.com/drive/folders/1ydHlKYoIYqc2QglPIBMSpDHeyS5skuln?usp=sharing.

The number of documents retrieved and filtered throughout this process is illustrated in Fig. 1. The performed search has led to **690 publications** in total and **495 publications** after removing duplicates. The following exclusion criteria (EC) were applied to eliminate irrelevant publications and to facilitate the subsequent steps: **EC-1:** Non-English publications; **EC-2:** Publications not related to the subject areas Computer Science or Engineering; **EC-3:** Publications with less than four or more than 60 pages; **EC-4:** Publications that are not accessible as full text or are non-scientific papers (e.g., posters, extended abstracts). After applying these ECs, we were left with **313** potentially relevant papers. Around 50% of them were published between the years 2015 and 2023.

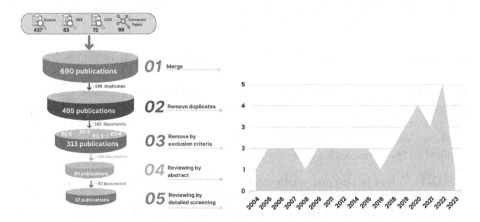

Fig. 1. Search and filtering steps   **Fig. 2.** Relevant documents per year

2.1   Screening of Publications

In this step, the goal was to identify publications that fit this research's purpose depending on their abstract. A first categorization of the possible relevant papers was conducted into the categories: **related to accessibility & conceptual modeling**; **related only to (web) accessibility**; and **not directly relevant to conceptual modeling**. The latter category was used if a publication or its subject area is not directly related to conceptual modeling but accessibility solutions are discussed which could also be useful for other domains.

After reading the abstracts, **94** out of the **313** potentially relevant publications remained potentially relevant. An initial grouping of these **94** publications indicates that exactly half of them (47) are related to topics about web accessibility. The other half can be split further: roughly half deal directly with accessibility in conceptual modeling (23 publications), and the remaining (24) are not directly related to conceptual modeling. Nevertheless, they were included because of their valuable insights that could be potentially useful in other areas if applied to this field. Eventually, we read the entire paper to select only the

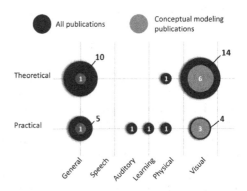

Fig. 3. Number of publications based on publication source and subject area.

Fig. 4. Overview of the disability types combined with the contribution type.

really relevant studies for our research scope. This led to a total of **37** eventually relevant publications. These papers have then been analyzed according to different aspects to respond to the research questions stressed at the outset. In Fig. 3 it can be observed that most publications deal with (web) accessibility in general. Only a few works have been published specifically in the field of conceptual modeling, especially if we consider that there was no restriction in the year of publication. Interestingly, the use of ConnectedPapers proved very valuable as it contributed additional potentially relevant publications.

2.2 Findings

The findings are categorized by the **article metadata** (i.e., year and subject area) to respond to RQ-1, the covered **disability types** to respond to RQ-2, and the **type of proposed solutions** to respond to RQ-3. For the latter, we distinguish **(Theoretical)** used for all publications which introduce discussions, methods, prototypes, and possible solution approaches without technical artifacts or implementations; and **(Practical)** used for all publications which propose implementations, tools, and similar technical artifacts.

RQ-1: The publications in the area of web accessibility have increased significantly over the years (cf. Fig. 2). The topic gains in relevance with an increasing number and diversity of available publications. Figure 3 show the distribution of the documents in specific subject areas and their source. It can be observed that around 84% of the eventually relevant papers originate from the search query while the other 16% originate from the search via ConnectedPapers. The majority of the documents were published in the subject areas of Web Engineering & Web Design & Web Content Generation (a total of 13), and Conceptual Modeling (a total of 10). It can be derived that our query was exhaustive with respect to the core focus on research at the intersection of disability and conceptual modeling, while several relevant works were found in adjacent domains like disability and web engineering through ConnectedPapers.

RQ-2: Fig. 4 shows a categorization of the state of the art of research on disability in conceptual modeling using the different disability categories (cf. Table 1) and the contribution type (i.e., theoretical or practical). The black bubbles represent the total number of publications selected as relevant, whereas the green bubbles present how many out of the total publications are related specifically to conceptual modeling. Notably, most relevant publications handle visual disabilities, with 14 theoretical publications and 4 with actual technical artifacts, including tools or implementations. About ten publications generally focus on disabilities without concentrating on a specific disability category. For the remaining four disability types almost no contributions exist. A majority of the publications provide a theoretical contribution. On the other hand, observing the publications related to conceptual modeling leads to the fact that only 11 of 37 selected papers are specifically handling modeling or modeling tools. Here, we can see that two contributions generally refer to disabilities without focusing on a particular type (marked in Fig. 4 as General, 1/10 & 1/5), and the rest explicitly targets visually disabled users (marked in Fig. 4 as Visual, 6/14 & 3/4). Furthermore, there was no existing research in the areas of *Physical*, *Auditory*, *Speech*, or *Learning* disabilities in the context of conceptual modeling.

RQ-3: The relevant papers have various foci. One central aspect of achieving accessibility is that this cannot be done additionally or at the end of a software development process. There is instead the need to address accessibility right from the beginning. Njangi et al. [26] present methods which should help to integrate the fulfillment of accessibility requirements into the software development phase. As Brophy et al. [5] presented in their publication, insufficient accessibility coverage can be detected using user-focused approaches to evaluate accessibility. This approach aims to ensure that disabled users are not overlooked. One reason for that, according to Kavicic et al. [15], is that traditional development processes assume that users do not possess any impairment.

Manual accessibility assessments are associated with increased effort. Weber et al. [43] therefore analyzed the potential for automation which yielded two significant limitations: *measuring readability* and *predictability of navigation* are subjective measures. This also leads to the question of whether there are existing features, especially in terms of Content Management Systems, that provide a more effortless and automatic way of achieving compliance with accessibility guidelines [31]. The authors state that this could be possible theoretically, however, they assess that the current technology is not prepared yet.

Some authors proposed the use of textual concrete syntaxes for visually impaired users (i.e., blended modeling). Luque et al. [19] discuss and evaluate how to make UML diagrams accessible for blind users and, therefore, evaluate the use of textual concrete syntaxes, as these textual models could be used in combination with screen readers and text-to-speech applications. An approach to using audio as a means to represent models was proposed by Metatla et al. [21].

The analysis shows, that the majority of the relevant publications (25 out of 37) mainly discuss different theories or propose potential methods. Only 12 out of 37 relevant publications present any existing tool or implementation (see Fig. 4). Furthermore, it is distinctly observable that the number of contributions specifically targeting conceptual modeling is relatively low, with only 11 out of 37 publications, with only four papers proposing practical input in this research field (see Fig. 4). Additionally, there is a clear gap regarding implementations and solution contributions specifically targeting physical, learning, auditory, and speech disabilities, as no relevant and suitable papers were found here.

RQ-4: This research question will be answered by examining ten well-known web modeling tools regarding the provided disability support. The analysis and findings of the assessment provide a comprehensive response to this research question. Section 3 elucidates these tools' strengths, limitations, and overall performance, offering insights into their effectiveness within the study's objectives.

2.3   Synopsis

The outcomes of this SLR show that accessibility is of increasing importance. While the web and software engineering communities made significant contributions with standards, methods, and tools, conceptual modeling research is currently scarce and focused on visual disabilities. Most existing papers on conceptual modeling analyze and present the detected issues that most disabled users have to deal with. This is achieved by providing evaluations and literature reviews, as done by e.g., Torres et al. [34] who reviewed the contributions in the field of accessibility in modeling for the visually impaired and found out that there is a research and solution gap in this field. Luque et al. [19] highlight the challenges visually impaired users may have while working with UML diagrams. Seifermann et al. [33] provide a survey that evaluates textual notation alternatives to replace existing graphical notations. On the other hand, some contributions provide systems that target specific disability types or solutions that only work for some modeling languages. As an example, several publications [8,16,18,32] target visually impaired and blind users and UML diagrams by presenting accessible systems or interfaces that make use of textual alternatives and editors. They aim to make the model content readable by screen readers or similar. Others provide auditory interfaces to allow operations via sound [21,35] and gestures [6], or want to avoid textual syntax as the only way and provide physically accessible prototypes [45].

In conclusion, the SLR has highlighted the research gaps in realizing more inclusive conceptual modeling. Based on the potential of web accessibility and the trend, that modeling tools move into the web, we review, in the following, current web modeling tools with respect to the extent to which they support modelers with disabilities.

3   Disability-Awareness in Web Modeling Tools

This section reports the findings of an in-depth evaluation of ten well-known current web-based UML modeling tools. The assessed tools serve as representatives of web modeling editors sourced from a curated list from the modeling community [22]. Naturally, the exhaustive examination of every existing modeling editor is unfeasible; thus, this compilation highlights ten web tools with a primary focus on UML, renowned for their widespread usage and established utility in modeling communities. Further details and references about the used web modeling tools can be observed in this submission's supplementary material(see footnote 1). When analyzing the tools, we used criteria proposed by the Web Accessibility Initiative (WAI) [39]. These criteria (see Table 2) provide a reasonable objective basis and summary of the most important aspects that should be provided by inclusive information systems like modeling tools. The criteria is structured along the disability dimensions *Visual Disabilities (V)*, *Cognitive, Learning, Neurological (CLN)*, and *Physical Disabilities (P)*. Finally, in Sect. 3.3, we describe the findings derived from assessing the tools with respect to the criteria.

3.1   Assessment Process

The evaluation has been conducted through *Observations* and *Experiments*. Each of the selected web modeling tools was evaluated according to whether it **satisfactorily**, **partially**, or **not** fulfills the evaluation criteria listed in Table 2. The tools were individually evaluated using the Google Chrome web browser. Consequently, the outcomes are based on the subjective judgment and expertise of the evaluator. Even if the evaluation would have been conducted with a group of disabled users, it would include subjective bias, as every person's disability is unique, and how they are affected by their limitations and barriers would influence the outcomes. A certain degree of bias is inevitable, but steps can be taken to mitigate its impact and ensure the analysis is as objective as possible. It is thus critical to establish well-defined evaluation criteria guiding the assessment in a transparent way and minimizing subjective bias through individual interpretation. The used evaluation criteria are based on objective evidence and standards, as their content is provided by the WAI, which is professionally dealing with accessibility and therefore has the necessary knowledge and experience in this particular area. Moreover, the evaluation was supported with various browser extensions for testing the accessibility of a given tool as described in Sect. 3.2. Furthermore, each step was noted in detail for better transparency. The following steps were followed for each of the assessed web modeling tools:

Check conditions of the evaluation criteria: The fulfillment for each criteria listed in Table 2 is assessed. Each assessment criteria is applied against *i*) the *Tool support & Graphical User Interface*, and *ii*) the *Canvas & Model* of the modeling tool. This step is supported by Browser extensions (cf. Sect. 3.2 for details on the tool and the assessment).

Check satisfaction of disability needs: This step is required to determine if a certain tool satisfies most of the disabled user needs for a disability type – a meta-assessment based on the fulfillment degree of each relevant criterion.

Determine Results: The end results were determined using a scoring system. *Satisfactorily fulfilled* is worth 1 point, *partially fulfilled* 0.5, and *not fulfilled* −1. The assessed web modeling tool *i*) **satisfies** the needs of a given disability type if the end score is positive, *ii*) **partially satisfies** the needs of a given disability type if the end score is zero, *iii*) **does not satisfy** the needs of a

Table 2. Applied evaluation criteria per disability dimension

V1-Customizing text and images size. The possibility to enlarge or reduce text or image sizes according to the user's needs. This criterion is partially fulfilled if only specific texts or images are resizable. It is not fulfilled if at least one visible element or area is not resizable.

V2-Customizing fonts, colors, and spacing. The color, spacing, and font impact the perception of specific visual impairments. This criterion is fulfilled or partially fulfilled if all or some of the mentioned features are customizable, respectively, or not fulfilled otherwise.

V3-Text-to-speech content synthesis. Visible elements should be recognizable by text-to-speech applications. The criterion is assessed as not fulfilled if at least the text-to-speech synthesizes of one visible element is not recognizable.

CLN1-Clearly structured content. This criterion describes the need for a structure that facilitates overview and orientation. This criterion is partially fulfilled if some element positions could be misleading. It is not fulfilled if the overall impression seems confusing and orientation is inefficient.

CLN2-Consistent labeling. The forms, buttons, and other content parts should have corresponding labels. This is important to make the content understandable, avoid misinterpretations, and make it accessible to text-to-speech readers. This criterion is not fulfilled if labels are missing. It is partially fulfilled if there are up to two elements without a label.

CLN3-Predictable interaction. This criterion describes that the outcomes of user interactions should be predictable, i.e., should do what it has indicated. This criterion is partially fulfilled if up to two interactions resulted in unexpected behavior and not fulfilled if this is more than three.

CLN4-Different navigating means. Using different navigational structures, e.g., hierarchical menu and search, allows users to use the most appropriate option for them. This criterion is fulfilled if at least two options, partially fulfilled if only one option is provided, and not fulfilled if e.g., only scrolling long options is available.

CLN5-Options to suppress distracting content. Animations or visual indicators, e.g., blinking and flashing, can be distracting. This criterion is fulfilled if there is an option to suppress distractions.

CLN6-Text supplemented by illustrations. Textual parts should have images, graphs, and similar supplements to improve comprehension. This criterion is only fulfilled if textual elements have a supplementary illustration.

P1-Full Keyboard Support. All possible interactions should be doable with the keyboard only (i.e., without a pointing device). The assessment of this criterion relies on the walkthrough option for manual accessibility checks, based on WCAG 2.1.

P2-Sufficient time limits to react. A person's reaction time should not lead to errors, interruption of the current task, or similar. This criterion was assessed by carrying out the same modeling actions at different speeds. This criterion is not fulfilled if at least one main modeling feature depends on the user's reaction time. It is partially fulfilled if this feature has corresponding alternatives for the same action or is not one of the main features.

P3-Controls, images, etc. with text alternatives. This criterion depends on alternative texts and ARIA labels to enable voice recognition. This criterion was not fulfilled if there were more than five (partially fulfilled if less than five) text alternatives or ARIA labels missing.

P4-Visual & non-visual orientation or navigational cues. This criterion is essential to navigate and make the current location/selection visible. It is not fulfilled if the cursor location or the marking of the elements is not visible, or there is no/only poor visual feedback or insufficient navigation support.

P5-Logical navigational mechanisms and page functions. This criterion describes that the page structure should not be misleading or that navigating does not show unexpected behavior. It is fulfilled if navigating is logical, i.e., in an expected and natural order.

P6-Large clickable areas. This criterion describes that the clickable area of action is large enough, so no fine motor skills are required. Additionally, the spaces between multiple elements are sufficient, so the probability of choosing the wrong one is low. This criterion is not fulfilled if there are multiple clickable traps.

P7-Error Correction Options. This criterion highlights the need of undo/redo or other correction options like deleting and renaming. This criterion is fulfilled if at least updating possibilities and redoing own actions is possible.

given disability type if the end score is negative. The assessment end result can be observed in Table 3. The detailed version of the table is available in this paper's submission supplementary material(see footnote 1).

3.2   Assessment Criteria and Evaluation Software

We now first describe the assessment criteria for evaluating the tool support and the canvas & model before we introduce the software supporting the evaluation.

First, we evaluated each web modeling tool with respect to the provided support for each criterion by the **tool and its graphical user interface**. Generally, these kinds of tools' GUI contain a menu header, footer, and different side or panel menus, which include different interaction types. The outcomes for each tool can be observed in column *T - Tool Support & GUI* of Table 3.

Next, the evaluation was focused on the interaction between the **canvas and the diagram or model**. As the tools can deal with different diagram types and modeling languages, a default workflow was set beforehand to ensure the same process for each tool, thereby ensuring comparable results. The outcomes for each tool can be observed in column *CM - Canvas & Model* of Table 3. The default workflow was about creating a simple test UML class diagram if applicable, i.e., two test classes with properties and a relationship between them with multiplicities as a starting point. An exception was made for two web modeling tools, namely Miro, which only supports UML class diagrams in the premium version and BPMN.io not supporting UML diagrams, so a diagram was created using similar shapes and relations. Secondly, Diagramo only supports UML state diagrams, so this was used instead. The basic workflow was to check the CRUD functionalities of the diagram.

As not every evaluation criterion can be manually checked, **additional software**, primarily browser extensions, were used to automate the assessment. References to the used software can be found online(see footnote 1). The overview below describes how each extension was applied and for which evaluation criteria it was used.

Magnifying Glass (Hover Zoom): This extension can be used on any page as an additional aid to increase the size of elements or text, especially if the web pages do not provide a (satisfying) resizing functionality. It was used for the evaluation of **V1** to check if additional zooming aids can be applied to the tool without any loss of information or unexpected behavior.

OneLine: This tool is a reading aid extension that highlights the first row of the corresponding web pages to help disabled or impaired users by increasing their focus and reading efficiency. It was used for the evaluation of **V1** and **V2** to check if the tool allows its usage in a reasonable and efficient way, without the loss of information or making the web content unusable.

Read Aloud: This browser extension is a text-to-speech tool and is applied to check whether the evaluation criterion **V3** is fulfilled. In that case, this extension can check if the provided model's content is suitably prepared and if the content can be read aloud to the user so that it makes sense and also if it is possible to use the tool sufficiently.

WAVE & Accessibility Insights for Web: Both extensions can automatically evaluate a given web page/web modeling tool and create an accessibility report for known accessibility issues. The results are used as a combination, especially for the evaluation criteria **V3**, **CNL2**, and **CNL6**, e.g., to check if contrast errors, missing alternative texts, or descriptions exist.

Table 3. Tool Support & GUI (TG) and Canvas & Model (CM) for Cognitive, Learning, Neurological (CLN), Visual (V), and Physical (P) Disabilities.

Tool	Lucidchart		GenMyModel		Gliffy		diagrams.net		Creately		Cacoo		UMLetino		Diagramo		miro		BPMN.io	
	TG	CM	TG	CM	TG	CM	TG	CM	TG	CM	TG	CM	TG	CM	TG	CM	TG	CM	TG	CM
CLN1	●	●	●	●	●	●	●	●	◐	●	●	●	●	●	●	●	●	●	●	●
CLN2	◐	◐	●	◐	◐	◐	◐	●	◐	◐	◐	◐	●	●	○	●	○	◐	◐	◐
CLN3	●	●	●	●	●	●	●	●	●	●	●	●	●	●	●	●	●	●	●	●
CLN4	●	○	●	◐	●	○	●	●	●	○	◐	○	○	○	○	○	○	○	○	○
CLN5	●	●	○	○	○	○	○	○	○	○	○	○	○	○	○	○	○	○	●	●
CLN6	●	●	●	●	●	●	●	●	●	●	●	●	●	●	●	●	●	●	●	●
V1	◐	●	●	●	◐	●	◐	●	◐	●	●	●	●	○	◐	●	◐	●	◐	●
V2	○	●	○	●	○	●	○	●	○	●	○	●	○	○	○	●	○	●	○	●
V3	○	○	●	◐	○	◐	○	○	○	○	○	○	○	○	○	○	○	○	○	○
P1	○	○	○	○	○	○	○	○	○	○	○	○	○	○	○	○	○	○	○	○
P2	●	●	●	●	◐	○	◐	◐	◐	◐	◐	●	◐	◐	◐	○	◐	●	●	●
P3	●	○	○	○	●	○	●	○	●	○	○	○	●	○	●	○	●	○	●	○
P4	◐	◐	◐	◐	◐	◐	◐	●	◐	◐	◐	◐	◐	◐	◐	◐	◐	◐	◐	◐
P5	◐	◐	◐	◐	◐	◐	◐	●	○	◐	●	●	◐	◐	●	◐	●	◐	●	◐
P6	●	◐	○	○	●	◐	●	◐	◐	◐	○	◐	●	●	●	◐	●	◐	●	●
P7	●	●	●	●	●	●	●	●	●	●	●	●	●	●	●	●	●	●	●	●

3.3   Findings

Table 3 shows the assessment results. It can be derived, that while there is sufficient support for cognitive, learning, neurological disabilities, support for physical and visual disabilities is insufficient if present at all in many tools.

Through this assessment, it is evident that especially the requirement *Full Keyboard Support (P1)* in the category of physical disabilities is not fulfilled at all by any of the evaluated web modeling tools. Furthermore, most tools could not return meaningful text-to-speech synthesizes if used with text-to-speech tools (*V3*). Moreover, the degree of customizability of tool settings, fonts, color, and contrast of the evaluated tools' GUI was unsatisfactory (*CNL5, V1, V2*).

It is also observable that some assessment criteria explicitly applied to the Canvas & Model perform differently than the GUI of the same tool, especially for the criteria *CNL2, CNL4*, and *V3*. The criterion *CNL2*, which assesses the sufficient labeling of the elements, shows that the labeling in the canvas or for the icons displayed together with the model elements is not sufficiently present. Furthermore, the criterion *CNL4*, which assesses the existence of different navigation types, is not fulfilled for the majority of the modeling tools in the area of canvas & model, as these tools do not offer a navigation option for created models. Furthermore, no tool offered a meaningful and helpful text-to-speech synthesis for the canvas & model (cf. *V3*). In conclusion, it can be said that especially for users with physical and visual disabilities dealing with the tools canvas and the created diagrams and models is not sufficiently possible.

4   Toward a More Inclusive Conceptual Modeling Future

The outcomes of the SLR (cf. Sect. 2) and the tool assessment (cf. Sect. 3) show that there is a blind spot in disability-aware conceptual modeling research aside from the apparent increasing importance and relevance. In the following, we present a research roadmap that aims to propose selected concrete avenues toward a more inclusive conceptual modeling future that would remove barriers for people with different disabilities and enable them to participate in modeling.

Visual Disabilities While there is research on e.g., improving visual notations of modeling languages [4,11,24] more research needs to be conducted and tools need to be improved to account for easy means to e.g., switch color schemes (color blindness), adjust font sizes and contrasts (visual impairment), or realize text-to-speech functionality such that alternative texts and ARIA labels for model elements can be read (blindness).

Physical Disabilities Research needs to address physical disabilities in conceptual modeling, especially because current modeling tools are heavily mouse-based. Virtual reality-based modeling (cf. [25,47]) tools might enable physically impaired people to engage in modeling. Additionally, advancing keyboard-only or audio-only interactions by smart support of complex modeling workflows (e.g., creation of edges) should be one area of future research.

Multiple and Complex Disabilities Disabilities are of course not binary. Different extents of e.g., visual impairment have different negative effects on the modelers. Moreover, problems increase when multiple impairments are given. Research needs to account for that by fine-tuning the techniques and tools to accommodate for the subjectivity adhering to disabilities.

Modeling Accessibility Assessment Research is necessary to prepare, similar to the web accessibility standards, frameworks, procedures, requirements, and tools for assessing the accessibility of conceptual modeling languages and tools. Thus, a revisiting of e.g., the seminal work by Moody [24] should be performed to assess a language's notation with respect to its accessibility.

Modeling Language & Tool Flexibility There has been a whole body of research on e.g., the flexibility in modeling tools, modeling notations, meta-modeling platforms, and the modeling process (cf. [3,9,13,14,27,30,46]). What is missing so far, and what our survey clearly shows, is flexibility with respect to e.g., alternative and customizable: i) representation of models (e.g., diagrammatic, audio, AR/VR, textual) and ii) interaction with models (e.g., keyboard-only, audio, AR/VR). The tool survey already showed a lack of basic customization features like changing font sizes, increasing contrast, etc.

Empirical Research Disability is per se human-centered. Consequently, a future research avenue needs to involve disabled persons. Languages and tools should be designed with disability in mind, and the resulting artifacts should, ideally, be tested for accessibility. This is of course not easy but necessary to truly involve disabled people in modeling.

The sketched research roadmap is by no means comprehensive. Instead, it should spark discussions by exploiting the research community in this very important but scarce researched area. Still, the few roadmap items already show the complexity of the many challenges toward disability-aware conceptual modeling. We believe convincing solutions to these challenges can only be achieved by collaborative measures, i.e., by building interdisciplinary teams composed of computer scientists (conceptual modeling, software engineering, human-computer interaction), social scientists, and maybe even medical scientists.

5   Toward Disability-Aware Web Modeling Tools - A Keyboard-Only Feasibility Study

When comparing the individual survey results, a research gap in the category of physical disabilities (see Fig. 4) and the missing fulfillment of the full keyboard support for all of the evaluated modeling tools (see *P1* in Table 3) inspired the implementation of a prototype in this area[2] This paper and the implemented prototype have an essential role as they form the building blocks for the first contribution in this direction, thus positively influencing further research and implementation in this area.

5.1   Motivation and Requirements

According to WAI [39], full-keyboard support for physically disabled persons is crucial, due to different types of mobility limitations, weaknesses, and limitations in muscular control and or pain that is involved in any kind of movement. Thus, using a keyboard over pointing devices, like a mouse, is often a better option as most of the needed movement, like dragging, moving, etc. is not applicable.

Our goal is not to improve efficiency, instead, we aim to realize a tool that enables persons with physical disabilities to fully engage in modeling. Modeling tools, traditionally heavily rely on a mouse for e.g., drag-and-drop interactions or the creation of edges, well-thought-through keyboard-only interaction possibilities are necessary. People with physical disabilities or impairments have difficulties or are even unable to use pointing devices (e.g., mouse), complex keyboard shortcuts, or to react fast in order to accomplish a task [15,39]. Thus, defining appropriate interactions require more awareness. Fortunately, keyboard interactions for HTML elements are already built-in [1] and developers can make use of it. This includes functionality like navigating through the page or interacting with controls by using the correct semantic HTML markup. However, not all developers pay attention to it, when developing custom functionality.

We developed our prototype together with the built-in functionalities and the keyboard accessibility developer guidelines by WebAIM [41] and MDN [20]. The following excerpt of the requirements was considered to fulfill the needs of keyboard-only web modeling.

- **Focus:** Only buttons, links, input fields, and custom interactive elements should be focusable to avoid leading users to elements, which cannot be interacted with and mislead or trap users in an unwanted state.
- **Navigation:** The tool should provide a mechanism to navigate through the model's content in a logical and intuitive way. Additionally, the focus from an element can be moved and is not trapped or locked there (cf. [37]).

---

[2] It should be noted that this prototype contribution does not necessarily mean that all people with physical disabilities can work entirely without limitations. Still, it should lower some essential barriers and therefore be more inclusive.

- **Shortcuts:** The selected shortcuts should allow easy and fast access to menus and functionalities. The shortcuts should be meaningfully designed, especially for frequently used actions and they should not conflict with standard keyboard shortcuts used by the operating system or assistive technologies (e.g., *CTRL+C* for Copying).
- **Visibility:** There should exist visual and non-visual orientation cues, page structure, and other navigational aids to help the user with better orientation and avoid misleading interactions. A clearly visible focus element should be ensured. This allows users to understand where they are and which element will receive their keyboard input next.
- **Consistency & Predictability:** Any interaction and functionality of the tool should provide the user with consistent and predictable behavior. Unexpected changes in behavior or focus can confuse or disorient users.
- **User Feedback:** In addition to providing keyboard shortcuts, there should be a mechanism that displays user feedback or information in real-time (e.g., short notifications about enabling/disabling a functionality), to keep the user informed about their interactions. These notifications should be clearly visible and not interfere with tool/model content or navigation.

Our prototype extends a Graphical Language Server Platform (GLSP) [12]-based workflow diagram editor with new keyboard interactions (see Sect. 5.2). GLSP is heavily used in industry and academia to realize web-based modeling tools with advanced visualization and interaction features (cf. [10]). The newly provided keyboard interactions aim to interact with the web modeling tool to accomplish a basic workflow of creating, editing, and observing a model.

5.2   Modeling Operations

This section presents the most common interactions when working with modeling tools. The keyboard interactions assigned for these functionalities need to be intuitive, easy to understand and handle. We will introduce first basic *modeling CRUD operators*, followed by the functionality to *navigate* and to *explore* a model. Please note that a demo video showcasing how these functionalities work, can be found in this paper's submission supplementary material(see footnote 1).

The following basic *modeling CRUD operators* have been conceptualized as keyboard-only interactions. The **tool palette** and its header menu are accessible using a shortcut (see Fig. 5a). Afterward, the entries can be chosen by using the character keys or the header menu options via the numeric keys. The single-key shortcuts allow easy access to these frequently used actions. **Grid and pointer for node creation:** After selecting a node in the tool palette, a grid turns visible, where the modeler can choose the starting point of the pointer (i.e., a cursor) on the screen by using the numeric keys (see Fig. 5b). Subsequently, moving the pointer using the arrow keys is possible, and finally, pressing the "enter" key finishes the node creation. The pointer also provides visual feedback on valid or invalid actions. **Edge auto-complete:** When creating an edge, an auto-complete palette appears that shows the valid source and target nodes of

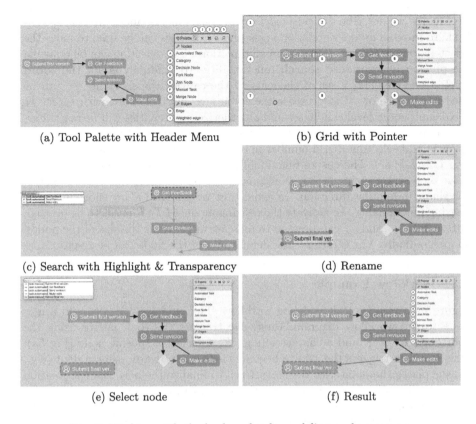

(a) Tool Palette with Header Menu   (b) Grid with Pointer

(c) Search with Highlight & Transparency   (d) Rename

(e) Select node   (f) Result

Fig. 5. Working with the keyboard-only modeling tool prototype

the selected edge and guides the user during the selection. The **search** functionality is one of the most essential interaction possibilities for a modeling tool, as models can get large quickly. Searching for specific labels, nodes, or edge types is a frequent task. In this particular prototype, one keyboard shortcut will reveal the search functionality and it is possible to intuitively search for nodes and edges. Afterward, the searched element will be focused and highlighted for further operations (e.g., renaming). The remaining elements of the model, which do not fulfill the search condition will become transparent (see Fig. 5c).

Next, we describe the two different **navigation** algorithms we conceptualized to navigate within a model using the keyboard-only. The **default navigation** can be enabled via the shortcut N and allows to iterate through the models' nodes and edges via the *arrow keys* depending on the direction of the given relations. The **position-based navigation** can be activated with $ALT+N$ and is used to iterate through the model via the *arrow keys* depending on their position in the canvas, i.e. their x and y coordinates without taking the relations and their directions into account.

Finally, we describe typical *model exploration* functionalities we conceptualized. To **move** a model's nodes or edges, the *arrow keys* can be used to move the selected node or the whole canvas in all directions. The selection can be done via the previously mentioned **search** functionality. To gradually adapt the **zoom** level of one element, a set of elements or the canvas, the shortcut '+' can be used to increase or '-' to decrease the zoom level. Additionally, with *CTRL+0* the default zoom level can be set and all other zoom activities will be reset. Furthermore, it is also possible to set the zooming level more refined, by displaying the grid and selecting a grid number in order to zoom in to the desired grid box (via *CTRL+'+'*). The **resize** functionality helps to set the size of the nodes. In most tools, the resizing action is accomplished by dragging the desired edge of the shape in another direction. To avoid this, we assigned a key shortcut to the resizing functionality. To activate the resizing mode *ALT+R* needs to be pressed. Afterward, '+' and '-' can be used to increase or decrease the size of the nodes' shape gradually. Via *CTRL+0* the default size of the node can be reset.

5.3   Workflow Example

Figure 5 shows a typical modeling workflow. The modeler wants to add a new node to the workflow diagram. First, she triggers the tool palette using the shortcut *ALT + P* and a character (e.g., *F*) to select a specific node (Fig. 5a). This selection triggers the grid to become visible. Afterward, using a digit (e.g., 7), she places the pointer to the correct cell to finalize the new element creation by *enter* (Fig. 5b). Now, she can use the search to focus the element and press *F2* to rename it (Fig. 5c-d). Lastly, she can connect the new element with the decision node by selecting the "weighted edge" in the tool palette and using the opened node selector to choose the source and target node for the new edge (Fig. 5e-f).

6   Conclusion

This article carries significant value by elaborating on the state of the art of accessibility research, and by sketching a research agenda for more inclusive, i.e., disability-aware conceptual modeling. Based on a systematic literature review of the literature and a selection of current web UML modeling tools, we establish a foundation for further research in this area. The observations showed that there are little to no contributions in research for the disability types physical, auditory, speech, and learning. Since this is the area where the most contribution is possible and the greatest need exists, a keyboard-only prototype was subsequently conceptualized and implemented, especially for users with physical disabilities. While the presented prototype is specific to a workflow modeling language, the generic implementation is currently under review to be integrated as a generic feature for the open-source Eclipse Graphical Language Server Platform. This enables other tool developers to easily plug-in our functionality to make their tool accessible for physically impaired modelers. In the future, we aim to invite impaired persons to empirically test our prototype. The current state of the prototype including a demo video is available online (see footnote 1).

References

1. Accessibility Developer Guide: How to implement websites that are ready for keyboard only usage (2018). https://www.accessibility-developer-guide.com/knowledge/keyboard-only/how-to-implement/. Accessed 23 May 2023
2. Albusays, K., et al.: The diversity crisis in software development. IEEE Softw. **38**(2), 19–25 (2021)
3. Bork, D., Alter, S.: Satisfying four requirements for more flexible modeling methods: theory and test case. Enterp. Model. Inf. Syst. Archit. Int. J. Concept. Model. **15**, 3:1–3:25 (2020). https://doi.org/10.18417/emisa.15.3
4. Bork, D., Roelens, B.: A technique for evaluating and improving the semantic transparency of modeling language notations. Softw. Syst. Model. **20**(4), 939–963 (2021). https://doi.org/10.1007/s10270-021-00895-w
5. Brophy, P., Craven, J.: Web accessibility. Libr. Trends **55**(4), 950–972 (2007)
6. de Carvalho, J.F., Amaral, V.: Towards a modelling workbench with flexible interaction models for model editors operating through voice and gestures. In: 2021 IEEE 45th Annual Computers, Software, and Applications Conference (COMPSAC), pp. 1026–1031. IEEE (2021)
7. ConnectedPapers. https://www.connectedpapers.com/. Accessed 15 May 2023
8. Cross, C., Cetinkaya, D., Dogan, H.: Transforming diagrams' semantics to text for visually impaired. In: Marcus, A., Rosenzweig, E. (eds.) HCII 2020. LNCS, vol. 12200, pp. 339–350. Springer, Cham (2020). https://doi.org/10.1007/978-3-030-49713-2_24
9. David, I., et al.: Blended modeling in commercial and open-source model-driven software engineering tools: a systematic study. Softw. Syst. Model. **22**(1), 415–447 (2023). https://doi.org/10.1007/s10270-022-01010-3
10. De Carlo, G., Langer, P., Bork, D.: Advanced visualization and interaction in GLSP-based web modeling: realizing semantic zoom and off-screen elements. In: Proceedings of the 25th International Conference on Model Driven Engineering Languages and Systems, MODELS 2022, Montreal, Quebec, Canada, 23–28 October 2022, pp. 221–231. ACM (2022)
11. De Carlo, G., Langer, P., Bork, D.: Rethinking model representation - a taxonomy of advanced information visualization in conceptual modeling. In: Ralyté, J., Chakravarthy, S., Mohania, M., Jeusfeld, M.A., Karlapalem, K. (eds.) ER 2022. LNCS, vol. 13607, pp. 35–51. Springer, Cham (2022). https://doi.org/10.1007/978-3-031-17995-2_3
12. Eclipse: GLSP. https://www.eclipse.org/glsp/. Accessed 23 May 2023
13. Gabrysiak, G., Giese, H., Lüders, A., Seibel, A.: How can metamodels be used flexibly. In: Proceedings of ICSE 2011 Workshop on Flexible Modeling Tools, Waikiki/Honolulu, vol. 22 (2011)
14. Guerra, E., de Lara, J.: On the quest for flexible modelling. In: Wasowski, A., Paige, R.F., Haugen, Ø. (eds.) Proceedings of the 21th ACM/IEEE International Conference on Model Driven Engineering Languages and Systems, MODELS 2018, Copenhagen, Denmark, 14–19 October 2018, pp. 23–33. ACM (2018). https://doi.org/10.1145/3239372.3239376

15. Kavcic, A.: Software accessibility: recommendations and guidelines. In: International Conference on "Computer as a Tool", pp. 1024–1027 (2005)
16. King, A., Blenkhorn, P., Crombie, D., Dijkstra, S., Evans, G., Wood, J.: Presenting UML software engineering diagrams to blind people. In: Miesenberger, K., Klaus, J., Zagler, W.L., Burger, D. (eds.) ICCHP 2004. LNCS, vol. 3118, pp. 522–529. Springer, Heidelberg (2004). https://doi.org/10.1007/978-3-540-27817-7_76
17. Kitchenham, B., et al.: Systematic literature reviews in software engineering-a tertiary study. Inf. Softw. Technol. **52**(8), 792–805 (2010)
18. Loitsch, C., Weber, G.: Viable haptic UML for blind people. In: Miesenberger, K., Karshmer, A., Penaz, P., Zagler, W. (eds.) ICCHP 2012. LNCS, vol. 7383, pp. 509–516. Springer, Heidelberg (2012). https://doi.org/10.1007/978-3-642-31534-3_75
19. Luque, L., Veriscimo, E.S., Pereira, G.C., Filgueiras, L.V.L.: Can we work together? on the inclusion of blind people in UML model-based tasks. In: Langdon, P.M., Lazar, J., Heylighen, A., Dong, H. (eds.) Inclusive Designing, pp. 223–233. Springer, Cham (2014). https://doi.org/10.1007/978-3-319-05095-9_20
20. MDN: Keyboard. https://developer.mozilla.org/en-US/docs/Web/Accessibility/Understanding_WCAG/Keyboard (2023). Accessed 23 May 2023
21. Metatla, O., Bryan-Kinns, N., Stockman, T.: Constructing relational diagrams in audio: the multiple perspective hierarchical approach. In: Proceedings of the 10th International ACM SIGACCESS Conference on Computers and Accessibility, pp. 97–104 (2008)
22. Modeling Languages: Top online UML modeling tools. https://modeling-languages.com/web-based-modeling-tools-uml-er-bpmn/. Accessed 01 May 2023
23. Monaco, F.: Color blind accessibility manifesto. Commun. ACM **65**(8), 7–7 (2022)
24. Moody, D.L.: The physics of notations: toward a scientific basis for constructing visual notations in software engineering. IEEE Trans. Software Eng. **35**(6), 756–779 (2009)
25. Muff, F., Fill, H.G.: Initial concepts for augmented and virtual reality-based enterprise modeling. In: ER Demos/Posters, pp. 49–54 (2021)
26. Nganji, J.T., Nggada, S.H.: Disability-aware software engineering for improved system accessibility and usability. Int. J. Softw. Eng. Appl. **5**(3), 47–62 (2011)
27. Ossher, H., van der Hoek, A., Storey, M.D., Grundy, J., Bellamy, R.K.E.: Flexible modeling tools (flexitools2010). In: Kramer, J., Bishop, J., Devanbu, P.T., Uchitel, S. (eds.) Proceedings of the 32nd ACM/IEEE International Conference on Software Engineering - Volume 2, ICSE 2010, Cape Town, South Africa, 1–8 May 2010, pp. 441–442. ACM (2010). https://doi.org/10.1145/1810295.1810419
28. Paiva, D.M.B., Freire, A.P., de Mattos Fortes, R.P.: Accessibility and software engineering processes: a systematic literature review. J. Syst. Softw. **171**, 110819 (2021)
29. Petersen, K., Vakkalanka, S., Kuzniarz, L.: Guidelines for conducting systematic mapping studies in software engineering: an update. Inf. Softw. Technol. **64**, 1–18 (2015)
30. Sandkuhl, K., et al.: From expert discipline to common practice: a vision and research agenda for extending the reach of enterprise modeling. Bus. Inf. Syst. Eng. **60**(1), 69–80 (2018). https://doi.org/10.1007/s12599-017-0516-y
31. Schulz, M., Pieper, M.: Web compliance management: barrier-free websites just by simply pressing the button? Accessibility and the use of content-management-systems. In: Stephanidis, C., Pieper, M. (eds.) UI4ALL 2006. LNCS, vol. 4397, pp. 419–426. Springer, Heidelberg (2007). https://doi.org/10.1007/978-3-540-71025-7_27

32. Seifermann, S., Groenda, H.: Towards Collaboration on Accessible UML Models. Mensch und Computer 2015-Workshopband (2015)
33. Seifermann, S., Groenda, H.: Survey on textual notations for the unified modeling language. In: 2016 4th International Conference on Model-Driven Engineering and Software Development (MODELSWARD), pp. 28–39. IEEE (2016)
34. Torres, M.J.R., Barwaldt, R.: Approaches for diagrams accessibility for blind people: a systematic review. In: 2019 IEEE Frontiers in Education Conference (FIE), pp. 1–7. IEEE (2019)
35. Torres, M.J.R., Barwaldt, R., Pinho, P.C.R., de Topin, L.O.H., Otero, T.F.: An auditory interface to workspace awareness elements accessible for the blind in diagrams' collaborative modeling. In: 2020 IEEE Frontiers in Education Conference (FIE), pp. 1–7. IEEE (2020)
36. W3: IPO Announcement (1997). https://www.w3.org/Press/IPO-announce. Accessed 23 May 2023
37. W3C: Web Content Accessibility Guidelines (WCAG) 2.1 (2018). https://www.w3.org/TR/WCAG21/. Accessed 18 Sept 2022
38. WAI: Accessibility Intro (2022). https://www.w3.org/WAI/fundamentals/accessibility-intro/. Accessed 22 May 2023
39. WebAIM: Diverse Abilities and Barriers (2017). https://www.w3.org/WAI/people-use-web/abilities-barriers/. Accessed 23 Nov 2022
40. WebAIM: WebAIM's WCAG 2 Checklist (2021). https://webaim.org/standards/wcag/checklist. Accessed 18 Sept 2022
41. WebAIM: Keyboard Accessibility (2022). https://webaim.org/techniques/keyboard/. Accessed 23 May 2023
42. WebAIM: The 2023 report on the accessibility of the top 1,000,000 home pages (2023). https://webaim.org/projects/million/. Accessed 23 May 2023
43. Weber, G., Weimann, K.: Editing a test suite for accessibility of interactive web sites. In: Stephanidis, C. (ed.) UAHCI 2007. LNCS, vol. 4556, pp. 193–201. Springer, Heidelberg (2007). https://doi.org/10.1007/978-3-540-73283-9_23
44. WHO: Disability (2023). https://www.who.int/news-room/fact-sheets/detail/disability-and-health. Accessed 22 May 2023
45. Wildhaber, F., Salloum, N., Gygli, M., Kennel, A.: Self-directed creation and editing of UML class diagrams on mobile devices for visually impaired people. In: Tenth International Model-Driven Requirements Engineering, pp. 49–57. IEEE (2020)
46. Wüest, D., Seyff, N., Glinz, M.: FlexiSketch: a lightweight sketching and meta-modeling approach for end-users. Softw. Syst. Model. 18(2), 1513–1541 (2017). https://doi.org/10.1007/s10270-017-0623-8
47. Zhang, B., Chen, Y.: Enhancing UML conceptual modeling through the use of virtual reality. In: 38th Hawaii International Conference on System Sciences (2005)

The Meta Level

A Terminological and Semiotic Review of the Digital Object Concept

Marcelo Jaccoud Amaral$^{(\boxtimes)}$ ⓘ, Vânia Borges ⓘ, and Maria Luiza M. Campos ⓘ

Programa de Pós-Graduação em Informática,
Universidade Federal do Rio de Janeiro, Rio de Janeiro, Brazil
jaccoud@ufrj.br

Abstract. The expression "digital object" is used in different initiatives dealing with the effects of exchanging and reusing information in scenarios with multiple standards and sources. However, born in different communities with distinct requirements, models, and vocabularies, the definitions of what is a digital object are usually incompatible, aggravating the interoperability problem they are trying to solve. As a contribution, this article reviews the historical and contemporary concepts of object, eliciting similarities and distinctions to result in a better understanding of the main framework proposals. Furthermore, we seek help in the Peircean concept of the semiotic sign to better understand how information flows in digital artifacts and media, and which are the relevant roles played by different agents, either human or not. We argue that, because computers can only deal with digital representations, it is irrelevant to the architecture of digital objects whether their data refers to real or virtual entities. Finally, we claim that a multipurpose definition should be broad enough to embrace new contexts and interpreters that cannot be prescribed a priori, in contrast to the usually rigid schemas found in object-oriented programming environments and relational database management systems.

Keywords: Digital Object · Semiotics · FAIR Digital Object Framework

1 Introduction

The escalation on the amount of data created using multiple standards leads to trust and interoperability issues, hampering the safe exchange of information and its reuse in other scenarios and knowledge domains. The increasing complexity of systems built to support these tasks aggravates the issues, demanding the automation of lexical and semantic compatibility checking. This is not a new problem, but understanding it well is crucial in providing solutions which are both effective and general.

Most proposals to mitigate such effects rely on the strategy of defining elementary data types and protocols to regulate the information exchange between systems, like the Protocol for Metadata Harvesting from the Open Archives Initiative (OAI-PMH) [1] and Dublin Core (DC) from the Dublin Core Metadata Initiative (DCMI) [2]. A recurrent concept that emerges in this search for a multipurpose solution is the Digital Object

J. P. A. Almeida et al. (Eds.): ER 2023, LNCS 14320, pp. 87–104, 2023.
https://doi.org/10.1007/978-3-031-47262-6_5

(DO). However, different definitions coming from different domains, result in similar but incompatible conceptual models, which, albeit temporarily, aggravates the problem in question. This review aims at pinpointing these conflicts, some terminological and others ontological in nature. As a base for this discussion, we use the Peircean semiotic model to aid in the convergence of proposals through a better understanding of the processes involved.

Our initial motivation sprang from our work with large repositories of clinical data in the Virus Outbreak Data Network Brazil (VODAN BR) Project [3], which brings together ontologies and frameworks from different origins. In order to put these to work together, precise and unambiguous definitions are needed in different interfaces. For example, it is critical to make clear if the object we are talking about is the raw data or the real-world entities they represent. This may seem evident when we are dealing with models of concrete, physical entities, but is not obvious when the named object in question only exists in cyberspace, such as a blog or a social network. Several questions arise which need objective and pragmatic answers. Concrete objects can be partially represented digitally, using models that profile the aspects relevant to the application at hand, but can we talk about real-world entities when we are dealing with abstract or imaginary entities? To which extent can we separate form and content if everything in a digital environment is a sequence of bits? How many levels of abstraction and encoding are needed to represent something and ensure it is correctly interpreted? Can and should we restrict the possible interpretations if we want to maximize reuse of the objects?

A central point to answer these questions is the interpretation process. Does it unfold the same way for humans and computers, and can we use linguistic theories regarding meaning and semantics together with the results offered by Computer Science? In his book "Language, Thought, and Logic" [4], the linguist J.M. Ellis argues that the schism between these domains leads to theories and practices that are, on their own, incomplete and poorly effective, but present great potential for synergy.

This work reviews the historical and contemporary concept of object comparing definitions to better understand the main framework proposals. As a contribution, the concept of semiotic sign, as defined by Peirce, is examined to see how it suits the current DO definitions, and check if DOs can effectively and efficiently work as complex signs in a computational scenario. Gaps provide insight in how to modify definitions and frameworks in order to improve current DO proposals.

This paper is organized as follows: Sect. 2 presents background on terminology, and Sect. 3 introduces the Peircean Sign Theory. Section 4 explores how signs apply to data interpretation, and Sect. 5 gives an example using a data catalog. Section 6 makes suggestions regarding DO models, and Sect. 7 draws some conclusions and proposes directions for future work.

2 Background

Object is a highly overloaded term whose proper meaning has been disputed for centuries. Even the existence of something called a *digital object* is still questioned. One would expect that in more formal and restricted domains like Computer Science and Conceptual Modeling there would be less disparity. However, if we look at the popular languages and foundational ontologies, there are different conceptions of what is an object: sometimes it represents a physical entity, as in the Basic Formal Ontology (BFO) [5]; sometimes it is just a continuant, as in the Unified Foundational Ontology (UFO) [6].

In the Web Ontology Language (OWL) [7] recommendation, *object* is defined as a synonym of resource as defined in the Resource Description Framework (RDF) [8]. The core structure of the RDF abstract syntax is the triple, which consists of a subject, a predicate, and an object. Here, the term *object* is defined simply as the third element of the triple. This object may be an IRI (a resource identifier), but also a blank node or a string literal, things that are not resources. Since OWL defines two disjunct predicates, ObjectProperty and DatatypeProperty, we conclude that resource and object are not used as synonyms. In OOP (Object Oriented Programming), sometimes *object* is the root class, as in Smalltalk [9] and Java [10], but also as a synonym to instance (of a class). Occasionally, it means the real-world entity represented in the source code or in the... object code. The adjective *digital* may also be used in different ways.

To better use ontologies, languages and frameworks that deal with DOs, it is vital to understand precisely and unequivocally their basic concepts. The DO is intended to be of general use and cannot be confused with other objects defined elsewhere. In common language, the most common use for *object* is that of a concrete, touchable thing, which is clearly not applicable to DOs. In particular, a DO must not be confused with an RDF object, because RDF is one of the languages of choice to represent a DO in frameworks. To contextualize the discussion, we shall examine definitions from different disciplines in this section.

2.1 Digital Object by Philosophers

In traditional Philosophy, a *natural object* is defined as something external to the thinking mind, in opposition to the subject, which is proper to the mind. In this sense, objects are determined by their essence and substance. They have existence in time, and ontologists call them continuants. We cannot use the word object to refer to events or any occurrent. Natural objects are characterized by their properties. At the beginning of the 20th Century, when we began to grow more conscious of the subatomic structure of matter, this realist view started to be questioned based on our limited perception of the real structure of any object.

An object, as defined by modern philosophers such as Martin Heidegger and Gilbert Harman, is usually known as a *technical object* [11]. This designation derives from the way it behaves in the world, from its function in the milieu. The object-oriented programming paradigm borrows from this idea, hiding the object essence (attributes) from the user and exposing only its behavior (methods). It is noticeable that most modern OOP languages have drifted from a strict attribute encapsulation in order to facilitate efficient reuse of the data.

According to Hui [12], Floridi defined an *informational object* in texts dealing with quantum mechanics, as what we know about it. Until something is known, the object can be seen as unstable and mutable. This is not very practical for quotidian tasks, as we usually learn about objects as we use them.

Hui [12] confronts these historical viewpoints and proposes a definition that returns us to a more traditional approach, seeing the digital object as a bundle of data and its regulating schemas, thus focusing on its essence. This means Hui's DO carries no embedded behavior like in OOP, only predefined recipes on ways to use the DO. This decoupling, as we will see, has a strong effect on interoperability.

2.2 Digital Object by Computer Practitioners

The expression *digital object* has been used for a while to refer to anything stored or manipulated in digital form [13]. Works to extend the current Internet standards with more support for interoperability started with Kahn and Wilensky in 2006 [14] and a formal definition: "A digital object is an instance of an abstract data type that has two components, data and key-metadata. [...] The key-metadata includes a handle, i.e., an identifier globally unique to the digital object." Further work on Kahn's framework continues today in the DONA Foundation [15]. Their DO is not any typed Internet resource, but one with an identifier that has time resilience and global applicability guaranteed by special infrastructure.

This idea gained a lot of momentum in 2022 with the venture of the FAIR Digital Object Framework (FDOF), that plans to deliver tools to work around a digital object model that adheres to the FAIR directives [16]. According to the FAIR Digital Object (FDO) Forum, as of May 2023, "A FAIR digital object is a unit composed of data that is a sequence of bits, or a set of sequences of bits, each of the sequences being structured (typed) in a way that is interpretable by one or more computer systems, and having as essential elements an assigned globally unique and persistent identifier (PID), a type definition for the object as a whole and a metadata description (which itself can be another FAIR digital object) of the object properties, making the whole findable, accessible, interoperable and reusable both by humans and computers for the reliable interpretation and processing of the data represented by the object." [17].

This definition has two essential points. First, the DO is considered a bundle of the main data with accompanying metadata, much in the spirit of Hui's model. This means the object is not what the data represents, but the data itself, plus some information that provides its sound interpretation. Second, it suggests that the reliable interpretations are limited to the FAIR ones prescribed by the metadata, which is not the case on an open-world scenario.

Another organization working on this problem for some time is the Research Data Alliance (RDA). According to it, a digital object is "[an entity] represented by a bit-stream [bit sequence], referenced and identified by a persistent identifier (PID), and has properties that are described by metadata." [18]. This definition is ontologically different from the previous one (apart from the FAIR-related requirements), because, in this case, the object relates to the representation by reference, implying the DO is not the representation, but what it refers to. This is aligned with the realism-based approaches of authors like [19]. RDA's DO has an identifier and properties of its own, like real-world objects [18]. In linguistic terms, RDA's DO is metonymical.

Some frameworks simply use the word *object* assuming its meaning is obvious. For example, the Research Object Crate (RO-Crate) project [20], which is focused on research data, describes a research object simply as an "object [that] aggregates a number of resources that are used and/or produced in a given scientific investigation". It does not explain the difference between an object and a resource nor defines what both are. Yet it defines entity as "an identified object, which has a given *type* and may be described using a set of *properties*". This looks like the inverse of the RDA definitions for entity and object. As of May 2023, technical proposals from RDA and the FDO Forum are already converging, but the terminology is still not settled.

2.3 A Digital Object we long for

We can observe in these examples the central idea of an object composed of data, a persistent ID, extensive type information, and characterizing metadata, although implementations may vary. Due to the continuous invention of new types, any solution must deal with all past and future ones. In order to gain momentum and displace their competitors, the best solution must offer clear advantages such as simplicity and ease of implementation. These same properties allowed TCP/IP to displace other network standards and become ubiquitous for most applications.

Proposals on persistent IDs are already advanced. Two other aspects of a DO — representing something accurately and interoperating with other DOs — are still at work in the framework proposals. In order to better understand how representation works, we will explore the concept of a sign according to Semiotics and show how it helps us understand more clearly the interaction of objects and their companions.

3 The Peircean Sign

Charles Sanders Peirce (1839–1914) was a philosopher, linguist, and mathematician known as the father of Pragmatism. His semiotic theory had a great impact in Linguistics and has been used with great success in Informatics in the development of human-machine interfaces by Souza [21] and Tanaka-Ishii [22], who described the semiotics of programming.

According to Peirce, information is transferred in a process called *semiosis*, that starts with an intentional human act for change and culminates in a resulting action that changes the state of something. Semiosis rarely involves a single sign, and can be highly complex, accumulating successive interpretations until it triggers a physical response. This resulting action may be a change of a mental state, as when we acquire knowledge about something, or a physical reaction to a command, such as moving something or storing information through symbolic codes. His theory may be applied to any domain where information is flowing, from common language to genomic DNA molecules. A compilation of Peirce's writings on signs can be found in [23].

Central in Peircean semiotics is the concept of sign. For simplicity, we will use a short definition from 1873: "A sign is something which stands for another to a mind" [24]. Although by this time he was dealing with signs exclusively in thought, by 1907 he had already admitted that it may emerge not only to a human mind, but anything capable of intentional interpretation [25]. Animals can do that, and so can machines properly and intentionally programmed by humans to mimic their behavior.

Peirce's sign differs from the one Saussure proposed in his seminal Linguistics work [26]. In contrast to the Saussure's dyadic sign (signified, signifier), Peirce's sign is a triad: representamen, (immediate) object, interpretant. Also, while Saussure's sign *is* the dyad, Peirce's sign is *of a* triad, meaning it emerges concomitantly to the triad. At this point, we should pause to clarify the terminological confusion among these terms. As we have seen, the word *object* is already a source of dispute. To be precise, Peirce later called this element the *immediate object*. Bateman [27] and Tanaka-Ishii [22] use different terms. We will stick to Peirce's late terms, because they help the reader to connect our arguments to other texts dealing with his semiotics. We will use *signified object* wherever it may raise confusion with the general idea of object or digital object. Table 1 presents a correlation between the terms used by Peirce, different authors, and this article.

Table 1. Sign terminology compared.

Peirce (triadic)	Representamen	Immediate Object	Interpretant
Saussure (dyadic)	signifier	signified	(not a part of the sign)
Tanaka-Ishii	signifier	content	use
Bateman	sign-vehicle	object	interpretant
In this article	representamen	[immediate or signified] object	interpretant

The sign embodies the phenomenon of representation, and for it to exist there must be always three components. They are not statically related to each other, but act together in the emergence of the sign. There is always something (the immediate object) being represented by another thing (the representamem) to a third thing (the interpretant), resulting in an effect. This is shown in Fig. 1. There has been a lot of controversy, even among Peirce's scholars, around what each element means. We do not presume to be conclusive but present an understanding that is prevalent.

It may cause some oddness when we say that the sign, which embodies representation, has an element that is a representation of something. In English and other languages, *representation* may be the action of representing something, the state of being so represented, or the depiction/description of the represented thing. The *representamen* is the latter, and not necessarily the whole thing, but only its relevant aspects. The same thing may represent different things to different persons in different situations, but in each case, the representamen embodies only the properties that make it possible. Confusion arises from the fact that the representamen role is played by things the anglophone community calls *signs*, such as traffic signs and storefront signs. Peirce changed some terms as his theory matured and started to call these *representamen* or *sign-vehicle* to avoid restriction to visual signs. We will use the later established terms and reserve the word *symbol* for arbitrary signs.

The *immediate object* stands for the relevant characteristics of something (whatever it may be) in the process of signification; it is not the object in its plenitude, which Peirce called the *dynamic object*.

The *interpretant* is the element that stands for knowledge in the triad, including knowledge of what links the representamen to the object, the context where this happens, and what effect is produced. It is a common misconception that the interpretant is an agent, an interpreter, that holds such knowledge. That is not the case, and Peirce never cared if the agent was a person, a group of persons, an animal, or a machine, which gives his theory a large applicability. The whole process, however, is intentional, i.e., the interpretation does not happen spontaneously and the interpretant indicates the action or effect produced by the emergence of the sign. This action may be a physical one (e.g. running from danger), creating a new object or storing information in a proper repository (the mind or a database). Such accumulation of knowledge may affect the result of further signs (thoughts or queries). It is understandable that many people consider the interpretant to be the effect, because "In general, Peirce referred to interpretants as the proper effects of signs, and not as that which produces effects; though, doubtless, such effects do have further effects." [25].

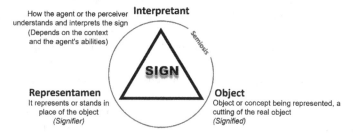

Fig. 1. The Peircean Sign – Adapted from [28].

In this paper, we will adopt a simpler approach, which is enough to identify these 3 elements in data interpretation: we will assume the interpretant determines the final effect of the sign, it is not the result. The 3 elements of the triad are roles, the sign itself is an event inside the semiosis process, and the effect is the result, which may lead to another sign — or not.

The way the interpretant connects characteristics from both representamen and object is the criterion behind the earliest classifications of sign. If there is some form of similarity or resemblance between them, like in a painting, the sign is an icon; if the representation only references the object by some means, like in an address (physical or logical), it is called an index; if the pairing is purely arbitrary, defined by convention or (as Peirce liked to say) habit, it is named a symbol. Further in the development of his theory, Peirce expanded this classification to 16, 28, and 66 subtypes (this last, incomplete), and renamed these primary types, but we will not delve into this here. It suffices to say that raw data is always a symbol, i.e., its meaning is always arbitrary. This seems settled among philosophers [29]. Also, these 3 subclasses are complete but not disjoint. Greenlee [30] shows that icons and indexes always have a symbolic portion, since there must be some prior conditioning or habit to learn how to identify resemblance or reference.

There are other models exploring relations for meaning that present other triangles which may confuse readers from different disciplines. Most of them start from Saussure's dyadic sign and introduce a third element to provide a glue between the signifier and the signified. This view is incompatible with Saussure's theory. Many of these triads were suggested, and a comparison of them can be found in [31]. We shall look into the triangle of Ogden and Richards [32].

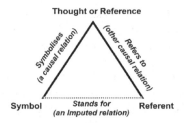

Fig. 2. The Triangle of Reference – adapted from [32].

The Triangle of Reference by Ogden and Richards in Fig. 2 depicts thought or reference as the mediator between a symbol (our representamen) and the referent (the signified object). Although not restricted to languages, the approach is clearly behaviorist and describes the process through engrams, a notion proposed by Semon, a Lamarckian biologist [33]. Engrams are mental impressions formed by habit and are specific to living organisms. Their intent was to show that the relationship between signifier and signified is not static, and it was created by the mind. We are tempted to equate "thought or reference" to Peirce's interpretant, but there are significant differences. Ogden's reference acts as an inference machine between the symbol and its referent, whereas the interpretant is more general, not dependent on the existence of rules or a human mind for interpretability. Initially tied to the thought process, Peirce later expanded the concept of interpretant to include non-thinking agents. Peirce's concepts of representamen and object are also more encompassing, including natural phenomena and abstract entities like logic propositions. Peirce's sign does not imply or enforce truth or correctness. Peirce considered semiosis a means to it. Additionally, Peirce emphasized that the elements and their relations to the sign are meaningful only when all three are present: a symbolic relation between symbol and thought requires a referent, and reference necessitates the triggering representation.

To end this section on the Peircean sign, some important aspects must be stressed. First, the sign model may be applied to a very large set of situations, including representations of many different forms in a plethora of media, immediate objects of any thinkable nature (concrete, abstract, virtual, and imagined things are all possible), and through various forms of association in the interpretant (logical rules, statistical models, guess, faith). It fits not only "correct" interpretations (whatever this means) but also misinterpretations. Second, the sign is not formed until all three elements are present, and no relations between two of the three components can produce the unique perspective of the triad. The sign is not decomposable. Third, the sign is not a continuant, it cannot be persisted, which is equivalent to say that the meaning momentarily attributed to some representation is not one of its properties. We will not attempt to define meaning, but it is not a mode that characterizes a continuant. The sign only embodies representation during semiosis, which is contextual and intentional. Expressions like "semantic encapsulation" or "to capture the semantics", even taken metaphorically, give a wrong impression that there is some aethereal, quintessential substance that infuses code with a static, prescribed meaning. There is not. Meaning only emerges during interpretation, when a representamen and an object are matched through an interpretant, and by no other way. Any bit sequence is meaningless until someone intentionally reads from it.

Being symbolic machines, computers can only work on representations, they cannot share concepts or engrams.

4 Interpreting Data

Examples of everyday signs can be found in linguistic textbooks. But what happens when the representamen at the start of the interpretation chain is always some form of digital data? Suppose that we are given the bit array □■□□□□■□□■■□□□□□■□■■■□■□□■□■■□■■□□■, materialized in some media. (That is the literal meaning of datum: something given.) Without any other knowledge, it is not possible to ascribe any meaning to it. If each □-state is interpreted as a zero digit and each ■-state is considered a one, and the 32-bit array is considered the binary representation of a natural number, it could be interpreted as meaning the same as 1113683309 in decimal notation, i.e., a specific number from the $\mathbb{N}$ set. We could also interpret it as a string of four ASCII characters, which leads us to B-a-u-m and, through another sign, to the word "Baum", which, to a German, could mean a plant with a trunk or a connected acyclic undirected graph. It could also mean anything else. Without the knowledge of the context in which the array is supposed to be used and what we use to call its type, it is not possible to match it to an object and arrive at any effect. Thus, a human or a machine programmed to act as an agent would face the same dilemma.

This example illustrates some important facts about digital data. First, the type/context knowledge necessary to decode the representation is never inside it and must be known a priori. Although some data types may contain embedded metadata or references to external resources, one must know the base format structure to extract such information. Second, computers are symbolic machines, i.e., they only work on representations, not on the things they represent. Consider integer arithmetic, which is accomplished by using logical operations on bits, and real numbers, which are only approximated by integer mantissas and exponents of fixed precision, profoundly impacting numerical algorithms. Any claim that a computer can operate on certain data types in the same way that a human would, should be carefully verified, because this is not true for all types and contexts.

Let us now focus on the signified object. It is common ground that real-world objects can only be represented through models, and these are, by definition, a simplified description of the object's relevant properties and behavior. In a sign, the immediate object is a cutting from the dynamic object, keeping only the characteristics relevant to the sign, and therefore its type is usually different. For example, in most network traffic, the devices are unaware of the contents of resources being carried around. Some protocols, however, are optimized for certain types, such as video or radar signals, and in this case higher types are used, which behave differently from bit arrays. From the semiotic angle, it is therefore irrelevant if the represented object is a "real world object" or a "virtual world object". There is no physical static link between a digital record and some concrete object it supposedly represents, only a logical and ephemeral one. What Hui calls digital objects are entities which are not models of real things but peculiar things on their own. But there is no semiotic difference between such models and models of real things, for their signs work in the same way.

It looks straightforward that the DO data may act as a representamen, and that some signs may reference immediate objects that are themselves other bit sequences. However, it is not obvious that software (a special case of data) may contribute to the role of the interpretant, incorporating knowledge of the context and type schemas that were either programmed by humans or acquired through previous stages in a semiosis. The intention grounding of this role is provided by those users in control of the software system, even if they sometimes are not fully aware of all its possible behaviors. Metadata descriptors can provide type information either in structural form or as additional parsers, i.e., extra knowledge representations that can be integrated into the interpretation chain. The existence of proper descriptors and schemas that can be statically or dynamically assimilated and brought into action by an agent is thus a precondition to achieve multiple acceptable interpretations of the same data.

Fig. 3. – René Magritte's «La trahison des images»

Consider René Magritte's surrealist painting named «La trahison des images» (The Treachery of Images), which is on display at the Los Angeles County Museum of Art. Figure 3 presents a picture of it. The semiotic chain that culminated in its creation was paused in 1929, when the painting was concluded. Still, it continues when the Wikipedia page containing its image [34] is selected in a web browser. The web server identifies it as a resource and sends it through the network, together with the information that its Media Type (formerly MIME-type) is image/jpeg. The web agent, which reflects the intention of the user operating it, causes a sign to emerge by matching the triad bits/type/image, which results in a matrix of pixels that reside in the device memory, encoded in a way the video board can understand. Notice that the machine recognizes that there is a picture that determines the sign but can only manipulate bit representations of it. In this case, the net effect is switching from a JPEG representation, which is optimized for storage, to a matrix representation suitable for display. The video board (another agent) interprets the matrix generating a video signal to display the image by means of a monitor. The user's visual cortex (yet another agent) interprets it as an image of a painting containing both the picture of a pipe and the sentence «Ceci n'est pas une pipe.» (this is not a pipe) in manuscript letters. He interprets the sentence image as words, and as a French literate, interprets the words and confronts their meaning with the meaning of the pipe image. The apparent contradiction continuously generates other mental signs until he reconciles the information with previous knowledge he has on pipes and pictures and learns a lesson: one should not mistake representations for the things they describe.

This example shows us that the full interpretation process extends well beyond the first step of decoding the data. It has been suggested [35] that a digital object should incorporate not only the type of information needed for the initial format decoding, but also more complex types that would allow the process to continue until an automated agent may have enough information to take action. This would be nice indeed, but the number of signs needed to perform such a complex task could be huge. It is important to notice that there is no predefined way to classify such signs in predefined layers, and sometimes a new sign may depend on results from more than one layer — they are far from sequential or hermetic. For example, textual and sound information come together in a song, and if we interpret them separately, the result is not equivalent. In the same way, text and images need to be interpreted together in things like Chinese calligraphy, concrete poetry, or ASCII art. The RDA, on the other hand, explicitly states that "The definition of a DO does not make statements about the content of the bit sequence, interpretation is left to other layers." [36].

We believe virtue is in the middle. Proving metadata only to the first layer equates DOs to web resources, where a media type suffices. But following all the way to the end of semiosis is unattainable to current computers. Adopting a less prescriptive and more incremental, pragmatic approach makes more sense. Low-level types are already covered by mature standards. But there is currently no consensus on how to provide information for higher level abstractions, and we doubt there will ever be. Hence it seems crucial that we provide DOs the capability to support static typing, rule engines or ontologies, and also other novel mechanisms such as heuristic models.

5 Object Interpretation in Data Catalogs

Data catalogs are curated collections of structured metadata for describing resources and pointing to data resources of interest [37]. They allow users to browse, search and organize these descriptors (metadata) and access the resource stored in repositories responsible for their curation [38]. For software systems that operate with catalogs, metadata are digital objects, the cataloged resources descriptors, organized through schemas such as the Data Catalog Vocabulary (DCAT). DCAT is a W3C-recommen-ded metadata schema that describes cataloged resources, particularly datasets and data services [39]. It was designed to facilitate interoperability between web catalogs.

According to our proposal, Peirce's sign can be employed to interpret data from cataloged resource descriptors. In this process, we can identify and analyze types and operations that should be performed/offered by the catalog software. As a result, in addition to types and subtypes, we identify properties that must be structured and standardized to provide machine-actionability, meeting the FAIR principles [16].

To illustrate, we present a simplified semiotic chain to interpret the access to a repository page based on information provided by a dataset descriptor in a catalog. This scenario commonly occurs in catalogs, directing users to the repository page referring to the described dataset.

Figure 4 shows our interpretation chain. This chain is composed of triads that represent the interpretation steps. Each triad presents a representamen, an object, and an interpretant. In the interpretation sequence from left to right, we observe that an object at a step becomes the representamen at the next step, demonstrating the different roles assumed. The interpretant provides knowledge that relates characteristics of the representamen and the object in the triad, the context where it happens, and the effect produced. Thus, each step has an action motivated by the sign.

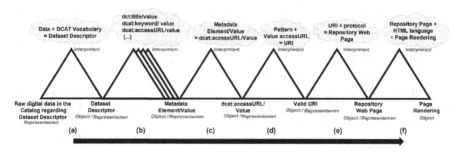

Fig. 4. Semiotic Chain Example

In step 4(a), the interpretant connects the raw digital data in the catalog (representamen) with the dataset descriptor (object), providing the knowledge for an agent to access, map, and translate the digital data to a particular dataset descriptor according to DCAT. The retrieval of this descriptor is the resulting action of this sign. In step 4(b), the retrieved descriptor is the representamen, and the interpreter provides the knowledge to identify and organize the different metadata element/value pairs (object) of it. As a result, the metadata/element pairs of the descriptor are obtained. The various metadata elements patterns are represented as interpretant in Fig. 4(b), employing DCAT (prefix dcat:) and DC (prefix dc:) schemas.

Once the metadata elements and their respective values are obtained, the next step should be to get the metadata element/value pair of interest, represented here by dcat:accessURL - "A URL of the resource that gives access to a distribution of the dataset. E.g. landing page, feed, SPARQL endpoint" [39]. So, in step 4(c), the object extracted in 4(b) becomes the representamen, and the interpretant represents the patterns needed to identify among its elements the one associated with the pair established by the object. The selection of the pair "dcat:accessURL/Value" is the resulting action. This pair is adopted in step 4(d), in which the interpreter holds the knowledge to identify the associated value and acquire a landing page web address, a valid URI.

Up to this point, all steps (interpretations), despite acting on different objects, were based on the descriptor of a specific dataset. However, we observe a contextual change in step 4(e). Now the representamen is a valid URL pointing to a repository web page (object) instead of its binary representation. Accessing and acquiring the HTML referring to the page is the result of step 4(e). To provide the page visualization, in step 4(f), the interpretant has the knowledge to render the accessed HTML. The resulting action is the HTML interpretation with the page image. The user's interpretation of information on the page establishes another interpretative chain.

In general, our semiotic chain presents a schema of interpretation through interpretants. It combines simple and complex sequences of bits (the representamina) to reference another (more or less complex) sequence of bits to the resulting immediate objects. In the end, from each interpretation, a usable object is obtained as a result.

In order for this chain to be realized automatically, the interpretants must be associated with the software, which operates as agents, and both representamen and object must be machine-readable and actionable elements. In addition, the context for each step should be clear, indicating whether the sequence is standard interpretation (known types) or specific interpretation (domain-specific types). Supplementary information should be provided for specific interpretations providing the interpreter with the necessary knowledge.

6   A Pragmatic Perspective on Digital Objects

We have seen that to engage in semiosis, the representamina must be matched to the objects they represent by interpretants which constitute knowledge provided in different ways through processes carried out by physical agents. Our focus is to clarify how this generic framework works with digital structures and, thus, how to define a DO model which preserves wide applicability and interoperability, while remaining lean, so that humans can relate to and manage it more easily. We shall identify which structures play each semiotic role during digital processing, then assert which should or should not be part of a DO, and how this fits into the current DO and FAIR DO proposals.

First, let us consider the representamen. All digital data are produced and manipulated either directly by humans or by machines that were designed by humans. Even if a sensor emits data regularly in response to changes in the environment, this happens by the intention of its user, and following a predefined rule. So, although signs may have natural representamina (e.g. a dark cloud interpreted as a sign of imminent rain), this is never the case in digital processing. There is no natural source of bit sequences. They are always the result of some artificial encoding. We are inclined to see digital encoding as radically different from the older analog methods such as writing, but their dependence on physical media and capacity for representing anything are the same. What makes the difference is the use of a uniform encoding — the bit sequence — that can be persisted in any media and represents any content. We argue that this is the actual DO. Sound waves will always be physical and analogue, only its MP3 representation is digital (i.e. binary encoded). Also, the prevailing sense of an object as something concrete, useful, and amenable to manipulation, persists in the form of identifiable bits used and exchanged through electronic devices. A proper definition for digital object should encompass this notion, and not twist it, in order to improve both technical and non-technical communication. So, a DO must denote, as proper part, its representamen, the bit sequence. Pointers are not the things they represent and if a DO were just a reference to another entity, the sign it generates would be an index, not a symbol. Also, in the same way, books are considered objects, independently of the literary work or subject they carry. The FAIR Digital Object Framework Conceptual Model (FDOF-CM) [35] distinguishes the FAIR Digital Media Object (the representamen) and the FAIR Digital Information Object (the immediate object or content). Still, we argue this use of the adjective *digital* may cause misinterpretation, since the media is always physical and analogue, and the information is abstract and therefore also not digital. This metonymical use is not grammatically wrong, but technically only the bit sequence should be considered digital.

Anything, concrete or abstract, existing or imaginable, may act in a sign as the immediate object. It embodies the interpretable aspects that are matched to the corresponding aspects in the representamen. The machine can represent anything, but operates solely on the symbolic level. So, for computers, the immediate object is also some bit sequence.

In the case of the interpretant, the knowledge used in the interpretation process may come from two different sources: the hardware, which contains many embedded rules in the circuitry design, and the software, a particular set of bit sequences which includes data that are interpreted as microprocessor commands. The hardware part must not be taken for granted, because in the same way numerical coprocessors and graphics processors were created to speed up highly reusable procedures, more and more algorithms are now being turned into highly specialized processing units. The software is the part which the technical user is empowered to alter more easily. It is composed of several layers of interpreting routines, starting down with drivers that deal with the hardware, passing through operational system routines, basic software frameworks, and reaching the application level that incorporates the higher semantic levels. These long sign chains happen in almost every application, and different programs follow different interpretation chains. For example, one can parse XML files with a SAX parser generating a series of events, or use a DOM parser producing a single object tree at the end.

Since the interpretant depends on previous knowledge regarding the context in which the interpretation happens, it uses not only auxiliary description data (usually called metadata) but also tacit knowledge that was incorporated in both hardware and software that drive this process. Because it is not possible to include all this a priori, we have to accept the fact that the metadata records may not be sufficient to describe all possible interpretations.

Therefore, we propose a simpler DO definition: *a finite bit sequence that is identified and has a set of assigned descriptors (also bit sequences) that support or aid in its interpretation*. This definition, albeit lean, has some advantages:

1. It embraces common use of the term as a noun for things made up of binary digits, thus opposed to analogue and concrete.
2. It is consistent with the general perception that when an object is copied, moved, or manipulated in any other way, all instance-related data is copied, moved, and manipulated as a single structure.
3. In Heidegger's terms, it is a technical object since it has at least an ascribed and described function.
4. It avoids the confusion between the DO and the thing it represents — to be used, the DO must be interpreted in some context. This should also discourage the production of questionable expressions that ignore this important distinction, like digital twins — twins are, by definition, a pair of things of the same type. The RDA definition does not fit ours, since it assigns the designation DO to the dynamical object (the represented entity) and not to the bit sequence. The RDF standard, on the other hand, properly refers to the represented entities as resources.
5. Allows for different implementations, as long as the DO and its descriptors are considered distinct. Since the FDO Forum definition provides further restrictions (e.g. it needs a PID), the FAIR DO should be considered a specialization of DO.
6. Allows for representations of anything, including proper random, encrypted, or yet untyped data, as long as it is described as such.
7. Allows the same DO to have different interpretations (and types) in different contexts.

8. Descriptors may be shared among DOs when they refer to universals and not particulars. The descriptor interpretation chains may grow quite large, and if they were a constitutive proper part of the DO, they could not be shared.
9. Does not enforce a single descriptor definition or schema for metadata. The descriptors may be DOs or not, as long as they provide knowledge that may be used as interpretants during semiosis. Even AI language models would fit here. These details are framework-dependent and should not affect the general DO definition.
10. It excludes infinite sequences because they cannot be properly distinguished or compared. Bitstream producers and consumers can be identified, but not the stream itself, only its finite bit slices are processed separately. We may have a DO stream, but the stream itself is not a DO.
11. This allows us to take common digital things, like files or internet resources, and turn them into DOs by assigning descriptors. Leaving the sequence unaltered assures everything will work as before, promoting an easier and quicker adoption of an alternative way to use the resource.

As aforementioned, a DO model that allows for novel interpretations is needed if we want it to be used in contexts far from the exact sciences. Literature and Arts are areas with complex semiotics, and modeling their content and context for such areas is a challenge.

DO descriptors may offer not only typing information, but also a palette of operations which may be applied to the current DO instance. A sensible architecture for systems organized among such semantic planes would be to provide microservices that implement the equivalent of parameterized signs. The sequencing of such services would stand for a complete interpretation chain, leading to a specific intended effect. Common and recurring chains could be optimized for performance on demand. This approach would fit nicely with architectures that seek to dissect information, like knowlets and their registries [40], to support the different interpretations that come with multiple perspectives [41], and to allow for the more complex signs that emerge in machine-learning models.

Following the sign-unfolding process in current systems helps us understand the different types of objects present in each layer, and segregate the semantic levels supported. It should also allow us to verify if the set of available metadata elements is enough to support human and automated agents in each task they intend to perform on the underlying resource. If the descriptors are represented using RDF or RDF-star, validation could be offered through SHACL code.

7 Conclusion and Future Work

This paper overviewed the evolution of the natural object concept to a digital object. Based on it, we discussed ongoing DO implementations, all with the common goal of increasing interoperability between systems. In addition, we highlighted the difficulties encountered in their processing, mainly when it is observed that the best solution must deal with a multitude of existing and emerging symbolic codes while trying to remain simple and easy to implement.

We have also shown that the Sign Theory allows us to identify some aspects of digital object models that need clarification and better separation of concerns. A systematization in the process of interpretation of DOs, with emphasis on descriptions and interoperability, should contribute to the convergence of proposals aiming at a generic model and facilitate implementation across platforms.

In particular, this work explored a small interpretation chain applied to descriptors of cataloged resources. Furthermore, the analysis of the semiotic chain highlights the different roles of objects, relevant attributes, and operations involved in the process. Thus, it contributes to identifying gaps in the metadata structure, providing clues on how to improve it to increase interpretability and reuse.

Metadata modeling can also benefit from a better investigation of Peirce's taxonomies of signs, which are related to essential properties. This approach has been explored previously by Bergman [42]. For future work, we will extend it. Furthermore, we intend to map these semiotic structures into a knowledge graph to support the generalization and adoption of DO models.

Another relevant aspect refers to information entities ontologies, which describe how content relates to the media formats that support it. They are still a topic of discussion, as presented by Sanfilippo [43]. We believe that Sign Theory can also help elucidate some aspects of denotation in symbolic systems.

Acknowledgments. This work has been partially supported with a student grant from CAPES (Process number 88887.613048/2021–00) and a research and development grant from RNP.

References

1. Logoze, C.: The open archives initiative protocol for metadata harvesting (2002). http://www.openarchives.org/OAI/2.0/openarchivesprotocol.htm
2. DCMI Homepage. https://www.dublincore.org/. Accessed 20 May 2023
3. Borges, V., de Oliveira, N.Q., Rodrigues, H.F., Campos, M.L.M., Lopes, G.R. (2023). Implementation Solutions for FAIR Clinical Research Data Management. In: Filipe, J., Śmiałek, M., Brodsky, A., Hammoudi, S. (eds) Enterprise Information Systems. ICEIS 2022. Lecture Notes in Business Information Processing, vol 487. Springer, Cham. https://doi.org/10.1007/978-3-031-39386-0_4
4. Ellis, J.M.: Language, thought, and logic (1993)
5. BFO Homepage. https://basic-formal-ontology.org/. Accessed 20 May 2023
6. UFO Project Homepage. https://nemo.inf.ufes.br/en/projetos/ufo/. Accessed 20 May 2023
7. OWL Homepage. https://www.w3.org/OWL/. Accessed 20 May 2023
8. RDF Homepage. https://www.w3.org/RDF/. Accessed 20 May 2023
9. Squeak/Smalltalk Homepage. https://squeak.org/. Accessed 20 May 2023
10. Java Homepage. https://docs.oracle.com/javase/8/docs/technotes/guides/language/index.html. Accessed 20 May 2023
11. Hui, Y.: What is a digital object? In:. Philosophical Engineering: Toward a Philosophy of the Web, pp. 52–67 (2013). https://doi.org/10.1002/9781118700143.ch4
12. Hui, Y.: On the Existence of Digital Objects. U of Minnesota Press (2016). 2016.80199571123.001.0001
13. Pearsall, J., Hanks, P., Soanes, C., Stevenson, A.: Oxford Dictionary of English (2010). https://doi.org/10.1093/acref/97
14. Kahn, R., Wilensky, R.: A framework for distributed digital object services. Int. J. Digit. Libr. 6(2), 115–123 (2006). https://doi.org/10.1007/s00799-005-0128-x
15. DONA Fundation Homepage. https://www.dona.net/index. Accessed 20 May 2023

16. Wilkinson, M.D., Dumontier, M., Aalbersberg, I.J., et al.: Comment: the FAIR guiding principles for scientific data management and stewardship. Sci. Data **3**(March), 2016 (2016). https://doi.org/10.1038/sdata.2016.18

17. Anders, I., et al.: FAIR digital object technical overview (2023). https://doi.org/10.5281/zenodo.78247

18. Berg-Cross, G., Ritz, R., Wittenburg, P.: Data foundation and terminology work group products (2015). https://doi.org/10.15497/06825049-8CA4-40BD-BCAF-DE9F0EA2FADF

19. Smith, B., Ceusters, W.: Ontological realism: a methodology for coordinated evolution of scientific ontologies. Appl. Ontol. **5**(3), 139–188 (2010)

20. Soiland-Reyes, S., et al.: RO-Crate community, paul groth, carole goble: packaging research artefacts with RO-crate. Data Sci. 5(2) (2022). https://doi.org/10.3233/DS-210053

21. De Souza, C.S.: The Semiotic Engineering of Human-Computer Interaction. MIT press, Cambridge (2005)

22. Tanaka-Ishii, K.: Semiotics of Programming. Cambridge University Press, Cambridge (2010)

23. Hoopes, J. (ed.): Peirce on Signs – Writings on Semiotic by Charles Sandrs Peirce. The University of North Carolina Press (1991). Project MUSE https://muse.jhu.edu/book/41103

24. Peirce, C. S.: Writings of Charles S. Peirce: A Chronological Edition, vol. 3: 1872 to 1878. Indiana University Press (1986)

25. Short, T. L.: Interpreting Peirce's Interpretant: A Response To Lalor, Liszka, and Meyers. Trans. Charles S. Peirce Soc. **32**(4), 488–541 (1996). http://www.jstor.org/stable/27794984

26. Saussure, F. de: Curso de Linguística Geral (Cours de linguistique générale) (Chelini, A., Paes, J.P. and Blikstein, I., Trans.). 28th. edn. Editora Cultrix (2012). ISBN 978-85-316-0102-6

27. Bateman, J. A.: Peircean Semiotics and Multimodality: Towards a New Synthesis. Multimodal Commun. **7**(1), 20170021 (2018). https://doi.org/10.1515/mc-2017-0021

28. Bergman, M.K.: What is Representation? AI3: Adaptive Information, pp. 8–15 (2017)

29. Crémier, L., Bonenfant, M., Lafrance St-Martin, L.: Raw data or hypersymbols? meaning-making with digital data, between discursive processes and machinic procedures. Semiotica **2019**(230), 189–212 (2019). https://doi.org/10.1515/sem-2018-0110

30. Greenlee, D.: Peirce's Concept of Sign. De Gruyter Mouton, Berlin (1973). https://doi.org/10.1515/9783110886443

31. Maculan, B.C.M.S., Lima, G.A.B.O.: Buscando uma definição para o conceito de "conceito" (Seeking a definition for the concept of concept). In: Perpectivas em Ciência da Informação, vol. 22, no. 2, pp. 54–87 (2017). https://doi.org/10.1590/1981-5344/2963

32. Ogden, C. K., Richards, I. A.: The Meaning of Meaning, Harcourt, Brace, and World, New York, 8th edn., p. 1946 (1923)

33. McElvenny, J.: Language and Meaning in the Age of Modernism – C. CK. Ogden and his Contemporaries. Edinburgh University Press (2018

34. Wikipedia. "The Treachery of Images." Wikimedia Foundation. (2023). https://en.wikipedia.org/wiki/The_Treachery_of_Images. Accessed 20 May 2023

35. Santos, L.O.B.D.S., Sales, T.P., Fonseca, C.M., Guizzardi, G.: Towards a conceptual model for the FAIR Digital Object Framework (2023). arXiv preprint arXiv:2302.11894

36. Wittenburg, P., Strawn, G., Mons, B., Bonino, L., Schultes, E.: Digital objects as drivers towards convergence in data infrastructures. Technical Paper (2019). https://doi.org/10.23728/b2share.b605d85809ca45679b110719b6c6cb11

37. Sheridan, H., et al.: Data curation through catalogs: a repository-independent model for data discovery. J. eSci. Librar. **10**(3), 4 (2021)

38. Connolly, D,: Catalogs: Resource Description and Discovery. W3C. (2014). https://www.w3.org/Search/catalogs.html. Accessed 24 Feb 2014

39. Albertoni, R. , Browning, D., Cox, S., Beltran, A. G., Perego, A., Winstanley, P.: Data Catalog Vocabulary (DCAT) - Version 2. W3C Recommendation. 4 February 2020. W3C Recommendation. (2020). https://www.w3.org/TR/vocab-dcat-2/

40. Kurfess, F., Jololian, L., Sebastian, D.: Knowlets: Components for Knowledge Management (2001)
41. Kropp, Y.O; Thalheim, B.: Modelling Perspectives to Support Multiple Information Demands. Inf. Model. Knowl. Bases XXXI **321**, 186–204 (2020). https://doi.org/10.3233/FAIA200015
42. Bergman, M.K.: A Knowledge Representation Practionary – Guidelines Based on Charles Sanders Peirce. Springer, Cham (2018). https://doi.org/10.1007/978-3-319-98092-8
43. Sanfilippo, E.M.: Ontologies for information entities: state of the art and open challenges. Appl. Ontol. **16**(2), 111–135 (2021)

The Ontology for Conceptual Characterization of Ontologies

Beatriz Franco Martins[1]([✉]) [iD], Renata Guizzardi[2] [iD],
José Fabián Reyes Román[1] [iD], Moshe Hadad[3] [iD], and Oscar Pastor[1]([✉]) [iD]

[1] Universitat Politècnica de València, VRAIN, Camino de Vera, 46022 Valencia,
Spain
{bmartins,jreyes}@vrain.upv.es, opastor@dsic.upv.es
[2] University of Twente, Twente, The Netherlands
r.guizzardi@utwente.nl
[3] Accenture LTD, Cyber R&D Lab, Ha-Menofim St 2, 4672553 Tel Aviv-Yafo, Israel
moshe.hadad@accenture.com

Abstract. Ontologies as computational artifacts have been seen as
a solution to FAIRness due to their characteristics, applications, and
semantic competencies. Conceptualizations of complex and vast domains
can be fragmented in different ways and can compose what is known
as ontology networks. Thus, the ontologies produced can relate to each
other in many different ways, making the ontological artifacts themselves
subject to FAIRness. The problem is that in the Ontology Engineering
Process, stakeholders take different perspectives of the conceptualizations, and this causes ontologies to have biases that are sometimes more
ontological and sometimes more related to the domain. Besides, usually, Ontology Engineers provide well-grounded reference ontologies, but
rarely are they implemented. At the same time, Domain Specialists produce operational ontologies storing large amounts of valid data but with
naive ontological support or even without any. We address this problem
of lack of consensual conceptualization by proposing a reference conceptual model (O4OA) that considers ontological-related and domain-
related perspectives, knowledge, and commitment necessary to facilitate
the process of Ontological Analysis, including the analysis of ontologies composing an ontology network. Indeed, O4OA is a (meta)ontology
grounded in the Unified Foundational Ontology (UFO) and supported by
well-known ontological classification standards, guides, and FAIR principles. We demonstrate how this approach can suitably promote conceptual
clarification and terminological harmonization in this area through our
framework proposal and its case studies.

Keywords: Interoperability · Reuse · FAIR · Ontological Analysis ·
Ontology Networks

The authors are grateful to the members of the PROS Center Genome group and
Ontology from UPV and Conceptual Modeling Research Group (NEMO) from UFES
for fruitful discussions.

J. P. A. Almeida et al. (Eds.): ER 2023, LNCS 14320, pp. 105–124, 2023.
https://doi.org/10.1007/978-3-031-47262-6_6

1 Introduction

The FAIR initiative proposes a series of principles to which data management practices should adhere to be considered adequate to meet the challenges of our times. These principles underlie the name of the initiative since FAIR means to be *Findable*, *Accessible*, *Interoperable*, and *Reusable* [66]. Ontologies as computational artifacts have been seen as a solution to FAIRness due to their characteristics, applications, and semantic competencies. In other words, it is possible to meet the aforementioned principles by using ontology to support data management. Consequently, more and more organizations are looking for ontology-based solutions to achieve these features. The usefulness of ontologies is vast, such as providing conceptual support for architectures (such as data mesh, data lake structuring, and big data solutions), and facilitating human-computer interaction through well-founded conceptual models, among others. All uses of ontologies have in common is the need to *interoperate and reuse conceptualizations and data*. This common trait requires that the semantics used be clear, and consensual; even more, these characteristics must last throughout the life cycle of the systems that use them. In other words, ontologies that describe complex, vast, and vital knowledge domains such as the cybersecurity domain, and the genetic domain, among others, require a suitable environment for them to comply with the FAIR Principles [66] and be effective in being FAIR [43]. In summary, ontological artifacts themselves are also subject to FAIRness.

Some applications lead to conceptualizations of complex and vast domains that can be fragmented in different ways, thus composing what is known as **Ontology Networks**. The capacity of ontologies to allow modelers to articulate abstractions of a particular state of affairs in reality [25] provides new possibilities for semantic interoperability and data reuse for more extensive and complex domains. However, our research identifies that those domains have characteristics that potentialize semantic misinterpretation that may occur when it is necessary to interoperate conceptualizations. Besides, ontologies covering these kinds of domains deal with data whose sources are strongly embraced by their community. The problem is that in the Ontology Engineering process, stakeholders take different conceptual perspectives, and this causes ontologies to have biases that are sometimes more ontological and sometimes more domain in nature. Indeed, the way domain specialists and ontology engineers seek to achieve FAIRness lacks a more robust semantic bond. Stakeholders usually adopt different perspectives (regarding their cognitive process - ontological commitment [23,24]) even about the same concept and its surroundings. This is why Ontology Engineers provide well-grounded reference ontologies, which are rarely implemented, while Domain Specialists produce operational ontologies storing large amounts of valid data but with naive ontological support or even without any. Actually, the *Ontological Perspective* must always comply with the *Domain Perspective*, throughout the whole conceptualization life cycle. In other words, ontology engineers must capture the domain notions provided by the domain specialists, returning them with conceptualization solutions through well-founded ontological artifacts (e.g., documents, models, and implementations) to support managing their data [51].

We address this problem of lack of consensual conceptualization by proposing a reference conceptual model named **Ontology for Ontological Analysis (O4OA)**. O4OA considers, at the same time, the ontological-related and the domain-related perspectives (along with their respective knowledge and commitment necessary to facilitate the process of ontological analysis). This is particularly useful when considering the analysis of the ontologies pertaining to an Ontology Network, which need to maintain consistency among many models to meet FAIR principles. By doing so, these ontology networks may serve the purpose of interoperating data and conceptualizations to their full potential. The presentation of the O4OA is the **main contribution** of this paper. The O4OA Reference Ontology is represented in OntoUML [6], along with its constraints formalized using OCL[1] rules. We implemented the O4OA as a REST-API over a NoSQL database [48] to support semi-automated ontological analysis.

We have organized the remaining of this paper as follows way: Sect. 2 walks through the FAIR Principles, showing the importance of homogenizing ontological artifacts' characterization to achieve FAIRness; Sect. 3 describes O4OA; Sect. 4 presents the verification and validation of O4OA; Sect. 5 discusses our proposal in face of related works; Sect. 6 concludes the paper, and discusses some further research directions.

2   Ontologies and FAIR Principles

The FAIR Principles proposed in [66] clarify data management and stewardship, providing a set of best-practice indicators to allow these processes to be effective. FAIR stands for Findable, Accessible, Interoperable, and Reusable [8,54]. The ontological notion that each individual *"thing"* has its own identity (*Identity Principle*) encompasses exactly the "F" principle, in a way that such identity serves the purpose of identification and, thus, allowing an object to be findable. Moreover, the notion of *Rigidity* guarantees that these individuals have a perennial identity, keeping the same *Identity Across Possible Worlds* [46]. The *Identity Principle* goes further from the notion of identification provided by computational artifacts because this kind of identification system only has a programmatic function. On the contrary, foundational ontologies like UFO [28,35], DOLCE [10], among others, can provide computational artifacts with that ontological identity support beyond their processable identification system. UFO provides *Identity Principle* and *Rigidity* through a clear definition of what is a *Kind* [33]. The "A" principle, best practices address this by exploring the (meta)characteristics ontologies must have in order to guarantee that the data it classifies is truly accessible. Examples of these approaches are [2,52], while [3] addresses mainly quantitative motivations, not exploring (meta)characteristics. Thus, as denoted in [57], for the security domain, achieving public availability and findability for domain ontologies is still an open issue.

---

[1] https://www.omg.org/spec/OCL/About-OCL/.

Reference domain ontologies [30] grounded over foundational ontologies provide conceptualizations that encompass the "I" and "R" principles. Moreover, implemented versions of these ontologies are computational artifacts that carry the necessary elements to be processable and semantically precise. However, this is only possible when ontologies fulfill the principles of being well-defined and well-grounded [51]. Guizzardi discusses this perception in depth in [34]. Mainly, well-founded ontologies are able to provide real-world semantics and are more prone to maintain consistency, making explicit the commitments of different conceptualizations.

However, Domain Ontologies (implemented or not) usually fail to accomplish interoperability requirements, mainly due to the different perspectives that Ontology Engineers and Domain Specialists have about standards and norms. These different perspectives are often a source of misinterpretations because they communicate through natural language, which is inherently ambiguous, besides being often governed by political decisions that rarely relate to semantics. Another problem with this divergence of perspective is embedding ontologies with different biases. Domain ontologies developed over the Ontology Engineers' bias usually are well-grounded reference ontologies, but are rarely implemented and the validation with data is limited. Instead, domain ontologies (following Domain Specialists' bias) are usually operational ontologies (i.e., implementations) storing large amounts of valid data but with naive ontological support or even without any [49]. Besides, in both cases, the lack of ontological grounding is a common issue [16,57]. We address this problem by providing a stable environment for ontological analysis through our proposal of an ontology and an associated framework and computational tool. We present the ontology in the next section. The framework is called **The Framework For Ontologies Classification** (F4OC) [50,51], and it uses O4OA to classify and analyze the ontologies meta-characteristics based on knowledge domain requirements. Finally, a computational tool (semi)automates the use of the framework.

3   A (Meta)Ontology to Describe Ontologies

The Ontology For Ontological Analysis (O4OA) models the foundational and domain-related concepts and relations that are necessary to facilitate the process of *Ontological Analysis* [22]. The goal (purpose) of O4OA is to clarify and homogenize the necessary (meta)ontological requirements, data, and characteristics to help stakeholders achieve awareness and common sense about conceptualizations (ontologies). Because O4OA covers the perspectives of both stakeholders (Ontology Engineer and Domain Specialist), it addresses the "Interoperability" and "Reusability" principles of FAIR, since it serves the purpose of correcting misalignment and miscommunication between the conceptualizations of each of these perspectives.

3.1 Methodology, Stakeholders and Research Questions

We advocate that every ontology must be developed in light of the best practices within the *Ontology Engineering Process*. Besides, we strongly recommend the adoption of a well-known methodology to drive the process; thus, we adopt the SABiO methodology [1]. According to it, we must define the ontology purpose and identify its users, i.e. their stakeholders. Therefore and taking into account the discussion in Sect. 2, two key responsibilities are part of the pursuit FAIR w.r.t. to the Ontology Engineering Process: While *Domain Specialists* are concerned with identifying the relevant knowledge aspects that are part of a conceptualization, *Ontology Engineers* aim at representing this ontology in a way that it expresses this knowledge with real-world semantics to be interpreted unequivocally, either by humans or by computational assets. Then we define the *Competence Questions* (CQs)[2] that are the pathway to define the ontology scope and provide its evaluation capabilities; complying with the stakeholder's expectations and requirements [20,21].

This set of CQs contemplates a cross-perspective of ontological and domain-related perspectives, extending them to consider ontology networks. In order to formulate these questions, and considering that they are the requirements engineering guidelines, we conducted the O4OA elicitation process in partnership with a multidisciplinary group of stakeholders and attended online meetings[3], providing different contributions. Our proposal is domain-agnostic, but our case studies are about the Cybersecurity domain; therefore, we are receiving advice from Cybersecurity specialists of our research group and others who are members of the project consortium we participate in[4]. The group comprises Cybersecurity Domain Specialists, Ontology Engineers, and Literature Review Specialists, among others. Also, it is essential to clarify that Ontology Engineers took on different roles, sometimes eliciting requirements and sometimes as project clients, depending on the context discussed and their roles in the group.

From the defined scope, purpose, commitment, and competence questions, and knowing the involved stakeholders, we proceeded with the ontology O4OA engineering process according to SABiO. We represent our proposal using the OntoUML language, which provides grounding over UFO.

3.2 Conceptual Characterization of Ontologies

In order to develop the Ontology Engineer perspective, we searched within the state of the art in ontology engineering to find the meta-features used to characterize an ontology. We found vast works within the context of ontology classification, such as the works [15,19,38,45,47,53,61,62,64]. These works use several

---

[2] Readers may find the complete description of O4OA competence questions at the following repository: https://bfmartins.gitlab.io/o4oa/.

[3] Part of the elicitation process happened during the COVID-2019 pandemic, so the remote strategy was mandatory.

[4] Our research is part of a research consortium to develop well-grounded knowledge graphs through a comprehensive solution within a project in collaboration with teams from several academic institutions, and Accenture LTD.

levels of abstraction to classify ontologies, for instance, according to the degree of formalization and/or axiomatization of ontologies, their applicability, generality, structure, and development among others. We adopt the most relevant and comprehensive classification criteria as the referential base for O4OA, they are [17,18,22,30,65]. However, we advocate that these dimensions must encompass a systematic ontology classification approach to guarantee the FAIRness of ontological artifacts. Therefore, O4OA uses a holistic approach that considers a set of dimensions to characterize ontologies.

The first dimension considers a classification based on the *level of applicability* proposed in [30]. This classification allows us to differentiate when an ontology is an "explicit and formal representation of a portion of reality for knowledge sharing" or an "implementation of this representation for knowledge computational management", i.e., and if it is a Reference or an Operational Ontology.

The second dimension deals with the *level of generality* (sometimes called knowledge kind) of ontologies that refer to a level of dependence on a specific point of view. Many proposals target this dimension, such as [15,38,62]; however, the proposal most accepted by the community is Guarino's [22], which complements the proposal of Mizoguchi and Ikeda [53]. This classification characterizes conceptualizations as *Foundational Ontologies* (which are independent of a particular problem or domain and express very general concepts and their relations like *things* and their properties, *events*, *relations*, etc. They are also known as High-level Ontologies or Upper Ontologies). Already, Non-Foundational Ontologies are *Domain Ontologies* (which provide conceptualizations for specific domains), *Task Ontologies* (which provide conceptualizations about domain tasks, processes, and activities), and *Application Ontologies* (which encompasses both contexts of Domain and Task Ontologies). Another widely accepted classification describes the *Core Ontologies* [65][5].

Figure 1 shows the classification approach adopted in O4OA, in which we describe the classification levels using OntoUML $<<subkind>>$, considering the aforementioned classification describes types of ontologies.

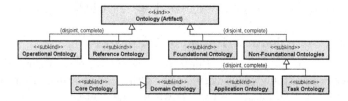

Fig. 1. Fragment of the O4OA as a (meta)ontology – Classifications according to [22,30,65].

---

[5] Which is more general than Domain, Task, and Application ontologies, but more specific than Foundational Ontologies.

We also consider the classification provided by Gomés-Peréz and Corcho [18] as additional dimensions for ontologies classification because it analyzes the ontologies based on their axiomatization level (and considers the limitations of the language) in order to identify its computational limitations when a conceptualization becomes an implemented ontology (i.e., an operational ontology). They divide ontologies by considering the expressiveness of the language used into two aspects: Lightweight and Heavyweight ontologies. A bi-dimensional classification [17], based on [63] and [18], provides a link between the axiomatization and formal levels, focusing on the approach and expressiveness of the language. In Subsect. 3.4 we detail how languages and ontologies are related, as well as the relational aspects that rely on this classification.

We opt for these works because are the most accepted classifications used by the Ontology Engineering community and cover the set of CQs related to the ontology engineering perspective (see previous section). The preference for these classification dimensions instead of others is based on the fact that they already combine the necessary meta-features for FAIRness and because other dimensions are not frequently used. For instance, some works provide a classification based on the nature of the real-world issue [45], the development method [61], and other bi-dimensional classifications [19,47]. However, due to their limited use and to avoid increasing the complexity of the proposed conceptualization, we do not use these additional classifications.

3.3 Domain Cloud of Concepts in Conceptual Characterizations

The O4OA responds to the domain-related CQs questions in terms of ontological artifacts. Thus, we center on the concepts belonging to a conceptualization that must be represented and described. However, to understand this, we need first to clarify the philosophical grounding of what encompasses a conceptualization, and precisely distinguish what a concept is (as an abstraction) and what is the concept representation (as an artifact).

In the philosophical context, a *Concept* is basically a building block of thoughts[6] and can be seen as a mental representation. UFO deals with this philosophical notion of what is a concept as *Tropes* [27,28]. However, we need to define artifacts belonging to ontologies used to represent concepts. Figure 2 presents the relation between concepts (`Concept`) and documentation sources (`Source`). In this situation, `Document` is defined as a *<<category>>* because it aggregates properties of individuals with different identity principles. Indeed, policies, standards, and any literature documentation exist with no dependence, having their own identity. Sources, as well as any other sort of element that provides relevant information for ontologies, are fluid (*<<rolemixin>>*). We also use `Term` as a syntactical artifact (an *Object Kind*) used to describe the notion of a *Concept* (as *Trope Kind*), thus we call `Concept` the role that a term assumes when is defined in an ontology. As a matter of fact, the notions of *Source* and *Term* as roles are relational-dependent [36]. Thus, we represent a `Concept Definition`

---

[6] https://plato.stanford.edu/entries/concepts/.

present in an ontology (`Domain Description`) as a building block used to clarify grammatically (terminologically) the notion of a *Concept* (as *Trope Kind*) according to some source of information. Note that we use the *OntoUML notion of Part/Whole* through the relation `componentOf` to represent the definitions that compose each domain description. We present more details about domain descriptions in Subsect. 3.4.

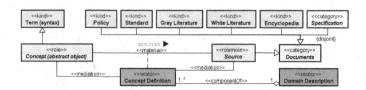

Fig. 2. Fragment of the O4OA as a (meta)ontology – Domain definitions.

3.4 Conceptual Characterization of Ontology Networks

From the conceptual characterization of ontologies as artifacts presented in Subsect. 3.2, we can extend it to identify the relationships among these ontologies (presented in Sect. 3.1). These are key elements regarding FAIR Principles, especially regarding the "I" and "R". Indeed, ontologies can relate in different ways in networks [1, 14], as demonstrated in initiatives like [9, 39], for example. Aside from that, ontology networks are not necessarily a set of isolated ontologies grouped together, merely because they act in a domain subdivided into smaller parts (subdomains). Instead, how ontologies relate to each other directly depends on how their building blocks relate; in this case, we are talking about relational (meta)characteristics that promote FAIRness.

Ontologies (meta)characteristics (i.e., their purpose, scope, generality, etc.), together with the definitions that compose a domain description applicable to these ontologies (and consequently its foundation), define the relationships present in this network [50]. The Applicability Level of ontologies goes beyond only classifying whether an ontology is implemented. This information follows the notion that a Reference Ontology should be a conceptualization that is constructed to make the best possible description of the domain concerning a certain level of generality and point of view and that an Operational Ontology is the actionable version of a Reference Ontology that uses the most appropriate language in order to guarantee desirable computational properties without compromising the previously defined ontological commitments [23, 30]. Therefore, there should not be any operational ontology without the existence of a previous reference ontology in which concepts and their relationships are *well-defined*. Figure 3 presents Reference and Operational Ontologies, their roles, and their relation.

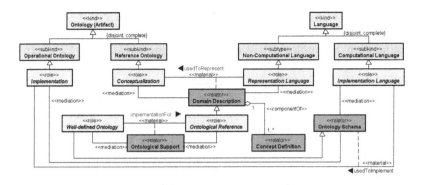

Fig. 3. Fragment of the O4OA as a (meta)ontology – Applicability Level.

Regarding the Application Level, a `Conceptualization` is a reference ontology that is represented through a `Modeling Language`; and an `Implementation` is an operational ontology that works through an `Implementation Language`. We use the *Relator Pattern* [32] to represent the relational aspects that appear in the characterization of ontologies. According to its Applicability Level, they are `Domain Description` and the `Ontology Schema`. Thus, the notion that an ontology is or has an implemented version (`implementationFor`, a <<*material*>> relation) derives from the fact that reference ontologies provide ontological support for ontological schemes. This relation allows us to evaluate the relational characteristics a Reference Ontology can provide to its implementations. Besides, this approach can also help ontology engineers deal with implementation language limitations by knowing which ontological aspects can (or can not) be implemented without losing ontological decidability.

Incidentally, a domain description is thought in some representation language (the `Modeling Language` role), usually an Ontology-Driven Modeling Language (ODML). Besides, as metamodels specify languages, an Ontology-Driven Metamodel specifies an ODML. From this perspective, an ontology drives an ODML, constraining philosophically its metamodel, denoting the `specifys` <<*material*>> relation, and defining the <<*Relator*>> `Ontology-driven Language Specification` as depicted in Fig. 4.

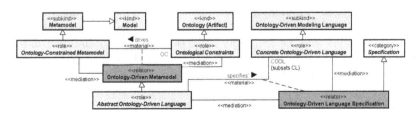

Fig. 4. Fragment of the O4OA as a (meta)ontology – Ontology-Driven Modeling Languages.

Any ontology can drive ODMLs. For instance, OASIS is an Ontology-Driven Domain Specific Language grounded over O^3 [59,60]; likewise, OntoUML is a Foundational Ontology-Driven Language grounded over UFO. In this case, an ontology is considered *Well-grounded*, if it is represented through a Foundational Ontology-Driven Language (as OntoUML, for instance), i.e. this language, is the bearer of the Ontological Foundation for the conceptualization. Thus, an indirect grounding is provided through the Ontology-driven Language Specification as depicted in Fig. 5.

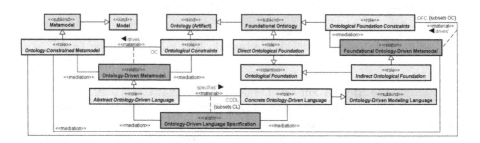

Fig. 5. Fragment of the O4OA as a (meta)ontology – Ontologies driving languages.

The notion of *Well-grounded* ontologies is based on the fact that the support of a Foundational Ontology helps to avoid semantic interoperability problems in more specific ontologies [26]. In other words, Foundational Ontologies are fundamental for Ontology-Driven Conceptual Languages used to produce Domain, Task, and Application, and Core Ontologies, as well as providing ontological analysis for not grounded conceptualizations. Therefore, we advocate that ontologies must be evaluated according to their grounding, separating ontologies that are driven by foundational ontologies (i.e., well-grounded) from ontologies without this support (i.e., not grounded) [51].

The classification according to the ontology generality level provides us the ability to study the impact that the lack of ontological foundation can produce when it is necessary to interoperate concepts of this type of ontologies and at the same time guarantee FAIRness when we put attention on this relationship among a Foundational Ontology, and the ontologies grounded by it. Therefore, we use O4OA to describe the grounding ontologies relationship. With this respect, we define the groundedOver <<*material*>> relation established through the Foundational Ontologies role, i.e. concepts defined in a non-foundational ontology specialize from more general conceptual (philosophical) notions from a Foundational Ontology, defining well-grounded ontologies and allowing stakeholders to make solid semantic considerations.

Figure 6 shows the (groundedOver) relation we define, as well as it also describes how the classification differentiates the ontologies through some of its characteristics. We use the *Relator Pattern* to describe how Foundational Ontologies ground the non-foundational ontologies.

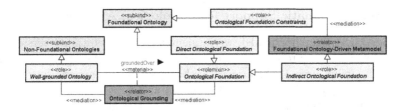

Fig. 6. Fragment of the O4OA as a (meta)ontology – Well-grounded ontologies.

Still chasing the FAIRness, O4OA characterizing ontologies according to their generality level provides another important feature. An ontology can reuse other ontologies; in this case, we are dealing directly with the "*R*" principle of FAIR. Different types of reuse can appear in this relation, depending on how the *Reuser Ontology* lays hold of and uses concepts of the *Reused Ontology*. The most usual reuse happens when concepts defined in an ontology can specialize into concepts defined in another ontology. Apart from this, concepts defined in non-foundational ontologies can specialize foundational notions (thought a `groundingOver` relation). Additionally, the reuse of ontologies can occur through the addition of stronger ontological grounding, however, maintaining the alignment of the domain definitions already adopted. This situation happens when the domain perspective about the definitions present in the related conceptualization is aligned, but the ontological perspective must be reinforced. In other words, this happens when the reused ontology lacks an ontological foundation and requires the grounding provided by a Foundational Ontology or the use of an ODML (provided by the reuser ontology), [13] is an example of this reuse.

Under the umbrella of ontology networks, stakeholders usually confuse the reuse of ontologies with the notion that ontologies can be composed of other ontologies. This is because the notion of a Whole/Part can be seen as a larger ontology using smaller ontologies, but this is not the same. This issue can be aggravated when these relationships occur simultaneously. For instance, UFO is composed of UFO-A, UFO-B, and UFO-C sub-ontologies, and at the same time, UFO-B and UFO-C reuse UFO-A. Indeed, the reuse of ontologies denotes an *Intersection* among ontologies while Whole/Part follows the *Weak Supplementation Pattern*, which states that every whole must be composed by at least two parts [29,31]. Figure 7 depicts the reuse of ontologies and how ontologies can be composed by other ontologies (sub-ontologies).

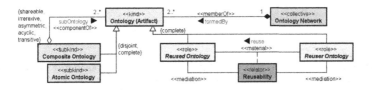

Fig. 7. Fragment of the O4OA as a (meta)ontology – Reuse a Whole/Part.

3.5   A Semi-automatic Support for Ontological Analysis

Given the O4OA reference model, we implemented an operational version and a frontend solution to provide easy, responsive, and multiplatform access. This operational version uses *Microservices Architecture* and composes data storage with *MongoDB*, a *REST-AP* made with *NodeJS* and *Express*, and the responsive frontend prototype implemented with *Angular Material*, all in *Docker* containers. We manually added the data collected about the ontologies belonging to our case studies [49]. Regarding the domain perspective, we loaded, verified, and validated the terminology of the domain in a study by using well-established standards. In this case, as our target domain is cybersecurity, our referential sources are the ISO/IEC 27032:2012 [40] and the ISO/IEC 27000:2018 [41]. Additionally, we use this referential to compare the cybersecurity terminology definitions from other sources, such STIX, MAEC, NIST, ITU, among others.

Up to now, we have assessed 161 concepts in the Cybersecurity domain, and many others obtained from the associated foundational and domain-correlated ontologies studied. Associated with these concepts (in the cloud of concepts), we registered 73 reliable sources, providing a burst of possible usage definitions in ontologies of this and its related domains. For instance, taking the concept of *Risk*, we found 18 definitions of *what it is a Risk*. Besides, we also found many other risk-related definitions, the ones for concepts such as *Level of Risk*, *Residual Risk*, *Risk Criteria*, and other 11 associated ones. In fact, this is a (regular expressions) recursive process because the O4OA operational ontology version is a graph. Although it is a syntactic process, these kinds of findings open the opportunity for the next step of research, which is reasoning the semantics of concepts, context, and ontological commitments[7]. This is possible because the concepts of Foundational Ontologies and their definitions are also registered in our data storage (as meta characteristics) through using ODML and grounding by specialization. We present findings about the analysis of the *Risk* and the analysis of the *Vulnerability* in the works [51] and [50] respectively, as part of our case studies.

The frontend solution of the tool is still under development, so we consider it as an *alpha* version. However, it has already demonstrated its potential in facilitating access to data and supporting the ontological analysis process with O4OA. For instance, Fig. 8 shows that we can trace the concept of *Vulnerability* from its definitions until the ontologies use them. We are working on a better graph presentation (dynamic) to allow dynamic navigation in the cloud of concepts as well as in ontology (meta)characteristics[8].

---

[7] The adoption of microservices allows API scaling adding reasoning capabilities, for this future possibilities.

[8] It is important to point out that we adopted an *Agile Development* approach in order to provide fast initial results meanwhile being scaled.

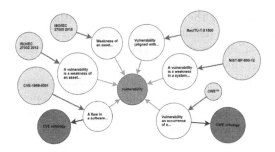

Fig. 8. Export image of the O4OA tool – fragment of the *Vulnerability* definitions.

O4OA deals with the (meta)characteristics of both the ontological and domain views, clarifying their relationship. Therefore, this allows tracing of how concepts are represented or implemented in ontologies that go beyond the presentation of the sub-ontologies walk graph, exemplified in Fig. 8. This allows navigating a graph starting from any concept within the cloud of concepts to the ontologies that use them, including access to the definitions adopted in each case. In fact, this is a feature already available in the API we developed and that will possibly gain relevance with the use of a graph-enhanced presentation in the frontend. Likewise, we can navigate through the ontological relations to find out the ontological grounding supporting a concept, even when it appears in different ontologies, and even compare it in one well-grounded ontology with another imprecise one, for instance.

4   Evaluation

According to SABiO, during the evaluation phase of the development process, the proposed CQs must be confronted with the ontology developed to guarantee that it complies with the requirements defined. Additionally, it is required that the reference model be analyzed through processes of model instantiation in order to explore possible issues or unexpected possibilities scenarios (branches or worlds). We adopted the Alloy analyzer tool [42] applying the OntoUML notions present in the work [7] to proceed with the validation; besides, this analysis is being performed concurrently with the development of the operational version of the ontology. Due to the O4OA model characteristics (size and complexity) and design decisions, we fragment the analysis, running the instantiation of each model package in an individual and modular way. In the validations process, we elicit the set of additional constraints (in addition to those already present in OntoUML) required, and we also check model cardinalities to ensure correct semantics. For example, when analyzing the instantiation of the contents of the **Reuse** package, because the reused and reuser ontology roles are not *disjoint*, we had to add a constraint to avoid cyclic reuses, i.e., a *Transitive Closure* predicate for the relations **reuses**. Note that some required constraints must be implemented directly in the persistence, while others in the API. See the complete model evaluation details in the repository of the ontology.

We also developed a framework for classifying and characterizing ontologies, which is composed of the presented reference ontology, its version implemented in NoSQL, and a prototype API that manipulates and manages the (meta)data obtained in the application of the framework. We proposed a sequence of five ontological-related and domain-related steps to identify and catalog the (meta)data regarding the ontology and the domain perspectives, respectively. As the framework is based on O4OA and was formulated to ensure compliance with FAIR principles, we obtained promising results in our case studies; for example, those we have presented in [49–51].

It is important to point out that although our case studies are within the Cybersecurity domain, O4OA and its associated framework are agnostic, allowing their use in any domain of knowledge. Indeed, in domains covering vast knowledge, which are extremely regulated (normalized) or complex, our proposal demonstrates its advantages more than those in lighter domains. This is because the complexity and expense of ontological analysis grow proportionally as the domain gets more vast and complex. We observe these phenomena during the course of the study done within the Cybersecurity domain, which has several of these characteristics; it is vast, highly regulated by norms and standards, constantly evolving, and difficult in its own right. One evidence of this is present in the work of [56], an example of which the O4OA-based framework can homogenize and contribute to the process of ontological analysis.

5 Related Works

Several initiatives deal with Ontology-Driven Interoperability (ODI), especially in areas of *Internet of Things* (IoT) and *Web of Things* (WoT), such as [5,55]. Their related ontologies SSN [4], oneM2M [58], and SAREF [11] are W3C standards. As in Cybersecurity, IoT and WoT are complex domains where stakeholders must commit agreement. However, these initiatives differ from ours. The first distinction is in the domain itself; while they deal with the core characteristics in the IoT/WoT domain[9], O4OA deals with (meta)characteristics present in any kind of ontological artifact created to represent any domain. Besides, O4OA rationalizes the notion of FAIRness over ontological analysis processes, while such ontologies rationalize ODI into their domain. Second, although they are well-example initiatives in the reuse of ontologies in themselves, they do not deal with the notion of a broad cloud of concepts (and their details) nor relations among ontologies in any networks. Indeed, they are data interoperability providers for IoT/WoT while O4OA is an interoperability provider for any ontologies[10]. Lastly, IoT/WoT ontologies have the same issues we detected in the cybersecurity ontologies, detailed in [49]; notably, lack of a grounding, making them require adaptations to interoperate or have proper reuse, with no

---

[9] SSN, oneM2M, and SAREF are *Core Ontologies* in the sense of [22,65].

[10] In O4OA, the relations and concepts of ontologies are data instances.

assuring semantic (grounding). The work [5] runs ODI by making ontological analysis and goes in line with the notion of FAIRness (like O4OA) under the ODI viewpoint (ontological perspective), but there is no mention of important domain-dependent aspects, i.e., domain (meta)characteristics (domain perspective). Instead, O4OA is domain-agnostic but not domain-indifferent since the purpose of performing an ontological analysis is to elicit knowledge in a consensual, reproducible, traceable, and formal way. Indeed, ODI is among many uses where ontological analysis is a key contributor.

The Ontology Metadata Vocabulary (OMV) [37] is a proposal for describing ontologies and related entities, and this is the only approach similar to ours that we could find in the state of the art. It focuses on metadata of ontologies intending to be the standard covering this domain. The proposal has demonstrated usefulness in initiatives such as [12]. The approach distinguishes between an ontology base (a conceptualization) and an ontology document (a realization of a conceptualization - an implementation). The ontology covers some of the metadata that is part of the FAIRness discussion, such as language, licensing, and quantitative data (number of classes, properties, and axioms). OVM also uses Guarino's classification [22] to classify ontologies. In this respect, OVM is similar but lighter than our proposal; however, as an ontology, OVM in itself is not FAIR. Besides, it does not have the support of a prior reference ontology; indeed, it is an ontology implemented in OWL without using any foundation ontology for grounding. Conversely, O4OA is grounded on UFO, has a well-defined reference model written in OntoUML, and is implemented in a NoSQL database; besides, it supports our framework proposal following a solid methodological approach (namely, SABiO).

The work [44] presents a study of the metadata of a vast number of ontologies. In this work, some works were more relevant in terms of being available to describe ontological metadata, such as Dublin Core, Ontology Metadata Vocabulary, VoID, etc. The study compared of these works and their implementations, demonstrating the lack of foundational grounding as an issue. This confirms the claim that "surprisingly, both in research and industry, ontologies as computational artifacts are very often built without the aid of any framework of this kind (citing our proposal), favoring recurrent modeling mistakes and gaps" [56].

6   Conclusions

The main contribution of this paper is proposing the Ontology for Ontological Analysis, a (meta)ontology that classifies and characterizes ontologies from their (meta)characteristics. We use the SABiO approach and OntoUML language (grounded in UFO) to develop O4OA. Additionally, our proposal is based on a series of well-established ontology classifications, as well as the best practices supported by FAIR Principles. This ontology is implemented and guides a framework for classifying and characterizing ontologies, providing a clear and reproducible environment that helps the Ontological Analysis Process. Our proposal stands out because in itself it is ontology-driven, well-defined, and well-grounded, i.e., it is FAIR.

Firstly, O4OA provides a conceptual analysis of the nature of the different (meta)characteristics present in the distinct stakeholders' perspectives by using of UFO's foundational categories present in OntoUML. We systematize the process of ontology classification using the most recognized works and with the best coverage of classification dimensions. Furthermore, this ontology is a reference model to study, manage, and maintain ontologies that describe real-world complex, extremely regulated, and data-sensible domains.

Secondly, as a (meta)ontological reference model, O4OA can provide operational versions to track, analyze, and provide reasoning about ontologies belonging to ontology networks. This kind of approach is a fertile field for managing conceptualizations that support industrial architectures such as data mesh, data lake structuring, big data solutions, facilitating human-computer interaction among enterprise stakeholders and teams, and many others.

Thirdly, O4OA establishes a common, stable, and systematic environment for improving communication among ontology engineers and domain experts, avoiding misinterpretations, misunderstandings, structural issues in ontologies, and communication problems that interfere with FAIRness.

Fourth, in addition to these uses, the O4OA prototype tool we are developing to support ontological analysis has been presenting interesting results despite its ongoing development. Its already-built features demonstrate its potential in allowing management and clarification of cloud-of-concepts in ontologies in a semi-automated way. Besides our implementation proposal, other initiatives can emerge; for instance, providing Analytics in a logical language such as Common Logic, OWL, or other reasoners. Moreover, these operational versions can evolve to provide reasoning, tools, and other features or automation. In particular, we intend to develop a web solution encompassing these resources.

Finally, we intend to define the full set of axioms (we did not include any axiom in this paper because of space limitations) to complete the formalization of O4OA. We plan to improve the evaluation of the ontology in other real-world industrial scenarios, including one focusing on the notion of **Ontological Technical Depth,** to prove that ontologies are promising for practical use. We also intend to strengthen the connection between the work developed in the Cybersecurity and Software Engineering domains to bring teams working in both areas closer to improve security in software systems. The objective is to promote practical results in industrial development environments. We also pretend to extend the number of (meta)characteristics covered in O4OA and provide Analytics with them.

Acknowledgments. This work has financial support of Accenture LTD with project Digital Knowledge Graph – Adaptable Analytics API, Generalitat Valenciana with the project CoMoDiD (CIPROM/2021/023), Spanish State Research Agency with projects DELFOS (PDC2021-121243-I00), SREC (PID2021-123824OB-I00), MICIN/AEI/10.13039/501 100011033, and co-financed by the European Union Next Generation EU/PRTR with ERDF.

References

1. de Almeida Falbo, R.: Sabio: systematic approach for building ontologies. In: Onto.Com/odise@ Fois (2014)
2. Amdouni, E., Bouazzouni, S., Jonquet, C.: O'faire: ontology fairness evaluator in the agroportal semantic resource repository. In: The Semantic Web: ESWC 2022 Satellite Events: Hersonissos, Crete, Greece, 29 May–2 June 2022, Proceedings, pp. 89–94. Springer, Heidelberg (2022). https://doi.org/10.1007/978-3-031-11609-4_17
3. Amdouni, E., Jonquet, C.: FAIR or FAIRer? an integrated quantitative FAIRness assessment grid for semantic resources and ontologies. In: Garoufallou, E., Ovalle-Perandones, M.-A., Vlachidis, A. (eds.) MTSR 2021. CCIS, vol. 1537, pp. 67–80. Springer, Cham (2022). https://doi.org/10.1007/978-3-030-98876-0_6
4. Atkinson, R., García-Castro, R., Lieberman, J., Stadler, C.: Semantic sensor network ontology. Technical Report. OGC 16–079, World Wide Web Consortium (2017)
5. Bauer, M., et al.: Towards semantic interoperability standards based on ontologies. In: AIOTI White paper (2019)
6. Benevides, A.B., Guizzardi, G.: A model-based tool for conceptual modeling and domain ontology engineering in OntoUML. In: Filipe, J., Cordeiro, J. (eds.) ICEIS 2009. LNBIP, vol. 24, pp. 528–538. Springer, Heidelberg (2009). https://doi.org/10.1007/978-3-642-01347-8_44
7. Benevides, A.B., Guizzardi, G., Braga, B.F.B., Almeida, J.P.A., et al.: Validating modal aspects of ontouml conceptual models using automatically generated visual world structures. J. Univ. Comput. Sci. **16**(20), 2904–2933 (2010)
8. Boeckhout, M., Zielhuis, G.A., Bredenoord, A.L.: The fair guiding principles for data stewardship: fair enough? Eur. J. Hum. Genet. **26**(7), 931–936 (2018)
9. Borges Ruy, F., de Almeida Falbo, R., Perini Barcellos, M., Dornelas Costa, S., Guizzardi, G.: SEON: a software engineering ontology network. In: Blomqvist, E., Ciancarini, P., Poggi, F., Vitali, F. (eds.) EKAW 2016. LNCS (LNAI), vol. 10024, pp. 527–542. Springer, Cham (2016). https://doi.org/10.1007/978-3-319-49004-5_34
10. Borgo, S., Masolo, C.: Ontological Foundations of DOLCE, pp. 279–295. Springer, Dordrecht (2010). https://doi.org/10.1007/978-90-481-8847-5_13
11. Daniele, L., Garcia-Castro, R., Lefrançois, M., Poveda-Villalon, M.: Smart applications reference ontology (saref) (2019). Accessed Aug 2023
12. d'Aquin, M., et al.: Watson: a gateway for the semantic web (2007)
13. Duarte, B.B., Falbo, R.A., Guizzardi, G., Guizzardi, R.S.S., Souza, V.E.S.: Towards an ontology of software defects, errors and failures. In: Trujillo, J.C., et al. (eds.) ER 2018. LNCS, vol. 11157, pp. 349–362. Springer, Cham (2018). https://doi.org/10.1007/978-3-030-00847-5_25
14. Euzenat, J.: Revision in networks of ontologies. Artif. Intell. **228**, 195–216 (2015)
15. Fensel, D.: Ontologies, pp. 11–18. Springer, Heidelberg (2001). https://doi.org/10.1007/978-3-662-04396-7_2
16. García S, A., Guizzardi, G., Pastor, O., Storey, V.C., Bernasconi, A.: An ontological characterization of a conceptual model of the human genome. In: Intelligent Information Systems: CAiSE Forum 2022, Leuven, Belgium, 6–10 June 2022, Proceedings, pp. 27–35. Springer, Heidelberg (2022). https://doi.org/10.1007/978-3-031-07481-3_4

17. Giunchiglia, F., Zaihrayeu, I.: Lightweight ontologies. University of Trento, Technical report (2007)
18. Gómez-Pérez, A., Corcho, O.: Ontology languages for the semantic web. IEEE Intell. Syst. **17**(1), 54–60 (2002)
19. Gomez-Perez, A., Fernández-López, M., Corcho, O.: Ontological Engineering: With Examples from the Areas of Knowledge Management, E-Commerce and the Semantic Web. Springer, Heidelberg (2004). https://doi.org/10.1007/b97353
20. Gruninger, M.: Methodology for the design and evaluation of ontologies. In: International Joint Conference on Artificial Intelligence (1995)
21. Gruninger, M.: Designing and evaluating generic ontologies. In: 12th European Conference of Artificial Intelligence, vol. 1, pp. 53–64. Citeseer (1996)
22. Guarino, N.: Formal ontology in information systems. In: Proceedings of the 1st International Conference, pp. 6–8. IOS Press, Trento (1998)
23. Guarino, N.: The ontological level. In: Philosophy and the Cognitive Sciences (1994)
24. Guarino, N.: The ontological level: Revisiting 30 years of knowledge representation. In: Conceptual Modeling: Foundations and Applications, pp. 52–67 (2009)
25. Guarino, N., Poli, R.: The role of formal ontology in the information technnology. Int. J. Hum Comput Stud. **43**(5–6), 623–965 (1995)
26. Guizzardi, G.: The role of foundational ontology for conceptual modeling and domain ontology representation, keynote paper. In: 7th International Baltic Conference on Databases and Information Systems (DB&IS). IEEE Press, Vilnius (2006)
27. Guizzardi, G., Masolo, C., Borgo, S.: In the defense of a trope-based ontology for conceptual modeling: an example with the foundations of attributes, weak entities and datatypes. In: 25th International Conference on Conceptual Modeling, Berlin (2006)
28. Guizzardi, G.: Ontological Foundations for Structural Conceptual Models. CTIT, Centre for Telematics and Information Technology (2005)
29. Guizzardi, G.: Modal aspects of object types and part-whole relations and the *de re/de dicto* distinction. In: Krogstie, J., Opdahl, A., Sindre, G. (eds.) CAiSE 2007. LNCS, vol. 4495, pp. 5–20. Springer, Heidelberg (2007). https://doi.org/10.1007/978-3-540-72988-4_2
30. Guizzardi, G.: On ontology, ontologies, conceptualizations, modeling languages, and (meta) models. Front. Artif. Intell. Appl. **155**, 18 (2007)
31. Guizzardi, G.: The problem of transitivity of part-whole relations in conceptual modeling revisited. In: van Eck, P., Gordijn, J., Wieringa, R. (eds.) CAiSE 2009. LNCS, vol. 5565, pp. 94–109. Springer, Heidelberg (2009). https://doi.org/10.1007/978-3-642-02144-2_12
32. Guizzardi, G.: Ontological patterns, anti-patterns and pattern languages for next-generation conceptual modeling. In: Yu, E., Dobbie, G., Jarke, M., Purao, S. (eds.) ER 2014. LNCS, vol. 8824, pp. 13–27. Springer, Cham (2014). https://doi.org/10.1007/978-3-319-12206-9_2
33. Guizzardi, G.: Logical, ontological and cognitive aspects of object types and cross-world identity with applications to the theory of conceptual spaces. In: Zenker, F., Gärdenfors, P. (eds.) Applications of Conceptual Spaces. SL, vol. 359, pp. 165–186. Springer, Cham (2015). https://doi.org/10.1007/978-3-319-15021-5_9
34. Guizzardi, G.: Ontology, ontologies and the "I" of FAIR. Data Intell. **2**, 181–191 (2020)
35. Guizzardi, G., Ferreira Pires, L., van Sinderen, M.: An ontology-based approach for evaluating the *domain appropriateness* and *comprehensibility appropriateness* of modeling languages. In: Briand, L., Williams, C. (eds.) MODELS 2005.

LNCS, vol. 3713, pp. 691–705. Springer, Heidelberg (2005). https://doi.org/10.1007/11557432_51

36. Guizzardi, G., Wagner, G.: What's in a relationship: an ontological analysis. In: Li, Q., Spaccapietra, S., Yu, E., Olivé, A. (eds.) ER 2008. LNCS, vol. 5231, pp. 83–97. Springer, Heidelberg (2008). https://doi.org/10.1007/978-3-540-87877-3_8

37. Hartmann, J., Sure, Y., Haase, P., Palma, R., Suarez-Figueroa, M.: OMV-ontology metadata vocabulary. In: ISWC, vol. 3729 (2005)

38. Hele-Mai, H., Tanel-Lauri, L.: A survey of concept-based information retrieval tools on the web. In: Proceedings of the 5thEast-European Conference AD BIS, pp. 29–41 (2001)

39. Hemberg, E., et al.: Linking threat tactics, techniques, and patterns with defensive weaknesses, vulnerabilities and affected platform configurations for cyber hunting (2021)

40. ISO Central Secretary: Information technology - security techniques - guidelines for cybersecurity. Standard ISO/IEC 27032:2012. International Organization for Standardization, Geneva (2012)

41. ISO Central Secretary: Information technology - security techniques - information security management systems - overview and vocabulary. Standard ISO/IEC 27000:2018–02, International Organization for Standardization, Geneva (2018)

42. Jackson, D.: Software Abstractions: Logic, Language, and Analysis. MIT press, Cambridge (2012)

43. Jacobsen, A., et al.: FAIR principles: interpretations and implementation considerations. Data Intell. **2**(1–2), 10–29 (2020). https://doi.org/10.1162/dint_r_00024

44. Jonquet, C., Toulet, A., Dutta, B., Emonet, V.: Harnessing the power of unified metadata in an ontology repository: the case of agroportal. J. Data Semant. **7**(4), 191–221 (2018)

45. Jurisica, I., Mylopoulos, J., Yu, E.: Using ontologies for knowledge management: an information systems perspective. In: Proceedings of the Annual Meeting-American Society For Information Science, vol. 36, pp. 482–496. Information Today; 1998 (1999)

46. Kripke, S.A.: Naming and Necessity. Harvard University Press, Cambridge (1980)

47. Lassila, O., McGuinness, D.: The role of frame-based representation on the semantic web. Linköping Electron. Articles Comput. Inf. Sci. **6**(5), 2001 (2001)

48. Martins, B.F., Serrano, L., Reyes, J.F., Panach, J.I., Pastor, O.: Towards the consolidation of cybersecurity standardized definitions: a tool for ontological analysis. In: Proceedings of the XXIV Iberoamerican Conference on Software Engineering, CIbSE 2021, San José, Costa Rica, 2021, pp. 290–303. Curran Associates (2021)

49. Martins, B.F., Serrano, L., Reyes, J.F., Panach, J.I., Pastor, O., Rochwerger, B.: Conceptual characterization of cybersecurity ontologies. In: Grabis, J., Bork, D. (eds.) PoEM 2020. LNBIP, vol. 400, pp. 323–338. Springer, Cham (2020). https://doi.org/10.1007/978-3-030-63479-7_22

50. Martins, B.F., Reyes Román, J.F., Pastor, O., Hadad, M.: Improving conceptual domain characterization in ontology networks. In: Research Challenges in Information Science: 17th International Conference, RCIS 2023, Corfu, Greece, 23–26 May 2023, Proceedings, pp. 187–202. Springer, Heidelberg (2023). https://doi.org/10.1007/978-3-031-33080-3_12

51. Martins, B.F., et al.: A framework for conceptual characterization of ontologies and its application in the cybersecurity domain. Softw. Syst. Model. **21**(4), 1437–1464 (2022)

52. Mazimwe, A., Hammouda, I., Gidudu, A.: Implementation of fair principles for ontologies in the disaster domain: a systematic literature review. ISPRS Int. J. Geo Inf. **10**(5), 324 (2021)
53. Mizoguchi, R., Ikeda, M.: Towards ontology engineering. J.-Jpn. Soc. Artif. Intell. **13**, 9–10 (1998)
54. Mons, B., Neylon, C., Velterop, J., Dumontier, M., da Silva Santos, L.O.B., Wilkinson, M.D.: Cloudy, increasingly fair; revisiting the fair data guiding principles for the European open science cloud. Inf. Serv. Use **37**(1), 49–56 (2017)
55. Murdock, P., et al.: Semantic interoperability for the Web of Things. Ph.D. thesis, Dépt. Réseaux et Service Multimédia Mobiles (Institut Mines-Télécom-Télécom (2016)
56. Ítalo Oliveira, E.G., et al.: Boosting D3FEND: ontological analysis and recommendations. In: Formal Ontology in Information Systems. IOS Press, Nieuwe Hemweg (2023)
57. Oliveira, Í., Fumagalli, M., Prince Sales, T., Guizzardi, G.: How FAIR are security core ontologies? a systematic mapping study. In: Cherfi, S., Perini, A., Nurcan, S. (eds.) RCIS 2021. LNBIP, vol. 415, pp. 107–123. Springer, Cham (2021). https://doi.org/10.1007/978-3-030-75018-3_7
58. oneM2M Partners: ONEM2M TECHNICAL SPECIFICATION. Technical Report. TS-0012-V3.7.3, oneM2M (2019). https://www.onem2m.org/images/pdf/TS-0012-Base_Ontology-V3_7_3.pdf. type 1 (ARIB, ATIS, CCSA, ETSI, TIA, TSDSI, TTA, TTC)
59. Pastor, O.: Diseño y Desarrollo de un Entorno de Producción Automática de Software basado en el modelo orientado a Objetos. Ph.D. thesis, Tesis doctoral dirigida por Isidro Ramos, DSIC, Universitat Politècnica de València (1992)
60. Pastor, O., Gómez, J., Insfrán, E., Pelechano, V.: The OO-method approach for information systems modeling: from object-oriented conceptual modeling to automated programming. Inf. Syst. **26**(7), 507–534 (2001). https://doi.org/10.1016/S0306-4379(01)00035-7. http://www.sciencedirect.com/science/article/pii/S0306437901000357
61. Simperl, E., Bürger, T., Hangl, S., Wörgl, S., Popov, I.: Ontocom: a reliable cost estimation method for ontology development projects. J. Web Semant. **16**, 1–16 (2012)
62. Studer, R., Benjamins, V.R., Fensel, D.: Knowledge engineering: principles and methods. Data Knowl. Eng. **25**(1–2), 161–197 (1998)
63. Uschold, M., Gruninger, M.: Ontologies and semantics for seamless connectivity. ACM SIGMOD Rec. **33**(4), 58–64 (2004)
64. Uschold, M., Gruninger, M., et al.: Ontologies: principles, methods and applications. Technical Report-University of Edinburgh Artificial Intelligence Applications Institute Aiai TR (1996)
65. Van Heijst, G., Schreiber, A.T., Wielinga, B.J.: Using explicit ontologies in kbs development. Int. J. Hum.-Comput. Stud., 183–292 (1997)
66. Wilkinson, M.D., et al.: The fair guiding principles for scientific data management and stewardship. Sci. Data **3**(1), 1–9 (2016)

ProMoTe: A Data Product Model Template for Data Meshes

Stefan Driessen[1]([envelope]) [ID], Willem-Jan van den Heuvel[1] [ID], and Geert Monsieur[2] [ID]

[1] Tilburg University, Sint-Janssingel 92, 's-Hertogenbosch, The Netherlands
s.w.driessen@jads.nl
[2] Eindhoven Unversity of Technology, Sint-Janssingel 92, 's-Hertogenbosch, The Netherlands

Abstract. As the shortcomings of monolithic data platforms such as data lakes are quickly becoming more grave and evident, many organisations are struggling to transition to data meshes, making data available for consumption in a decentralised manner. However, the emerging data mesh paradigm fails to provide sufficient (modelling) support to effectively create, manage, and describe data products, the architectural quanta of a data mesh. In this work, we introduce the data Product Model Template (PROMOTE): a formal meta-model of data products that is fully aligned with a data mesh. PROMOTE was devised, explored and partially validated based on industry requirements in tandem with academic literature and is currently being used by a major Dutch Telecom company to enable their data mesh transition.

Keywords: Data Product · Data Mesh · Modelling · Industry Report

1 Introduction

Despite the promises of big data to revolutionise the way companies do business, many organisations still grossly fail to fully capitalise on the data they are generating. Data Meshes are being developed as alternatives to the traditional monolithic architectures-e.g., data lakes and warehouses-that are the norm for dealing with big data and which critics have pointed to as bottlenecks in big data management [7,9]. The main downside of these monolithic approaches is that they fail to scale with the number of data sources on the one hand and data science and analytics use cases on the other [9,19]. Data meshes, which are domain-oriented alternatives that revolve around data products, in theory, provide a solution to this problem of scalability because each data product offered in a data mesh is provided by an owner responsible for optimising the data for consumption. Data Products can be defined as the combination of all responsibilities and functionalities required to optimally exchange data on a platform. When viewed from this perspective, data products mirror the successful transition in software development from monolithic software solutions to (micro)services [3].

J. P. A. Almeida et al. (Eds.): ER 2023, LNCS 14320, pp. 125–142, 2023.
https://doi.org/10.1007/978-3-031-47262-6_7

Because of these shortcomings, data meshes have attracted significant interest from industry, as can be observed from the amount of grey literature that is becoming available online on'the topic [6]. However, a persistent theme in these sources is that there are no instances of completed data meshes populated with mature data products. We find four main reasons for this lack of maturity. First is the topic's novelty: The term data mesh was first coined by Zhamak Dehghani and posted in a blog [19] in 2019 and has only recently gained widespread attention in the scientific and industrial community. Second, the greatest challenges with transitioning from a monolithic data platform to a data mesh are probably organisational rather than technical [2]. Shifting the necessary responsibilities and capabilities from centralised teams to the domains that generate the data is an immense task that comes on top of the technical challenges. A third problem we see is that building data products, and consequently data meshes, is a holistic problem. Existing data mesh (reference) architectures include a self-service layer for creating data products with at least a dozen components [6]. This complexity leads to a chicken-and-egg problem. On the one hand, well-developed self-service components are desired for creating and maintaining data products. On the other hand, these same data products are necessary for the agile development of self-service components. Moreover, the functionality of the different components frequently depends on each other. Finally, there is ambiguity surrounding the concept of data products, and a clear definition appears to be missing. The term data product has been around much longer than data meshes and has meant different things in different contexts. For example, some authors take the view of a data product as data that can be bought or sold on a market (see e.g., [8]). However, such a view does not suffice for data products in a data mesh, which are generally exchanged *within* an organisation[1].

At the same time, data products in data meshes bear an undeniable resemblance to the concept of data as a service (DaaS), which has been around as a concept since around 2010 [11]. One could argue that data products are the natural successors to DaaS, with one crucial difference being that they live in a completely different environment; i.e., one that is designed for *data* (the mesh) and not as a generic software service in a service-oriented architecture.

In this paper, we introduce the data Product Model Template (PROMOTE), which is a technology-agnostic meta-model to specify and define data products in a data mesh (like) environment whilst embracing and extending existing standards for modelling (meta-)data. The rest of this paper is organised as follows. The next section introduces the study design that has been systematically applied for the development and application of PROMOTE. In Sect. 3, we then discuss data products and the non-functional requirements they should meet. Based on these requirements, Sect. 4 discusses existing standards and their suitability for describing data products in a data mesh. Then, in Sect. 5, we introduce the main concepts of PROMOTE and illustrate these with an example data product. Afterwards, Sect. 6 discusses our validation efforts and lessons learned

---

[1] Although they can be extended to external data markets or data spaces [12].

by highlighting how PROMOTE is leveraged in an industrial setting at a major Telco company. Finally, in Sect. 7, we discuss the paper's main takeaways and propose future work.

2 Study Design

From a high-level perspective, our research methodology for the development and evaluation of PROMOTE consists of four phases, as shown in Fig. 1. A fifth phase is currently being executed, whereby a standardised methodology for building data products uses PROMOTE to design blueprints of data products before instantiating them and will be presented in future work. As the first step, we established (non-functional) requirements from both literature and industry. These guided the development of PROMOTE, because a useful meta-model is such that data products that comply with it meet these requirements. Then, we looked at existing (metadata) model standards to evaluate their suitability for describing and modelling data products that meet the functional requirements. Since we concluded that none of these models was a good fit for data products, we then based PROMOTE on the Data Catalog Vocabulary (DCAT), which is one of the more general, well-established standards, paying special attention to new industry-proposed standards for comparison. Finally, we demonstrate the applicability of PROMOTE in two ways: first, by explicitly linking its components to the established non-functional requirements, and secondly, by constructing technical prototypes based on PROMOTE in an industrial context at a large Telco provider in the Netherlands.

Fig. 1. Methodology Overview.

2.1 Establish Non-functional Requirements

One of the goals for the development of PROMOTE is to make it easier for organisations to formulate relevant functional requirements for their data products by relating non-functional requirements to architectural components. As a starting point for the non-functional requirements for data products, we used the so-called DAUTNIVS usability properties proposed by Dehghani [2], described below in Sect. 3. To ensure relevance for the industry and to make it easy to use our standard for metadata management, we extended these requirements through collaborations with two industrial partners, where we conducted interviews with various stakeholder experts.

Our first collaboration was with a major German automotive company and yielded a new set of industry-driven requirements for data products [3]. More recently, in order to extend the external validity of these requirements, we set up a new collaboration with a major Dutch TelCo provider, where we interviewed 20 expert stakeholders. The interviews were semi-structured and followed the same methodology described in our previous work [3]. Both companies operate with over a billion euros in revenue and have thousands of employees organised across different departments with their own IT systems and data landscape. Furthermore, both companies are in the early stages of transitioning away from their monolithic data landscape towards a data product-based data mesh-like architecture.

2.2 Comparative Analysis of Existing Standards

After establishing the requirements for data products, we examined existing standards to assess their applicability for describing data products in a corporate data market or data mesh. Section 4 discusses the models that were considered and their potential for describing data products.

2.3 Developing PROMOTE

We selected the DCAT[2] ontology as a basis for creating PROMOTE. DCAT offers two advantages for our purposes:

- DCAT is a well-established standard for describing data catalogues. One of the explicit steps of creating a data product is to ensure that it is well-described in a data catalogue for potential consumers to find it.
- Many existing standards for describing data product-like entities are DCAT compliant. By ensuring that PROMOTE is DCAT compliant, we promote its interoperability with other standards that exist e.g., to describe data sets [21] or data contracts [16].

We extended the DCAT concepts of resources, distributions and datasets with the new concepts and relations necessary for describing data products that meet the requirements established in step 1. This led to the inclusion of input-, output- and control ports, as well as explicit use case modelling. Finally, we created a mapping from the entities in the meta-model to the requirements they address. This mapping makes it easier for data providers to understand which components to build for their data product and how to prioritise them according to the product's context. For example, for a data product with unknown value, it can be relevant to focus first on establishing and describing use cases, whereas a data product resulting from a new business process might concentrate on discoverability first and focus on accessibility and interoperability later.

2.4 Derive and Implement Metadata Template from PROMOTE

In order to evaluate the usefulness of PROMOTE we collaborated with KPN[3], a major Dutch Telco company. The company has started a transition to a data

---

[2] https://www.w3.org/TR/vocab-dcat-2/.
[3] https://www.kpn.com/.

mesh and is in the process of setting up a data catalogue in which data from all of its many different data platforms will be available for discovery. The data catalogue is implemented in DataHub[4], which allows both push-based and pull-based metadata ingestion from a wide variety of sources such as data lakes, DBMS, data warehouses, etc.

In addition to making data sets discoverable on the data catalogue, a concerted effort is made to promote the creation of data products which should be registered on the same data catalogue. For this process, we have created a metadata template based on PROMOTE and implemented this with a proof-of-concept within the DataHub business glossary, where it is used by new data providers. Filled-out instantiations of this template then populate the data catalogue and feed into the workflow of the centralised data governance team. Section 6 discusses these applications in more detail.

3 Data Product Requirements

Considering the lack of well-defined data products in literature that can be used as a reference, we consider good data products to be those that meet the needs of

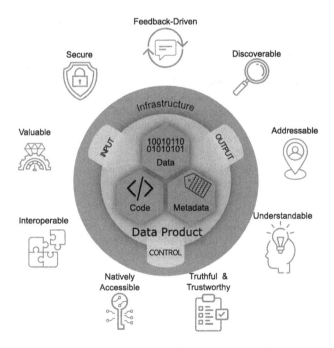

Fig. 2. A Data Product is a combination of data, code, metadata, and infrastructure. Data products are exposed through ports and aim to achieve several non-functional requirements.

---

[4] https://datahubproject.io/.

their stakeholders. To ensure that our model can be used as a reference for such data products[5], we used the DAUTNIVS usability attributes defined by Zhamak Dehghani [2] to evaluate potential models for describing data products, which we verified through interviews as described below. These attributes are the golden standard for data product requirements in industry, and academia. DAUTNIVS is an acronym standing for Discoverable, Addressable, Understandable, Trustworthy & Truthful, Natively Accessible, Interoperable, Valuable and Secure (see Fig. 2). An extensive description of these requirements is beyond the scope of this work and can be found in the original source [2].

To ensure the grounding of our work both in academia and industry, we additionally interviewed 30 stakeholders from our two industrial partners transitioning from a centralised monolithic data architecture to a decentral data product-driven architecture. Through these interviews, several additional requirements were identified, as shown in Table 1, which extends our previous work that established requirements for metadata management for data products [3]. We found that most of the requirements in Table 1 can be directly explained by

Table 1. Seven industry-driven requirements for any practical formal data product meta-model were established. All of these can be related to the DAUTNIVS+ non-functional requirements.

Req.	Industry-Driven Requirement for Meta-Models	DAUTNIVS+
R1.	The model should serve as a baseline for creating standardised data products or assets and, consequently, provide a complete overview of different data product components with direct relations to DAUTNIVS+	D, A, U, T, N, I, V, S, Feedback-Driven
R2.	Data products should be related semantically, even when crossing domain- or organisational boundaries. when crossing domain- or organisational boundaries. The model should incorporate relations with other (existing) business ontologies	D, U, I
R3.	Data in data products should be related on a technical level whenever possible. The model should incorporate schema relations to reflect this	D, U, I
R4.	The model should show the lineage of the data assets	D, A, U
R5.	The model should incorporate the promises and agreements between the data provider and the consumer. Either as separate promises or in a data contract	T, S
R6.	Data consumer feedback should be an explicit part of the model	V, Feedback-Driven
R7.	Data products should shorten the lines between providers and consumers. The model should demonstrate this relation by containing both actors	Feedback-Driven
R8.	The model should be applicable for data products at different levels of maturity	D,A, U, T, N, I, V, S, Feedback-Driven

---

[5] and consequently, for describing such data products.

trying to achieve the DAUTNIVS, for example: **R2.** states that data should be related to (existing) business ontologies. This requirement can easily be explained as wanting to make the data product more Discoverable, Understandable, and Interoperable.

One interesting conclusion that we drew from our interviews was a clear need to establish and model one or more feedback loops between data providers and data consumers. This feedback can be part of the effort required for establishing data product value (**R6**), but more importantly, it can help organisations to prioritise data assets to turn into data products (**R8**) and improve existing data products (**R7**). Moreover, stakeholders expressed concerns over the expected resource investments required to build data products that do not weigh up against their uncertain value. We believe an agile, feedback-driven approach should work best when developing and maintaining data products, similar to best practices in software development [1]. For these reasons, we take as nonfunctional requirements the DAUTNIVS usability attributes + being feedback-driven. In the rest of this paper, we will refer to these requirements as the DAUTNIVS+ requirements. Figure 2 shows a visualisation of the data product as defined by Dehghani as a combination of data,code, metadata and infrastructure which aims to achieve several non-functional requirements.

4 Related Standards

This section discusses two types of related literature. First, we briefly introduce existing academic coverage of data mesh and data markets, which has focused mainly on architectural aspects. Afterwards, we discuss tangentially related standards for describing and defining data that can be exchanged, similar to data products in a data mesh.

4.1 Data Markets and Data Mesh

Data markets, which facilitate the exchange of data products between independent parties, have received significant attention from the academic community [4]. However, internal data marketplaces and data meshes appear more obscure, and most of the academic work related to these platforms focuses on establishing architectures and architectural patterns [5,9,10]. Additionally, there is the work by Dehghani [2], who first coined the term data mesh and who provides both an excellent conceptual overview of the topic and notes the need for standardised description models for data products. As far as the authors are aware, only one (grey) literature survey exists, which is in pre-print at the time of writing and extensively covers the data mesh topic [6]. In this survey, Goedegebuure et. al. identify research challenges for data mesh, which include a need for: 1) Standardisations, 2) Tools for Data Mesh development and operation, and 3) Data Product Lifecycle Management. In this work, we make steps towards addressing these requirements by providing a meta-model for describing data products that can help describe and develop data products in a mesh and facilitate the collection of information needed for data product lifecycle management.

4.2 Work on Data Standards

Standards and vocabularies for describing data are well-researched and under-stood in today's age of big data. Among the most comprehensive of these standards are the Data Catalog Vocabulary (DCAT)[6] Dublin Core Terms (DCT)[7] and Simple Knowledge Organization System (SKOS)[8], which can serve as the basis for describing almost any type of data. Even though these standards generally do not consider data *products*, the DCAT vocabulary is especially interesting because it focuses on describing data in the context of data catalogues, which are a crucial part of data mesh architectures [6].

Other standards have been developed for describing data, specifically in data markets. These are often specific to the field in which they are developed, such as the FIESTA-IOT ontology [18], the Common Vehicle Information Model (CVIM) [14] and the spatial standard developed by Sakr [15]. However, like most of the standards above, these focus heavily on describing only data in a standardised manner rather than describing the *product* aspects of data products.

Finally, we note that there have been previous initiatives to describe data as well as the context in which it can be exchanged. An excellent standard for describing data as a service is DEMODS, which was introduced by Vu et. al. in 2012 [20]. One of the main benefits of DEMODS is that it explicitly combines the service aspects of data as a service, such as API descriptions, and the data aspects, such as different field descriptions. These aspects are, of course, still very relevant when describing data products. However, as previously argued, data products are more than just data as a service, and DaaS standards are insufficient for our purposes. More recently, there have been some attempts to describe data products on commercial data markets (e.g., [13,17]). These standards add descriptions for formal agreements and prices to data products; however, they often neglect the service aspects and consider almost no aspects for describing the data.

In addition to academic work, several industry standards exist. Besides vendor-specific standards (e.g., Google[9], Amazon[10], Microsoft[11]) two open-source, generalised data product standards aim to describe data products in a data mesh environment. The Data Product Specification (DPS) was developed by agile-lab[12] to provide a technology-independent standard for defining data products, much like PROMOTE. However, it is unclear how the standard was developed, and some crucial entities, such as input ports, are missing. Additionally, the data product descriptor specification (DPDS)[13] is an excellent standard

---

[6] https://www.w3.org/TR/vocab-dcat-2/.

[7] https://www.dublincore.org/specifications/dublin-core/dcmi-terms/.

[8] https://www.w3.org/TR/skos-reference/.

[9] https://cloud.google.com/architecture/describe-organize-data-products-resources-data-mesh#the_data_product_template.

[10] https://docs.aws.amazon.com/marketplace/latest/userguide/data-products.html.

[11] https://learn.microsoft.com/en-us/azure/cloud-adoption-framework/scenarios/cloud-scale-analytics/architectures/what-is-data-product.

[12] https://github.com/agile-lab-dev/Data-Product-Specification.

[13] https://dpds.opendatamesh.org/resources/specifications/1.0.0-DRAFT/.

that builds on the OpenAI initiative. However, while the DPDS is more extensive than the DPS, how it was developed and whether or how it relates to *any*
non-functional properties (such as DAUTNIVS+) is unclear. More importantly,
DPDS was not built to be interoperable- or compliant with existing ontologies
such as DCAT and DCT, which could prove to be a crucial benefit for PROMOTE
in terms of extensibility and interoperability with other existing standards.

Although each of these standards offers valuable perspectives on describing
data in specific environments, we can conclude that no standard currently exists
that: 1) describes and defines data products in a data mesh (like) environment,
2) is technology-independent, and 3) extends existing standards for modeling
(meta-)data. PROMOTE addresses all these points and refers explicitly to the
DAUTNIVS+ non-functional requirements for data products. This means it can
be used to define and describe data products in a data mesh, as illustrated in
the next section.

5 PROMOTE

In this section, we introduce PROMOTE by discussing a hypothetical yet realistic
data product use case in a Telco company. Figure 3 below shows an overview in
UML of the (meta)classes and relations in PROMOTE. A full specification and
explicit linkage to the DAUTNIVS+ requirements can be found in our online
repository[14].

5.1 Overview

ProMoTe extends the dcat:Resource class with a subclass: pmt:Resource. These
pmt:Resources come in three varieties: the pmt:Dataset, which is a subclass of
dct:Dataset; the pmt:Dataproduct, which is the architectural quantum of a data
mesh and the main focus of ProMoTe; and the pmt:UseCase, that describes
how the data is consumed. Data Products make available one or more datasets.
Each dataset has one or more physical representations (distributions), which are
exposed through output ports.

Each resource is managed within a pmt:Domain that maintains semantic
domain knowledge in pmt:InstitutionalKnowledge. Data products ingest data
through one or more pmt:InputPorts and are governed through pmt:policies managed through pmt:ControlPorts. Finally, data products make available one or
more dct:Distributions of pmt:Datasets through an associated pmt:OutputPort.
For each output port, an associated pmt:DataContract establishes the conditions
that apply when consuming the underlying data.

5.2 Modelling Data Products with PROMOTE

The customer data product is created and maintained by the company's
customer service department and instantiates the diagram of PROMOTE,

---

[14] https://github.com/Stefan-Driessen/ProMoTe.

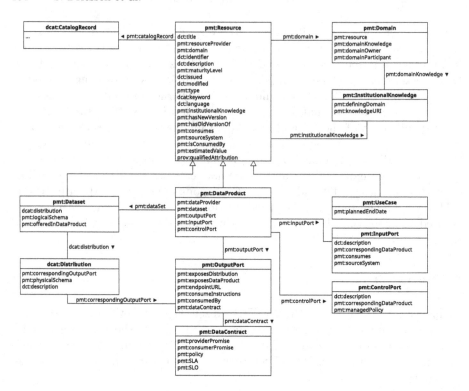

Fig. 3. A UML-representation of PROMOTE

depicted in Fig. 3. The customer service department handles the onboarding of **customers** who **subscribe** to a **product** and keeps this information in a pmt:Dataset consisting of three tables. Figure 4 shows a simple pmt:logicalSchema with these three tables and their internal relations.

Following PROMOTE, the data product needs to be described with relevant aspects from the pmt:Resource and pmt:DataProduct. This begins by assigning "Alice" from the customer service pmt:domain as the pmt:dataProvider. Alice then chooses the dct:title "Subscription Data Product" and fills out relevant metadata for the data catalogue, such as a short dct:description and some dcat:keywords, and assigns the dct:language to "English". Moreover, in their description, Alice explicitly references the business glossary of the customer service domain through pmt:institutionalKnowledge, which contains standardised semantic definitions of what customers, products, and subscriptions mean in the customer service pmt:Domain.

The dataset itself is stored physically in a SQL-based database during the customer onboarding process. Every dcat:Distribution of the pmt:Dataset that will eventually be offered by the customer of the pmt:DataProduct will source its data from this database. Alice describes this using PROMOTE in the pmt:sourceSystem property when describing their data product's pmt:InputPort.

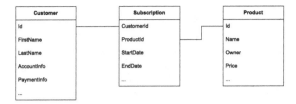

Fig. 4. The pmt:logicalSchema of the dataset in the customer data product.

It quickly becomes apparent that the customer data product has three potential pmt:UseCases with corresponding consumers. These use cases are the first major components that make the data product sensitive to feedback (from the consumers). Use case A is presented by Bob, who is from a different team in the customer service pmt:Domain and wants to use the data to allow customers to cancel their subscriptions. Use case B comes from Charlie, in the marketing pmt:Domain, who wants to run a targeted advertisement campaign and needs to perform customer segmentation. Finally, use case C is presented by Dave from the website pmt:Domain that builds and maintains the company's website. Here, customers can log in, find information about their subscriptions, and update the information they provided when they subscribed. Based on these pmt:UseCases, Alice builds and describes her data product using PROMOTE. Figure 5 illustrates this process as an instantiation of the PROMOTE meta-model.

Use Case A. Normally, there would be no need to create a data product for a consumer from the same domain. Presumably, Bob is familiar with the pmt:sourceSystem (i.e., the SQL database) of the customer service pmt:Domain. However, since Alice knows there are other consumers, they decide to put in the effort of creating an output port that can be reused for future use cases. They describe the dcat:Distribution of this pmt:Dataset through the pmt:physicalSchema as it exists on their SQL database. Moreover, they create a pmt:OutputPort that pmt:exposesDistribution this distribution through an API that data consumers can call if they follow the pmt:consumeInstructions. In addition to the pmt:OutputPort, they create a pmt:DataContract. In this data contract, they describe the terms of service in a pmt:SLA and any quality checks already performed in the customer service pmt:Domain's database as pmt:providerPromises. Moreover, the company has a pmt:policy that any personally identifiable information (PII) can only be shared in compliance with the GDPR. Therefore, Alice will have to add a clause to the pmt:DataContract in the form of a pmt:consumerPromise that this data can only be consumed for purposes for which the data subject has given consent.

At the same time, Alice asks Bob to describe their use case. This is useful for improving the Discoverability and Understandability of the data product by providing useful information for other potential data consumers. However, Alice is also interested in feedback from their consumers in the form of the

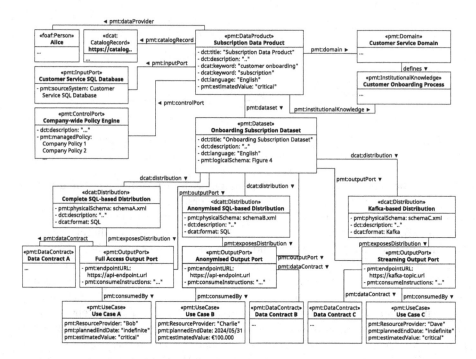

Fig. 5. The subscription data product, described with ProMoTe. Some aspects, such as data contracts, have been abbreviated for improved legibility.

pmt:estimatedValue of Bob's use case, which justifies their effort for creating the data product. In the same vein, Alice wants to know how long Bob plans to consume the data product. Since customers should always be able to cancel their subscriptions, Bob tells Alice that their intended pmt:plannedEndDate is "indefinite".

Use Case B. For use case B, Alice realises Charlie cannot use the same output port as Bob because of the aforementioned pmt:policy, which only allows the processing of customer data for marketing purposes if they have specifically opted in. Because of this, Alice creates another dcat:Distribution of the pmt:Dataset in their SQL-based database. In this distribution, customers who have not opted-in to targeted marketing or segmentation are anonymised by removing all values in their columns. Alice makes sure to describe how the pmt:physicalSchema includes anonymised data and creates another pmt:OutputPort to expose this distribution at the same pmt:endpointURL (e.g., an API) as for use case A, but with different access rights. The access rights are captured in the pmt:DataContract. Moreover, the data contract notes that this output port is suitable for any use case that consumes the data for marketing purposes in a pmt:consumerPromise. Finally, Charlie describes their pmt:UseCase in much the same manner as Bob did for use case A.

Use Case C. Based on customer interviews, Dave tells Alice that timeliness is an essential pmt:SLO for their use case: it's more important that data is quickly available, even if it might take a while to update the customer information. Therefore, Alice decides to create a Kafka dcat:Distribution for streaming that prioritises speed and completeness over accuracy. The pmt:endpointURL of the corresponding output port refers to a topic that pmt:exposesDistribution this distribution, and Dave (or any other data consumer) can subscribe to this topic following the pmt:consumeInstructions. Alice describes all the pmt:providerPromises they make over this output port, such as the timeliness pmt:SLO constraint in a pmt:DataContract. Additionally, since the customer data contains the same personally identifiable information (PII) as use case A, Alice includes the same limitation in a pmt:consumerPromise. Finally, just like in the previous use cases, Alice asks Dave to describe their use case for improved discoverability and understandability of the data product and establish its pmt:estimatedValue.

Throughout the process of creating the customer data product, Alice is supported by the infrastructure-as-a-service that the platform providers of her company provide as part of the data mesh ecosystem, such as a data catalogue for registering the dcat:CatalogRecord of her data product and access management tools for her output port. In particular, the company offers tools that help measure and enforce the pmt:policies captured in the pmt:DataContract. Updating and managing these tools is done through the pmt:ControlPorts, which can be accessed both by Alice as the data provider and also by members of the federated data governance team. This makes the control port the second major component that makes Alice's data product sensitive to feedback (from the platform providers).

6   Validation

In order to validate that PROMOTE can accurately, consistently and robustly describe data products, we employed validation through formalisation, validation through experimentation and validation through construction.

Firstly, we have formally specified and verified PROMOTE in UML (see, for example, Fig. 3 and its instantiation Fig. 5), and RDF (see GitHub)(See footnote 14). This has allowed us to ascertain internal and construct validity. Moreover, we have formalised the relation between the components of PROMOTE and the non-functional requirements in the formal specification provided online(See footnote 14).

As mentioned above, the fact that PROMOTE is technology independent is an advantage, as it allows organisations to implement its logic to fit their own architecture, organisational structure, and technical infrastructure. We envision different organisations having different physical implementations of data policies, data contracts, data storage infrastructure, metadata storage, etc. To validate that PROMOTE can help develop such physical implementations, we created several technical prototypes within the company based on PROMOTE. Specifically, metadata entities were created for data products, use cases, and output ports on

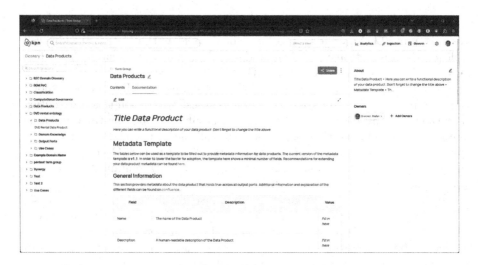

Fig. 6. A screenshot of the PROMOTE-based technical prototype data product meta-data template implemented in the KPN data catalogue.

the company's data catalogue. These entities came with corresponding metadata templates that aspiring data product providers can fill out to help them describe new data (and existing) data products. These metadata entries then enabled the development of new prototypes, such as an early data governance dashboard for tracking ownership of the various data products.

The company uses the Datahub (See footnote 4) data catalogue to gather metadata about its datasets and distributions from various source platforms across the company. For each dataset and distribution, metadata is ingested and stored in an entry within the DataHub model, which runs on a GraphQL backend. To implement the metadata entry for data products, output ports and use cases, we used the business glossary functionality of DataHub, Fig. 6 shows a screenshot of the template in DataHub. This approach had several advantages over editing DataHub's GraphQL model: 1) It allowed for rapid changes based on user feedback; 2) It resulted in an intuitive, interactive environment for users to fill out the template and create their own metadata entries; 3) Whenever entities were not yet implemented in the catalogue, or existed on external platforms (such as the companies institutional knowledge) hyperlinks could be easily leveraged to reference these external resources.

The data product metadata template also came with instructions on how to relate to other metadata entries, such as owners, domains, datasets, use cases, output ports and institutional knowledge. Figure 7 shows an example data product and its relations to a dataset metadata entry, an owner and a domain. Relations to other entries, such as use cases, output ports and institutional knowledge, are captured in the same manner on different tabs of the data product metadata entry.

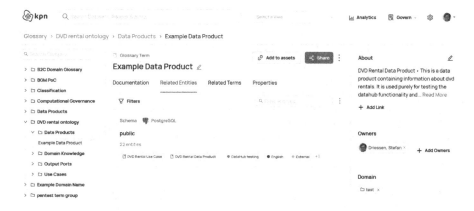

Fig. 7. An anonymised screenshot of a filled-out metadata template in DataHub and how it relates to distributions.

Another application of ProMoTe that feeds directly from the metadata template is the construction of a prototype governance dashboard. The dashboard, shown in Fig. 8, runs in Power BI and feeds directly off the GraphQL backend of the data catalogue. Having a formal meta-model of data products in ProMoTe allows the company's governance team to keep track of the status of important data product characteristics. In the prototype, this translates to keeping track of (domain- and individual) ownership and encouraging new data providers to provide, at minimum, a description of their data product.

6.1 Lessons Learned

Based on the implementations described above, we present a brief overview of the lessons learned when applying ProMoTe in practice in industrial settings and how these lessons affected the (use of) ProMoTe.

Lesson 1. Set maturity levels for developing and describing data products. The industrial partners wanted to categorise existing data entities and data products under construction in different maturity levels. We addressed this by relating

Fig. 8. An anonymised screenshot of the Power BI dashboard technical prototype used by the centralised data governance team in the company.

maturity levels to non-functional requirements: level 1 focusing on Discoverable and Addressable, level 2 focusing on Understandable, level 3 focusing Native Accessability, Value and Feedback-Driven, and level 4 focusing on Truthfulness & Trustworthiness, Interoperability and Security. Moreover, we added a pmt:maturityLevel to the PROMOTE meta-model so it can be described.

Lesson 2. Emphasise relevant components first. When describing and developing the first data products, the full PROMOTE meta-model came across as overwhelmingly much for new data providers. To address this, we organised information sessions with relevant stakeholders and only used a subset of the fields in PROMOTE for the metadata template described above.

Lesson 3. Address interoperability top-down and bottom-up. Achieving interoperability between data products has proven challenging. Nevertheless, we have found two ways to address this problem. The first relies on interoperability between pmt:InstitutionalKnowledge entities, e.g., through the use of knowledge graphs, and the second relies on traditional techniques for achieving interoperability between datasets such as the use of foreign keys [3].

Lesson 4. Integrate PROMOTE with data mesh architecture. Despite demonstrating which components must be built, PROMOTE cannot be used out-of-the-box for *building* data products. For this, a clear overview of the various tools and infrastructure-as-a-service components (e.g., as described by Goedegebuure et. al. [6]) and how they relate to the individual components of PROMOTE is necessary.

7   Conclusion

In this paper, we have introduced PROMOTE (See footnote 14), a technology-agnostic meta-model for specifying, developing and managing data products in a data mesh. PROMOTE is DCAT-compliant and can be easily combined with existing data catalogues for describing data. Moreover, PROMOTE is explicitly linked to non-functional requirements gathered from academia and industry, making it more likely to describe valuable data products. We believe PROMOTE can be used to instantiate the different components of data products in various organisational settings. To validate this, we instantiated the metadata entries of data products and their components in a data catalogue in an industrial environment at a large Telco company.

The results in this paper are core results in nature; more extensions and refinements are needed in various directions. Firstly, we wish to establish external validity by testing our approach in other industrial settings. Moreover, we intend to demonstrate the applicability of PROMOTE by developing instantiations of all its components, not just metadata entries on a data catalogue. Eventually, we hope to extend this approach to define a method and/or patterns that assist data product developers in effectively creating, maintaining and improving data products. Finally, another aspect for future work is to focus on the integration with the larger data mesh architecture by considering the different architectural components (e.g., from the reference architecture provided by Goedegebuure et. al. [6]) and their relation to the data product.

References

1. Beck, K., Beedle, M., Bennekum, A.V., Cockburn, A.: The agile manifesto (2001). https://www.agilealliance.org/wp-content/uploads/2019/09/agile-manifesto-download-2019.pdf
2. Dehghani, Z.: Data Mesh: Delivering Data-Driven Value at Scale, 1st edn. O'Reilly (2022)
3. Driessen, S., Monsieur, G., van den Heuvel, W.J.: Data product metadata management: an industrial perspective (2022)
4. Driessen, S., Monsieur, G., Heuvel, W.V.D.: Data market design: a systematic literature review. IEEE Access **10**, 1 (2022). https://doi.org/10.1109/access.2022.3161478
5. Eichler, R., Gröger, C., Hoos, E., Schwarz, H., Mitschang, B.: From data asset to data product - the role of the data provider in the enterprise data marketplace. In: Barzen, J., Leymann, F., Dustdar, S. (eds.) Service-Oriented Computing, SummerSOC 2022. Communications in Computer and Information Science, vol. 1603, pp. 119–138. Springer, Cham (2022). https://doi.org/10.1007/978-3-031-18304-1_7
6. Goedegebuure, A., et al.: Data mesh: a systematic gray literature review (2023)
7. Hooshmand, Y., Resch, J., Wischnewski, P., Patil, P.: From a monolithic PLM landscape to a federated domain and data mesh, pp. 713–722 (2022)
8. Kennedy, J., Subramaniam, P., Galhotra, S., Fernandez, R.C.: Revisiting online data markets in 2022. ACM SIGMOD Rec. **51**, 30–37 (2022). https://doi.org/10.1145/3572751.3572757
9. Loukiala, A., Joutsenlahti, J.-P., Raatikainen, M., Mikkonen, T., Lehtonen, T.: Migrating from a centralized data warehouse to a decentralized data platform architecture. In: Ardito, L., Jedlitschka, A., Morisio, M., Torchiano, M. (eds.) PROFES 2021. LNCS, vol. 13126, pp. 36–48. Springer, Cham (2021). https://doi.org/10.1007/978-3-030-91452-3_3
10. Machado, I.A., Costa, C., Santos, M.Y.: Data mesh: concepts and principles of a paradigm shift in data architectures, vol. 196, pp. 263–271. Elsevier B.V. (2021). https://doi.org/10.1016/j.procs.2021.12.013
11. Olson, J.A.: Data as a service: are we in the clouds? J. Map Geography Libr. **6**, 76–78 (2009). https://doi.org/10.1080/15420350903432739
12. Otto, B., Steinbuß, S., Teuscher, A., Lohmann, S.: IDSA reference architecture model. International Data Spaces Association (2019). https://internationaldataspaces.org/download/16630/
13. Ozyilmaz, K.R., Dogan, M., Yurdakul, A.: IDMoB: IoT data marketplace on blockchain. In: Proceedings - 2018 Crypto Valley Conference on Blockchain Technology, CVCBT 2018, pp. 11–19 (2018). https://doi.org/10.1109/CVCBT.2018.00007
14. Pillmann, J., Sliwa, B., Schmutzler, J., Ide, C., Wietfeld, C.: Car-to-cloud communication traffic analysis based on the common vehicle information model, pp. 1–5 (2018)
15. Sakr, M.: A data model and algorithms for a spatial data marketplace. Int. J. Geograph. Inf. Sci. **32**, 2140–2168 (2018). https://doi.org/10.1080/13658816.2018.1484124

16. Shakeri, S., et al.: Modeling and matching digital data marketplace policies. In: Proceedings - IEEE 15th International Conference on eScience, eScience 2019, pp. 570–577 (2019). https://doi.org/10.1109/eScience.2019.00078

17. Spiekermann, M., Tebernum, D., Wenzel, S., Otto, B.: A metadata model for data goods. In: MKWI 2018 - Multikonferenz Wirtschaftsinformatik 2018-March, pp. 326–337 (2018)

18. Sánchez, L., et al.: Federation of internet of things testbeds for the realization of a semantically-enabled multi-domain data marketplace. Sensors (Switzerland) **18**, 3375 (2018). https://doi.org/10.3390/s18103375, https://www.mdpi.com/1424-8220/18/10/3375

19. (Thoughtworks), Z.D.: How to move beyond a monothilitic data lake to a distributed data mesh (2019). https://martinfowler.com/articles/data-monolith-to-mesh.html

20. Vu, Q.H., Pham, T.V., Truong, H.L., Dustdar, S., Asal, R.: DEMODS: a description model for data-as-a-service. In: Proceedings - International Conference on Advanced Information Networking and Applications, AINA, pp. 605–612 (2012). https://doi.org/10.1109/AINA.2012.91

21. Yuan, J., Li, H.: Research on the standardization model of data semantics in the knowledge graph construction of oil & gas industry. Comput. Stand. Interfaces **84**, 103705 (2023). https://doi.org/10.1016/J.CSI.2022.103705

Model-Based Analysis
and Implementation

Using a Conceptual Model
in Plug-and-Play SQL

Shubham Swami[1], Santosh Aryal[1], Sourav S. Bhowmick[2],
and Curtis Dyreson[1(✉)]

[1] Department of Computer Science, Utah State University, Logan, UT 84322, USA
{a02345936,curtis.dyreson}@usu.edu
[2] School of Computer Engineering, Nanyang Technical University,
Singapore, Singapore
assourav@ntu.edu.sg
https://www.usu.edu/cs/people/CurtisDyreson ,
https://personal.ntu.edu.sg/assourav/

Abstract. We propose using a conceptual model for a database query's input type. The input type is the shape of the data needed by a query. Pairing a conceptual model with a query creates a plug-and-play query that can be type matched to a database's schema to determine whether the query can be safely evaluated. Plug-and-play queries are portable, easier to write, and are type safe. We describe a simple conceptual model based on virtual hierarchies, show how a virtual hierarchy is type matched to a relational schema, and how to transform an SQL query into one that can be evaluated on the matched schema.

Keywords: SQL · query evaluation · hierarchical data · query guards

1 Introduction

This paper proposes using a conceptual model to improve database queries. More specifically we propose using a conceptual model as the query's *input type*. In a broad sense a database query has an input type and an output type; the query transforms data from the input to the output type. The input type is either a generic type, *e.g., Any*, or (a subset of) a database's schema. In languages for schemaless databases, like XQuery and Cypher, the input type is generic. There is no compiler type check for the input type, instead a query will evaluate on any data collection, producing an empty result if a path expression in the query fails to navigate to desired data.[1] In languages for databases that have a schema, such as SQL, the input type is the names of tables and columns that appear in the query, which is a subset of a schema. The compiler checks the input type and generates an error if there is a mismatch.

Suppose that instead of a generic type or a subset of the schema we used a conceptual model as the input type. The conceptual model describes the *mini-world* in which the query needs to be evaluated. The idea is depicted in Fig. 1.

---

[1] XML and Graph schema specifications are used and checked for data modification, rather than (read) query evaluation.

J. P. A. Almeida et al. (Eds.): ER 2023, LNCS 14320, pp. 145–161, 2023.
https://doi.org/10.1007/978-3-031-47262-6_8

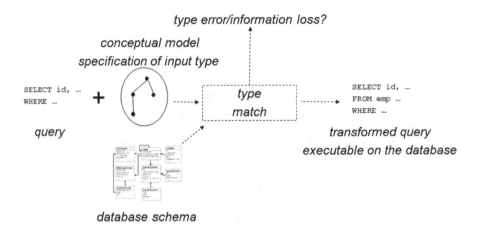

Fig. 1. Using a conceptual model as the input type

A query together with the conceptual model of the data needed by the query is type matched to the schema of the database. The match produces a transformed query that is executable against the schema as well as a report on type errors or potential information loss in the transformation. There are several benefits that potentially accrue.

- *Type Safety* - A query that ignores the input type is said to *lack type safety*. The evaluation of the query cannot determine whether the query is mal-formed, *e.g.,* a name in a path expression is misspelled, or whether there is no data that matches the query since both cases produce the empty set. A type safe query, on the other hand, evaluates the structure of the input to determine if it conforms to that expressed by the conceptual model, *i.e.,* needed by the query.
- *Portability* - A query is *portable* if it can be type safely evaluated on different data collections. The conceptual model is not only critical to describing the input type to safeguard the query, but the model can be used to transform the query so that it can adapt to the data's type.
- *Simplicity* - A key challenge for query writers, especially novice query writers, is understanding the (conceptual model of a) database. It is simpler and easier for writers to express their conceptual understanding of the data needed by the query and let the compiler match the input type to the data's type, transforming the query to adapt to the data's type as needed.
- *Resilience* - Queries written with respect to a specific schema are brittle in the sense that if the schema changes, even small changes, the query may fail. To make a query resilient to schema evolution it is best to capture in a conceptual model what the query needs to evaluate and match the conceptual model to the current schema.

In summary using a conceptual model as the input type potentially makes a query type safe, portable, easier to code, and more resilient to schema changes.

This paper describes a system that has these potential benefits and specifically does not address the issue of determining *what is the best conceptual model to use as the input type*. We address instead the research question of *what are the potential benefits of using a conceptual model as the input type*. We chose to use the hierarchical model as the input type, surprisingly, for queries in SQL, a relational query language. The advantages of the hierarchical model are simplicity and prior research by others in *virtual hierarchies*, which are hierarchies that are not stored, rather they are constructed during query evaluation.

In his 1970 seminal paper on the relational model, E. F. Codd argued in favor of the relational model by describing important drawbacks of the popular (at that time) hierarchical model [7]. One of the drawbacks of the hierarchical model that Codd identified was *access path dependence*. Codd pointed out that queries in a hierarchical (or network) model necessarily have to use access paths ("dot" operators) to navigate to desired data. The access paths tightly couple the query to a specific hierarchy, which is problematic since the same data could be organized in different hierarchies, so a query written for one hierarchy would fail if the same data were organized differently. Access path dependence decreases query portability and increases the brittleness of queries to changes in the structure of the data.

But hierarchical data also makes some aspects of querying easier. First, access paths in hierarchical queries are simpler and more straightforward to express than joins in a relational database, an advantage also present in graph queries in languages such as Cypher and GQL, and in SQL for SurrealDB, which uses a RELATE clause to build relationships between tables that can be navigated by path expressions. Joins are implicitly embedded in a hierarchical data structure, performed when creating the data model, and these embedded joins in the data are easily navigated with a path expression. Second, grouping and aggregation can be more naturally expressed in hierarchical data. Their expression in SQL has been shown to be cognitively challenging for many users, especially programmers learning SQL [1,17,18]. Third, Codd's critique of access path dependence applies only to *stored* hierarchies. *Virtual hierarchies* are dynamically constructed as needed for query evaluation, hence have no such dependence.

This paper leverages virtual hierarchies as a conceptual model to support *plug-and-play* SQL. We propose coupling a query to a hierarchical specification of its input type, we call the specification a *query guard*, to create a plug-and-play query. A plug-and-play query is similar to a plug-and-play device. Such a device can be plugged into any socket and if the socket provides the necessary electrical input or other required input, then the device will play. Similarly, a plug-and-play query can be plugged into any data source and, if the data source provides data in a sufficient structure specified by its input type or guard, it will "play" producing a desired result.

We motivate the utility of query guards with an example. Suppose that we have a relational database with data about biological specimens collected in the field. A user could query the database using the query in Fig. 2 to retrieve the names of botanists who collected *Asteraceae* (plants in the Daisy family)

```
SELECT collectors.name
FROM taxa, occurrences, collectors
WHERE taxa.tid = occurrences.tid AND collectors.id = occurrences.collid
  AND taxa.family = 'Asteraceae' AND occurrences.year = 2023
```

Fig. 2. Retrieve the names of botanists who collected *Asteraceae* specimens in 2023

```
GUARD collectors {
        name,
        occurrences {
          family,
          year
        }
      }
SELECT name
WHERE family = 'Asteraceae' AND year = 2023
```

Fig. 3. Retrieve the names of those who collected *Asteraceae* specimens in 2023

specimens in 2023. The query does a join between the `taxa`, `occurrences`, and `collectors` tables, applies the appropriate selection conditions, and projects the name of the botanist. The query explicitly uses logical pointers (foreign key to key associations) from the `taxa` table to the `occurrences` and `collectors` tables. We can rewrite the query as a plug-and-play SQL query using a query guard as shown in Fig. 3. The guard specifies the *shape* or type of the *input* to the query. The guard stipulates that the query can be evaluated on any data collection that has this hierarchy, or that can be converted or transformed to the desired shape (within information loss guarantees).

One big advantage of plug-and-play SQL queries is that they are *portable*. The query in Fig. 3 is portable to data collections that have different shapes (*i.e.*, we do not care how many steps are involved in "joining" the tables to construct the hierarchy). A second advantage is that the hierarchy naturally *groups* the data, and the grouping can be exploited in a query for aggregation. Suppose for instance we only wanted those collectors who collected more than 40 specimens then we could modify the query as shown in Fig. 4. Querying against a hierarchy simplifies grouping and aggregation (as in XQuery and Cypher).

This paper focuses on matching and transforming the *shape* of the data. We are agnostic about the *semantic* matching of labels between the guard and the source, *e.g.*, does `person` in the guard mean the same as `person` in the data, because the *semantic matching problem* is already being researched by other communities, *e.g.*, work on ontologies in the Semantic Web community. The focus of our research is on the shape of the data and because the problem is orthogonal we can add Semantic Web solutions to plug-and-play queries to address the problem of semantic mismatch. Note that the table names in the query guard in Fig. 3 are present to help in the semantic matching. The guard

```
GUARD collectors {
      name,
      occurrences {
        family,
        year
      }
    }
SELECT name
WHERE family = 'Asteraceae' AND year = 2023 AND COUNT(*) > 40
```

Fig. 4. Retrieve the names of botanists who collected more than 40 *Asteraceae* specimens in 2023

```
GUARD name {
           family,
           year
         }
SELECT name
WHERE family = 'Asteraceae' AND year = 2023
```

Fig. 5. Simplified guard for the query in Fig. 3

could be simplified to that shown in Fig. 5. To better combine the output of any semantic matching technique with the guard, a MATCH clause could be added that maps names in the schema to those in the guard.

This paper makes the following contributions.

- We describe using a conceptual model as the input type for an SQL query. We call the model a query guard.
- We show how to match the query guard to the schema of a relational database.
- We give a denotational semantics for converting a plug-and-play query to SQL.
- We report on the implementation of plug-and-play SQL.

This paper is organized as follows. The next section describes how an input type specification is matched to a schema hierarchy and how the match is used to rewrite the query to one that can be evaluated. We then explain how we implemented query guards and give a brief evaluation. Section 5 covers related work. The paper concludes with a short summary and gives some avenues for continuing the research in future.

2   Model

In this section we describe, at an abstract level, how the virtual hierarchy is constructed for a guard when evaluated on a relational database. The key ideas are to model *data-relatedness* using a multigraph of associations among relations. A spanning tree in the multigraph determines how to best relate names in a hierarchical context. The tree is used to construct an SQL query to extract data for formatting in the shape specified by a guard.

2.1   Guard

A *guard* is a specification or declaration of the structure of the data needed by the query.

Definition 1 (Guard). *Let database, D, consist of names $N = n_1, \ldots, n_k$. Then guard $G = (M, E)$ where $M \subseteq N$ and*

$$E = \{(n_p, n_c) \mid n_p, n_c \in M\}$$

forms a connected, acyclic graph. ∎

Essentially a guard is a tree of database column or table names.

We assume that a guard is specified using JSON-like syntax, as is common in other tools, *e.g.*, GraphQL.

Definition 2 (Guard JSON Specification). *A guard conforms to the EBNF grammar given below.*

```
guard  ← GUARD pair
pair   ← name obj?
name   ← TABLE_NAME | COLUMN_NAME
obj    ← { pair (, pair)* }
```
∎

The tree of names in a guard is built from the nested values of name/obj pairs in the guard specification. For example, the guard in Fig. 3 is the tree consisting of nodes {collectors, occurrences, name, family, and year} and edges { (collectors, name), (collectors, occurrences), (occurrences, family), (occurrences, year) }.

2.2   Association Multigraph

For our purposes a relational database, D, is a set of relations, $\{R_1, \ldots, R_n\}$, and a set of *associations* among attributes in the relations $K = f_1, \ldots, f_m$, *e.g.*, K could be a set of foreign key constraints, inclusion dependencies, or user specified "edges" (such as specified by the RELATE clause in SurrealDB SQL). Each relation in D has some number of attributes, that is, the schema for relation R_i is $(A_1, \ldots, A_k)$ and each relationship in K is of the form $R_j \rightarrow R_m$, that is, relation R_j is related to R_m, *e.g.*, there is a foreign key from R_j to R_m.

Definition 3 (Association Multigraph). *The association multigraph, $G = (V, E)$, for D is an undirected multigraph where $V = \{R_1, \ldots, R_n\}$ is the set of vertices and $E = \{(R_j, R_m, i) \mid f_i \in K \wedge f_i = R_j \rightarrow R_m\}$ is the set of edges (i is the label of the edge).* ∎

Note that there is one edge per association. The edge is labelled with the identifier for the association. As there could be more than one association, *e.g.,* more than one foreign key, between a pair of relations, there can be more than one edge between nodes, but each edge will have a different label.

As an example consider the relational schema depicted in Fig. 6. The schema is for Symbiota, a commonly used biodiversity data management system [11]. The schema depicted is a small part of Symbiota's schema, which has 74 tables and 97 foreign keys. Symbiota stores specimen biodiversity data such as occurrences of `taxa` that are part of `collections` housed in herbaria, natural history museums, and private collections. A collection may involve various `collectors` and `images` of the specimens. The `taxa` table is the taxonomic hierarchy of scientific names that may be synonyms (recorded in the `statuses` table) as stipulated by taxonomic `authorities`. The `taxa` records also have `descriptions` derived from taxonomic treatments. The `taxa` table has a foreign key to itself that associates child to parent taxa. The association multigraph for the schema in Fig. 6 is given below and depicted in Fig. 7.

- $V = \{$`statuses, descriptions, authorities, taxa, occurrences,`
  `collections, images, collectors`$\}$
- $E = \{$(`authorities, statuses`, 1), (`authorities, descriptions`, 2),
  (`statuses, taxa`, 3), (`descriptions, taxa`, 4), (`occurrences, taxa`, 5),
  (`collections, occurrences`, 6), (`taxa, images`, 7),
  (`collectors, occurrences`, 8), (`taxa, taxa`, 9)$\}$

In general in this paper we will utilize foreign keys for the associations. We focus on foreign keys not only because foreign keys describe important semantic connections between tables, but also because the keys are stored in the schema and so can be automatically read and used. But the multigraph could be constructed by computing other associations among relations, *e.g.,* inclusion dependencies, and the techniques described in this paper would be the same.

2.3   Relating Data Through Names

The association multigraph can be used to relate names in a guard based on the notion of *closeness* [20]. Closeness can be described as the property that two data items are *related* if they are connected (by a path) and that no shorter paths that connect items of the same *type* exists. In the context of relational databases the *type* of a datum is the domain (an attribute in a relation) to which it belongs.

Suppose that a guard specifies that `affiliation` should be related to `scientific name`. The `affiliation` type exists in the `collectors` relation, while `scientific name` is part of `taxa`. There is a path of length two that connects `collectors` to `taxa` as well as paths of length greater than two (by traversing the link from `taxa` to itself). Closeness stipulates that the shortest path is preferred.

Definition 4 (Parent/Child Closeness). *Let plug P have parent p with child c where p is an attribute of relation R_p and c is an attribute of relation R_c.*

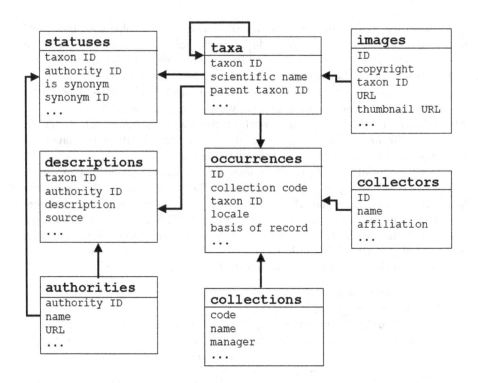

Fig. 6. Reduced schema of the Symbiota2 database

Closeness stipulates that a path from R_p to R_c makes p closest to c if and only if there is no shorter path between R_p and R_c in a association multigraph, F, that is,

$$\otimes(F, P, p, c) = \{(R_p, R_1, i_1), \dots, (R_n, R_c, i_n)\}$$

$\otimes$ *is the closest operator and* $(R_p, R_1, i_1), \dots, (R_n, R_c, i_n)$ *is a shortest path.* ∎

As an example assume the pattern contains `affiliation` (in relation `collectors`) and `description` (in relation `descriptions`), then the shortest path is below.

```
{(collectors, occurrences, 8), (occurrences, taxa, 5),
 (taxa, descriptions, 4)}
```

Parent/child closeness relates a pair of names in a guard, but a guard could contain many names. Closeness for the guard is built from parent/child closeness.

Definition 5 (Guard Closeness). *Let P be the set of parent child relationships, (p, c), in a guard. Then for association multigraph F the data relationship operator, $\bigotimes$, is defined as follows.*

$$\bigotimes(F, P) = \bigcup_{\forall(p,c)\in P} \otimes(F, P, p, c)$$

■

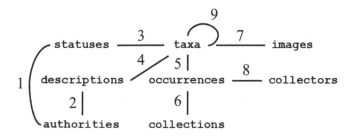

Fig. 7. Association multigraph for the Symbiota2 database

Guard closeness defines a spanning tree within the graph over the nodes corresponding to relations that have attributes in the guard. To relate data in a guard, P, the paths on the plug are joined using an in-order walk of the tree for $\otimes(F, P)$.

Definition 6 (Relating Data). *Given a guard, P, and an association multi-graph, F, with spanning tree, C, for $\otimes(F, P)$ that relates names $x_1, \ldots, x_k$ in P, let an inorder walk of the spanning tree yield the list of relations $[R_1, \ldots, R_n]$. Then the data relationship operator, $\bowtie_P$, is defined as follows.*

$$\bowtie_P(C, [x_1, \ldots, x_k]) = \pi_{x_1, \ldots, x_k}(\bowtie[R_1, \ldots, R_n])$$

where $\bowtie$ is the left outer join (on the attributes in the foreign keys). ∎

For example, to relate `affiliation` to `scientific name`, the inorder walk for the spanning tree is [collectors, occurrences, taxa]. The data relationship operator applied to this list yields the query given below.

$$\pi_{\text{affiliation,scientific name}}(\text{ collectors} \bowtie \text{occurrences} \bowtie \text{taxa })$$

2.4 Potential Information Loss

There may be more than one closeness spanning tree that connects pairs of names. For instance there are two paths of length two from `authorities` to `taxa`, one through `statuses` and one through `descriptions`. To determine which spanning tree to use, we rank the trees by their *potential information loss*.

Definition 7 (Loss Ranking). *Let spanning trees $T_1, \ldots, T_n$ connect names $x_1, \ldots, x_k$. Then T_i is the most complete spanning tree if the data relatedness of the tree produces the most tuples, i.e.,*

$$|\otimes(T_i, [x_1, \ldots, x_k])| = \max_{1 \le j \le n} |\otimes(T_j, [x_1, \ldots, x_k])|.$$

∎

```
taxa {
  name {
    manager
  }
}
```

Fig. 8. Taxa and the managers who manage collections of them

The idea of loss ranking is to choose the spanning tree that produces the most tuples since such a join represents the most complete connection among the set of relations. Note that the loss ranking is an instantaneous measure, that is, it produces a ranking with respect to the state of a database as of when the query is evaluated. Since relations change over time an alternative path may represent the most complete connection at some future time. To compute a measure of the completeness the association multigraph can be annotated with *join selectivity*. Suppose foreign key f is from relation R to relation S, that is, R borrows a key from S. Then the join selectivity for f be $L_f = |S \bowtie R|/|S|$. Note that $S \bowtie R$ using f will produce between 0 and $|S|$ tuples. We can annotate the association multigraph with join selectivities and multiply the selectivities along branches in a spanning tree to get total completeness; alternative spanning trees can be ranked by their total completeness.

Completeness factors can also be used to categorize plugs by the amount of information loss. A completeness factor of 1 for a plug represents that the construction of a hierarchy loses no information, *i.e.*, it is *complete* in the sense that every value at a leaf can be reached from the root. A completeness factor of less than 1 indicates that some leaf values might not be represented. For example, consider the guard specified in Fig. 8. which relates `taxa` to `collections`. The guard specifies joins along the following path: `taxa`, `occurrences`, and `collections`. If the completeness factor is 1 then every taxon is part of some collection that has a manager. On the other hand, a completeness factor less than 1 indicates that some `taxa` may be unrelated to a `manager` (are not in a collection). Note that because we are using outer joins to compute the hierarchy those `taxa` will still be present in the hierarchy, but the `manager` will be a null value.

Guard closeness as defined above is based on the closeness of parent/child relationships in a guard rather than the minimal number of relationships overall in a guard. An alternative is to use the Steiner tree, which is a minimal spanning tree among a subset of nodes in the multigraph. Computing the Steiner tree is NP-complete [14], even for an unweighted multigraph. Though approximation techniques exist [5], it is unclear if the Steiner tree gives a better intuitive solution to the data-relatedness problem since a guard designer may construct a guard by reasoning about parent/child relationships in a hierarchy rather than overall minimality of the edges in a guard.

$[\![$ GUARD G
  SELECT $s_1, \ldots, s_n$
  WHERE Q
$]\!](D) \equiv$
  SELECT A.s_1, ..., A.s_n
  FROM (
    SELECT $s_1, \ldots, s_n$
    FROM $\bowtie_P(C, s_1, \ldots, s_n)$ where C is the spanning tree derived from G for D
    WHERE Q
) A

Fig. 9. Denotational rule for translating a plug-and-play query into SQL

```
SELECT A.name
FROM (SELECT name
      FROM collectors
          LEFT OUTER JOIN occurrences ON collectors.id = occurrences.collid
          LEFT OUTER JOIN taxa ON occurrences.'taxon ID' = taxa.'taxon ID'
      WHERE family = 'Asteraceae' AND year = 2023) A
```

Fig. 10. SQL for retrieving who collected *Asteraceae* specimens in 2023

2.5 Combining the Guard with the Query

In this section we give the denotational semantics of a plug-and-play query. There are two cases: with and without an aggregate function. We consider the without case first.

If a query does not have an aggregate function then the transformation is relatively straightforward using the data-relatedness operator, $\bowtie_P$. In the rule given in Fig. 9, D is the database on which the query is evaluated. As an example, the transformation of the query in Fig. 3 is given in Fig. 10. Note that the outer join operator generates a path from collectors to taxa through occurrences to relate name to family, hence the final hop in the path back to occurrences is not needed in the join expression.

A query with an aggregate function has to add grouping (more than one aggregate is a repetition of this case). In the denotation rule given in Fig. 11 we assume a is an aggregate applied to a name at level k in the tree (with ancestor names g_1 to g_k). We further assume a is both in the SELECT and the WHERE clause. As an example, the transformation of the query in Fig. 4 is given in Fig. 12.

3   Implementation

In this section, we describe the code structure for our application. Most of the code is written in Java. We used ANTLR for parsing and translation and modified the grammar for SQLite. The code structure for the application is shown

⟦ GUARD G
    SELECT $s_1, \ldots, s_n, a$ where a is an aggregate
    WHERE Q AND Q_A where Q_A is the predicate part of the aggregate
⟧$(D) \equiv$
    SELECT A.s_1, ..., A.s_n, A.a
    FROM (
        SELECT $s_1, \ldots, s_k, a$
        FROM $\bowtie_P(C, s_1, \ldots, s_n)$ where C is the spanning tree derived from G for D
        WHERE Q
        GROUP BY $s_1, \ldots, s_k$
) A
    WHERE Q_A

Fig. 11. Denotational rule for translating a plug-and-play query with an aggregate into SQL

```
SELECT A.name
FROM (SELECT name, count(*) as C
      FROM collectors
              LEFT OUTER JOIN occurrences ON collectors.id = occurrences.collid
              LEFT OUTER JOIN taxa ON occurrences.'taxon ID' = taxa.'taxon ID'
      WHERE family = 'Asteraceae' AND year = 2023
      GROUP BY name) A
WHERE A.C > 40
```

Fig. 12. SQL for retrieving who collected *Asteraceae* specimens in 2023

in Fig. 13. It consists of five modules. The **database** module is handles database communication We used JDBC for communicating. The **grammar** module contains the lexer and parser rules for the SQL and query guard, and a custom listener to implement the denotational semantics for the translation of a plug-and-play SQL query into SQL. The **data pull** module contains the logic to evaluate a query and display results. The **join graph** module builds and maintains the association multigraph. Lastly, the **tree module** communicates with the listener and the data pull module to generate the queries.

    Figure 14 shows a screenshot of our JavaFX application that displays the generated query (the guard and query are in the context of a baseball database). As shown in Fig. 15, the user selects the query they want to execute and hits the **Execute Query** button to generate the result.

4   Plug-and-Play Evaluation

We provide a comparative analysis of the run-time cost of ordinary SQL queries with plug-and-play queries. Of course the plug-and-play queries were easier to write, but in this evaluation we focus on the run-time cost. We wrote six plug-and-play queries on a baseball database with 2GB of data (the Lahman baseball

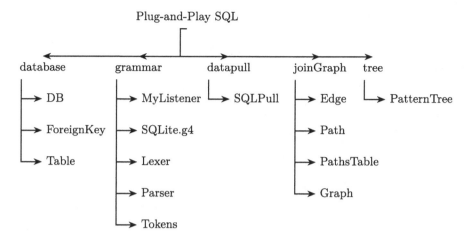

Fig. 13. Plug and Play SQL- Code Structure

Table 1. Cost Analysis

Query No.	Manual Query Cost	Generated Query Cost
Query 1	318.61	2009.71
Query 2	3684.72	3684.72
Query 3	0.29	709
Query 4	3906.91	3924.3
Query 5	2500.25	2677.22
Query 6	3040.94	3040.94
Query 7	2004.75	8958.4

database is publicly available). We ran the queries using Postgres version 14.7 on a Linux system running Ubuntu with 16GB of RAM. Table 1 shows the cost comparison of the manually created SQL queries compared to the queries generated by the plug-and-play application. We observe that the plug-and-play queries are often the same cost as the hand-crafted queries, but sometimes incur higher cost due to the cost of left outer joins versus inner joins. We plan to focus on optimizing queries to consider edge cases in future work.

5   Related Work

To the best of our knowledge, there is no previous work in querying SQL using hierarchies, in fact, the relational model replaced the hierarchical model and is widely considered an improved successor. But there has been previous research in querying with input types that can be broadly classified into several categories.

Query Relaxation/Approximation. One way to loosen the tight coupling of the input type to the data is to relax the path expressions in a query or

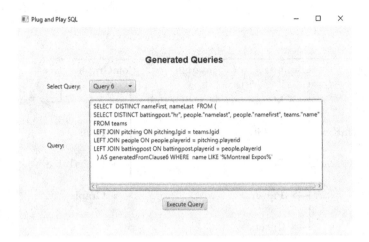

Fig. 14. Generated Queries

approximately match them to the data within a given edit distance [2, 3, 13]. Though such techniques work well for small variations in data structure or values, there can be a *very large* edit distance among the same data organized in different structures, which we would like to consider as the same data. Relaxing a query to explore all data shapes within a large edit distance is overly permissive, and includes many shapes which do not have the same data. Query correction [8] and refinement [4] approaches are also best at exploring only small changes to the data.

Declarative Transformations. There are declarative languages for specifying transformations of (hierarchical) data [15, 16]. However, each transformation depends on the hierarchy of the input and would have to be re-programmed for a different hierarchy. It would be more desirable if a programmer could simply declare the desired hierarchy in a single guard.

Schema Integration. Data can be integrated from one or more source schemas to a target schema by specifying a mapping to carry out a specific, fixed transformation of the data [6]. Once the data is in the target schema, there is still the problem of queries that need data in some schema other than the target schema. In some sense schema mediators integrate data to a fixed schema, which is the starting point for what query guards do. The different problem leads to a difference in techniques used to map or transform the data. For instance, tuple-generating dependencies (TGDs) are a popular technique for integrating schemas [9, 12]. Part of a TGD is a specification of the source structure from which to extract the data. Specifying the source schema will not work for a query guard, a query guard must be agnostic about the schema and work for any given schema (work in the sense that the input type can be matched or the matching produces information about potential data loss or errors). A second concern for query guards is that the transformation must be fully auto-

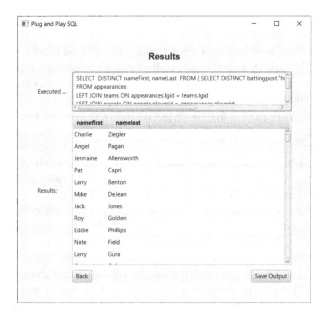

Fig. 15. Results

matic. A third difference is the need to determine potential information loss, which is an important part of a query guard, but absent from such mappings for data integration. For schema mediation, if a programmer programs a data transformation that loses information, that information is gone and subsequent queries on the transformed data will never know about the information loss. Fan and Bohannon explored preserving information in data integration, namely by describing schema embeddings that ensure invertible mappings that are query preserving [10]. Query guards focus on an important special case of the mappings they investigated. Query preservation concerns all possible queries, while query guards are designed to check a single query. Our approach for quickly determining whether a mapping is invertible (or in our terminology reversible) is based on the concept of *closeness*, and in those cases where mapping is not reversible we can identify weaker, but still useful classes of mappings that permit some information loss.

Finally we note that our research focuses only on the *structure, not the semantics,* of the data because Semantic Web technologies, *i.e.,* ontologies, already address the orthogonal semantic matching problem. Hence, solutions developed by the Semantic Web community can be used to semantically match in plug-and-play queries.

6   Conclusions and Future Work

This paper describes how to pair a query with a conceptual model, which we call a query guard. The query guard is a specification of the query's input type, that is, the structure or shape of the data that the query needs in order to correctly evaluate. The combination of query guard and query creates a plug-and-play query. Plug-and-play queries are more portable, more reliable because they are input type safe, and are potentially easier to write.

In this paper we chose a very simple conceptual model for expressing a query guard, namely, a hierarchical specification. We used this specification for a relational query language, thereby demonstrating that the model for the input type can be independent of the data model for the query. Though we focused on how to run a plug-and-play query on a relational database, a plug-and-play query could be equally run on JSON data or graph data. But the input type must be matched to a given data model. We described how to match the query guard to a relational schema. Once the schema is matched the query can be transformed to a query that can be safely evaluated on the relational database.

In future we plan to investigate whether there is a better way to express a query guard, *i.e.,* what is the best conceptual model to use? Concurrent with this effort we will conduct a user survey to help evaluate the effectiveness of plug-and-play SQL in lowering the time and effort to write queries. The user survey will investigate the use of different conceptual models using a randomized approach [19]. The user survey requires a separate treatment than this paper, which focuses on conceptual modeling. We also plan to expand the range of queries we handle to include subqueries, relational operations (union, intersection, and difference), and data modification. Another direction of future research is guard inference. Relying on programmers to specify query guards for plug-and-play queries has two problems: First, a programmer may change a query but forget to change the guard. Second, a programmer may give an incorrect guard, for instance, specify a guard that is in the wrong shape for a query. The best way to solve both problems is to automatically infer a guard, Q_p, from a query Q. Ideally, Q_p, will be minimal, that is we will infer Q_p such that there does not exist another guard, Q'_p, for Q, which is tighter than Q_p.

Acknowledgements. This work was supported in part by the National Science Foundation under Award No. DBI-1759965, *Collaborative Research: ABI Development: Symbiota2: Enabling greater collaboration and flexibility for mobilizing biodiversity data.* Opinions, findings and conclusions or recommendations expressed in this material are those of the author(s) and do not necessarily reflect those of NSF.

References

1. Ahadi, A., Prior, J., Behbood, V., Lister, R.: A quantitative study of the relative difficulty for novices of writing seven different types of SQL queries. In: Proceedings of the 2015 ACM Conference on Innovation and Technology in Computer Science Education, ITiCSE 2015, pp. 201–206 (2015). https://doi.org/10.1145/2729094.2742620

2. Amer-Yahia, S., Cho, S., Srivastava, D.: Tree pattern relaxation. In: EDBT, pp. 496–513 (2002)
3. Augsten, N., Böhlen, M.H., Gamper, J.: The q-gram distance between ordered labeled trees. ACM Trans. Database Syst. **35**(1), 1–36 (2010)
4. Balmin, A., Colby, L.S., Curtmola, E., Li, Q., Ozcan, F.: Search driven analysis of heterogenous XML data. In: CIDR (2009)
5. Beyer, S., Chimani, M.: Strong Steiner tree approximations in practice. J. Exp. Algorithmics **24**(1), 1.7:1–1.7:33 (2019)
6. Bhide, M., Agarwal, M., Bar-Or, A., Padmanabhan, S., Mittapalli, S., Venkat-achaliah, G.: XPEDIA: XML processing for data integration. PVLDB **2**(2), 1330–1341 (2009)
7. Codd, E.F.: A relational model of data for large shared data banks. CACM **13**(6), 377–387 (1970)
8. Cohen, S., Brodianskiy, T.: Correcting queries for XML. Inf. Syst. **34**(8), 690–710 (2009)
9. Fagin, R., Haas, L.M., Hernández, M., Miller, R.J., Popa, L., Velegrakis, Y.: Clio: schema mapping creation and data exchange. In: Borgida, A.T., Chaudhri, V.K., Giorgini, P., Yu, E.S. (eds.) Conceptual Modeling: Foundations and Applications. LNCS, vol. 5600, pp. 198–236. Springer, Heidelberg (2009). https://doi.org/10.1007/978-3-642-02463-4_12
10. Fan, W., Bohannon, P.: Information preserving XML schema embedding. ACM Trans. Database Syst. **33**(1), 1–44 (2008)
11. Gries, C., Gilbert, E., Franz, N.: Symbiota - a virtual platform for creating voucher-based biodiversity information communities. Biodivers. Data J. **2**, e1114 (2014)
12. Jiang, H., Ho, H., Popa, L., Han, W.S.: Mapping-driven XML transformation. In: WWW, pp. 1063–1072 (2007)
13. Kanza, Y., Sagiv, Y.: Flexible queries over semistructured data. In: PODS (2001)
14. Karp, R.M.: Reducibility among combinatorial problems. In: Proceedings of a Symposium on the Complexity of Computer Computations, pp. 85–103 (1972)
15. Krishnamurthi, S., Gray, K.E., Graunke, P.T.: Transformation-by-example for XML. In: PADL, pp. 249–262 (2000)
16. Pankowski, T.: A high-level language for specifying XML data transformations. In: ADBIS, pp. 159–172 (2004)
17. Poulsen, S., Butler, L., Alawini, A., Herman, G.L.: Insights from student solutions to SQL homework problems. In: Proceedings of the 2020 ACM Conference on Innovation and Technology in Computer Science Education, pp. 404–410 (2020). https://doi.org/10.1145/3341525.3387391
18. Taipalus, T., Siponen, M., Vartiainen, T.: Errors and complications in SQL query formulation. ACM Trans. Comput. Educ. **18**(3), 1–29 (2018)
19. Uesbeck, P.M., Peterson, C.S., Sharif, B., Stefik, A.: A randomized controlled trial on the effects of embedded computer language switching. In: 28th ACM Joint European Software Engineering Conference and Symposium on the Foundations of Software Engineering, ESEC/FSE 2020, Virtual Event, USA, 8–13 November 2020, pp. 410–420. ACM (2020). https://doi.org/10.1145/3368089.3409701
20. Zhang, S., Dyreson, C.E.: Symmetrically exploiting XML. In: WWW, pp. 103–111 (2006)

Sanity-Checking Multiple Levels of Classification

A Formal Approach with a ConceptBase Implementation

Thomas Kühne[1(✉)] [iD] and Manfred A. Jeusfeld[2] [iD]

[1] Victoria University of Wellington, Wellington, New Zealand
thomas.kuehne@vuw.ac.nz
[2] University of Skövde, IIT, Skövde, Sweden
manfred.jeusfeld@acm.org

Abstract. Multiple levels of classification naturally occur in many domains. Several multi-level modeling approaches account for this and a subset of them attempt to provide their users with sanity-checking mechanisms in order to guard them against conceptually ill-formed models. Historically, the respective multi-level well-formedness schemes have either been overly restrictive or too lax. Orthogonal Ontological Classification has been proposed as a foundation that combines the selectivity of strict schemes with the flexibility afforded by laxer schemes. In this paper, we present a formalization of Orthogonal Ontological Classification, which we empirically validated to demonstrate some of its hitherto only postulated claims using an implementation in CONCEPTBASE. We discuss both the formalization and the implementation, and report on the limitations we encountered.

Keywords: multi-level modeling · well-formedness · integrity constraints

1 Introduction

Modeling languages intended to support conceptual modeling differ to the extent by which they support modeling domains with multiple classification levels; specifically how explicitly they represent such domain classification within models. A long history of modeling mechanisms that attempt to support the modeling of multiple classification domain levels includes materialization [29] and power-types [27], both implying concepts that go beyond individuals and their types. Telos [25] pioneered support for an unbounded number of classification levels and DeepTelos [18] added support for *deep characterization* [6].

Unfortunately, having to manage more than two classification levels increases the potential of creating ill-formed models, i.e., models that cannot be given a sound interpretation. It has been argued that the complexity of contemporary conceptual modeling is akin to the complexity of programming large computer systems and therefore analog complexity management strategies are needed [14]. A well-known discipline within the area of multi-level modeling [8] for enforcing sound models is "strict metamodeling" [3], which is widely accepted to be highly selective, but has been equally widely criticized for being too inflexible [12,13,24].

© The Author(s), under exclusive license to Springer Nature Switzerland AG 2023
J. P. A. Almeida et al. (Eds.): ER 2023, LNCS 14320, pp. 162–180, 2023.
https://doi.org/10.1007/978-3-031-47262-6_9

Multi-dimensional multi-level modeling (MDM), based on the notion of "Orthogonal Ontological Classification" [21], has been proposed as a multi-level modeling paradigm that claims to enjoy the same selectivity as "strict meta-modeling" but without incurring the latter's downside of requiring modelers to employ workarounds for several commonly occurring modeling scenarios. However, to this date, MDM has only been described informally, making it difficult to verify or validate its claims.

Since CONCEPTBASE had been successfully used to formalize the multi-level modeling approaches DDI [26], DeepTelos [18], and MLT* [16], we set out to

- develop a formalization of MDM,
- investigate whether CONCEPTBASE' specification language is sufficiently expressive to support this formalization,
- examine CONCEPTBASE's efficiency when supporting MDM, and
- empirically validate some of the MDM claims.

In this paper, we first further motivate the need for well-formedness checking of models featuring multiple levels of domain classification and then briefly compare two existing approaches to MDM [21] in Sect. 2. We subsequently present an MDM formalization using many-sorted first-order logic in Sect. 3 and follow with a description of an implementation of the formalization using CONCEPTBASE in Sect. 4. We finally, before concluding, discuss the formalization, its implementation, and lessons learned in Sect. 5.

2   Sanity Checking

Enforcing well-formedness requirements on models or programs is a well-established technique to ensure that the latter have a sound semantics. In particular, well-formedness requirements have been effectively used as preconditions to the analysis, interpretation, execution, etc., of models, protecting semantics implementations to trip over problematic structures such as circular or dangling references, to name just two of many sources for ill-formed scenarios.

Beyond serving this purpose, however, well-formedness constraints may also be used to alert users to structures that would not necessarily create problems for semantics implementations, but instead contain conceptual issues such as performing a category mistake. Multi-level models, in particular, provide a richer source for conceptual issues in user models, compared to traditional two-level counterparts. In general, such conceptual issues are harder to find than violations of straightforward structural requirements since they involve the semantics of concepts.

Providing respective solutions is becoming increasingly important due to the dependence of societies on reliable data and the significant amount of higher-order concepts naturally arising not only in specialized domains such as biology, or process metamodeling, but also in such commonplace domains as covered by UNICLASS classifications [28] and Wikidata [9,10]. Brasileiro et al. report that in 2016 Wikidata contained 6,963,059 elements involved in instantiation chains of lengths three [9].

2.1   Detecting Ill-Conceived Conceptualizations

Consider Fig. 1 which shows a condensed version of a modeling scenario that was part of Wikidata in 2016 [9, Figs. 3 & 4]. The rightmost "instance-of" relationship can be derived from two Wikidata claims: First, that Tim Berners-Lee is a scientist and, second, that "Scientist" is a subtype of "Profession". From these claims one can conclude that Tim Berners-Lee is a profession, which obviously does not make sense. Dadalto et al. observed that Wikidata no longer supports this particular incorrect inference, but that this is not a result of applying a general solution to eradicate all such issues. Equivalently ill-formed model fragments, e.g., a certain "Frank Hilker" being inferable as a "Position" are still pervasive in Wikidata, affecting many areas including biology, gastronomy, awards, professions, and sports [10]. Regarding the three "Anti-Patterns" Brasileiro et al. identified as characterizing ill-formed model fragments, they found that 15,177 Wikidata elements were involved in "Anti-Pattern 1", and 7,082 were involved in "Anti-Pattern 3" [9].

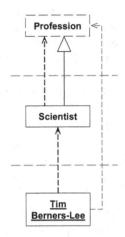

Fig. 1. Semantically Flawed Model

In general, such nonsensical inferences cannot be mechanically detected without attaching semantics to the concepts involved and, based on those semantics, computing that a claim is made involving incompatible concepts.

Fortunately, however, nonsensical models like that in Fig. 1 can still be mechanically detected without having to attach rich semantics to the concepts involved. For instance, by associating "order"-values to the concepts, e.g., by categorizing Tim Berners-Lee as an order-0 concept and Profession as an order-2 concept, it becomes apparent that the former cannot be a direct instance of the latter. Likewise, a specialization relationship between an order-1 concept Scientist and an order-2 concept Profession is equally unsound with respect to a set-theoretic interpretation of the model fragment.

Having to manually assign order values to each model element would be onerous, however even in the absence of such information, the scenario in Fig. 1 can still be detected to make unsound claims based on its inconsistent relationships. The "instance-of" relationship between Scientist and Profession is necessarily incompatible with the simultaneous claim that the former is a subtype of the latter, regardless of the absolute order values associated to these concepts. There is an inherent contradiction in instantiation requiring the two orders to differ by one and specialization requiring that the two orders are identical.

The above explains the call for "Ontological Anti-Patterns" that can be used to detect such ill-formed scenarios [9,14]. In contrast, the approach underlying this paper was not arrived at by mining data for problematic patterns; rather the well-formedness constraints we are considering originated from the motivation to ensure that models have a sound set-theoretic interpretation.

2.2   Previous Attempts

The original attempt to exclude ill-formed user models in the context of modeling with multiple levels of abstraction was "strict metamodeling" [3,4]. Based on a single principle, it rules out a huge class of conceptual errors, including those characterized by anti-patterns AP1–AP3 in [9]. The downside of its very conservative nature is that it also forbids users from adequately modeling a number of naturally occurring domain scenarios. These force users to employ workarounds that lead to "unnatural" solutions [23, section 8.1] or a duplication of elements [22], which not only add complexity of their own but also necessitate the introduction of additional constraints.

Many approaches aim to avoid the aforementioned downsides by using various concepts. The one most founded on ontological correctness is Almeida et al.'s MLT* which supports the adequate modeling of more demanding domain scenarios through the use of *orderless types* [2,11]. While a disciplined use of the approach retains sanity-checking abilities for a large proportion of a user model, the remaining part, involving orderless types, cannot be fully checked anymore. Some users may hence unintentionally exploit orderless types to create unsound models, thus undermining the rigor that MLT* otherwise supports.

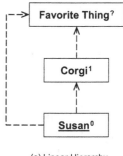

(a) Linear Hierarchy

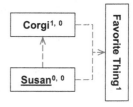

(b) Multi-Dimension Hierarchy

Fig. 2. Traditional vs Orthogonal Classification

2.3   Orthogonal Ontological Classification

"Multi-Dimensional Modeling" (MDM) based on the notion of "Orthogonal Ontological Classification" claims to fully retain the sanity-checking capabilities of "strict metamodeling" without incurring its downsides, while avoiding to create loopholes that can be exploited [21]. It claims to retain the same rigor for local hierarchies, referred to as "classification clusters", and argues that inter-cluster relationships cannot give rise to conceptually ill-formed models. It addresses challenging scenarios in which elements are ostensibly classified by multiple classifiers of different order (cf. Fig. 2(a)), by maintaining that such overlapping classifications are best understood as occurring from different separate dimensions (cf. Fig. 2(b)), using a "separation of concerns" approach.

Although MDM is inherently focused on precise well-formedness criteria for models and its description elaborates on a number of constraints to be enforced, the respective descriptions are informal and to date no complete publicly available implementation of the ideas has been available. We therefore set out to investigate the suitability of CONCEPTBASE for realizing an MDM implementation, both in terms of the expressiveness of its specification language and the efficiency of its optimized deductive database engine.

3 Formalization

Our formalization of MDM in CONCEPTBASE is based on TELOS (see Sect. 4), but for better accessibility we present a technology-independent formalization in this section. It not only covers a deliberately restrictive version of MDM, as outlined in [21, section 4.3], but also includes characterization potency [20]. We do not include well-formedness rules concerning element features (e.g., attributes), since our focus is on validating MDM's main principles, which is possible while making very little reference to element features. In the following, due to space restrictions, we only present our formalization of the aforementioned MDM version without elaborating on the rationales behind the original constraints. However, wherever we deviated from the original, informally described, constraints, we state our motivation and reasoning.

The model structures we are concerned with are graphs over elements. The latter are sometimes referred to as "clabjects" [3], because they can play the role of a class or an object, or both at the same time. These elements are connected with relationships, of which we only cover classification and generalization here, as other relationships are not restricted by MDM. Since elements have potencies that belong to dimensions (cf. Fig. 2) and relationships belong to dimensions as well, we use the many-sorted signature of Eq. 1.

We denote an element e with a potency p in dimension d as e^{p_d}. If e_2 classifies e_1 in dimension d, we use $e_1 :_d e_2$. If e_2 generalizes e_1 in dimension d, we use $e_1 \prec_d e_2$. The combination $e_1 :\prec_d e_2$ is used as a shortcut for representing that e_2 is either a classifier or a generalization of e_1. We use a "+" super-

$$\Sigma = (E, D, A, \rho) \quad (1)$$
$$E = \{e_i \mid e_i \in Elements\} \quad (2)$$
$$D = \{d_i \mid d_i \in Dimensions\} \quad (3)$$
$$A = \{a_i \mid a_i \in Attributes\} \quad (4)$$
$$\rho = \{:^d, \prec^d, :\prec^d, .\} \quad (5)$$

script to denote sequences of relationships of at least length one. For instance, $e_s :^+ e_e$ represents the scenarios $e_s : e_e$, $e_s : e_1 : e_e$, $e_s : e_1 : e_2 : e_e$, etc.

In the following, we use labels for our well-formedness constraints that correspond to the labels C_1-C_4 suggested in [21, section 4.3]. Since the latter do not cover characterization potency, we use a C_0 prefix for our respective constraints.

The first characterization potency constraint C_{0a} covers two aspects: First, upon instantiation potency must decrease, and second, only non-zero potency elements can be instantiated.

C_{0a}: *Instances must have a potency that is strictly lower than that of their classifiers and classifiers must have potencies greater than zero.*

$$\forall e_{1,2}, p_2, d: \quad e_1 :_d e_2^{p_{2d}} \quad \rightarrow \quad \exists p_{1d}: e_1^{p_{1d}} \ \wedge \ 0 \leq p_{1d} < p_{2d} \qquad (C_{0a})$$

Note the omission of any potency information on e_1 in the premiss. Underspecification with respect to element potency is allowed, however, we deemed it to be appropriate to enforce the specification of a potency value in case an element has a classifier with an explicit potency. We thus require all instance-classifier pairs where the classifier specifies a potency to obey the rules of characterization potency, not just those where both participants have explicit potencies.

The second characterization potency constraint C_{0b} requires that subtypes must not have a potency that is lower than the supertype potency.

C_{0b}: *Subtypes must have an equal or higher potency than their supertypes.*

$$\forall e_{1,2}, p_{1,2}, d: \quad e_1^{p_{1d}} \prec e_2^{p_{2d}} \quad \rightarrow \quad p_{1d} \geq p_{2d} \qquad (C_{0b})$$

Constraint C_1, named *disjoint feature sets* and informally described in [21], is designed to avoid having to disambiguate access to element features in case multiple classifiers of an element define a feature with the same name. In the constraint definition below, the pattern $(e_1.a) : e_2$ represents, w.r.t. e_1, the existence of a feature a with the type e_2.

C_1: *Elements that classify or generalize the same element, must not define features with the same name.*

$$\forall e_{0,1,2,3,4}, a_{1,2}:$$
$$(e_0 : e_1 \ \vee \ e_0 \prec^+ e_1) \wedge (e_0 : e_2 \ \vee \ e_0 \prec^+ e_2) \wedge \qquad (C_1)$$
$$(e_1.a_1) : e_3 \wedge (e_2.a_2) : e_4 \ \wedge \ a_1 = a_2 \quad \rightarrow \quad e_1 = e_2$$

Even though we exclude multiple classification and multiple generalization within one dimension (via constraints C_{3a} & C_{3b}), we still need the above constraint to account for potential name clashes produced by multiple classification/generalizations from different dimensions.

Constraint C_2, named *bottom-level overlapping* in [21], ensures that there is a unique dimension in which an element that is classified from multiple dimensions can be instantiated into. We cover this aspect with our constraint C_{2a}.

C_{2a}: *Elements with potencies in more than one dimension must not have more than one non-zero potency value.*

$$\forall e_0, p_{1,2}, d_{1,2}: \quad e_0^{p_{1d_1}} \ \wedge \ e_0^{p_{2d_2}} \ \wedge \ d_1 \neq d_2 \ \wedge \ p_{1d_1} > 0 \quad \rightarrow \quad p_{2d_2} = 0 \qquad (C_{2a})$$

Note that potency values of zero prevent instantiation (cf. constraint C_{0a}), and that we do not specify a classifier for e_0 since we want to allow for e_0 to be a top-level element with a manually assigned potency. We thus deviate from the "*bottom-level* overlapping" focus of the original C_2 constraint since we deemed that the constraint was in essence about preventing the potential of instantiation into more than one dimension, as opposed to only achieving this for elements that have explicit classifiers.

Since it is possible to omit potency specifications for the purposes of under-specification, an element could potentially be instantiated into multiple dimensions without constraint C_{2a} preventing such a scenario, since it (in combination with constraint C_{0a}) only covers cases featuring explicitly specified potencies. Constraint C_{2b} below addresses this by ensuring that instantiation may only occur into one dimension only even in the absence of any potency information.

C_{2b}: *All instantiations from a classifier must be into the same dimension.*

$$\forall e_{1,2,3}, d_{1,2} : e_1 :_{d_1} e_3 \wedge e_2 :_{d_2} e_3 \rightarrow d_1 = d_2 \qquad (C_{2b})$$

Constraint C_{2c} below is not part of the original MDM well-formedness suggestions, however, we felt that an analog to constraint C_{2a} was needed that addressed the reception of type facets through specialization, thus complementing the classification focus of the original C_2. Since constraint C_{2a} restricts elements to instantiation into one dimension only, it seemed inappropriate to allow elements to receive type facets from other dimensions via specialization.

C_{2c}: *Elements participating in multiple dimensions must not entertain generalization relationships in their potency-zero dimensions.*

$$\begin{aligned} \forall e_{1,2}, d_{1,2} : & \\ & e_1 \prec_{d_1} e_2 \wedge \mathrm{member}(e_1, d_2) \wedge \\ & d_1 \neq d_2 \rightarrow \exists p_{d_1} : e_1^{p_{d_1}} \wedge p_{d_1} > 0 \end{aligned} \qquad (C_{2c})$$

$$\begin{aligned} \text{where } \mathrm{member}(e, d) = & \\ & \exists e_1 : (e :_d e_1 \vee e_1 :_d e \vee e \prec_d e_1 \vee e_1 \prec_d e) \end{aligned}$$

Note that the "member"-predicate does not require an element to have an explicit potency in a dimension. Dimension membership is solely acquired via respective relationships. This supports the underspecification of potency values, while simultaneously allowing checking for inappropriate type facet acquisition from dimensions that an element cannot be instantiated into anyhow.

The C_3 constraint, named *connected classification clusters* in [21] requires all elements within a dimension to form a single tree-shaped "classification cluster". It prohibits disjoint clusters, containing instanceOf relationships, that declare the same dimension. Since the single cluster needs to be tree-shaped, we rule out multiple classification within a dimension with constraint C_{3a}.

C_{3a}: *Elements must not have more than one classifier within a dimension.*

$$\forall e_{0,1,2}, d : e_0 :_d e_1 \wedge e_0 :_d e_2 \rightarrow e_1 = e_2 \qquad (C_{3a})$$

Note that ruling out multiple classification within a dimension does not represent nearly as much of a limitation as it would in an approach that did not support multiple classification from multiple dimensions.

Although the original C_3 formulation does not imply it, we also rule out multiple generalization (aka, multiple inheritance). It acknowledges that our implied language design currently does not support any merging mechanisms and/or semantics that a useful approach to multiple generalization should feature.

C_{3b}: *Elements must not have more than one supertype within a dimension.*

$$\forall e_{0,1,2}, d: \; e_0 \prec_d e_1 \; \land \; e_0 \prec_d e_2 \; \rightarrow \; e_1 = e_2 \qquad (C_{3b})$$

We take a liberal approach to allowing multiple generalizations of different dimensions since they may be regarded as non-overlapping, i.e., do not require merging mechanisms.

The main "tree-shaped" aspect of the original C_3 constraint is taken care of by our constraint C_{3c} below.

C_{3c}: *Within a dimension, there must be only one classification cluster root.*

$$\forall d: \; (\exists e_3: \; (\forall e_{1,2}: \; e_1 :_d e_2 \; \rightarrow \; e_1 :_d^+ e_3)) \qquad (C_{3c})$$

It ensures that each dimension only has a single classification cluster, by ruling out classification forests that feature multiple roots.

The final original constraint C_4, named *sound meta-hierarchies*, concerns general well-formedness requirements that would apply outside a multi-dimensional approach as well and correspond to, in spirit but not as restrictively, the regiment established by "strict metamodeling".

The graphs implied by models must be free of cycles with respect to classification and generalization relationships.

C_{4a}: *The graph of instanceOf and specializationOf relations must be acyclic.*

$$\forall e: \; \neg(e :\prec^+ e) \qquad (C_{4a})$$

Note that through the use of $:\prec^+$ we require every path with mixed classification and generalization relationships edges to be acyclic, as opposed to imposing the constraint only on pure classification and pure generalization paths respectively. Unlike the original C_4 constraint suggests, we do not restrict the context of the constraint to a single dimension only. In combination, these two choices lead to the rejection of a wider range of models with circular definitions, which we deem to be obviously ill-formed.

We do not need a constraint that establishes the *level-respecting*-property for classification hierarchies since a prerequisite for establishing respective ill-formed scenarios, is the ability of an element to be an instance of multiple classes in the same dimension and we rule out multiple classification scenarios via constraint C_{3a}.

An important component of the original C_4 constraint is that generalization relationships must not occur between elements of different order (i.e., of different set-theoretic classification power). We do not explicitly formalize element order but can infer when element orders must necessarily be different. If two elements are in the same classification branch, i.e., related to each other by one or more classification relationships, they must necessarily have different order values. Any such pair must not participate in the same generalization hierarchy, regardless of their relative positions in that hierarchy.

C_{4b}: *Elements in a classification path must not share a generalization hierarchy.*

$$\forall e_{1,2}, d: e_1 :_d^+ e_2 \rightarrow \neg specConnected(e_1, e_2, d) \qquad (C_{4b})$$

where $specConnected(e_1, e_2, d) =$
$\quad (e_1 \prec_d e_2 \lor e_2 \prec_d e_1) \lor$
$\quad (\exists e_3 : (e_1 \prec_d e_3 \lor e_3 \prec_d e_1) \land specConnected(e_3, e_2, d))$

Constraint C_{4b} could be generalized to cover all sources of order differences between elements but here we simply document what we were able to implement using CONCEPTBASE.

Before sharing our findings on the above eleven constraints in Sect. 5, we first present our respective CONCEPTBASE implementation.

4   Implementation

4.1   ConceptBase

CONCEPTBASE [15] is a deductive database system for managing models and metamodels. Its data model is based on the TELOS language [19] and its predicative specification language is based on Datalog with negation [1]. The latter uses a closed world assumption and guarantees terminating evaluations of –

rules: predicates that can infer information, similar to PROLOG predicates,
constraints: model integrity conditions which must always be satisfied, and
queries: supporting the identification of instances of custom query classes.

Around 30 rules and constraints in CONCEPTBASE define the TELOS semantics for instantiation, specialization, attribution, and relationships. TELOS is similar to the OMG's MOF, in that TELOS can both be used to (in an extended variant or as is) directly represent user models, or to support the definition of modeling languages, which in turn are used to represent user models [7].

4.2   Realizing Multi-Dimensional Modeling with TELOS

A fundamental design decision we had to make was to either build on TELOS's definitions for instantiation and specialization, or to define a new language definition with custom instantiation and specialization relationships. We opted for the first alternative for the following reasons:

– MDM's classification and generalization notions are compatible with TELOS,
– it minimized the effort, allowing us to focus on MDM-specific rules, and
– it allows a seamless adoption of MDM principles to TELOS.

Adding MDM well-formedness to TELOS well-formedness criteria can be achieved cleanly by employing CONCEPTBASE's module system. A so-called oHome module, which defines relation semantics, provides the basis on which our Multi-Dim submodule builds on, to add potencies to elements, dimensions to relationships, rules, constraints, etc.

Early on in our experiments we learned that subjecting all TELOS objects to the MDM well-formedness principles resulted in undesirable performance. This is due to MDM's inclusion of classification well-formedness and the fact that around 50% of predefined facts in CONCEPTBASE are classification-related. To address the lack of performance, we confined the application of MDM-specific constraints to MDM-specific elements by letting respective quantified variables in the constraints range over a custom-defined Element instead of the TELOS type Individual (cf. Sect. 5.2). Element represents the notion of a Clabject, i.e., a concept that can be an instance, a type, or both at the same time [3,5].

We use a total of 18 CONCEPTBASE rules to define the relations in Eq. 5, e.g., instanceOf/lab and specializationOf/lab. Note the use of lab rather than dim which reflects the fact that the dimension properties attached to these relationships are dimension *labels*. These can be user-defined and our validation scenarios include labels such as Products, Favorites, Activities, Assets, etc. These are labels of explicit dimension objects Products, Favorites, etc. which TELOS relationships link to (cf. Listing 1.1).

The "member" predicate used in constraint C_{2c} (see Sect. 3) is defined by two mdrules, one of which is shown in Listing 1.1, with the other one analogously taking care of specialization relationships.

```
1 $ forall inst/InstanceOf x/Element dim/Dimension
2     (inst dimension dim) and (From(inst, x) or To(inst, x))
3     ==> (x memberOf dim) $
```

Listing 1.1. Rule mdrule1

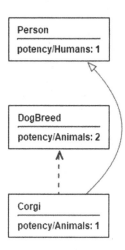

The TELOS class InstanceOf referenced in line 1 of Listing 1.1 classifies all explicit instantiation relationships. Likewise, Dimension classifies all dimension objects. With (inst dimension dim) we establish that the inst relationship is linked to a dim dimension object.

The next two premises (line 2 of Listing 1.1) establish that element x participates in the instantiation relationship inst. From these it follows (in line 3) that element x is a member of dimension dim.

Of the eleven constraints we defined, we show our implementation of constraint C_{2c} in Listing 1.2, since it

Fig. 3. C_{2c}-violating model

- shows a usage of the custom-defined memberOf predicate (cf. Listing 1.1).
- is one of the richer constraints but still nicely demonstrates how readable CONCEPTBASE constraints are.
- exhibits the slight implementation inelegance of dealing with both dimension objects and dimension labels.

```
1 c2c: $ forall x,c/Element lab/Label dim/Dimension
2         (x specializationOf/lab c) and
3         (x memberOf dim) and not Label(dim,lab)
4         ==> exists p/Integer (x potency/lab p) and (p > 0) $
```

Listing 1.2. Constraint C_{2c}

Figure 3 shows a CONCEPTBASE screenshot of a model which is rejected due to violating constraint C_{2c}. Here, Corgi cannot claim to simultaneously be a classifier for both the Animals and the Humans dimensions.

The implementation of constraint C_{4b} in Sect. 3, shown in Listing 1.3, shows in line 2 how to use an operator like :$^+$ in CONCEPTBASE.

```
1 c4b: $ forall x,y/Element lab/Label
2         (x instanceOf_trans/lab y)
3         ==> not (x specConnected/lab y) $
```

Listing 1.3. Constraint C_{4b}

Line 2 in Listing 1.3 establishes that an element x is in the same instantiation branch as another element y, through any non-zero number of "instanceOf" relationships, in which case those two elements must not be in the same generalization hierarchy, i.e., must not be connected via any specialization relationships. The symmetric and transitive specConnected relationship is concisely defined by rules mdrule17 & mdrule18, each rule fitting in one line.

We separated constraint- from rule definitions by using two separate Telos source files since it is often desirable to not enforce constraints, e.g., when developing models where intermediate editing states are not well-formed or when defining negative validation examples. We were thus able to include constraints only if and when we wanted to demonstrate that it passes or fails validation.

We implemented constraint C_{3c} as a CONCEPTBASE query rather than as a constraint since we wanted to avoid being forced to have all of our validation scenarios conform to constraint C_{3c}. A query allows one to check a model for a property on request, and

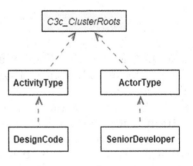

Fig. 4. Queries in CONCEPTBASE

unlike a constraint, can point out culprits in a visual manner. Figure 4 shows a CONCEPTBASE screenshot in which our query representing constraint C_{3c} was used to identify multiple classification cluster roots in a model. From a usability standpoint it can be argued that such visual support can be helpful compared to having to scan CONCEPTBASE error messages for the respective Element names.

4.3   ConceptBase Visualization Support

Beyond supporting the representation of MDM models and allowing them to be checked against well-formedness rules, we also implemented some visualization support. Note the colored relationships in the CONCEPTBASE screenshots (Figs. 3 & 4). Modelers can specify arbitrary RGB colors when defining dimensions such

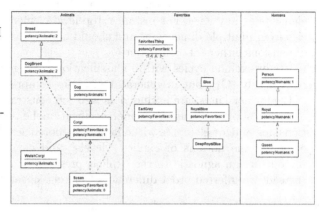

Fig. 5. Explicit dimensions in CONCEPTBASE

as Animals. Element attributes and potencies are rendered below an Element's name, instead of the standard CONCEPTBASE approach that visualizes every attribute on its own and draws links between them and their owning elements.

Finally, we support the visualization of dimensions as such, using colored backgrounds, which are semantics-free but visually structure model content. Figure 5 shows a sample model featuring three dimensions. We omitted associations and links but note that these could have of course crossed dimension boundaries. We have made our CONCEPTBASE implementation source files and a set of models we used for validation purposes–in source format but also as PNG files–available at https://conceptbase.sourceforge.net/mdm-er2023/ [17].

5   Discussion

In the following, we first discuss our formalization choices and the consequences resulting from them. In Sect. 5.2 we then discuss the merit of CONCEPTBASE as a supporting tool.

5.1   Formalization Discussion

The MDM paper our work is based on [21], proposes C_1–C_4 "constraints" that informally describe one possible realization of the approach and are rather constraint categories, each often requiring multiple formal constraints to be covered, hence the use of our $_a$, $_b$, etc. sublabels. Whenever constraint definitions called for precision that was not in the informal descriptions or suggested generalizations, we often were able to improve or expand on the informal design: We

- generalized the exclusion of classifier feature clashes (C_1) to include supertype feature clashes (cf. constraint C_1).

- generalized the prohibition to instantiate a "bottom-level" element participating in multiple dimensions into more than one dimension (C_2), to include elements at any level. For instance, top-level elements may entertain potencies from multiple dimensions and should not be instantiatable into multiple dimensions either (cf. constraint C_{2a}).
- not only exclude cycles within classification- and generalization hierarchies respectively (C_4), but in general, i.e., cycles comprising mixed relationships of the former kinds, are excluded as well (cf. constraint C_{4a}).
- explicitly support dimension underspecification, i.e., allow dimensionless relationships and/or elements without explicit potencies.
- eschewed the notions of explicit "levels" and element-"order", thus making our design agnostic to the explicit presence or absence of such notions. Instead, we inferred order differences from classification relationships.

Note that the latter choice elegantly targets the root cause of soundness violations and could be regarded as avoiding overspecification in comparison to a level-based approach. However, this design choice obviously means that we do not support manual "order" assignments or "level" allocations. Respective values are always inferred from relationships, i.e., we currently do not support any modeler-supplied claims about such values that could be checked for accuracy.

Generality. Note that our CONCEPTBASE implementation does not cover all inferable order differences. Constraint C_{4b} identifies order-differences for elements in the same classification branch but, for instance, does not account for elements in different branches with known different path lengths to a shared root.

We still have to begin a quite involved investigation into whether CONCEPTBASE's expressiveness is sufficient to infer a larger set of elements with order-differences. It is clear already, though, that the readability and execution efficiency of constraint C_{4b} would significantly suffer. An enhanced version of constraint C_{4b} would have to compare edge counts between different paths, which may be beyond what CONCEPTBASE can provide. The current syntax definitely does not support an extra edge-count parameter in addition to our "/lab" dimension label parameter.

For now, we are satisfied with the coverage our current version of constraint C_{4b} achieves for the following reasons:

- The constraint can be concisely formulated and is very readable.
- It does not require the use of CONCEPTBASE queries and/or functions which are more complex, i.e., require a much deeper skill set to develop.
- Whether CONCEPTBASE supports a better version is unclear at this stage.
- The discrimination power of our current constraint C_{4b} compares very favorably to approaches based on a small set of anti-patterns and is already optimal with respect to recognizing specialization connectivity.

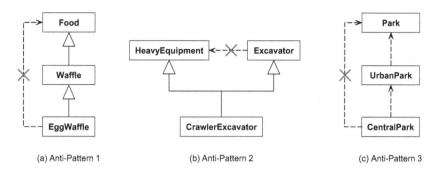

(a) Anti-Pattern 1   (b) Anti-Pattern 2   (c) Anti-Pattern 3

Fig. 6. Wikidata Anti-Pattern Scenarios (cf. [9, Fig. 6, Fig. 8, Fig. 10])

MDM Well-Formedness vs Anti-patterns. Although our current implementation does not infer all possible element order differences that could potentially give rise to unsound generalization hierarchies, it easily covers all scenarios detected by the Anti-Patterns AP1–AP3 defined in [9], plus many more. Figure 6 shows three Wikidata model fragments, which exemplify violations of three Anti-Patterns Brasilero et al. used to detect ill-formed modeling scenarios. In general, Anti-Patterns represent schemata, i.e., will detect a wide range of unsound model fragments, not just very specific configurations. For instance, the generalization hierarchy involving Food and EggWaffle in Fig. 6(a), could involve arbitrarily many generalization relationships; as long as a classification relationship between the bottom and top elements exists, the model is not sound.

Note that there is a single reason as to why AP1 & AP2 appropriately reject offending models: Elements, that are connected via generalization relationships, must have the same order; otherwise, no sound set-theoretic interpretation of the respective model exists. Our constraint C_{4b} simultaneously covers AP1 & AP2 since it targets the root cause that underlies the validity of these two anti-patterns. Unlike AP1, for instance, constraint C_{4b} also correctly rejects models like that in Fig. 6(a) where the classification relationship is reversed, i.e., where Food is declared to be an instance of EggWaffle.

Our constraint C_{3a} takes care of AP3 violations, again, in a very general manner, i.e., the constraint is (trivially, in this case) agnostic to the number of classification edges involved. A less trivial detection, that does not simply rule out multiple classification, would have required the implementation of the "*level-respecting*" property mentioned in [21]. Since this property would require the comparison of classification path lengths, it belongs to the same "unclarified" category as the extension of constraint C_{4b} (see above).

We observed that anti-pattern scenario variations we considered in our validation sometimes violated more than one constraint. This appears to testify to an increased robustness of a sanity-checking approach that covers multiple soundness principles. For instance, the aforementioned variation of AP1 in Fig. 6(a), violates both constraint C_{4a} & C_{4b}.

We acknowledge that the Anti-Patterns used in [9,10] were solely used as queries to search for ill-formed model fragments and hence should not be judged as integrity specifications. However, we note that for the purposes of ensuring the well-formedness of models, an approach based on constraints that embody fundamental soundness principles seems more suited than a collection of schemata that were devised on the basis of found integrity violations.

Overall, we did not attempt to create a full-fledged language design that resolves all possible design choices, e.g., we did not impose limitations on generalizations into multiple dimensions even though the respective semantics are undefined at this stage. We only attempted, and almost entirely succeeded, to capture the constraint categories C_1–C_4. CONCEPTBASE might support a full coverage but ascertaining whether that is the case is less than trivial and any respective measures would affect constraint readability and execution efficiency.

5.2   Implementation Discussion

Expressiveness. It is remarkable how close CONCEPTBASE constraint implementations such as Listing 1.3 are to a concise logic formulation (cf. constraint C_{4b}). There is some contamination due to the need to distinguish between dimension objects and their corresponding labels but overall the CONCEPTBASE constraints are very readable and very well supported experimentation with variants.

As mentioned in Sect. 5.1, we did not implement the *"level-respecting"* property of C4 (addressing it trivially by excluding multiple classification) and our constraint C_{4b} is not as general as it theoretically could be. We plan to investigate whether there is a real hard limitation of CONCEPTBASE expressiveness or whether a rather involved implementation may be feasible after all.

Efficiency. CONCEPTBASE's evaluation of rules and constraints is not sufficiently performant to support all MDM constraints at the TELOS level. We therefore had to let our constraints range over a dedicated Element class instead of the TELOS class Individual, and let one rule range over DimensionLabel instead of Label, to achieve typical evaluation times of less than one second per instance of Element. Given those domain restrictions, our validation scenarios are checked very swiftly, in particular when incremental changes to existing models are made.

Usability. Our emphasis was on exploring the feasibility of formalizing MDM constraints using CONCEPTBASE and we therefore paid little attention to usability concerns. For instance, we could have formulated all constraints as queries, which would have allowed them to be evaluated on demand only–thus decreasing model loading times and supporting intermediate invalid models–and produce visual pointers to offending elements (cf. Fig. 4). However, the readability of our implementation would have suffered as a consequence. As an exception, we implemented constraint C_{3c} as a query because enforcing it on all models seemed limiting to users while the benefits of enforcing this particular integrity condition were not obvious to us.

We also considered implementing part of constraint C_{0a} as a query, giving users the chance to omit potency values and only providing them with a warning mechanism in case the underspecification is unintended (cf. Sect. 3). However, we eschewed the formulation of an additional query as we deemed the enforcement of the constraint to be appropriate.

Overall, we treated CONCEPTBASE mainly as a user model storage backend as opposed to an environment with optimal support for interactive modeling. We support visual presentation of dimensions (cf. Fig. 5) but so far did not pursue further visualization support, e.g., rendering potencies as superscript values.

Utility for Formalization. As expected, CONCEPTBASE proved to be invaluable for validating our formalization. In many cases, subjecting select modeling scenarios to our constraints simply confirmed the latter's adequacy and/or the claimed properties of MDM. In some cases, however, CONCEPTBASE supported experimenting with variants, e.g., to explore alternative formulations or achieve better evaluation efficiency. By defining a validation suite of model scenarios that target all constraints respectively, we were able to trial tweaks and either confirm or disprove that they were still reporting ill-formed models and not reporting sound models and/or measure respective evaluation times.

Note that our suggested amendment to the original C_2 formulation in the form of a slightly wider constraint C_{2a} definition was arrived at during such constraint validation experiments. While working with respective validation scenarios, it seemed odd to forbid the clashing of multiple potency values greater than zero only for elements that have explicit classifiers (cf. Sect. 3).

Our regression validation suite (not including further scenarios that we used in general development) and a log of evaluating the respective models is part of the data we provided at [17].

6   Conclusion

The more critical the reliance on the conceptual integrity of a model is, the higher the need to eliminate avoidable conceptual mistakes. It is concerning that modeling concepts of societal importance, such as "gene", "protein", and "disease" are used inconsistently in models [10, Table 1]. Ontological sanity-checking of models is not a novel concept, but for multi-level models, it has in the past translated to users either needing to complicate their models as a result of having to work around overly strict well-formedness requirements, or users being subjected to loopholes that they may inadvertently exploit with ill consequences.

In this paper, we presented the first formalization of an approach [21] that reliably and independently of the modeling domain prevents a large class of ill-conceived conceptualizations without requiring modelers to explicitly provide semantic descriptions of the concepts they are using, or forcing them to work around unnecessary limitations imposed by overly strict well-formedness criteria when modeling naturally occurring domain scenarios. Our formalization does not rely on explicit "order" or "level" constructs, making it widely applicable, i.e., a candidate for adoption by other multi-level modeling approaches. While an implementation challenge has so far prevented us from realizing the full discrimination potential of the MDM paradigm, our implementation is very faithful to MDM principles and has more discriminative power than the anti-patterns in [9,10]. Being based on fundamental soundness principles, rather than attempting to match ill-formed model fragments, our implementation is not dependent on a comprehensive schematic capturing of such fragments.

We have empirically validated MDM claims and our implementation by using numerous sample models of which the most essential form a regression validation test suite that we resorted to any time we explored a constraint variant, e.g., to increase evaluation efficiency. In many cases we additionally created a systematic exploration of scenarios, in which, for instance, all combinations of relationship directions in specific scenarios were explored. Our slight modification of constraint C_{2a} and our introduction of constraint C_{2c} were the direct result of following such a tool-supported, scenario-based exploration approach.

We demonstrated that CONCEPTBASE is capable of supporting a concise, intuitive and sufficiently performant implementation of MDM well-formedness principles that did not require any coding at any stage. Even without prioritizing usability, we achieved decent notation support, including the rendering of UML-like attributes, colored relationships, and explicit dimension containers.

Despite that fact that future work remains with respect to exploring the expressiveness of CONCEPTBASE, which could potentially improve the coverage of constraint C_{4b}, we are convinced that our work is a suitable foundation for a further exploration of the MDM paradigm, allowing richer variants–such as supporting instantiation into multiple dimensions from a single element–to be considered and validated. Our formalization and public implementation open up these avenues not only for us, but also for any other researchers who may want to extend or adopt the approach to fit their frameworks.

References

1. Abiteboul, S., Hull, R.: Data functions, datalog and negation. SIGMOD Rec. **17**(3), 143–153 (1988). https://doi.org/10.1145/971701.50218
2. Almeida, J.P.A., Fonseca, C.M., Carvalho, V.A.: A comprehensive formal theory for multi-level conceptual modeling. In: Mayr, H.C., Guizzardi, G., Ma, H., Pastor, O. (eds.) ER 2017. LNCS, vol. 10650, pp. 280–294. Springer, Cham (2017). https://doi.org/10.1007/978-3-319-69904-2_23
3. Atkinson, C.: Meta-modeling for distributed object environments. In: Enterprise Distributed Object Computing, pp. 90–101. IEEE (1997)
4. Atkinson, C., Gerbig, R.: Melanie: Multi-level modeling and ontology engineering environment. In: Proceedings of Modeling Wizards 2012. ACM (2012)
5. Atkinson, C., Kühne, T.: The essence of multilevel metamodeling. In: Gogolla, M., Kobryn, C. (eds.) UML 2001. LNCS, vol. 2185, pp. 19–33. Springer, Heidelberg (2001). https://doi.org/10.1007/3-540-45441-1_3
6. Atkinson, C., Kühne, T.: Rearchitecting the UML infrastructure. ACM Trans. Model. Comput. Simul. **12**(4), 290–321 (2003)

7. Atkinson, C., Kühne, T.: Concepts for comparing modeling tool architectures. In: Briand, L., Williams, C. (eds.) MODELS 2005. LNCS, vol. 3713, pp. 398–413. Springer, Heidelberg (2005). https://doi.org/10.1007/11557432_30

8. Atkinson, C., Kühne, T.: Reducing accidental complexity in domain models. Softw. Syst. Model. **7**(3), 345–359 (2008). https://doi.org/10.1007/s10270-007-0061-0

9. Brasileiro, F., Almeida, J.P.A., Carvalho, V.A., Guizzardi, G.: Applying a multi-level modeling theory to assess taxonomic hierarchies in Wikidata. In: Proceedings of the 25th International Conference Companion on World Wide Web, pp. 975–980. WWW '16 Companion, International World Wide Web Conferences Steering Committee (2016). https://doi.org/10.1145/2872518.2891117

10. Dadalto, A.A., Almeida, J.P.A., Fonseca, C.M., Guizzardi, G.: Type or individual? evidence of large-scale conceptual disarray in Wikidata. In: Ghose, A., Horkoff, J., Silva Souza, V.E., Parsons, J., Evermann, J. (eds.) ER 2021. LNCS, vol. 13011, pp. 367–377. Springer, Cham (2021). https://doi.org/10.1007/978-3-030-89022-3_29

11. Fonseca, C.M., Almeida, J.P.A., Guizzardi, G., Carvalho, V.A.: Multi-level conceptual modeling: from a formal theory to a well-founded language. In: Trujillo, J.C., et al. (eds.) ER 2018. LNCS, vol. 11157, pp. 409–423. Springer, Cham (2018). https://doi.org/10.1007/978-3-030-00847-5_29

12. Frank, U.: Multilevel modeling. Bus. Inf. Syst. Eng. **6**(6), 319–337 (2014). https://doi.org/10.1007/s12599-014-0350-4

13. Gitzel, R., Merz, M.: How a relaxation of the strictness definition can benefit MDD approaches with meta model hierarchies. In: Proceedings of the 8th World Multi-Conference on Systemics, Cybernetics & Informatics, vol. IV, pp. 62–67 (2004)

14. Guizzardi, G.: Ontological patterns, anti-patterns and pattern languages for next-generation conceptual modeling. In: Yu, E., Dobbie, G., Jarke, M., Purao, S. (eds.) ER 2014. LNCS, vol. 8824, pp. 13–27. Springer, Cham (2014). https://doi.org/10.1007/978-3-319-12206-9_2

15. Jeusfeld, M.A.: Metamodeling and method engineering with ConceptBase. In: Metamodeling for Method Engineering, pp. 89–168. MIT Press (2009)

16. Jeusfeld, M.A., Almeida, J.A.P.A., Carvalho, V.A., Fonseca, C.M., Neumayr, B.: Deductive reconstruction of MLT* for multi-level modeling. In: Proceedings of the 23rd ACM/IEEE International Conference on Model Driven Engineering Languages and Systems: Companion Proceedings. MODELS 2020 (2020). https://doi.org/10.1145/3417990.3421410

17. Jeusfeld, M.A., Kühne, T.: ConceptBase implementation of MDM. Project Web Site (2023), https://conceptbase.sourceforge.net/mdm-er2023/

18. Jeusfeld, M.A., Neumayr, B.: DeepTelos: multi-level modeling with most general instances. In: Comyn-Wattiau, I., Tanaka, K., Song, I.-Y., Yamamoto, S., Saeki, M. (eds.) ER 2016. LNCS, vol. 9974, pp. 198–211. Springer, Cham (2016). https://doi.org/10.1007/978-3-319-46397-1_15

19. Koubarakis, M., et al.: A retrospective on Telos as a metamodeling language for requirements engineering. Requirements Eng. **26**(1), 1–23 (2020). https://doi.org/10.1007/s00766-020-00329-x

20. Kühne, T.: Exploring potency. In: ACM/IEEE 21th International Conference on Model Driven Engineering Languages and Systems (MODELS 2018). ACM (2018). https://doi.org/10.1145/3239372.3239411

21. Kühne, T.: Multi-dimensional multi-level modeling. Softw. Syst. Model. **21**(2), 543–559 (2021). https://doi.org/10.1007/s10270-021-00951-5

22. Kühne, T., Lange, A.: Melanee and DLM: a contribution to the MULTI collaborative comparison challenge. In: Proceedings of the 25th International Conference

on Model Driven Engineering Languages and Systems: Companion Proceedings, pp. 434–443. MODELS 2022, ACM, NY, USA (2022). https://doi.org/10.1145/3550356.3561571

23. Lange, A., Atkinson, C.: Multi-level modeling with LML – a contribution to the multi-level process challenge. Int. J. Conceptual Model. **17**, 6–1 (2022). https://doi.org/10.18417/emisa.17.6. special Issue: Multi-Level Process Challenge

24. de Lara, J., Guerra, E., Cobos, R., Moreno-Llorena, J.: Extending deep meta-modelling for practical model-driven engineering. Comput. J. **57**(1), 36–58 (2012). https://doi.org/10.1093/comjnl/bxs144

25. Mylopoulos, J., Borgida, A., Jarke, M., Koubarakis, M.: Telos: representing knowledge about information systems. Inf. Syst. **8**(4), 325–362 (1990)

26. Neumayr, B., Jeusfeld, M.A., Schrefl, M., Schütz, C.: Dual deep instantiation and its conceptbase implementation. In: Jarke, M., et al. (eds.) CAiSE 2014. LNCS, vol. 8484, pp. 503–517. Springer, Cham (2014). https://doi.org/10.1007/978-3-319-07881-6_34

27. Partridge, C., de Cesare, S., Mitchell, A., Odell, J.: Formalization of the classification pattern: survey of classification modeling in information systems engineering. Softw. Syst. Model. **17**(1), 167–203 (2016). https://doi.org/10.1007/s10270-016-0521-5

28. Partridge, C., et al.: Implicit requirements for ontological multi-level types in the uniclass classification. In: Proceedings of the 23rd ACM/IEEE International Conference on Model Driven Engineering Languages and Systems: Companion Proceedings. MODELS 2020 (2020). https://doi.org/10.1145/3417990.3421414

29. Pirotte, A., Zimányi, E., Massart, D., Yakusheva, T.: Materialization: a powerful and ubiquitous abstraction pattern. In: Proceedings of the 20th International Conference on Very Large Data Bases (VLDB 1994), pp. 630–641. Morgan Kaufman (1994)

A Safari for Deviating GoF Pattern Definitions and Examples on the Web

Apostolos V. Zarras[(✉)] and Panos Vassiliadis

Department of Computer Science and Engineering, University of Ioannina,
Ioannina, Greece
zarras@cs.uoi.gr

Abstract. The Gang of Four (GoF) patterns have been around for many years now. People use them to solve object-oriented design problems. The main source to consult for the GoF patterns is the seminal book published by Gamma, Helm, Johnson, and Vlissides in 1994. However, today there is also a large amount of information about the GoF patterns on the Web. There, the developers can find pattern definitions and code examples.

In this paper, we assess the compliance of pattern definitions and examples found on the Web to the original GoF pattern definitions. We study a corpus of definitions and examples, gathered from 4 well-known sites. According to our findings, most of the provided pattern definitions comply with the original GoF pattern definitions. However, there are some intent deviations that result in incorrect definitions. There are also a few deviations that concern missing and incomplete participants. When it comes to the patterns examples, the situation is quite different. Deviations in the examples are much more frequent and include missing participants, incomplete participants, and erroneous participants. The paper concludes with a discussion of the practical implications of our findings for the developers.

Keywords: GoF design patterns · deviating definitions · deviating examples

1 Introduction

In the mid-nineties, Gamma, Helm, Johnson and Vlissides introduced the Gang of Four (GoF) patterns catalog [8]. The GoF catalog documents reusable object-oriented solutions to common development problems. The authors employ a unified form for the specification of the patterns. A pattern specification includes the name of the pattern, the intent of the pattern, a motivating scenario, a discussion of the pattern applicability, a diagrammatic description of the pattern structure, the responsibilities of the participants (i.e., classes or interfaces) involved in the pattern structure, a description of how the participants collaborate to carry out their responsibilities, the consequences of the pattern, implementation guidelines, sample code, known uses of the pattern, and, a discussion concerning other related patterns. The patterns are divided in three different categories:

J. P. A. Almeida et al. (Eds.): ER 2023, LNCS 14320, pp. 181–197, 2023.
https://doi.org/10.1007/978-3-031-47262-6_10

creational patterns that deal with the creation of objects, structural patterns that concern the composition of classes or objects and behavioral patterns that focus on the interaction between objects and the distribution of responsibilities.

Nowadays, the GoF catalog is a significant part of object-oriented design theory and practice. Many people like students, junior developers and more experienced developers search on the Web for information about the GoF patterns, for a variety of reasons. Popular Web sites provide definitions of the patterns and examples that illustrate instances of the patterns in specific contexts. The patterns definitions range from brief statements of the patterns intent to more detailed ones that specify the patterns structure and other details.

The story behind this paper starts a couple of years ago, when an undergraduate student came to complain about his grade on a software engineering quiz. Specifically, the student claimed that his answer to a question about a design pattern was correct. While discussing the issue, the student said that he had studied the pattern very well and that he had also used in his study additional sources that he found on a Web site. When we looked again at the information given about the pattern on that site we found out that both the definition and the examples of the pattern deviated from the original GoF pattern definition. In fact, we discovered that several examples were entirely wrong!

So, sometimes the information we find on the Web about the GoF patterns deviates from the original definitions of the patterns that are given in the GoF catalog.

This observation is the main motivation of this paper. The overall **research goal** of the paper is **to assess the compliance of pattern definitions and examples that we find on the Web to the original GoF pattern definitions**. To this end, we study a corpus of pattern definitions and examples, gathered from four different well-known Web sites. At first, we identify the **kinds of deviations** that occur in the **pattern definitions** and **examples**. To highlight the issues that arise from the different kinds of deviations, we discuss in detail characteristic examples. Then, we study the **amount of deviations**, the **percentage** of deviating definitions and examples, and the **density** of deviations in the patterns definitions and examples. Finally, we discuss the implications of our findings for the developers who seek information about GoF patterns on the Web.

The rest of this paper is structured as follows. In Sect. 2 we discuss related work. In Sect. 3 we provide details regarding the setup of this study. In Sect. 4, we report the different kinds of deviations that occur in pattern definitions and examples. In Sect. 5, we assess the compliance of the pattern definitions and examples to the original GoF patterns. In Sect. 6, we conclude with the practical implications of our findings.

2   Related Work

Design patterns have been an active area of research and practice for decades. The state of the art is vast with dedicated communities and venues for researchers and practitioners[1,2]. An interesting systematic mapping of the state of the art is provided by Mayvan et al. [10]. According to this study, research efforts in the area of design patterns can be divided in 5 major sub-areas that concern pattern development, specification, usage, mining, and quality evaluation.

Our study falls in the area of pattern quality evaluation. This area includes efforts that investigate the impact of pattern usage on software quality and efforts that assess the soundness of pattern instances.

The impact of design pattern usage in software quality has been the subject of several interesting empirical studies. For instance, Prechelt et al. [12] found that the use of design patterns provides flexibility, which facilitates maintenance. In another study, Prechelt et al. [11] observed that the use of design patterns, along with specialized comments related to these patterns is helpful towards performing maintenance tasks. According to Vokac [14], the use of patterns by itself does not guarantee few defects. Bieman et al. [4] observed that pattern classes are prone to changes. Aversano et al. [3] observed that pattern classes are more prone to changes than classes that depend on the pattern classes. Walter and Alkhaeir [15] and Alfadel et al. [1] observed that classes participating to design patterns are less prone to code smells than classes not participating to design patterns. A detailed systematic literature review of works that concern the relation between design patterns and code smells has been performed by Almadi et al. [2].

Regarding the soundness of design patterns, Izurieta and Bieman [9] introduced the notions of design pattern rot and grime. Design rot is the breakdown of the structural integrity of a design pattern instance, as a result of changes in subsequent software releases. Design pattern grime is a decay due to unrelated features added in classes that participate in a design pattern instance. These features do not jeopardize the intent of the pattern. In a study of 3 software systems, Izurieta and Bieman did not find evidence of design rot. However, they found evidence of design pattern grime. In further studies, Dale and Izurieta [5] observed that certain kinds of design grim results in higher technical debt, while Reimanis and Izurieta [13] investigated possible correlations between different kinds of grime. In a study of five software systems, Feitosa et al. [7] found a linear accumulation of design grime that depends on the design patterns and the developers, while in a subsequent study [6] the same authors observed correlations between the accumulation of grime and decreased performance, security and correctness.

Still, regarding the soundness of design patterns, Zarras [17] observed frequent mistakes in the usage of the Command pattern, during the project of a software engineering course. The observed mistakes concern the configuration of command objects and invalidate the benefits of the Command pattern. The author further introduced a pattern for the proper configuration of command objects. In a similar effort, Zarras [16] reported mistakes in the usage of Strategy pattern and introduced respective solutions in the form of patterns.

---

[1] hillside.net.

[2] www.europlop.net.

Going beyond the state of the art, this paper evaluates the compliance of patterns definitions and examples found on the Web to the original GoF pattern definitions in a study that involves a large number of definitions and examples gathered from different sites.

3   Setup of the Study

Our study considers four popular Web sites that provide information for several software development topics like refactoring, UML, design principles and patterns. In particular, we focus on pattern definitions and examples from Source Making[3], Refactoring Guru[4], Tutorials Point[5] and Java T Point[6].

Table 1. Corpus of patterns definitions and examples.

Corpus Patterns' Definitions and Examples		Source Making		Refactoring Guru		Tutorials Point		Java T Point		ALL	
		Definition	Example(s)	Definition	Example(s)	Definition	Example(s)	Definition	Example(s)	Definitions	Examples
Creational	Abstract Factory	✓	7	✓	10	✓	1	✓	1	4	19
	Builder	✓	5	✓	10	✓	1	✓	1	4	17
	Factory Method	✓	6	✓	10	✓	1	✓	1	4	18
	Prototype	✓	7	✓	10	✓	1	✓	1	4	19
	Singleton	✓	4	✓	10	✓	1	✓	1	4	16
Sructural	Adapter	✓	6	✓	10	✓	1	✓	1	4	18
	Bridge	✓	5	✓	10	✓	1	✓	1	4	17
	Composite	✓	9	✓	10	✓	1	✓	1	4	21
	Decorator	✓	8	✓	10	✓	1	✓	1	4	20
	Façade	✓	5	✓	10	✓	1	✓	1	4	17
	Flyweight	✓	7	✓	10	✓	1	✓	1	4	19
	Proxy	✓	6	✓	10	✓	1	✓	1	4	18
Behavioral	Chain of Responsibility	✓	6	✓	10	✓	1	✓	1	4	18
	Command	✓	8	✓	10	✓	1	✓	1	4	20
	Interpreter	✓	5	✗	0	✓	1	✓	1	3	7
	Iterator	✓	6	✓	10	✓	1	✓	1	4	18
	Mediator	✓	6	✓	10	✓	1	✓	1	4	18
	Memento	✓	5	✓	10	✓	1	✓	1	4	17
	Observer	✓	8	✓	10	✓	1	✓	1	4	20
	State	✓	9	✓	10	✓	1	✓	1	4	21
	Strategy	✓	5	✓	10	✓	1	✓	1	4	17
	Template Method	✓	5	✓	10	✓	1	✓	1	4	17
	Visitor	✓	6	✓	10	✓	1	✗	0	3	17
	Total	**23**	**144**	**22**	**220**	**23**	**23**	**22**	**22**	**90**	**409**

During the data-gathering process we visited each Web site. For each GoF pattern, we looked for the pattern definition and examples that illustrate the usage of the pattern. We downloaded local copies of the pattern definition and examples. At the end of the gathering process, we reviewed the retrieved definitions and examples to make sure that we did not omit any relevant definitions and examples.

---

[3] sourcemaking.com.
[4] refactoring.guru.
[5] www.tutorialspoint.com/design_pattern.
[6] www.javatpoint.com/design-patterns-in-java.

The corpus of our study consists of 90 pattern definitions and 409 examples that concern a variety of programming languages. The corpus and the raw data of the compliance evaluation are available online[7]

Table 1 provides further details concerning the corpus. More specifically, Source Making provides definitions for all of the GoF patterns and a total number of 144 examples. There is at least one example for every GoF pattern. Most of the examples are in Java and C++. However, there are also several examples in Delphi, PhP and Python. Refactoring Guru covers all, but the Interpreter pattern. Therefore the corpus includes 22 definitions and 220 examples. The examples are in Pseudo code, Java, C#, C++, PhP, Python, Ruby, Swift, Typescript, and Go. Tutorials Point and Java T Point focus only on Java. Tutorials Point covers all of the GoF patterns, while Java T Point covers all but the Visitor pattern. Thus, Tutorials Point and Java T Point add 23 and 22 patterns definitions and examples to the corpus, respectively.

To assess the compliance of a set of pattern definitions (respectively examples) to the original GoF pattern definitions we rely on three basic statistics:

- The *number of deviations* that occur in the examined set.
- The *percentage* of *deviating pattern definitions* (respectively, *examples*) in the examined set.
- The *density of deviations* in the examined set, defined as the number of deviations, over the cardinality of the examined set.

In all our deliberations, the diagrams that we use are made by us, for copyright purposes, with respect to the diagrams that accompany the GoF pattern definitions, the diagrams that accompany the pattern definitions of the sites and the source code of the pattern examples given in the sites.

The deviation analysis that concerns *pattern definitions* relies on the combination of text and diagrams of the site contrasted to the GoF definition text and diagrams. The comparison protocol involves the following sequence of checks:

- The first check concerns whether the intent of the pattern definition given in the site is inline with the intent of the GoF pattern definition.
- The second check concerns whether the participants specified in the GoF pattern definition are present in the pattern definition of the site.
- The third check concerns whether the participants specified in the pattern definition of the site provide the methods of the corresponding participants of the GoF pattern definition.

The deviation analysis that concerns the *pattern examples* is based on the text and the source code of the pattern examples given in the sites, contrasted to the GoF definition text and diagrams. The comparison protocol involves the following steps:

---

[7] Due to their volume, data are available in a non-monitored, anonymous google drive (https://drive.google.com/file/d/1vAn58ul7whaXM01TMFcj1er5UcCSzrYN/view?usp=sharing), to become eponymously public at github upon acceptance of the paper.

- The first check concerns whether the participants specified in the GoF pattern definition are present in the pattern example.
- The second check concerns whether the participants in the pattern example provide the methods of the corresponding participants of the GoF pattern definition.
- The third check concerns whether the implementation of the participants in the pattern example is inline with the behavior of the corresponding participants of the GoF pattern definition.

4   Kinds of Deviations

In the corpus, we identified four different kinds of deviations. Specifically, we found intent deviations, missing participants, incomplete participants and erroneous participants. In the rest of this section, we discuss each kind of deviations in more detail, along with respective examples.

Table 2. Intent deviations found in the corpus.

Web site	Pattern	Deviating intent	Original intent
Tutorials Point	Abstract Factory	"Abstract Factory patterns work around a super-factory which creates other factories. This factory is also called as factory of factories. This type of design pattern comes under creational pattern as this pattern provides one of the best ways to create an object. In Abstract Factory pattern an interface is responsible for creating a factory of related objects without explicitly specifying their classes. Each generated factory can give the objects as per the Factory pattern."	"Provide an interface for creating families of related or dependent objects without specifying their concrete classes."
Tutorials Point	Builder	"Builder pattern builds a complex object using simple objects and using a step by step approach. This type of design pattern comes under creational pattern as this pattern provides one of the best ways to create an object. A Builder class builds the final object step by step. This builder is independent of other objects."	"Separate the construction of a complex object from its representation so that the same construction process can create different representations."
Tutorials Point	Visitor	"In Visitor pattern, we use a visitor class which changes the executing algorithm of an element class. By this way, execution algorithm of element can vary as and when visitor varies. This pattern comes under behavior pattern category. As per the pattern, element object has to accept the visitor object so that visitor object handles the operation on the element object."	"Represent an operation to be performed on the elements of an object structure. Visitor lets you define a new operation without changing the classes of the elements on which it operates."
Java T Point	Observer	"An Observer Pattern says that "just define a one-to-one dependency so that when one object changes state, all its dependents are notified and updated automatically."	"Define a one-to-many dependency between objects so that when one object changes state, all its dependents are notified and updated automatically."

4.1   Intent Deviations

In the corpus, we identified certain pattern definitions that do not reflect the purpose of the corresponding patterns, as specified in the GoF catalog. Hereafter, we call these issues, **intent deviations**. Obviously an intent deviation is very important, as it always results in an incorrect definition. Table 2, illustrates the deviating pattern definitions that we found in the corpus. Specifically, the table gives the Web site that provides each pattern definition, the deviating intent of the pattern, and the original intent of the pattern, as specified in the GoF catalog.

At a glance, in Tutorials Point the intent of Abstract Factory is defined quite differently from the original definition of the pattern. According to the original GoF definition, an abstract factory is an interface that defines methods for creating families of related objects, without having to specify their concrete classes, while according to the Tutorials Point definition the abstract factory is an interface that defines methods for creating other factories.

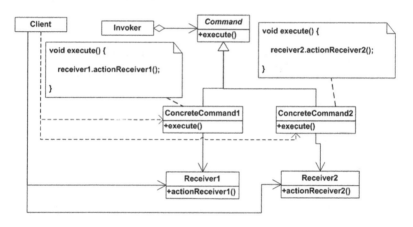

Fig. 1. Command structure, as defined in the GoF catalog.

In the Tutorials Point definition of Builder, the main issue is that there is absolutely no mention of the separation between the construction process of a complex object and the different representations of the object, which is the key benefit of the pattern. The intent of Visitor in the Tutorials Point definition is also very different from the original definition. According to the Tutorials Point definition, the purpose of a visitor class is to change the algorithm of another class, while in the latter the focus is on extensibility, and specifically the addition of new operations that operate on an hierarchy of objects, without having to change this hierarchy. Finally, in the Java T Point definition of Observer the intent of the pattern is incorrect as it refers to one-to-one, instead of one-to-many, dependencies between subscribers and observers.

4.2 Missing Participants

In the corpus, we encountered pattern definitions and examples that do not include all the participants, specified in the structure of the original pattern definitions. Hereon, we use the term **missing participants** to refer to these participants. The criticality of missing participants depends on the pattern and on who these participants are. In some cases, missing participants may result in incorrect pattern definitions and examples. In other cases, missing participants may result in incomplete pattern definitions and examples that partially illustrate the original pattern concepts.

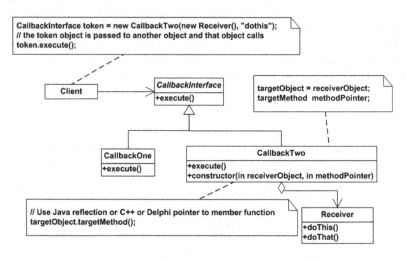

Fig. 2. Command structure, as defined in Source Making.

Figure 1, gives the structure of the Command pattern, as specified in the GoF patterns catalog. The intent of Command is to *"encapsulate a request as an object, thereby letting you parameterize clients with different requests, queue or log requests, and support undoable operations"*. Command defines a common interface for executing different commands. ConcreteCommand1 and ConcreteCommand2 are different classes that implement the Command interface. Client creates Command objects that belong to the different implementation classes. Invoker is parameterized with Command objects. To execute a command, Invoker invokes the execute() method on a particular Command object.

Figure 2, gives the structure of the Command pattern, as defined in Source Making. In particular, Client, CallbackInterface, CallbackOne and CallbackTwo, correspond to Client, Command, ConcreteCommand1 and ConcreteCommand2, in the original pattern structure, respectively. Apparently, in the Source Making definition, the Invoker participant is missing. The Client participant creates Command objects and invokes the execute() method to execute the corresponding commands. The lack of `Invoker` is important here because the pattern definition does not reflect the concept of parameterization of objects with different commands.

4.3   Incomplete Participants

The corpus includes patterns definitions and examples involving **incomplete participants** that do not provide a complete and exact set of methods, as they should according to the original pattern definitions. Specifically, some methods may be missing, or some methods may be merged with others in larger methods that have more responsibilities than they should.

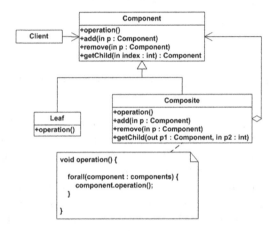

Fig. 3. Composite structure, as defined in the GoF catalog.

The impact of incomplete participants depends on the methods that are actually missing. In some cases, the lack of certain methods is very important (e.g. the lack of certain creation methods in creational patterns), resulting in incorrect pattern definitions and examples, while in other cases the missing methods result in incomplete definitions and examples that partially illustrate the concepts of the original pattern.

Figure 3, shows the original structure of the Composite pattern. The purpose of the pattern is to *"compose objects into tree structures to represent part-whole hierarchies"*. `Component` is a class that defines a uniform interface for both primitive and composite objects. The interface includes domain-specific methods (like `operation()`) and methods for managing the structure of composite objects. Specifically, `add()` serves for adding a `Component` object to a `Composite` object, while `remove()` allows removing a `Component` object from the `Composite` object. The `getChild()` method allows retrieving a `Component` object that is part of the `Composite` object, based on a given index. The interesting point in the pattern is that `Component` not only defines the uniform interface, but also provides default

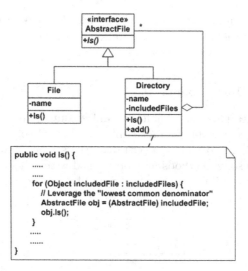

Fig. 4. Example of Composite from Source Making.

implementations for the defined methods. `Leaf` represents primitive objects that do not consist of other objects. `Leaf` provides its own implementations for the domain-specific methods and inherits the default implementations of the structure management methods, defined in `Component`. `Composite` represents composite objects. It provides implementations for both the domain-specific methods and the structure management methods, defined in `Component`. `Client` manipulates objects that conform with the aforementioned composite structure, via the uniform `Component` interface.

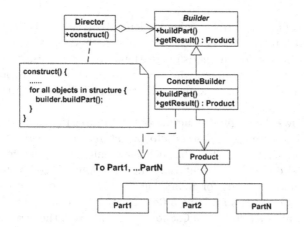

Fig. 5. Builder structure, as defined in the GoF catalog.

Figure 4, gives an example of Composite from Source Making. `AbstractFile`, `File` and `Directory`, correspond to `Component`, `Leaf` and `Composite`. `Directory` is an incomplete participant because it does not provide methods for the removal and the retrieval of `AbstractFile` objects.

4.4 Erroneous Participants

In the corpus, we also found **erroneous participants** that do not behave as dictated in the original definitions of the patterns. Typically, the deviations of the participants' behaviors are such that they jeopardize the intent of the pattern. We observed erroneous participants only in the pattern examples. Erroneous participants have a direct impact on the correctness of the examples in which they appear. In all cases, the examples are wrong.

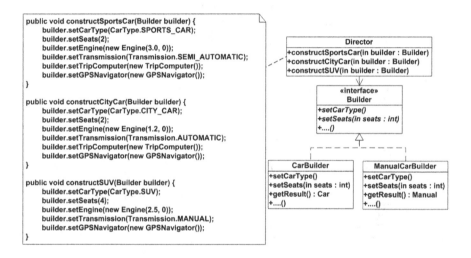

Fig. 6. Example of Builder from Refactoring Guru.

Figure 5 gives the original structure of Builder. The intent of this pattern is to *"separate the construction of a complex object from its representation so that the same construction process can create different representations"*. Consequently, the same construction process can be reused to create objects with different internal representations. `Builder`, defines an interface that provides operations for the creation of the constituents parts of a `Product` object. `ConcreteBuilder`, is an implementation of the `Builder` interface that constructs and assembles the parts of the `Product` object. In general, `Builder` can have different alternative implementations that correspond to different internal `Product` object representations. `ConcreteBuilder` further provides a method for retrieving the resulting `Product` object. `Director`, realizes the overall `Product` object construction process, by invoking methods of the `Builder` interface.

Figure 6 details an example of Builder from Refactoring Guru. In the example, the `Builder` interface has two alternative implementations, namely, `CarBuilder` and `ManualCarBuilder`. The products of `CarBuilder` and `ManualCarBuilder` are `Car` and `Manual` objects, respectively. The constituent parts of `Car` and `Manual` objects are `Engine`, `Transmission`, `TripComputer` and `GPSNavigator` objects. `Director` realizes the object construction process. However, the `Director` class is not correct with respect to the pattern specification. The main problem is that the `Director` class implements three different construction processes, instead of one. The different construction processes are similar, in fact they are code clones, and depend on the internal representation of the objects under construction.

Table 3. Assessing the compliance of pattern definitions.

Patterns	Deviations in pattern definitions			
	Source Making	Refactoring Guru	Tutorials Point	Java T Point
Abstract Factory	0	0	1	0
Builder	0	0	1	0
Factory Method	0	0	0	0
Prototype	0	0	0	0
Singleton	0	0	0	0
Adapter	0	0	0	0
Bridge	0	0	0	0
Composite	1	1	0	0
Decorator	0	0	0	0
Façade	0	0	0	0
Flyweight	1	2	0	0
Proxy	0	0	0	0
Chain of Resp	1	0	0	0
Command	1	0	0	0
Interpreter	0		0	0
Iterator	0	2	0	0
Mediator	2	1	0	0
Memento	0	0	0	0
Observer	1	1	0	1
State	0	0	0	0
Strategy	0	0	0	0
Template Method	0	0	0	0
Visitor	1	0	1	
Sum	8	7	3	1
Density of deviations in pattern definitions	0.35	0.32	0.13	0.05
% Patterns with deviating definitions	30.43%	27.27%	13.04%	9.09%

The two classes that implement the `Builder` interface are also incorrect. In particular, the two classes do not construct the parts of the resulting objects, as dictated by the pattern. Instead, `Director` constructs the parts and gives them to the `Builder` implementation classes as parameters of respective methods. Consequently, `Director` is not independent from the internal representation of the objects under construction. Overall, the example fails to communicate the intent of the Builder pattern.

5   Compliance of Pattern Definitions and Examples

In this section, we assess the compliance of pattern definitions and examples to the original GoF pattern definitions.

We begin our assessment from the **pattern definitions** that we consider in this study. Table 3, summarizes the results of the assessment. Specifically, for each site the table provides (1) the number of deviations that we observed in the definition of each pattern, and in total, (2) the density of deviations in the pattern definitions, defined as the total number of deviations in pattern definitions, divided by the number of pattern definitions, and (3) the percentage of patterns with deviating definitions. The empty cells in the table concern patterns for which there are no definitions in the respective sites.

Overall, we observe that **patterns with deviating definitions do not occur very often**. In the sites that we examined, the percentage of patterns with deviating definitions varies from 9.09% to 30.43%. The **density of deviations in the pattern definitions is low**, ranging from 0.05 deviations per definition to 0.35 deviations per definition. In practice, this means that most definitions adhere to the original GoF definitions. In Source Making we observe the highest density of deviations, followed by Refactoring Guru, Tutorials Point and Java T Point. In all sites, there are eleven patterns with deviation-free definitions.

Next, we investigate the compliance of the **pattern definitions** that we consider in our study, in relation to the **different kinds of deviations** that occur in the definitions. To this end, for each site, Table 4 gives the number of deviations of each kind that occur in the definitions, and the density of the deviations of each kind.

Table 4. Compliance of pattern definitions for the different kinds of deviations.

	Kinds of deviations in pattern definitions							
	Source Making		Refactoring Guru		Tutorials Point		Java T Point	
	# deviations	density	# deviations	density	# deviations	density	# deviations	density
Intent Deviations	0	0.00	0	0.00	3	0.13	1	0.05
Missing Participant	7	0.30	4	0.18				
Incomplete Participant	1	0.04	3	0.14				

In the results, we observe a **low density of intent deviations** in the patterns definitions. In Source Making and Refactoring Guru, there are no intent deviations. In Source Making and Refactoring Guru, **the density of missing participants is higher than the density of incomplete participants**. The cells that concern missing and incomplete participants in Tutorials Point and Java T Point are empty because the pattern definitions in these sites are very brief, consisting only of the intent of the patterns. The structure of the patterns is not part of the provided definitions. The brevity of the definitions is also the reason for the relatively small number of deviations and the respective low deviation density values in Tutorials Point and Java T Point. Despite the low deviation density values, in these two sites we observe the only occurrences of intent deviations, which result in entirely incorrect pattern definitions. Moreover, 3 of the 11 occurrences of missing participants also result in incorrect pattern definitions that do not reflect the original purpose of the patterns. The rest of the deviations, result in incomplete definitions that partially specify the structure of the original GoF patterns.

Table 5. Assessing the compliance of pattern examples.

	Deviations in pattern examples							
	Source Making		Refactoring Guru		Tutorials Point		Java T Point	
Patterns	# deviations	# examples	# deviations	# examples	# deviations	# examples	# deviations	# examples
Abstract Factory	12	7	0	10	2	1	3	1
Builder	1	5	1	10	3	1	3	1
Factory Method	5	6	1	10	1	1	1	1
Prototype	5	7	7	10	0	1	1	1
Singleton	1	4	0	10	0	1	0	1
Adapter	8	6	7	10	1	1	1	1
Bridge	0	5	0	10	0	1	0	1
Composite	19	9	20	10	4	1	3	1
Decorator	2	8	1	10	0	1	0	1
Façade	0	5	0	10	0	1	0	1
Flyweight	13	7	20	10	1	1	0	1
Proxy	3	6	0	10	0	1	0	1
Chain of Resp	10	6	0	10	1	1	1	1
Command	9	7	1	10	0	1	0	1
Interpreter	8	5			0	1	3	1
Iterator	17	6	23	10	2	1	2	1
Mediator	15	6	0	10	3	1	2	1
Memento	3	5	11	10	1	1	1	1
Observer	16	8	12	10	2	1	1	1
State	4	9	0	10	0	1	2	1
Strategy	3	5	0	10	0	1	0	1
Template Method	0	5	0	10	0	1	0	1
Visitor	0	6	0	10	0	1		
Sum	154	143	104	220	21	23	24	22
Density of deviations in pattern examples	1.08		0.47		0.91		1.09	
% Patterns with deviating examples	86.36%		52.17%		50.00%		63.64%	

We move on to the assessment of the **pattern examples** that we consider in our study. The results of the assessment are given in Table 5. In particular, for each site the table reports (1) the number of examples for each pattern, (2) the number of deviations that we observed in the examples, (3) the density of deviations in the examples, defined as the total number of deviations, divided by the number of pattern examples, and (4) the percentage of patterns with deviating examples. The empty cells in the table signify the lack of pattern examples in the corresponding sites.

In the results, we observe that **patterns with deviating examples are quite frequent**. Specifically the percentage of patterns with deviating examples

Table 6. Compliance of pattern examples for the different kinds of deviations.

	Kinds of deviations in pattern examples							
	Source Making		Refactoring Guru		Tutorials Point		Java T Point	
	# deviations	density	# deviations	density	# deviations	density	# deviations	density
Missing Participant	108	0.76	49	0.22	14	0.61	15	0.68
Incomplete Participant	28	0.20	45	0.20	4	0.17	5	0.23
Errorneous Participant	17	0.12	10	0.05	3	0.13	6	0.27

in the examined sites ranges from 50% to 86.6%. The **density of deviating examples is medium-high**, varying from 0.47 to 1.09 deviations per example. In all sites, there are only **three patterns** with **deviation-free examples**. In three out of the four sites, the density of deviations in the examples is greater than 0.9. Practically this means that **in many pattern examples we have multiple deviations**. Among the sites, Source Making is the one with the highest density of deviations, followed by Java T Point, Refactoring Guru and Tutorials Point. In all sites, **the percentage of patterns with deviating examples is higher than the percentage of patterns with deviating definitions**.

Regarding the **different kinds of deviations**, Table 6 gives the number of deviations of each kind that occur in the examples, and the density of deviations of each kind. Among the different kinds of deviations, **missing participants are the ones that occur more often, followed by incomplete participants and erroneous participants**. In all sites, **the number and the density of missing participants is high**. On the other hand, **the numbers and the densities of incomplete and erroneous participants are low**. Overall, 60 of the 186 occurrences of missing participants and 20 of the 82 occurrences of incomplete participants, result in incorrect examples. The same holds for all the occurrences of erroneous participants. The rest of the deviations, result in examples that partially illustrate the structure of the original GoF patterns.

Threats to Validity: The retrieval of the examined definitions and examples has been done manually. The identification of deviations and the compliance assessment of the retrieved pattern definitions and examples has also been done manually. This is a possible threat to the construct validity of the study. To mitigate this risk and reduce the probability of human mistakes the gathering and the assessment of the data have been done in multiple iterations. Internal validity, is not an issue in our study because we do not attempt to establish any particular cause-effect relationships regarding the deviations that occur in the examined pattern definitions and examples. Regarding external validity, the scope of our study is pattern definitions and examples that we find on the Web. In this context, we studied pattern definitions and examples gathered from four well-known sites. Therefore, we are confident that our findings are representative of the scope of the study.

6   Takeaway Messages for the Developers

In this paper, we assessed the compliance of the pattern definitions and examples that we find on the Web, to the original GoF pattern definitions. Our study brought out the following key messages for the developers:

- The developers should know that the definitions and examples that we find on the Web deviate from the original definitions.
- The pattern definitions that we find on the Web may involve intent deviations, missing participants and incomplete participants, while the pattern examples may involve missing participants, incomplete participants and erroneous participants.
- The impact of the different kinds of deviations to the correctness of the pattern definition and examples varies. Intent deviations and erroneous participants always result in incorrect definitions and examples. Missing participants and incomplete participants may also result in incorrect pattern definitions and examples. However, most of these deviations do not entirely jeopardize the involved pattern definitions and examples. Typically, these deviations result in definitions and examples that partially illustrate the original pattern concepts.
- The developers should be more concerned about deviating examples than deviating definitions, since the frequency of the former is much higher than the frequency of the latter.
- Finally, the developers should be aware that the choice of the site in which they seek information about GoF patterns is important. Certain sites appear more suitable for developers who are looking for pattern definitions and examples that fully comply to the original GoF pattern definitions, while other sites may be more appropriate for developers looking for simplified pattern variants. In any case, the developers should be very careful and crosscheck the information they find on the Web with the original GoF pattern information.

Besides the aforementioned takeaway messages, our study opens up a number of directions for future research. Specifically, a more detailed analysis of the specific deviations that occur in the definitions and the examples of each pattern would be interesting for the developers who seek information about specific patterns. Additional studies that involve the assessment of further sites and pattern collections would also be interesting. Finally, another issue worth investigating in the future is the (semi)automated validation of pattern definitions and examples that we find on the Web.

References

1. Alfadel, M., Aljasser, K., Alshayeb, M.: Empirical study of the relationship between design patterns and code smells. PLoS ONE **15**, e0231731 (2020)
2. Almadi, S.H.S., Hooshyar, D., Ahmad, R.B.: Bad smells of gang of four design patterns: a decade systematic literature review. Sustainability **13**, 10256 (2021)

3. Aversano, L., Canfora, G., Cerulo, L., Grosso, C.D., Penta, M.D.: An empirical study on the evolution of design patterns. In: Proceedings of the 6th Joint Meeting of the European Software Engineering Conference and the ACM SIGSOFT International Symposium on Foundations of Software Engineering (ESEC-FSE), pp. 385–394. ACM (2007)

4. Bieman, J.M., Straw, G., Wang, H., Munger, P.W., Alexander, R.T.: Design patterns and change proneness: an examination of five evolving systems. In: Proceedings of the 9th IEEE International Software Metrics Symposium (METRICS), pp. 40–49 (2003)

5. Dale, M.R., Izurieta, C.: Impacts of design pattern decay on system quality. In: Proceedings of the 8th ACM/IEEE International Symposium on Empirical Software Engineering and Measurement ESEM, pp. 37:1–37:4 (2014)

6. Feitosa, D., Ampatzoglou, A., Avgeriou, P., Nakagawa, E.Y.: Correlating pattern grime and quality attributes. IEEE Access **6**, 23065–23078 (2018)

7. Data are available at https://drive.google.com/file/d/1vAn58ul7whaXM01TMFcj1er5UcCSzrYN/view?usp=sharing

8. Gamma, E., Helm, R., Johnson, R., Vlissides, J.: Design Patterns - Elements of Reusable Object-Oriented Software. Addison-Wesley (1994)

9. Izurieta, C., Bieman, J.M.: A multiple case study of design pattern decay, grime, and rot in evolving software systems. Softw. Qual. J. **21**(2), 289–323 (2013). https://doi.org/10.1007/s11219-012-9175-x

10. Mayvan, B.B., Rasoolzadegan, A., Yazdi, Z.G.: The state of the art on design patterns: a systematic mapping of the literature. J. Syst. Softw. **125**, 93–118 (2017)

11. Prechelt, L., Unger, B., Philippsen, M., Tichy, W.F.: Two controlled experiments assessing the usefulness of design pattern documentation in program maintenance. IEEE Trans. Softw. Eng. **28**(6), 595–606 (2002)

12. Prechelt, L., Unger, B., Tichy, W.F., Brössler, P., Votta, L.G.: A controlled experiment in maintenance comparing design patterns to simpler solutions. IEEE Trans. Softw. Eng. **27**(12), 1134–1144 (2001)

13. Reimanis, D., Izurieta, C.: Behavioral evolution of design patterns: understanding software reuse through the evolution of pattern behavior. In: Peng, X., Ampatzoglou, A., Bhowmik, T. (eds.) ICSR 2019. LNCS, vol. 11602, pp. 77–93. Springer, Cham (2019). https://doi.org/10.1007/978-3-030-22888-0_6

14. Vokác, M.: Defect frequency and design patterns: an empirical study of industrial code. IEEE Trans. Softw. Eng. **30**(12), 904–917 (2004)

15. Walter, B., Alkhaeir, T.: The relationship between design patterns and code smells: an exploratory study. Inf. Softw. Technol. **74**, 127–142 (2016)

16. Zarras, A.: The strategy configuration problem and how to solve it. In: Proceedings of the ACM European Conference on Pattern Languages of Programs (EuroPLoP), pp. 9:1–9:11. ACM (2021)

17. Zarras, A.V.: Common mistakes when using the command pattern and how to avoid them. In: Proceedings of the ACM European Conference on Pattern Languages of Programs (EuroPLoP), pp. 4:1–4:9. ACM (2020)

Process Mining and Abstraction

Object-Centric Alignments

Lukas Liss[✉][iD], Jan Niklas Adams[✉][iD], and Wil M. P. van der Aalst[✉][iD]

RWTH Aachen University, Aachen, Germany
{liss,niklas.adams,wvdaalst}@pads.rwth-aachen.de

Abstract. Processes tend to interact with other processes and operate on various objects of different types. These objects can influence each other creating dependencies between sub-processes. Analyzing the conformance of such complex processes challenges traditional conformance-checking approaches because they assume a single-case identifier for a process. To create a single-case identifier one has to flatten complex processes. This leads to information loss when separating the processes that interact on some objects. This paper introduces an alignment approach that operates directly on these object-centric processes. We introduce alignments that can give behavior-based insights into how closely related the event data generated by a process and the behavior specified by an object-centric Petri net are. The contributions of this paper include a definition for object-centric alignments, an algorithm to compute them, a publicly available implementation, and a qualitative and quantitative evaluation. The qualitative evaluation shows that object-centric alignments can give better insights into object-centric processes because they correctly consider inter-object dependencies. Findings from the quantitative evaluation show that the run-time grows exponentially with the number of objects, the length of the process execution, and the cost of the alignment. The evaluation results motivate future research to improve the run-time and make object-centric alignments more applicable for larger processes.

Keywords: Process mining · Object-centric process mining · Alignments

1 Introduction

Process mining analyzes event data to provide insights into processes, using a variety of conceptual models. One standard pipeline for this includes data extraction, process model discovery, and conformance checking [14]. The insights of each step are bound by the expressiveness of the used models. This paper proposes to use more expressive models for conformance checking to correctly handle inter-object dependencies, for which traditional methods fail to give correct insights. We introduce object-centric alignments that can model deviations in interacting subprocesses with multiple objects. Traditional methods use representations that model a process using a single case notion meaning that all

J. P. A. Almeida et al. (Eds.): ER 2023, LNCS 14320, pp. 201–219, 2023.
https://doi.org/10.1007/978-3-031-47262-6_11

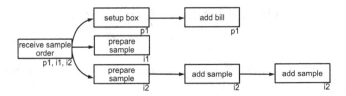

Fig. 1. A process execution of our running examples. Events are associated with objects of type package (prefix p) or item (prefix i). The process execution describes the partial order of events induced by the individual objects.

actions created for one object define a process execution. Real-world processes often do not fit that assumption. For example, a supply chain process involves multiple subprocesses operating on varied objects like raw materials, products, orders, and customers. One execution of the supply chain is not defined by a single object.

Recently, *object-centric process mining* [21] was introduced to generalize the notion of a process so that one can follow multiple objects through multiple, connected sub-processes. In object-centric process mining a process execution is a graph showing the partial order between sub-process events [7] So far, replay-based fitness has been proposed for object-centric conformance checking [5]. However, process owners are typically interested in aligning observed behavior to modeled behavior, to identify deviations, i.e., using alignments [8]. The notion, calculation, implementation, and feasibility analysis for alignments on object-centric process mining are, so far, missing.

The running example is the process execution in Fig. 1 belonging to a packaging process with cross-object dependencies between a package and multiple items. This process is described using the object-centric Petri net in Fig. 2, which differs from traditional ones by introducing place types with typified tokens and variable arcs (highlighted in red). Tokens of a type can only occupy places of the same type, and variable arcs can consume multiple tokens at once. There are two types here: item (green) and package (blue). In this process, the paths of the package and items depend on each other. The first event involves all objects and decides whether it is a sample or product order which defines the following allowed behavior for the package and the items. If a process owner would like to find deviations in their object-centric processes today, they would need to *flatten* [2] the observed process executions and apply traditional alignments to the object-centric Petri net's subnets of the same type. We show this for our example process execution of Fig. 1 in Fig. 2. If flattened to one trace per object, the three resulting traces get aligned to the type's subnet in a way that is not possible in the composed model. Activity *receive sample order* and *receive product order* can never happen both in one process execution since the de-jure model forces a decision between product orders and sample orders. But the flattened alignments do not agree on which activity should happen. The alignment for *p1* has *receive product order* in the model part whereas the alignments for *i1*

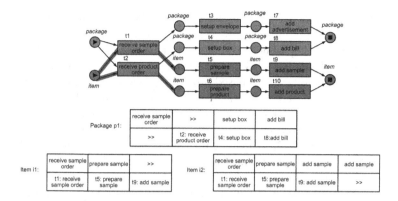

Fig. 2. Top: De-jure model as an object-centric Petri net. Variable arcs are marked red. Bottom: The process execution of Fig. 1 is flattened to the individual objects and aligned to the de-jure model's subnet of the object's types. (Color figure online)

and *i2* have *receive sample order* in their model part. As shown by the running example, computing alignments on object-centric processes requires more than just finding alignments for each object individually. Aligning the sub-processes for all objects by respecting their object dependencies creates a computationally complex problem that we tackle in this paper.

This paper presents four contributions to enable and investigate object-centric alignments. First, we generalize the notion of an alignment to object-centric processes. Second, we present an algorithm to compute optimal object-centric alignments. Third, we implemented our algorithm and make it publicly accessible as an open-source project[1] based on the open-source object-centric process mining library OPCA [6]. Fourth, we evaluate the quality and the computation time of object-centric alignments on real-world event data. Thereby, we gain insights into the scalability and suitability of the approach.

This paper is structured in the following way. We present related work in Sect. 2 and preliminaries in Sect. 3. Then, we define object-centric alignments in Sect. 4. Our algorithm to compute alignments consists of two parts: constructing the synchronous product net (Sect. 5) and finding an optimal alignment in the synchronous product net (Sect. 6). In this paper, we give a declarative description of our algorithm. The formal definitions for all the steps in Sect. 5 and Sect. 6 are presented in the extended pre-print [26]. We present a qualitative and quantitative evaluation in Sect. 7 and conclude the paper in Sect. 8.

2 Related Work

Process mining includes discovery, conformance checking, and enhancement of business processes [1]. Our approach belongs to conformance checking, where

---

behavior from the event log is compared to allowed behavior that is specified by a de-jure model [14]. For traditional processes, there exists a variety of conformance checking approaches [20], which mainly use token-based replay [29] approaches, or alignments [8]. Both have been used to derive quality metrics like precision [9] and fitness [10]. Unlike token-based replay, alignments are independent of the structure of the de-jure model [8]. Like our calculation, the traditional alignment calculation defined by Adriansyah et al. uses a two-step algorithm to compute alignments [8]. Adriansyah et al.'s approach creates a synchronous product net such that finding optimal alignments relates to finding a shortest path in that net. This is a well-studied problem that can be solved with the Dijkstra [17] or A^* [15] algorithm. Different ways to speed up the calculation have been researched [19, 31]. However, the alignment algorithm assumes the process to have a single case identifier and can therefore not be used directly with object-centric processes.

Multiple extensions to the traditional alignment algorithm use higher-order nets to consider additional dimensions together with the workflow dimension [12,13]. The data and resource-aware conformance checking approach from de Leoni et al. uses data Petri nets [25]. Felli et al. use data Petri nets together with satisfiability modulo theories to compute data-aware alignments [22]. Sommers et al. constructed a ν-Petri net to calculate resource-constrained alignments [30]. But all of the approaches above assume the process to have a single-case identifier. There are approaches that lift this generalization and model processes as interacting sub-processes. Multi-agent process models describe the behavior of agents and their interaction by composing Petri nets [27]. Conceptual models like business artifacts [28] and GSM [23] can model the interactions between multiple process entities but can not be generated automatically from real-world event data. Thus, we use model notations from object-centric process mining [2] to model processes with a variety of objects from different types that interact with each other. Object-centric Petri nets can be discovered directly from event data from current information systems [4]. Adams et al. defined the notion of cases and variants for object-centric processes [7] as event graphs instead of event sequences. The defined process executions serve as input for our alignment calculation as well as object-centric Petri nets [4] that can describe allowed behavior. Precision and fitness metrics to evaluate the quality of a model have, recently, been proposed [5]. However, techniques to check conformance to a de-jure model and spot deviations, such as object-centric alignments, are so far missing.

3   Preliminaries

Object-centric process mining deals with events that operate on a variety of objects of different types. Events are activities that happen at a timestamp for a number of objects of different types. $\mathbb{U}_{event}$ is the Universe of event identifiers. The universe $\mathbb{U}_{act}$ contains all visible activities. $\mathbb{U}_{typ}$ is the universe of all object types. The universe of objects is $\mathbb{U}_{obj}$. Each object has exactly one type associated with it $\pi_{type} : \mathbb{U}_{obj} \rightarrow \mathbb{U}_{typ}$. $\mathbb{U}_{time}$ is the universe of all timestamps.

Definition 1 (Event Log). $L = (E, O, OT, \pi_{act}, \pi_{obj}, \pi_{time}, \pi_{trace})$ *is an event log with:*

- $E \subseteq \mathbb{U}_{event}$ *is a set of events,* $O \subseteq \mathbb{U}_{obj}$ *is a set of objects,*
- $OT = \{\pi_{type}(o) | o \in O\}$ *is a set of object types,*
- $\pi_{act} : E \to \mathbb{U}_{act}$ *maps each event to an activity,*
- $\pi_{obj} : E \to \mathcal{P}(\mathbb{U}_{obj}) \setminus \{\emptyset\}$ *maps each event to at least one object,*
- $\pi_{time} : E \to \mathbb{U}_{time}$ *maps each event to a timestamp, and*
- $\pi_{trace} : O \to E^*$ *maps each object onto a sequence of events such that* $\pi_{trace}(o) = \langle e_1, ..., e_n \rangle$ *with* $\{e_1, ..., e_n\} = \{e \in E | o \in \pi_{obj}(e)\}$ *and* $\forall_{i \in \{1,...,n-1\}} \pi_{time}(e_i) \leq \pi_{time}(e_{i+1})$

Event logs can contain events from multiple process executions. When analyzing the behavior we want to extract one process execution.

Definition 2 (Process Execution). *Let* $L = (E, O, OT, \pi_{act}, \pi_{obj}, \pi_{time}, \pi_{trace})$ *be an object-centric event log. The object graph* $OG_L = (O, I)$ *with* $I = \{\{o, o'\} | \exists_{e \in E} \{o, o'\} \subseteq \pi_{obj}(e) \land o \neq o'\}$ *connects objects that share events. The connected components* $con(L) = \{X \subseteq O | X$ *is a connected component in* $OG_L\}$ *of the object graph are sets of inter-dependent objects. Each set* $X \in con(L)$ *defines a process execution of* L. *A process execution is a graph* $P_X = (E_X, D_X)$ *with nodes* $E_X = \{e \in E | X \cap \pi_{obj}(e) \neq \emptyset\}$ *and edges* $D_X = \{(e, e') \in E_X \times E_X | \exists_{o \in X, 1 \leq i < n} \langle e_1, ..., e_n \rangle = \pi_{trace}(o) \land e = e_i \land e' = e_{i+1}\}$. *The set* $px(L) = \{P_X | X \in con(L)\}$ *contains all process executions of event log* L.

Figure 1 shows the example process execution with one package and two items. Object-centric Petri nets describe object-centric behavior by using types like colored Petri nets [24]. $\mathcal{B}(A)$ is used to represent all multisets for a set A.

Definition 3 (Object-centric Petri Net [4]). *An object-centric Petri net is a tuple* $ON = (N, pt, F_{var})$ *where* $N = (P, T, F, l)$ *is a labeled Petri net with places* P *and transitions* T. $F \in \mathcal{B}((P \times T) \cup (T \times P))$ *is the multiset of arcs between places and transitions. Transitions are labeled with activities or* τ *by* $l : T \to \mathbb{U}_{act} \cup \{\tau\}$ *with invisible activity* $\tau \notin \mathbb{U}_{act}$. $pt : P \to \mathbb{U}_{typ}$ *maps places to object types and* $F_{var} \leq F$ *is the sub-multiset of variable arcs.*

Note that we label all transitions to activities or τ *with function* l. *Other common definitions for object-centric Petri nets define* l *as a partial function. This can be translated into our definition by assuming* $l(t) = \tau$ *for all* t *without a label. We define the following derived notations for object-centric Petri nets*

- $\bullet t = \{p \in P | (p, t) \in F\}$ *is the preset of transition* $t \in T$.
- $t \bullet = \{p \in P | (t, p) \in F\}$ *is the post set of transition* $t \in T$.
- $pl(t) = \bullet t \cup t \bullet$ *are the input and output places of* $t \in T$, $pl_{var}(t) = \{p \in P | \{(p, t), (t, p)\} \cap F_{var} \neq \emptyset\}$ *are places that are connected through variable arcs and* $pl_{nv}(t) = \{p \in P | \{(p, t), (t, p)\} \cap (F \setminus F_{var}) \neq \emptyset\}$ *are places that are connected through non-variable arcs.*
- $tpl(t) = \{pt(p) | p \in pl(t)\}$, $tpl_{var}(t) = \{pt(p) | p \in pl_{var}(t)\}$, *and* $tpl_{nv}(t) = \{pt(p) | p \in pl_{nv}(t)\}$ *are object types related to transitions.*

The object-centric Petri net in Fig. 2 models the running example using typed places and has variable arcs for *receive sample order* and *receive product order*. The variable arcs model that multiple items can be part of one package.

Definition 4 (Well-Formed Object-Centric Petri Net [4]). *Let $ON = (N, pt, F_{var})$ be an object-centric Petri net with $N = (P, T, F, l)$. ON is well-formed if for each transition $t \in T : tpl_{var}(t) \cap tpl_{nv}(t) = \emptyset$.*

In a well-formed object-centric Petri net arcs, connected to the same transition and places with the same object type, are either all variable or none of them is. We assume for the following that all the object-centric Petri nets we use are well-formed. Similar to colored Petri nets, object-centric Petri nets use the notion of markings and bindings to describe the semantics of a Petri net.

Definition 5 (Marking of object-centric Petri Net [4]). *Let $ON = (N, pt, F_{var})$ be an object-centric Petri net with $N = (P, T, F, l)$. $\mathcal{Q}_{ON} = \{(p, o) \in P \times \mathbb{U}_{obj} | pt(p) = \pi_{type}(o)\}$ is the set of possible tokens. A marking M of ON is a multiset of tokens $M \in \mathcal{B}(\mathcal{Q}_{ON})$.*

A binding describes which transition fires and the consumed and produced objects per object type. For example, a binding for the object-centric Petri net in Fig. 2 can define that *t1* fires using objects *p1*, *i1*, and *i2*.

Definition 6 (Binding of object-centric Petri Net [4]). *Let $ON = (N, pt, F_{var})$ be an object-centric Petri net with $N = (P, T, F, l)$. The set of all possible bindings is $B = \{(t, b) \in T \times (\mathbb{U}_{type} \nrightarrow \mathcal{P}(\mathbb{U}_{obj})) | dom(b) = tpl(t) \wedge \forall_{ot \in tpl_{nv}(t)} \forall_{p \in pl_{nv}(t), pt(p) = ot} |b(ot)| = F(p, t)\}$. A binding $(t, b) \in B$ corresponds to firing transition t in Petri net ON. The object map b describes what object instances are consumed and produced. The multiset of consumed tokens given binding $(t, b) \in B$ is $cons(t, b) = [(p, o) \in \mathcal{Q}_{ON} | p \in \bullet t \wedge o \in b(pt(p))]$. The multiset of produced tokens given binding $(t, b) \in B$ is $prod(t, b) = [(p, o) \in \mathcal{Q}_{ON} | p \in t \bullet \wedge o \in b(pt(p))]$.*

Binding $(t, b) \in B$ is enabled in marking $M \in \mathcal{B}(\mathcal{Q}_{ON})$ if $cons(t, b) \leq M$. Applying binding (t, b) in marking M leads to new marking $M' = M - cons(t, b) + prod(t, b)$. We use the notation $M \xrightarrow{(t,b)} M'$ for applying (t, b) in M. This implies that (t, b) was enabled in M and M' is the result of applying (t, b) in M.

This notation can be extended to a sequence of bindings $\sigma = \langle (t_1, b_1), (t_2, b_2), ..., (t_n, b_n) \rangle \in B^*$ such that $M_0 \xrightarrow{(t_1, b_1)} M_1 \xrightarrow{(t_2, b_2)} M_2 ... \xrightarrow{(t_n, b_n)} M_n$. We use the notation $M \xrightarrow{\sigma} M'$ to show that M' can be reached from M by applying the bindings in σ after another. The transitions can be mapped to activities using the label function l. This results in the visible binding sequence $\sigma_v = \langle (l(t_1), b_1), (l(t_2), b_2), ..., (l(t_n), b_n) \rangle$ where $(l(t_i), b_i)$ is omitted if $l(t_i) = \tau$.

Definition 7 (Accepting object-centric Petri Net [4]). *An accepting object-centric Petri net is a tuple $AN = (ON, M_{init}, M_{final})$ where $ON = (N, pt, F_{var})$ is a well-formed object-centric Petri net. $M_{init} \in \mathcal{B}(\mathcal{Q}_{ON})$ and $M_{final} \in \mathcal{B}(\mathcal{Q}_{ON})$ indicate the initial and final markings of the net.*

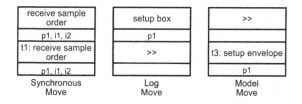

Fig. 3. One synchronous, one log, and one model move for the running example.

Accepting object-centric Petri nets accept some binding sequences and some not. The set of all binding sequences that are accepted form a language.

Definition 8 (Language of an Accepting Petri Net [4]). *The language* $\phi(AN) = \{\sigma_v | M_{init} \xrightarrow{\sigma} M_{final}\}$ *of an accepting object-centric Petri net* $AN = (ON, M_{init}, M_{final})$ *contains all the visible binding sequences starting in* M_{init} *and ending in* M_{final}.

4   Alignment

Alignments are a conceptual model to describe how observed (log) behavior and normative (model) behavior relate. It consists of moves that represent whether something occurs in the process execution, the de-jure model, or both of them.

Definition 9 (Moves). *Let* $L = (E, O, OT, \pi_{act}, \pi_{obj}, \pi_{times}, \pi_{trace})$ *be an object-centric event log and* $P_X = (E_X, D_X) \in px(L)$ *a process execution. Let* $AN = (((P, T, F, l), pt, F_{var}), M_{init}, M_{final})$ *be an accepting object-centric Petri net. The set of all moves is* $moves(P_X, AN) \subseteq (\{\pi_{act}(e)|e \in E_X\} \cup \{\gg \}) \times \mathcal{P}(O) \times (T \cup \{\gg\}) \times \mathcal{P}(O)$ *with skip symbol* $\gg \notin \mathbb{U}_{act} \cup T$. *A move* $(a_{log}, o_{log}, t_{mod}, o_{mod}) \in moves(P_X, AN)$ *is one of the following three types:*
Log move - for an $e \in E_X$*:* $a_{log} = \pi_{act}(e)$, $o_{log} = \pi_{obj}(e)$, $t_{mod} = \gg$, *and* $o_{mod} = \emptyset$.
Model move - for a $(t, b) \in \sigma$ *with* $\sigma_v \in \phi(AN)$*:* $t_{mod} = t$, $o_{mod} = \bigcup_{o \in range(b)} o$, $a_{log} = \gg$, *and* $o_{log} = \emptyset$.
Synchronous move - for an $e \in E_X$ *and a* $(t, b) \in \sigma$ *with* $\sigma_v \in \phi(AN)$*:* $a_{log} = \pi_{act}(e) = l(t)$, $t_{mod} = t$, *and* $o_{log} = o_{mod} = \pi_{obj}(e) = \bigcup_{o \in range(b)} o$.

Figure 3 shows the three types of moves. Log and model moves model deviations, whereas synchronous moves model conforming behavior. For synchronous moves, activities and objects of model and log part have to be exactly the same. For log and model moves, only one part has an activity and objects while the other parts are skipped, represented by skip symbol $\gg$. The upper part is the log part a_{log} and o_{log}. The lower block is the model part that contains t_{mod}, the activity $l(t_{mod})$ it is labeled with, and o_{mod}. We define the following projections on moves.

Definition 10 (Move Projections).
Given a move $m = (a_{log}, o_{log}, t_{mod}, o_{mod}) \in moves(P_X, AN)$ *with process execution* P_X *and accepting object-centric Petri Net* $AN = (((P, T, F, l), pt, F_{var}),$ $M_{init}, M_{final})$. *We use the following projections to map moves to their attributes:*

$\pi_{la}(m) = a_{log}$ *maps moves to their log activity.*
$\pi_{lo}(m) = o_{log}$ *maps moves to their log objects.*
$\pi_{mt}(m) = t_{mod}$ *maps moves to their model transition.*
$\pi_{ma}(m) = l(t_{mod})$ *maps moves to the activity the transition is labeled with.*
$\pi_{mo}(m) = o_{mod}$ *maps moves to their model objects.*

An alignment, which we define in Definition 12, is a directed acyclic graph of moves. We need to reason about the model and log behavior individually to define alignments. Therefore, we introduce the following reductions that remove moves with skipped behavior in a given part from a directed acyclic graph of moves while maintaining the partial order defined by the acyclic graph.

Definition 11 (Reduction to Log and Model Part). *Let* $MG = (M, C)$ *be a directed acyclic graph with vertices* $M \subseteq moves(P_X, AN)$ *and edges* $C \subseteq M \times M$ *with process execution* P_X *and accepting object-centric Petri Net* AN. *The reduction to moves with visible activity in the log part is* $MG_{\downarrow log} = (M_{\downarrow log}, C_{\downarrow log})$ *and the reduction to moves with visible activity in the model part is* $MG_{\downarrow mod} = (M_{\downarrow mod}, C_{\downarrow mod})$ *with:*

- $M_{\downarrow log} = \{m \in M | \pi_{la}(m) \neq \gg\}$ *synchronous and log moves.*
- $C_{\downarrow log} = \{(m_1, m_n) \in M_{\downarrow log} \times M_{\downarrow log} | \exists_{<m_1,\ldots,m_n> \in M^*} \forall_{1 \leq i < n} (m_i, m_{i+1}) \in C \wedge \forall_{1 < i < n} \pi_{la}(m_i) = \gg\}$ *edges between synchronous and log moves and new edges where model moves were removed.*
- $M_{\downarrow mod} = \{m \in M | \pi_{ma}(m) \neq \gg\}$ *synchronous and model moves*
- $C_{\downarrow mod} = \{(m_1, m_n) \in M_{\downarrow mod} \times M_{\downarrow mod} | \exists_{<m_1,\ldots,m_n> \in M^*} \forall_{1 \leq i < n} (m_i, m_{i+1}) \in C \wedge \forall_{1 < i < n} \pi_{ma}(m_i) = \gg\}$ *edges between synchronous and model moves and new edges where log moves were removed.*

In Fig. 4 both $MG_{\downarrow log}$ and $MG_{\downarrow model}$ are visualized for a directed acyclic graph of moves. $MG_{\downarrow log}$ describes a directed acyclic graph after removing all model moves and related edges. New edges are added when two movements used to be connected via removed model moves in the movement graph. $MG_{\downarrow model}$ behaves simultaneously for the model part. An alignment is a directed acyclic graph of moves that requires the log part to contain the process execution and the model part to be in the language of the de-jure model.

Definition 12 (Alignment). *Let* $L = (E, O, OT, \pi_{act}, \pi_{obj}, \pi_{times}, \pi_{trace})$ *be an object-centric event log and* $P_X = (E_X, D_X) \in px(L)$ *a process execution. Let* $AN = (((P, T, F, l), pt, F_{var})M_{init}, M_{final})$ *be an accepting object-centric Petri net. An alignment* $AL_{P_X, AN} = (M, C)$ *is a directed acyclic graph on* $M \subseteq moves(P_X, AN)$ *such that:*

The alignment contains the process execution behavior in the log parts: P_X *is isomorphic to* $AL_{P_X, AN_{\downarrow log}}$ *with bijective function* $f : E_X \to M_{\downarrow log}$ *such that* $\forall_{e \in E_X} \pi_{act}(e) = \pi_{la}(f(e)) \wedge \pi_{obj}(e) = \pi_{lo}(f(e))$.

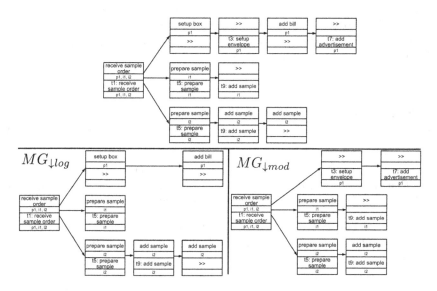

Fig. 4. Optimal object-centric alignment for the running example and reductions $MG_{\downarrow log}$ and $MG_{\downarrow model}$.

The alignment contains behavior that is accepted by the Petri net in the model parts: There exists a binding sequence $\sigma = \langle (t_1, b_1), (t_2, b_2), ..., (t_n, b_n) \rangle \in B^*$ with $\sigma_v \in \phi(AN)$ and a bijective function $f' : B \to M_{\downarrow mod}$ such that:

- $\forall_{(t,b) \in \sigma} t = \pi_{mt}(f'(t,b)) \wedge \bigcup_{o \in range(b)} o = \pi_{mo}(f'(t,b))$
- $\forall_{m_1, m_2 \in M_{\downarrow mod}} (m_1, m_2) \in C_{\downarrow mod} \Rightarrow \exists_{1 \leq i < j \leq n} m_1 = f'(t_i, b_i) \wedge m_2 = f'(t_j, b_j)$

There can be multiple alignments for a process execution and an accepting object-centric Petri net. $al(P_X, AN)$ is the set of all these alignments.

Figure 4 shows an alignment for the running example. Its reduction to log and synchronous moves $MG_{\downarrow log}$, is isomorphic to the given process execution in Fig. 1. This ensures that the alignment contains the process execution behavior. The reduction to the model part relates to a binding sequence that is in the language of the de-jure model in Fig. 2. This ensures that the model part describes behavior that is accepted by the model. We want to find deviations between the process execution and the most similar allowed behavior. Thus, we want an alignment to have as few model or log moves as possible. By giving model and log moves higher costs than synchronous moves, we can prefer synchronous behavior.

Definition 13 (Standard Cost of Move Function).
Let $AL_{P_X, AN} = (M, C) \in al(P_X, AN)$ be an alignment with process execution P_X and accepting object-centric Petri Net AN. The cost function $cost_{move}$: $moves(P_X, AN) \to \mathbb{R}$ is defined as:

$$cost_{move}(m) = \begin{cases} 0 \text{ if } m \text{ is a synchronous move,} \\ |\pi_{lo}(m) \cup \pi_{mo}(m)| \text{ if } m \text{ is a model or log move} \wedge \pi_{ma}(m) \neq \tau, \\ \varepsilon \text{ if } \pi_{ma}(m) = \tau \wedge a_{log} =\gg, \\ +\infty \text{ else} \end{cases}$$

With ε being a positive very small number. The cost of a complete alignment is the sum over all alignment moves: $cost_{alignment}(AL_{P_X,AN}) = \sum_{m \in M} cost_{move}(m)$.

The cost of the alignment in Fig. 4 is 6 because there are 3 model and 3 log moves that have one object each. The lower the cost the fewer deviations are in the alignment. We call one of the cheapest alignments an optimal alignment.

Definition 14 (Optimal Alignment). *Let L be an object-centric event log and $P_X \in px(L)$ be a process execution. Let AN be an accepting object-centric Petri net. An alignment $AL_{P_X,AN} = (M,C) \in al(P_X, AN)$ is optimal if $\forall_{a \in al(P_X,AN)} cost_{alignment}(AL_{P_X,AN}) \leq cost_{alignment}(a)$.*

Note that there can be multiple optimal alignments with the same cost for a given process execution and a de-jure Petri net. Also, practitioners can modify the cost function to weight deviations according to domain-specific knowledge. Figure 4 shows the optimal object-centric alignment for the running example. The inter-object dependencies that are defined in the object-centric Petri net in Fig. 2 are respected by the object-centric alignment. For example, the object-centric alignment agreed on one shared start activity for *p1, i1,* and*i2* which keeps the alignment consistent with inter-object dependencies. This differentiates object-centric alignments and traditional alignments which can violate this requirement.

5   Object-Centric Synchronous Product Net

This section presents a declarative description of the first part of our optimal alignments algorithm. Additional formal definitions for each presented step can be found in the extended pre-print [26]. This first part creates a synchronous product net that can generate all possible alignments. It consists of three parts, each relating to a move type. In the synchronous product net in Fig. 7 the log, model, and synchronous parts are marked. First, we construct the log part from the process execution. Then, we pre-process the de-jure model to finally merge them together to the synchronous product net and add the synchronous part. We assume the model to use the same objects that are in the process execution.

5.1   Process Execution Net Construction

The process execution net is the part of the synchronous product net that ensures that the process execution is contained in the alignment. The construction relates to Petri net runs [16] and causal nets [3]. The process execution

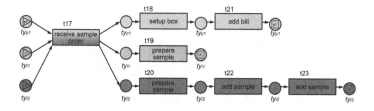

Fig. 5. Process Execution Net

contains *directly follows* relations on the level of objects. For example, the running example process execution in Fig. 1 shows that on item *i1* *add sample* never happens, whereas on item *i2* activity *add sample* happens twice. Although they both have the same object type, the process execution differentiates them. An accepting object-centric Petri net is under-specified in that regard because it only differentiates places by type and not by object. This differentiation is important because otherwise, deviations in one object could compensate for a contrary deviation in another. For example, the missing *add sample* activity on *i1* could be compensated by the additional *add sample* activity on *i2* if one would not strictly separate which event happened on which object. To seperate each object, we have to create a new individual type for each object in the process execution. Since objects can only have one type, we also create a new object for each object from the process execution to use them with the new types. We create the process execution net with the new objects and types. The conditions defined in the process execution are the *directly follows* relation per object. For each condition, the Petri net contains a place. Also, start and end places are added for each object. The transitions relate to the events of the process execution. Thereby, the process execution net precisely models the process execution behavior.

5.2   Pre-processing of the Object-Centric Petri Net

The pre-processed de-jure modes will be the part of the synchronous product net that guarantees that allowed behavior is contained in the model part of the alignment. The pre-processing replaces variable arcs in the de-jure model. For transitions with variable arcs, we do not know beforehand how many objects they use. This information is needed to find synchronous transitions when creating the synchronous product net because two transitions can only be synchronous if they use the same objects which implies using the same number of objects.

As aforementioned, we assume that the set of objects for the model part of the alignment is defined by the process execution. Thus, these objects form the initial and final marking. For a predefined set of objects, the number of objects a variable arc can use is finite. Therefore, we can replace transitions with variable arcs with a set of transitions without variable arcs. For each combination of how many objects a variable arc could consume we add a new transition to the Petri net that uses exactly that number of objects, but by replacing the variable arc with a number of non-variable arcs. When doing this for the Petri net in

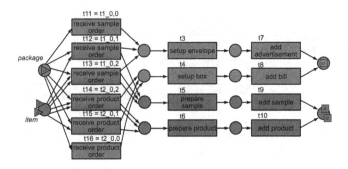

Fig. 6. Pre-processed accepting object-centric Petri net without variable arcs

Fig. 2 the result will be the Petri net without variable arcs in Fig. 6. We call the pre-processed accepting object-centric Petri net a de-jure net.

5.3   Creating the Synchronous Product Net

The synchronous product net models possible alignments. The two nets without variable arcs from the previous steps represent the model and log part of the synchronous product net. In an alignment, either process execution or de-jure parts advance individually, or they progress synchronously. Activities can occur simultaneously in both parts if they involve the same activity on identical object instances. We add a synchronous transition for each pair of transitions from the model and log part that have the same activity label and use the same number of objects per type. For comparing types between the model and log part, we first map the newly created types in the process execution net to their original types. To ensure that in the model and log part the same objects and not only the same types are used by a synchronous transition, we add ν-net requirements. The ν net requirement function assigns variables to the in-going arcs of the synchronous transitions. Arcs with the same variable have to consume the same objects. This refers to the original objects not the newly created ones in the process execution net. For each in-going arc from the process execution net, there has to be one arc from every place that has the same original type, so that those arcs have the same unique variable assigned by Var. This requires the synchronous transition to use the same object instance in the process execution net and the de-jure net. Figure 7 shows the resulting synchronous Petri net for the running example.

6   Alignments from Synchronous Product Net

This section describes the second part of our approach to finding object-centric alignments in a declarative way. Additional formal definitions and proofs can be found in the extended pre-print [26]. The input is a synchronous product net in which every binding relates to a move of an alignment. The activity and the set of objects of the move are given by the label of the transition and

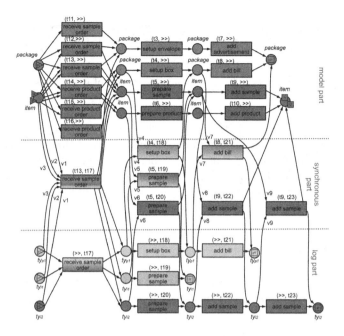

Fig. 7. Synchronous product net for the process execution net in Fig. 5 and accepting object-centric Petri net in Fig. 6

the objects that are defined in the binding. The type of the move depends on whether the transition in the binding is from the log, model, or synchronous part. All binding sequences from the initial marking to the final marking in the synchronous product net relate to an alignment because the log part ensures that the process execution is contained in the log part of the alignment and the model part ensures that the model part of the alignment describes allowed behavior. Therefore, searching for an optimal alignment relates to searching for an optimal binding sequence from the initial to the final marking of the synchronous product net. Interpreting markings as nodes and bindings as edges between markings, we can set up the search space. The cost of the edges is given by the cost of the move that relates to the binding. This is a well-defined search problem we can solve with standard search algorithms for finding the cheapest or shortest path in a graph.

As shown in the extended version, the search space is finite given that the event log and the de-jure model have a finite size [26]. Thus, the Dijkstra algorithm [15] can find the cheapest path. If there is no cheapest path, there is no path at all. So the de-jure model has no option to complete for the set of objects of the process execution meaning it does not contain any related allowed behavior. In this case, there can be no alignment and the user is informed that the de-jure model does not match the process execution. This is similar to traditional alignments with a de-jure model that has no option to complete. In the normal case where the de-jure model describes behavior related to the given pro-

Fig. 8. A process execution from [18] and a variation of it that has some noise.

cess execution, the cheapest path relates to the optimal alignment. The resulting shortest path is a binding sequence from the initial to the final marking. It relates directly to an optimal object-centric alignment for the given process execution and the de-jure model. For the running example Fig. 4 shows the optimal object-centric alignment. If there are multiple binding sequences with the same cost, it depends on the implementation which one is found.

7   Evaluation

We conducted an evaluation with real-world data from the BPI2017 challenge [18]. The evaluation is split into a qualitative part and a quantitative evaluation.

7.1   Qualitative

The qualitative evaluation aims to assess if object-centric alignment can give better insights into object-centric processes compared to traditional alignments. We used BPI2017 data, one of few public event logs convertible into an object-centric format. Its process includes two object types: application and offer. For this evaluation, we selected only the 4 most dominant variants that made up 19.6% of process executions, excluding the activities *Submit, Complete*, and *Accept* for clarity. We discovered the de-jure Petri net from those 4 variants using the python library ocpa [6] which implements the discovery approach from van der Aalst and Berti [4]. We then introduced noise to the log by removing and replacing events. Figure 8 shows the original accepted process execution and the one with noise. For object *application 1, Cancel application* is removed and *Cancel offer* is replaced with *Accept offer*. This creates deviations from the de-jure model behavior. For instance, it is impossible to accept an application without accepting an offer, which is an inter-object dependency one wants to be respected. Also, *Cancel application* and *Cancel offer* events, now only recorded for an offer, represent unwanted behavior. We applied our object-centric alignment approach and the traditional one with flattening to the evaluation data. The optimal object-centric alignment and traditional alignment for each object can be found in Fig. 9.

The traditional alignment failed to detect that application 1 should not have been accepted. This is because the traditional alignment does not consider the inter-object dependency that there has to be a matching offer to accept. This isolated view results in the traditional alignment suggesting *Validate* and *Pending* activities are missing, reinforcing the false acceptance of *application 1*. However,

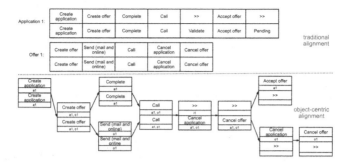

Fig. 9. Traditional and object-centric alignments for the variant with noise and the evaluation de-jure model.

our approach, considering all inter-object dependencies, identifies *Accept Offer* as a log move. Additionally, the traditional alignment doesn't indicate any deviation for *offer 1*, creating a contradiction between alignments of *offer 1* and *application 1*. Such contradictions can not occur in an object-centric alignment because the whole process execution is considered at once. The more inter-object dependencies a process has, the bigger the benefit of object-centric alignments.

7.2   Quantitative

To evaluate the scalability of our approach, we performed a quantitative analysis of the run time, comparing our method with traditional alignment methods.

Evaluation Setup. As the data source we used BPI2017 event data [18]. Only the most frequent 50% of activities were used. All other activities were filtered out. Afterward, the log consisted of 755 variants. We used a Petri net designed so that the given log contains some dis-aligned process executions. The used Petri net is available on GitHub (See Footnote 1). It has 6 visible transitions and 4 silent transitions. There are 10 places in the net. We aligned all the 755 variants with the model and tracked their properties and the resulting alignment calculation time. For comparison with current methods, we also tracked the run time of flattening and then computing optimal alignments for the separate objects using PM4Py [11]. The raw results of that evaluation can be found at GitHub (See Footnote 1). The evaluation was performed on a 3.1 GHz Dual Core Intel Core i5 with 8 GB of RAM.

Results. We computed 755 alignments with costs ranging from 0 to a maximum of 5. Process executions had 3 to 20 events, mostly having 11 to 14 events. Object instances varied from 2 to 7. The calculation time ranged from 0.007 s to 1051.8 s. Results at the end of the attribute range are less resistant to outliers due to fewer data points. Moreover, the correlation coefficient between events and objects is 0.59, while the correlation between events and cost is -0.38. We

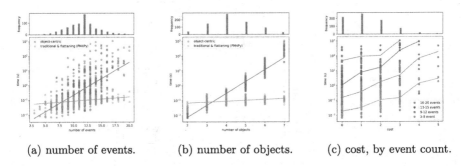

(a) number of events.   (b) number of objects.   (c) cost, by event count.

Fig. 10. Computation time on a logarithmic scale over input parameters. (Color figure online)

plotted the calculation time against the number of events (Fig. 10a), number of objects (Fig. 10b), and alignment cost (Fig. 10c), with a logarithmic scale for the time. To mitigate the effect of the negative correlation, we grouped data points in Fig. 10c by the number of events. The computation time for object-centric alignments grows exponentially across all three dimensions.

This result can be explained by the structure of the search space. More events increase the size of the process execution net and potentially the number of synchronous transitions which creates more potential markings resulting in a bigger search space. Similarly, more objects add parallel behavior, again increasing the search space. The run time of the Dijkstra algorithm is on average exponential in the size of the search space [17]. Therefore, the computation time grows exponentially for the number of events and objects. For an alignment with a higher cost, a bigger portion of the search space is explored, resulting in exponential growth for the cost of the alignment. For small process executions, object-centric alignments (blue graph) can be faster than traditional ones (orange graph) because of the overhead of flattening, but the traditional method has better scalability, as one can see in Fig. 10a and Fig. 10b.

8   Conclusion

This paper presented four contributions for conformance checking in object-centric process mining. First, we defined object-centric alignments generalizing traditional alignments to graphs of moves. Second, we provided an algorithm to calculate them. The two-step approach creates a synchronous product net and searches for the optimal binding sequence from initial marking to final marking. Third, we implemented this algorithm using the open-source library OCPA [6] and made it publicly available on GitHub (See Footnote 1). There are some limitations of the provided model notation and implementation. The notation does not include additional perspectives to the workflow dimension, which makes it less expressive in that regard. But it also makes the notation and implementation applicable to any domain with normative and observed workflow information. If there are multiple cheapest alignments, it depends on the implementation which one is returned. The presented algorithm does not detect missing or redundant objects although the alignment notation would support that. Finally, we evaluated our approach. The qualitative evaluation shows the benefits of object-centric alignments in detecting deviations because they respect inter-object dependencies. Our quantitative evaluation indicates an exponential computation time in the number of object instances and cost of the alignment. This suggests, that an alignment of a whole object-centric event log to a moderately fitting model might be too time-consuming. In those scenarios, one might use object-centric alignments to get specific diagnostics for individual process executions or variants.

There are two directions for future work based on object-centric alignments. On the one hand, one can investigate lifting limitations of the current approach, like finding missing or redundant objects. On the other hand, one can work towards decreasing the complexity and run time: Heuristics, using the A^* algorithm, and defining relaxations of the problem are all promising directions to decrease the computation time.

Acknowledgment. We thank the Alexander von Humboldt (AvH) Stiftung for supporting our research.

References

1. van der Aalst, W.M.P.: Process mining. Commun. ACM **55**(8), 76–83 (2012). https://doi.org/10.1145/2240236.2240257
2. Aalst, W.M.P.: Object-centric process mining: dealing with divergence and convergence in event data. In: Ölveczky, P.C., Salaün, G. (eds.) SEFM 2019. LNCS, vol. 11724, pp. 3–25. Springer, Cham (2019). https://doi.org/10.1007/978-3-030-30446-1_1
3. van der Aalst, W., Adriansyah, A., van Dongen, B.: Causal nets: a modeling language tailored towards process discovery. In: Katoen, J.-P., König, B. (eds.) CONCUR 2011. LNCS, vol. 6901, pp. 28–42. Springer, Heidelberg (2011). https://doi.org/10.1007/978-3-642-23217-6_3
4. van der Aalst, W.M.P., Berti, A.: Discovering object-centric Petri nets. Fundam. Informaticae **175**(1–4), 1–40 (2020). https://doi.org/10.3233/FI-2020-1946
5. Adams, J.N., van der Aalst, W.M.P.: Precision and fitness in object-centric process mining. In: 3rd International Conference on Process Mining, ICPM 2021, Eindhoven, The Netherlands, 31 October–4 November 2021, pp. 128–135. IEEE (2021). https://doi.org/10.1109/ICPM53251.2021.9576886
6. Adams, J.N., Park, G., van der Aalst, W.M.P.: ocpa: a python library for object-centric process analysis. Softw. Impacts **14**, 100438 (2022). https://doi.org/10.1016/j.simpa.2022.100438
7. Adams, J.N., Schuster, D., Schmitz, S., Schuh, G., van der Aalst, W.M.P.: Defining cases and variants for object-centric event data. In: 4th International Conference on Process Mining, ICPM 2022, Bolzano, Italy, 23–28 October 2022, pp. 128–135. IEEE (2022). https://doi.org/10.1109/ICPM57379.2022.9980730
8. Adriansyah, A.: Aligning observed and modeled behavior (2014). https://doi.org/10.6100/IR770080

9. Adriansyah, A., Munoz-Gama, J., Carmona, J., van Dongen, B.F., van der Aalst, W.M.P.: Alignment based precision checking. In: La Rosa, M., Soffer, P. (eds.) BPM 2012. LNBIP, vol. 132, pp. 137–149. Springer, Heidelberg (2013). https://doi.org/10.1007/978-3-642-36285-9_15

10. Adriansyah, A., Sidorova, N., van Dongen, B.F.: Cost-based fitness in conformance checking. In: 11th International Conference on Application of Concurrency to System Design, ACSD 2011, Newcastle Upon Tyne, UK, 20–24 June 2011, pp. 57–66. IEEE Computer Society (2011). https://doi.org/10.1109/ACSD.2011.19

11. Berti, A., van Zelst, S.J., van der Aalst, W.M.P.: Process mining for python (PM4Py): bridging the gap between process- and data science. CoRR abs/1905.06169 (2019)

12. Borrego, D., Barba, I.: Conformance checking and diagnosis for declarative business process models in data-aware scenarios. Expert Syst. Appl. **41**(11), 5340–5352 (2014). https://doi.org/10.1016/j.eswa.2014.03.010

13. Burattin, A., Maggi, F.M., Sperduti, A.: Conformance checking based on multi-perspective declarative process models. Expert Syst. Appl. **65**, 194–211 (2016). https://doi.org/10.1016/j.eswa.2016.08.040

14. Carmona, J., van Dongen, B.F., Solti, A., Weidlich, M.: Conformance Checking - Relating Processes and Models. Springer, Cham (2018). https://doi.org/10.1007/978-3-319-99414-7

15. Dechter, R., Pearl, J.: Generalized best-first search strategies and the optimality of A*. J. ACM **32**(3), 505–536 (1985). https://doi.org/10.1145/3828.3830

16. Desel, J., Reisig, W.: Place/transition Petri nets. In: Reisig, W., Rozenberg, G. (eds.) ACPN 1996. LNCS, vol. 1491, pp. 122–173. Springer, Heidelberg (1998). https://doi.org/10.1007/3-540-65306-6_15

17. Dijkstra, E.W.: A note on two problems in connexion with graphs. Numer. Math. **1**, 269–271 (1959). https://doi.org/10.1007/BF01386390

18. van Dongen, B.: BPI Challenge 2017 (2017). https://doi.org/10.4121/UUID:5F3067DF-F10B-45DA-B98B-86AE4C7A310B

19. Dongen, B.F.: Efficiently computing alignments. In: Weske, M., Montali, M., Weber, I., vom Brocke, J. (eds.) BPM 2018. LNCS, vol. 11080, pp. 197–214. Springer, Cham (2018). https://doi.org/10.1007/978-3-319-98648-7_12

20. Dunzer, S., Stierle, M., Matzner, M., Baier, S.: Conformance checking: a state-of-the-art literature review. In: Proceedings of the 11th International Conference on Subject-Oriented Business Process Management, S-BPM ONE 2019, Seville, Spain, 26–28 June 2019, pp. 4:1–4:10. ACM (2019). https://doi.org/10.1145/3329007.3329014

21. Fahland, D.: Process mining over multiple behavioral dimensions with event knowledge graphs. In: van der Aalst, W.M.P., Carmona, J. (eds.) Process Mining Handbook. LNBIP, vol. 448, pp. 274–319. Springer, Cham (2022). https://doi.org/10.1007/978-3-031-08848-3_9

22. Felli, P., Gianola, A., Montali, M., Rivkin, A., Winkler, S.: CoCoMoT: conformance checking of multi-perspective processes via SMT. In: Polyvyanyy, A., Wynn, M.T., Van Looy, A., Reichert, M. (eds.) BPM 2021. LNCS, vol. 12875, pp. 217–234. Springer, Cham (2021). https://doi.org/10.1007/978-3-030-85469-0_15

23. Hull, R., et al.: Introducing the guard-stage-milestone approach for specifying business entity lifecycles. In: Bravetti, M., Bultan, T. (eds.) WS-FM 2010. LNCS, vol. 6551, pp. 1–24. Springer, Heidelberg (2011). https://doi.org/10.1007/978-3-642-19589-1_1

24. Jensen, K., Kristensen, L.M.: Colored Petri nets: a graphical language for formal modeling and validation of concurrent systems. Commun. ACM **58**(6), 61–70 (2015). https://doi.org/10.1145/2663340

25. de Leoni, M., van der Aalst, W.M.P., van Dongen, B.F.: Data- and resource-aware conformance checking of business processes. In: Abramowicz, W., Kriksciuniene, D., Sakalauskas, V. (eds.) BIS 2012. LNBIP, vol. 117, pp. 48–59. Springer, Heidelberg (2012). https://doi.org/10.1007/978-3-642-30359-3_5

26. Liss, L., Adams, J.N., van der Aalst, W.M.P.: Object-centric alignments (2023). https://doi.org/10.48550/arXiv.2305.05113

27. Nesterov, R., Bernardinello, L., Lomazova, I.A., Pomello, L.: Discovering architecture-aware and sound process models of multi-agent systems: a compositional approach. Softw. Syst. Model. **22**(1), 351–375 (2023). https://doi.org/10.1007/s10270-022-01008-x

28. Nigam, A., Caswell, N.S.: Business artifacts: an approach to operational specification. IBM Syst. J. **42**(3), 428–445 (2003). https://doi.org/10.1147/sj.423.0428

29. Rozinat, A., van der Aalst, W.M.P.: Conformance checking of processes based on monitoring real behavior. Inf. Syst. **33**(1), 64–95 (2008). https://doi.org/10.1016/j.is.2007.07.001

30. Sommers, D., Sidorova, N., van Dongen, B.F.: Aligning event logs to resource-constrained ν-Petri nets. In: Bernardinello, L., Petrucci, L. (eds.) PETRI NETS 2022. LNCS, vol. 13288, pp. 325–345. Springer, Cham (2022). https://doi.org/10.1007/978-3-031-06653-5_17

31. Song, W., Xia, X., Jacobsen, H., Zhang, P., Hu, H.: Efficient alignment between event logs and process models. IEEE Trans. Serv. Comput. **10**(1), 136–149 (2017). https://doi.org/10.1109/TSC.2016.2601094

Transforming Event Knowledge Graph to Object-Centric Event Logs: A Comparative Study for Multi-dimensional Process Analysis

Shahrzad Khayatbashi[1]([✉]), Olaf Hartig[1], and Amin Jalali[2]

[1] Linköping University, Linköping, Sweden
{shahrzad.khayatbashi,olaf.hartig}@liu.se
[2] Stockholm University, Stockholm, Sweden
aj@dsv.su.se

Abstract. Process mining has significantly transformed business process management by introducing innovative data-based analysis techniques and empowering organizations to unveil hidden insights previously buried within their recorded data. The analysis is conducted on event logs structured by conceptual models. Traditional models were defined based on only a single case notion, e.g., order or item in the purchase process. This limitation hinders the application of process mining in practice for which new data models are developed, a.k.a, multi-dimensional Event Knowledge Graph (EKG) and Object-Centric Event Log (OCEL). While several tools have been developed for OCEL, there is a lack of process mining tooling around the EKG. In addition, there is a lack of comparison about the practical implication of choosing one approach over the other. To fill this gap, the contribution of this paper is threefold. First, it defines and implements an algorithm to transform event logs represented as EKG to OCEL. The implementation is then used to transform five real event logs based on which the approach is evaluated. Second, it compares the performance of analyzing event logs represented in these two models. Third, it reveals similarities and differences in analyzing processes based on event logs represented in these two models. The results highlight ten important findings, including different approaches in calculating directly-follows relations when analyzing filtered event logs in these models and issues that need to be considered in analyzing event lifecycle and inter-log relations using OCEL.

Keywords: Event Knowledge Graph · Object-Centric Event Log · Object-Centric Process Mining · Neo4j · Graph database

1 Introduction

Business process analysis is important in modern organizations because it enables comprehension, optimization, and enhancement of operational processes based on recorded data [38]. These processes are complex due to the complex nature of the business domain. To address this complexity, log file formats and standards have emerged as conceptual models that capture the essential information required to support the analysis [2,14,21,33]. These conceptual models drive the development of algorithms and facilitate the processing and analysis of recorded data.

J. P. A. Almeida et al. (Eds.): ER 2023, LNCS 14320, pp. 220–238, 2023.
https://doi.org/10.1007/978-3-031-47262-6_12

Process mining is a research area that facilitates data-driven business process analysis based on recorded event logs [38]. Log files are crucial for analyzing business processes. Thus, extensive efforts have been made to define conceptual models, in the forms of log file formats and standards, that enable the analysis of recorded data using different software systems [21,23,34]. These formats and standards ensure compatibility and interoperability across various systems while providing a consistent and structured format for recording process-related information.

Traditionally, event log formats assume a single case notion as an obligatory element based on which the rest of the information could be correlated. For example, a purchase order event log could be extracted using either the order or the item notions, while the process contains both objects as potential cases. In reality, business processes deal with different perspectives, which may require several case notions. Hence, restricting log formats to a single case notion limits the applicability of process mining in practice.

To circumvent this limitation, researchers and practitioners flattened the recorded event log to perform process analysis, which introduces its limitations, including false behavior and false analysis results [16] (which result from so-called divergence and convergence problems [39]). For example, one order may contain many items. In the log extraction, if we consider the "item" as the case notion, events like "create order" must be repeated for each item. The mapping of events based on one case notion, like this example, is called flattening. One consequence is that we will get false statistics when retrieving the number of orders which are created. If the log is flattened around the "order" case notion, the relation between the "select item" and "approve item" in the process can be lost because all items can be stored around one order resulting in losing information about relations between items. The lack of these relations could introduce loops between the activities of these two events in discovering process models, which is considered false behavior. These issues compromise the accuracy of the analysis [39].

The Object-Centric Event Log (OCEL) [21] has been proposed to address the limitation of having only one case notion when extracting log files, and it is part of a new and emerging paradigm in process mining called Object-Centric Process Mining (OCPM) [39]. This paradigm aims to support analyzing business processes considering multiple case notions that require developing algorithms, techniques, and methods to support multi-dimensional process analysis. Although OCPM has started recently, due to the highly relevant problem that it targets, several algorithms, tools, and libraries have been developed to support such analysis, e.g., [3,4,6,11,26,34,35,39,40]. This development can also be observed in commercial tools like Celonis[1], showing the relevancy of the problem in practice.

Another recent alternative to recording event logs is knowledge graphs, which unleash their power within information systems, showcasing their ability to support various data sources, scalability, semantic reasoning, and adaptable schema evolution [24]. Thus, it is recently used to record and process event logs with multiple case notions, called multi-dimensional Event Knowledge Graph (EKG) [14]. However, the lack of process mining tools for analyzing EKG limits the practical application of this approach. Additionally, there is a lack of comparative analysis in terms of performance, strengths, weaknesses, limitations, and differences between the processing of data rep-

---

[1] https://www.celonis.com/.

resented using these two approaches (EKG and OCEL). Therefore, this paper aims to address the following research questions:

RQ1) How can an event knowledge graph be transformed into an object-centric event log?

RQ2) How does the performance of processing event knowledge graph compare to processing object-centric event log in process mining?

RQ3) What are the differences and similarities in applying process mining on an event knowledge graph compared to an object-centric event log?

To answer the first research question, we define an algorithm that transforms it into a set of OCELs. We implemented an algorithm as a part of a Python library, called neo4pm, that can be used to perform the transformation. In this paper, we use this implementation to transform five real EKGs into OCEL files, which are available publicly [28–32]. In addition, we compare similarities and differences in analyzing processes based on event logs represented in EKG and transformed OCELs, which helped us answer the third research question.

The structure of the paper is as follows. Section 2 gives an overview of related work. Section 3 provides preliminaries which are used in Sect. 4, where we define the algorithm formally. Section 5 reports the results and discusses the findings. Finally, Sect. 6 concludes the paper by giving future direction.

2   Related Work

In this section, we provide an overview of the research that offers tool support for processing event logs represented in multi-dimensional Event Knowledge Graph (EKG) and Object-centric Event Log (OCEL). Table 1 summarizes the process mining tools developed for OCEL and EKG. The table categorizes the level of support into eight use cases: transformation, exploration, monitoring, performance analysis, discovery, conformance checking, enhancement, and predictive process monitoring.

The tool support for EKG focuses on transforming traditional log files into the EKG data model [14]. A recent study has proposed a method for transforming OCEL to EKG [16]; however, the existing implementation does not yet support the transformation from the serialized standard OCEL files. Furthermore, there is a lack of support for EKG in other use cases. In contrast to EKG, the existing contributions to OCEL varies in different use cases. These categories are represented as columns in Table 1.

In the *transformation* use case, we have identified three sub-categories of transformation. Firstly, there are approaches focused on transforming traditional log to OCEL [37]. Secondly, there are methods for transforming data recorded in databases or Enterprise Resource Planning (ERP) systems to OCEL [10,42]. Lastly, there are techniques available for flattening OCEL to traditional log [11,21]. In the *exploration* use case, we have identified four sub-categories of exploration. This includes support for filtering events based on certain criteria [11], identifying concept drift in event data [8], supporting variant analysis on event logs [5,7], and splitting the log into several clusters based on similarity in underlying behaviour [26].

Table 1. Summary of studies providing tool support for OCEL or EKG

Approach	UC_1	UC_2	UC_3	UC_4	UC_5	UC_6	UC_7	UC_8
OCEL	[10,11,21,37,42]	[5,7,8,11,26]	[36]	[11,35,36]	[4,26,40]	[4,6,11]	[3,4]	[4,22]
EKG	[14,16]							

UC_1: Transformation, UC_2: Exploration, UC_3: Monitoring, UC_4: Performance Analysis, UC_5: Discovery

UC_6: Conformance Checking, UC_7: Enhancement, UC_8: predictive process monitoring

In the *monitoring* use case, Park and van der Aalst present a tool for monitoring object-centric constraints [36]. In the *performance analysis* use case, a tool called OC-PM is available for calculating the duration time of objects [11]. Additionally, performance metrics computation is supported by [36] and [35]. In the *discovery* use case, the discovery of object-centric Petri nets is supported by [40] and [4]. In addition, the discovery of Markov Directly-Follow Multigraphs is supported by [26] by extending the discovery of Markov Directly-Follow Graphs [27]. In the *conformance checking* use case, Berti and van der Aalst provide a tool for conformance checking [11]. Also, tool support is provided for calculating precision and fitness [4,6]. In the *enhancement* use case, tool support is provided for enhancing process models through feature extraction [3,4]. In the *predictive process monitoring* use case, Adams et al. [4] provide a tool for predictive monitoring, and Gherissi et al. [22] offer a tool for predicting the next event time, activity, and remaining sequence time.

3   Preliminaries

This section introduces the notions of the Event Knowledge Graph (EKG) and the Object-Centric Event Log (OCEL), which serve as the foundation for defining the transformation algorithm in Sect. 4. We explain the EKG definition using a running example, which will also be utilized to demonstrate the approach and algorithm in the subsequent sections of this paper.

Figure 1 illustrates a running example that is used to explain the components of EKG. The figure represents recorded information in an EKG for a fictitious business process involving a customer order (o1) with two items (i1 and i2). Orders and items are depicted as ovals (annotated with : Entity), while events are represented as rectangles (annotated with : Event). Each event has an activity name and a timestamp (e.g., Submit Order and 15 : 00 for e1, respectively). Some events have the performing resource (e.g., Elin for e3). The figure illustrates the chronological sequence of events: Submit Order, two instances of Check Availability (one for each item), and Pick Items. The following definitions will define the elements within this graph based on which we can define the transformation algorithm.

Definition 1 (Universes). We define the following universes to be used throughout the paper, some of which are adopted from [39]:

- $\mathbb{U}_{lbl}$ is an infinite set of strings representing labels,
- $\mathbb{U}_{att}$ is an infinite set of strings representing attribute names,
- $\mathbb{U}_{val}$ is an infinite set of strings representing attribute values containing the following disjoint subsets:

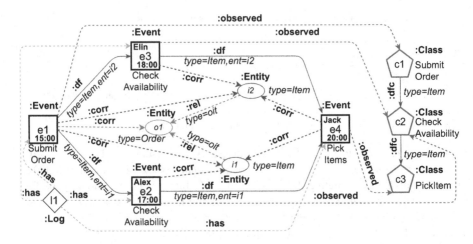

Fig. 1. Running example showing event log represented in an EKG

- $\mathbb{U}_{eid} \subset \mathbb{U}_{val}$ represents the universe of event identifiers,
- $\mathbb{U}_{time} \subset \mathbb{U}_{val}$ represents the universe of timestamps,
- $\mathbb{U}_{act} \subset \mathbb{U}_{val}$ represents the universe of activity names,
- $\mathbb{U}_{ot} \subset \mathbb{U}_{val}$ represents the universe of object types,
- $\mathbb{U}_{oid} \subset \mathbb{U}_{val}$ represents the universe of object identifiers,
- $type : \mathbb{U}_{oid} \rightarrow \mathbb{U}_{ot}$ is a function that assigns exactly one object type to each object identifier,
- $\mathbb{U}_{omap} = \{omap : \mathbb{U}_{ot} \rightarrow \mathcal{P}(\mathbb{U}_{oid}) \mid \forall_{ot \in dom(omap)} \forall_{oid \in omap(ot)} \ type(oid) = ot\}$ is the universe of all object mappings indicating which object identifiers are included per object type[2],
- $\mathbb{U}_{vmap} = \{vmap : \mathbb{U}_{att} \nrightarrow \mathbb{U}_{val}\}$ is the universe of value assignments,[3] and
- $\mathbb{U}_{event} = \mathbb{U}_{eid} \times \mathbb{U}_{act} \times \mathbb{U}_{time} \times \mathbb{U}_{omap} \times \mathbb{U}_{vmap}$ is the universe of events.

Definition 2 (Labeled Property Graph (LPG)). An LPG (adopted from [9,16]) is a tuple $G = (N, R, \gamma, \lambda, \rho)$, where:

- N and R are finite sets of nodes and relations, respectively,
- $\gamma : R \rightarrow N \times N$ is a total function assigning a pair of nodes (representing the source and target, respectively) to a relation,
- $\lambda : (R \cup N) \rightarrow \mathbb{U}_{lbl}$ is a total function assigning a label to a node or a relation,
- $\rho : (N \cup R) \times \mathbb{U}_{att} \nrightarrow \mathbb{U}_{val}$ is a partial function assigning a value to an attribute of a node or a relation.

Given an LPG $G = (N, R, \gamma, \lambda, \rho)$, we call $E = N \cup R$ the set of elements in the graph containing both nodes and relations. Considering a Label $l \in \mathbb{U}_{lbl}$, we write E^l to

---

[2] $\mathcal{P}(\mathbb{U}_{oid})$ is the powerset of the universe of object identifiers, i.e., objects types are mapped onto sets of object identifiers.

[3] $\mathbb{U}_{att} \nrightarrow \mathbb{U}_{val}$ is the set of all partial functions mapping a subset of attribute names onto the corresponding values.

denote the subset of E consisting of all the elements with Label l. Formally, we show this as $E^l = \{e \in E \mid \lambda(e) = l\}$. We use the same notation for the subsets N and R of E (e.g., N^l). Moreover, for every element $e \in E$ and every attribute name $a \in \mathbb{U}_{att}$, if $(e, a) \in dom(\rho)$, we write $e.a$ to refer to the value $v \in \mathbb{U}_{val}$ for which it holds that $\rho(e, a) = v$; if $(e, a) \notin dom(\rho)$, then $e.a$ denotes a special value $\bot$ that is not in $\mathbb{U}_{val}$.

Example 1. In Fig. 1, we can see ten nodes. One is annotated with e1, where we refer to it by n and its activity name by act in this example. Thus, we can say $\rho(n, act) =$ SubmitOrder representing that the activity name of this event is SubmitOrder. We can also write $n.act = $ SubmitOrder. As this node is labeled with Event, we can say $\lambda(n) = $ Event or $n \in N^{\text{Event}}$. This node has a relation to another event annotated with e2. We refer to this event by n' and to its relation to n' by r. We can say $\gamma(r) = (n, n')$. This relation is labeled with df, so $\lambda(r) = $ df or $r \in R^{\text{df}}$.

After defining LPG, we now introduce a special kind of LPG that uses a specific schema named Event Knowledge Graph. We define the schema as $\mathcal{S} = \{(\text{has}, (\text{Log}, \text{Event})), (\text{observed}, (\text{Event}, \text{Class})), (\text{rel}, (\text{Entity}, \text{Entity})), (\text{df}, (\text{Event}, \text{Event})), (\text{dfc}, (\text{Class}, \text{Class}))\}$. This schema specifies the possible label of the source and the target node in each relation based on the relation's label. Each member of the set is a tuple, where the first element indicates a possible relation's label, and the second element indicates the label of source and target nodes, respectively. In the Event Knowledge Graph definition, we restrict the universe of labels as $\mathbb{U}_{lbl} = \bigcup_{(l,(s,t)) \in S} \{l\} \cup \{s\} \cup \{t\}$, meaning that $\mathbb{U}_{lbl} = \{$Event, Entity, Class, Log, observed, has, rel, df, dfc, corr$\}$. Note that an EKG can have multiple nodes labeled as Log, meaning that it can record events related to multiple logs in one graph.

Definition 3 (Event Knowledge Graph (EKG)). An EKG is an LPG $G = (N, R, \gamma, \lambda, \rho)$, that has the following properties[4].

a) $\forall_{e \in N^{\text{Event}}} (e.id \in \mathbb{U}_{eid} \wedge e.act \in \mathbb{U}_{act} \wedge e.time \in \mathbb{U}_{time})$ indicating that each node with the label Event has attributes called id, act, and $time$ with the value of an event identifier, an activity name, and a timestamp, respectively,

b) $\forall_{e \in N^{\text{Entity}}} (e.id \in \mathbb{U}_{oid} \wedge e.type \in \mathbb{U}_{ot})$ indicating that each node with the label Entity has an attribute called id and $type$ with the value of an object identifier and object type, respectively,

c) The relations between nodes can be specified as $\forall_{(l,(s,t)) \in S,\ r \in R \text{ with } \gamma(r)=(e,e')} (e \in N^s \wedge e' \in N^t) \Leftrightarrow r \in R^l$ indicating that a relation can be labeled as specified in schema if and only if the source and target nodes are labeled accordingly,

d) $\forall_{r \in R^{\text{rel}}} r.type \in \mathbb{U}_{ot} \cup \{\text{Reified}\}$ indicating that each relation with the label rel has attributes called $type$ with the value of an object type or a special value called Reified. The Reified type is used to model the relation between derived entities to other entities.

We keep the definition of EKG to a minimum in this paper without elaborating on detailed properties that are not needed for the transformation algorithms. For example, we omit details on properties that should be held by df and dfc relations. More details can be found in [14, 16].

---

[4] The definition is aligned with definitions in [14, 16].

Example 2. Our running example graph fulfills the properties stated in Definition 3 (a-b). As required by Definition 3 (a), each event in our graph has an event identifier (e.g., e1), an activity name (e.g., SubmitOrder for e1), a timestamp (e.g., 15 : 00 for e1). Also, all entities have an identifier as well as a type as required by Definition 3 (b), e.g., the mustard-colored oval has an identifier with the value of o1 and type of Order.

Our running example graph fulfills the properties stated in Definition 3 (c-d). As required by Definition 3 (c), every relation that its source and target are labeled with Log and Event respectively are labeled with has, e.g., the relation between l1 and e1. The same applies to other relations such as observed, rel, df, and dfc, where their source and target nodes are labeled as indicated in the defined set. As required by Definition 3 (d), every relation which is labeled by rel has an attribute named type, e.g., the relation between i1 and o1 which has a type with the value of oit.

The following two definitions are adopted from [39] describing an OCEL, the target format to which we will transform the described EKG.

Definition 4 (Event Projection (adopted from [39])). An *event* e is a tuple $(eid, act, time, omap, vmap)$ where $eid \in \mathbb{U}_{eid}$, $act \in \mathbb{U}_{act}$, $time \in \mathbb{U}_{time}$, $omap$ is an object mapping, and $vmap$ is a value assignment. For each such event $e = (eid, act, time, omap, vmap)$, we write $\pi_{eid}(e)$ to denote eid, $\pi_{act}(e)$ denotes act, $\pi_{time}(e)$ to denote $time$, $\pi_{omap}(e)$ to denote $omap$, and $\pi_{vmap}(e)$ denotes $vmap$.

Definition 5 (Object-Centric Event Log (OCEL) [39]). An event log L is a pair $(E, \leq_E)$ with $E \subseteq \mathbb{U}_{event}$ and $\leq_E \subseteq E \times E$ such that:

- $\leq_E$ defines a partial order (reflexive, antisymmetric, and transitive),
- $\forall_{e_1, e_2 \in E} \pi_{eid}(e_1) = \pi_{eid}(e_2) \Rightarrow e_1 = e_2$, and
- $\forall_{e_1, e_2 \in E} e_1 \leq_E e_2 \Rightarrow \pi_{time}(e_1) \leqslant \pi_{time}(e_2)$.

4 Approach

This section introduces a transformation algorithm that enables transforming an Event Knowledge Graph (EKG) into a set of Object Centric Event Logs (OCELs), addressing RQ1. In this algorithm's definition, the following Design Choices (DC) have been made:

DC1. EKG with Multiple Logs: The algorithm converts an EKG with multiple logs (i.e., an EKG with multiple nodes with the label Log) into a set of OCEL files. This choice aligns with the OCEL standard, allowing one global log element per file [21]. An alternative option would be to include all of events in one log file and mark events related to a log file using a *vmap*. However, this alternative deviates from the standard, as the *vmap* value does not represent logs according to the standard. Our approach can easily support the second design choice by merging the generated OCELs into one with a new *vmap* indicating the log file.

DC2. Event Lifecycles: Unlike XES, OCEL does not explicitly define event lifecycles which specifies events representing different states of an operational task in a business process. As a result, we chose to omit to transform event classes (representing lifecycles in EKG) to OCEL. Event classes in EKG can be related to multiple lifecycle states, and the explicit definition of the event lifecycle in a log file can enable the development of lifecycle-aware algorithms, similar to algorithms developed for XES. If OCEL is extended to support lifecycles in the future, our transformation algorithm can easily include the transformation logic. As an alternative design choice, it is possible to transform the lifecycle as event attributes or related objects, yet this still will not help in the definition of lifecycle-aware algorithms as this information needs to be explicitly supported by standards so that algorithms can take them into account.

DC3. Relations Between Entities: The algorithm also omits to transform EKGs' reified entities. OCEL does not support these relations, leaving them out of the transformation process.

By making these design choices, the algorithm ensures compliance with the current version of the OCEL standard while accommodating potential future extensions for lifecycle support and other entity transformations. Algorithm 1 describe the transformation logic, where the input is an EKG, and the output is a set of OCELs.

Algorithm 1. Converting EKG to OCELs

1: **Input:** A event knowledge graph $G = (N, R, \lambda, \gamma, \rho)$
2: **Output:** A set of OCELs $\mathcal{O}$
3: **Begin**
4: $\mathcal{O} \leftarrow \varnothing$
5: $\mathcal{R} \leftarrow N^{Entity} \backslash \{n \in N^{Entity} \mid \exists_{n' \in N^{Entity}} (n, n') \in R^{Rel} \wedge \exists_{r \in R^{Rel}} \gamma(r) = (n, n') \wedge r.type = \mathsf{Reified}\}$
6: **for each** $l \in N^{Log}$ **do**
7:      $E \leftarrow \varnothing$
8:      **for each** $e \in N^{Event}$ **do**
9:          $omap \leftarrow \varnothing$
10:          $vmap \leftarrow \varnothing$
11:          **if** $\exists_{r \in R^{Has}} \gamma(r) = (l, e)$ **then**
12:              $\mathcal{E}_{\mathcal{R}} \leftarrow \{n \in \mathcal{R} \mid \forall_{r \in R^{Corr}} \gamma(r) = (e, n)\}$
13:              $\mathcal{OT} \leftarrow \bigcup_{n \in \mathcal{E}_{\mathcal{R}}} n.type$
14:              **for each** $ot \in \mathcal{OT}$ **do**
15:                  $omap(ot) \leftarrow \bigcup_{n \in \mathcal{E}_{\mathcal{R}} \wedge (n.type=ot)} n.id$
16:              **end for**
17:              **for each** $att \in \mathbb{U}_{att} \backslash \{id, act, time\}$ **do**
18:                  **if** $e.att \neq \perp$ **then**
19:                      $vmap(att) \leftarrow e.att$
20:                  **end if**
21:              **end for**
22:              $E \leftarrow E \cup \{(e.id, e.act, e.time, omap, vmap)\}$
23:          **end if**
24:      **end for**
25:      $\leq_E \leftarrow \{(e, e') \mid e, e' \in E \wedge e \neq e' \wedge \pi_{time}(e) \leq \pi_{time}(e')\}$
26:      $\mathcal{O} \leftarrow \mathcal{O} \cup \{(E, \leq_E)\}$
27: **end for**

Here, we elaborate on this algorithm. Line 5 assigns the set of non-reified entities to $\mathcal{R}$. In our running example, $\mathcal{R} = \{i1, i2, o1\}$. We exclude reified entities in EKG as OCEL does not capture relations among entities. Thus, we only need the set of non-reified entities. Then, the algorithm starts iterating around each log node. It defines a set for capturing all events of the log, i.e., E (line 7). Then, for each event, it defines two empty functions (lines 9 and 10) that will be configured accordingly: if the log has a has relation to the event, the algorithm i) retrieves all non-reified entities to which the event has a *corr* relation and assigns them to $\mathcal{E}_\mathcal{R}$ (line 12), and ii) retrieves the type of all retrieved entities and assigns them to $\mathcal{OT}$ (line 13). If we look at our running example, this algorithm sets the mentioned variables for e1 accordingly: $\mathcal{E}_\mathcal{R} = \{i1, i2, o1\}$, $\mathcal{OT} = \{\text{Order}, \text{Item}\}$.

Then, the algorithm sets *omap* and *vmap* through two loops. The first loop configures the *omap* function by relating each retrieved object type to a set of related object identifiers (line 15). This means that, $omap(\text{Order}) = \{o1\}$ and $omap(\text{Item}) = \{i1, i2\}$ for e1. The second loop configures the *vmap* function by assigning all event's attributes (except for *id*, *act*, and *time*) to *vmap* (line 19). For event e1, *vmap* will be empty as the event has no other attributes. However, if we consider e3, $vmap(\text{Resource}) = \text{Elin}$.

Finally, the algorithm updates the variable capturing all events within the processing log, i.e., E (line 22). For our example when processing e1, $E = ($e1, SubmitOrder, 15:00, $\{omap(\text{Order}) = \{o1\}, omap(\text{Item}) = \{i1, i2\}\}, \{\})$. Iterating all these steps will produce an OCEL, and line 26 retrieves the set of OCELs transformed from the EKG.

5   Evaluation

This section presents the evaluation results of comparing transformed OCEL with EKG. Through this evaluation, we analyze the differences and similarities between these two approaches. A comparative performance analysis is also conducted between EKG and OCEL, further investigating the disparities and similarities between these approaches.

5.1   Data Processing

The transformation algorithm was implemented as part of an open-source Python library[5], called neo4pm[6]. For evaluation, EKG was transformed to OCEL using our implemented algorithm, and the transformed logs are available publicly at [28–32]. Due to the large size of the log files, the transformation was performed on a server. Subsequently, EKG and OCEL were evaluated and compared on a laptop, replicating the environment typically used by analysts.

Data Transformation: To evaluate our approach, we transformed five open-access real-world EKG: BPIC14 [17], BPIC15 [18], BPIC16 [19], BPIC17 [20], and BPIC19 [15]. As a result, we obtained nine OCELs (one OCEL file for each EKG, except for BPIC15, which produced five OCEL files).

---

[5] The library can be installed using !pip install neo4pm.
[6] The source code is available at https://github.com/neo4pm/neo4pm.

Evaluation Setup: For the evaluation setup, we used a laptop with the following specifications: two 6-core Intel Core i9 CPUs running at 2.90 GHz, 32 GB of RAM, a 1 TB HDD, and a 64-bit Windows 11 Enterprise operating system. Docker (v.4.17.1) was installed on the laptop to host the running evaluations. Neo4j (community edition 3.5) and PM4Py (v.2.7.3) were utilized for the evaluations [12,13].

5.2 Information Preserving Evaluation

Table 2 illustrates the information-preserving evaluation results, comparing the number of different elements in the EKG and the transformed OCEL. This table captures the count of Logs, Events, non-reified Entities (objects in OCEL), Classes (activity names in OCEL), Observed relations (showing the activity lifecycles), corr relations, and direct-follow relations (df), shown as columns in the table. The rows represent the evaluation result for different BPICs. BPIC15 consists of multiple logs, so the numbers are given in detail for each log for OCEL, and they are aggregated to be compared with EKG. In the subsequent discussion, we will explore the differences observed in these elements.

As can be seen in the table, information preservation is evident for all BPICs except BPIC15 and BPIC17, which exhibit some differences compared to the others. BPIC15 involves process data associated with multiple log files, leading to the transformation of EKG into multiple OCEL log files (as followed based on DC1.). EKG for BPIC17, on the other hand, captures information regarding the lifecycle of each event. Further elaboration on these differences will be provided below.

Table 2. Information preserving evaluation result

		# Log	# Event	# Entity*	# Class	# observed	# corr*	# df
BPIC 14	OCEL	1	690,622	228,885	330	690,622	2,732,213	2,503,328
	EKG	1	690,622	228,885	330	690,622	2,732,213	2,503,328
BPIC 15	OCEL$_1$	1	52,217	1,269	289	52,217	208,868	207,599
	OCEL$_2$	1	443,54	859	304	44,354	177,416	176,557
	OCEL$_3$	1	59,681	1,465	277	59,681	238,724	237,259
	OCEL$_4$	1	47,293	1,084	272	47,293	189,172	188,088
	OCEL$_5$	1	59,083	1,202	285	59,083	236,332	235,130
	OCEL	Sum:	262,628	5,879	1,427	262,628	1,050,512	1,044,633
	EKG	5	262,628	5,862	356	262,628	1,050,512	1,044,650
BPIC 16	OCEL	1	7,360,146	748,913	620	7,360,146	36,430,880	35,681,967
	EKG	1	7,360,146	748,913	620	7,360,146	36,430,880	35,681,967
BPIC 17	OCEL	1	1,202,267	106,162	26	1,202,267	2,404,534	2,298,372
	EKG	1	1,202,267	106,162	92	2,404,534	2,404,534	2,298,372
BPIC 19	OCEL	1	1,595,923	330,685	42	1,595,923	5,984,602	5,653,917
	EKG	1	1,595,923	330,685	42	1,595,923	5,984,602	5,653,917

#: Number of, $*$: Non-Reified, OCEL$_n$: nth sublog

Differences in BPIC 15: Three differences can be observed when comparing the EKG with the generated OCELs, i.e., the difference in the total number of Entities (referred to as Objects in OCEL), Classes, and directly-follows relations.

The difference in the total number of Entities and Classes is the result of splitting the data to multiple OCELs for BPIC15, as shown in the Table 2, which is due to the limitation of OCEL to capture multiple logs. Consequently, some entities are repeated across different log files, leading to double counting when aggregating the numbers. The same applies to the count of classes. However, these differences do not affect the analysis, as each OCEL represents a subset of the log.

An additional disparity lies in the number of directly-follows relations. These relations significantly impact process discovery and conformance-checking algorithms, warranting a detailed analysis to ascertain the reasons behind the difference. We identified 860 missing directly-follows relations after transforming the EKG BPIC15 into OCEL. Notably, this number does not align with the difference reported in the table. The reason is that directly-follows relations need to be calculated at runtime for a given OCEL. This is different from EKG which materializes these relations. Hence, additional directly-follows relations may be inferred in OCEL that were not present in the source EKG. To illustrate this case, Fig. 2 presents a sub-graph extracted from the EKG for BPIC15, which allows us to delve deeper into the aforementioned issue.

In Fig. 2, we can observe two types of directly-follows (DF) relations: intra-log and inter-log directly-follows relations. The two red DF flows represent intra-log relations, indicating that these relations exist among events within a single log, i.e., events related to BPIC15_1. Additionally, there is one intra-log directly-follows relation involving events related to BPIC15_3, denoted by a thin mustard-colored (DF) relation. The figure's two thick mustard-colored DF relations represent inter-log directly-follows relations. These relations occur when the source and target events are associated with different logs in the graph.

Figure 3 showcases the directly-follows relations discovered using PM4Py python library [12] with the transformed OCEL specifically for BPIC15_1. Several similarities and differences can be observed in comparison to Fig. 2. i) The two intra-log directly-follows relations for BPIC15_1 are preserved in the transformed OCEL. ii) However, the two inter-log directly-follows relations are lost, indicating that they are not captured in the transformed OCEL. iii) An additional intra-log directly-follows relation is introduced between the register submission date request and enter senddate acknowledgement events for the Case_R object type. Please note that we omit to discuss the intra-log directly-follows relation for BPIC15_3 in this context, as it is present in the other log file.

The absence of the two inter-log relations in the transformed OCEL is indeed expected, as OCEL does not support multi-log event storage. Based on this observation, we can conclude that:

- **Finding 1.** Analyzing a process using multiple OCEL logs (as followed based on DC1.) can result in missing the inter-log relations. On the one hand, an Event Knowledge Graph (EKG) supports analyzing multiple logs simultaneously, meaning it will

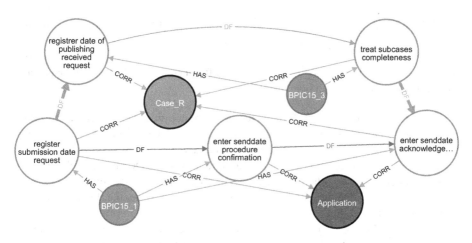

Fig. 2. Intra- and inter- log directly-follows relations (shown by thin and thick flows respectively) for a part of BPIC15_1 & for BPIC15_3 in the Event Knowledge Graph

Fig. 3. Inter-log directly-follows relations for a part of BPIC15_1 equivalent to Fig. 2

not miss these relations; on the other hand, merging multiple logs into one OCEL and keeping the log information as event attributes can be considered as a technique to handle this shortcoming.

As previously mentioned, some directly-follows relations in the transformed log were not present in the original EKG. For instance, the relation between register submission date request and enter senddate acknowledgement for the Case_R object type was not captured in the EKG. The reason behind this discrepancy lies in the runtime computation of directly-follows relations in Object-Centric Process Mining. In the EKG, two other events were occurring between these two events, resulting in the absence of a direct relation. However, when we project events related to a specific event log, events from other logs are removed, leading to different computations of directly-follows relations among events.

The addition of directly-follows relations can also be observed when filtering event logs based on certain event attributes. An important difference arises when filtering out specific events, such as the enter senddate procedure confirmation event in the EKG (as depicted in Fig. 2). In this case, there would be no directly-follows (DF) relation between the register submission date request and enter senddate acknowledgement events for the Application entity. However, applying the same filter in OCEL would result in a new directly-follows (DF) relation between these two events.

This difference arises because directly-follows relations in OCEL are calculated at run-time based on existing timestamps.

It is important to note that we do not conclude which approach is correct or incorrect. However, this discrepancy is a significant difference that analysts should be aware of to avoid drawing incorrect conclusions.

– **Finding 2.** Inter-log directly-follows relations are not preserved when transforming an EKG to multiple OCELs (as followed based on DC1.). If those relations matter in the analysis, an analyst may follow the alternative design choice stated in DC1.
– **Finding 3.** Analyzing processes with multiple logs using OCEL can include additional directly-follows relations due to the absence of inter-log directly-follows relations. The alternative design choice can be followed to overcome this challenge as stated in DC1.
– **Finding 4.** Filtering OCEL event logs based on specific events can introduce extra directly-follows relations due to the lack of filtered events, similar to the case of filtering traditional logs. These relations are not added when analyzing event knowledge graphs, as all directly-follows relations are pre-calculated.

Differences in BPIC 17: In the EKG, each event is associated with two classes. For instance, event 9 with the activity name O_Created is linked to two classes in the EKG, both of which have the same name as the activity. One class has the type Activity with the same name, while the other class has the type Activity+Lifecycle with the lifecycle value of COMPLETE. However, when transforming to OCEL, the information regarding the lifecycle is not taken into transformation since the OCEL standard does not include lifecycle specifications.

– **Finding 5.** The OCEL standard does not include support for the event lifecycle, but it is supported in EKG. One option to overcome this limitation is to map this information as event's values or related objects as explained in alternative choice for DC2.

5.3 Performance Evaluation

Table 3 shows the performance comparison result of processing event data in EKG and OCEL. The column labeled "Loading Time" in the table represents the time required to prepare the log file for analysis. For OCEL, it indicates the time taken to load the log file into memory. For the EKG, it refers to the time required to load the dump file into Neo4j.

– **Finding 6.** Analyzing OCEL using PM4Py requires the log file to fit within the computer's memory. In contrast, EKG (stored in Neo4j) can handle large data sizes without such memory limitations because a part of graph content is loaded into memory as needed and processed on demand [1], as also demonstrated in [25]. This distinction is crucial when dealing with big data in process analysis as it can enable scaling process mining in practice.

Table 3. Performance comparison (in seconds)

		Loading Time	Query Execution Time						
			#Log	#Event	#Entity*	#Class	#observed	#corr*	#df
BPIC 14	OCEL	24.86	0.00	0.00	0.00	0.16	0.20	0.00	124.12
	EKG	53.59	0.02	0.02	2.37	0.02	0.02	2.79	0.03
BPIC 15	OCEL	9.52	0.00	0.00	0.00	0.05	0.04	0.00	37.59
	EKG	25.97	0.02	0.02	0.41	0.01	0.01	1.52	0.03
BPIC 16	OCEL	349.95	0.00	0.00	0.00	2.19	2.44	0.00	1845.80
	EKG	166.02	0.02	0.02	7.32	0.01	0.01	67.71	0.03
BPIC 17	OCEL	38.96	0.00	0.00	0.00	0.28	0.33	0.00	181.44
	EKG	45.03	0.02	0.02	3.24	0.01	0.01	3.53	0.03
BPIC 19	OCEL	57.96	0.00	0.00	0.00	0.22	0.24	0.00	277.14
	EKG	62.48	0.02	0.02	2.87	0.02	0.02	7.23	0.03

*: Non-Reified

- **Finding 7.** Loading logs into EKG is a one-time process, similar to loading data into databases. Once the data is loaded, multiple analyses can be performed without reloading the data. However, with OCEL and PM4Py, the analyst needs to consider the loading time for every new analysis. Keeping large datasets in memory for extended periods may not be efficient, requiring careful consideration for each analysis conducted with OCEL and PM4Py when dealing with big data.

The columns labeled #Log, #Event, and #Entity* represent the query execution times for retrieving the number of logs, events, and non-derived entities in OCEL and EKG, respectively. The queries on OCEL are extremely fast, with execution times rounded to zero. On the other hand, the query execution time for EKG is also reasonable. In the worst case, it takes approximately 7 seconds for BPIC16, which is a substantial EKG. Similar observations can be made for #Class, and #observed. However, there is one exception for BPIC16 in the case of #corr. Retrieving the number of #corr elements takes around one minute due to the size of the EKG, and the additional filtering of #corr relations for non-reified entities significantly increases the query execution time.

Considering the execution query times, a significant difference is observed in calculating the number of directly-follows relations in the log file. These relations play a crucial role as fundamental information for many process mining algorithms. EKG outperforms OCEL in this aspect. This is because all directly-follows relations are materialized in EKG, whereas in OCEL, these relations are computed at runtime during processing. Based on this observation, we can conclude that:

- **Finding 8.** Discovering directly-follows relations on the entire log file is more efficient (performance-wise) in the EKG than OCEL. This is because the relations are materialized in EKG, whereas in OCEL, they are computed at runtime. The precalculation of directly-follows relations in the EKG enhances the efficiency and performance of process mining analyses.

Table 4. Execution time by filtering (in seconds)

Filters on:

		timestamp	Entity Type		Entity	
				timestamp		timestamp
BPIC 14	OCEL	0.73	0.10	0.13	0.10	0.13
	EKG	12.19 (0.16)	0.46 (0.45)	0.17 (0.07)	0.15 (0.07)	0.12 (0.08)
BPIC 15	OCEL	0.27	0.10	0.08	0.06	0.10
	EKG	3.97 (0.18)	0.07 (0.09)	0.09 (0.07)	0.12 (0.07)	0.09 (0.09)
BPIC 16	OCEL	8.59	1.85	1.75	1.77	1.78
	EKG	109.03 (0.16)	1.99 (1.28)	0.45 (0.07)	0.11 (0.07)	0.10 (0.08)
BPIC 17	OCEL	1.49	0.20	0.23	0.21	0.22
	EKG	15.89 (0.18)	0.53 (0.51)	0.20 (0.08)	0.12 (0.09)	0.09 (0.11)
BPIC 19	OCEL	1.26	0.15	0.16	0.14	0.18
	EKG	31.26 (0.16)	0.77 (0.79)	0.26 (0.08)	0.13 (0.07)	0.10 (0.10)

The numbers in parentheses are execution time after creating an index on the timestamp.

Applying process mining without appropriate filters can lead to unhelpful and complex process models, often called "spaghetti" models, which is considered a fundamental weakness in most early process mining algorithms [41]. Hence, filtering event logs and focusing on a subset of directly-follows relations is common practice. In our paper, we compare the performance of retrieving different subsets of directly-follows relations from EKG and OCEL on all listed BPICs. We employ common filtering operations such as i) dicing the log based on a timestamp, ii) slicing the log based on an entity type, iii) slicing and dicing the log based on a timestamp and an entity type, iv) slicing the log based on an entity, and v) slicing and dicing the log based on a timestamp and an entity. The performance of slicing and dicing based on timestamp can be improved in neo4j if an index is defined for the timestamp. However, this solution may not be applicable for all attribute types, e.g., if we slice or dice based on the similarity of a textual attribute. Thus, we will test both approaches here. For the timestamp, we follow a pessimistic approach by selecting a timestamp and an entity type that does not exist in the data, which mandates traversing the whole graph when it has no index. Table 4 shows the performance comparison result of retrieving directly-follows relations by applying the above filtering. The numbers in the parenthesis represent the total query time execution after creating an index on the timestamp.

From the third column, it is evident that the performance of retrieving directly-follows relations using PM4Py is significantly better compared to EKG when applying a filter solely based on the event's timestamp without the index. If the index can be defined, EKG has better performance. The main reason behind this difference is that applying such a filter in the EKG without the index necessitates traversing all nodes in the graph, resulting in a time-consuming operation. If the index can be used, EKG will not need to traverse the whole graph. On the other hand, PM4Py executes this operation by processing data in memory.

As observed from the remaining columns, the disparity mentioned above becomes less significant when filtering the log based on other log elements, such as entity type (referred to as object type in OCEL) and entities (referred to as objects). In summary, we can conclude with the following findings:

- **Finding 9.** Analyzing a process using an OCEL log is much more efficient than an EKG without a relevant index when filtering only by dicing the data. In case that index can be defined, EKG has better performance.
- **Finding 10.** There is no significant performance difference when analyzing a process using sliced data for an OCEL or EKG.

There are some limitations and threats to validity that shall be discussed as well. We shall emphasize that some findings can get affected by following alternative design choices as discussed in this section. Currently, we limit the comparison to taken design choices, but we will extend the comparison by considering alternative choices in the future. Also, we shall emphasize that our analysis is based on the current version of the OCEL standard. Our findings and other investigation can influence the extension of this standard in the future, which can relax or change some of the identified findings.

6   Concluding Remarks

This study conducted a comparative analysis of multi-dimensional process analysis using two contemporary conceptual models, namely Object-Centric Event Log (OCEL) and Event Knowledge Graph (EKG). A novel algorithm was introduced to transform EKG into the set of OCEL, which was implemented in Python as part of an open-source library. Five real log files represented in EKG were transformed into OCEL using this algorithm, and the resulting log files were utilized for the comparative analysis.

A total of ten findings emerged from this study, with several noteworthy ones highlighted here. The research shows that transforming EKG containing multiple log files into separate OCELs can cause a loss of inter-log relations between events. Moreover, the study demonstrated differences in analyzing directly-follows relations, attributing them to the materialization of these relations in the EKG while requiring runtime calculations for OCEL. Additionally, it was found that analyzing a process using an OCEL log exhibited higher efficiency compared to an EKG without any index when only dicing the data. Also, it shows how the possibility of applying an index can shift the advantage toward EKG.

As a future direction, it will be interesting to investigate how the OCEL standard can be extended to address some of the reported limitations. It is also interesting to evaluate the difference between these two approaches in calculating directly-follows relations in real use cases where we can have access to stakeholders to evaluate those relations with the help of process experts.

Acknowledgements. Khayatbashi's and Hartig's contributions to this work were funded by Vetenskapsrådet (the Swedish Research Council, project reg. no. 2019-05655).

References

1. The neo4j operations manual v5: Performance: Disks, ram and other tips. https://neo4j.com/docs/operations-manual/current/performance/disks-ram-and-other-tips. Accessed 05 Aug 2023
2. IEEE Task Force on Process Mining. XES Standard Definition (2013). http://www.xes-standard.org
3. Adams, J.N., Park, G., Levich, S., Schuster, D., van der Aalst, W.M.P.: A framework for extracting and encoding features from object-centric event data. In: Troya, J., Medjahed, B., Piattini, M., Yao, L., Fernandez, P., Ruiz-Cortes, A. (eds.) ICSOC 2022. LNCS, vol. 13740, pp. 36–53. Springer, Cham (2022)
4. Adams, J.N., Park, G., van der Aalst, W.M.P.: ocpa: a python library for object-centric process analysis. Softw. Impacts **14**, 100438 (2022)
5. Adams, J.N., Schuster, D., Schmitz, S., Schuh, G., van der Aalst, W.M.P.: Defining cases and variants for object-centric event data. In: 2022 4th International Conference on Process Mining (ICPM), pp. 128–135. IEEE (2022)
6. Adams, J.N., van der Aalst, W.M.P.: Precision and fitness in object-centric process mining. In: 2021 3rd International Conference on Process Mining (ICPM), pp. 128–135. IEEE (2021)
7. Adams, J.N., van der Aalst, W.M.P.: Oc π: object-centric process insights. In: Bernardinello, L., Petrucci, L. (eds.) PETRI NETS 2022. LNCS, vol. 13288, pp. 139–150. Springer, Cham (2022). https://doi.org/10.1007/978-3-031-06653-5_8
8. Adams, J.N., van Zelst, S.J., Rose, T., van der Aalst, W.M.P.: Explainable concept drift in process mining. Inf. Syst. **114**, 102177 (2023)
9. Angles, R., Arenas, M., Barceló, P., Hogan, A., Reutter, J., Vrgoč, D.: Foundations of modern query languages for graph databases. ACM Comput. Surv. (CSUR) **50**(5), 1–40 (2017)
10. Berti, A., Park, G., Rafiei, M., van der Aalst, W.M.P.: An event data extraction approach from SAP ERP for process mining. In: ICPM Workshops, vol. 433, pp. 255–267 (2021)
11. Berti, A., van der Aalst, W.M.P.: OC-PM: analyzing object-centric event logs and process models. Int. J. Softw. Tools Technol. Transfer **25**(1), 1–17 (2023)
12. Berti, A., van Zelst, S., Schuster, D.: PM4Py: a process mining library for Python. Softw. Impacts **17**, 100556 (2023)
13. Berti, A., Van Zelst, S.J., van der Aalst, W.M.P.: Process mining for python (pm4py): bridging the gap between process-and data science. arXiv preprint arXiv:1905.06169 (2019)
14. Esser, S., Fahland, D.: Multi-dimensional event data in graph databases. J. Data Semant. **10**(1–2), 109–141 (2021)
15. Fahland, D.: Event Graph of BPI Challenge 2019 (2021). https://data.4tu.nl/articles/dataset/Event_Graph_of_BPI_Challenge_2019/14169614/1
16. Fahland, D.: Process mining over multiple behavioral dimensions with event knowledge graphs. In: van der Aalst, W.M.P., Carmona, J. (eds.) Process Mining Handbook. LNCS, vol. 448, pp. 274–319. Springer, Cham (2022). https://doi.org/10.1007/978-3-031-08848-3_9
17. Fahland, D., Esser, S.: Event graph of BPI challenge 2014 (2021). https://data.4tu.nl/articles/dataset/Event_Graph_of_BPI_Challenge_2014/14169494/1
18. Fahland, D., Esser, S.: Event Graph of BPI Challenge 2015 (2021). https://data.4tu.nl/articles/dataset/Event_Graph_of_BPI_Challenge_2015/14169569/1
19. Fahland, D., Esser, S.: Event Graph of BPI Challenge 2016 (2021). https://data.4tu.nl/articles/dataset/Event_Graph_of_BPI_Challenge_2016/14164220
20. Fahland, D., Esser, S.: Event Graph of BPI Challenge 2017 (2021). https://data.4tu.nl/articles/dataset/Event_Graph_of_BPI_Challenge_2017/14169584/1

21. Ghahfarokhi, A.F., Park, G., Berti, A., van der Aalst, W.M.P.: OCEL: a standard for object-centric event logs. In: Bellatreche, L., et al. (eds.) ADBIS 2021. CCIS, vol. 1450, pp. 169–175. Springer, Cham (2021). https://doi.org/10.1007/978-3-030-85082-1_16

22. Gherissi, W., El Haddad, J., Grigori, D.: Object-centric predictive process monitoring. In: Troya, J., et al. (eds.) ICSOC 2022. LNCS, vol. 13821, pp. 27–39. Springer, Cham (2023)

23. Gunther, C.W., Verbeek, H.: Xes-standard definition (2014)

24. Hogan, A., et al.: Knowledge graphs. ACM Comput. Surv. (CSUR) **54**(4), 1–37 (2021)

25. Jalali, A.: Graph-based process mining. In: Leemans, S., Leopold, H. (eds.) ICPM 2020. LNBIP, vol. 406, pp. 273–285. Springer, Cham (2021). https://doi.org/10.1007/978-3-030-72693-5_21

26. Jalali, A.: Object type clustering using Markov directly-follow multigraph in object-centric process mining. IEEE Access **10**, 126569–126579 (2022)

27. Jalali, A.: dfgcompare: a library to support process variant analysis through Markov models. BMC Med. Inf. Decis. Making **21**(1), 1–13 (2021)

28. Khayatbashi, S., Hartig, O., Jalali, A.: BPI Challenge 2014 (OCEL) (2023). https://doi.org/10.4121/7d097cec-7304-4b85-9e78-a3ca1cc44c40

29. Khayatbashi, S., Hartig, O., Jalali, A.: BPI Challenge 2015 (OCEL) (2023). https://doi.org/10.4121/110d2fcf-b5e1-494a-a588-896a0a21e60a

30. Khayatbashi, S., Hartig, O., Jalali, A.: BPI Challenge 2016 (OCEL) (2023). https://doi.org/10.4121/95613fb2-29a5-49dc-b196-0948cf96cd7c

31. Khayatbashi, S., Hartig, O., Jalali, A.: BPI Challenge 2017 (OCEL) (2023). https://doi.org/10.4121/6889ca3f-97cf-459a-b630-3b0b0d8664b5

32. Khayatbashi, S., Hartig, O., Jalali, A.: BPI Challenge 2019 (OCEL) (2023). https://doi.org/10.4121/46a7e15b-10c7-4ab2-988d-ee67d8ea515a

33. Li, G., de Carvalho, R.M., van der Aalst, W.M.P.: Automatic discovery of object-centric behavioral constraint models. In: Abramowicz, W. (ed.) BIS 2017. LNBIP, vol. 288, pp. 43–58. Springer, Cham (2017). https://doi.org/10.1007/978-3-319-59336-4_4

34. Li, G., de Murillas, E.G.L., de Carvalho, R.M., van der Aalst, W.M.P.: Extracting object-centric event logs to support process mining on databases. In: Mendling, J., Mouratidis, H. (eds.) CAiSE 2018. LNBIP, vol. 317, pp. 182–199. Springer, Cham (2018). https://doi.org/10.1007/978-3-319-92901-9_16

35. Park, G., Adams, J.N., van der Aalst, W.M.P.: Opera: object-centric performance analysis. In: Ralyté, J., Chakravarthy, S., Mohania, M., Jeusfeld, M.A., Karlapalem, K. (eds.) ER 2022. LNCS, vol. 13607, pp. 281–292. Springer, Cham (2022). https://doi.org/10.1007/978-3-031-17995-2_20

36. Park, G., van der Aalst, W.M.P.: Monitoring constraints in business processes using object-centric constraint graphs. In: Montali, M., Senderovich, A., Weidlich, M. (eds.) ICPM 2022. LNBIP, vol. 468, pp. 479–492. Springer, Cham (2023). https://doi.org/10.1007/978-3-031-27815-0_35

37. Rebmann, A., Rehse, J.R., van der Aa, H.: Uncovering object-centric data in classical event logs for the automated transformation from XES to OCEL. In: Di Ciccio, C., Dijkman, R., del Río Ortega, A., Rinderle-Ma, S. (eds.) BPM 2022. LNCS, vol. 13420, pp. 379–396. Springer, Cham (2022). https://doi.org/10.1007/978-3-031-16103-2_25

38. van der Aalst, W.M.P.: Process Mining: Data Science in Action, vol. 2. Springer, Heidelberg (2016)

39. van der Aalst, W.M.P.: Object-centric process mining: dealing with divergence and convergence in event data. In: Ölveczky, P.C., Salaün, G. (eds.) SEFM 2019. LNCS, vol. 11724, pp. 3–25. Springer, Cham (2019). https://doi.org/10.1007/978-3-030-30446-1_1

40. van der Aalst, W.M.P., Berti, A.: Discovering object-centric petri nets. Fundamenta informaticae **175**(1–4), 1–40 (2020)

41. van der Aalst, W.M.P., Gunther, C.W.: Finding structure in unstructured processes: The case for process mining. In: Seventh International Conference on Application of Concurrency to System Design (ACSD 2007), pp. 3–12. IEEE (2007)
42. Xiong, J., Xiao, G., Kalayci, T.E., Montali, M., Gu, Z., Calvanese, D.: A virtual knowledge graph based approach for object-centric event logs extraction. In: Montali, M., Senderovich, A., Weidlich, M. (eds.) ICPM 2022. LNBIP, vol. 468, pp. 466–478. Springer, Cham (2023). https://doi.org/10.1007/978-3-031-27815-0_34

Ontology-Based Abstraction of Bot Models in Robotic Process Automation

Maximilian Völker$^{(\boxtimes)}$ and Mathias Weske

Hasso Plattner Institute, University of Potsdam, Potsdam, Germany
{maximilian.voelker,mathias.weske}@hpi.de

Abstract. Robotic Process Automation is a technology for lightweight task automation that empowers business users to build their own software bots by combining predefined operations in a graphical user interface. However, due to the detailed nature of these operations, which are comparable to single code instructions, the graphical models become complex and hard to understand. This complicates the sharing, discussion, and maintenance of these software bots. At the same time, RPA projects typically require extensive documentation of the process and its automation aspects that must be kept in sync during the maintenance phase. This paper presents a foundation for bot model abstraction in RPA that leverages semantic information. It proposes an abstraction method to generate smaller but still expressive bot models in an automated fashion. These abstract bot models can be used for documentation purposes and to foster process understanding, as they convey key activities while hiding operational details that are not relevant to perceiving the overall automation goal.

Keywords: Robotic Process Automation · Model Abstraction · Ontology

1 Introduction

Despite recent advancements in computer technology, repetitive and tedious tasks are still the order of the day for many employees. These tasks are not only costly due to the many working hours spent, they also increase the risk of silently introducing errors by slips. Robotic Process Automation (RPA) enables companies and employees to automate such computer-based tasks by employing software robots: scripts that can operate on user interfaces but that can also make use of programming interfaces, e.g., to access databases directly [9,10,25].

As opposed to traditional process automation, often considered costly and laborious, RPA is a rather lightweight automation technique with its unintrusive approach based on user interfaces [11]. Additionally, common tools for RPA focus on business users and thus offer no-code or low-code solutions for building RPA bots [2]. Their graphical interfaces allow users to select and connect predefined operations, such as opening a program or entering text in an input field, resulting in an automation workflow displayed in process model-like notations [4,9,11].

© The Author(s), under exclusive license to Springer Nature Switzerland AG 2023
J. P. A. Almeida et al. (Eds.): ER 2023, LNCS 14320, pp. 239–256, 2023.
https://doi.org/10.1007/978-3-031-47262-6_13

While such graphical representations enable business users to create RPA bots, they entail a major drawback: The atomic level of the individual operations quickly results in large graphical models. Whereas in business processes the level of abstraction and, to this extent, the complexity of the model can be chosen according to the model's purpose and will most likely hide complexity, the individual nodes in RPA bot models represent specific work instructions, e.g., the assignment of a value to a variable. Consequently, even smaller use cases can result in large, confusing models. While they serve the purpose of automation, they are hard to comprehend or reason about, hindering maintenance and communication tasks at later stages.

Similar to business process models, some RPA tools offer sub-process-like constructs to better structure the model. However, just as with process models, such representations are highly dependent on the modeler, who must manually specify the desired levels of abstraction that are then "cast" into the model. Furthermore, it does not help with already existing models or when using an RPA software that does not support such constructs.

This paper addresses the challenge of extensive RPA bot models by proposing an abstraction technique that automatically generates reduced and condensed models that can be used for documentation and communication purposes. Unlike traditional abstraction techniques, it does not rely on syntactic features, but rather considers the semantics of the model elements grounded on the ontology of RPA operations. With that, the goal is to create an abstract model that conveys the overall purpose and main tasks of a bot model. Additionally, a slider-based solution is devised that allows the user to control the level of abstraction.

The importance of model abstraction in RPA is motivated in Sect. 2. Subsequently, Sect. 3 presents related work on business process model abstraction and introduces RPA and the ontology of RPA operations in more detail. Section 4 elaborates on the devised abstraction technique for RPA bot models, which is extended in Sect. 5 to allow different levels of abstraction. A prototypical implementation of the approach, its application to an example, and current limitations are discussed in Sect. 6, before the paper is concluded in Sect. 7.

2   Motivating Example

During execution, RPA bots follow a sequence of work instructions that was previously modeled by a user. The available "building blocks" are predefined by the respective RPA tool provider [9] and are rather atomic operations, such as clicking a button or inserting a string into a text field [21]. Consequently, even simpler tasks may require numerous instructions. Since most RPA tools provide a graphical way to define these workflows, the created models can become accordingly large. This section illustrates this issue with an example.

In the scenario, a common task suitable for RPA should be carried out. Orders are received as PDF files attached to e-mails, and need to be populated to multiple systems. Once the relevant data has been extracted from the PDF file, it must first be entered into the company's browser-based order management

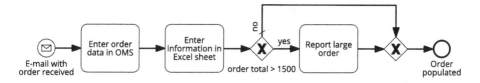

Fig. 1. High-level process model capturing the scenario

system (OMS), which returns an identifier for the order. Subsequently, some information and the identifier need to be appended to a specific spreadsheet used for reporting. Lastly, if the order surpasses a certain threshold, an e-mail needs to be generated. Figure 1 shows a business process model with the described steps.

While this scenario is not overly complex, its realization using RPA requires certain intermediate steps. For example, the text extracted from the PDF file needs to be analyzed, and the results must be cached locally, such as the address or the list of order items. The web-based OMS may require a login, and the bot occasionally needs to wait until certain UI elements are loaded. In Fig. 2, a possible sequence of RPA operations is presented, demonstrating the complexity. While all the steps shown are necessary to execute the bot properly, the model's complexity impedes communication and maintenance[1].

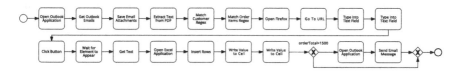

Fig. 2. RPA bot model for the described scenario (intentionally not readable)

The goal of this work is to derive from an inherently detailed bot model an abstract, yet meaningful, business process-like model, similar to the one shown in Fig. 1. That is, the abstract representation should convey the overall purpose and main functionality of the bot while hiding specific and intermediate steps. This is also in line with the main purpose of abstraction for business process models, providing a quick overview, as reported by Smirnov et al. [18]. In summary, the developed approach should address the following requirements:

R1 Reduce the size of the model.
R2 Preserve information that is vital to understand the bot's purpose.
R3 The level of abstraction should be adjustable by the user.

---

[1] Due to the lack of a modeling standard in RPA [22], we use BPMN for visualization.
   A high-resolution version can be found here: https://github.com/bptlab/onto-rpa-platform/raw/main/components/abstraction/figures/BotModelExample.svg.

R3 recognizes that there will not be a single level of abstraction that fits all needs, e.g., a coarse abstraction may be sufficient for a quick overview, while a more detailed version may be required for documentation and discussion.

3   Related Work and Preliminaries

To the best of the authors' knowledge, the topic of automated abstraction of RPA bot models has not been addressed in research so far. However, the related discipline of business process management has developed several approaches to business process model abstraction (BPMA), some of which are summarized in this section together with ontology-based approaches to model abstraction. This is followed by a brief introduction to Robotic Process Automation in general and the ontology of RPA operations in particular. In addition, two general abstraction methods used in the paper are outlined.

3.1   Business Process Model Abstraction

Business process models define a workflow consisting of activities which outline the process' steps [24], like in Fig. 1. Unlike RPA, there are no predefined activities to choose from (cf. Sect. 2) due to the complexity and diversity of the business domains. Instead, the purpose of an activity is defined by a natural language label, often without directly linking structured information [16].

Consequently, many abstraction approaches focus only on structural features of the process model, like aggregating activities of "single entry single exit" (SESE) fragments in the model [13] or applying abstraction techniques only to manually selected parts of the model to create personalized views on the process model [3]. In [19], the authors propose an abstraction approach that not only considers activities for abstraction, but that also handles aspects like roles, data objects, and messages based on a set of abstraction rules they provide.

Other approaches make use of external data not included in the model, such as execution times or costs of certain model parts [12]. Based on this information, Polyvyanyy et al. [12] propose the use of a slider that allows users to set a custom threshold for those values and to abstract model elements with a lower value.

Another abstraction approach advises the use of a vector space model to cluster activities of the process model regarding their similarity with respect to different information available in the model, such as data objects, IT systems, or roles [17]. Adding to this approach, Wang et al. [23] recently proposed a semi-supervised clustering approach that not only considers the semantic similarity, but also takes the consistency of the control flow more into account.

Theoretically, these abstraction techniques developed for business process models could be applied to RPA bot models, as they exhibit similar syntactical features and can be regarded as (part of) a business process model [7]. However, RPA with its limited set of possible operations, captured by the ontology of RPA operations presented below, offers semantic information about each task that could be exploited for abstraction, which shall be the focus of this paper.

3.2   Ontology-Based Abstraction

The lack of structured semantic information in common models hampers the development of an abstraction technique that goes beyond purely syntactical properties of the model [8]. This also applies to business process models, which have no semantic information embedded by default, but rely on text-based labels to convey their meaning, as noted above. However, since using only structural information is not always sensible, as it likely combines model parts that are semantically unrelated [16], Smirnov et al. [16] propose a semi-automated approach for BPMA that is based on ontological knowledge, more specifically, that utilizes a part-of relation defined between process activities. Groups of activities in the model that are strongly related based on this relation can be aggregated and replaced by their lowest common ancestor in the relation. As the approach requires the existence of such an ontology of the specific business environment of the process, it is not easily applicable to every business process model.

Apart from process models, there also are ontology-based abstraction techniques that aim to reduce the complexity of conceptual domain models. For example, Guizzardi et al. [8] present a rule-based abstraction approach for conceptual models that are created using the ontology-based modeling language OntoUML and which consequently can make use of semantic information. The provided rules exploit the ontological underpinning and modify the graph of the class diagram-like model to create a more abstract version of the model, for example, to abstract from classes that describe relations. Related to the idea of generating views on process models as described above, Figueiredo et al. [6] define an abstraction approach that extracts views from OntoUML models based on the ontology-induced semantics to reduce the complexity.

3.3   The Ontology of RPA Operations

Companies resort to Robotic Process Automation (RPA) for a fast and, compared to traditional approaches, cheap process automation [11]. By combining predefined automation operations, users can define automation routines that can operate on the user interface, imitating the user's behavior, and also access, for example, web services and databases [1,9].

Compared to business processes with their plenitude of application domains and user-defined activities, workflows in robotic process automation are restricted to the predefined set of RPA operations provided by the respective RPA tool vendor [9,21]. Völker and Weske [21] introduced the *ontology of RPA operations (ORPAO)*, that provides a vendor-agnostic view on *RPA operations* and relates them to the *software* and the *data* that can be automated. It defines a taxonomy (type-of relationship) of operations that classifies the available operations regarding their purpose, differentiating three main types of operations: `AutomationOperations` that actually operate on the computer, such as accessing data, performing mouse clicks, or starting software; `InternalOperations` that are used for local data storage and checks; and `ControlFlowOperations`, such as decisions that affect the execution [21]. Instances of the operations-taxonomy,

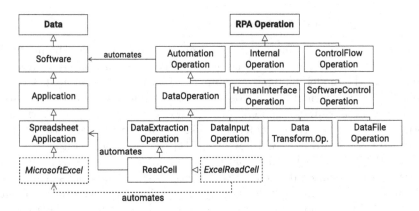

Fig. 3. Excerpt of the operations-taxonomy in the ontology of RPA operations, showing its main concepts and the branch for the *ExcelReadCell* operation with its connection to the concept of `Software` in the ORPAO. Adapted from [21].

such as *ExcelReadCell*, represent a specific operation that is available for building an RPA bot [21]. Traversing the taxonomy, partly depicted in Fig. 3, reveals that *ExcelReadCell* belongs to the concept (class) `ReadCell`, which in turn is a `DataExtractionOperation`, and so on. Figure 3 also depicts the `automates` relation, that connects `AutomationOperations` and `Software`.

In this paper, we refer to the operations-taxonomy as a rooted tree T_O with `RPAOperation` as its root r_O. Let o be an element (node) in T_O, then we define $type : T_O \rightarrow T_O \cup \{\perp\}$ as the function that returns for each element in the taxonomy its parent element and undefined ($\perp$) for $type(r_O)$. For example, $type(\text{ExcelReadCell}) = \text{ReadCell}$. Furthermore, we denote the set of all specific operations (instances in the taxonomy) as $\mathcal{O}$, which are the leafs in T_O. Likewise, we introduce $\mathcal{S}$ as the set of all specific software programs in the ORPAO, including, for example, *MicrosoftExcel*.

3.4 Abstraction Methods

While the different abstraction approaches address different goals and consider different information for abstraction, they usually rely on the same two methods on *how* to abstract elements in the model, i.e., how the model itself is pruned: *elimination* and *aggregation* [3,5,14,15,18,19]. Likewise, the abstraction approach presented in this paper makes use of these two methods, which is why they and their effects on process models are introduced in more detail.

Dimensions of Abstraction. Smirnov et al. [18] characterize the effects of elimination and aggregation operations on the model and highlight two dimensions to consider: *granularity* and *coverage*. The degree of granularity describes how detailed the model's activities are. At a high level of granularity, the model consists of many very detailed activities, whereas at lower levels, it consists of only a few activities that outline the process. Coverage in turn considers the

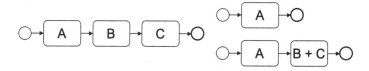

Fig. 4. Application of the abstraction methods *elimination* (top right) and *aggregation* (bottom right) to B and C.

amount of information included in the model. A high degree of coverage means that most of the available information is represented, while a lower level results in a loss of information.

Elimination. Elimination removes elements from the model and thus decreases its complexity. The level of coverage is reduced because the information carried by the eliminated elements is no longer included and cannot be recovered from the abstract model. Figure 4 illustrates the effect with a simple example. Assuming activities B and C are supposed to be eliminated from the original model at the left, the resulting abstracted model is depicted at the top right. Any information about the eliminated activities is lost. The granularity remains unchanged, as the level of detail (of the remaining activities) is unaffected.

Aggregation. The goal of aggregation is to combine a number of connected elements of the original model and represent them as a new, single element in the abstract model. The new element describes the subsumed parts in more general, resulting in a lower degree of granularity. However, by reducing the granularity, some detailed information may also be lost, slightly decreasing the coverage of the model. Aggregating activities B and C in the example in Fig. 4 results in the abstract model shown at the bottom right. Instead of two activities, a new activity representing both is incorporated.

4 Generating Abstract RPA Bot Models

With the goal of creating an abstract bot model that conveys the bot's key functionality as motivated in Sect. 2, this section discusses the application of the two abstraction methods, elimination and aggregation, in the context of RPA. By leveraging ontological knowledge, the presented abstraction approach focuses on the content of the model instead of syntactic features, with the aim of providing a more meaningful abstraction.

Similar to business processes, RPA bots follow a well-defined sequence of operations to achieve their automation goal [21]. This order is, as with business processes, typically defined graphically using a notation based on workflow graphs.

In previous work, we introduced the notion of a conceptual RPA bot as "a vendor-independent representation of an RPA bot that is based on the concepts of the ontology of RPA operations" [22]. Along this line, we introduce the concept of a *conceptual RPA bot model* in Definition 1 as a workflow graph whose nodes are connected to instances in the ontology of RPA operations and thus yields semantic information for each of its nodes.

Definition 1 (Conceptual RPA Bot Model). A conceptual RPA bot model B is a tuple $(N, F, concept)$, where

- N is a finite and nonempty set of nodes in the model;
- $F \subseteq N \times N$ is the flow relation between operations, so that (N, F) is a weakly connected graph; and
- $concept : N \to \mathcal{O}$ maps each node in the model to the corresponding individual in the operations-taxonomy T_O, part of the ORPAO.

Existing, vendor-specific RPA bot models can be linked to the ontology using the knowledge base of RPA operations which connects implementations of operations by the various RPA vendors to their conceptual counterparts in the ontology, thus enabling an automated transformation to conceptual RPA bot models that can also be applied to text-based RPA bot models [21, 22].

The central idea of the abstraction approach detailed in this section is built on two pillars described in Sect. 4.1. First, it requires a mapping that assigns (classes of) RPA operations in the ontology an abstraction method to apply. Second, the bot model is analyzed to determine the execution context of each node in the model, which is used to constrain and scope aggregation operations during the abstraction. Both, the general mapping and the model-specific context analysis, are prerequisites for performing the abstraction as described in Sect. 4.2.

4.1   Prerequisites and Preparation of the Abstraction

To be able to perform the abstraction, we introduce two new concepts: the abstraction mapping and the operation context analysis. While the abstraction mapping is independent of bot models, the automatic context analysis must be performed on the model prior to abstraction.

Abstraction Mapping. The abstraction mapping determines how specific operations should be treated during abstraction based on their importance regarding the abstraction goal of creating a smaller model for communication purposes (cf. Sect. 2). As defined in Definition 2, (classes of) operations in the operations-taxonomy can be assigned one of the abstraction methods, *elimination* or *aggregation*.

Definition 2 (Abstraction Method Mapping). Let T_O be the taxonomy of operations in the ontology of RPA operations as introduced in Sect. 3.3. α is a partial mapping that assigns elements in the taxonomy an abstraction method:

$$\alpha : T_O \rightharpoonup \{elimination, aggregation\}$$

Based on the partial mapping, the abstraction method that should be applied to any element $o \in T_O$ can be determined as follows:

$$abs(o) = \begin{cases} \alpha(o) & \text{if } \alpha(o) \text{ is defined} \\ abs(type(o)) & \text{elseif } type(o) \neq \bot \\ \bot & \text{else} \end{cases}$$

As each node n in a conceptual bot model is linked to the ontology via the model's *concept* function, the appropriate abstraction method to apply can be retrieved using $abs(concept(n))$. According to the definition of $abs(o)$, the function either returns the abstraction method directly assigned to o (case 1) or the method of the nearest ancestor of o in T_O that has a method assigned by applying the function recursively to the parent in T_O (case 2). Otherwise, $abs(o)$ will return $\bot$ to indicate that o and none of its ancestors are assigned an abstraction method and thus o is not to be abstracted (case 3). Inheriting the abstraction method (case 2) allows assigning a method to classes of operations conveniently instead of having to specify a method for each operation in $\mathcal{O}$. At the same time, it is still possible to overwrite the inherited method by assigning it directly (case 1).

For the mapping, we differentiate operations that (a) are essential for understanding the bot's purpose and hence should not be affected by the abstraction, (b) convey important information and whose semantics should therefore be preserved as well as possible (both relate to **R2**), and (c) operations that do not contribute to understanding and thus can be concealed in the abstract model (**R1**). Operations of type (a) are not assigned a method and consequently will not be modified by the abstraction. This applies, for example, to `ControlFlowOperations`, which are essential to understand the execution logic.

Operations of type (b) are, in their sum, important for the understanding and are therefore assigned *aggregation*, i.e., they can be merged and represented at a higher level of abstraction, but should not be removed (**R2**). This applies primarily to `DataOperations`, since data processing is the essence of RPA. In addition, certain interactions with the UI may be relevant to understanding the purpose of the bot. In the example, the operations performed in the OMS are not that important individually, but taken together they convey that data is being entered into this system.

Operations of type (c) are assigned *elimination*, reducing the size of the model (**R1**) and focussing the attention to more important parts. Regarding the example, this applies, among others, to the operations concerning the internal data structure of the bot, such as matching a regular expression. While it is essential for the bot to be functional, it is not necessary for grasping its purpose, and is therefore also not included in the high-level process model presented in the motivation (Fig. 1). Other examples include operations that resize windows, wait for UI elements to appear, or navigating in the UI to a specific point.

In this paper, we establish the theoretical foundation for the abstraction approach, but do not elaborate on a specific mapping. The development of such a mapping is beyond the scope of this paper and should be done in collaboration with domain experts (cf. Sect. 6.3).

Operation Context Analysis. Like in the motivating example, an RPA bot will most likely automate different software and access various data during its execution as defined in the bot model. Thus, each of its nodes is performed in a specific *context*, defined in Definition 3. It comprises the specific application on which the operation will be executed, and, if applicable, the data on which the operation is being performed. For example, after opening the browser once (application context), the bot navigates to and operates on different websites (data context) within this browser instance.

Definition 3 (Operation Context). Let $B = (N, F, concept)$ be a conceptual bot model. The contexts of B, C_B, is a tuple $(c_{software}, c_{data})$, where:

- $c_{software} : N \rightharpoonup S$ where S are the specific software programs (instances) in the ORPAO, and
- $c_{data} : N \rightharpoonup D$ where D is the set of strings describing all possible data contexts, such as file names or URLs.

As some nodes and their respective operations are not executed in a specific context, such as `InternalOperations` that have no effect outside the bot, the context is defined as a partial mapping.

To be able to assign the correct context to nodes in the model, it needs to be analyzed for *context switches*, i.e., points where the active software or data changes during the bot's execution. As there should be no external influence on the context (only the bot operates the computer), context switches can be determined by analyzing the operations linked in the bot model.

For this, we differentiate between two types of operations, application-specific and generic operations. For application-specific operations, i.e., operations that are tailored to a certain application, the software context can be directly derived from their *automates* relation to a software in the ontology (cf. Sect. 3.3). In contrast, generic operations can be applied to various applications, such as *Get-Text*. Therefore, we also explicitly analyze the model for preceding operations that change the active application to determine their software context, such as `SoftwareControlOperations`. The software context can either be derived by their *automates* relation as well, or, in the case of a generic `SoftwareControl-Operation`, by analyzing the operation's configuration. Generic operations are then assigned to the context previously started by such an operation.

For the data context, we similarly analyze for operations that change the data context, such as operations that open a file. As the data context is very specific to each RPA bot, e.g., a URL or file path, the data context needs to be derived from the specific configurations of the operations, i.e., the configured inputs and outputs. If this is not possible, a unique string can be used to identify a new data context and thus a context switch.

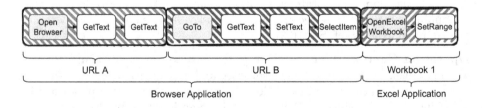

Fig. 5. Exemplary bot model sequence with annotated context

In Fig. 5, an excerpt of a bot model is shown, highlighting the different contexts in which operations are executed. The *OpenBrowser* operation causes a context switch to the browser application and a specific configured URL, on which the subsequent two operations are performed. *GoTo* is a browser-specific operation and navigates to a new URL, i.e., the data context is changed. Finally, *OpenExcelWorkbook* causes another context switch.

4.2   Performing the Abstraction

With the abstraction mapping and the results of the context analysis at hand, the given (conceptual) bot model B can be abstracted by applying first elimination operations and then aggregation operations as described below.

In the **elimination** step, all nodes $n_e \in N$ in the model B that reference an operation that should be eliminated according to the abstraction method mapping, i.e., $abs(concept(n_e)) = elimination$, are removed from the set of nodes N. At the same time, the flow relation F needs to be adjusted so that the predecessor and successor of n_e are now directly connected, thus omitting n_e. As `ControlFlowOperations` are neither considered for elimination nor aggregation, n_e cannot have multiple incoming or outgoing control flow arcs.

Compared to elimination, which only removes individual nodes, **aggregation** requires determining suitable groups of nodes in the model.

Techniques for BPMA typically aggregate regions or fragments (cf. Sect. 3.1), since the models' complexity often stems from the involvement of multiple roles, nested choices, and parallel execution, in addition to the overall intricacy of the processes themselves. RPA processes, in turn, rarely exhibit parallel behavior, do not have the concept of roles, and also do not feature too many choices, as the behavior to automate would become too complex to handle and maintain. Consequently, we focus only on the abstraction of sequences of nodes in this work (cf. Sect. 6.3). This focus also ensures that ordering constraints are preserved, as parallel or exclusive operations will not be aggregated.

An aggregation group $A \subseteq N$ consists of the nodes that form a (maximal) sequence of nodes in the model B according to its flow relation F, where for all nodes $n_{a1}, n_{a2} \in A$ the following constraints hold.

Constraint 1 $abs(concept(n_{a1})) = abs(concept(n_{a2})) = aggregation$
Constraint 2 $c_{software}(n_{a1}) = c_{software}(n_{a2})$
Constraint 3 $c_{data}(n_{a1}) = c_{data}(n_{a2})$

Accordingly, each sequence of maximal length of nodes in the model that reference an operation intended for aggregation and that are performed in the same software context and the same data context forms an aggregation group. Thus, since only nodes in the same context are considered together, the aggregation is context-preserving.

The nodes of an aggregation group A will then be replaced by a common abstract node n_A in the model. To maintain the connection to the ontology and thus retain semantic information, n_A is linked to the lowest common ancestor of

Fig. 6. Example sequence after applying elimination and aggregation

the operations referenced by the abstracted nodes in the operations-taxonomy T_O. By this, n_A refers to the class of operations that describes the aggregated operations as specific as possible.

Considering the example in Fig. 5 again, after performing the elimination on the nodes marked gray and the aggregation step for each context present, three abstract activities remain, as shown in Fig. 6.

4.3 Semantic Label Generation

Structural abstraction approaches often have problems providing meaningful labels for aggregated activities [18]. Here, the semantic underpinning of the abstract bot model can facilitate the automatic generation of labels.

To generate labels, the approach makes use of the ontology connection as well as the context. It is composed of the brief natural language description of the class in the ORPAO, the name of the software program of the context ($c_{software}$), and the string describing the data context (c_{data}).

In the example (Fig. 5), the two operations found in the first context are the same (*GetText*). Thus, this operation name can be used to describe the abstracted operations as well. The second context comprises three different operations, their lowest common ancestor in the taxonomy being `DataOperation`, as we observe both, reading and writing operations. Instead of the class name, its description in the ontology, "Handle Data", is used for the label. The third context consists of only one operation that can be used directly again for the description. The labels are then enriched with the respective context information, i.e., in which application and on which data they are performed, as shown in Fig. 6.

In sum, this allows the reader of the abstract bot model to comprehend which applications are being automated and what types of operations are being performed on them.

5 Slider-Driven Abstraction

The ontology-based abstraction technique introduced in the previous section already satisfies **R1** and **R2** by removing unimportant operations and grouping detailed work instructions to more high-level tasks. But it only provides a single level of abstraction, which is potentially too fine or too coarse for certain use cases. Therefore, we introduce an extension to this technique which allows the user to adjust the degree of abstraction using a "slider approach" and that addresses **R3**.

To match the two different employed abstraction methods, elimination and aggregation, this dynamic approach utilizes two sliders. One for determining the level of coverage, and a second for adjusting the granularity.

5.1   Coverage Slider

The *coverage slider* gives the user control over how much information should be removed from the model, i.e., how extensive operations should be eliminated, based on weights. To enable an incremental elimination, an element o in the operations-taxonomy T_O can be assigned not only the abstraction method but, if $abs(o) = elimination$, also a relevance weight w. Similar to abs, the weight of an element $o \in T_O$, $w_{elim}(o)$, is either directly annotated at the element or inherited from the closest ancestor in the operations-taxonomy that features such a value.

Using the slider, the user can now set a minimum weight w_{min}. Nodes referencing operations o with $abs(o) = elimination$ and $w_{elim}(o) < w_{min}$ are eliminated in the abstract model.

This enables a step-wise reduction of the model and allows differentiating the various concepts that are marked for elimination, but are not necessarily of the same importance. For example, internal operations that are used to set up and check the bot's internal data structure could now be removed first, as they might be considered less relevant than other types of operations.

5.2   Granularity Slider

The aggregation technique described in the previous section aggregates nodes that occur in the same context. In Fig. 5, for example, the combination of input and extraction operations results in a very abstract element, which might be too coarse in some cases.

The *granularity slider* controls the extent of the aggregation by setting a maximum depth d in the operations-taxonomy to which nodes will be aggregated. Let $concept_d(n)$ be the function that returns for a node n the ancestor of $concept(n)$ in T_O at the depth d. With the granularity slider, an additional constraint for determining the aggregation groups at a slider value d is added to the constraints presented for aggregation in Sect. 4.2:

Constraint 4 $concept_d(n_{a1}) = concept_d(n_{a2})$, i.e., nodes refer to the same operation (type) at currently set taxonomy depth d

That is, for each operation referenced in the model, its ancestor at the currently set depth in the taxonomy is determined. Sequential nodes intended for aggregation that are performed in the same context and that have the same ancestor at that depth are aggregated and replaced with that ancestor. The aggregation groups grow larger with each step in the slider as the considered depth in T_O decreases, elements become more abstract and cover more descendants.

At the very first, the operations-taxonomy is considered to full extent, and the aggregation is performed as prescribed by the constraints, i.e., only for the nodes referring to the very same operations intended for abstraction. Applied to the model in Fig. 5, this results in model 1 depicted in Fig. 7 where only the two *GetText* operations in the first context are aggregated (elimination is applied as well, concealing the operations marked in gray).

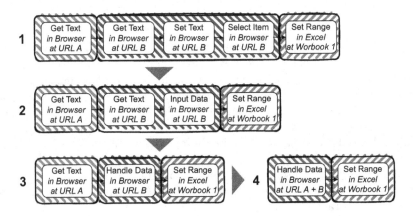

Fig. 7. Different levels of aggregation applied to the example in Fig. 5

For each slider step hereinafter, the depth of the operations-taxonomy to which the operations are abstracted is reduced stepwise and the aggregation groups determined using the given constraints. To ensure that each slider step entails a change, the slider range is set to the depth of the operations-taxonomy pruned to the branches with operations that are actually referenced in the model.

In Fig. 7, this causes *SetText* and *SelectItem* to be combined next, as both are of the type `DataInputOperation` (model 2). At the next level in the taxonomy, all three operations in the original model are `DataOperations` and, consequently, they are aggregated with the next slider step. The resulting model 3 corresponds to the abstracted model of the static approach in Fig. 6.

As soon as no further aggregation is possible, as in model 3, the next slider step will lift constraint 3, i.e., only the software context is considered and operations can be aggregated across different data contexts (see model 4). While relaxing constraint 3 enables an even more compact abstract model, aggregating data contexts may result in the loss of the corresponding information.

The label for the nodes is created similarly to the previous approach. As each links to a concept, its brief description is used for label generation, along with the respective context information, as described in Sect. 4.3.

Building on the abstraction approach presented in the previous section, the slider extension provides a considerably more flexible solution that can generate both less and more abstract models, depending on the current needs of the user and thus satisfying **R3**.

6   Evaluation

To demonstrate the applicability and usefulness of the abstraction approach, we provide a prototypical implementation of the slider approach presented in Sect. 5 and report on the application of the abstraction to the motivating example. Additionally, we briefly discuss current limitations of the presented approach.

Fig. 8. Application of abstraction method to motivating example

6.1 Prototype

The described abstraction technique has been implemented as an open-source prototype[2], extending the conceptual RPA bot modeler described in [22]. The prototype features two interactive sliders, one for the elimination threshold and one for the aggregation level, as introduced in Sect. 5, and displays the corresponding abstracted bot model to the user. Internally, the conceptual bot model is translated into a process tree [20] first, which then undergoes the context analysis (cf. Sect. 4.1). The result is an enriched version of the process tree, whose leafs, i.e., the operations, are annotated with the respective application and data context, if applicable. After the elimination candidates are determined, the process tree is pruned and all sequences of operations are analyzed to determine the aggregation groups. Based on the list of candidates for elimination and aggregation, specific model transformations are derived and applied to the bot model, more specifically which operations to remove and which to rename, since aggregation is performed by renaming the first operation of the aggregation group using the abstract label and removing the other operations from the group.

6.2 Application to Motivating Example

Figure 8 shows the bot model of the motivating example introduced in Sect. 2, abstracted using the slider approach. Here, the coverage slider was set high to remove many not-so-relevant operations, and the granularity slider was configured to match the level of abstraction of step 2 in Fig. 7, e.g., `DataOperations` may be aggregated up to the main data classes that differentiate between input and extraction of data, and the data context is preserved. Overall, it provides an overview of what is happening in each application, while reducing the number of elements from 20 to 6 (also counting *if*, as it is a control-flow operation [22]).

6.3 Current Limitations

This work provides a first step towards a more complex framework for abstraction of RPA bot models. In the following, some current assumptions for simplification made by the presented approach and points for improvement that should be addressed in the future are discussed.

First, this work focuses on linear RPA workflows and does not consider parallel and exclusive behavior. While not too common, especially parallel behavior,

---

[2] https://github.com/bptlab/onto-rpa-platform/tree/main/components/abstraction.

it poses interesting challenges and opportunities to further improve the abstraction. For one, abstracted models could contain empty branches in case every node on them is eliminated, which should be removed from the model in a post-processing step. In addition, the relation between the branches could be analyzed. For example, adjacent branches could involve different types of operations in the same context (e.g., different ways to achieve the same based on certain conditions) or the same operations in slightly different contexts (e.g., crawling different documents simultaneously), opening up new opportunities for aggregation.

Another aspect is the detection of patterns that can be observed in RPA bot models, such as alternating operations or contexts. For example, alternating read and write operations in two contexts implementing a data transfer would currently not be abstracted at all. They could be replaced by a node representing the data transfer between the two contexts, or by a loop construct.

Regarding the context analysis, implicit context switches are currently not considered. For example, the software context could also be changed by starting a software using a sequence of UI commands, or the data context could be affected by clicking a hyperlink or a button in a browser. Detecting such sequences could be incorporated in the future to improve the context analysis.

Also, the paper does not provide a specific abstraction method mapping. While it is intended as a flexible solution that can be adapted to specific needs, expert interviews and user studies could yield a reasonable basis to start with.

7   Conclusion

Generating abstract views on process models is a crucial step to improve understanding and to get a quick overview of the process goal without having to work through all the details. In this paper, we motivated and established the foundations for the abstraction of RPA bot models that leverage contextual and semantic information provided by the ontology of RPA operations. In addition, we contributed a prototype that realizes the described abstraction approach.

Some RPA tools offer constructs similar to sub-processes in BPMN to structure the bot process. Our approach, however, is vendor-independent, can be applied to existing bot models, and the level of abstraction can be dynamically adjusted to the current needs thanks to the slider extension.

In the future, it is conceivable to extend the abstraction approach by more facets, such as highlighting important areas or, making more use of the ontology, focusing on specific applications or the flow of data. Other ideas for future work include considering control-flow constructs besides sequences, such as decisions or loops. In addition, certain RPA-specific patterns of operations could be explored and addressed in the abstraction, such as interleaving read and write operations. The generation of labels that are more model-specific than the solution in this paper should also be further investigated, as they convey the semantic information to the reader. Finally, the abstraction approach and different mappings should be evaluated in a user study to analyze the perceived usefulness and quality of the abstraction.

References

1. van der Aalst, W.M.P., Bichler, M., Heinzl, A.: Robotic process automation. Bus. Inf. Syst. Eng. **60**(4), 269–272 (2018). https://doi.org/10.1007/s12599-018-0542-4

2. Aguirre, S., Rodriguez, A.: Automation of a business process using robotic process automation (RPA): a case study. In: Figueroa-García, J.C., López-Santana, E.R., Villa-Ramírez, J.L., Ferro-Escobar, R. (eds.) WEA 2017. CCIS, vol. 742, pp. 65–71. Springer, Cham (2017). https://doi.org/10.1007/978-3-319-66963-2_7

3. Bobrik, R., Reichert, M., Bauer, T.: View-based process visualization. In: Alonso, G., Dadam, P., Rosemann, M. (eds.) BPM 2007. LNCS, vol. 4714, pp. 88–95. Springer, Heidelberg (2007). https://doi.org/10.1007/978-3-540-75183-0_7

4. Enriquez, J.G., Jimenez-Ramirez, A., Dominguez-Mayo, F.J., Garcia-Garcia, J.A.: Robotic process automation: a scientific and industrial systematic mapping study. IEEE Access **8**, 39113–39129 (2020). https://doi.org/10.1109/ACCESS.2020.2974934

5. Eshuis, R., Grefen, P.: Constructing customized process views. Data Knowl. Eng. **64**(2), 419–438 (2008). https://doi.org/10.1016/j.datak.2007.07.003

6. Figueiredo, G., Duchardt, A., Hedblom, M.M., Guizzardi, G.: Breaking into pieces: an ontological approach to conceptual model complexity management. In: 2018 12th International Conference on Research Challenges in Information Science (RCIS), pp. 1–10. IEEE (2018). https://doi.org/10.1109/RCIS.2018.8406642

7. Flechsig, C., Völker, M., Egger, C., Weske, M.: Towards an integrated platform for business process management systems and robotic process automation. In: Marrella, A., et al. (eds.) BPM 2022. LNBIP, vol. 459, pp. 138–153. Springer, Cham (2022). https://doi.org/10.1007/978-3-031-16168-1_9

8. Guizzardi, G., Figueiredo, G., Hedblom, M.M., Poels, G.: Ontology-based model abstraction. In: Kolp, M., Vanderdonckt, J., Snoeck, M., Wautelet, Y. (eds.) 2019 13th International Conference on Research Challenges in Information Science (RCIS), pp. 1–13. IEEE (2019). https://doi.org/10.1109/RCIS.2019.8876971

9. Hofmann, P., Samp, C., Urbach, N.: Robotic process automation. Electron. Mark. **30**(1), 99–106 (2019). https://doi.org/10.1007/s12525-019-00365-8

10. Lacity, M.C., Willcocks, L.P.: A new approach to automating services. MIT Sloan Manag. Rev. **58**(1), 41–49 (2016)

11. Penttinen, E., Kasslin, H., Asatiani, A.: How to choose between robotic process automation and back-end system automation? In: Bednar, P.M., Frank, U., Kautz, K. (eds.) ECIS 2018 Proceedings. AIS (2018)

12. Polyvyanyy, A., Smirnov, S., Weske, M.: Process model abstraction: a slider approach. In: 12th International IEEE Enterprise Distributed Object Computing Conference, pp. 325–331. IEEE (2008). https://doi.org/10.1109/EDOC.2008.17

13. Polyvyanyy, A., Smirnov, S., Weske, M.: On application of structural decomposition for process model abstraction. In: Abramowicz, W., Maciaszek, L., Kowalczyk, R., Speck, A. (eds.) Business Process, Services Computing and Intelligent Service Management. LNI, pp. 110–122. Gesellschaft für Informatik e.V. (2009)

14. Polyvyanyy, A., Smirnov, S., Weske, M.: Business process model abstraction. In: vom Brocke, J., Rosemann, M. (eds.) Handbook on Business Process Management 1. IHIS, pp. 147–165. Springer, Heidelberg (2015). https://doi.org/10.1007/978-3-642-45100-3_7

15. Smirnov, S.: Structural aspects of business process diagram abstraction. In: Wilde, O. (ed.) 2009 IEEE Conference on Commerce and Enterprise Computing, pp. 375–382. Wiley (2009). https://doi.org/10.1109/CEC.2009.18

16. Smirnov, S., Dijkman, R., Mendling, J., Weske, M.: Meronymy-based aggregation of activities in business process models. In: Parsons, J., Saeki, M., Shoval, P., Woo, C., Wand, Y. (eds.) ER 2010. LNCS, vol. 6412, pp. 1–14. Springer, Heidelberg (2010). https://doi.org/10.1007/978-3-642-16373-9_1

17. Smirnov, S., Reijers, H.A., Weske, M.: From fine-grained to abstract process models: a semantic approach. Inf. Syst. **37**(8), 784–797 (2012). https://doi.org/10.1016/j.is.2012.05.007

18. Smirnov, S., Reijers, H.A., Weske, M., Nugteren, T.: Business process model abstraction: a definition, catalog, and survey. Distrib. Parallel Databases **30**(1), 63–99 (2012). https://doi.org/10.1007/s10619-011-7088-5

19. Tsagkani, C., Tsalgatidou, A.: Process model abstraction for rapid comprehension of complex business processes. Inf. Syst. **103**(C) (2022). https://doi.org/10.1016/j.is.2021.101818

20. van Zelst, S.J., Leemans, S.J.J.: Translating workflow nets to process trees: an algorithmic approach. Algorithms **13**(11), 279 (2020). https://doi.org/10.3390/a13110279

21. Völker, M., Weske, M.: Conceptualizing bots in robotic process automation. In: Ghose, A., Horkoff, J., Silva Souza, V.E., Parsons, J., Evermann, J. (eds.) ER 2021. LNCS, vol. 13011, pp. 3–13. Springer, Cham (2021). https://doi.org/10.1007/978-3-030-89022-3_1

22. Völker, M., Weske, M.: Ontology-supported modeling of bots in robotic process automation. In: Ralyté, J., Chakravarthy, S., Mohania, M., Jeusfeld, M.A., Karlapalem, K. (eds.) ER 2022. LNCS, vol. 13607, pp. 239–254. Springer, Cham (2022). https://doi.org/10.1007/978-3-031-17995-2_17

23. Wang, N., Sun, S., OuYang, D.: Business process modeling abstraction based on semi-supervised clustering analysis. Bus. Inf. Syst. Eng. **60**(6), 525–542 (2016). https://doi.org/10.1007/s12599-016-0457-x

24. Weske, M.: Business Process Management: Concepts, Languages, Architectures, 3 edn. Springer, Heidelberg (2019). https://doi.org/10.1007/978-3-662-59432-2

25. Willcocks, L.P., Lacity, M., Craig, A.: The IT function and robotic process automation: the outsourcing unit working research paper series (15/05) (2015). http://eprints.lse.ac.uk/64519/

Modeling Events and Processes

Shards of Knowledge – Modeling Attributions for Event-Centric Knowledge Graphs

Florian Plötzky[1]([✉]) [iD], Katarina Britz[2], and Wolf-Tilo Balke[1] [iD]

[1] Institute for Information Systems, TU Braunschweig, Braunschweig, Germany
{ploetzky,balke}@ifis.cs.tu-bs.de
[2] CAIR, Stellenbosch University, Stellenbosch, South Africa
abritz@sun.ac.za

Abstract. Recently the usage of narratives as a means of fusing information from large knowledge graphs (KGs) into a coherent line of argumentation has been proposed. Narratives are especially useful in event-centric knowledge graphs in that they provide a means to categorize real-world events by well-known narrations. However, specifically for controversial events a problem in information fusion arises. Namely, the existence of multiple viewpoints regarding the validity of certain event aspects, e.g., regarding the role a participant takes in an event. Expressing those viewpoints into large KGs is challenging, because disputed information provided by different viewpoints may introduce *inconsistencies*. Hence, most KGs only feature a single view on the contained information, hampering the effectiveness of narrative information access. In this paper, we introduce *attributions*, i.e., parameterized predicates that allow for the representation of facts that are only valid in a certain viewpoint. For this, we develop a conceptual model that allows for the representation of viewpoint-dependent information and further describes how such information can be fused for querying and reasoning consistently.

Keywords: Attributions · Events · Knowledge Graphs · Viewpoints

1 Introduction

Narratives play a big role in understanding and interpreting information [17]. On the one hand, narratives allow for an intuitive understanding of knowledge by framing facts or events in a way that is close to human information processing [11]. On the other hand, a narrative constructs a coherent line of argumentation, oftentimes by connecting a chain of events with participating entities. Especially in the case of knowledge graphs, where information usually extracted from a variety of sources is fused into one big structure, narratives can be used to make sense of connected subgraphs [15]. Such narratives often take the form of substitutions for prototypical narrative patterns, i.e., established patterns are isomorphically matched against some bigger knowledge graph, and for each match nodes can be

J. P. A. Almeida et al. (Eds.): ER 2023, LNCS 14320, pp. 259–276, 2023.
https://doi.org/10.1007/978-3-031-47262-6_14

filled with concrete instances (entities or literal values), fleshing out the actual narrative(s). This is especially useful in the area of event-centric KGs (e.g., EvenTKG [4] or OEKG [5]). For instance, real-world conflicts might be categorized by well-known narrations like the biblical David vs. Goliath story [20].

However, such an approach will quickly lead to the problem of *inconsistency* with respect to the information needed in a KG. In particular, when working with heterogeneous data sources and in controversial areas, multiple *viewpoints* on a topic can exist. Viewpoints may concern a participant's role in an event, the cause of an event, or its actual type. Take for instance the Russo-Ukrainian War in Wikidata [31].[1] Regarding the predicate has_cause there are two conflicting entries "Russian Colonialism" vs. "Eastward Expansion of NATO", where the latter is qualified by "supported by Vladimir Putin and by the Government of Russia". Therefore, two different viewpoints on the same fact (war cause) exist. As an implication, the role of Russia in this conflict depends on the viewpoint. If the cause of the war is declared to be "Russian Colonialism", Russia's role in the war would be that of a "conqueror" while in the second case, Russia's role would rather be seen as a "defender" against ongoing aggression. Both cases are examples of facts in a KG that are only valid in specific viewpoints.

Although the aforementioned causes are conflicting, one could argue that there is actually some truth in both and thus, they might be utilized in the same argumentation. However, we argue that they can not be used arbitrarily in this regard but must be contained in their respective viewpoints. This observation leads to the question: what do these different viewpoints and attributions mean with respect to later information fusions for querying and reasoning? Matching narratives over information provided from several viewpoints might lead to inconsistent arguments and thus, in the worst case might completely invalidate the explanatory power that should be provided by narrative argumentation patterns.

The problem of inconsistent information with respect to different viewpoints is a general problem that does not only occur in the described scenario. Prior approaches in this area, however, separate disputed information from the KG by either explicitly casting it as an extraction problem [20] or as a downstream enrichment of KG data [21]. Other works on models for event-centric KGs (ECKGs) mention the idea of assigning different roles to participants [9], but neither provide a conceptual model on this mechanism nor explain the implications of such roles for downstream tasks. None of them solves the problem of representing viewpoint-related information in real-world KGs.

In this paper we develop a conceptual model that allows for the representation of facts in a ECKG that may only be valid in certain viewpoints. We call those facts *attributions* since they can be seen as properties of an event, that are attributed from a certain point of view. The model is designed to incorporate different viewpoints and also guide information fusion for downstream tasks. Additionally, the model is grounded on stance detection [1]. Thus, it provides a natural means of information extraction and is therefore tailored for practical usage scenarios.

---

[1] https://www.wikidata.org/wiki/Q15860072.

2   A Motivating Example

As a motivation, we revisit the ongoing war between Russia and Ukraine. We refer to this event as RUvsUKR for the remainder of this paper. For now, we focus on the Wikidata representation of the actual invasion of Ukraine in 2022.[2] Wikidata is not only one of the largest freely available knowledge repositories but also offers a convenient way of adding meta-data to facts, i.e., *qualifiers*.[3] In this example, we take a closer look at the usage of such qualifiers for RUvsUKR.

2.1   Views on Event Attributes

The invasion is an instance of five different classes. One of those is "military operation" and it is qualified as being supported by Russia and disputed by Ukraine. Additionally, the statement is qualified by a special item that explicitly describes the euphemism "special military operation" as used by Vladimir Putin to describe the invasion. This example shows on the one hand that it is disputed, whether the event can be seen as a military operation or not. On the other hand, by referencing the "special military operation" entity, one can infer that the statement is not actually a military operation but framed as such.

The intention here might be to incorporate Vladimir Putin's framing while at the same time adhering to the notion that the event is in fact an invasion. That is, at least Vladimir Putin (and possibly the government of Russia) attributes the event in this way; other individuals or groups disagree with this notion. We can observe this kind of annotation in the same event in multiple cases, e.g., regarding the cause and goal of the event. However, shoehorning in different views like this leads to modeling and interpretation problems.

For the first problem, we refer again to the disputed event type "military operation", which is annotated with a "statement supported by" and "statement disputed by" qualifier regarding the respective entities Russia and Ukraine. However, both entities represent the respective countries in terms of both states. It is not clear what constitutes this viewpoint, or in other words, which view exactly is the "Russian" and if it is the view of multiple groups, how is it composed. Therefore, the first problem concerns the *viewpoint constitution*.

Taking this into account, the questions arise, which viewpoints are actually important to model, and who are the representatives of the groups behind a viewpoint? For instance, regarding the goals of the invasion, the view of the head of the Chechen Republic is annotated in Wikidata, but it is not clear whether this is his personal opinion or his opinion as head of state. In other words, who are the *viewpoint representatives* that influence a viewpoint?

The last problem concerns practical implications regarding other event attributes, especially the role of participants in the event. If we adopt the Russian view of framing the event as a military operation, Russia's role significantly differs from its role in an invasion. The next section is specifically focusing this problem.

---

[2] https://www.wikidata.org/wiki/Q110999040.
[3] https://www.wikidata.org/wiki/Help:Qualifiers.

2.2   Views on Roles of Event Participants

Wikidata supports an "object has role" qualifier. In our example this is used to assign roles to the invasions' participants, e.g., it is used to cast Russia as an aggressor, Ukraine as a war victim, and Belarus as a staging area. However, as discussed before, this assignment is not universally agreed on. If we assume that this event is a military operation with the goal of denazification, Ukraine can not be seen as a war victim in the same line of argumentation. The relation between event participants and events is, however, of high interest and often debated. Therefore, role assignments should also include the respective viewpoint of the assigner. This is especially true if we introduce roles that bear moral dimensions like Russia being a liberator in the event (cf. [21]). We call those assignments *attributions*. Regarding attributions, again, some questions must be answered for practical use.

Firstly, the set of available attributions must be determined. This relates to the problem of the choice of event types. For instance, the role of an aggressor is plausible in wars but not in football matches. Secondly, attributions may include participant roles that are not typical in knowledge graphs, like the role of an underdog or the aforementioned liberator.

Additionally, some attributions have a specific relationship with each other. For instance, a nation that is attributed to be a conqueror in one view can not be a liberator in the same event and according to the same view. This means, that the attributions must not contradict themselves from a single point of view.

3   Modeling World Views

Before we can conceptualize attributions, we address one of the core problems in the motivating example. That is, we provide a conceptual model for viewpoints and their composition. Additionally, we connect viewpoints to stance detection to ensure compatibility with current extraction methods.

3.1   Viewpoints and Stances

Generally, we argue that a viewpoint should always represent the view of either an individual or a group of entities towards a given target. Hence, a group in this sense is a finite set of entities constituted by a given criterion, e.g., political parties, a set of newspapers sharing the same political ideology, or interest groups like non-government organizations. Along these lines a target is a *fact* about an event, like the role a participant played or the kind of happening itself. Therefore, we can define viewpoints as follows:

Definition 1 (Viewpoints). *A viewpoint $v \in V$ is a consensual stance $s \in \{valid, invalid\}$ towards a fact $f \in KG$ expressed by a group G.*

The constitution criterion of G is subject to the modeling domain or extraction method (cf., for example, [22]). We will, however, later in this paper provide some intuition regarding the selection of viewpoints.

It is possible that the group only consists of a single member to allow viewpoints of individual entities. Finally, the target of the viewpoint is a fact f from an ECKG, e.g., whether Russia can be seen as an aggressor in RUvsUKR.

In order to determine whether a group G does in fact accept f as valid, we rely on the notions of stance detection. Stances are usually defined as attitudes, standpoints, and judgments of a speaker regarding a given proposition [1]. In our case, the proposition is the fact in question and the speaker is the group where the stance, according to [1], expresses agreement, disagreement, or neutrality towards the facts' validity. We define a function $stance(g, f) \mapsto \{0, 1\}$ with $g \in G$ and f being the fact in question. The function returns a truth value whether g sees f as valid or not. Note, that the second case includes both neutrality and disagreement regarding the validity of f. The latter case implies that $stance(g, \neg f)$ must hold.

Please also note that setting a fact to be invalid in v if the underlying group stance is neutral leads to several implications. On the one hand, it prevents neutrality to be interpreted as acceptance. We argue that facts should only be valid in a viewpoint if an actual majority agrees on it. Especially in groups with a silent majority (i.e., absence of stances for a majority of group members), this would otherwise lead to viewpoints where facts are valid although being agreed upon by a minority only. On the other hand, this decision weakens negative stances. This is because the reason for a negative stance is ignored and hence, the notion of disagreement of the group proxied by the viewpoint is lost. In this paper, we argue, that the benefit of combining the neutral and negative stances is greater than having the ability to differentiate between them.

To construct a viewpoint for a group we need the individual stances of each group member. This implies that every $g \in G$ must be capable of expressing such a stance. Additionally, we defined any v to be a *consensual* stance of the group and hence, we need a measure for consensus. For this paper we define consensus as:

Definition 2 (Consensus). *A* consensus *in a group G is reached, if a weighted consensus measure $\phi_W(G, f)$ with weights W, surpasses a given threshold θ.*

The choice of consensus measure depends on the domain it is used in. A typical choice would be a simple majority vote surpassing a threshold $\theta = 0.5$. However, rigorous measures like a necessary majority of two-thirds are also possible. Since ϕ is a weighted consensus measure it allows us to boost certain individuals in G, e.g., in cases where a dedicated speaker or otherwise higher-ranked individual exists. For instance, in the case of the US senate, it might be suitable to assign a higher weight to the respective party speaker.

With those preliminaries we can define the stance of a group as:

$$stance(f, G, W) = \begin{cases} \text{valid} & \phi_W(G, f) \geq \theta, \\ \text{invalid} & \text{otherwise.} \end{cases}$$

If the stance regarding f is valid for G, we say that f *is valid in v*, where v is the viewpoint representing G.

3.2 Viewpoint Hierarchies

Until now, we have a notion of viewpoints and consensus to construct a viewpoint for a given group. Different viewpoints are, however, not generally disjoint but can be combined in various cases, i.e., a fact f might be valid in two viewpoints $v_1, v_2 \in V$. Hence, those viewpoints are compatible with respect to f and can be *aggregated* into a new viewpoint v^*. In other words, v^* subsumes v_1 and v_2 with respect to f, and only with respect to f. For other facts, aggregation might not be possible.

Research in the area of viewpoint discovery has shown, that similar groups show similar stances on the same topic, e.g., groups constituted by homophily [22]. That means that we can define typical viewpoints in the sense of common aggregations to prevent a combinatorial explosion of viewpoint aggregations. One instance of such a viewpoint was already visible in our motivational example, i.e., the Russian and Ukrainian viewpoints.

Additionally, those common aggregated viewpoints can further be refined into different sub-viewpoints. We argue, that viewpoints form an aggregation hierarchy. For instance, the viewpoint of Vladimir Putin as president of Russia is subsumed by the general Russian viewpoint along with the viewpoint of the Russian government.[4] Analogously, the viewpoints of the US Congress, senate, and President of the United States (POTUS) may be aggregated by a US viewpoint. Figure 1 depicts an example of a tree-shaped like viewpoint hierarchy. Formally, we define viewpoint hierarchies as follows:

Definition 3 (Viewpoint Hierarchy). *A viewpoint hierarchy is a directed acyclic graph $H(N, A)$ with $N = V \cup \{ALL\}$ being a set of viewpoints and A a set of arcs indicating aggregation relationships.*

In this hierarchy, we illustrate typical aggregations, like common political viewpoints. The shape of the hierarchy depends on the usage domain, e.g., viewpoint hierarchies for political issues will include other viewpoints than those tailored for sports events. Regardless of the shape, we set ALL to be the *virtual top* of the hierarchy. If a fact is valid in ALL it is also valid in all other viewpoints of the hierarchy. In other words, a fact valid in ALL is said to be universally agreed upon. In all other cases, a fact is only valid in some viewpoints.

Arranging viewpoints in a hierarchy has practical advantages. On the one hand, the hierarchy defines which viewpoints should actually be represented and which are implicitly co-represented. On the other hand, such a hierarchy exemplifies which information from a knowledge graph can be fused without introducing inconsistencies.

However, besides defining the shape of the hierarchy, the main problem is the definition of suitable aggregation functions and consensus measures between the viewpoints. A weighted consensus measure, analogous to Definition 2, can be used in this respect. For instance, the UN viewpoint in Fig. 1 is derived from the US viewpoint, the Russian viewpoint, and various others. In reality, however,

---

[4] Note, that the president of Russia is not a member of the Russian government.

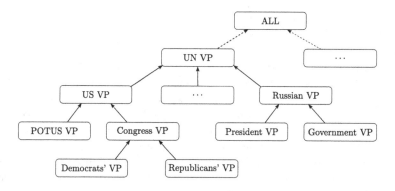

Fig. 1. An example for a viewpoint aggregation hierarchy.

the UN viewpoint might not be influenced by all of its constituting viewpoints equally. Instead, the viewpoints of larger nations like the USA might impose more weight than that of Germany or Ethiopia.

Using such a hierarchy also requires a choice on how to handle non-agreeing viewpoints during aggregation. For instance assume, that the Democratic viewpoint has a higher weight than the Republican view. In this case, a fact might be valid according to the Democratic view and the Congress but not for the Republican viewpoint. Therefore, inconsistencies in the hierarchy may appear and the viewpoint of the congress can not be seen as representative of all parts it is aggregated from. We propose two hierarchy variants to approach this problem.

View-Preserving Hierarchies (VPH). We allow for dissenting viewpoints in the (sub) hierarchy. In the example, this means that a fact f can be valid in the Democratic viewpoint and the Congress viewpoint but invalid according to the Republican viewpoint. The benefit of this approach is that minority viewpoints can exist, especially in larger hierarchies. Typically, democratic systems work by majority votes, and hence, it is inevitable that a minority exists. VPH allows us to preserve those minorities. Note, however, that if f is valid in ALL it must also be valid in all other viewpoints, i.e., for those facts, no minorities exist. A major downside is the practicability with respect to downstream tasks like reasoning and querying. In both cases, it is not possible to derive for instance the US viewpoint on a fact without considering all subtrees of this viewpoint for minorities. This is possible, for instance by using defeasible logic for reasoning, where a fact is valid according to the US viewpoint with exception to the republican view.

Winner Takes all Hierarchies (WTAH). This variant assumes that after aggregation the fact in question is valid in all viewpoints of the subtree. In our example, this means that if a fact is valid in Congress viewpoint, it is also valid in the Democratic and the Republican viewpoint, even though it was not valid in the Republican viewpoint before the aggregation. This leads to benefits in practicability of downstream tasks since it reduces the overall complexity of the model. For instance, it is possible to safely combine facts from different subtrees if the fact is valid in the roots of those subtrees. However, this simplification can also lead to a representation paradox in larger hierarchies. Assume, for example, the fact "Russia is a war criminal in RUvsUKR" and the example hierarchy as depicted in Fig. 1. Obviously, this fact would not be valid in the Russian viewpoint. If, however, it is valid in enough viewpoints on the same hierarchy level, due to the aggregation it would be valid in the UN viewpoint and hence, in the whole subtree including Russia. Of course, this effect is by design but would lead to a situation where Russia was a war criminal according to the Russian view. One can easily observe that this would hamper information fusion from a Russian point of view. A solution approach to mitigate this problem could be boosting the weights according to a fact or increasing the consensus threshold in higher levels of the hierarchy. The first option could, for example, be implemented in a way, where viewpoints of groups represented in the fact in question are boosted.

In the end, a trade-off between a plurality of viewpoints and the complexity of using the hierarchy in downstream tasks prevails. It is up to the domain, which configuration should be used. We argue that both variants provide a solid ground for the representation of viewpoints. In the next section, we discuss how a viewpoint hierarchy can be used in the context of attributions.

4   Attributions in Event-Centric Knowledge Graphs

In this section, we provide our notion of attributions and their entanglement with viewpoints. Before that, we formally introduce events and ECKGs.

4.1   Event-Centric KGs

ECKGs have gained traction over the last years, either by means of constructing specialized KGs [4,5] or by using portions of general knowledge graphs [24]. Events themselves have been studied extensively from an ontological perspective [2,6,25] and from a semantic web perspective [9]. Mostly agreed upon here is the notion that an event has a temporal as well as a spatial component and connects participants in a certain situation. Also, a notion of hierarchy is often described, i.e., the aggregation of single events to form complex events. For our purposes, we rely on the following, simple definition:

Definition 4 (Events). *Events are interactions between participants $p \in P$ that take place at a given location $l \in L$ at a specific time $t \in T$. We denote $\mathcal{E}$ to be the set of events.*

The definition includes the aforementioned typical components of events. Each event must at least provide attributes for specifying the time and location it takes place in. We do not specify the granularity of time and space since for our purposes, the existence is enough. Further properties might exist but are not mandatory.

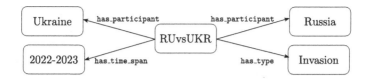

Fig. 2. Example ECKG for an excerpt of the motivational example.

At the core, each event describes an interaction between participants, the latter being entities. Typically, the event *label* describes this interaction, as it is the case for practical ECKGs. Additionally, we assign an *event type* to each event, denoted by *event_type(ev)* with *ev* ∈ $\mathcal{E}$. With that, we can formally define ECKGs.

Definition 5 (Event-Centric Knowledge Graphs). *An* event-centric knowledge graph *is a* knowledge graph, *represented by RDF triples (subject-predicate-object), where each subject is an event.*

In other words, ECKGs are star-shaped knowledge graphs with events at their centers. A knowledge graph here is nothing more than a graph following the RDF standard recommendations [13]. Events may also be present in a triple's object, e.g., for sub-event relationships. Subjects, however, must be events. Predicates in ECKG either denote attributes of an event (e.g., the time and location) or connect entities as participants to the event. In the most general case, this is done with a `has_participant` predicate. Objects can either be entities, events, time, locations, or literal values (with $\mathcal{L}$ denoting the set of literals). Figure 2 depicts an example ECKG based on an excerpt of the motivational example. We rely on this graph for the remainder of this section for illustration purposes.

4.2 Predicate Parameterization and Refinements

Refering back to our motivational example, we can observe that the relationships between events and participants are a key part of ECKGs. In this regard, we can derive multiple information from the respective event type, including:

1. Role predicates for the participants. For instance, invasions must have a participant that is in role *invader*.
2. The information, whether the time attribute of an event is a point in time or a time span. Events like wars are typically characterized by time spans while sports events like football matches are characterized by the start time.
3. Additional domain restrictions like the type of permissible participants.

For our example graph in Fig. 2 we can derive that Russia and Ukraine should in fact be war parties and hence, the predicates connecting them to RUvsUKR should be `has_war_party`. We call the concept of specializing predicates according to the event type a *refinement*. To indicate that a predicate in a triple can

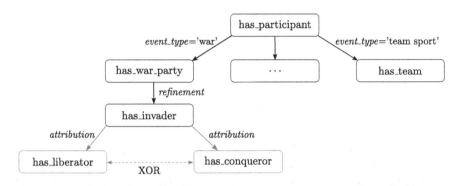

Fig. 3. Example for a predicate hierarchy featuring a specialization operation and mutual exclusiveness constraint (XOR).

be refined, we denote *et* as a parameter to it, i.e., the triple becomes $\langle s, p_{et}, o \rangle$. Given the predicate vocabulary $\mathcal{P}$ of a ECKG, the parameterized predicates, with respect to the event type, are a proper subset $\mathcal{P}^{ET} \subset \mathcal{P}$. For the "regular" predicates $\mathcal{P}^{REG} \subset \mathcal{P}$, i.e., predicates that can be applied to all event types, we set $\mathcal{P}^{ET} \cap \mathcal{P}^{REG} = \varnothing$. Hence, any regular predicate can not be used as a parameterized predicate.

We additionally allow for multiple refinements. For instance, a war party may also have the role of an invader for one participant. In this case we may refine `has_war_party` to `has_invader`. Therefore, the predicates can be arranged in a hierarchy. Figure 3 illustrates an example predicate hierarchy in its upper, black colored portion.

In accordance to the refinement, the event type may also impose constraints on the former. For instance, an event with type "invasion" should have at least two participants. One of them should be an invader and the other one the invaded country. Additionally, invader and invaded country can not be the same participant.

4.3 Attributions

In the last section, we introduced parameterized predicates to indicate possible refinements based on the event type. Those refinements are helpful to add precisifications to event-related facts, i.e., they specialize the relationships between the events and their attributes and participants. However, in the motivational example, we have seen a second class of those precisifications that can not be expressed by refinements. For instance, the notion that Russia is the aggressor in RUvsUKR and Ukraine is a war victim. As discussed before, such roles are not necessarily agreed upon by all viewpoints. This is especially true for roles incorporating moral dimensions like being a "liberator" in an invasion instead of a "conqueror". Also, disputed information like RUvsUKR being a military operation belongs to this class that is characterized to include facts only valid in a specific viewpoint. We call those facts *attributions* and define them as follows:

Definition 6 (Attributions). *An* attribution *is a parameterized predicate with a parameter* $v \in V$, *i.e.*, $\langle s, p_v, o \rangle$.

While parameterized predicates, as introduced in Sect. 4.2, are solely dependent on the event type, attributions depend on a viewpoint. Attributions allow us to introduce a set of predicates $\mathcal{P}^{ATT} \subset \mathcal{P}$ with $\mathcal{P}^{ET} \cap \mathcal{P}^{REG} \cap \mathcal{P}^{ATT} = \varnothing$ that describes such disputed information. This features both, disputes regarding event attributes (like the goal of RUvsUKR) and regarding roles assigned to participants (like Ukraine being a war victim). Again, we can utilize the structure of ECKGs and define a set of *permissible viewpoints* $V^{ET} \subseteq V$ based on the event type. The intuition is that in general only a subset of viewpoints is sensible for certain event types. For example, the viewpoint hierarchy depicted in Fig. 1 is sensible for events concerning international relations but rather not for a local sports event.

Attributions regarding participant roles can be described as further refinements, i.e., as a specialization of a parameterized predicate. This case is illustrated in blue color in Fig. 3. After two refinements, `has_invader` can be further specialized in the attributions `has_liberator`$_v$ and `has_conqueror`$_v$. Both attributions add a moral judgment to the role of an invader. The first attribution bears a justification for the invasion, the second one condemns the event. Note that those attributions are mutually exclusive with respect to a viewpoint. That is, it is not possible to describe an invader both as liberator and conqueror from the same viewpoint. Therefore, a set of constraints can apply to $\mathcal{P}^{ATT}$. We suggest two kinds of constraints, *mutual exclusiveness* and *inverse role enforcement*.

The first constraint applies to two attributions that can not be applied to the same participant in the same viewpoint. For instance, one can not be "liberator" and "conqueror" at the same time from a certain point of view. Inverse role enforcement introduces pairs of attributions that are mutually exclusive but always co-occur. Hence, if a participant is assigned to an attribution with inverse role enforcement, another participant is attributed to the counterpart. This is, for example, the case for "underdog" and "topdog" attributions. If a participant is attributed as "underdog" in a conflict, the other participant is automatically attributed as "topdog".

Attributions regarding attributes of an event are described as *transformations* of regular predicates. Take, for instance, the notion of different causes for RUvsUKR from our motivational example. One viewpoint claims the eastward expansion of NATO as a reason while another one claims Russian colonialism as the root cause. In such cases we transform the `has_cause` predicate into `has_attrib_cause`. That is, we apply a transformation function that maps a regular predicate $p \in \mathcal{P}^{REG}$ to an attribution $p' \in \mathcal{P}^{ATT}$ while preserving the semantics of p.

One special case, however, is a transformation of the `has_event_type` predicate. Such a transformation could be suitable if the event type itself is subject to debate like in our motivational example. Those transformations would have an impact on all other attributions and also on parameterized predicates. Given that RUvsUKR is a military operation and not an invasion, attributions like an `has_aggressor` may not be defined for this event type. In those cases, according to the viewpoint assuming RUvsUKR to be a military operation, all attributions that are not defined in the attribution vocabulary for it are invalid. The opposite direction is also true. According to all remaining viewpoints, attributions only defined for military operations are invalid since according to those viewpoints, the event was an invasion after all.

5   Implementation and Limitations

In this section we discuss, how attributions can be implemented in KGs. We focus on how reification can be utilized and exemplify the effect of the model on information fusion for downstream tasks. Finally, we discuss the benefits and limitations of our model.

5.1   Implementation and Materialization in ECKGs

Parameterizing predicates to represent attributions allows for direct integration in knowledge graphs. That means that both generally agreed-upon facts and disputed information, can co-exist in the same graph. We rely on RDF reification [26] to represent attributions in RDF. Specifically, we utilize *Singleton Properties* [18] as a reification technique in this example. At the core, singleton properties model reification with the idea of representing one specific relationship between two entities. This can be seen analogously to the idea of an attribution that is specific to one viewpoint. Additionally, singleton properties generate fewer triples than standard RDF reification and have been shown to represent reified knowledge as well as other techniques like named graphs in a large-scale study on Wikidata [12].

As an example, consider ECKG depicted in the left portion of Fig. 4. It contains two attributions, one regarding the role of Russia in RUvsUKR (1) and one regarding the cause of the latter (2). The attributions can be written as parameterized predicates, i.e.:

$$\langle \text{RUvsUKR}, \texttt{has\_conqueror}_{\text{NATO}}, \text{Russia} \rangle \tag{1}$$

$$\langle \text{RUvsUKR}, \texttt{has\_attrib\_cause}_{\text{RU}}, \text{NATO East. Exp} \rangle \tag{2}$$

Both attributions can be expressed directly in Singleton Properties. The translation for (1) is:

$$\langle \text{RUvsUKR}, \texttt{has\_conqueror\#1}, \text{Russia} \rangle$$

$$\langle \text{has\_conqueror\#1}, \texttt{singleton\_property\_of}, \text{has\_conqueror} \rangle$$

$$\langle \text{has\_conqueror\#1}, \texttt{acc\_to\_vp}, \text{NATO} \rangle$$

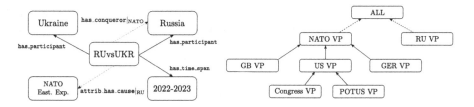

Fig. 4. Example ECKG with attributions and a corresponding viewpoint hierarchy.

Attribution (2) can be translated analogously. Note that in this case the constraint that an ECKG only contains triples with an event as the subject is slightly relaxed to allow also reified attributes. Additionally, this example shows that both attributions and transformed regular predicates, are reified in the same way. Hence, dividing those concepts does not increase the implementation complexity.

A downside of reification is that, even by using a reification technique that generates only two triples per fact instead of the regular four, the size of the knowledge graph increases significantly. However, the necessary amount of materialized reified triples depends on the viewpoint hierarchy and its variant (winner takes all vs. view-preserving hierarchies). For instance, WTAHs only require the materialization of the highest common viewpoints since the triple is also valid for all subtrees of those viewpoints. Considering the viewpoint hierarchy in the left portion of Fig. 4, both attributions only require one respective reification. If attribution (1) is materialized as shown above, it is clear from the viewpoint hierarchy that the triple is also valid in the whole subtree, i.e., including the viewpoints GB, US, GER, and transitively Congress and POTUS. Additionally, if an attribution is valid in all viewpoints on the highest hierarchy level, i.e., in ALL, no materialization is necessary.

Reifying attributions for the same hierarchy in VPHs, however, requires a different approach. We reduced the viewpoints to binary stances and thus, as an implication, we have to materialize the attributions for all viewpoints in which they are valid. The absence of an attribution for a specific viewpoint is then interpreted as invalidity for this attribution with respect to the viewpoint.

5.2   Information Fusion

Attributions also impact information fusion, in the sense of information combination or aggregation, as a precursor for downstream tasks like querying and reasoning in viewpoint-enabled ECKGs. One can not merely fuse them arbitrarily since their validity is bound to the viewpoint if not agreed upon in general. In order to prevent inconsistencies, any information fusion, i.e., the aggregation of facts and attributions for usage in downstream tasks, must be *viewpoint-compatible*. That means, since each attribution adds introduces a viewpoint to the task, it must be ensured that all attributions are valid in all viewpoints intro-duced (again, this is controlled by the hierarchy variant chosen). To exemplify this in our model, assume the hierarchy given in the right portion of Fig. 4 and a set of attributions in a ECKG:

$$EKG = \{f_1|_{\text{ALL}}, f_2|_{\text{US}}, f_3|_{\text{POTUS}}, f_4|_{\text{RU}}, f_5|_{\text{RU}}\}$$

Assume an arbitrary reasoning task on EKG. If we want to fuse facts in this KG, e.g. to check whether two facts satisfy a given rule, we have to ensure viewpoint-compatibility between them. To do that, we again differentiate the two hierarchy variants introduced in Sect. 3.2.

WTAH. In a winner-takes-all hierarchy, a fact is valid in all viewpoints of a subtree with root v, if it is valid in v. Given EKG this means we can fuse facts f_1, f_2, and f_3 arbitrary, and f_4 can be fused with f_1 and f_5. All facts can be fused with general facts, i.e., facts valid in ALL. Hence, every fact in EKG can be fused with f_1. Additionally, facts can always be fused with facts along the same viewpoint and hence, the fusion of f_4 and f_5 is valid. Due to the winner takes all principle, all facts in the subtree spanned by US can be combined with facts valid in US. Hence, f_3 can be fused with f_2 since f_2 is guaranteed to also be valid in POTUS. As an implication, f_3 may also be fused with facts valid in Congress, if the respective facts are valid in US. This is, however, not guaranteed reciprocally. Facts valid in US can only be combined with facts valid in POTUS and Congress, if they are also valid in US. Otherwise, it is not guaranteed that the consensus between POTUS and Congress is high enough for an aggregation on those specific facts. In consequence, all facts in EKG can be fused with f_1 but f_1 can only be fused with other general facts.

VPH. In a viewpoint-preserving hierarchy, facts can be invalid in a viewpoint v even if they are valid in an aggregated viewpoint containing v. Contrasting WTAH, this means that facts can only be fused with facts valid in ALL and facts valid in the same viewpoint. For our example knowledge base this means that every fact can be fused with f_1 (since it is a general fact), f_4 and f_5 can be fused but f_3 can only be fused with f_2, if f_2 is also valid in POTUS. Since we do not assume "winner takes all", this is not guaranteed. For practical reasoning, this requires either to only use facts valid in the same viewpoint (or in ALL) or to rely on a variant of defeasible logic. The latter case in our example would assume that f_2 is valid for all viewpoints in the subtree spanned by US except for some viewpoints.

5.3   Discussion and Model Limitations

Attributions can be used to include disputed information in ECKGs. We argue that they solve portions of the inconsistency problem arising especially for con-troversial events, as shown in the motivational example. The proposed model of

attributions along with a viewpoint hierarchy allows for such disputed information to co-exist in the same KG while combining information is guided by the
hierarchy without enforcing global consistency. Additionally, the model can be
implemented by only using established semantic web technologies, e.g., Singleton
Property for reification and SHACL [16] to ensure the attribution constraints
like mutual exclusiveness. The choice of hierarchy variant, i.e., WTAH or VPH,
has a direct impact on the degree of materialization and complexity of reasoning.
Of course, the model has limitations that are discussed in the following.

Choice of Hierarchy Variant. The viewpoint hierarchy and respective variant
must be known in advance. Like with all explicit models, this requirement can
be hard to fulfill. More research in the area of (semi-)automatic construction of
such hierarchies is necessary to either assist modelers with this task or automate
it completely.

Requirement of Same Conceptual Views. As discussed before, this model is
designed to allow for representing viewpoint-dependent *validity* of facts. This
requires, however, the same conceptual understanding of the attributions in
all viewpoints. In other words, inserting an attribution like has_liberator$_v$
requires a shared conceptualization of a "liberator" for all $v \in V$. While this
might be the case for most parts, this might be a problem for extraction algorithms, since primary sources sometimes utilize framing techniques to present
the facts in a specific context. Thus, it must be ensured during fact extraction
that the attribution semantics is indeed guaranteed.

Rarity of Positive Stances. One design decision concerned the fusion of neutral
and negative stances to imply the invalidity of a fact. We already argued, why
this is beneficial for this model. However, this again constrains the extraction
process, since in reality, a lot of viewpoints may stay neutral. In this case, the
model can be slightly tuned in three ways. Firstly, it is possible to define finer-
grained hierarchies to adapt for extraction sparsity. Secondly, the weights of the
consensus measures might be adapted in a way that allows for faster consensus.
Finally, the neutral stance regarding a fact from a viewpoint can be interpreted
as agreement and hence, the fact be treated as valid in this viewpoint. The latter
option comes with all benefits and flaws we already discussed.

6   Related Work

Viewpoint Discovery. Research in the area of discovery and description of viewpoints is mostly done concerning document collections or social media (e.g., [8]).
Discovering viewpoints on controversial topics in social media, for example, has
been done by clustering users based on interaction graphs [22] or by applying
variants topic modeling [30]. Additionally, advances in stance detection [1] and
a growing understanding of the difference between stance and sentiment [3] may
soon allow for more fine-grained methods of collecting viewpoints from text cor-
pora. Our work contributes to this area by providing a means to represent those
different viewpoints by using established formats for downstream applications.

Viewpoints in ECKGs. Current ECKGs, either constructed from general-purpose knowledge graphs [4,5] or from news [23], do not support different views on facts. Their underlying RDF schema, the simple event model (SEM) [9], however, intend the use of different views but does not describe in detail how those views work in terms of their composition or implications for downstream tasks. Other works have suggested fusing factual knowledge from KGs with viewpoint-dependent knowledge from other sources in downstream tasks either at query time by using a hybrid query-processor [20] or by designing transformation pipelines on top of a graph query [21].

Multiple Viewpoints in Ontologies and Conceptual Modeling. Related areas of conceptual modeling, like requirements engineering and enterprise modeling, have adopted notions of multiple viewpoints in the past [14,27,29]. In contrast to our work, those views limit the model to certain aspects that are relevant in it but do not modify the underlying facts or assumptions based on the view taken. More similar to our work are approaches of ontology integration [19] and specialized description logics allowing for reasoning with different ontology vocabularies (e.g., [7,10,28]). The difference of those works to our approach is that information fusion in our model seeks sufficient agreement between different viewpoints, in order to aggregate knowledge graphs representing the different viewpoints. The graph structure representing all the facts from a specific viewpoint can be viewed as an input ontology, but instead of matching equivalences between entities from different input ontologies in order to create an ontology alignment which then guides the ontology integration, the viewpoint hierarchy is used to guide the aggregation of viewpoint-compatible facts.

7   Conclusion

Overall, attributions based on viewpoint hierarchies can improve the utility of ECKGs. On the one hand, they allow for the representation of disputed and morally charged information. Both kinds of knowledge would otherwise either not be available in an ECKG or reasoning tasks in this regard would suffer since fusing information in a meaningful way is only possible with a clear conceptual understanding. On the other hand, all conceptualizations shown in this paper can be implemented by using already available techniques orchestrated by the models developed here. However, future work is necessary to put this model into practice, e.g., to actually enrich available ECKGs with attributions and test the practicability at scale. Finally, the development of efficient information fusion algorithms is subject to future work on this topic.

Acknowledgement. Supported by the Leibniz-ScienceCampus Postdigital Participation funded by the Leibniz Association (Leibniz-Gemeinschaft).

References

1. AlDayel, A., Magdy, W.: Stance detection on social media: state of the art and trends. J. Inf. Process. Manag. **58**(4), 102597 (2021). https://doi.org/10.1016/j.ipm.2021.102597
2. Almeida, J.P.A., Falbo, R.A., Guizzardi, G.: Events as entities in ontology-driven conceptual modeling. In: Laender, A.H.F., Pernici, B., Lim, E.-P., de Oliveira, J.P.M. (eds.) ER 2019. LNCS, vol. 11788, pp. 469–483. Springer, Cham (2019). https://doi.org/10.1007/978-3-030-33223-5_39
3. Bestvater, S., Monroe, B.: Sentiment is not stance: target-aware opinion classification for political text analysis. Polit. Anal. **31**(2), 235–256 (2023). https://doi.org/10.1017/pan.2022.10
4. Gottschalk, S., Demidova, E.: EventKG: a multilingual event-centric temporal knowledge graph. In: Gangemi, A., et al. (eds.) ESWC 2018. LNCS, vol. 10843, pp. 272–287. Springer, Cham (2018). https://doi.org/10.1007/978-3-319-93417-4_18
5. Gottschalk, S., et al.: OEKG: the open event knowledge graph. In: International Workshop on Cross-Lingual Event-centric Open Analytics Co-located with the Web Conference (CLEOPATRA@WWW). CEUR Workshop Proceedings. CEUR-WS.org (2021). https://ceur-ws.org/Vol-2829/paper5.pdf
6. Guizzardi, G., Wagner, G., de Almeida Falbo, R., Guizzardi, R.S.S., Almeida, J.P.A.: Towards ontological foundations for the conceptual modeling of events. In: Ng, W., Storey, V.C., Trujillo, J.C. (eds.) ER 2013. LNCS, vol. 8217, pp. 327–341. Springer, Heidelberg (2013). https://doi.org/10.1007/978-3-642-41924-9_27
7. Gómez Álvarez, L., Rudolph, S., Strass, H.: How to agree to disagree - managing ontological perspectives using standpoint logic. In: Sattler, U., et al. (eds.) ISWC 2022. LNCS, vol. 13489, pp. 125–141. Springer, Cham (2022). https://doi.org/10.1007/978-3-031-19433-7_8
8. Hada, R., et al.: Beyond digital "echo chambers": the role of viewpoint diversity in political discussion. In: International Conference on Web Search and Data Mining (WSDM). ACM (2023). https://doi.org/10.1145/3539597.3570487
9. van Hage, W.R., Malaisé, V., Segers, R., Hollink, L., Schreiber, G.: Design and use of the simple event model (SEM). J. Web Semant. **9**(2), 128–136 (2011). https://doi.org/10.1016/j.websem.2011.03.003
10. Hemam, M., Boufaïda, Z.: MVP-OWL: a multi-viewpoints ontology language for the Semantic Web. Int. J. Reason. Based Intell. Syst. (2011). https://doi.org/10.1504/IJRIS.2011.043539
11. Herman, D.: Narrative theory and the cognitive sciences. Narrative Inq. **11**(1) (2001). https://doi.org/10.1075/ni.11.1.01her
12. Hernández, D., Hogan, A., Krötzsch, M.: Reifying RDF: what works well with Wikidata? In: International Workshop on Scalable Semantic Web Knowledge Base Systems Co-located with International Semantic Web Conference (SSWS@ISWC). CEUR-WS.org (2015). https://ceur-ws.org/Vol-1457/SSWS2015_paper3.pdf
13. Klyne, G., Carroll, J., McBride, B.: RDF 1.1 concepts and abstract syntax (2014). https://www.w3.org/TR/rdf11-concepts/
14. Kotonya, G., Sommerville, I.: Requirements engineering with viewpoints. Softw. Eng. J. **11**(1), 5–18 (1996). https://doi.org/10.1049/sej.1996.0002
15. Kroll, H., Nagel, D., Balke, W.-T.: Modeling narrative structures in logical overlays on top of knowledge repositories. In: Dobbie, G., Frank, U., Kappel, G., Liddle, S.W., Mayr, H.C. (eds.) ER 2020. LNCS, vol. 12400, pp. 250–260. Springer, Cham (2020). https://doi.org/10.1007/978-3-030-62522-1_18

16. Kublauch, H., Kontokostas, D.: Shapes constraint language (SHACL) (2017). https://www.w3.org/TR/shacl/

17. László, J.: The Science of Stories: An Introduction to Narrative Psychology. Routledge, Oxfordshire (2008). https://doi.org/10.4324/9780203894934

18. Nguyen, V., Bodenreider, O., Sheth, A.: Don't like RDF reification?: making statements about statements using singleton property. In: International World Wide Web Conference (WWW). ACM (2014). https://doi.org/10.1145/2566486.2567973

19. Osman, I., Yahia, S.B., Diallo, G.: Ontology integration: approaches and challenging issues. Inf. Fusion **71**, 38–63 (2021). https://doi.org/10.1016/j.inffus.2021.01.007

20. Plötzky, F., Balke, W.: It's the same old story! Enriching event-centric knowledge graphs by narrative aspects. In: Web Science Conference (WebSci). ACM (2022). https://doi.org/10.1145/3501247.3531565

21. Porzel, R., Pomarlan, M., Spillner, L., Bateman, J., Mildner, T., Santagiustina, C.: Narrativizing knowledge graphs. In: International Workshop on AI Technology for Legal Documentations and International Workshop on Knowledge Graph Summary Co-located with the International Semantic Web Conference (AI4LEGAL/KGSum@ISWC). CEUR Workshop Proceedings, CEUR-WS.org (2022). https://ceur-ws.org/Vol-3257/paper11.pdf

22. Quraishi, M., Fafalios, P., Herder, E.: Viewpoint discovery and understanding in social networks. In: Web Science Conference (WebSci). ACM, Amsterdam (2018). https://doi.org/10.1145/3201064.3201076

23. Rospocher, M., et al.: Building event-centric knowledge graphs from news. J. Web Semant. (2016). https://doi.org/10.1016/j.websem.2015.12.004

24. Rudnik, C., Ehrhart, T., Ferret, O., Teyssou, D., Troncy, R., Tannier, X.: Searching news articles using an event knowledge graph leveraged by Wikidata. In: Companion of World Wide Web Conference (WWW). ACM (2019). https://doi.org/10.1145/3308560.3316761

25. Scherp, A., Franz, T., Saathoff, C., Staab, S.: F - a model of events based on the foundational ontology DOLCE+DnS ultralite. In: International Conference on Knowledge Capture (K-CAP). ACM (2009). https://doi.org/10.1145/1597735.1597760

26. Schreiber, G., Raimond, Y.: RDF 1.1 Primer (2014). https://www.w3.org/TR/rdf11-primer/

27. Sommerville, I., Sawyer, P., Viller, S.: Managing process inconsistency using viewpoints. IEEE Trans. Softw. Eng. **25**(6), 784–799 (1999). https://doi.org/10.1109/32.824395

28. Stuckenschmidt, H.: Toward multi-viewpoint reasoning with OWL ontologies. In: Sure, Y., Domingue, J. (eds.) ESWC 2006. LNCS, vol. 4011, pp. 259–272. Springer, Heidelberg (2006). https://doi.org/10.1007/11762256_21

29. Sultan, M., Miranskyy, A.: Ordering stakeholder viewpoint concerns for holistic enterprise architecture: the W6H framework. In: Proceedings of the 33rd Annual ACM Symposium on Applied Computing, (SAC), pp. 78–85. ACM (2018). https://doi.org/10.1145/3167132.3167137

30. Thonet, T., Cabanac, G., Boughanem, M., Pinel-Sauvagnat, K.: Users are known by the company they keep: topic models for viewpoint discovery in social networks. In: Conference on Information and Knowledge Management (CIKM) (2017). https://doi.org/10.1145/3132847.3132897

31. Vrandecic, D., Krötzsch, M.: Wikidata: a free collaborative knowledgebase. Commun. ACM **57**(10), 78–85 (2014). https://doi.org/10.1145/2629489

A Characterisation of Ambiguity in BPM

Marco Franceschetti[1]([✉])⬤, Ronny Seiger[1]⬤, Hugo A. López[2]⬤,
Andrea Burattin[2]⬤, Luciano García-Bañuelos[3]⬤, and Barbara Weber[1]⬤

[1] Institute of Computer Science, University of St.Gallen, St. Gallen, Switzerland
{marco.franceschetti,ronny.seiger,barbara.weber}@unisg.ch
[2] Technical University of Denmark, Kgs. Lyngby, Denmark
{hulo,andbur}@dtu.dk
[3] Department of Computer Science, Tecnológico de Monterrey, Puebla, Mexico
luciano.garcia@tec.mx

Abstract. Business Process Management is concerned with *process-related artefacts* such as informal specifications, formal models, and event logs. Often, these process-related artefacts may be affected by ambiguity, which may lead to misunderstandings, modelling errors, non-conformance, and incorrect interpretations. To date, a comprehensive and systematic analysis of ambiguity in process-related artefacts is still missing. Here, following a systematic development process with strict adherence to established guidelines, we propose a taxonomy of ambiguity, identifying a set of concrete ambiguity types related to these process-related artefacts. The proposed taxonomy and ambiguity types help to detect the presence of ambiguity in process-related artefacts, paving the road for improved processes. We validate the taxonomy with external process experts.

Keywords: Ambiguity · Business Process Management · Taxonomy

1 Introduction

The Business Process Management (BPM) lifecycle iterates through a number of phases, each operating on different representations of a process. These representations include informal process specifications, formal process models, and event logs [15]; hereinafter, we refer to them as *process-related artefacts*. The presence of ambiguity in these process-related artefacts, however, might undermine the success of the BPM initiative these artefacts are part of [1].

According to the Cambridge dictionary[1], ambiguity is *"a situation or statement that is unclear because it can be understood in more than one way"*. In the context of software, authors in [13] relate ambiguity to the existence of multiple possible interpretations (e.g., of a software requirements specification). In the context of BPM, ambiguity is a quality issue (cf. [27]) that can be found in various process-related artefacts, namely informal specifications, formal models, and

---

[1] https://dictionary.cambridge.org/dictionary/english/ambiguity.

© The Author(s), under exclusive license to Springer Nature Switzerland AG 2023
J. P. A. Almeida et al. (Eds.): ER 2023, LNCS 14320, pp. 277–295, 2023.
https://doi.org/10.1007/978-3-031-47262-6_15

event logs, yielding multiple artefact interpretations. Nevertheless, sometimes ambiguity may be the result of a deliberate choice to allow multiple interpretations, for instance, to avoid overly complicated models, or to guarantee flexibility in the application of rules and principles in legal systems, or to facilitate explorative BPM initiatives [20,24,39]. Here, we regard a process-related artefact as ambiguous if it admits multiple interpretations, and regard ambiguity as an artefact characteristic making it ambiguous. Ambiguity has high relevance in BPM; surprisingly enough, it has received only marginal attention to date.

Prior works studied ambiguity in the aforementioned process-related artefacts to some extent: [4] analysed it in user stories used to elicit process requirements, while [1,43] studied it in textual process descriptions. Ambiguity emerging when comparing a process model against its specification was studied in [5]. Authors analysed the manifestation of ambiguity in event logs in the form of uncertainty in [35] and of imperfection patterns in [44]. These previous works acknowledged the presence of ambiguity in process-related artefacts; however, they focused on some particular manifestation of ambiguity, such as linguistic ambiguity in textual process descriptions in [1], and lack a comprehensive and systematic analysis of ambiguity in relation to the different process-related artefacts.

The goal of this work is to reach a first characterisation of ambiguity. From a conceptual standpoint, this characterisation helps to better understand the notion of ambiguity in process-related artefacts and expose its relation with these artefacts. From an operational standpoint, the characterisation indicates process designers and analysts where to look for the presence of which forms of ambiguity in relation to the specific artefact. The main advantage is that it becomes easier to detect the presence of ambiguity in the artefacts, pinpointing potential misunderstandings, modelling errors, non-conformance, incorrect interpretations, as well as the risk of cascading ambiguities across the BPM lifecycle. It also becomes possible to systematically define general remedies rather than remedies specific to particular manifestations of ambiguity, which prior works do (cf. [4]).

Here, we address two research questions: *RQ1:* Where and in what form might ambiguity emerge in process-related artefacts? *RQ2:* What are potential causal relations between ambiguities observed in different process-related artefacts?

To answer *RQ1*, we propose a characterisation of ambiguity in the form of a taxonomy, whose purpose is to identify where specific ambiguity types may emerge in process-related artefacts. The taxonomy was built with a rigorous adherence to the taxonomy development guidelines for Information Systems research following the Design Science Research paradigm proposed in [29] and was evaluated by BPM experts. To answer *RQ2*, we present a relational characterisation of ambiguity across various process-related artefacts in the BPM lifecycle, highlighting potential causal relations. Our results enable further studies more focused on specific ambiguity types and on developing disambiguation strategies.

In Sect. 2, we establish the scope of our study revising process-related artefacts; in Sect. 3, we present the methodology and the resulting ambiguity characterisation; in Sect. 4, we report on the evaluation; in Sect. 5, we discuss implications; in Sect. 6, we discuss related work; Sect. 7 concludes the paper.

2   Process-Related Artefacts

We contextualise our study of ambiguity in the process-related artefacts describing processes managed in the BPM lifecycle. The BPM lifecycle is composed of the phases of process identification, process discovery, process analysis, process redesign, process implementation, and process monitoring and controlling [15]. We recall the artefacts describing a process usually associated with these phases on which we focus: informal specifications, formal models, and event logs [15].

Typically, a number of artefacts describing (fragments of) a process, data, requirements, key performance indicators, and goals are involved in the identification, discovery, and analysis phases [15]. Some of these artefacts might be preexisting; others might be produced in these phases, e.g., as the outcome of a workshop. Due to heterogeneity in sources, viewpoints, concerns, and formats and despite reconciliation efforts, these artefacts might exhibit ambiguity [25]; however, they are out of the scope of this study, since they are not a process description. Nevertheless, from these artefacts, analysts may distil an *informal* process specification in natural language (cf. [15]), which, as we study here, is an artefact potentially exhibiting ambiguity, too [1,7]. Extending the definition in [13], we call an informal process specification ambiguous if it admits multiple alternative interpretations in the form of process models, each model being consistent with the specification but mutually incompatible with any other model.

To facilitate communication or as a result of automated discovery techniques, an outcome of the aforementioned phases may also be a *formal* process model, represented in a formal language (e.g., Business Process Model and Notation, BPMN [2]). A formal process model is also the outcome of the phases of the process (re-)design and implementation [15]. These phases are concerned with enabling the enactment of the process, hence the resulting executable formal model may include additional information to support deployment to and execution by a BPM system (BPMS) [45]. As prior work indicates, ambiguity might emerge also in formal process models [36]. We say that a formal process model is ambiguous if elements in one or more of its perspectives can be interpreted in more than one way, also regarding the operational semantics [12]. For an example found in a publicly available process dataset, a gateway with a non-exclusive condition followed by activities whose labels indicate mutual exclusion can be interpreted in several ways, as confirmed by the evaluation reported in Sect. 4.

The lifecycle phase of process monitoring and controlling is related to the enactment of process model instances; it refers to tasks of analysis of data describing these enactments such as conformance checking [11]. The phase of process discovery may also analyse these data with automated approaches for process mining [15]. Typically, these tasks are performed on event logs, i.e., collections of timestamped events that occurred in the process enactments. In Sect. 3, we will show that also event logs might exhibit ambiguity. We say that an event log is ambiguous if it admits multiple interpretations of how the process enactment unfolded. For an example used in the evaluation, an event log may lead to different interpretations if the event timestamps have a too-coarse granularity, admitting multiple possible orderings of events, assuming an unordered log.

3   Characterisation of Ambiguity

3.1   Methodology

In order to reach a characterisation of ambiguity fostering an understanding of its relation with process-related artefacts, we developed a taxonomy of ambiguity following the principles of Design Science Research (DSR). Such an endeavour requires a sound and rigorous methodological approach, hence we selected the taxonomy development guidelines in Information Systems research recently proposed in [29], which revise and extend the well-known and widely adopted ones originally proposed in [34], as the methodological framework for our work. Accordingly, we followed an iterative development process, which started by establishing the following definitions as prescribed by the guidelines:

Observed Phenomenon: Ambiguities in BPM have been investigated by previous research works, however, each focuses on some specific ambiguity manifestation without a systematic analysis. Thus, a structured characterisation of ambiguity is missing. This characterisation has the potential of building a common understanding of ambiguity and supporting the further development of strategies for managing ambiguities in BPM.

Taxonomy Purposes: Here, we propose a characterisation of ambiguity in the form of a taxonomy whose purposes are: (i) to shed light on various possible types of ambiguity that might affect informal process specifications, formal models, and event logs; (ii) to support the detection and identification of these types of ambiguity in process-related artefacts in BPM.

Target User Groups: We expect that process designers and process analysts will benefit from the proposed taxonomy by gaining a clearer understanding of which types of ambiguity emerge in various process-related artefacts, which inter-dependencies exist between these ambiguity types, and which particular elements they affect. In turn, this might help to define type-specific strategies for managing ambiguities during BPM tasks such as modelling, conformance checking, and process discovery.

Meta-characteristic: Defining the meta-characteristic is crucial for taxonomy development since it is the most comprehensive characteristic supporting the identification of characteristics and dimensions, which reflect the taxonomy purpose [29]. With our study, we aim at identifying potential sources of ambiguity in process-related artefacts, i.e., where ambiguity might be observed. Thus, we defined the source of ambiguity as the meta-characteristic of the proposed taxonomy. Our choice is motivated by the stance that for properly dealing with ambiguity it is essential to know where it might emerge.

Building Approach: Following [29], two non-mutually exclusive taxonomy building approaches exist: empirical-to-conceptual and conceptual-to-empirical. The former is more suitable when the taxonomy designers have limited domain knowledge, but have a large number of concrete cases to analyse and abstract from. The latter is more suitable when the taxonomy designers are knowledgeable in the taxonomy domain and do not require a large number of concrete cases to analyse; concrete cases can be used to validate the taxonomy. Based on the six authors' expertise in the BPM domain, the proposed taxonomy was constructed following a conceptual-to-empirical approach for most iterations, with intermediate empirical-to-conceptual iterations to validate newly introduced concepts. Publicly available collections of process-related artefacts were used for these empirical-to-conceptual iterations, as well as for the evaluation (cf. Sect. 4).

Ending Conditions: The guidelines in [29] define both objective and subjective ending conditions, which collectively establish the completion of the taxonomy development process. According to the guidelines, objective ending conditions state that the taxonomy encodes a mutually exclusive and collectively exhaustive classification and that stability (a fixpoint) is reached within the development iterations. Subjective ending conditions state that the taxonomy is concise, robust, comprehensive, extendable, and explanatory.

Evaluation Goals: After meeting the ending conditions (end of the development phase), an evaluation should be performed with the goal of determining the usefulness of the taxonomy. The taxonomy should clearly describe ambiguity for the target users, and it should facilitate the identification of ambiguity types in concrete use cases. We will report on the evaluation in Sect. 4.

The proposed taxonomy was reached after 8 iterations (cf. [18]), each of which incrementally refined the taxonomy. Each iteration involved and was evaluated by different, disjoint subsets of the authors. The iterative process ended when it was ultimately agreed by all authors that no structural or terminological changes were required anymore and that the subjective ending conditions were met.

3.2   Ambiguity Taxonomy

The taxonomy development process resulted in the taxonomy shown in Fig. 1. In line with the discussion in Sect. 2, we identify three main classes of artefacts in which ambiguity might emerge and which correspond to the first level of the taxonomy. The first class of artefacts is that of unstructured representations of a process, such as requirements documents, laws, guidelines, and informal specifications in natural language. Here, ambiguity leads to multiple possible interpretations of the process, hence multiple possible process models: we refer to this ambiguity as *descriptive* ambiguity. The second class of artefacts comprises representations of the process model in (possibly executable) formal languages. Here, ambiguity leads to multiple possible interpretations of the model semantics: in this case, we have *representational* ambiguity. The third class of artefacts comprises event logs, in which ambiguity leads to multiple possible interpretations of the executed process: in this case, we have *observational* ambiguity. We now discuss ambiguity in detail and provide brief yet focused examples for ambiguity types we identified; larger examples are available in [19].

Descriptive ambiguity relates to characteristics of the specification of a process in natural language, which lead to multiple interpretations of the process by a reader. More specifically, descriptive ambiguity may be determined by *linguistic* ambiguity or *epistemic* ambiguity.

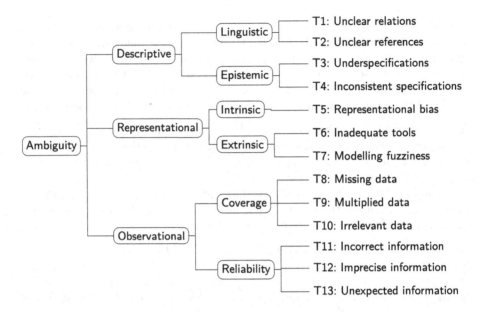

Fig. 1. Ambiguity taxonomy with possible ambiguity types as leaves of the tree

Linguistic ambiguity emerges from lexical, syntactic, semantic, pragmatic ambiguity, or vagueness in the language constructs forming the process specification [23], as well as polysemy. Generalising the findings in [1], which studies linguistic ambiguity with respect to the specification of the control flow only, we identify *unclear relations* and *unclear references* as possible linguistic ambiguity types occurring in a specification and affecting various process perspectives, e.g., functional or organisational.

- **T1: Unclear Relations:** A process specification may fail to express in a sufficiently clear manner the relations between some process elements. The process model resulting from such a specification may include or exclude constructs or concepts, in contrast to the intended model. For instance, the guidelines for the process of hypokalaemia treatment in [41] state: *"Treat any underlying cause (. . .) and/or review medication."* With this specification, it is unclear whether between the tasks of treatment and medication reviewing there exists a precedence, mutually exclusive or parallel execution relation.
- **T2: Unclear References:** In an informal process specification, it might be unclear what relevant process element is being described by a given statement. The resulting process model may contain erroneous elements or concepts, lack relevant elements, or include elements not matching the specification. For instance, the hotel service process specification in [21] states: *"Eighty per cent of room-service orders include wine or some other alcoholic beverage."* Also considering the whole specification, the relation between this statement and any process element that might relate to the mentioned orders is unclear and might result in a model excluding such element, like in [37].

Epistemic ambiguity reflects an insufficient knowledge of the process or its domain when developing a process specification, which results in knowledge gaps or inconsistencies in various perspectives of the specification. These gaps and inconsistencies may lead to a number of possible interpretations when reading the specification. We identify *underspecifications* and *inconsistent specifications* as epistemic ambiguity types.

- **T3: Underspecifications:** The term underspecification refers to the omission of certain features from a representation [22]. In a process specification, it refers to the deliberate or unintentional exclusion of some characteristics or the partial specification of one or more process perspectives. Underspecifications may exist due to the need to cope with flexible process specifications without cluttering, limited domain or process knowledge, or to negligence. The resulting process model might exhibit some "conceptual gaps". For instance, the "MCT finalise SCT warrant possession" process studied in [21] states: *"After that, some other MC internal staff receives the physical SCT file (out of scope)."* Here, there is a deliberate omission of details around a resource, which makes it unclear who should receive the file and how this should be modelled.
- **T4: Inconsistent Specifications:** A process specification might present conflicting requirements, which cannot be satisfied altogether. In this case, either the modelling language allows including all such requirements into an inconsistent process model, or the process designer has to decide which of these requirements to retain, resp. to discard. Consider the excerpt from the specification of exercise 4 in [47], stating: *"If the combined design fails the test, then they are both sent back (...). If the designs pass the test, then they are deemed complete and are then sent to the manufacturing Process (...)"*. Here, it is not clear whether the condition is based on a single compound data object or on two separate data objects, which requires deciding how to model both the data and the condition.

Representational ambiguity is associated with a formal process model expressed in some modelling language such as BPMN or Petri nets. It refers to the possibility that the process model is formalised in a way that leads to multiple different interpretations of its semantics. Note that here we do not consider erroneous formal models with invalid syntax or that could not be executed by a process engine. We consider syntactically valid formal models that can be executed, but whose execution or interpretation have uncertain semantics. Representational ambiguity may be *intrinsic* or *extrinsic*.

Intrinsic ambiguity refers to inherent characteristics of the modelling language that may enforce or prevent certain modelling constructs, patterns, and styles, which are in contrast to the specific modelling objectives. A possible type of intrinsic ambiguity is *representational bias*:

- **T5: Representational Bias:** Process modelling languages have intrinsic characteristics that may limit the expression of certain process elements, altering or curbing the process semantics. For instance, with classical Petri nets, it is impossible to model the organisational aspect of a process: the resulting model would lead to uncertainty in interpreting the assignment of tasks to roles if these were relevant to the process. Additional examples based on BPMN 2.0 can be found in [2].

Extrinsic ambiguity does not stem from characteristics of a specific modelling language but derives from the modelling task. This can be due to limitations of the modelling tool used, e.g., lack of support for certain modelling constructs – for which case *inadequate tools* is a possible ambiguity type. Alternatively, a lousy use of the modelling language may be attributed to the human process designers – here, *modelling fuzziness* is a possible ambiguity type.

- **T6: Inadequate tools:** Process modelling tools may have limitations in the support to modelling languages, excluding certain constructs allowed by a given language from a process model, or allowing the inclusion of constructs or relations forbidden by the language. For an example, consider Camunda Platform 8: it allows modelling BPMN 2.0 process models, but (currently) does not allow defining signal events. Using other events as a workaround might result in confusion in interpreting such events.
- **T7: Modelling fuzziness:** A process designer might deviate from established modelling best practices, producing process models that are syntactically valid, but that still exhibit uncertain semantics. For an example based on BPMN, consider that a designer may associate several activities with the same name. If these activities are not identical, their interpretation would be unclear and might induce one to consider them to be the same.

Observational ambiguity might affect the representation of a process execution, which is usually in the form of an event log describing activities, roles, and so on. In line with the criteria at the basis of the event log maturity levels indicated in [3], observational ambiguity may relate to both the completeness of data describing a process execution and the trustworthiness of the information such data conveys about the process execution. Therefore, we distinguish between *coverage* ambiguity and *reliability* ambiguity.

Coverage ambiguity refers to the presence, resp. absence, and the amount of data describing an execution, and may result from ambiguity types such as *missing data, repeated data,* and *irrelevant data.* Missing data and irrelevant data reflect general data quality issues affecting event logs identified in [10]. Repeated data does not refer to redundancy, i.e., multiple identical occurrences, but repetitions of the same data with variations in the values, which make it unclear which data values should be considered correct.

- **T8: Missing Data:** Process logs may be incomplete due to the absence of certain data in log entities, such as missing case id or timestamp. Missing data can be attributed to a number of reasons, such as nonconforming behaviour, faults in sensors generating process data, resource unavailability, or negligence. Additional examples of missing data are presented in [10].
- **T9: Multiplied Data:** An event log may contain multiple occurrences of the same event, i.e., of the same happening, with variations in the values of

some attributes. Possible causes might be non-conformance of the execution with the process model, or faults in the logging. For instance, in the log of a storage process instance used for the evaluation (see Sect. 4), an event for the single occurrence of an activity "Read colour" reading the colour of a workpiece occurs twice, first reporting that the workpiece is blue, then red.

- **T10: Irrelevant Data:** If no adequate filtering methods are adopted, more data than required is retained about the execution of a process, which may be erroneously considered relevant and lead to erroneous interpretations of the executed process [10]. For instance, the log for a smart factory process may include large amounts of environmental data continuously generated by sensors and stored as events: process discovery based on such an unfiltered log may result in a very large model cluttered with irrelevant activities.

Reliability ambiguity refers to the trust that can be put in the logged information describing a process execution. An event log might lead to multiple interpretations of how an execution unfolded if a trace does not conform to a known process model. It is also possible that the analysis of the traces alone, without any knowledge of the underlying process model, might lead to multiple interpretations. Here, possible ambiguity types are *incorrect information*, *imprecise information*, and *unexpected information*.

- **T11: Incorrect Information:** Information representing the execution of a process instance might be misaligned with the known process model, representing facts that do not hold true as per the model. Wrong interpretations of how the process unfolded are thus possible. For instance, in the log of a storage process used for the evaluation (see Sect. 4), an activity *"Store Workpiece"* is performed by resource *"VGR"*, while according to the corresponding BPMN process model used for the enactment, the activity is assigned to resource *"HBW"*. Thus, it is not clear whether a different resource took over, or there was a logging error.
- **T12: Imprecise Information:** Information may be recorded at a coarse granularity (e.g., due to data anonymisation), losing relevant information about a process execution. For instance, if events in an event log are recorded with minute precision, there might be uncertainty regarding the exact order of execution of consecutive activities, and one could infer several different traces. Additional examples of imprecise information are discussed in [10].
- **T13: Unexpected Information:** Logged execution information might deviate from the values expected as per the analysis of the process log, making it unclear how to interpret the execution against a discovered model. For example, consider the case of a monitored push-down hand sanitiser dispenser: the log usually reports an amount of 5–10 ml of sanitiser per dispensing event; however, if an event with 20 ml is recorded, it might be unclear whether multiple nurses used the dispenser together, or just one with double the amount.

3.3   Relational Characterisation

Ambiguity may propagate across the process-related artefacts, i.e., ambiguity affecting one artefact might induce cascading ambiguity in the same or other

Table 1. Relational characterisation of ambiguity assuming a transition from a specification to a model and from the model to an event log. → denotes potential direct causal relation, ⤳ indirect, ↻ reflexive.

	Descriptive	Representational	Observational
Descriptive	↻	→	⤳
Representational		↻	→
Observational			↻

artefacts. For a systematic analysis of these relations between ambiguities across artefacts, the artefacts need to be anchored to the respective BPM lifecycle phases and the transitions between the phases need to be established. Here, we give an example for this analysis assuming the case in which a given informal specification is used to design and implement an executable formal model, whose enactment in a BPMS generates an event log. Other cases (for instance, starting from an event log, deriving a formal model with process mining, and from this model generating a textual description) will be analysed in future work. Table 1 summarises the potential causal relations between descriptive, representational and observational ambiguities in this case.

We observe that each ambiguity might cause additional ambiguities of the same kind, which we indicate as *potential reflexive* causal relationship and denote with ↻. Descriptive ambiguity might cause representational ambiguity, and representational ambiguity might induce observational ambiguity: we refer to these as *potential direct* causal relationships (denoted with →). For transitivity, descriptive ambiguity might cause observational ambiguity, which we refer to as *potential indirect* causal relationship and denote with ⤳.

Descriptive ↻: This is the case, for instance, when a linguistic ambiguity causes epistemic ambiguity. Consider, for example, the excerpt from the description of the phylogenetic analysis process in [31]: *"Similarly, alignments were examined and investigated by an MP approach with heuristic search in MEGA"*. The relation between the data object *alignments* and its origin is not introduced in the specification: a *T1: Unclear Relations* ambiguity type. In turn, this causes the process fragment responsible for producing the data object as output to be underspecified: a *T3: Underspecifications* ambiguity type.

Descriptive → Representational: This is the case, for instance, when an inconsistent specification is translated into a formal process model affected by modelling fuzziness. Consider the following fragment of a process specification from [15]: *"(...) once the license is granted, this is sent by EPA directly to the applicant. (...) Once the required permit and/or license have been obtained, the assessment manager notifies the applicant of the final approval"*. Here, the ambiguity type in the informal specification is *T4: Inconsistent Specifications*, since the first sentence states that the applicant receives the license (not the manager); however, the second sentence states that the manager informs the applicant of the reception and subsequent approval. The second sentence implies that it is the manager who receives the permit and license, in contrast with the first sentence.

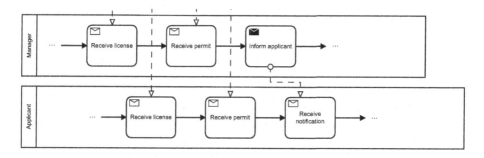

Fig. 2. BPMN fragment for a land development applications process from [15]

One may formalise this specification fragment as the BPMN fragment in Fig. 2, with the same *receive* tasks for both manager and applicant, which generates confusion in the interpretation of these tasks and the subsequent notification.

Representational ↻**:** This is easily observed, for instance, when ambiguity type *T6: Inadequate Tools* leads to *T7: Modelling Fuzziness*. For example, some BPMN modelling tools allow defining message flows connecting elements in different lanes of the same pool, making it unclear whether the lanes are meant to refer to different organisations, or whether it is the message flow to be incorrect.

Representational → Observational: This is the case when the execution of an ambiguous process model generates a log trace that can be interpreted in multiple possible ways. As an example, consider the case in which the same name is assigned to multiple different activities in a BPMN model (*T7: Modelling Fuzziness* ambiguity). The log describing the execution of an instance of this process model would include multiple events associated with the same name, one for each executed activity (*T9: Multiplied Data* ambiguity). Here, due to modelling fuzziness, it is unclear whether the same activity was executed several times, or the logged events refer to different activities with the same name.

Observational ↻**:** An example for this case is a coverage ambiguity causing a cascading coverage ambiguity. For instance, consider the case of a smart factory in which all case id attributes are missing from the log (*T8: Missing Data*) due to a malfunctioning of the communication bus during a given time period when parallel process instances were executed. This results in the impossibility of establishing the right activity-instance associations for all tasks carried out during the malfunctioning of the communication bus (*T12: Imprecise Information*).

4   Evaluation

The guidelines in [29] remark that it is not sufficient to evaluate a taxonomy *ex-ante* by assessing the ending conditions, but also an *ex-post* evaluation should be performed after the design process is completed. This evaluation checks *"based on the feedback of (potential) users whether the completed version of a taxonomy fulfils the sufficient condition and evaluation criteria to be a useful taxonomy"* [29].

4.1   Method, Participants, and Dataset

Several evaluation methods for taxonomies exist: for the proposed taxonomy, we deem the *illustrative scenario with real-world objects* the most suitable one. The method aims at demonstrating the usefulness of the taxonomy by applying it to synthetic or real-world situations (here: informal specifications, formal models, and event logs), and is the most frequently adopted evaluation method [29].

We involved four participants with several years of expertise in BPM; none of the authors acted as participants. Each participant had a training session, in which (s)he was educated on the taxonomy. Afterwards, the participant was asked to individually analyse 13 process-related artefacts–for each of which the authors had detected the presence of one ambiguity type–and to identify the specific ambiguity type with the help of the taxonomy, motivating the answer.

For a comprehensive evaluation, we needed a set of realistic examples from various domains, covering all artefacts and ambiguity types from Sect. 3; we considered only artefacts in English to accommodate the diverse nationalities of the participants. For informal specifications, we analysed the set of 47 pairs process specification–model studied in [21], which comes from academic and industrial sources and has been used in several other studies; we also analysed the process specifications from the exercises in [15], which is a well-known textbook in the BPM community. For formal models, we analysed the models from the BPM Academic Initiative in [46], which also comes from academia and industry and is well-known in the community. For event logs, we analysed the BPI Challenge 2012 log in [14], the Road Traffic Fine Management Process log in [30], and logs from a smart factory simulation environment [42]. In the end, we selected 13 artefacts, in each of which we identified a distinct ambiguity type from Sect. 3.

4.2   Results

The dataset, results, and demographics of participants are publicly available [19]. Out of 52 total identifications of ambiguity types by the participants, 43 matched those by the authors. The 43 matching identifications support the usefulness of the taxonomy. In the case of a mismatch, at most two participants disagreed with the authors' identified ambiguity type. Only in one case one participant firmly argued that there was no ambiguity, while another identified a different type. These mismatches demonstrate the possibility of different interpretations among the participants, indeed underpinning the presence of ambiguity.

What emerged from the discussions with the participants is that different interpretations may stem from the different mental models and frames. For example, a case of *T1: Unclear relations* between activities due to multiple possible interpretations of the term "and" (also identified in [1] as such), was identified by one participant as *T3: Underspecifications*, since in the participant's view the meaning of the term "and" was not further specified; on the other hand, another participant could not detect any ambiguity, with the motivation that the term "and" in that context necessarily denotes a sequential relation. For another example, when analysing a formal model specified in Event-driven Process Chain

(EPC) notation, one participant, for historic reasons, held an interpretation of EPC as an informal language, hence identified a descriptive (*T3: Underspecifications*) instead of a representational ambiguity (*T5: Representational bias*).

Overall, while the evaluation proved the usefulness of the taxonomy for identifying ambiguity in process-related artefacts, it also asserted the need to investigate, in future work, the role played by the mental model of the consumers (i.e., those supposed to use) of these artefacts in detecting and identifying ambiguity.

5   Discussion

The taxonomy proposed in Sect. 3 gave an answer to *RQ1* on where ambiguity might emerge in process-related artefacts. The discussion on the relational characterisation addressed *RQ2* on possible causal relations. Here, we outline some applications and further research directions, and discuss threats to validity.

5.1   Ambiguity Detection

In the spirit of open science, datasets composed of process-related artefacts are being increasingly shared and reused among the BPM community. However, there is the risk that they are used unaware of the potential presence of ambiguity. Reusing ambiguous processes in experiments without acknowledging and managing ambiguity poses a threat to the validity of these experiments. For example, the PET dataset from [7] is built by annotating the specifications from [21], which we have found to exhibit various ambiguity types. Indeed, in [7] the authors report on the need to discard some processes from the dataset due to the impossibility of reaching a consensus on the interpretation.

We propose our ambiguity taxonomy as a tool for analysing process-related artefacts and detecting ambiguity types in these datasets. Such a systematic analysis is beyond the scope of this paper; however, we expect this paper to trigger further analysis of existing datasets to improve the quality of future experimental evaluations based on these datasets. In general, we envision the proposed taxonomy to raise awareness of the presence of ambiguity in BPM, and to support new research directions such as prompt engineering for BPM.

5.2   Analysis of the Affected Elements

Analysing ambiguity in process-related artefacts in-depth requires examining which specific elements of these artefacts may be affected by ambiguity.

Descriptive ambiguity emerges in informal process specifications whose interpretation results in multiple possible process models. Thus, in order to measure the effect of descriptive ambiguity, it makes sense to determine which process model perspectives are affected by it. The BPM literature identifies several process perspectives, four of which are most agreed upon: control flow, data, organisational, and operational [38]. A systematic analysis should consider at least these perspectives; when relevant, also other perspectives might be considered.

In our experience and preliminary observations, we found all descriptive ambiguity types identified in Sect. 3 to potentially affect each of these four perspectives.

Representational ambiguity affects formal process models, and results in different possible model interpretations. These interpretations are relative to the aforementioned process perspectives; hence we argue that these process perspectives should be the object of analysis of formal process models, too.

Observational ambiguity affects event logs, hence analysing its effects requires examining the affected event log entities. Prior work (cf. [44]) identified and studied the following event log entities: Case, Event, Belongs_to (event–case association), Case attribute, Position, Activity name, Timestamp, Resource, Event attributes. These entities constitute a good starting point for analysis.

An in-depth analysis of ambiguity should inspect the above-indicated elements in relation to the artefact at hand. In light of the relational characterisation discussed in Sect. 3, the analysis should also study the potential cascading effects of ambiguity across the elements of the process-related artefacts.

5.3   Ambiguity Reduction Strategies

A reduction of descriptive ambiguity in informal process specifications could be achieved combining different strategies. One possible strategy might be to adopt a controlled language (e.g., the *Attempto* controlled language [40]), as controlled languages impose restrictions on the available linguistic constructs, reducing the risk of linguistic ambiguity. Ontology annotations and glossaries have also been proposed to tackle descriptive ambiguity (e.g., in [4]). Additionally, involving domain experts could help to alleviate epistemic ambiguity.

To reduce representational ambiguity in formal models, it is critical to put great care into the modelling task, starting from the choice of the prospective modelling language [9]. This choice should consider criteria such as expressive power, tool support, and familiarity of the process designer. Additionally, assisted modelling (e.g., [17,33]) and checking (cf. [48]) approaches, as well as ontology-based modelling (cf. [16]) might help to reduce representational ambiguity.

Possible strategies to reduce observational ambiguity require employing *a priori* adequate methods and tools to record process executions comprehensively and faithfully. To this end, the recent idea of integrating Internet of Things (IoT) technologies with BPM to collect rich datasets (cf. [26]) shows great potential for disambiguation and is worth investigating.

The approaches outlined above are examples of possible unstructured strategies to reduce ambiguity. However, if dependencies between ambiguities across artefacts can be identified (cf. Sect. 3), more structured strategies may be achieved by exploiting these dependencies to achieve cascading reductions. For example, reducing descriptive ambiguity in an informal specification may lead to a cascading reduction of representational ambiguity in the formal model derived from the specification. A detailed study of type-specific reduction strategies and of more structured approaches exploiting dependencies will be addressed in future work.

5.4   Threats to Validity

The evaluation confirmed that all ambiguity types identified in the taxonomy are indeed ambiguities. Regarding the taxonomy structural completeness, it can be seen that it is met at the first level, since the taxonomy covers all the artefacts describing processes typically identified in the literature in relation to BPM lifecycle phases and process mining tasks [3,15] (cf. Sect. 2). New ambiguity types for these artefacts, which may be discovered in the future, could find a position in lower levels of the taxonomy in relation to the pertaining artefact, in line with the extensibility principle [29]. Regarding external validity and the generalisability of our findings, strictly adhering to the development guidelines in [29] ensures that the scope of applicability is clearly defined within BPM. The evaluation results indicate applicability and usefulness of the taxonomy in a broad set of domains, suggesting general applicability across domains where BPM is applied. As part of a first step towards a comprehensive understanding of ambiguity, the evaluation involved academics only: in follow-up work, we will involve practitioners for further evaluation, and also investigate the generalisability beyond BPM.

6   Related Work

Prior work recognised ambiguity as a quality issue [13,27]; here, we identified several ambiguity types as its manifestations in process-related artefacts. As not every quality issue is an ambiguity, these ambiguity types can be seen as a *proxy* for a subset of quality issues of process-related artefacts, i.e., analysts can investigate certain quality issues by detecting ambiguity types. For instance, completeness quality issues (cf. [6]) take the form of coverage ambiguity; issues in semantic validity (cf. the SEQUAL framework [27]) take the form of *T7: Modelling fuzziness*; incorrect data issues (cf. [10]) take the form of *T11: Incorrect information*. A systematic analysis of the relations between quality issues and ambiguity types is beyond the scope of this paper and invites further research.

Prior work studied ambiguity in informal documents to elicit requirements or to describe business processes. In [4], authors conduct a systematic literature review focusing on user stories to elicit requirements. They identify four ambiguity problems (vagueness, inconsistency, insufficiency, and duplicates), which can be related to the descriptive ambiguity types identified here. They also summarise proposed solutions to these problems, such as algorithmic solutions, ontologies, and controlled languages: while these are proposed to resolve particular manifestations of ambiguity, our taxonomy identifies ambiguity types as abstractions of particular manifestations, enabling designing type-specific resolution strategies.

The work in [1] studies what we identified here as linguistic ambiguity in textual process descriptions. Based on the concept of behavioural space, the authors design a technique to deal with ambiguity in the context of conformance checking; however, the scope is limited to the control flow. As Sect. 5 indicates, ambiguity might affect all major process perspectives: we foresee that by extending the concept of behavioural space, one might be able to deal with ambiguity in these perspectives. Ambiguity in textual descriptions is studied also in [43], where it is identified based on sentence templates, resulting in six ambiguity issues, which can all be related to the descriptive ambiguity types we identified.

The work in [8] presents a qualitative analysis of the state of the art in the task of process extraction from texts. Related to this, the work in [32] discusses challenges in the discovery of legal processes arising from the analysis of the natural language. Complementing these works with our study on ambiguity could result in further insights to guide the process of process extraction from text.

In line with our indications from Sect. 5, the work in [36] proposes an automated technique to assist the modelling task and resolve representational ambiguity due to activity labels. Representational ambiguity might result in inconsistencies between a process model and the corresponding specification: the work in [5] studies how to detect such inconsistencies with respect to role associations.

The work in [44] studies imperfection patterns in event logs with the goal of cleaning event logs for process mining. Imperfection patterns are quality issues, in line with the results of [10], which result in the observational ambiguity types presented here. By detecting these ambiguity types, analysts can discover the presence of imperfection patterns and quality issues. Potential ambiguity in object-centric event logs is highlighted in [28]: we expect this recent log format to benefit from our taxonomy for the identification of ambiguity, and to potentially extend the taxonomy with new ambiguity types. A related problem is uncertainty in process logs, i.e., the lack of precise knowledge about certain process aspects [35], e.g., in relation to task durations and event data. Here, we interpret uncertainty as a consequence of ambiguity, aligning with the work in [1,35].

7   Conclusion

Ambiguity in BPM can be found in various process-related artefacts, namely informal specifications, formal models, and event logs. In order to shed first light on ambiguity in these artefacts, we proposed a taxonomy of ambiguity, identifying 13 concrete ambiguity types in it; for each ambiguity type, we provided real examples. Additionally, we studied potential causal relations between ambiguities in relation to the affected artefacts and proposed a relational characterisation of ambiguity. An evaluation with process experts confirmed the usefulness of the proposed taxonomy. We regard these contributions as a tool for helping to detect the presence of ambiguity in process-related artefacts. Detecting ambiguity is the first step towards achieving increased quality of process-related artefacts.

In future work, we will perform further evaluations involving academics and practitioners. We further plan to study the effect of ambiguity on process-related artefact elements. Moreover, we plan to define ambiguity reduction strategies. We expect this work to foster further reflection on how to deal with unresolvable ambiguity, as well as on how to generalise the presented concepts beyond BPM.

Acknowledgement. This work has received funding from the Swiss National Science Foundation under Grant No. IZSTZ0_208497 (*ProAmbitIon* project). The authors thank the anonymous reviewers and the evaluation participants.

References

1. van der Aa, H.: Dealing with ambiguity in textual process descriptions. In: van der Aa, H. (ed.) Comparing and Aligning Process Representations. LNBIP, vol. 323, pp. 77–101. Springer, Cham (2018). https://doi.org/10.1007/978-3-319-94634-4_5
2. Aagesen, G., Krogstie, J.: BPMN 2.0 for modeling business processes. In: vom Brocke, J., Rosemann, M. (eds.) Handbook on Business Process Management 1. IHIS, pp. 219–250. Springer, Heidelberg (2015). https://doi.org/10.1007/978-3-642-45100-3_10
3. van der Aalst, W., et al.: Process mining manifesto. In: Daniel, F., Barkaoui, K., Dustdar, S. (eds.) BPM 2011. LNBIP, vol. 99, pp. 169–194. Springer, Heidelberg (2012). https://doi.org/10.1007/978-3-642-28108-2_19
4. Amna, A.R., Poels, G.: Ambiguity in user stories: a systematic literature review. Inf. Softw. Technol. **145**, 106824 (2022)
5. Aysolmaz, B., Iren, D., Reijers, H.A., et al.: Detecting role inconsistencies in process models. In: Proceedings of the ECIS 2019 (2019)
6. Batini, C., Scannapieco, M.: Data Quality: Concepts, Methodologies and Techniques. Data-Centric Systems and Applications. Springer, Heidelberg (2006). https://doi.org/10.1007/3-540-33173-5
7. Bellan, P., van der Aa, H., Dragoni, M., Ghidini, C., Ponzetto, S.P.: PET: an annotated dataset for process extraction from natural language text tasks. In: Cabanillas, C., Garmann-Johnsen, N.F., Koschmider, A. (eds.) BPM 2022. LNBIP, vol. 460, pp. 315–321. Springer, Cham (2022). https://doi.org/10.1007/978-3-031-25383-6_23
8. Bellan, P., Dragoni, M., Ghidini, C.: A qualitative analysis of the state of the art in process extraction from text. In: DP@ AI* IA, pp. 19–30 (2020)
9. Bork, D., Karagiannis, D., Pittl, B.: A survey of modeling language specification techniques. Inf. Syst. **87**, 101425 (2020)
10. Bose, R.J.C., Mans, R.S., van der Aalst, W.M.: Wanna improve process mining results? In: 2013 IEEE Symposium on Computational Intelligence and Data Mining (CIDM), pp. 127–134. IEEE (2013)
11. Carmona, J., van Dongen, B., Solti, A., Weidlich, M.: Conformance Checking. Springer, Heidelberg (2018). https://doi.org/10.1007/978-3-319-99414-7
12. Christiansen, D.R., Carbone, M., Hildebrandt, T.: Formal semantics and implementation of BPMN 2.0 inclusive gateways. In: Bravetti, M., Bultan, T. (eds.) WS-FM 2010. LNCS, vol. 6551, pp. 146–160. Springer, Heidelberg (2011). https://doi.org/10.1007/978-3-642-19589-1_10
13. Davis, A.M., et al.: Identifying and measuring quality in a software requirements specification. In: Proceedings of the METRICS 1993, pp. 141–152. IEEE Computer Society (1993)
14. van Dongen, B.: BPI challenge 2012 (2012). https://doi.org/10.4121/uuid:3926db30-f712-4394-aebc-75976070e91f
15. Dumas, M., La Rosa, M., Mendling, J., Reijers, H.A.: Fundamentals of Business Process Management. Springer, Heidelberg (2018). https://doi.org/10.1007/978-3-662-56509-4

16. Fan, S., Hua, Z., Storey, V.C., Zhao, J.L.: A process ontology based approach to easing semantic ambiguity in business process modeling. Data Knowl. Eng. **102**, 57–77 (2016)

17. Ferreira, R.C.B., Thom, L.H., de Oliveira, J.P.M., Avila, D.T., dos Santos, R.I., Fantinato, M.: Assisting process modeling by identifying business process elements in natural language texts. In: de Cesare, S., Frank, U. (eds.) ER 2017. LNCS, vol. 10651, pp. 154–163. Springer, Cham (2017). https://doi.org/10.1007/978-3-319-70625-2_15

18. Franceschetti, M., Seiger, R., Lopez, H., Burattin, A., Garcia-Banuelos, L., Weber, B.: Ambiguity taxonomy development iterations (2023). https://doi.org/10.5281/zenodo.8268074

19. Franceschetti, M., Seiger, R., Lopez, H., Burattin, A., Garcia-Banuelos, L., Weber, B.: A characterization of ambiguity in BPM (2023). https://doi.org/10.5281/zenodo.7944319

20. Freedman, D.S., Singer, B., Swain, F.S.: The regulatory flexibility act: orienting federal regulation to small business. Dick. L. Rev. **93**, 439 (1988)

21. Friedrich, F., Mendling, J., Puhlmann, F.: Process model generation from natural language text. In: Mouratidis, H., Rolland, C. (eds.) CAiSE 2011. LNCS, vol. 6741, pp. 482–496. Springer, Heidelberg (2011). https://doi.org/10.1007/978-3-642-21640-4_36

22. Frisson, S.: Semantic underspecification in language processing. Lang. Linguist. Compass **3**(1), 111–127 (2009)

23. Gleich, B., Creighton, O., Kof, L.: Ambiguity detection: towards a tool explaining ambiguity sources. In: Wieringa, R., Persson, A. (eds.) REFSQ 2010. LNCS, vol. 6182, pp. 218–232. Springer, Heidelberg (2010). https://doi.org/10.1007/978-3-642-14192-8_20

24. Hall, J.M., Johnson, M.E.: When should a process be art, not science? Harv. Bus. Rev. **87**(3), 58–65 (2009)

25. Hoppenbrouwers, S.J.B.A., Proper, H.A.E., van der Weide, T.P.: A fundamental view on the process of conceptual modeling. In: Delcambre, L., Kop, C., Mayr, H.C., Mylopoulos, J., Pastor, O. (eds.) ER 2005. LNCS, vol. 3716, pp. 128–143. Springer, Heidelberg (2005). https://doi.org/10.1007/11568322_9

26. Janiesch, C., et al.: The internet of things meets business process management: a manifesto. IEEE Syst. Man Cybern. Mag. **6**(4), 34–44 (2020)

27. Krogstie, J.: Quality in Business Process Modeling. Springer, Heidelberg (2016). https://doi.org/10.1007/978-3-319-42512-2

28. Kumar, A., Soffer, P., Tsoury, A.: Normalizing object-centric process logs by applying database principles. Inf. Syst. **115**, 102196 (2023)

29. Kundisch, D., et al.: An update for taxonomy designers. Bus. Inf. Syst. Eng. **64**(4), 421–439 (2022)

30. de Leoni, M.M., Mannhardt, F.: Road traffic fine management process (2015). https://doi.org/10.4121/uuid:270fd440-1057-4fb9-89a9-b699b47990f5

31. Liang, L., et al.: Combining spatial-temporal and phylogenetic analysis approaches for improved understanding on global H5N1 transmission. PLoS One **5**(10) (2010)

32. López, H.A.: Challenges in legal process discovery. In: ITBPM@ BPM, pp. 68–73 (2021)

33. López, H.A., Marquard, M., Muttenthaler, L., Strømsted, R.: Assisted declarative process creation from natural language descriptions. In: 23rd International Enterprise Distributed Object Computing Workshop, pp. 96–99. IEEE (2019)

34. Nickerson, R.C., Varshney, U., Muntermann, J.: A method for taxonomy development and its application in information systems. Eur. J. Inf. Syst. **22**(3), 336–359 (2013)
35. Pegoraro, M.: Probabilistic and non-deterministic event data in process mining: embedding uncertainty in process analysis techniques. arXiv preprint arXiv:2205.04827 (2022)
36. Pittke, F., Leopold, H., Mendling, J.: Automatic detection and resolution of lexical ambiguity in process models. IEEE Trans. Softw. Eng. **41**(6), 526–544 (2015)
37. Rosa, L.S., Silva, T.S., Fantinato, M., Thom, L.H.: A visual approach for identification and annotation of business process elements in process descriptions. Comput. Stand. Interfaces **81**, 103601 (2022)
38. Rosa, M.L., Dumas, M., ter Hofstede, A.H.M., Mendling, J.: Configurable multi-perspective business process models. Inf. Syst. **36**(2), 313–340 (2011)
39. Rosemann, M.: Explorative process design patterns. In: Fahland, D., Ghidini, C., Becker, J., Dumas, M. (eds.) BPM 2020. LNCS, vol. 12168, pp. 349–367. Springer, Cham (2020). https://doi.org/10.1007/978-3-030-58666-9_20
40. Schwitter, R., Fuchs, N.E.: Attempto - from specifications in controlled natural language towards executable specifications. CoRR cmp-lg/9603004 (1996)
41. Seddon, H., Rea, R.: Derbyshire shared care pathology guidelines - hypokalaemia in adults (2012). https://www.uhdb.nhs.uk/shared-care-pathology-guidelines. Accessed 02 May 2023
42. Seiger, R., Franceschetti, M., Weber, B.: An interactive method for detection of process activity executions from IoT data. Future Internet **15**(2), 77 (2023)
43. Silva, T.S., Thom, L.H., Weber, A., de Oliveira, J.P.M., Fantinato, M.: Empirical analysis of sentence templates and ambiguity issues for business process descriptions. In: Panetto, H., Debruyne, C., Proper, H.A., Ardagna, C.A., Roman, D., Meersman, R. (eds.) OTM 2018. LNCS, vol. 11229, pp. 279–297. Springer, Cham (2018). https://doi.org/10.1007/978-3-030-02610-3_16
44. Suriadi, S., Andrews, R., ter Hofstede, A.H., Wynn, M.T.: Event log imperfection patterns for process mining: towards a systematic approach to cleaning event logs. Inf. Syst. **64**, 132–150 (2017)
45. Weske, M.: Business Process Management - Concepts, Languages, Architectures, 3rd edn. Springer, Heidelberg (2019). https://doi.org/10.1007/978-3-662-59432-2
46. Weske, M., Decker, G., Dumas, M., La Rosa, M., Mendling, J., Reijers, H.A.: Model collection of the business process management academic initiative (2020). https://doi.org/10.5281/zenodo.3758705
47. White, S.A., Miers, D.: BPMN Modeling and Reference Guide: Understanding and Using BPMN. Future Strategies Inc. (2008)
48. Winter, K., van der Aa, H., Rinderle-Ma, S., Weidlich, M.: Assessing the compliance of business process models with regulatory documents. In: Dobbie, G., Frank, U., Kappel, G., Liddle, S.W., Mayr, H.C. (eds.) ER 2020. LNCS, vol. 12400, pp. 189–203. Springer, Cham (2020). https://doi.org/10.1007/978-3-030-62522-1_14

Dealing with the Evolution of Event-Based Choreographies of BPMN Fragments: Definition and Proof of Concept

Jesús Ortiz[✉] [iD], Victoria Torres [iD], and Pedro Valderas [iD]

PROS Research Centre, Universitat Politècnica de València, Valencia, Spain
{jortiz,vtorres,pvalderas}@pros.upv.es

Abstract. Organisations usually use Business Processes (BPs) to describe their goals. However, the decentralisation found nowadays in many organisations forces them to coordinate fragmented BPs to achieve their goals. In this context, microservices architectures are an excellent choice to coordinate such fragments. To maintain a lower coupling among microservices, they are usually composed through event-based choreographies. This makes it hard to analyse business requirements since the composition flow is split among microservices. Our previous work improves this issue with an approach to implement microservice compositions based on the global definition in a BPMN collaboration model and its further execution through an event-based choreography of BPMN fragments. In this work, we extend this approach by facing the challenge of evolving these choreographies from the local perspective of one microservice. Each microservice oversees the execution of its BPMN fragment. If one microservice changes its fragment locally, the rest of the microservices should adapt theirs to maintain the functional integrity of the composition. We have formally defined a catalogue of adaptation rules that must be applied when a local change is performed to adapt the affected microservices. We have proposed a new microservice architecture that integrates a MAPE-K control loop to automate the application of the adaptation rules. Finally, we have evaluated both the architecture and the adaptation rules through the implementation of a proof-of-concept prototype.

Keywords: Microservices · composition · BPMN · MAPE-K · evolution

1 Introduction

Business processes (BPs) are the key instrument to organize and understand the interrelationships of the different activities in an organization in order to describe their goals [1]. When these activities are performed in a decentralized way, e.g., by different departments within the same organization, microservice architectures turn into a very interesting and convenient way to implement such processes due mainly to their decoupling nature. Microservice architectures [2] propose the decomposition of applications into small independent building blocks (the microservices) that focus on single business capabilities. When we want to support the goals defined in the business processes of organisations that use such architecture, microservices need to be composed. Within this context,

J. P. A. Almeida et al. (Eds.): ER 2023, LNCS 14320, pp. 296–313, 2023.
https://doi.org/10.1007/978-3-031-47262-6_16

to keep a lower coupling and independence among microservices for deployment and evolution, these compositions are usually implemented by means of event-based choreographics. However, choreographies split the control flow of compositions among the different participant microservices, which makes them hard to analyse and understand when requirements change. Our previous work [3] improves this problem by proposing a microservices composition approach based on the choreography of BPMN fragments. In this approach, business process engineers create a global view of the microservice composition through a BPMN collaboration diagram. Then, this diagram is split into BPMN fragments which are executed through an event-based choreography. This composition approach is supported by a microservice architecture developed to achieve that both descriptions of a composition, the *global composition view* and the one split into *BPMN fragments*, coexist simultaneously in the same system.

This solution introduces two main benefits regarding the microservice composition. First, it facilitates business engineers to analyse the control flow if the composition's requirements need to be modified since they have available the *global composition view* of the composition. Second, it provides a high level of decoupling among the microservices that participate in a composition, since it is implemented as an event-based choreography of independent BPMN fragments. However, this solution introduces a new challenge to be faced: how to evolve a microservice composition that is globally defined in a BPMN collaboration diagram but executed through a choreography of BPMN fragments.

In this work, we face the evolution of a microservice composition from a bottom-up perspective, i.e., when a participant introduces a local change in an individual BPMN fragment. To achieve this, we present a formal specification of adaptation rules that describe how the BPMN fragments of microservices must evolve to maintain the functional integrity of the composition when another microservice introduces a local change. In particular, we focus on those changes that can affect the collaboration among microservices as we discuss further. Additionally, we propose an extension of the architecture presented in [3] to integrate the presented adaptation rules through a new microservice component that implements a MAPE-K control loop. This new microservice oversees automating the characterisation of local changes done by a microservice and selecting the adaptation rule that must be applied to keep, as much as possible, the participation of all partners. We evaluate the extended architecture with a proof-of-concept validation through the implementation of a prototype. Considering the major problems identified by the BPM community [4], the contribution of this paper focuses on improving the problem of automating the redesign of processes, which currently remains as a manual and cognitively demanding task, making it time-consuming, labour-intensive and error-prone.

The rest of this paper is organised as follows: Sect. 2 presents the previous work required to understand the current proposal and states the problem being addressed. Section 3 formally defines an event-based choreography of BPMN fragments and proposes, based on this definition, a set of adaptation rules to face the evolution of the choreography when a local change occurs. Section 5 presents the microservice architecture solution designed to support our proposal and Sect. 7 evaluates a prototype implementing it. Section 8 analyses the related work. Finally, conclusions are commented on in Sect. 8.

2   Previous Work and Problem Statement

To properly understand our current work, this section presents an overview of the approach presented in [3] to create a microservice composition based on the event-based choreography of BPMN fragments. This approach proposes to create a microservice composition in two main steps: (1) by creating the *global composition view* of the composition in a BPMN collaboration diagram following an orchestration approach and (2) by splitting this model into *BPMN fragments* that are deployed into separated microservices and executed through an event-based choreography.

We use BPMN collaboration diagrams since they allow us to separate the functional responsibilities of the different microservices and to represent the interaction between the microservices. In addition, we can describe the internal behaviour of each microservice together with the behaviour of the composition from a global perspective [21].

As a representative example, we define a scenario based on the e-commerce domain, which describes the process of placing an order in an online shop. We use this simple example since we aim to explain the basic concepts of our approach, and because this paper focuses on characterising all the changes that can occur in the different BPMN elements that compose a microservice process. The different tasks and events that make up this process are distributed by responsibilities in four different lanes: *Customers*, *Inventory*, *Payment*, and *Shipment* (see Fig. 1).

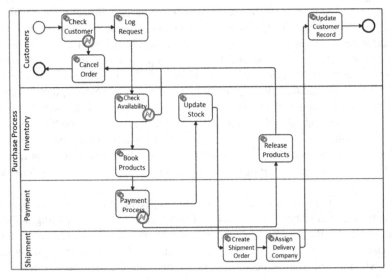

Fig. 1. Global composition view of a microservice composition based on BPMN fragments.

After creating the *global composition view* of the composition, the second step consists in splitting it by responsibilities into independent BPMN fragments that will be managed by different microservices. This split is performed automatically by a tool we developed in [3] where each BPMN fragment is created as a pool with the tasks that are defined in the corresponding lane and a list of catch/throw events that are automatically added to support the event-based choreography. The microservices managing each fragment are endowed with a process engine that oversees the execution of their respective BPMN fragment to execute (1) the tasks defined in the pool (what we call *functional requirements*), and (2) the catch/throwing events to either receive or publish asynchronous events in a communication bus to support the collaboration with the rest of participants (what we call *coordination requirements*). Thus, the microservice composition is executed by means of an event-based choreography of BPMN fragments in which microservices wait for specific events to execute their corresponding piece of work (see Fig. 2).

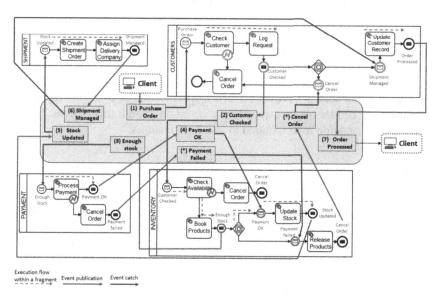

Fig. 2. Example of an event-based choreography of BPMN fragments.

Problem Statement. Our approach allows evolving the composition following either a top-down or a bottom-up approach. On the one hand, a top-down approach proposes to address the changes from a global perspective by modifying the *global composition view* of the composition and splitting it again into BPMN fragments. This evolution is natively supported in our previous work [3]. On the other hand, a bottom-up approach implies modifying a BPMN fragment from the local perspective of a microservice. This requires synchronising changes with both the BPMN fragments of the rest of the microservices that are affected by the change and the *global composition view* of the composition. Allowing local changes in a microservice reinforces the independence among development teams that is demanded by this type of architecture. Note that a change may affect a *functional requirement* (e.g., modifying a BPMN task) or a *coordination requirement* (e.g., modifying a throwing/catch event). While local changes in *functional requirements* only affect the internal behaviour of a microservice and do not require the adaptation of the rest of the participants [3], local changes in *coordination requirements* can have an impact on the composition (eventually causing its failure), affecting the participation of the rest of microservices. For instance (see Fig. 2), if the *Customers* microservice deletes the throwing event that sends the message *Customer Checked*, the *Inventory* microservice, which is waiting for it, will never start, and the microservice composition will never continue. Therefore, changes in these types of requirements imply coordinated actions in two or more microservices in such a way a correct communication between microservices is ensured. In this work, we focus on supporting the bottom-up evolution of coordination requirements found in such distributed compositions.

3   Formalisation of the Evolution of Microservice Compositions

As explained above, the main goal of this work is to support the evolution of event-based choreographies of BPMN fragments when a local change is introduced in the *coordination requirements* of a fragment. To achieve this, we precisely describe independently from any implementation technology, the adaptations to be done when local changes are produced. First, Sect. 3.1 presents a formal specification of concepts related to the choreography of BPMN fragments; and then, based on these formalisations, Sect. 3.2 introduces the adaptation rules required to face local changes.

3.1   Formal Definitions for the Choreography of BPMN Fragments

Definition 1. *Local Fragment (Lf).* As we can see in Fig. 2, the local fragment of a microservice is defined as a BPMN process that is made up of a set of tasks and interaction activities, which are coordinated by control nodes that define a sequence of nodes (*SEQ*), a choice (based on a condition) between two or more nodes (*CHC*), a parallel execution of nodes (*PAR*), and an iteration over several nodes (*RPT*). In addition, the start of a BPMN process must be associated with at least one start *ReceiveEvent* (can be one or more) and the end with at least one end *SendEvent* (can be one or more). Thus, the *Lf* of a microservice m is formalised as follows:

$Lf_m ::= \{ReceiveEvent(Message)\}, [\{PNode\}], \{SendEvent(Message)\}$
$PNode ::= Activity \mid ControlNode$
$Activity ::= Task \mid Interaction$
$Interaction ::= SendEvent(Message) \mid ReceiveEvent(Message)$
$ControlNode ::= SEQ(\{PNode\}) \mid PAR(\{PNode\}) \mid CHC(\{PNode\}) \mid RPT(\{PNode\})$

For example, the local BPMN fragment of the *Shipment* microservice can be represented as follow:

$Lf_{Shipment} = ReceiveEvent(Stock\ Updated), SEQ(Task(Create\ Order), Task(Assign\ Driver)), SendEvent(Shipment\ Managed)$

Associated to the definition of *Lfm*, we define two functions: (1) *getMessage(i, Lfm)* which returns the *Message* of the interaction element *i* that is being sent/received by the fragment *Lfm*; and (2), *putMessage(i, newMessage, Lfm)* which sets the message *newMessage* in the interaction element *i* in the fragment *Lfm*, changing the message that *i* sends/receives. For instance, the function *getMessage(ReceiveEvent(Stock Updated), Lf Shipment)* returns the message *Stock Updated*; and the function *setMessage(ReceiveEvent(Payment Ok), Success Payment, Lf Inventory)* changes the *ReceiveEvent* of the *Inventory*'s Local Fragment to start listening to the message *Success Payment* instead of *Payment Ok*.

Definition 2. *Choreography.* As we can see in Fig. 2, an event-based choreography of BPMN fragments is defined by the participant microservices, their local fragments, and the coordination among them, which is defined by the messages they publish and/or expect to receive.

Thus, a choreography *C* is defined as a tuple *(M, L, InputI, OuputI, Coord)* where:

- *M = {m1, m2, ... mn}* is the set of all participant microservices.
- *L = {Lfm}ₘ∈M* is the set of the participant microservices' local fragments (c.f. Definition 1).
- *InputI: Lfm∈ L → {ReceiveEvent(Message) ∈ Lfm}*, for each microservice, is the set of *ReceiveEvent* elements of its *Local Fragment*, i.e., the input interface of the fragment.
- *OutputI: Lfm∈ L → {SendEvent(Message) ∈ Lfm}*, for each microservice, is the set of *SendEvents* elements of its *Local Fragment*, i.e., the output interface of the fragment.
- *Coord: InputI(Lfma)ma∈ M ↔ OuputI(Lfmb)mb∈ M* is a partial mapping function between the input interface of a microservice *ma* and the output interface of a microservice *mb*, in such a way the message received by a *ReceiveEvent* in *ma* is the same message sent by a *SendEvent* in *mb*. This represents the coordination between two microservices. This function is a partial mapping, since it can return a subset of *SendEvents* for a message received by a *ReceiveEvent* and a subset of *ReceiveEvents* for a message sent by a *SendEvent*.

For example, a partial formalisation of the choreography presented in Fig. 2 is the following:

M={Customers, Inventory, Payment, Shipment}

L={Lfcustomers(ReceiveEvent(Process Purchase Order), SEQ(Task(Check Customer), CHC({
Task(Log Request), SendEvent(Customer Checked), ...}), Lfinventory (..), Lfshipment (...), Lfpayment (...) }}

InputI(LfCustomers)={ReceiveEvent(Process Purchase Order), ReceiveEvent(Shipment Managed)}
InputI(Lfinventory)={ReceiveEvent(Customer Checked),ReceiveEvent(Payment OK),... }
[...]
OutputI(LfCustomers)={SendEvent(Customer Checked), SendEvent(Order Processed)}
OutputI(Lfinventory) = { SendEvent(Stock Updated), { SendEvent(Cancel Order)}
[...]
Coord = { ReceiveEvent(Customer Checked) ∈ InputtI(Lfinventory) = SendEvent(Customer Checked)
∈ OutputI(lfcustomer), ...}

Definition 3. *Change in a Local Fragment Lfm.* We consider three different types of changes: (1) *Delete*, which consists of removing a *PNode* in a local fragment *Lfm*; (2) *Insert*, which consists of adding a new *PNode* in a local fragment *Lfm*; and (3) *Update*, which consists of replacing one *PNode* (*Old PNode*) with a new one (*New PNode*) in a local fragment *Lfm*.

> $Change ::= Delete(PNode, Lfm) \mid Insert(PNode, Lfm) \mid Update(Old\ PNode,\ New\ PNode,$
> $Lfm)$

Besides the above definitions, we also propose the following three auxiliary functions to support the adaptation of the BPMN fragments when a local change is done in a coordination requirement.

Definition 4. *Complement Function.* Assume that ia_1 corresponds to an interaction activity (*SendEvent* or *ReceiveEvent*) in a local fragment Lf_n. Then, the complement of ia_i corresponds to the list of counterparts defined in the partial mapping *Coord* of a specific choreography (c.f. Definition 2).

> $Complement\ (ia_i,\ Lf_n) = \{ai_j \in Lf_m \mid \exists\ (ia_i,\ ia_j) \in Coord\}$

For instance in Fig. 2, this function over the interaction activity *SendEvent(Customer Checked)* of the local fragment *Customers* returns the interaction activity *ReceiveEvent(Customer Checked)* of the local fragment *Inventory*. Note that this function can return a set of interaction activities since, for instance, a message sent by a local fragment can be received by several ones.

Definition 5. *PresetReceive Function.* The *PresetReceive* of a *SendEvent(Message) se* in a fragment *Lfm* corresponds to the set of *ReceiveEvent(Message)* in *Lfm* that are executed before *se* in a sequence flow.

> $PresetReceive\ (se,\ Lfm) = \{re \in Lfm \mid re \in InputI_{Lfm}\ \&\ \exists SEQ(re,\ se) \in Lfm\}$

For instance in Fig. 2, this function over the *SendEvent(Stock Updated)* of the local fragment *Inventory* returns *ReceiveEvent(Payment OK)* and *ReceiveEvent(Customer Checked)* of the same fragment.

Definition 6. *PrecedingReceive Function.* The *preceding* of a *SendEvent(Message) se* in a fragment *Lfm* corresponds with the *ReceiveEvent(Message) re* in *Lfm* that is executed immediately before *se* in a sequence flow.

> $PrecedingReceive(se,\ Lfm) = \{\ re \in PresetReceive(se,\ Lfm) \mid \nexists\ re' \in Pre\text{-}$
> $setReceive(se,\ Lfm)\ \&\ SEQ(re,\ re') = true\ \}$

For instance in see Fig. 2 this function over the *SendEvent(Stock Updated)* of the local fragment *Inventory* returns *ReceiveEvent(Payment OK)* of the same fragment.

3.2 Adaptation Rules

Based on the formal definitions presented above, we have defined a catalogue of adaptation rules that describe how a local change must be managed to maintain, when possible, the functional integrity and the compatibility of the choreography. By *functional integrity*, we mean that all the tasks defined in each microservice must be completed. Consequently, there must be at least one potential *SendEvent* that sends a message to be received by a corresponding *ReceiveEvent*. By *compatibility*, we mean that all BPMN fragments of the choreography must end safe and terminate in an acceptable state. However, these rules do not ensure properties such as deadlock-free and fault-tolerance in composition. These problems have been extensively researched by the BPM community [23, 24] and to face them we propose to apply the change patterns identified in [22] to ensure the correctness of the composition after the change and the adaptation rules are applied.

A total amount of 14 rules have been defined. However, due to space issues, this paper only presents two representative examples. The complete description of the catalogue of rules can be found in [6]. In this paper, we extend our previous contributions by formalizing the adaptation rules through the description of algorithms that can be executed independently of the implementation technology used to compose the choreography. Based on our previous work [5] we have identified every add, delete, and update modification that can be applied in an interaction activity (*SendEvent* or *ReceiveEvent*). We only focus on these types of modifications as they are challenging by themselves, and any further change can be written as a combination of them. We have applied all the modifications identified in three different case studies, and we have analysed the actions required to maintain the functional integrity and compatibility of the composition. This was done following an iterative and incremental process [7] in such a way the adaptation rules were progressively developed and tested in the case studies, refining previous definitions when some errors or objections were detected.

6 out of 14 rules are defined to support delete changes (3 affect *SendEvents*, and 3 *ReceiveEvents*). 6 out of 14 rules are defined to support update changes (3 affect *SendEvents*, and 3 *ReceiveEvents*). Finally, the 2 remaining rules are defined to support insert changes. In this case just for changes that affect *ReceiveEvents* since add changes that affect *SendEvents* do not introduce inconsistencies between microservices but extend instead the possibilities of the composition by adding new throw. In the following paragraphs we explain two representative rules and characterize them.

The first rule presented in this paper faces the removal of a $SendEvent(msg_1)$ in the local fragment *Lf* of the microservice *m*. This change modifies the output interface (*OutputI*, see Definition 2) of *Lfm*. Thus, it affects all the microservices that include a $ReceiveEvent(msg_1)$ in its input interface (*InputI*), which will never start or continue since their execution depends on the triggering of such message (msg_1).

To support this change, we propose the Adaptation Rule #1 (see below) that adapts the affected microservices to start listening to the message triggered just before the deleted one. This rule receives as input a *Delete* local change (see Definition 3) and uses the *precedingReceive()* function to search for the *ReceiveEvent preRec* that is executed immediately before the deleted *SendEvent se*. Then, the *Complement()* function is used to obtain a list *reList* with all the *ReceiveEvents* affected by the change. Finally, for each *ReceiveEvent*, the *Update()* function is executed to replace them with *preRec*.

Adaptation Rule #1
Input *Delete(se, lf1)	se ∈ lf1 & se ∈ OutputI$_{lf1}$*
preRec = PrecedingReceive(se, lf1)
reList = Complement(se, lf1)
For each *element re of reList	re ∈ lfn & re ∈ InputI$_{lfn}$*
Update(re, preRec, lfn)
End for

Figure 3 shows a graphical example of the application of this rule. If the *SendEvent(Customer Checked)* is removed from the local fragment of *Customers*, the *Inventory* microservice, which is waiting for it, will never start. To allow the *Inventory* microservice to complete its tasks, it is modified to wait for the message previously caught by the modified fragment, i.e., to wait for the *Process Purchase Order* message instead. This adaptation of the affected local fragment maintains the functional integrity of the choreography (i.e., all the tasks executed before the local change are executed afterwards). However, two microservices that initially worked sequentially (e.g., first, *Customers* checks the customer information, and then *Inventory* checks the availability of the purchased products) are now executed in parallel (e.g., after the adaptation, the start of the *Customers* microservice and the *Inventory* microservice are executed when the client sends the message *Process Purchase Order*). As we explain in Sect. 7 (execution phase), applying this rule requires human supervision since the order of execution of the microservices has changed. However, as described in [5], depending on the magnitude of the change, we find adaptation rules that may or may not require human supervision. For instance, the second rule presented next can be automatically applied without human supervision.

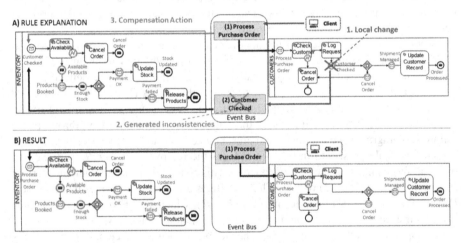

Fig. 3. Example of Adaptation Rule #1.

This second rule faces the update of a *SendEvent(msg$_1$)* in the local fragment *Lfm* of the microservice *m* to send a new message (*msg2*) that does not exist in the context of the composition. This change modifies the output interface (*OutputI*, see Definition 2) of *Lfm*. Thus, it affects all the microservices that include a *ReceiveEvent(msg$_1$)* in its input interface (*InputI*), which will never start since their execution depends on the triggering of *msg$_1$*.

To support this change, we propose the Adaptation Rule #7 (see below) that adapts the affected microservices to start listening to the new message triggered (*newMsg*). This rule receives as input an *Update* local change (see Definition 3) that contains the *SendEvent* *se* that is being updated and the new *SendEvent se'* that will replace it. The algorithm obtains the new message that is being sent with the *getMessage()* function. Then, the *Complement()* function obtains a list (*reList*) with all the *ReceiveEvent*s affected by the change. For each of them, the *putMessage()* function is executed to receive the new message.

Adaptation Rule #7
Input *Update(se, se', lf1)	se ∈ lf1 & se ∈ OutputI$_{lf1}$ & ∀lf ∈ L: ∄se' ∈ lf*
newMsg = getMessage(se', lf1)
reList = Complement(se, lf1)
For each *element re of reList	re ∈ lfn & re ∈ InputI$_{lfn}$*
putMessage(re, newMsg, lfn)
End for

Figure 4 shows a graphical example of the application of this rule. If the *SendEvent(Payment OK)* is replaced with a new *SendEvent* called *SendEvent(Success Payment)*, the *Inventory* microservice will not continue its tasks since it is waiting for a message that is no longer sent. Therefore, the *Inventory* microservice can be modified to wait for the new message sent, i.e., to wait for the message *Success Payment*. Even though in this case there is only one affected microservice, note that this adaptation rule will be executed for every microservice that is waiting for receiving the updated message. This adaptation rule maintains the functional integrity and compatibility of the choreography and the coordination between microservices without altering the order of execution of the microservices. Consequently, as we explain in Sect. 7, this type of rule can be applied automatically without human supervision.

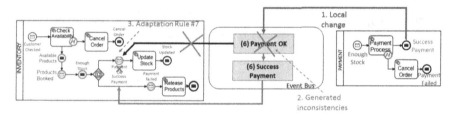

Fig. 4. Example of Adaptation Rule #7.

4 Supporting Microservice Architecture

In this section, we describe an extension of the microservice architecture presented in [3] to integrate the adaptation rules presented above. The objective of this architecture is to automate the application of the adaptation rules presented above as much as possible when a change in coordination requirements is done from a local perspective.

We have extended our microservice architecture by implementing a MAPE-K control loop, which is typically used to manage the adaptation of autonomic systems [10]. A MAPE-K control loop consists of four phases: the 1) **M**onitoring phase; the 2) **A**nalysis phase; the 3) **P**lanning phase; and the 4) **E**xecution phase. In addition, the MAPE-K control loop includes a **K**nowledge base that stores properties to describe the past and present state of the system and its environment [11].

The extended version of the architecture is shown in Fig. 5. Initially, the architecture was designed with the following components: (1) the business microservices that participate in the composition (i.e., *Customers, Inventory, Payment,* and *Shipment* microservices); (2) the *Global Manager* microservice that oversees the BPMN collaboration diagram that represents the *global composition*; and (3) an event bus that supports the exchange of messages among microservices at execution time. In this work we have revised the architecture by: (1) introducing the *MAPE-K Controller* a new microservice introduced to control the three first phases of the MAKE-K loop; (2) endowing the *Global Manager* microservice with the adaptation rules and a new component that oversees the execution phase of the MAKE-K loop; and (3) introducing the *Knowledge Base* component to register the local changes that occur in the system.

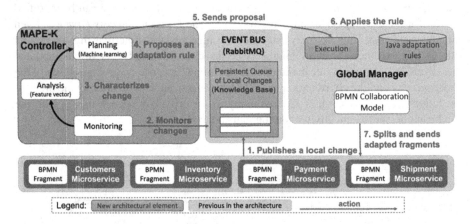

Fig. 5. Representation of the extended architecture.

To properly understand the MAPE-K loop implemented in our architecture, let us give additional details first about the Knowledge Base and then about the MAPE-K.

Knowledge Base: In this work, we want to evolve a microservice composition that is implemented as an event-based choreography of BPMN fragments when a local change is done. Thus, we need a Knowledge Base that represents and stores the local changes that occur in the system to be able to react to them. Thus, each time a microservice performs a local change in its BPMN fragment, the change is published in the event bus (Step 1 in Fig. 5). The change is described according to Definition 3 (cf. Sect. 3.1). Thus, the log of local changes registered in the Knowledge Base would look like:

Delete(Task (CheckCustomer), Customers), Insert(Task(VIPCusomter), Customers), Delete(SendEvent(Stock Updated), Inventory), Update(Task (CheckAvailability), Task (CheckStock), Inventory), etc.

Monitoring phase: This phase identifies when a published local change can introduce inconsistencies in the coordination requirements (Step 2 in Fig. 5). If we analyse the log of local changes shown above, we can see that only one registered change, the

Delete(SendEvent(Stock Updated), Inventory), produces inconsistencies in the coordination requirements. The others affect only the internal functionality of each microservice without affecting the rest of the partners, i.e., they do not modify the output interface (*OutputI*, see Definition 2), which do not require the application of any adaptation rule. In a previous work [5], we analysed in detail the changes that can produce inconsistencies in coordination requirements. In general terms, inconsistencies appear when a *ReceiveEvent* or *SendEvent* of a BPMN fragment is altered. Thus, each time one of these changes is detected, the next phase of the MAPE-K loop, the Analysis phase, is performed.

Analysis phase: This phase collects and analyses all the necessary information to characterise a local change in detail. The information required to perform such characterisation is collected from the local change registered in the Knowledge Base (Step 3 in Fig. 5). Specifically, part of the information collected includes the following features: (F1) the type of the modified element (*SendEvent* or *ReceiveEvent*); (F2) the type of change that has been done (delete, update, or insert); (F3) whether or not the change results in the publication of a new message in the choreography; (F4) whether or not a BPMN throwing event is affected; or (F5) whether or not a BPMN catch event is affected. Besides this information, as shown in [8], more data is collected to characterise the change. For simplification purposes, we only present the above-introduced five ones. Note that this characterisation of the local change is done to be interpreted by a machine learning algorithm used in the Planning phase. Thus, derived data is explicitly included to improve the performance of the machine learning algorithm (e.g., a BPMN catch event is affected (F5) when the modified element (F2) is a *SendEvent* and the type of change (F1) is delete or update; thus, F5 is derived from F1 and F2). When all this information is collected, it is encoded as a feature vector [12]. As a representative example, Table 1 represents a partial characterisation of the local change presented in Fig. 3 (*Delete(SendEvent(Stock Updated), Inventory)*): the modified element (F1) is a *SendEvent* (represented by the value 1), the action done (F2) is a deletion (represented by the value 0); the change (F3) does not result in the publication of a new message since is a deletion (represented by the value 0); a BPMN throwing event (F4) is not affected (represented by the value 0), and a BPMN catch event (F5) is affected (represented by the value 1).

Table 1. A partial feature vector characterising the delete change is illustrated in Fig. 3

F1	F2	F3	F4	F5	...
1	0	0	0	1	...

Planning phase: Once a local change has been characterised in a feature vector, the planning phase must select one of the rules contained in the catalogue of adaptation rules to solve the inconsistencies created by the change (Step 4 in Fig. 5). Thus, in this phase, a machine learning algorithm processes the feature vector, and depending on how the change has been characterized, selects one of the rules from the catalogue. We propose using an algorithm based on machine learning techniques since it provides us with several benefits: note that by manually implementing an algorithm to predict an adaptation rule, we need to code a vast amount of complex conditions, which is a time-consuming and error-prone task. In addition, this turns its further redesign difficult. Using a machine learning algorithm, this process is automatically done by a prediction model that just needs to be trained with data. Also, we can re-train the prediction model or change the technique used to predict either to improve the predictor's performance or to add more adaptation rules in the future.

Execution phase: Once the machine learning algorithm has selected an adaptation rule to be applied, the *Global Manager* microservice is informed (Step 5 in Fig. 5) to apply it in the BPMN collaboration diagram that represents the *global composition view* (Step 6). To do so, we proposed in [5] an application protocol that classifies the adaptation rules into *automatic adaptation* or *adaptation with acceptance*. Depending on this classification, the way of applying the adaptation rules changes.

An adaptation rule classified as *automatic adaptation* can be applied automatically without human supervision. An example of this adaptation is the one proposed by Adaptation Rule #7 (see Fig. 4). In these cases, the *Global Manager* can automatically apply an adaptation rule to the *global composition view* and synchronise the performed adaptations with the affected microservices (Step 7 in Fig. 5).

An adaptation rule classified as *adaptation with acceptance* implies some alterations in the order of execution of the affected microservices. Thus, it must be manually accepted by business engineers. An example of this type of adaptation is the one proposed by Adaptation Rule #1 (see Fig. 3). This adaptation implies that some microservices that were initially defined in a sequential way are executed now in parallel. Consequently, business engineers need to accept the proposed adaptation.

5   Prototype Evaluation

According to [13], a way of preliminary evaluating the proposal of a new architecture is through developing a prototype. Next, we introduce a realisation of the proposed architecture and the adaptation rules formalised in Sect. 3 as a prototype involving mapping technology choices onto the solution concepts[1].

Adaptation rules implementation. Each rule is implemented as a transformation between two models (the original BPMN fragment and the adapted one) expressed in the same language. For instance, considering Adaptation Rule #1 (see Fig. 3), it can be implemented as a model transformation that, when applied to the original BPMN fragment of a microservice (*Inventory* in the presented example), transforms it into a new version that adapts the Start *ReceiveEvent* to wait for another message (in the example, the *Customer Checked* message should be replaced by the *Process Purchase Order* message). Currently, there are several solutions to implement model transformations [14]. In this work, we have used a direct manipulation approach based on the Java BPMN parser provided by the Camunda platform. We have selected this option since it is supported by other Java tools that facilitate the integration of the adaptation rules with our proposed microservice architecture [3].

---

[1] Source code available at: https://github.com/MicroservicesResearch/MAPE-K-Loop.git.

Microservice architecture. All microservices are implemented by using the Spring Boot Java framework; business microservices are endowed with a Camunda BPMN engine to execute their BPMN fragment; the event bus is supported by a RabbitMQ message broker; and communication among the Global Manager and the MAPE-K Controller is done through REST APIs.

MAPE-K implementation. Regarding the technology used to implement the different phases of the MAPE-K loop, we took the following decision:

- The Knowledge Base is implemented as a persistent queue in a RabbitMQ message broker. Consequently, the monitoring phase is achieved by subscribing the *MAPE-K Controller* microservice to this queue.
- In the planning phase, we want to predict a nominal value, i.e., the adaptation rule to be applied. Thus, we used a supervised machine-learning technique focused on classification tasks [9]. In order to train algorithms of this type, we need a dataset. We used a synthetic dataset with a total of 272^2 input cases. We have simulated 272 local changes in coordination requirements in four different microservice composition based on our approach, selecting manually the adaptation rule required to solve the inconsistencies generated. We trained different classifiers with different techniques, and in the end, the k-NN technique was the classifier that obtained better results for our purpose in terms of precision (the obtained rule is correct) and recall (the rule is correctly retrieved). Further details about the training and testing of these techniques and the justification of their selection can be found in [8]. The algorithm can only return one rule, and as a consequence, there are no scenarios where two different rules can be applied.
- In the execution phase, the adaptation rules implemented with the BPMN Camunda parser are applied to the *global composition view*. To achieve this, we faced two main technological decisions:

  - How to interact with business engineers when an adaptation needs a manual acceptance (e.g., Rule #1, see Fig. 3). To support this, we have developed a web tool[3] that graphically shows the performed local change and the result of applying the proposed adaptation [5].
  - How to manage running instances of BPMN fragments when an adaptation rule must be applied. To solve this, we used the versioning strategy implemented by the Camunda engine deployed into the microservices to synchronise the adaptation with the instances executed after the adaptation. The running instances of the BPMN fragments that are being executed when the adaptation is applied are not affected.

5.1 Testing the Prototype

Once the proposed architecture was implemented, we did a preliminary test to evaluate the feasibility of evolving a microservice composition with the technology choices we did. To do so, we implemented the running example of this paper and perform different

---

[2] Available at https://github.com/microserviceresearch/ml-microservice-composition-evolution.

[3] A video demo of this tool can be found at: https://microserviceresearch.github.io/

local changes that affect coordination requirements[4]. In particular, the changes we did were the ones described in Table 2. These changes considered the three type of changes defined in Definition 3 (cf. Sect. 3.1) and the two types of interaction activities (*Receive Event* and *SendEvent*) defined in Definition 1 (cf. Sect. 3.1). Each scenario was performed three times. In the Table 2, in the outcome column, the result of each execution is presented. C represents correct, and in these cases the MAPE-K selected the correct rule to integrate the local change. F represents failed, and in these cases the MAPE-K chose an incorrect rule and consequently, the change was not correctly integrated. According to the obtained results, the MAPE-K successfully integrate the introduced change in approximately 80% of the executions. In [8], we present a preliminary test that reinforces the results obtained in this evaluation. Some minor adjustments were made so that the MAPE-K avoids making the errors made in this evaluation in the future. In terms of the correctness, in the executions where the local changes were correctly integrated in the composition, the BPMN collaboration diagram generated as a result was functional, i.e., the application of the rule did not introduce errors on the BPMN processes. In the executions where the selected rule was not correct, the resulting BPMN collaboration diagram was not functional since the change was not correctly integrated. Finally, the adaptation process times were minimal. They lasted for milliseconds and were no relevant differences between different types of changes.

Table 2. Local changes in coordination requirements used to test the architecture.

Mod.	Element	Micro	Out
Delete	*SendEvent(Customer Checked)*	Customers	C/C/C
	SendEvent(Payment OK)	Payment	C/F/C
	ReceiveEvent(Stock Updated)	Shipment	C/C/F
	ReceiveEvent(Enough Stock)	Payment	C/F/C
Update	*SendEvent(Customer Checked)* to throw *VIP Customer*	Customers	F/C/C
	SendEvent(Payment OK) to throw *Success Payment*	Payment	C/C/C
	ReceiveEvent(Customer Checked) to catch *VIP Customer*	Inventory	C/C/F
	ReceiveEvent(Enough Stock) to catch *Available Items*	Payment	C/F/C
Insert	*SendEvent(VIP Customer)*	Customers	C/C/C
	SendEvent(Available Products)	Inventory	C/C/C
	ReceiveEvent(Success Payment)	Customers	C/C/C
	ReceiveEvent(VIP Customer)	Inventory	C/C/F

---

[4] The change of deleting the Send Event *Customer Checked* in the BPMN fragment of the *Customers* microservice was included in the video demo of the web tool (from 1'40")

6   Related Work

In service compositions, [15] provides a formal method for representing syntactic properties of orchestrations and a set of axioms/invariants to align the orchestration model syntactically and semantically. In their work, the orchestration and the choreography are considered two different elements with different representations and consequently, to propagate the changes it is required to apply transformations between the two models. Our proposal implements an architecture to automate the evolution process when a change is introduced from the perspective of one microservice, and we also make it easier to understand the impact that the change and the adaptations have on the composition, since we have a visual representation of the global composition and the fragments.

In flexible business processes, [16] proposes an approach to model business scenarios as a set of small fragments and use data object states to combine them at runtime. Their work differs from ours in that they cover major changes in fragments such as adding new one, while we consider changes that affect specific elements inside the process of a BPMN fragment, such as tasks or interaction elements (throw/catch).

In object-centred process coordination, [26] presents a concept where multiple coordination processes are used to coordinate a relational process structure. In our work, the coordination is distributed between the microservices and thus, we offer a high degree of decoupling between them for its development and evolution. In addition, their work does not consider the evolution of the different objects. [27] presents an artefact that encapsulates process logic and data into objects that, at run-time, are represented as microservices. Their work focuses on scalability and considers the propagation of smaller changes, such as attribute value changes, which do not require coordinated adaptations.

Finally, in change management, [17] proposes change propagation algorithms to ensure the behavioural and structural soundness of choreography partners in cross-organizational processes. We go a step further and propagate and adapt the changes to guarantee the participation of every partner in a composition based on a microservice architecture. Unlike their work, we use a MAPE-K component to automate the evolution process, characterise the produced changes in detail and be able to select an adaptation rule from a catalogue. [18] explains a negotiation phase to apply a change, but no mechanism is proposed to ensure all partners have applied the change. [19] presents an approach to apply incremental changes (modify, add, and delete) to the choreography participants, but it does not consider mechanisms to ensure the propagation of the changes. Our approach follows a protocol that ensures that local changes and adaptations are propagated and implemented in the global composition and to each affected participant. [20] defines a set of rules to ensure the correctness of change operations. Their work is a formalisation of an event-based process and its refinement, but it is unclear how this refinement can be done from a participant's perspective. Furthermore, their proposal has not been put in practice, while ours has been implemented. [25] presents a method to compute different variants of ecosystems if a module rejects an adaptation, maintaining two versions of the ecosystem simultaneously. We follow a protocol to ensure that the change and the adaptation must be agreed with all affected participants in order to be implemented.

7 Conclusions and Further Work

In this paper, we have proposed a strategy to support a bottom-up evolution of microservice compositions that are implemented as event-based choreographies of BPMN fragments. We have formally defined a set of adaptation rules that describe how microservices must adapt their BPMN fragments when one of them introduces a local change. This formalisation allows us to present an evolution strategy that is precisely specified independently of any technology. This facilitates its integration with different infrastructures that can support the choreography of BPMN fragments.

In addition, we propose a new version of an event-based microservice architecture that includes a MAPE-K loop to integrate the adaptation rules. As a proof-of-concept, we have developed a prototype to evaluate the implementation. This allowed us to demonstrate that the proposed evolution strategy can be successfully implemented from a pragmatic point of view. In addition, the presented proof-of-concept implementation constitutes a promising result that reinforces the idea of integrating IA techniques with microservice architectures to support their evolution.

As ongoing work, we are extending this work by considering local changes that affect the data exchanged by the microservice. We are working on its formalisation [6] and integration in the architecture. As further work, we want to study the application of online machine learning techniques so the classifier used in the planning phase of the MAPE-K loop can be automatically re-trained from the different results obtained progressively.

References

1. Weske, M.: Business Process Management: Concepts, Languages, Architectures. Springer, Heidelberg (2007)
2. Lewis, J., Fowler, M.: Microservices (2014). https://martinfowler.com/articles/microservices. html (Accessed April 2023)
3. Valderas, P., Torres, V., Pelechano, V.: A microservice composition approach based on the choreography of BPMN fragments. Inf. Soft. Technol. **127** (2020)
4. Beerepoot, I., et al.: The biggest business process management problems to solve before we die. Comput. Industry **146**, 103837 (2023)
5. Ortiz, J., Torres, V., Valderas, P.: Microservice compositions based on the choreography of BPMN fragments: facing evolution issues. Computing 1–42 (2022)
6. Ortiz, J., Torres, V., Valderas, P.: Formalisation of evolution issues in microservice compositions implemented as a choreography of BPMN fragments. Research Report. https://github. com/MicroservicesResearch/Catalogue-of-Adaptation-Rules/blob/main/Catalogue%20of% 20Adaptation%20Rules.pdf (Accessed May 2023)
7. Larman, C., Basili, V.R.: Iterative and incremental development: a brief history. Computer **36**(6), 47–56 (2003)
8. Ortiz, J., Torres, V., Valderas, P.: A machine learning approach to support a bottom-up evolution of microservice compositions based on the choreography of BPMN fragments. Research Report. https://github.com/MicroservicesResearch/Machine-Learning/blob/main/Machine% 20Learning.pdf (Accessed May 2023)
9. Mohammed, M., Khan, M.B., Bashie, E.B.M.: Machine learning: algorithms and applications. Machine Learning: Algorithms and Applications, pp. 1–204 (2016)

10. Jahan, S., et al.: MAPE-K/MAPE-SAC: an interaction framework for adaptive systems with security assurance cases. Futur. Gener. Comput. Syst. **109**, 197–209 (2020)
11. Garlan, D., Cheng, SW., Schmerl, B.: Increasing system dependability through architecture-based self-repair. In: de Lemos, R., Gacek, C., Romanovsky, A. (eds.) Architecting Dependable Systems. LNCS, vol. 2677, pp. 61–89. Springer, Heidelberg (2003). https://doi.org/10.1007/3-540-45177-3_3
12. Miao, J., Niu, L.: A Survey on Feature Selection. In Procedia Computer Science **91**, 919–926 (2016)
13. Völter, M.: Software architecture-a pattern language for building sustainable software architectures. In: EuroPLoP, pp. 31–66 (2006)
14. Czarnecki, K., Helsen, S.: Classification of model transformation approaches. In: Proceedings of the 2nd OOPSLA Workshop on Generative Techniques in the Context of the Model Driven Architecture, vol. 45, pp. 1–17. USA (2003)
15. Wombacher, A.: Alignment of choreography changes in BPEL processes. In: 2009 IEEE International Conference on Services Computing, pp. 1–8. IEEE (2009)
16. Hewelt, M., Weske, M.: A hybrid approach for flexible case modelling and execution. In: Business Process Management Forum: BPM Forum, Proceedings 14, pp. 38–54. Brazil (2016)
17. Fdhila, W., Indion, C., Rinderle-Ma, S., Reichert, M.: Dealing with change in process choreographies: design and implementation of propagation algorithms. Inf. Syst. 49 (2015)
18. Fdhila, W., Indiono, C., Rinderle-Ma, S., Vetschera, R.: Multi-criteria decision analysis for change negotiation in process collaborations. In: 2017 IEEE 21st International Enterprise Distributed Object Computing Conference (EDOC), pp. 175–183. IEEE (2017)
19. Mukkamala, R.R., Hildebrandt, T., Slaats, T.: Towards trustworthy adaptive case management with dynamic condition response graphs. In: 2013 17th IEEE International Enterprise Distributed Object Computing Conference, pp. 127–136. IEEE (2013)
20. Debois, S., Hildebrandt, T., Slaats, T.: Safety, liveness and run-time refinement for modular process-aware information systems with dynamic sub processes. In: Bjørner, N., de Boer, F. (eds.) FM 2015: Formal Methods. LNCS, vol. 9109, pp. 143–160. Springer, Cham (2015). https://doi.org/10.1007/978-3-319-19249-9_10
21. Corradini, F., Morichetta, A., Polini, A., Re, B., Tiezzi, F.: Collaboration vs. choreography conformance in BPMN 2.0: from theory to practice. In: IEEE 22nd International Enterprise Distributed Object Computing Conference (EDOC), pp. 95–104 (2018)
22. Weber, B., Reichert, M., Rinderle-Ma, S.: Change patterns and change support features–enhancing flexibility in process-aware information systems. Data Knowl. Eng. **66**(3), 438–466 (2008)
23. Fakhfakh, F., Kacem, H.H., Kacem, A.H.: Ensuring the correctness of adaptive business processes: a systematic literature review. Int. J. Comput. Appl. Technol. **62**(3), 189–199 (2020)
24. Vaca, A.J.V., Gasca, R.M.: OPBUS: fault tolerance against integrity attacks in business processes. In: Herrero, Á., Corchado, E., Redondo, C., Alonso, Á. (eds.) Computational Intelligence in Security for Information Systems 2010. AISC, vol. 85, pp. 213–222. Springer, Heidelberg (2010). https://doi.org/10.1007/978-3-642-16626-6_23
25. Manousis, P., Vassiliadis, P., Papastefanatos, G.: Automating the adaptation of evolving data-intensive ecosystems. In: Conceptual Modeling: 32th International Conference, ER 2013. Proceedings 32, pp. 182–196. China (2013)
26. Steinau, S., Andrews, K., Reichert, M.: Coordinating large distributed relational process structures. Softw. Syst. Model. **20**, 1403–1435 (2021)
27. Andrews, K., Steinau, S., Reichert, M.: Engineering a highly scalable object-aware process management engine using distributed microservices. In: On the Move to Meaningful Internet Systems. Confederated International Conferences. Proceedings, Part II, pp. 80–97. Malta (2018)

Conceptual Modeling in Context

Safety Analysis of Human Robot Collaborations with GRL Goal Models

Marian Daun$^{(\boxtimes)}$ [ID], Meenakshi Manjunath [ID], and Jeshwitha Jesus Raja [ID]

Center Robotics, Technical University of Applied Sciences Würzburg-Schweinfurt, Schweinfurt, Germany
marian.daun@thws.de

Abstract. Currently, we see a rapid digitization of manufacturing processes using robotic systems. However, not all work can be automatized at reasonable cost in the foreseeable future. As a consequence, human-robot collaborations are defined for complex work tasks. In human-robot collaborations, humans and robots share the same working space and work in parallel in close vicinity. In addition, humans and robots work at the same time on the same task. Per definition, human-robot collaborations must be considered safety-critical and be treated as such. Therefore, not only must the adaptive behavior of the robot be specified to perfectly align with the expected human behavior, but safety analyses are mandated to specify potential hazards harming the human, the robot, or the work product. To support meaningful safety analyses and thereby the identification of needed monitoring and safety mechanism to be implemented as early as possible, we investigate the use of GRL goal models to specify safety threats in human robot collaboration and foster the definition of safety tasks.

Keywords: Safety Analysis · Goal Modeling · GRL · Human Robot Interaction · Human Robot Collaboration

1 Introduction

A robot is programmed to automatically execute complex sequences of actions. However, robotic systems are undergoing rapid development and with increasing complexity, rendering them one of the most intricate types of cyber-physical systems (CPS). This is due to an increasing demand for service robots in residential and industrial settings, which has catalyzed the creation of advanced robots that are equipped with proprioception sensing and precise actuation control [1]. In addition, robots in future manufacturing scenarios are expected to adapt their behavior due to real time sensed human behavior in their vicinity and, furthermore, to collaborate with humans on complex work tasks [35].

As a point of distinction, it is important to note that human-robot interaction (HRI) and human-robot collaboration (HRC) are related yet distinct concepts. HRI pertains to the communication and interaction between humans and robots,

© The Author(s), under exclusive license to Springer Nature Switzerland AG 2023
J. P. A. Almeida et al. (Eds.): ER 2023, LNCS 14320, pp. 317–333, 2023.
https://doi.org/10.1007/978-3-031-47262-6_17

which may involve one-way or two-way communication. On the other hand, HRC pertains to situations where humans and robots work together towards a shared objective, with both parties sharing tasks and responsibilities. In HRI, it is also important to design safe and socially acceptable robot interactions with humans [5].

However, in various domains we rely on collaborations not only as collaborative robots between robots [5] but in particular between robots and humans. Such human-robot collaborative systems are designed to combine the potential of human work and automated machines, some examples are observable in manufacturing, healthcare, and service industries [13].

As HRC becomes more widespread, ensuring the safety of human operators in such collaborations has become a pressing concern [36]. Therefore, for defining proper human robot collaborative systems, it is important to adequately consider the safety of the human already in the early development phases [17].

In software and systems engineering, model-based engineering approaches have established to cope with complex system development [8] as is the case for collaborative embedded systems [4]. In recent years, model-based engineering has also proven useful and beneficial for industry automation systems [6,27]. Goal models provide an easy language to specify complex specifications already in requirements engineering [20]. Particularly, goal models cannot only be used for specification in early phases but provide a profound foundation for early analyses [7,21]. This has already been shown useful for collaborative cyber-physical systems [12].

In this paper, we investigate the application of goal models for specifying and conducting early safety analyses of human-robot collaborative systems. In doing so, we define a goal modeling extension for specifying and analyzing the safety of the human-robot collaborative system. Therefore, we combine and adapt two unrelated extensions for the goal modeling languages, iStar [10] and GRL (goal oriented requirement language, [2]). We build upon previous work proposing an extension to model collaborative cyber-physical systems [11] and work by Ribeiro et al. for modeling safety hazards [33]. We evaluated the approach using a human-robot collaborative systems' case examples from the industry automation domain. In summary, this paper contributes:

- a GRL modeling approach for human robot collaborations
- a GRL modeling approach for safety analysis in human robot collaborations
- a case study evaluation showing applicability and usability

The paper is outlined as follows. Section 2 discusses the related work and introduces the relevant foundations of goal modeling, human-robot collaboration, and Safety analysis with goal models. Further on, we introduce our approach for goal modeling of human robot collaborations and safety threats in Sect. 3. Section 4 illustrates the applicability of the approach using an industrial case study. Finally, Sect. 5 concludes the paper.

2   Foundations and Related Work

2.1   Goal Modeling

Goal modeling techniques play a critical role in the requirements engineering process, facilitating the elicitation of requirements while also helping to identify potential problems and constraints within a system [24]. Initially, goal modeling approaches focused on modeling the requirements of different stakeholders and highlighting dependencies and conflicts [18]. In recent years, goal modeling approaches have been used for modeling and analyzing various problem situations in different domains (see [20] for a recent review of the field of goal modeling in requirements engineering).

Among recent approaches, the idea to not only model stakeholders but to model systems as actors and reason about dependencies in the goal fulfillment of systems became popular. This way, realizability of a requirements specification can already be determined early in the development. Furthermore, collaborative CPSs can be investigated [11,30] or safety analyses can be supported [33]. Approaches in this area commonly build upon and extend the iStar goal modeling language [10] or the goal oriented requirement language (GRL, [22]), which is a simplified and standardized version of iStar.

2.2   Modeling Human-Robot Collaborations

Human behavior is intricate and challenging to distill, necessitating the integration of different modeling approaches such as mathematical, structural, and conceptual [23]. HRC is typically modeled using behavioral models [34]. In doing so, the collaboration can be described rather abstractly, for instance, using statecharts [3] or sequence diagrams [16], or in very detailed fashion using mathematical models [31] or simulation models [26] such as Gazebo or OpenRAVE [19].

As HRC is a widespread term, as the interactions and the level of robot autonomy varies greatly. At one extreme are fully autonomous robots like RUMBA, while at the other extreme are robots that rely solely on operator inputs, such as the line-of-sight search and rescue UAVs [36]. As a result, modeling human behavior can be either overly complex or overly simplistic, depending on the extent to which behavior needs to be modeled. Hence, modeling human behavior is still a challenge [25].

In model-based software engineering, often models of different perspectives are combined and related to a coherent view on the system [4]. Thus, combining modeling approaches such as structural with behavioral modeling, one can integrate the complexities of human behavior into the system design [36]. This can, also, be applied for goal modeling and relating behavioral models to goal models. However, goal reasoning and other analyzes can no longer be executed on the goal model alone. In addition, the overall size and complexity of models easily get too complex to adequately support stakeholder discussions.

2.3   Collaboration Goal Modeling

CPSs are characterized by the integration of physical and computational processes, where embedded computers and networks monitor and control physical processes through feedback loops [14]. In addition, collaborative CPSs have the ability to create networks in real-time to achieve goals that cannot be achieved by individual systems alone. This is accomplished through the exchange of information that facilitates the coordination of their behaviors to achieve shared goals [11]. To ensure that CPSs meet their intended requirements, it is essential to systematically elicit, specify, and analyze the goals and objectives of the system, along with their relationships. This process, known as goal modeling [28], provides a basis for verifying and validating the system's behavior.

In previous work, we proposed a GRL extension to model collaborative CPS [11]. The meta-model shown in Fig. 1 highlights the changes of the extension. Actors are categorized into collaborative CPS, collaborative CPS network, and roles. Collaborative actors are integral to the dynamics of collaborative CPSs. Representing distinct entities collaborating to achieving shared objectives. Therefore, real-time coordination and adaptation mechanism are needed. This also plays a pivotal role when defining HRC relationships, since they are collaborative and both entities work towards achieving the same goal. Moreover, relationships between actors are defined as Is-a, Collaborates-in, and Is-assigned relationships. In addition, three types of dependencies, namely AND, XOR, and IOR, have been incorporated into the model. This extension enables the modeling of bidirectional and self-dependencies. These dependencies are crucial for capturing the complex interactions between different collaborative CPSs, and for ensuring that the system is designed and developed to meet the intended requirements.

Figure 2 shows a modeling example using the extension for collaborative CPS. It is shown the collaboration of a transport robot fleet. By condensing a complex goal modeling diagram into an easily digestible format, the extension simplifies the task of understanding these relationships, requiring only a basic level of knowledge.

2.4   Safety Goal Modeling

When humans are involved in any system, ensuring safety is a major concern that requires immediate attention. In the context of HRC, where humans and robots work collaboratively in a controlled environment, it is still necessary to model the safety and analyze potential hazards or unexpected situations that could arise. This is especially important since human-robot collaborative systems involve dynamic and uncertain interactions between humans and robots, making it difficult to ensure complete safety and predictability [15].

Ribeiro et al. present the iStar4Safety extension to foster safety analyses with goal models already in early development phases. The meta-model is shown in Fig. 3. The iStar4Safety extension allows for modelling hazard and safety threats

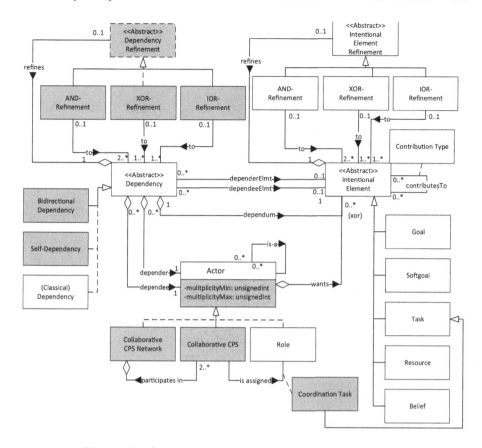

Fig. 1. GRL/iStar extension for collaborative CPS from [11]

in iStar. Therefore, introduces new elements to model *safety hazards*, *safety goals*, *safety tasks*, and *safety resources*.

To model the impact of hazards on safety goals, iStar4Safety introduces *obstruct links* that represent the relationship between hazards and safety goals. Additionally, safety goals have five levels of accident impact levels, which can be assigned to them when they are obstructed by safety hazards. This feature allows designers and developers to evaluate the severity of a safety hazard's impact on the safety goals of the system and prioritize their mitigation efforts accordingly.

3   Modeling Human Robot Collaborations and Safety Threats with GRL

In this paper, we apply the GRL to model human robot collaborations and document the results of safety analyses within the goal model. Therefore, some extensions to the GRL are needed to match the goal of adequately capturing

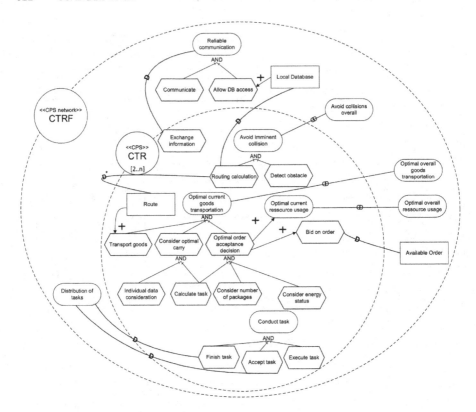

Fig. 2. Goal model for a fleet of collaborating transport robots [11]

human robot collaborations and to foster safety analyses of human robot collaborations. In this section, we define our modeling approach, whose application and usefulness we illustrate later in Sect. 4.

Our approach extends the GRL with two general ideas:

1. Explicitly model the human robot collaboration. To do so, we build upon the work by we [11] that proposed a GRL-compliant iStar extension to model collaborative CPS. In this paper, we show that this approach can in principle also be used to model human robot collaborations but is missing specific aspects. Therefore, we extend this approach with collaboration relations, that explicitly differentiate human robot collaboration related dependencies from common dependencies.

2. Explicitly model safety threats and safety goals related to human robot collaboration. To do so, we build upon the work by Ribeiro et al. [33] that proposed a iStar extension to model safety hazards.

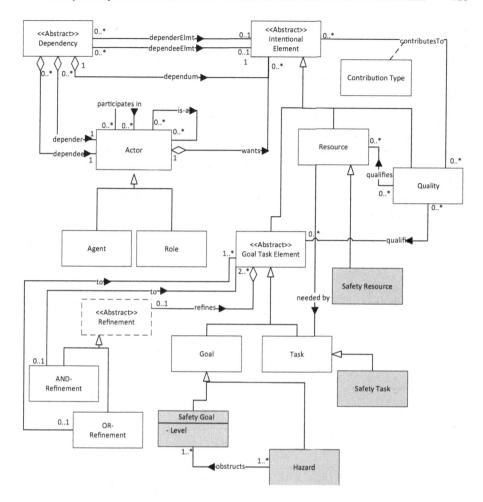

Fig. 3. iStar4Safety Extension from [33]

3.1   Modeling Human Robot Collaborations

As a simple but very common example for human robot collaborations in manufacturing, we use a pick and place scenario, as is often emphasized for future manufacturing use cases [29]. Collaborative robots (cobots) are specifically engineered to work alongside humans in a coordinated manner [9,32]. These cobots excel at executing pick and place operations within controlled setups. Unlike their larger industrial counterparts, cobots are compact, facilitating easy maneuverability and allowing for swift emergency response without disrupting the entire production line.

The pick and place scenarios are typically placed in a controlled environment where a human and a cobot assemble a product. In our example, the product is assembled by the human. The human is supported by the cobot that identifies the needed parts in a storage box, picks the needed part and places it in a sequence on a work counter, after which the human assembles them at a secondary work counter.

The cobot follows a specific process pattern to assemble the product collaboratively with the human.

1. The cobot begins by scanning and identifying the required parts for the product assembly process.
2. It then navigates to the storage area to pick up the first required part.
3. The cobot moves to the work counter and places the part on the empty slot for that specific part.
4. The cobot repeats steps 2–3 for all the required parts until the work counter is fully equipped.
5. The human proceeds with assembling each part on the work counter.
6. Once the human completes assembly of one product, the robot starts step 1–4.

Figure 4 shows the derived goal model for the cobot. The goal model is designed such that all tasks are explicitly stated at the bottom of the model, which will better support safety analysis – as the safety is imminent to the tasks – and, thus, allows later on easier documentation of the safety goals, hazards, and tasks in relation to the causing tasks of the goal model.

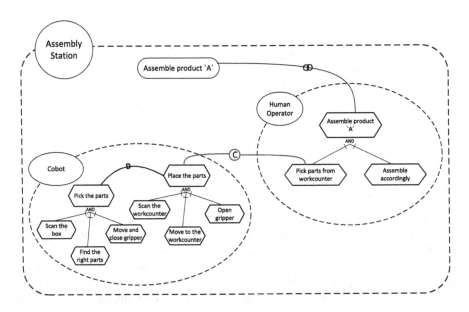

Fig. 4. Goal model of HRC in an assembly station

The task of the human *pick different parts* and the task of the cobot *place parts* is a special case of bidirectional dependency that occur adjacently within the same controlled environment. To effectively highlight the collaborative nature between the human and the cobot, the use of bidirectional or unidirectional dependencies alone was not sufficient. Therefore, we introduce a new type of dependency called *Collaboration dependency*. This collaboration dependency, specifically emphasizes and represents the collaborative relationship and interaction between the human and the cobot, which aids in providing an accurate and comprehensive sketch of their collaborative tasks in the model.

3.2 Modeling Safety Threats in Human Robot Collaboration

Modeling the collaboration dependency, is a first step towards safety analysis, as the majority of safety threats is due to the collaboration between human and the cobot. Based on the goal model from Fig. 4, we conduct a safety analysis. This, leads us to the identification of potential safety hazards, which we exemplarily show in Table 1.

Table 1. Excerpt of Safety Analysis Results

Safety Hazard	General Resolution Approach
Human operator in the vicinity of the cobot	Check if the human operator is within the safe distance of cobot operation. If yes, continue and keep monitoring. If no, stop any operation
Execution of pick-and-place leads to a collision?	Predict any possible collision and stop any operation if necessary
Human operator gets tired	Monitor the efficiency of human operation. For reduced efficiency, advise change of operators or inform the operator to take a break

As can be seen from Table 1, safety hazards either relate to the tasks of the cobot, or to the collaboration dependency between human and cobot. We extended, the goal model from Fig. 5 to include the various safety hazards. Furthermore, we defined in accordance with the approach from Ribeiro et al. [33] safety goals and safety tasks to mitigate these hazards.

In our exploration of HRC safety threats, we identified different threat categories based on their origin. System-specific threats arise directly from malfunctions within the system, such as a cobot. Human-system interaction threats emerge from the dynamics between humans and robots, like in pick-and-place scenarios. Inter-system collaboration threats stem from interactions between multiple robotic systems.

For the **safety threats related to the tasks of the robot**, we documented, for instance, that the safety task *Gripper closed correctly?* is an elementary safety task. If the gripper is not completely closed, this can lead to potential falling objects. This should be monitored through the gripper sensors that constantly monitor the position of the actuator that moves the gripper jaws. The same applies to when the cobot places the part on the work station for the human to pick. The part should be placed in its respective position on the work station. If the cobot fails to do so, the part could again be a potential fall hazard that can be avoided through constant monitoring via optical sensors and gripper sensors.

In addition, major **safety hazards related to the collaboration dependency** exist. These relate to potential safety hazards to humans and can generally be placed into three main categories:

1. **Physical Injuries.** The interaction between human and the cobot can lead to physical injuries such as collisions, crushing, trapping, or impact-related accidents. To address this, it is crucial to continuously monitor both actors in the environment, namely the human and the cobot, for instance, using a 3D camera. By monitoring human and cobot positions and movements, any violations of safety rules, such as maintaining a safe distance, can be detected. If such violations occur, the safety manager activates a response where the cobot immediately stops all movements to prevent any potential hazards from occurring.

2. **Strain.** Humans may experience discomfort or pain due to prolonged or repetitive motions, awkward postures, or excessive force exertion. This leads to reduced efficiency. To address this hazard, the solution proposed involves monitoring the efficiency of the human's work performance. This includes tracking the speed at which tasks are being carried out and the frequency of errors made. For instance, if the human operator is consistently working at a significantly slower pace than expected and is making a substantial number of mistakes, it indicates a potential risk of physical strain. In such cases, the safety manager should intervene and determine that the human to be unfit to continue working at that moment. The recommended course of action would be to advise the operator to take a rest period or to have another human operator take over the task to prevent further strain and potential injuries.

3. **Unsynchronized Communication and Coordination.** Ineffective communication and/or coordination between the human and the cobot can result in misunderstandings, misinterpretation of signals, or lack of synchronization. One specific scenario is when the cobot's sensor, responsible for detecting humans in its vicinity, is blocked or damaged. In such cases, it is imperative that the safety manager is immediately notified to take appropriate action. This ensures that the cobot's movements and operations are adjusted to prevent any accidental collisions or unsafe interactions with the human operator. Furthermore, variations in workflow speed between the human operator and the cobot can also pose a safety hazard. If the human operator is working at a substantially slower pace compared to the cobot or vice versa, it can create potential risks. In these situations, the safety manager should intervene and adjust the cobot's pace to align with the workflow of the human operator, ensuring proper synchronization and minimizing the chances of accidents or errors.

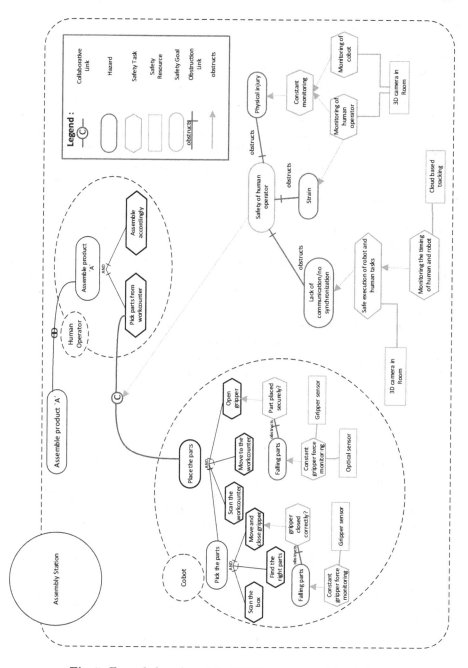

Fig. 5. Extended goal model of HRC in an assembly station

3.3   Meta-model of the Extension

The meta-model of our extension is given by Fig. 6. It combines the already existing iStar extensions by we and Ribeiro et al., which build upon the original iStar meta-model by Dalpiaz et al. [10]. To ensure compatibility with GRL, we integrated the iStar4Safety extension into the extension for collaborative CPS, which was already tailored to GRL. Aside from this consolidation, we introduce a new dependency type *collaboration dependency* to explicitly document tasks of two actors that are executed in collaboration. Thus, they not only depend on the result as is the case for common dependencies, but we see some kind of physical collaboration that is potentially prone to safety hazards. Furthermore, the obstruction link is invariably associated with a collaboration link, as it signifies the joint efforts of two entities striving towards a mutual objective. This inherent association strongly suggests the presence of safety hazards.

The imperative need for safety analysis in this context led us to seamlessly integrate *iStar4Safety* with our extension from previous work (see Fig. 1 and [11]). As a result, we incorporated the element of *hazard* and its corresponding *safety task*, which, when executed, mitigates potential complications. To bolster this framework, we introduced specific resources and objectives, termed as *safety resource* and *safety goal* respectively. These elements play a pivotal role in "obstructing" or actively preventing the actualization of the identified hazard, ensuring a robust safety mechanism throughout the system's operation. Additionally, we introduced the concept of *collaboration dependency*.

4   Evaluation

We evaluated the approach using common human robot collaboration scenarios from manufacturing. We applied the extension to a human-robot collaborative system for an industrial case study involving two cobots, collaborating with one another and with a human. One cobot is responsible for pick and place tasks, utilizing its autonomous capabilities to handle part movement within the assembly station. This cobot operates based on predefined instruction sets. The second cobot serves as a collaborative assistant, providing support in the assembly process with minimal human intervention. Thus, the first cobot conducts typical pick and place tasks as pre-processing support for the human and the other cobot. The human and the other cobot then take the placed work pieces to assemble them independently, but on the same product, thus, in close vicinity with the risk of collisions.

With this case study highlighting a more complex HRC, we could show that the approach is applicable. Figure 7 shows the results. As can be seen, the figure defines the multiple collaboration actions between human and cobot as well as between cobot and cobot. This helps in identifying potential safety hazards. These are also shown in Fig. 7, as the approach was able to adequately model safety hazards, relate them to safety goals and derive safety tasks to be implemented.

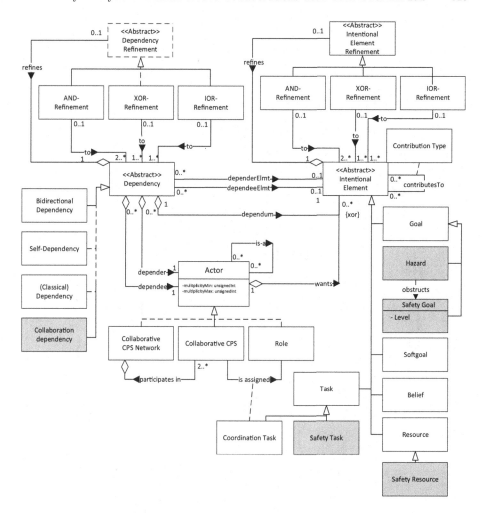

Fig. 6. Extended meta-model of GRL

As described in Fig. 7, there are three collaboration dependencies, namely between the human and two cobots as well as between cobot and cobot. The safety threats posed due to human cobot collaboration remain similar with respect to both cobots involved, but with minor changes. The human operator will not be necessarily strained when working with Cobot 2, as they are called for assistance only when the cobot is unable to assemble the part on its own. Whereas when we observe the relation between Cobot 1 and the human operator, the human operator is bound to have some strain due to constant attention and precision needed when assembling. There are a number of safety hazards when it comes to the cobot collaboration. A major hazard is collision of the two cobots, which further leads to human physical injury caused due to flying parts or broken parts or due to loud collision noise or short-circuiting due to

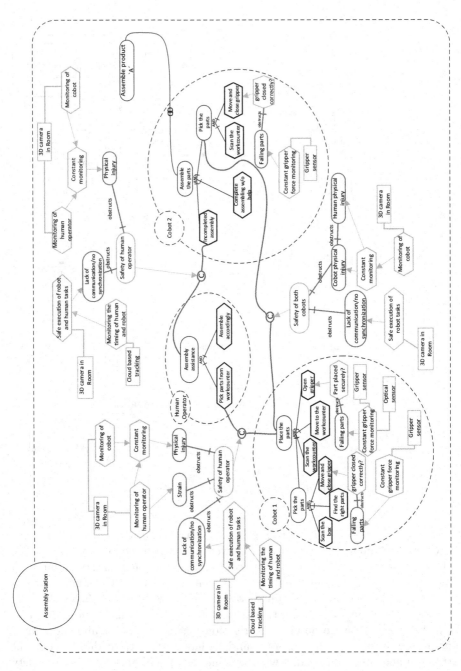

Fig. 7. Goal model of 2 cobots in a controlled environment

broken wires. Furthermore, due to the unsynchronized working pattern of both cobots, this could lead to further hazards that need to be carefully monitored.

Thus, the model successfully captured the safety requirements and dependencies between the cobots and the human operator, allowing for comprehensive safety analysis. Hence, the goal model can already serve in early development phases to support systematic safety analysis of HRC. However, it is important to acknowledge that further evaluation is needed to assess the generalizability and validity of the proposed extension. Future investigations should explore various scenarios, such as multiple human and one cobot collaboration, multiple cobots and one human collaboration, or even multiple robots and multiple human collaboration. These evaluations will provide a comprehensive understanding of the extended GRL model's applicability, robustness, and effectiveness across diverse collaborative setups, ultimately ensuring the reliability and safety of human-robot collaborative systems in different industrial contexts.

5   Conclusion

The objective of this research paper is to enable safety analysis, particularly for human robot collaborations, during the conceptual planning phase using GRL.

Goal modeling plays a vital role in representing requirements in a concise and comprehensible manner, making it well-suited for conducting safety analysis of HRC systems. The primary challenge in modeling HRC systems lies in the unpredictable behavior of the human operator involved. To address this issue, an iStar extension was introduced by we [11] specifically for cyber-physical systems. Moreover, the iStar4Safety extension proposed by Ribeiro et al. [33] was another crucial component for safety analysis.

Building upon these extensions, we have shown that the extension for collaborative CPS is in principle also able to sketch human robot collaboration. Also, the iStar4Safety extension has shown applicable to analyze and model safety threats in HRC systems. Furthermore, both extensions could seamlessly be integrated to adequately consider safety threats in human robot collaborations. In addition, we extended the resulting combined meta-model with a *collaboration dependency* to make tasks of two actors that collaborate closely and pose considerable safety threats explicit.

By applying the combined extension to the modelling and analysis of an industrial case example showing a common collaboration scenario for future manufacturing in the context of Industry 4.0, we could show applicability and usefulness of the approach to document safety hazards and relate safety tasks to them. Thus, future work will need to consider more complex case examples involving different types of robots. In addition, future work should deal with linking the early safety results documented in the goal model to safety analyses of the later phases and combining them to make up the final safety case of HRC systems.

References

1. Ajoudani, A., Zanchettin, A.M., Ivaldi, S., Albu-Schäffer, A., Kosuge, K., Khatib, O.: Progress and prospects of the human-robot collaboration. Auton. Robot. **42**, 957–975 (2018)
2. Amyot, D., Mussbacher, G.: User requirements notation: the first ten years, the next ten years. J. Softw. **6**(5), 747–768 (2011)
3. An, D., Liu, J., Chen, X., Li, T., Yin, L.: A modeling framework of cyber-physical-social systems with human behavior classification based on machine learning. In: Ait-Ameur, Y., Qin, S. (eds.) ICFEM 2019. LNCS, vol. 11852, pp. 522–525. Springer, Cham (2019). https://doi.org/10.1007/978-3-030-32409-4_37
4. Böhm, B., et al.: Engineering of Collaborative Embedded Systems. Springer, Cham (2021). https://doi.org/10.1007/978-3-030-62136-0
5. Breazeal, C., Hoffman, G., Lockerd, A.: Teaching and working with robots as a collaboration. In: AAMAS, vol. 4, pp. 1030–1037 (2004)
6. Brings, J., et al.: Model-based documentation of dynamicity constraints for collaborative cyber-physical system architectures: Findings from an industrial case study. J. Syst. Architect. **97**, 153–167 (2019)
7. Brings, J., Daun, M., Weyer, T., Pohl, K.: Goal-based configuration analysis for networks of collaborative cyber-physical systems. In: Proceedings of the 35th Annual ACM Symposium on Applied Computing, pp. 1387–1396 (2020)
8. Casalaro, G.L., Cattivera, G., Ciccozzi, F., Malavolta, I., Wortmann, A., Pellicione, P.: Model-driven engineering for mobile robotic systems: a systematic mapping study. Softw. Syst. Model. **21**(1), 19–49 (2022)
9. Colgate, J.E., Wannasuphoprasit, W., Peshkin, M.A.: Cobots: robots for collaboration with human operators. In: Proceedings of the 1996 ASME International Mechanical Engineering Congress and Exposition (1996)
10. Dalpiaz, F., Franch, X., Horkoff, J.: iStar 2.0 language guide. arXiv preprint arXiv:1605.07767 (2016)
11. Daun, M., Brings, J., Krajinski, L., Stenkova, V., Bandyszak, T.: A GRL-compliant iStar extension for collaborative cyber-physical systems. Requirements Eng. **26**(3), 325–370 (2021)
12. Daun, M., Stenkova, V., Krajinski, L., Brings, J., Bandyszak, T., Weyer, T.: Goal modeling for collaborative groups of cyber-physical systems with GRL: reflections on applicability and limitations based on two studies conducted in industry. In: Proceedings of the 34th ACM/SIGAPP Symposium on Applied Computing, pp. 1600–1609 (2019)
13. De Simone, V., Di Pasquale, V., Giubileo, V., Miranda, S.: Human-robot collaboration: an analysis of worker's performance. Procedia Comput. Sci. **200**, 1540–1549 (2022)
14. Derler, P., Lee, E.A., Vincentelli, A.S.: Modeling cyber-physical systems. Proc. IEEE **100**(1), 13–28 (2011)
15. El-Shamouty, M., Wu, X., Yang, S., Albus, M., Huber, M.F.: Towards safe human-robot collaboration using deep reinforcement learning. In: 2020 IEEE International Conference on Robotics and Automation (ICRA), pp. 4899–4905. IEEE (2020)
16. Guiochet, J.: Hazard analysis of human-robot interactions with Hazop-UML. Saf. Sci. **84**, 225–237 (2016)
17. Halme, R.J., Lanz, M., Kämäräinen, J., Pieters, R., Latokartano, J., Hietanen, A.: Review of vision-based safety systems for human-robot collaboration. Procedia CIRP **72**, 111–116 (2018)

18. Hassine, J., Amyot, D.: An empirical approach toward the resolution of conflicts in goal-oriented models. Softw. Syst. Model. **16**(1), 279–306 (2017)
19. He, L., Glogowski, P., Lemmerz, K., Kuhlenkötter, B., Zhang, W.: Method to integrate human simulation into gazebo for human-robot collaboration. In: IOP Conference Series: Materials Science and Engineering, vol. 825, p. 012006. IOP Publishing (2020)
20. Horkoff, J., et al.: Goal-oriented requirements engineering: an extended systematic mapping study. Requirements Eng. **24**, 133–160 (2019)
21. Horkoff, J., Yu, E.: Comparison and evaluation of goal-oriented satisfaction analysis techniques. Requirements Eng. **18**, 199–222 (2013)
22. ITU International Telecommunication Union: Recommendation itu-t z.151: User Requirements Notation (URN). Technical report (2018)
23. Karwowski, J., Dudek, W., Wegierek, M., Winiarski, T.: Hubero: a framework to simulate human behaviour in robot research. J. Autom. Mob. Robot. Intell. Syst. **15**(1), 31–38 (2021)
24. Kavakli, E., Loucopoulos, P.: Goal modeling in requirements engineering: analysis and critique of current methods. In: Information Modeling Methods and Methodologies: Advanced Topics in Database Research, pp. 102–124. IGI Global (2005)
25. Kindler, E.: Model-based software engineering: the challenges of modelling behaviour. In: Proceedings of the Second International Workshop on Behaviour Modelling: Foundation and Applications, pp. 1–8 (2010)
26. Malik, A.A., Bilberg, A.: Digital twins of human robot collaboration in a production setting. Procedia Manuf. **17**, 278–285 (2018)
27. Mohagheghi, P., Gilani, W., Stefanescu, A., Fernandez, M.A., Nordmoen, B., Fritzsche, M.: Where does model-driven engineering help? Experiences from three industrial cases. Softw. Syst. Model. **12**, 619–639 (2013)
28. Mylopoulos, J., Chung, L., Yu, E.: From object-oriented to goal-oriented requirements analysis. Commun. ACM **42**(1), 31–37 (1999)
29. Najafi, E., Ansari, M.: Model-based design approach for an industry 4.0 case study: a pick and place robot. In: 2019 23rd International Conference on Mechatronics Technology (ICMT), pp. 1–6. IEEE (2019)
30. Nazarenko, A.A., Camarinha-Matos, L.M.: Towards collaborative cyber-physical systems. In: 2017 International Young Engineers Forum (YEF-ECE), pp. 12–17. IEEE (2017)
31. Nikolaidis, S., Forlizzi, J., Hsu, D., Shah, J., Srinivasa, S.: Mathematical models of adaptation in human-robot collaboration. arXiv preprint arXiv:1707.02586 (2017)
32. Peshkin, M., Colgate, J.E.: Cobots. Ind. Robot: Int. J. **26**, 335–341 (1999)
33. Ribeiro, M., Castro, J., Pimentel, J.: iStar for safety-critical systems. In: iStar@ ER (2019)
34. Uchitel, S., Brunet, G., Chechik, M.: Behaviour model synthesis from properties and scenarios. In: 29th International Conference on Software Engineering (ICSE 2007), pp. 34–43. IEEE (2007)
35. Wang, L., Liu, S., Liu, H., Wang, X.V.: Overview of human-robot collaboration in manufacturing. In: Wang, L., Majstorovic, V.D., Mourtzis, D., Carpanzano, E., Moroni, G., Galantucci, L.M. (eds.) Proceedings of 5th International Conference on the Industry 4.0 Model for Advanced Manufacturing. LNME, pp. 15–58. Springer, Cham (2020). https://doi.org/10.1007/978-3-030-46212-3_2
36. Yagoda, R.E., Coovert, M.D.: How to work and play with robots: an approach to modeling human-robot interaction. Comput. Hum. Behav. **28**(1), 60–68 (2012)

A Domain-Specific Visual Modeling Language for Augmented Reality Applications Using WebXR

Fabian Muff$^{(\boxtimes)}$ and Hans-Georg Fill

Research Group Digitalization and Information Systems, University of Fribourg,
Fribourg, Switzerland
{fabian.muff,hans-georg.fill}@unifr.ch

Abstract. Augmented reality (AR) is a technology that overlays digital information onto real-world objects using devices like smartphones, tablets, or head-mounted displays to enrich human comprehension and interaction with the physical environment. The creation of AR software applications requires today advanced coding skills, particularly when aiming to realize complex, multifaceted scenarios. As an alternative, we propose a domain-specific visual modeling language for designing AR scenarios, enabling users to define augmentations and AR workflows graphically. The language has been implemented on the ADOxx metamodeling platform, together with a software engine for running the AR applications using the W3C WebXR Device API for web-based augmented reality. The language and the AR application are demonstrated through a furniture assembly use case. In an initial evaluation, we show, via a comprehensive feature comparison, that the proposed language exhibits a more extensive coverage of AR concepts compared to preceding model-based approaches.

Keywords: Augmented Reality · Domain-specific modeling language · Metamodeling

1 Introduction

Augmented reality (AR) plays an important role in the ongoing convergence of the physical and the digital world [28]. At its core, augmented reality enhances the user's perception by superimposing visual information such as images, videos, or three-dimensional (3D) visualizations onto real-world environments in real time [2,39]. It uses computer vision techniques to align objects in the virtual and physical worlds and displays the virtual information using see-through displays or screens, e.g., on smartphones or head-mounted displays [32]. AR reverts to markers or detectors of real-world objects to determine their location and orientation in three-dimensional space to accurately map visual information onto

Financial support is gratefully acknowledged by the Smart Living Lab funded by the University of Fribourg, EPFL, and HEIA-FR.

them. For realizing complex AR workflows in practical work scenarios, additional concepts such as the integration of external data sources in combination with triggers, conditions, and actions to process this data become necessary.

Recent technological advances have made augmented reality affordable via its availability on standard smartphones and tablets [38]. In addition, the future open W3C standard WebXR Device API is being developed for accessing AR devices on the web across a wide variety of hardware form factors [18]. In terms of industrial applications, market research by Gartner [27] and PwC [7] indicates that AR is a highly promising technology allowing for broad usage in industrial scenarios such as maintenance tasks or training [15].

Creating augmented reality applications requires today advanced programming skills, e.g., for platforms and APIs such as Vuforia[1], ARKit[2], Google ARCore[3], or MRTK[4]. For easing the creation of AR applications, several proposals have been made in model-driven engineering (MDE) and conceptual modeling. This includes, for example XML and JSON schemas for describing AR scenes in generic, platform-independent formats [21,30] or with a focus on learning experiences [37]; domain-specific languages for creating AR model editors using Vuforia, ARKit, or MRTK [6,29,33]; or a BPMN extension for representing process information in AR using the Unity platform [15]. In addition, commercial low-code and no-code tools are offered that aim to empower non-technical users to create AR applications. This includes tools such as UniteAR[5], or Adobe Aero[6]. However, these tools are mostly designed for creating a single AR scene or very simple workflows.

What is missing so far is a visual modeling approach that can represent complex AR workflows for diverse application scenarios, that can be easily adapted to new requirements, and that is based on open standards. To facilitate the creation of AR applications that take advantage of the accessibility, portability, interoperability, and openness of the web, we propose a domain-specific modeling language (DSML) based on models conforming to the W3C WebXR Device API recommendation, thereby enabling the definition of different scenarios such as assembly processes, maintenance tasks, or learning experiences. The development of the language follows guidelines for DSML development proposed by Frank [13]. The DSML has been implemented on the ADOxx metamodeling platform and applied to a furniture assembly use case [11]. For a first evaluation, we conduct a feature comparison with similar languages in the area of augmented reality [34].

The remainder of the paper is organized as follows. Section 2 describes fundamental concepts in AR and the most important development platforms for achieving a common understanding. In Sect. 3, we analyze previous related work

---

[1] https://library.vuforia.com/.
[2] https://developer.apple.com/augmented-reality/arkit/.
[3] https://developers.google.com/ar.
[4] https://github.com/Microsoft/MixedRealityToolkit-Unity.
[5] https://www.unitear.com/.
[6] https://adobe.com/products/aero.html.

in MDE and conceptual modeling in the context of AR. From these insights, we derive generic and specific requirements for a domain-specific visual modeling language for AR applications and present its specification and implementation in Sect. 4. This is followed by a use case in Sect. 5. In Sect. 6, we evaluate the language through a feature comparison. Finally, in Sect. 7, we conclude the paper and point to future work.

2   Foundations

As augmented reality relies on a range of specific techniques from computer vision to achieve the intended user experience, we will briefly explain the most important concepts in the following for ensuring a common understanding.

2.1   Augmented Reality

Augmented reality is a technology that allows computer-generated virtual images to be embedded in the real environment [39], thereby creating a three-dimensional alignment between virtual and real objects that allows for interaction in real-time [2].

Augmented reality relies on three core concepts from the field of computer vision [32]: (1) *Detectables/Trackables*, (2) *Coordinate Mappings*, and (3) *Augmentations*. First, for determining the location and orientation of the real-world environment, computer vision algorithms are used to estimate the position and orientation based on two-dimensional (2D) or 3D sensor information, e.g., from a camera stream or a LiDAR scanner [9,31]. This detection can either revert to *detectables* in the form of *natural features* or *markers* such as QR codes as surrogates for simplifying the detection and tracking [32]. Coordinate mappings are then needed to align objects in the real and the virtual world to each other. Thereby, a *real world origin reference* position, e.g., stemming from global positioning system (GPS) coordinates, must be mapped to the *global coordinate system* of the virtual environment. Further, *local coordinate systems* are used for any real-world or virtual object. These permit to define *reference points* for placing virtual objects relative to other objects, independent of the current global coordinates. Finally, virtual information is superimposed on the real world through so-called *augmentations*. These can be animations, 2D images, videos, audio, text labels, 3D objects, hyperlinks, checklists, or forms. By defining *anchors*, augmentations can be fixed at a particular position in real space.

For more complex AR scenarios, further concepts are necessary. This includes in particular the integration and processing of additional data that is acquired throughout the life-cycle of an AR scenario via sensors or user interactions. To enable dynamic changes in the AR environment, at least basic workflow concepts such as *triggers, conditions*, and *actions* need to be foreseen [37]. Thereby, triggers include: click, detection, sensor, or timer events; voice commands; entry/exit of defined spatial areas; or, gestures. Conditions specify the branchings into different process flows and actions refer to any change applied to the virtual objects such as the appearance and disappearance of objects or transformations, i.e., rotation, scaling, and positioning.

2.2 Implementation Platforms

For creating AR applications, several development platforms and software development kits (SDK) are provided. Most of them require significant programming skills and are either commercial or closed-source. Examples include the Unity runtime and development environment, Apples ARKit, Wikitude, Vuforia, Kudan, Unreal Engine, or Adobe Aero. In addition, open source platforms and SDKs are available, such as Google ARCore, ARToolKit+, OpenXR, or Holokit.

An alternative to the above platforms and SDKs is the WebXR Device API [18]. It specifies a web Application Programming Interface (API) that provides browser-based access to handheld or head-mounted augmented reality and virtual reality devices, including sensors. This allows AR content to be rendered by any compatible WebXR-enabled browser without the need to install additional software or use SDKs. As of today, WebXR is supported, for example, by Chromium-based browsers on the Android operating system[7], including handheld smartphones and tablets, as well as *head-mounted displays*, e.g., the Microsoft HoloLens 2[8]. Further, WebXR is already included in the WebKit engine used by iOS Safari[9] and will be supported by the Apple Vision Pro[10]. WebXR does not facilitate the development of technical applications, but applications developed with it are more accessible.

3 Related Work

Several approaches have explored the application of conceptual modeling and model-driven engineering for augmented reality applications. In a comprehensive literature analysis, we previously identified 201 relevant papers at the intersection of conceptual modeling and *virtual reality/augmented reality* and derived the major research streams in these areas [26]. From the results of this study, we selected the most important contributions in the area of model-driven engineering and conceptual modeling for AR which are related to our approach. These will be briefly characterized in the following.

Ruminski and Walczak [30] describe a text-based declarative language for modeling dynamic, contextual augmented reality environments called *CARL*. They claim that CARL can simplify the creation of AR experiences by allowing developers to create reusable, modular components. Their development approach is based on textual modeling and does not include a visual representation.

Wild et al. [37] focused on data exchange formats for AR experiences in manufacturing workplaces. They propose two textual modeling languages that include the definition of learning activities (activityML) and the definition of workplaces (workplaceML). Based on this work, a new IEEE standard for *Augmented Reality Learning Experience Models* has been developed [36], which includes a reference

---

[7] https://caniuse.com/webxr.
[8] https://microsoft.com/en-us/hololens.
[9] https://github.com/WebKit/WebKit/tree/main/Source/WebCore/Modules/webxr.
[10] https://www.apple.com/apple-vision-pro/.

implementation[11]. It enables the direct definition of learning workflows within an AR context. However, the textual models for these workflows are stored only at runtime, precluding a definition outside the tool.

A similar approach has been developed by Lechner [21]. He proposes the XML-based *Augmented Reality Markup Language* (ARML 2.0) for describing virtual objects, their appearance, and anchors in an AR scene in relation to the real world. ARML 2.0 has been included in a standard issued by the *Open Geospatial Consortium*[12] in the form of an XML grammar.

Ruiz-Rube et al. [29] proposed a model-driven development approach for creating AR-based model editors, aiming at more efficient means of creating and editing conceptual models in AR. Thus, the generated applications target modeling itself. They demonstrate their approach by a tool called *ARE4DSL*[13]. It only allows for the definition of AR-based modeling applications and not for the definition of other types of AR applications.

Seiger et al. [33] presented *Holoflows*, a modeling approach for creating *Internet of Things* (IoT) processes in augmented reality environments. The approach includes an interface allowing non-experts to design IoT processes without process or modeling knowledge. The approach is specific to the IoT domain and modeling is only possible within the provided AR application.

Grambow et al. [15] introduced an approach called *BPMN-CARX*. It stands for a solution integrating context-awareness, visual AR support, and process modeling in BPMN of *Industrial Internet of Things* (IIoT) processes. The approach allows to extend business process management software with AR and IIoT capabilities. Further, it supports the modeling of context-aware and AR-enabled business processes. BPMN-CARX extends BPMN with new elements including a graphical notation. The approach is specific to business process modeling and does not seem applicable to other scenarios.

Campos-Lopez et al. [6] and Brunschwig et al. [5] proposed an automated approach for constructing AR-based interfaces for information systems using model-driven and software language engineering principles without the need for coding knowledge. They introduced a model-driven approach for AR interface construction, where the interface is automatically generated from a high-level domain metamodel of the system and includes AR features like augmentations, a mechanism for anchors based on real-world position, or the recognition of barcodes and quick response (QR) codes. Additionally, it is possible to define API calls to be performed upon certain user interactions, e.g., the creation of objects. The approach is mainly designed for modeling systems that use AR, however, there is no possibility to define states or executable workflows. They demonstrate the feasibility of their approach through a prototypical iOS app called *AlteR* that is based on Apple's ARKit[14].

In summary, approaches exist for (1) generating specific AR applications based on models and schemata, (2) generating AR-based modeling tools based

---

[11] https://github.com/WEKIT-ECS/MIRAGE-XR.

[12] http://docs.opengeospatial.org/is/12-132r4/12-132r4.html.

[13] https://github.com/spi-fm/ARE4DSL.

[14] https://alter-ar.github.io/.

on MDE, and (3) AR modeling applications based on conceptual modeling languages. However, to the best of our knowledge, there is no visual modeling approach available so far for representing executable AR workflows for diverse application scenarios and that is based on open AR standards. Therefore, we advance in the next section to the definition of the requirements of such a modeling language and its implementation, as well as an exemplary use case.

4   Derivation of the Visual Modeling Language

Domain-specific languages in general provide constructs that are tailored to a specific field of application with the goal of gaining expressiveness and ease of use to increase productivity [22]. In the area of model-driven software development, typically languages with a visual notation are proposed, which we will denote in the following as *domain-specific visual modeling languages*, cf. [13,19]. Related to this is a trend found today in industrial software development with the rise of low-code and no-code approaches which aim at empowering users to develop software with less or no programming expertise [3,8]. We will thus derive a domain-specific visual modeling language for creating augmented reality applications.

4.1   Methodology

Several guidelines and methodologies have been proposed for the development of domain-specific languages, cf. [13,17,20,35]. We will mainly follow the macro process proposed by Frank [13], who describes seven phases including details for each phase - see Fig. 1. For the language specification and the creation of the modeling tool we further considered the methodology by Visic et al. [35], which focuses on the interplay between a modeling language and algorithms and the deployment of the modeling tool.

Fig. 1. Seven Phases for Domain-Specific Language Development [13] [p. 8]

In terms of *scope and purpose*, we aim for a language that permits users with no programming expertise to create augmented reality applications that include complex workflows and run in a web browser without further plugins or software components on a broad range of devices.

4.2   Requirements

Frank distinguishes between *generic* and *specific* requirements that need to be analyzed prior to the language specification [13]. As Gulden and Yu pointed out, these requirements have to be carefully balanced for considering trade-offs between different design alternatives [16], especially in terms of simplicity, comprehensibility, and convenience of use of the language [13].

Thus, we defined the following seven **generic requirements** (GR_{1-7}) for our language as proposed by Frank [13] and in similar fashion by Karsai et al. [20], as well as Jannaber et al. [17]: GR_1: The language should allow the specification of AR applications of various types without programming skills, making AR application development more intuitive and user-friendly than traditional approaches. GR_2: The modeling language shall use concepts that a potential user is familiar with, i.e., concepts that are either common in everyday life or related to AR environments. GR_3: The modeling language shall contain special constructs that are tailored to the domain of augmented reality. These terms need to be understood in the same way in all situations and by all users. GR_4: The constructs of the language should allow modeling at a level of detail sufficient for all foreseeable AR applications. GR_5: The language shall provide different levels of abstraction to avoid overloading and thus compromising the proper interpretation of a model. GR_6: There shall be a clear association between the language constructs and the constructs of the relevant target representations in the AR application. GR_7: In addition, Frank describes the requirement of choosing an appropriate metamodeling language that is consistent with the generic requirements described, which we will consider later for the language specification.

Further, we added twelve specific requirements SR_{1-12} that originate from: (a) our analysis of the domain of augmented reality in the form of fundamental concepts and existing software platforms and approaches – see Sect. 2, (b) previously identified academic approaches in the area of model-driven engineering for AR [26], and (c) requirements concerning the implementation of the language in terms of satisfying the purpose of platform-independent execution using WebXR [18]. The specific requirements have been further grouped into three categories: *Domain*, *Abstraction*, and *Implementation*.

The category *Domain* refers to specific requirements that emerge from the domain of augmented reality applications. SR_1: Superimposing virtual objects on the real world (*Augmentation*) is the main functionality of augmented reality applications [6,15,21,29,30,33,37]. The domain-specific modeling language must allow the user to represent virtual augmentations in various forms such as images, text labels, animations, or 3D objects. SR_2: To create a realistic AR experience, the digital augmentations superimposed on the physical world must align with the real world [6,29,37]. A virtual augmentation placed on a real object should remain in its original position relative to the real object, even as the user moves around. Therefore, the modeling language must provide a concept for creating a local real-world origin to provide a reference point at application runtime (*World Origin Reference*). SR_3: It must be possible to specify the location of virtual augmentations in relation to other objects or the world origin in real or virtual space during model specification (*Reference Point*) [6,21,37]. SR_4: It must be possible to specify real-world objects that can be tracked during application runtime (*Detectable/Trackable*) [6,15,21,29,30,37]. Therefore, a concept is required to create such detectable objects during modeling. These detectables should not only specify the existence of a real-world object, but also provide data to recognize these objects at runtime, for example using images or 3D object data. SR_5: Specifying the modification of different objects based on different *actions* is a critical functionality of AR applications [21,29,30,33,37]. Thus, the modeling language should permit to define transitions to subsequent actions and to directly manipulate and transform augmentations. SR_6: For realizing complex AR workflows [15,33,37], *triggers and conditions* are required to enable dynamic branchings in AR applications [6,15,29,30,33,37].

The category *Abstraction* refers to a general aspect for creating an AR modeling language and contains only one specific requirement, which details the generic requirement of different abstraction levels (GR_5). SR_7: To reduce complexity and to separate the different roles required during the specification of AR scenarios, the modeling language shall include concepts for abstraction, e.g., model decomposition, and separation of concerns to allow task sharing among stakeholders with different responsibilities [21,29,30,37]. For example, a designer could work on visualizing augmentations, while a domain expert could specify the application workflow.

The final category, *Implementation*, considers the requirements that must be supported in terms of language specification and implementation. SR_8: Due to the nature of modeling languages, an abstract and a concrete syntax in textual notation needs to be provided [13,20], also for easing future interoperability with previous approaches [6,15,21,29,30,33,37]. In addition, as visual notations are more intuitive and user-friendly than text-based notations, a two-dimensional graphical notation needs to be specified [15]. Finally, since the AR domain reverts largely to 3D content, specifying models directly in a 3D environment is useful to facilitate spatial imagination [6,33,37]. Thus, a domain-specific modeling language should consider concepts for text-based, 2D visual, and 3D spatial modeling. SR_9: To allow for an easy and rapid adaptation of the language as requirements change, the modeling language shall be based on *metamodeling* [6,13,29]. SR_{10}: It should be possible to directly feed the model into an AR application for the *execution* of the modeled AR scenario [15,29,30,37]. Thus, a domain-specific modeling language for AR applications shall provide a data format that can be processed by an AR engine during runtime [10] or generate code for creating the AR application itself from the models [15]. SR_{11}: AR applications are often built using commercial SDKs such as Apple ARKit, Wikitude, or Vuforia, most of which depend on the closed-source Unity platform. To make the modeling language widely applicable on a large range of devices and enable non-commercial long-term research, the modeling language (*specification*) and code generated from it (*execution*) shall be based on open standards, such as the WebXR Device API [18]. SR_{12}: To ensure reproducibility and accessibility, the implementation of the domain-specific modeling language shall be made openly available [29,33,37].

4.3   Language Specification

According to Frank the phase of *language specification* contains several parts [13]. The first step is to create a glossary containing all the concepts that are considered relevant to the domain of discourse. These terms were derived from the

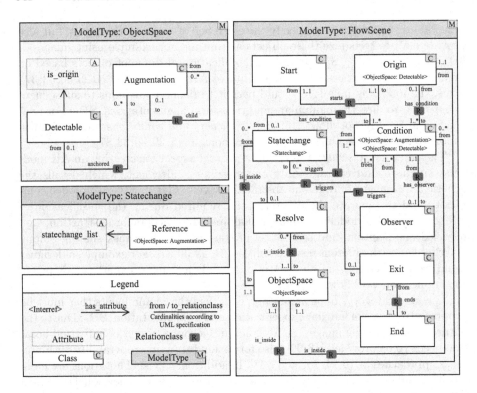

Fig. 2. Metamodel of the DSML for augmented reality applications with the three modeltypes ObjectSpace, Statechange, and FlowScene, as well as a legend.

requirements shown above, e.g., *augmentation*, *detectable*, or *condition*. Next, for each concept in the glossary, it has to be decided whether it shall be part of the modeling language and how it will be expressed with the language during instantiation. Further, it needs to be decided which *metamodeling language* or $meta^2$ model shall be used. Subsequent to the language specification, Frank foresees a separate phase for the design of the graphical notation. First, an overview of the language concepts and the abstract syntax is presented in the form of a metamodel. Thereafter, we show the graphical notation and details on the semantics of the constructs.

For the definition of the modeling language, we used the metamodeling language of ADOxx [11]. ADOxx was chosen due to its wide usage within projects of the OMiLAB network [14] and the availability of an open platform for the implementation of model editors. The main metamodeling concepts in ADOxx are [11,12]: *ModelType* (**M**) , *Class* (**C**) , *Relationclass* (**R**) , and *Attribute* (**A**). Modeltypes contain one or more classes, which may be connected by relationclasses. Modeltypes, classes, and relationclasses may have attributes. Instances of classes and relationclasses can only be contained in one particular instance of a modeltype. Special attributes of type <Interref> act as pointers to other class instances or model instances. In the metamodel introduced in the following, each concept will be marked with the icons introduced above ((Ⓜ), (Ⓒ), (Ⓡ), (Ⓐ)) to indicate the corresponding meta²-concept.

Figure 2 shows the metamodel of the new domain-specific modeling language. The modeling language is divided into three separate *ModelTypes* (Ⓜ): *ObjectSpace*, *Statechange*, and *FlowScene*. This results from requirements **GR₂**, **GR₅** and **SR₇**. An *ObjectSpace* (Ⓜ) defines the real world of an AR environment. It contains the two classes *Augmentation* (Ⓒ) and *Detectable* (Ⓒ) as defined by requirements **SR₁** and **SR₄**. Further, augmentations can include other augmentations, indicated by the *child* (Ⓡ) relationclass and they may be connected to Detectables via *anchored* (Ⓡ) relations (**SR₃**). A *Detectable* has an attribute *is_origin* (Ⓐ), specifying if a *Detectable* references the world origin (**SR₂**).

Statechanges are described in the separate ModelType *Statechange* (Ⓜ) - **SR₅** and **SR₇**. Within such models, Augmentations from the *ObjectSpace* model are referenced (*Reference* (Ⓒ)) and changes on their attributes - e.g., a rotation transformation - are expressed via the attribute *statechange_list* (Ⓐ).

The *FlowScene* (Ⓜ) ModelType defines the workflow of the AR application and how it reacts to different environmental conditions (**GR₄**, **SR₆**). Every *FlowScene* contains exactly one *Start* (Ⓒ) and one *End* (Ⓒ) instance (**SR₆**). Each *FlowScene* contains an *ObjectSpace* (Ⓒ) instance, which references an instance of the *ObjectSpace* ModelType. Inside this *ObjectSpace* class instance, the *FlowScene* model defines an *Origin* (Ⓒ), one or multiple *Statechanges* (Ⓒ), *Conditions* (Ⓒ), and *Resolves* (Ⓒ) (**SR₂**, **SR₆**). They are linked to the *ObjectSpace* with the *is_inside* (Ⓡ) relationclass, specifying that these concepts are linked to one specific *ObjectSpace*. The *Origin* is used to define the world origin of the AR environment. Thus, it references a *Detectable* in the *ObjectSpace* model. *Conditions* (Ⓒ) define requirements which are necessary to trigger the subsequent *Statechanges*, or to trigger *Resolves*, if there are no consecutive *Statechanges* (**SR₆**). Thus, *Statechanges* and *Resolves* are connected to *Conditions* by the *triggers* (Ⓡ) relationclass. *Conditions*, on the other hand, follow an *Origin* or *Statechange* via the *has_condition* (Ⓡ) relationclass. Furthermore, *Conditions* can be associated with an *Observer* (Ⓒ) using the *has_observer* (Ⓡ) relationclass. *Observers* can be used to monitor sensor data or APIs (**SR₆**).

For each of the classes and relationclasses, we added a graphical notation and details about the meaning of each construct in the form of a semantic definition, as shown in Table 1. Thereby, we considered principles from graphical notation design by Moody as far as possible [23]. In particular we aimed for *Semiotic Clarity, Perceptual Discriminability, Semantic Transparency, Complexity Management, Cognitive Integration, Visual Expressiveness, Dual Coding, Graphic Economy,* and *Cognitive Fit.* The further development of the graphical notation including more advanced methods such as recently described by Bork and Roelens is planned for the future [4].

4.4 Implementation and Execution

Subsequently, the modeling language has been implemented using the freely available and open ADOxx metamodeling platform and will be made available

Table 1. Semantics and notation of the modeling language. For each ModelType, the semantic definition of the contained constructs is explained and the visual notation is shown.

	Concept	Semantic Definition	Notation
ObjectSpace	Detectable	Supplying configuration information to sensory processing and computer vision systems, guiding them to identify physical objects. *Detectables* are an integral component of the AR environment and may be affixed to real-world objects.	
	Augmentation	Virtual, visual, or acoustic content that is fueled into the AR environment with a given position and orientation relative to its parent *Augmentation*, a *Detectable*, or the world origin of the AR environment. Can be of the type image, animation, 3D object, video, audio, label, or link.	PNG
	Anchored	Relationship type that allows connecting *Augmentations* with a *Detectable*. This is used to specify the position of *Augmentations* based on the position of real-world objects, independent of *Statechanges*. A *Detectable* can have multiple anchored *Augmentations*, but an *Augmentation* can be anchored to a maximum of one detectable.	
	Child	Relationship type used for the hierarchical structuring of *Augmentations*. An *Augmentation* can have multiple children, which in turn can have children. Useful for specifying the transformation of multiple *Augmentations*, based on a common point.	
Statechange	Reference	*Reference* is the only class of the *Statechange ModelType*. It is used to define a transformation of an *Augmentation* at a given state. It references an *Augmentation* in the *ObjectSpace* model and specifies the *Augmentation's* position, rotation, and visibility at the time of this particular *Statechange*.	PNG
FlowScene	ObjectSpace	*ObjectSpace* is a part of the *FlowScene* model. It points to an instance of an *ObjectSpace* model. Each *ObjectSpace* instance can contain *Condition*, *Statechange*, and *Resolve* instances. All contained instances are dependent on the referenced *ObjectSpace* model.	
	Start	Indicates the start of a *FlowScene* model. There can be only one *Start* object in a model.	
	End	Indicates the end of a *FlowScene* model. There can be only one *End* object in a model.	
	Statechange	Defines a *Statechange* in the AR environment at a given point in time. *Statechanges* are triggered by *Conditions*. A *Statechange* instance references a *Statechange* model that specifies transformations of *Augmentations* at that given *Statechange*. A *Statechange* is followed again by a *Condition*. The icon (S) represents a reference to a *Statechange*.	Ⓢ
	Origin	Defines the world origin of the AR environment. An *Origin* depends on an instance of an *ObjectSpace* model. It must be placed on the border of an *ObjectSpace* instance and references a *Detectable* in the *ObjectSpace* model on which it depends. The *Origin* always follows a *Start* instance and is followed by one or more *Conditions* that are triggered when the referenced *Detectable* is detected in the AR environment. The icon (+) represents a reference to an *ObjectSpace* model instance.	Origin ⊕
	Condition	Defines what *Condition* must be met to move to the next instance, which can be a *Statechange*, a *Resolve*, or an *Exit* instance. There are four types of *Conditions*, including user-driven actions (click and voice condition), visibility of *Detectables* (detect condition), conditions driven by *Observers* (observer condition), e.g., based on sensor data, and time conditions (timer condition). A *Condition* can follow multiple preceding instances of *Origin* and *Statechange*, and can have multiple subsequent instances of *Statechange*, *Resolve*, or *Exit*. To show the reference between a *Detectable* or an *Augmentation* (object) and its corresponding instance, icons (D) and (O) are used next to the triangle.	Ⓓ Ⓞ
	Resolve	Resolves an open sequence of *Statechanges*. Since it is possible to have multiple parallel sequences of *Statechanges*, it is possible to resolve a sequence without using an *Exit* instance, thus exiting the entire model. A *Resolve* instance can follow multiple *Conditions* and has no succeeding instances.	
	Observer	Additional conditional information, always being attached to a *condition* instance. *Observers* specify an observer call that can return a result at runtime. For example, an *observer* can monitor a temperature sensor and trigger a *condition* at a certain threshold.	
	Exit	*Exit* depends on an *ObjectSpace* and must be placed on the border of an *ObjectSpace* instance. It indicates that the sequences specified in the *ObjectSpace* have ended. An *Exit* instance can follow several *Condition* instances. It is always followed by exactly one *End* instance.	
	Starts	Relationship type for the entry of an *ObjectSpace* instance by an *Origin* instance. There is always exactly one *Starts* relation.	
	Has Condition	Relationship type to enter a *Condition* instance. A *Has Condition* relation can connect an *Origin* or a *Statechange* instance to a *Condition* instance.	
	Triggers	Relationship type used to trigger an action after a *Condition* is satisfied. A *Triggers* relationship can connect a *Condition* instance to a *Statechange* instance, a *Resolve* instance, an *Exit* instance, or another *Condition*.	
	Has Observer	Relationship type to connect a *Condition* instance to an *Observer* instance.	
	Ends	Relationship type for the exit of an *ObjectSpace* instance by an *Exit* instance. There is always exactly one *Ends* relation.	

via Zenodo [25]. The platform allows the easy definition and adaptation of meta-models based on the ADOxx meta^2 model and the creation of model instances in automatically generated model editors ($\mathbf{SR_9}$). ADOxx provides several text-based formats for defining metamodels and models, as well as a DSL for graphical notation ($\mathbf{SR_8}$). In this way, the models can be exported manually or program-matically in XML format for processing them in other applications.

The ADOxx XML interface has been chosen as a basis for enabling the execution of the modeling language ($\mathbf{SR_{10}}$). For this purpose, a software compo-nent has been designed in the form of an AR engine to interpret the models. The engine is implemented as a platform-independent web application using the 3D JavaScript library *three.js*[15] and the VR/AR immersive web standard *WebXR* [18]. The application can be accessed through a WebXR-compatible web browser on any mobile device, such as smartphones or *head-mounted dis-plays* in line with requirement $\mathbf{SR_{11}}$. For starting an AR experience, the engine processes the models selected by the user and monitors the user's environment for potentially relevant changes. Based on these environmental changes and user interactions, the application adapts the environment according to the specified workflows specified through triggers, conditions, and actions ($\mathbf{SR_6}$).

5   Use Case

To demonstrate the use of the modeling language and showcase a practical appli-cation, we have developed a use case involving augmented reality-assisted assem-bly of a bedside table. The goal of this use case is to guide a user through the assembly of a bedside table using an augmented reality application instead of traditional 2D instructions on paper. Figure 3 shows a screenshot of the imple-mentation in ADOxx. It includes an excerpt of a *FlowScene* model (1), the referenced *ObjectSpace* model (2), and two *Statechange* models (3, 4).

In the upper part of Fig. 3, the excerpt of the *FlowScene* model shows how to define the process for assembling the piece of furniture step by step. This includes steps such as turning the pieces into the correct position and attaching them piece by piece. It is important to note that no static flows are defined here but rather *trigger-condition-action* sequences. The *FlowScene* model references one *ObjectSpace* model (2) and several *Statechange* models (3 & 4).

In the lower left part of Fig. 3, the *ObjectSpace* model is shown (2). It includes ten *Detectables* that contain images of markers that are well-suited for computer vision detection algorithms. These act as surrogates for more advanced 3D object recognition algorithms that would permit the direct detection of physical objects. Further, the model includes *Augmentation* instances for each part of the furniture piece, e.g., "TopPlate 1". These *Augmentations* are provided as GLTF files[16], which is a common format for 3D objects and their textures. The *Augmentations* are connected by *is_child* relations to facilitate positioning and can be assigned

---

[15] https://github.com/mrdoob/three.js/.

[16] https://registry.khronos.org/glTF/specs/2.0/glTF-2.0.html.

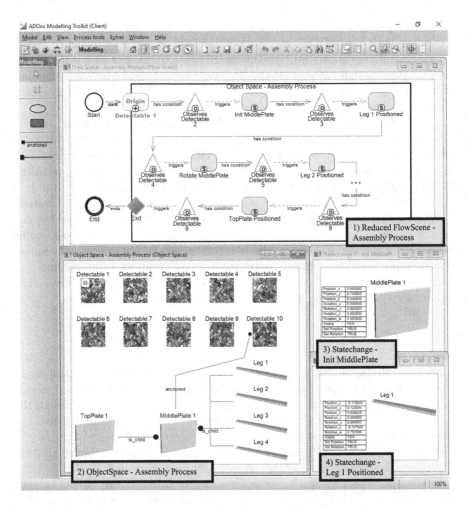

Fig. 3. Screenshot of the ADOxx implementation showing model excerpts for supporting an assembly process in augmented reality: 1) *FlowScene* model of the assembly process. 2) *ObjectSpace* model of the necessary augmentations and detectables using markers. 3) and 4) showing two exemplary *Statechange* models.

Detectables to use them as reference points by *anchored* relations. The *Augmentations* and *Detectables* defined in the *ObjectSpace* model are then referenced in the *FlowScene* model.

Furthermore, the *FlowScene* model (1) includes *Statechange* instances - e.g., "Init MiddlePlate" - which reference *Statechange* models. In the lower right of Fig. 3, two examples of *Statechange* models "Init MiddlePlate" (3) and "Leg 1 Positioned" (4) are shown. They reference one or more *Augmentations* from the *ObjectSpace* model and define the state of the position, rotation, and visibility parameters during the execution of the *FlowScene* model. These parameters are also displayed as a table. A detailed description of the semantics and notation of each language concept is available in Table 1.

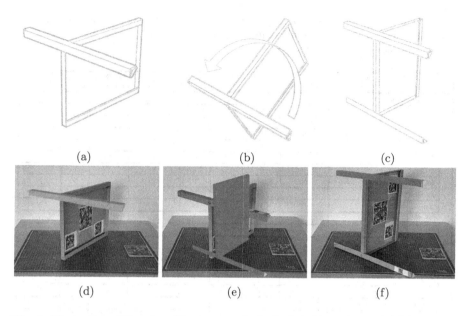

(a)   (b)   (c)

(d)   (e)   (f)

Fig. 4. Illustration of the assembly process of a bedside table – cf. IKEA [1] (a–c), and the support through AR based on the visual models (d–f).

The execution of the models of the use case is shown in Fig. 4 by using parts from an IKEA table [1]. Subfigures (a)–(c) illustrate the traditional 2D assembly instructions for (a) "attaching Leg 1", (b) "turning MiddlePlate 90° counterclockwise", and (c) "attaching Leg 2". Subfigures (d)–(f) illustrate the same steps of the instructions in augmented reality using the aforementioned models [25] and the WebXR AR engine. The screenshots were taken while using the WebXR AR engine in the Chrome browser on a *Samsung Galaxy Tab S7* tablet. Subfigure (d) shows the *Statechange* "Leg 1 Positioned". It superimposes an image of *Leg 1* on top of the real *MiddlePlate*, whose existence, position, and orientation are detected via a marker – *Detectable 10*. The *Statechange* "Rotate MiddlePlate", where the virtual object is rotated according to the desired position for further assembly of the table is shown in Subfigure (e). Subfigure (f) shows the *Statechange* "Leg 2 Positioned". The augmentation shows where the next leg shall be attached. As can be seen in subfigures (d), (e) and (f), several colored markers are placed on the real object at strategic points and according to the *ObjectSpace* model. Once a marker is detected, it is decided based on the current state of the workflow defined by the *FlowScene* model if it triggers an action or not. If an action is triggered, the workflow moves on and waits until the next detectable (marker) in line is detected. The flexible structure of the DSML allows multiple workflow paths to be active at the same time by checking for multiple detectables simultaneously. Detectables are also tracked when they are not part of the *FlowScene*. To avoid making the use case unnecessarily complex, the concepts of *Resolves* and *Observer* were not used.

Table 2. Feature comparison of the new domain-specific visual modeling language ARWFML based on twelve specific requirements SR_{1-12}. (Y): Requirement met. (N): Requirement not met. (-): Not specified.

Approach / Requirement	Ruminski & Walczak 2014	Grambow et al. 2021	Seiger et al. 2021	Lechner 2013	Campos-Lopez et al. 2021	Ruiz-Rube et al. 2020	Wild et al. 2014	ARWFML
SR1: Augmentation								
Animations	N	N	N	Y	N	N	Y	N
Images	N	Y	N	Y	Y	Y	Y	Y
Videos	N	Y	N	Y	Y	N	Y	Y
Audio	N	N	N	Y	N	N	Y	Y
Labels	Y	Y	Y	Y	Y	Y	Y	Y
3D Object	Y	Y	Y	Y	Y	Y	Y	Y
Link	N	N	Y	Y	Y	Y	N	N
Checklist	N	Y	N	N	N	N	N	N
Form	N	Y	N	N	N	N	N	N
SR2: World Origin Reference	N	N	N	N	Y	Y	Y	Y
SR3: Reference Point	N	N	N	Y	Y	N	Y	Y
SR4: Detectables / Trackables								
Anchor	N	N	-	N	Y	N	Y	Y
Marker / Image	Y	Y	-	Y	Y	Y	Y	Y
3D Object	N	N	-	Y	N	N	N	Y
SR5: Action	Y	N	Y	Y	N	Y	Y	Y
SR6: Triggers and Conditions								
Click	Y	-	Y	-	Y	Y	Y	Y
Detect	N	-	N	-	Y	Y	Y	Y
Sensor	N	-	Y	-	N	Y	Y	Y
Voice	N	-	N	-	N	Y	Y	Y
Timer	N	-	N	-	N	Y	N	Y
Area	Y	-	N	-	N	N	N	N
Gesture	N	-	Y	-	Y	Y	N	Y
Workflow	N	Y	Y	N	N	N	Y	Y
SR7: Levels of Abstraction								
Decomposition	N	N	N	N	N	Y	Y	Y
Separation of Concerns	Y	N	N	Y	N	Y	N	Y
SR8: User Interaction								
Text-based Modeling	Y	Y	Y	Y	Y	Y	Y	Y
2D Visual Modeling	N	Y	N	N	N	N	N	Y
3D Spatial Modeling	N	N	Y	N	Y	N	Y	N
SR9: Metamodeling	N	N	N	N	Y	Y	N	Y
SR10: Model Execution	Y	Y	N	-	N	Y	Y	Y
SR11: Open 3D Standard Support								
Specification	N	N	N	N	N	N	N	N
Execution	N	N	N	N	N	N	N	Y
SR12: Openly Available	N	N	Y	N	N	Y	Y	Y
Σ of supported requirements	9	11	11	13	16	18	21	26

6   Evaluation

Several techniques can be chosen to evaluate the new modeling language, including feature comparisons, theoretical and conceptual investigations, and empirical evaluations [34]. Thereby we opted for a feature comparison to previous approaches along the specific requirements that we had formulated. The previous approaches we considered were the ones from Ruminski and Walczak [30],

Grambow et al. [15], Seiger et al. [33], Lechner [21], Campos-Lopez et al. [6], Ruiz-Rube et al. [29], and Wild et al. [37].

For each specific requirement that we had formulated, we conducted a detailed comparison using multiple dimensions, as shown in Table 2. This provides a detailed overview of the features supported by previous approaches and our new modeling language in terms of augmented reality concepts, levels of abstraction, user interaction, metamodeling capabilities, model execution, support for open standards, and availability of according implementations. Thereby, we can show that our new modeling language denoted as *ARWFML* (AR Workflow Modeling Language) currently supports 26 out of 33 dimensions of requirements, whereas the next runner-up only supports 21 dimensions.

In regard to *Augmentations* (SR_1), features such as animations, links, checklists, and forms are not yet supported by our language. However, this is more of a technical than a conceptual issue and will be addressed in future versions. The same holds true for area triggers (SR_6). Concerning *User Interaction* (SR_8), the current implementation of our language only supports text-based and 2D visual modeling, which is due to limitations of the ADOxx platform, which is not yet available as open source. 3D spatial modeling, such as in a 3D-capable modeling tool or directly in AR, is not yet supported. For enabling 3D spatial modeling, the adaptation of current metamodeling platforms would be necessary, e.g., for directly supporting open 3D standards such as WebXR [18] (SR_{11}). This would certainly facilitate the specification of models, as 3D modeling greatly facilitates spatial imagination.

7   Conclusion and Outlook

In this paper, we presented a domain-specific visual modeling language that is capable of representing complex augmented reality workflows for diverse application scenarios and that can be executed using the open WebXR standard. The modeling language allows designers to specify three different types of visual models: (1) for defining the AR environment, (2) the AR workflow, and (3) different statechanges within this workflow. Thus, the language emphasizes a high level of abstraction and separation of concerns. This abstraction bridges potentially missing knowledge about the technical implementation for AR environments and allows the user to focus on the content and functionality of AR applications. The technical feasibility was demonstrated by implementing the modeling language using the ADOxx platform and a prototypical web application for executing the models. A first evaluation has been conducted through a feature comparison to previous approaches and indicated the high coverage of the defined requirements.

In future research, we plan a further evaluation of the DSML and the AR application by means of a user study, which allows to identify bottlenecks or blind spots of the DSML. Furthermore, the 2D modeling approach presented here has some limitations due to modeling 3D environments in 2D modeling tools. For example, specifying the position of the legs in the application use case described above requires a good understanding of three-dimensional space. It is almost impossible to define position and rotation vectors in 3D space without visualizing them in 3D. Therefore, a new metamodeling platform is currently being developed to incorporate the third dimension during visual modeling, enabling 3D modeling in three-dimensional space [24]. Once the approach has gained further maturity, it will be possible to evaluate it empirically.

References

1. IKEA Online Shop (2023). https://www.ikea.com/us/en/p/knarrevik-nightstand-black-30381183/. Accessed 28 Apr 2023
2. Azuma, R.T.: A survey of augmented reality. Presence Teleoperators Virtual Environ. **6**(4), 355–385 (1997)
3. Bock, A.C., Frank, U.: Low-code platform. Bus. Inf. Syst. Eng. **63**(6), 733–740 (2021). https://doi.org/10.1007/s12599-021-00726-8
4. Bork, D., Roelens, B.: A technique for evaluating and improving the semantic transparency of modeling language notations. Softw. Syst. Model. **20**(4), 939–963 (2021). https://doi.org/10.1007/s10270-021-00895-w
5. Brunschwig, L., Campos-Lopez, R., Guerra, E., de Lara, J.: Towards domain-specific modelling environments based on augmented reality. In: 2021 IEEE/ACM 43rd International Conference on Software Engineering: New Ideas and Emerging Results (ICSE-NIER), Madrid, ES, pp. 56–60. IEEE (2021). https://doi.org/10.1109/ICSE-NIER52604.2021.00020
6. Campos-López, R., Guerra, E., de Lara, J.: Towards automating the construction of augmented reality interfaces for information systems. In: Insfrán, E., et al. (eds.) Information Systems Development: Crossing Boundaries Between Development and Operations (DevOps) in Information Systems (ISD2021 Proceedings), Valencia, Spain, 8–10 September 2021. Universitat Politècnica de València/Association for Information Systems (2021). https://aisel.aisnet.org/isd2014/proceedings2021/hci/6
7. Dalton, J., Gillham, J.: Seeing is believing (2019). https://www.pwc.com/gx/en/industries/technology/publications/economic-impact-of-vr-ar.html. Accessed 09 Mar 2023
8. Di Ruscio, D., Kolovos, D., de Lara, J., Pierantonio, A., Tisi, M., Wimmer, M.: Low-code development and model-driven engineering: two sides of the same coin? Softw. Syst. Model. **21**(2), 437–446 (2022). https://doi.org/10.1007/s10270-021-00970-2
9. Doerner, R., Broll, W., Grimm, P., Jung, B. (eds.): Virtual and Augmented Reality (VR/AR). Springer, Cham (2022). https://doi.org/10.1007/978-3-030-79062-2
10. Fill, H.-G., Härer, F., Muff, F., Curty, S.: Towards augmented enterprise models as low-code interfaces to digital systems. In: Shishkov, B. (ed.) BMSD 2021. LNBIP, vol. 422, pp. 343–352. Springer, Cham (2021). https://doi.org/10.1007/978-3-030-79976-2_22
11. Fill, H., Karagiannis, D.: On the conceptualisation of modelling methods using the ADOxx meta modelling platform. Enterp. Model. Inf. Syst. Archit. Int. J. Concept. Model. **8**(1), 4–25 (2013). https://doi.org/10.18417/emisa.8.1.1
12. Fill, H.-G., Redmond, T., Karagiannis, D.: Formalizing meta models with FDMM: the ADOxx case. In: Cordeiro, J., Maciaszek, L.A., Filipe, J. (eds.) ICEIS 2012. LNBIP, vol. 141, pp. 429–451. Springer, Heidelberg (2013). https://doi.org/10.1007/978-3-642-40654-6_26

13. Frank, U.: Domain-specific modeling languages: requirements analysis and design guidelines. In: Reinhartz-Berger, I., Sturm, A., Clark, T., Cohen, S., Bettin, J. (eds.) Domain Engineering, Product Lines, Languages, and Conceptual Models, pp. 133–157. Springer, Heidelberg (2013). https://doi.org/10.1007/978-3-642-36654-3_6

14. Götzinger, D., Miron, E.-T., Staffel, F.: OMiLAB: an open collaborative environment for modeling method engineering. In: Domain-Specific Conceptual Modeling, pp. 55–76. Springer, Cham (2016). https://doi.org/10.1007/978-3-319-39417-6_3

15. Grambow, G., Hieber, D., Oberhauser, R., Pogolski, C.: A context and augmented reality BPMN and BPMS extension for industrial Internet of Things processes. In: Marrella, A., Weber, B. (eds.) BPM 2021. LNBIP, vol. 436, pp. 379–390. Springer, Cham (2022). https://doi.org/10.1007/978-3-030-94343-1_29

16. Gulden, J., Yu, E.: Toward requirements-driven design of visual modeling languages. In: Buchmann, R.A., Karagiannis, D., Kirikova, M. (eds.) PoEM 2018. LNBIP, vol. 335, pp. 21–36. Springer, Cham (2018). https://doi.org/10.1007/978-3-030-02302-7_2

17. Jannaber, S., Riehle, D.M., Delfmann, P., Thomas, O., Becker, J.: Designing a framework for the development of domain-specific process modelling languages. In: Maedche, A., vom Brocke, J., Hevner, A. (eds.) DESRIST 2017. LNCS, vol. 10243, pp. 39–54. Springer, Cham (2017). https://doi.org/10.1007/978-3-319-59144-5_3

18. Jones, B., Goregaokar, M., Cabanier, R.: WebXR device API. W3C candidate recommendation draft, work in progress, World Wide Web Consortium (2023). https://www.w3.org/TR/2023/CRD-webxr-20230303/

19. Karagiannis, D., Mayr, H.C., Mylopoulos, J. (eds.): Domain-Specific Conceptual Modeling, Concepts, Methods and Tools. Springer, Cham (2016). https://doi.org/10.1007/978-3-319-39417-6

20. Karsai, G., Krahn, H., Pinkernell, C., Rumpe, B., Schneider, M., Völkel, S.: Design guidelines for domain specific languages. In: Rossi, M., Sprinkle, J., Gray, J., Tolvanen, J.P. (eds.) Proceedings of the 9th OOPSLA Workshop on Domain-Specific Modeling (DSM 2009), Orlanda, vol. B-108, pp. 7–13. Helsingin Kauppakorkeakoulu (2009)

21. Lechner, M.: ARML 2.0 in the context of existing AR data formats. In: Latoschik, M.E., Reiners, D., Blach, R., Figueroa, P.A., Wingrave, C.A. (eds.) 6th Workshop on Software Engineering and Architectures for Realtime Interactive Systems, SEARIS 2013, Orlando, FL, USA, 17 March 2013, pp. 41–47. IEEE Computer Society (2013). https://doi.org/10.1109/SEARIS.2013.6798107

22. Mernik, M., Heering, J., Sloane, A.M.: When and how to develop domain-specific languages. ACM Comput. Surv. **37**(4), 316–344 (2005). https://doi.org/10.1145/1118890.1118892

23. Moody, D.L.: The physics of notations: toward a scientific basis for constructing visual notations in software engineering. IEEE Trans. Softw. Eng. **35**(6), 756–779 (2009). https://doi.org/10.1109/TSE.2009.67

24. Muff, F., Fill, H.: Initial concepts for augmented and virtual reality-based enterprise modeling. In: Lukyanenko, R., Samuel, B.M., Sturm, A. (eds.) Proceedings of the ER Demos and Posters 2021 Co-Located with 40th International Conference on Conceptual Modeling (ER 2021), St. John's, NL, Canada, 18–21 October 2021. CEUR Workshop Proceedings, vol. 2958, pp. 49–54. CEUR-WS.org (2021). https://ceur-ws.org/Vol-2958/paper9.pdf

25. Muff, F., Fill, H.: ADOxx Library and UseCase Models for the ER23 Publication: A Domain-Specific Visual Modeling Language for Augmented Reality Applications Using WebXR (2023). https://doi.org/10.5281/zenodo.8207639

26. Muff, F., Fill, H.: Past achievements and future opportunities in combining conceptual modeling with VR/AR: a systematic derivation. In: Shishkov, B. (ed.) BMSD 2023. LNBIP, vol. 483, pp. 129–144. Springer, Cham (2023). https://doi.org/10.1007/978-3-031-36757-1_8

27. Nguyen, T.: 4 impactful technologies from the gartner emerging technologies and trends impact radar for 2021 (2021). https://www.gartner.com/smarterwithgartner/4-impactful-technologies-from-the-gartner-emerging-technologies-and-trends-impact-radar-for-2021. Accessed 09 Mar 2023

28. Roo, J.S., Hachet, M.: One reality: augmenting how the physical world is experienced by combining multiple mixed reality modalities. In: Gajos, K., Mankoff, J., Harrison, C. (eds.) Proceedings of the 30th Annual ACM Symposium on User Interface Software and Technology, UIST 2017, Quebec City, QC, Canada, 22–25 October 2017, pp. 787–795. ACM (2017). https://doi.org/10.1145/3126594.3126638

29. Ruiz-Rube, I., Baena-Pérez, R., Mota, J.M., Sánchez, I.A.: Model-driven development of augmented reality-based editors for domain specific languages. IxD&A 45, 246–263 (2020). https://doi.org/10.55612/s-5002-045-011

30. Ruminski, D., Walczak, K.: Dynamic composition of interactive AR scenes with the carl language. In: Bourbakis, N.G., Tsihrintzis, G.A., Virvou, M. (eds.) IISA 2014, The 5th International Conference on Information, Intelligence, Systems and Applications, Chania, Crete, Greece, pp. 329–334. IEEE (2014). https://doi.org/10.1109/IISA.2014.6878808

31. Saxena, D., Verma, J.K.: Recreating reality: classification of computer-assisted environments. In: Verma, J.K., Paul, S. (eds.) Advances in Augmented Reality and Virtual Reality. SCI, vol. 998, pp. 3–9. Springer, Singapore (2022). https://doi.org/10.1007/978-981-16-7220-0_1

32. Schmalstieg, D.: Augmented Reality: Principles and Practice. Addison-Wesley, Boston (2016)

33. Seiger, R., Kühn, R., Korzetz, M., Aßmann, U.: HoloFlows: modelling of processes for the Internet of Things in mixed reality. Softw. Syst. Model. 20(5), 1465–1489 (2021). https://doi.org/10.1007/s10270-020-00859-6

34. Siau, K., Rossi, M.: Evaluation techniques for systems analysis and design modelling methods - a review and comparative analysis. Inf. Syst. J. 21(3), 249–268 (2011). https://doi.org/10.1111/j.1365-2575.2007.00255.x

35. Visic, N., Fill, H., Buchmann, R.A., Karagiannis, D.: A domain-specific language for modeling method definition: from requirements to grammar. In: 9th IEEE International Conference on Research Challenges in Information Science, RCIS 2015, Athens, Greece, 13–15 May 2015, pp. 286–297. IEEE (2015). https://doi.org/10.1109/RCIS.2015.7128889

36. Wild, F., Perey, C., Hensen, B., Klamma, R.: IEEE standard for augmented reality learning experience models. In: Mitsuhara, H., et al. (eds.) IEEE International Conference on Teaching, Assessment, and Learning for Engineering, TALE 2020, Takamatsu, Japan, 8–11 December 2020, pp. 1–3. IEEE (2020). https://doi.org/10.1109/TALE48869.2020.9368405

37. Wild, F., et al.: Towards data exchange formats for learning experiences in manufacturing workplaces. In: Kravcik, M., Mikroyannidis, A., Pammer, V., Prilla, M., Ullmann, T.D., Wild, F. (eds.) Proceedings of the 4th Workshop on Awareness and Reflection in Technology-Enhanced Learning in conjunction with the 9th European Conference on Technology Enhanced Learning: Open Learning and Teaching in Educational Communities, ARTEL@EC-TEL 2014, Graz, Austria, 16 September 2014. CEUR Workshop Proceedings, vol. 1238, pp. 23–33. CEUR-WS.org (2014). http://ceur-ws.org/Vol-1238/paper2.pdf

38. Yin, K., He, Z., Xiong, J., Zou, J., Li, K., Wu, S.T.: Virtual reality and augmented reality displays: advances and future perspectives. J. Phys. Photonics **3**(2), 022010 (2021). https://doi.org/10.1088/2515-7647/abf02e

39. Zhou, F., Duh, H.B., Billinghurst, M.: Trends in augmented reality tracking, interaction and display: a review of ten years of ISMAR. In: 7th IEEE and ACM International Symposium on Mixed and Augmented Reality, ISMAR 2008, Cambridge, UK, 15–18 September 2008, pp. 193–202. IEEE Computer Society (2008). https://doi.org/10.1109/ISMAR.2008.4637362

An Ontology for Context Modeling in Smart Spaces

Leonardo Vianna do Nascimento[1,2](✉) and José Palazzo Moreira de Oliveira[1]

[1] Informatics Institute, Federal University of RS, Porto Alegre, Brazil
palazzo@inf.ufrgs.br
[2] Federal Institute of Education, Science and Technology of Rio Grande do Sul (IFRS), Campus Alvorada, Porto Alegre, Brazil
leonardo.nascimento@alvorada.ifrs.edu.br

Abstract. Smart environments are one of the hot topics in the recent scientific literature in computer science. An essential aspect of these applications is how to obtain data about their users and understand them. Context-aware approaches proved to be successful in understanding these data. Therefore, user context representation is one of the problems to address in this domain. Context information can contain multidimensional information. This paper presents an ontology for representing context in smart environments called SpaceCOn. This ontology contains a definition of several context-related concepts. This ontology can be a strategic tool to integrate context data from different sources in large smart environments, such as smart universities and cities. Tests carried out in a case study demonstrated the developed ontology's potential.

Keywords: Ontology · Context modeling · Smart spaces · IoT

1 Introduction

Ubiquitous computing defines that computing must be present in environments to assist the user in performing their daily tasks efficiently. For this to happen, systems considered ubiquitous must be context-aware. They must adapt their behavior to the contexts obtained from the environment. One of the recent topics in ubiquitous computing deals with the definition and construction of smart environments using technologies, methodologies, and models adapted to ubiquitous computing.

In smart environments, systems may acquire and apply contextual data to improve users' experience [16]. Context-Awareness (CA) is a research area directly related to ubiquitous computing. The information exchange between systems is an important issue when dealing with context-aware systems. Is contextual information shared between systems in a representation pattern understandable to all concerned agents? For instance, a middleware present in a smartphone can provide information about its user's activities to the recommendation and monitoring applications. Therefore, it is necessary to have some standard for exchanging context information between such applications.

J. P. A. Almeida et al. (Eds.): ER 2023, LNCS 14320, pp. 354–371, 2023.
https://doi.org/10.1007/978-3-031-47262-6_19

In this context, the concept of ontology stands out. An ontology defines a common vocabulary within a specific domain. It includes a set of semantic definitions that are interpretable by computer programs where the concepts of a domain and the relationships among them are defined [19].

This paper aims to present an ontology called SpaceCOn that allows semantically representing context information in smart environments. This research is part of a project to develop an architecture for context integration in smart cities. The ontology evaluation used a case study based on a scenario previously described in the literature.

The remainder of this article is organized as follows. Section 2 presents some essential concepts related to context and used in constructing the ontology. Section 3 presents the formal definition of context used in this work. Section 4 presents the analysis of some related works found in the literature. Section 5 contains the presentation of the proposed ontology. A case study is presented in Sect. 6 to evaluate the ontology and demonstrate its potential. Section 7 presents an overview of the architecture that uses SpaceCOn to integrate context sources in smart cities. Finally, Sect. 8 concludes the article.

2 Background

Context is an object of study for researchers in different areas of computer science. Each of these areas presents a different view on the definition of context. The term conceptualization varies when considering its application in different domains [6]. The most used definition in the scientific literature is the one presented by [1], where context is *"any information useful to characterize the situation of an entity (a person, object or place) that can affect the interaction between users and systems."*

Thus, context exists only when related to another entity and contains a set of items (concepts, rules, propositions) associated with such entity. Such items can be part of the context of an entity only if they help solve the addressed problem. Such items are called *contextual elements*. A contextual element is *"any piece of data or information that allows characterizing an entity in a given domain"* [24].

A system is context-aware when it uses context to provide relevant information or services to its users [1]. An example of a context-aware system is a smartphone application that recommends restaurants to its user based on location and locomotion mode (walking, driving, on a bus). The location and locomotion mode information characterize the entity "user", and the application uses them to provide recommendations. Thus, the location and locomotion mode are contextual elements that compose the user context.

2.1 Context Categorization

It is common to classify context information according to specific categories or types. Categorizing context allows computer application designers to more easily identify which contextual elements will be useful in their applications. The work of [27] presents an interesting classification for such schemes into two types:

- *Operational Categorization*, whose objective is to categorize context information based on how it was acquired, modeled, and treated.
- *Conceptual Categorization*, where context information is categorized based on meaning and conceptual relationships.

An example of an operational categorization scheme can be found in [20]. This scheme uses two categories to classify context:

- *Primary Context*: any information obtained without using other existing context information or applying data merging operations. Examples: latitude obtained from a GPS receptor, an acceleration value obtained from an accelerometer.
- *Secondary Context*: any context information computed from primary context information. Information of this type includes that obtained through data fusion operations, inference, or database query operations.

The work in [7] presents another operational categorization scheme classified into three levels:

- *Low Level*: data collected directly from environmental sensors.
- *Intermediate Level*: context information with a higher level of abstraction obtained from inference and aggregation of another context. Examples of intermediate context include activities (such as running or walking), derived from low-level acceleration data, and places like "at home" or restaurants, derived from geographic coordinates.
- *High Level*: context information is aggregated with semantic relations to relate it to other information, such as time and location.

Several works propose different conceptual categorization schemes [1, 25, 28]. The work in [18] describes a new conceptual categorization scheme combining elements already presented in previous proposals. The scheme defines six categories: individual (that includes anything observed about an entity, including user preferences and user identification), location, time (information that specifies when some action takes place), activity (refers to tasks performed by entities), relational (corresponds to social relationships that arise from the circumstances that they are involved), the context of interest (that describes the information about things around an entity, such as objects, sounds, weather, and temperature, that may interest it at a specific moment).

It is challenging to devise an ideal context categorization scheme. Combining different categorization schemes can complement their strengths and mitigate their weaknesses [20]. For example, a geographic position by latitude and longitude coordinates obtained from a GPS reader can be classified as a low-level primary context corresponding to the location of an entity. Another example is the action performed by a person (walking, standing, lying down, running) obtained from an inference engine that uses data from different sensors as input. In this case, the information obtained can be categorized as activity and intermediate-level secondary context. Thus, in this work, categories specified in complementary schemes are expected to categorize each contextual element instance.

2.2 Quality of Context

Approaches to context management must deal with situations where the data obtained must be more accurate. Sensor data are subject to imperfection, given their technical limitations, availability, and possible malfunctions [3]. Furthermore, intermediate or high-level context inference mechanisms may present a greater or lesser degree of precision and accuracy. Furthermore, these mechanisms are trained using a subset of possible contexts and are not adapted to deal with all types of situations that may occur.

Inaccurate context information can lead an application to fail to meet its functional and non-functional requirements. Serious problems can occur due to wrong decisions made according to incorrect context information provided by a system.

Considering this scenario, mechanisms of quality assurance in context information must be used by applications in order to minimize the impact of inaccuracy in the data. As a result, the concept of *Quality of Context* (*QoC - Quality of Context*) was proposed in order to measure the quality of any contextual information. A more comprehensive and precise definition of the term is given in [14], where QoC *indicates the degree of compliance of the collected/inferred context with the prevailing situation in the environment and the requirements of a particular context consumer.*

Some QoC metrics have already been proposed in the literature [3,14]. There are two basic types of metrics: *objective parameters* (which are independent of the requirements of the context-consuming application) and *subjective parameters* (dependent on non-functional requirements of the application). Some examples of QoC parameters are Reliability, Timeliness, and Accuracy.

2.3 Context History

Some applications need not only the current context of an entity but also past context information. Historical context data are interesting in identifying trends and predicting future context-related values. Examples of applications that use context history include [5,23], and [15].

Some issues arise when manipulating [11] context histories:

- *Storage.* A fundamental point for handling a context history is the possibility of storing such information.
- *Reading.* Should data be obtained from contextual sources even when no consumers are interested? Future applications may be interested in this information that is currently not needed. How to reconcile these accesses with issues such as saving energy and resources? Thus, defining when context information will be read and stored is important for historical context data management.

- *Granularity*. Ideally, the context storage should consider storing this information at the finest possible degree of granularity to fulfill any future requests for context information. However, other issues arise related to this, such as the depletion of storage spaces. Therefore, defining the level of granularity of the stored context information is also extremely relevant.

3   Formal Context Definition Used in This Work

Based on the concepts presented in the previous section, each contextual element instantiated is considered a tuple γ, defined as:

$$\gamma = (e, v, Q, t, C) \tag{1}$$

where e is the contextual element associated with the instance, v is the value of this contextual element, Q is a set of QoC values associated with the instance, t is its creation time, and C is a set of context categories associated with the instance.

Each contextual element e is a tuple:

$$e = (\beta, \alpha) \tag{2}$$

where β is the entity characterized by the contextual element and α corresponds to the aspect of the entity related to the contextual element. Examples of aspects would be acceleration, the latitude of a geographic location, and the ambient temperature. As examples, one could define a contextual element $(PersonA, Latitude)$, corresponding to the latitude of the geographical position of $PersonA$. Another contextual element could be $(HappyCity, Temperature)$, representing the temperature in the city of HappyCity.

Each element in the set of Q quality values, in turn, can be defined as a q tuple:

$$q = (p, v) \tag{3}$$

where p is any QoC parameter and v is the associated value.

In this way, defining examples of contextual element instances is possible. For example, an instance that defines the value $Walking$ for the $Activity$ aspect of the person $PersonA$ obtained at the instant of time t_1, could be defined as:

$$((PersonA, Activity), Walking, \{(Accuracy, 0.89)\}, t_1, \{Secondary\}) \tag{4}$$

where it is possible to see the definition of a QoC value (0.89 for accuracy) and the $Secondary$ context category(the context is of the secondary type, obtained from other contexts, as defined in Sect. 2.1).

Entities, aspects, contextual elements, categories, and QoC parameters represent terms whose semantics need to be clearly defined so that agents in a smart space can exchange information based on a common vocabulary. For that, a high-level ontology is necessary to define more generic terms of the model any application domain shares. Applications can extend such an ontology to define specific terms and individuals of a domain. For instance, a domain can define specific context categories, entities, and aspects.

Thus, the ontology should:

- be able to represent the concepts defined in this section;
- be generic enough to allow its extension to different domains within smart spaces;
- enable the modeling of different types of possible entities and aspects in smart spaces;
- make it possible to associate different categories with contextual information.

4   Related Works

The first step in this work was the analysis of existing high-level ontologies for context representation. A review of the existing scientific literature identified some of these ontologies. See below a brief presentation of each one.

The ontology *CONtext ONtology* (CONON) models contextual information from four basic concepts related to computational entities, location, people, and activities [29]. Therefore, despite defining high-level concepts related to context, the CONON ontology limits the representation of such information to the categories of location, activity, individual, and representation of the context of computational interest. In addition, it is not possible to relate temporal information with modeled context.

The ontology *CoBrA-ONT* (*Context Broker Architecture Ontology*) was developed to define terms used in agent communication, where a multi-agent architecture manages context information [9]. However, the high-level concepts are limited to location, individual, and activity categories. Several terms defined in this ontology are related to meeting room applications that limit the possibilities of environments and context models.

The ontology *CoOL* (*Context Ontology Language*) models context at three levels: *look, scale,* and *context information* [26]. The ontology's main domain is a distributed system for discovering and executing services on the Web, but it is possible to adapt its concepts in other domains.

SOUPA (*Standard Ontology for Ubiquitous and Pervasive Applications*) was designed to support pervasive applications [10]. It consists of two ontologies: *SOUPA Core* (generic vocabulary common to different applications) and *SOUPA Extension* (support for different application domains). The *Core* ontology defines groups of concepts that describe people, agents, actions, security and privacy policies, time, space, and events. Although SOUPA has a set of several concepts for context modeling in multi-agent applications, it cannot represent entities that are not people, places, or agents (such as physical or virtual objects, for example) and the context of interest.

The ontology used in the CoDAMoS project (*Context-Driven Adaptation of Mobile Services* presents four main high-level concepts: user, environment, platform, and service [21]. It allows its extension to several subdomains, even in smart spaces. However, the representation of activities that go beyond the use of applications on mobile devices is quite limited.

The CACOnt ontology (*Context-Aware Computing Ontology*) allows representing concepts related to users, devices, services, location, and environment [30]. It is possible to represent several different context categories without associating temporal information, making implementing context history difficult.

A three-level approach is used by 3LConOnt (*Three-Level Context Ontology*): a higher level ontology (more generic concepts), an intermediate level ontology, and a lower level ontology (domain ontologies). The top-level ontology defines two concepts: context and entity information. Context information concept has seven subclasses: Activity, Location, States, Role, Environment, Profile, and Time [8]. Thus, this ontology can represent several categories of conceptual context.

Finally, the ontology CAMeOnto (*Context Awareness Meta Ontology*) was defined in two levels: a first level where high-level concepts were defined, and a second level for domain-specific ontologies [2]. The first level presents six key concepts: User, Activity, Time, Device, Services, and Location.

As shown above, several high-level ontologies claim to model context-related concepts. These ontologies generally bring solutions to represent many context-related concepts, but they must be richer to represent essential aspects in pervasive environments such as smart spaces:

1. Some of these ontologies, even if they claim to be high-level, were modeled with specific environments in mind (such as smart rooms), which limits their applicability.
2. They need concepts for modeling important information in smart spaces, such as contexts of interest and entities.
3. Applications can classify contextual information by combining operational and contextual categories. The analyzed ontologies do not support this feature.

5   SpaceCOn - Smart Spaces Context Ontology

Considering the specified requirements for the needed ontology, and the limitations of the existing ontologies, the authors decided to elaborate a new ontology for context modeling called *SpaceCOn: Smart Spaces Context Ontology*. For the development of this model, the methodology proposed by [19] called *Ontology Development 101* was used. The methodology contains seven main steps.

The first step is the definition of the scope and domain of the ontology. This ontology describes concepts agents use to represent contextual elements and their instances. Therefore, this ontology should provide a high-level representation of context, leaving the representation of more specific concepts and their relationships to derived domain ontologies. Therefore, this ontology aims to be extensible to any subdomain within smart spaces. The scope of the ontology encompasses the concepts and terms to be used and shared between agents concerning contextual elements and their instances. The ontology must also support the representation of historical contexts.

The second step of the methodology considers the reuse of other ontologies. As already analyzed in Sect. 4, no specific pre-existing high-level ontology was used in this work. However, some of these ontologies can represent domain-specific concepts in subdomains. In addition, this work considered other ontologies for reuse, such as the ontology *DOLCE+DnS Ultralite* (DUL)[1] for representing entities in general, the ontology *Time*[2] for representing temporal concepts, and the ontology $QUDT$[3] for specifying quantities and units of measure.

The third step concerns the enumeration of terms related to the ontology's application domain. By the definitions already mentioned in this work, it was possible to identify the following terms: *contextual element, contextual element instance, entity, context value, instant of time, aspect, context quality, QoC parameter, QoC value, context category*.

Steps four, five, and six are related, respectively, to defining the hierarchy and relationships between classes, defining properties, and constraints. After applying these steps, the set of classes shown in Fig. 1 was obtained. The presented diagram uses OntoUML language to model the ontology [12].

The main class in this ontology is *ContextualElementInstance*, which represents a contextual element instance. Each of these instances is associated with a specific instant of time (represented by an individual of the *Instant* class defined in the *Time* ontology), which indicates the instance instant of creation. Furthermore, every instance has a contextual element associated with it, an optional set of corresponding QoC values, and an optional set of associated context categories. The latter allows relating operational and conceptual categories to instances of contextual elements. For example, it is possible to define that a contextual element instance related to the *latitude* aspect of a person, obtained from a GPS receiver, is related to the categories *location* (conceptual category) and *context primary* (operational category). Latitude information obtained from processing a GSM signal from a cell phone tower could receive the categories *location* and *secondary context*.

QoC information related to contextual element instances has a parameter (an instance of the *QoCParameter* class) and a value (an instance of the *Quantity* class, defined in the QUDT ontology). An instance of the *Quantity* class has a value and a unit associated with it, supporting the conversion of values between different units.

---

[1] http://ontologydesignpatterns.org/wiki/Ontology:DOLCE+DnS_Ultralite.

[2] https://www.w3.org/TR/owl-time/.

[3] https://qudt.org/.

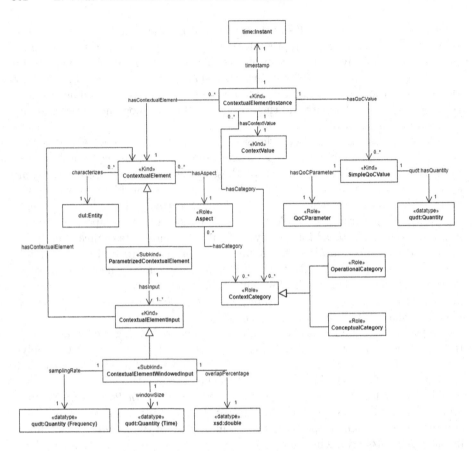

Fig. 1. SpaceCOn context concepts

The *ContextValue* class allows representing any value associated with a contextual element instance. These values can be defined more precisely in derived domain ontologies. Possibilities include, for example, values obtained from observing sensors (for example, instances of the class *Observation* defined in the ontology *SOSA - Sensor, Observation, Sample, and Actuator*[4]) or higher-level values represented in the form of other domain-specific context ontologies.

ContextualElement class represents contextual elements. Each contextual element is related to an entity (represented as an instance of the *Entity* class defined in the *DUL* ontology) and to an aspect (instance of the *Aspect* class). Each aspect can be directly related to context categories. For example, latitude and longitude coordinates will always receive a *location* category. Categories related to an aspect will automatically be associated with all instances of contextual elements related to that aspect.

---

[4] https://www.w3.org/TR/vocab-ssn/.

Input contextual elements can provide additional information that characterizes some derived contextual elements. An example of such a situation would be the average of the X-axis component of the acceleration of a given *smartphone*. Such a contextual element is associated with an entity (smartphone) and an aspect (average), but another input contextual element (X component of smartphone acceleration) is necessary to characterize it completely. The class *ParametrizedContextualElement* can represent such contextual elements in the ontology. Instances of this class must be associated with at least one input represented by an instance of the *ContextualElementInput* class. A given input may be a set of values from an observation window. The *ContextualElementWindowedInput* class can represent input sets of values by specifying a sampling frequency, size (in time units), and percentage of overlap.

6   Evaluation

The ontology was implemented in OWL language using Protégé software [17], version 5.5.0. The implementation used the *gUFO* [4] as base ontology. The implementation of each class is summarized below.

1. *ContextualElement*
   – Subclass of: *gufo:Kind*
   – Restrictions:
     • spacecon:characterizes **exactly** 1 dul:Entity
     • spacecon:hasAspect **exactly** 1 spacecon:Aspect
2. *ContextualElementInstance*
   – Subclass of: *gufo:Kind*
   – Restrictions:
     • spacecon:hasContextElement **exactly** 1 spacecon:ContextualElement
     • spacecon:hasContextValue **exactly** 1 spacecon:ContextValue
     • time:hasTime **exactly** 1 time:Instant
3. *ContextualElementInput*
   – Subclass of: *gufo:Kind*
   – Restrictions:
     • spacecon:hasCtxElement **exactly** 1 spacecon:ContextualElement
4. *ContextValue*
   – Subclass of: *gufo:Kind*
   – Restrictions: -
5. *SimpleQoCValue*
   – Subclass of: *gufo:Kind*
   – Restrictions:
     • qudt:hasQuantity **exactly** 1 qudt:Quantity
     • spacecon:hasQoCParameter **exactly** 1 spacecon:QoCParameter
6. *ContextualElementWindowedInput*
   – Subclass of: *gufo:SubKind, spacecon:ContextualElementInput*
   – Restrictions:
     • spacecon:samplingRate **exactly** 1 qudt:Quantity

- spacecon:windowOverlapPercentage **exactly** 1 xsd:double
- spacecon:windowSize **exactly** 1 qudt:Quantity

7. *ParametrizedContextualElement*
   - Subclass of: *gufo:SubKind, spacecon:ContextualElement*
   - Restrictions:
     - spacecon:hasInput **some** spacecon:ContextualElementInput

8. *Aspect*
   - Subclass of: *gufo:Role*
   - Restrictions: -

9. *ContextCategory*
   - Subclass of: *gufo:Role*
   - Restrictions: -

10. *ConceptualCategory*
    - Subclass of: *gufo:Role*, spacecon:ContextCategory
    - Restrictions: -

11. *OperationalCategory*
    - Subclass of: *gufo:Role*, spacecon:ContextCategory
    - Restrictions: -

12. *QoCParameter*
    - Subclass of: *gufo:Role*
    - Restrictions: -

The classes *ContextualElement, ContextualElementInstance, ContextValue, SimpleQoCValue, ContextualElementInput* are disjoint. Similarly, the classes *OperationalCategory, ConceptualCategory* are also disjoint.

To evaluate the capacity of the ontology to represent real-world situations, we used a case study based on the scenario presented in [22]. The described scenario involves recognizing people's activity by capturing data from motion sensors while performing routine day-to-day tasks. A dataset called *Opportunity* was generated from the data collected through the execution of sequences of activities by volunteers in a room simulating a small apartment. Four activities related to modes of locomotion were performed by the volunteers: standing, walking, lying, and sitting.

The wearable sensors each volunteer used generated the data to obtain the activities. Figure 2 shows the sensors' location. The sensors include twelve 3D accelerometers (shown in yellow in the figure) and seven IMU (*Inertial Measurement Unit*) inertial systems identified in red in the figure. The five IMUs on the volunteers' upper body (RLA, RUA, LUA, LLA, and BACK) can generate nine movement-related parameters (3D acceleration, 3D rotation, and 3D magnetic field). The IMUs on each volunteer's feet (R-SHOE and L-SHOE) provide another 32 parameters. In total, 113 parameters were generated by these sensors and recorded in the *dataset*.

The described scenario still contained sensors in objects scattered throughout the environment. However, the inference process to obtain the considered activities do not use data from these sensors. Thus, the evaluation process described here does not present models for these data.

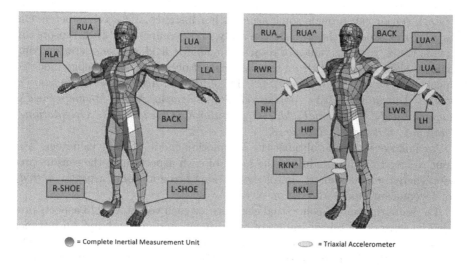

= Complete Inertial Measurement Unit   = Triaxial Accelerometer

Fig. 2. Location of sensors to capture data for the *Opportunity* dataset [22]

Each volunteer in the scenario was modeled using the *dul:Entity* class. Each sensor obtains data from different body parts, and they were also modeled as entities that are constituents of each volunteer. An example of entity modeling using the proposed ontology in the described scenario is shown in Fig. 3. The volunteer *S1* is a *dul:Entity* instance, and its constituents are other entities that model parts of the body with sensors.

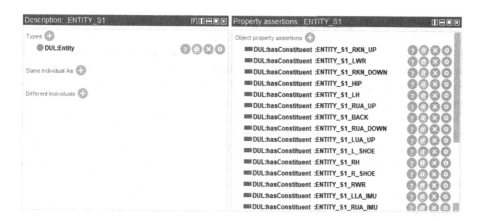

Fig. 3. Example of entity modeling a volunteer

Each sensor can provide some aspects. For instance, 3D accelerometers can provide three aspects: the acceleration's x, y, and z components. IMU sensors can provide the x, y, and z values of rotation, magnetic field, and acceleration components. Sixteen instances from the class *Aspect* of SpaceCOn ontology modeled aspects in the scenario: *AccelerationX, AccelerationY, AccelerationZ, AngularVelocityX, AngularVelocityY, AngularVelocityZ, CompassAngle, MagneticFieldX, MagneticFieldY, MagneticFieldZ, OrientationX, OrientationY, OrientationZ, RotationX, RotationY, RotationZ.*

An inference module obtains the locomotion mode of each volunteer. The input received by this module is the mean of each aspect value the sensors provide. Therefore, the scenario ontology contains two additional aspects: *Activity* (for locomotion mode) and *Mean*.

The scenario has 227 contextual elements for each volunteer: 113 aspects provided by sensors, 113 mean values of each aspect, and one activity. An instance of the *ContextualElement* class modeled each contextual element provided in the considered scenario. Figure 4 shows an example of a contextual element defined to model the activity of the *S1* volunteer.

Fig. 4. Example of a contextual element that models the activity of the S1 volunteer

Figure 5 shows another example of a contextual element. In this example, an individual of the *ParametrizedContextualElement* models the mean value of the acceleration x component from the back sensor of the S1 volunteer. The top part of the figure shows the contextual element that models the mean value. The bottom part of the figure shows the model of the input value that points to the contextual element that models the acceleration x component of the back of S1. The input models a window of acceleration value with the specified sampling rate, window size, and overlap percentage.

Eight individuals model context categories: two operational categories (*PrimaryContext* and *SecondaryContext*) and six conceptual categories (*ActivityCategory, ContextOfInterestCategory, IndividualCategory, LocationCategory, RelationalcCategory*, and *TimeCategory*. Each aspect receives one or more related categories. For instance, aspects related to sensors receive the category *PrimaryContext*, while the *Activity* aspect receives the *ActivityCategory* and *SecondaryContext* categories. The scenario ontology contains a QoC parameter, *Accuracy*, as an instance of the *QoCParameter* class.

In this scenario, the *ContextValue* class has been extended in four new concepts (see Fig. 6): *Observation, WindowedValue, AggregatedValue*, and *ActivityValue*. The *Observation* class models a value obtained from a sensor. An instance

Fig. 5. Example of a contextual element that models the mean value of acceleration x-axis from the S1 volunteer back.

of the QUDT *Quantity* class models the observation value. A *WindowedValue* is a value in a set of observations representing a window of values with a sampling rate, size (in a time unit), and an overlapping percentage. The *AggregatedValue* class models a value obtained after calculating the mean of a window of observations. Finally, the *ActivityValue* class models an inferred locomotion mode.

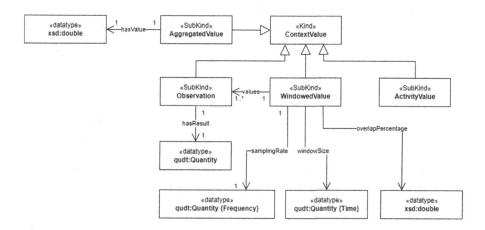

Fig. 6. Extension of ContextValue concept created in the case study.

Figure 7 shows an example of a contextual element instance. The instance *EXAMPLE_CTX_ELEM_INSTANCE_1_TIME* is an individual of the class *Instant* of W3C *Time* ontology. The *ACTIVITY_WALKING_VALUE* instance is an individual of *ActivityValue* class.
Finally *EXAMPLE_CTX_ELEM_INSTANCE_1_QOC_VALUE* is an instance of the *SimpleQoCValue* class.

Situation modeling is a limitation of SpaceCOn. Situations, as defined in [13], are a set of contexts that hold in a time interval. For example, *John is*

Fig. 7. Example of contextual element instance modeled with the ontology.

traveling to Portugal to attend ER conference is an example of a situation with a specific duration. It is possible to model relations between context instances in SpaceCOn through the specialization of *ContextValue* concept. For instance, a situation instance value can be a set of other instances that compose it. However, SpaceCOn relates a specific time instant to each contextual element instance and does not support the association of time intervals, and situation modeling is a limitation of the ontology. Even so, a situation modeling ontology can use SpaceCOn to model contextual instances that compose a specific situation.

7   Context Integration Architecture

The SpaceCOn ontology has been used in an architecture for context integration described in Fig. 8. Each agent encapsulates a context source (such as a sensor, an inference engine, a database, or a web service). The whole model is a large society where agents can come and go. Agents can enter society by providing access to new sources of context. These agents can leave if their capabilities are no longer needed.

Logical sets called *nodes* aggregate agents. An agent can be part of only one node. Each node works as a federation, where an agent called *broker* acts as a facilitator and manages all the information that enters and leaves the node. Intermediary agents are responsible for carrying out the exchange of information between nodes. These agents are organized in a *peer-to-peer* network to connect nodes without needing a centralizing entity. Teams of agents can be formed, even between agents from different nodes, to cooperate in providing the contextual elements requested by an application.

Each application is a context consumer managed by the model. An application must insert itself inside a node and access its context information. Applications can send query requests or subscribe to brokers to receive instances of contextual elements. These requests contain a set of contextual elements that the architecture must provide. To answer these requests, the brokers consult other agents in the node or in other nodes to obtain all the requested information.

Agents communicate using messages. The messages use terms defined by the SpaceCOn ontology. For example, query requests contain a set of instances of the ContextualElement class, and responses to applications contain a set of instances of contextual elements modeled through the ContextualElementInstance class.

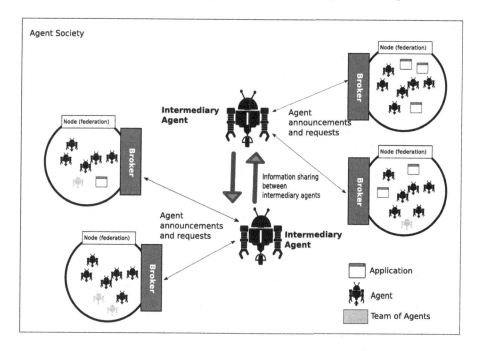

Fig. 8. The context integration architecture that uses SpaceCOn.

8   Conclusion

This paper describes an ontology called SpaceCOn for representing context in smart environments. Classes for context-related concepts were analyzed in the context recognition literature and included in the ontology. An analysis of the existing high-level ontologies for context representation showed that SpaceCOn covers aspects other models do not support.

A case study based on the literature showed that ontology had reached the intended purpose of consistently representing context information. SpaceCOn can be used with success to represent contextual elements and their instances. Furthermore, domain ontologies can extend SpaceCOn to represent domain-specific concepts.

We intend to model context in other scenarios and domains in future work. We intend to use the ontology in a context-aware application based on the integration architecture shown in this work.

Acknowledgments. This study was supported by CNPq/MCTI/FNDCT Nº 18/2021 grant n. 405973/2021-7, and by the Federal Institute of Education, Science and Technology of Rio Grande do Sul (IFRS).

References

1. Abowd, G.D., Dey, A.K., Brown, P.J., Davies, N., Smith, M., Steggles, P.: Towards a better understanding of context and context-awareness. In: Gellersen, H.-W. (ed.) HUC 1999. LNCS, vol. 1707, pp. 304–307. Springer, Heidelberg (1999). https://doi.org/10.1007/3-540-48157-5_29

2. Aguilar, J., Jerez, M., Rodríguez, T.: CAMeOnto: context awareness meta ontology modeling. Appl. Comput. Inform. **14**(2), 202–213 (2018)

3. Al-Shargabi, A., Siewe, F., Zahary, A.: Quality of context in context-aware systems (2017)

4. Almeida, J., Guizzardi, G., Falbo, R., Sales, T.P.: gUFO: a lightweight implementation of the unified foundational ontology (UFO) (2019). http://purl.org/nemo/doc/gufo

5. Aranda, J.A.S., Bavaresco, R.S., de Carvalho, J.V., Yamin, A.C., Tavares, M.C., Barbosa, J.L.V.: A computational model for adaptive recording of vital signs through context histories. J. Ambient Intell. Humanized Comput. 1–15 (2021)

6. Bazire, M., Brézillon, P.: Understanding context before using it. In: Dey, A., Kokinov, B., Leake, D., Turner, R. (eds.) CONTEXT 2005. LNCS (LNAI), vol. 3554, pp. 29–40. Springer, Heidelberg (2005). https://doi.org/10.1007/11508373_3

7. Bettini, C., et al.: A survey of context modelling and reasoning techniques. Pervasive Mob. Comput. **6**(2), 161–180 (2010)

8. Cabrera, O., Franch, X., Marco, J.: 3LConOnt: a three-level ontology for context modelling in context-aware computing. Softw. Syst. Model. **18**(2), 1345–1378 (2019)

9. Chen, H., Finin, T., Joshi, A.: An ontology for context-aware pervasive computing environments. Knowl. Eng. Rev. **18**(3), 197–207 (2003)

10. Chen, H., Perich, F., Finin, T., Joshi, A.: SOUPA: standard ontology for ubiquitous and pervasive applications. In: The First Annual International Conference on Mobile and Ubiquitous Systems: Networking and Services, MOBIQUITOUS 2004, pp. 258–267. IEEE (2004)

11. Dey, A.K., Abowd, G.D., Salber, D.: A conceptual framework and a toolkit for supporting the rapid prototyping of context-aware applications. Hum.-Comput. Interact. **16**(2–4), 97–166 (2001)

12. Guizzardi, G., Fonseca, C.M., Benevides, A.B., Almeida, J.P.A., Porello, D., Sales, T.P.: Endurant types in ontology-driven conceptual modeling: towards OntoUML 2.0. In: Trujillo, J.C., et al. (eds.) ER 2018. LNCS, vol. 11157, pp. 136–150. Springer, Cham (2018). https://doi.org/10.1007/978-3-030-00847-5_12

13. Gundersen, O.E.: Situational awareness in context. In: Brézillon, P., Blackburn, P., Dapoigny, R. (eds.) CONTEXT 2013. LNCS (LNAI), vol. 8175, pp. 274–287. Springer, Heidelberg (2013). https://doi.org/10.1007/978-3-642-40972-1_21

14. Manzoor, A., Truong, H.L., Dustdar, S.: Quality of context: models and applications for context-aware systems in pervasive environments. Knowl. Eng. Rev. **29**(2), 154–170 (2014)

15. Martini, B.G., et al.: IndoorPlant: a model for intelligent services in indoor agriculture based on context histories. Sensors **21**(5), 1631 (2021)

16. Morandi, C., Rolando, A., Di Vita, S.: From Smart City to Smart Region: Digital Services for an Internet of Places. SAST, Springer, Cham (2016). https://doi.org/10.1007/978-3-319-17338-2

17. Musen, M.A.: The protégé project: a look back and a look forward. AI Matt. **1**(4), 4–12 (2015)

18. do Nascimento, L.V., Machado, G.M., Maran, V., de Oliveira, J.P.M.: Context recognition and ubiquitous computing in smart cities: a systematic mapping. Computing **103**(5), 801–825 (2021)

19. Noy, N.F., McGuinness, D.L., et al.: Ontology development 101: a guide to creating your first ontology (2001)

20. Perera, C., Zaslavsky, A., Christen, P., Georgakopoulos, D.: Context aware computing for the internet of things: a survey. IEEE Commun. Surv. Tutor. **16**(1), 414–454 (2014). https://doi.org/10.1109/SURV.2013.042313.00197

21. Preuveneers, D., et al.: Towards an extensible context ontology for ambient intelligence. In: Markopoulos, P., Eggen, B., Aarts, E., Crowley, J.L. (eds.) EUSAI 2004. LNCS, vol. 3295, pp. 148–159. Springer, Heidelberg (2004). https://doi.org/10.1007/978-3-540-30473-9_15

22. Roggen, D., et al.: Collecting complex activity datasets in highly rich networked sensor environments. In: 2010 Seventh International Conference on Networked Sensing Systems (INSS), pp. 233–240. IEEE (2010)

23. da Rosa, J.H., Barbosa, J.L., Ribeiro, G.D.: ORACON: an adaptive model for context prediction. Expert Syst. Appl. **45**, 56–70 (2016)

24. dos Santos, V.V.: CEManTIKA: a domain-independent framework for designing context sensitive systems (2008)

25. Schilit, B., Adams, N., Want, R.: Context-aware computing applications. In: 1994 First Workshop on Mobile Computing Systems and Applications, pp. 85–90. IEEE (1994)

26. Strang, T., Linnhoff-Popien, C., Frank, K.: CoOL: a context ontology language to enable contextual interoperability. In: Stefani, J.-B., Demeure, I., Hagimont, D. (eds.) DAIS 2003. LNCS, vol. 2893, pp. 236–247. Springer, Heidelberg (2003). https://doi.org/10.1007/978-3-540-40010-3_21

27. Van Bunningen, A.H., Feng, L., Apers, P.M.: Context for ubiquitous data management. In: International Workshop on Ubiquitous Data Management, pp. 17–24. IEEE (2005)

28. Villegas, N.M., Müller, H.A.: Managing dynamic context to optimize smart interactions and services. In: Chignell, M., Cordy, J., Ng, J., Yesha, Y. (eds.) The Smart Internet. LNCS, vol. 6400, pp. 289–318. Springer, Heidelberg (2010). https://doi.org/10.1007/978-3-642-16599-3_18

29. Wang, X.H., Zhang, D.Q., Gu, T., Pung, H.K.: Ontology based context modeling and reasoning using OWL. In: Proceedings of the Second IEEE Annual Conference on Pervasive Computing and Communications Workshops, pp. 18–22. IEEE (2004)

30. Xu, N., Zhang, W.S., Yang, H.D., Zhang, X.G., Xing, X.: CACOnt: a ontology-based model for context modeling and reasoning. In: Applied Mechanics and Materials, vol. 347, pp. 2304–2310. Trans Tech Publications (2013)

Applications of Conceptual Modeling

A Reference Meta-model to Understand DNA Variant Interpretation Guidelines

Mireia Costa[1]([⊠])[iD], Alberto García S.[1][iD], Ana Leon[1][iD], Anna Bernasconi[2][iD], and Oscar Pastor[1][iD]

[1] PROS Group, Valencian Research Institute (VRAIN) Universitat Politècnica de València, Valencia, Spain
micossan@vrain.upv.es, {algarsi3,aleon,opastor}@pros.upv.es
[2] Politecnico di Milano, Milan, Italy
anna.bernasconi@polimi.it

Abstract. Determining the role of a DNA variant in patients' health status – a process known as *variant interpretation* – is highly critical for precision medicine applications. Variant interpretation involves a complex process where, regrettably, there is still debate on how to combine and weigh diverse available evidence to achieve proper and consistent answers. Indeed, at the time of writing, 22 different variant interpretation guidelines are available to the scientific community, each of them attempting to establish a framework for standardizing the interpretation process. However, these guidelines are qualitative and vague by nature, which hinders their streamlined application and potential automation. Consequently, more precise definitions are needed. Conceptual modeling provides the means to bring clarification within this domain. This paper presents our efforts to define and use a UML meta-model that describes the main concepts involved in the definition of variant interpretation guidelines and the constructs they evaluate. The precise conceptual definition of the guidelines allowed us to identify four common misinterpretation patterns that hamper the correct interpretation process and that can consequently affect classification results. In several proposed examples, the use of the meta-model provides support in identifying the inconsistencies in the observed process; this result paves the way for further proposing reconciliation strategies for the existing guidelines.

Keywords: Conceptual Modeling · Genomics · Variant Interpretation Guidelines · Standards

1 Introduction

Precision medicine has emerged as a disruptive medical approach aiming to transform historically reactive medicine into a proactive one. To do so, this new perspective prioritizes individualized clinical actions based on each patient's

---

M.C. and A.G.S. should be regarded as Joint First Authors.

J. P. A. Almeida et al. (Eds.): ER 2023, LNCS 14320, pp. 375–393, 2023.
https://doi.org/10.1007/978-3-031-47262-6_20

unique characteristics [53]. The most distinguishing characteristic of an individual is its DNA sequence, which slightly differs among individuals.

Individual DNA sequences are compared to a DNA reference sequence that reflects an "ideal" individual, leading to the identification of differences. These differences among individuals are known as DNA variants[1], and they determine our physical characteristics, predisposition to disorders, or a different response to treatments.

Identifying variants in an individual's DNA sequence has become easier and faster thanks to Next-Generation Sequencing (NGS) [41]. This technique uses massive parallelization to obtain the entire DNA sequence of an individual; the connected technological advancement has significantly improved our ability to identify and analyze DNA variants [41]. However, the scientific community must overcome numerous challenges (costs, ethics, security of the shared data, and data integration and interpretation, among others) [34] before achieving the paradigm shift that precision medicine proposes. In the data integration and interpretation context, one of the most difficult challenges is determining a DNA variant's role in our health status (i.e., whether it will cause a particular disorder or affect treatment response), a process known as *variant interpretation.*

Variant interpretation is a complex process that involves weighing various factors, such as the variant's frequency among the population, whether it has previously been linked to a disorder, etc. Geneticists and clinical experts are still debating on how to correctly weigh this evidence in order to achieve proper variant interpretation. To address this issue, several authors have developed *variant interpretation guidelines.* A variant interpretation guideline is a set of instructions designed to guide the interpretation process by assessing whether or not a variant meets specific criteria. These guidelines have quickly been embraced by geneticists [37] and they have been adapted to the peculiarities of several disorder-causing genes [30].

However, several issues have arisen due to the vague definition of these guidelines and their application, which depends on the subjective interpretations of domain experts [50]. In this context, clinical experts argue that more concrete definitions are needed to standardize the variant interpretation process and reduce inconsistencies [2]. A suitable approach to clarify this complex domain is Conceptual Modeling. Conceptual Modeling techniques have proven to be effective to achieve high levels of concreteness and standardization in genomics [7, 15, 38, 42, 45].

In this work, we report on our use of Conceptual Modeling to achieve a systematized definition of the main concepts involved in the definition of variant interpretation guidelines and the constructs they evaluate. For this purpose, we created a meta-model using the Unified Modeling Language [10]. Twenty-two well-known variant interpretation guidelines were carefully analyzed. Based on these analyses, we were able to characterize the differences and similarities between these guidelines. This allowed us to identify the common conceptual

---

[1] https://www.cancer.gov/publications/dictionaries/genetics-dictionary/def/variant.

structure that underpins all of these guidelines and to consolidate our findings via the meta-model.

The contribution of our work is to show how using a conceptual meta-model to represent the concepts and constructs behind variant interpretation guidelines can provide the following benefits: (a) Definition of the underlying structure that different interpretation guidelines share, resulting in the development of a common framework for representing various types of guidelines; (b) Identification of patterns of misinterpretation of variants due to inconsistencies or conflicts within or between existing guidelines; (c) Disentanglement of the intricate details of existing clinical guidelines by resolving aspects whose definitions are left implicit or ambiguous, requiring clarification.

Prospectively, our contribution can support a shared effort to define clinical guidelines more consistently and objectively, reducing variant interpretation inconsistencies. In parallel, it offers the possibility to improve variant interpretation automation because tools will be based on a precise and concrete definition to guide their implementation rather than relying on personal interpretations.

The remainder of the paper is organized as follows. Section 2 provides the background that has motivated our work. Section 3 overviews related work. Section 4 describes the proposed conceptual meta-model, instantiating it on a simple example of use (contributing to benefit (a)). Section 5 proposes to use the above-mentioned conceptual meta-model to define a set of misinterpretation patterns (contributing to benefit (b)). Section 6 discusses lessons learned (regarding benefit (c)) and, finally, Sect. 7 concludes the paper with a future outlook.

2   Background

At the time of writing, 22 DNA variant interpretation guidelines have been proposed. Some examples are the ACMG/AMP 2015 guidelines [43], the Ambry Genetics 2015 guidelines [17], or the ACGS for Rare Disease 2020 guidelines [23]. The current guidelines support Mendelian disorders (disorders caused by variants in a single gene), Rare disorders (disorders affecting a small percentage of the population), X-linked disorders (disorders caused by variants in the X chromosome), and Recessive or Autosomal dominant disorders (disorders with a specific inheritance pattern). Some guidelines are only applicable to somatic variants (variants that occur after conception in specific body tissues), mitochondrial variants (variants affecting the mitochondrial DNA), or copy number variants (variants that affect the number of copies of a specific gene). Finally, some guidelines present generic applicability, i.e., they are theoretically applicable to any kind of variant or disorder.

Even though these guidelines attempted to improve and standardize the variant interpretation process, they are far from being a shared and widely-adopted solution. Indeed, distinct works [13,21] have highlighted a number of issues that arise when using variant interpretation guidelines. The most frequently expressed concern is that the guidelines are qualitative in nature without providing the needed specificity [24,28]; as a consequence, their practical application is left open to expert interpretation [22]. In this context, inconsistent interpretations among experts become common, leading to serious consequences in healthcare applications.

Consider for instance a case where an initial assessment in prenatal care reveals that an unborn child is at high risk of developing Muscular Dystrophy disorder. The assessment was later revised by a different team of experts, finally determining that it was incorrect [40]. Because often these families have to make decisions on pregnancy management within a limited timeframe, the improperly classified variant could have had irreversible consequences. Furthermore, the more complex the disorder (e.g., cancer), the more inconsistencies in variant classification usually emerge [14].

In an effort to provide more exact definitions and streamline the process by lowering the complexity and time needed to complete the interpretation, several tools have been created to automate the variant interpretation process [26,29,35,46,49,52]. Among these, VarSome [26], InterVar [29], and CharGer [46] aim to operate within a broad scope, i.e., with variations associated with any kind of disorder. Instead, CardioVAI [35] and CardioClassifier [52] focus on inherited cardiac conditions. All of them assign a label representing the disorder-causing potential of the variants based on a set of applied criteria from the ACMG/AMP 2015 guidelines. Following a different approach, Tavtigian et al. [49] modeled the ACMG/AMP 2015 guidelines as a Bayesian framework, which allowed the authors to provide a probabilistic score of pathogenicity associated with each variation.

These tools are meant to provide automated support for the variant interpretation process; this is supposed to be more effective than human application and reduce reproducibility issues. However, the qualitative nature and insufficient specificity of variant interpretation guidelines cause different tools to make assumptions and interpret the data in discordant ways. Furthermore, some guideline criteria are frequently omitted by these tools because of the heterogeneous information required for their application [36]. Overall, the inconsistencies that naturally rise in a "manual" variant interpretation process are inevitably reiterated. Automation of the interpretation process does not provide additional value when it is not based on precise and concrete definitions. This further motivates the effort described next.

3   Related Works

In the last years, several works have targeted specific domains all united by the lack of a solid and well-founded conceptual characterization of their characteristics. This was accomplished by proposing conceptual meta-models that provide general clarification and guidance on the understanding of the said domain. For instance, we report recent work in the context of fake news [6,51], Virtual Network Function Marketplaces [20], FAIR scientific datasets [8], or FAIR Digital Objects [47].

In the field of genomics, the use of conceptual models for specifying genomics-related processes has been explored. More specifically, conceptual modeling techniques have proven to be an effective tool to achieve high levels of concreteness and standardization. A recent work [7], has considered general genomic data types represented in datasets for analysis and connected them to an abstract conceptual representation, with the purpose to resolve their heterogeneity. Other modeling efforts have targeted the inherent temporal dimension associated with genomics data by mapping their evolution over time [15]; such an approach is particularly sensitive in cases of changes in variant interpretation due to gene-related data being updated [48]. Conceptual models have also been proposed to target other specific aspects in the use of multi-omics data for precision medicine [45] and for the identification of relevant and high-quality data records [38].

Aside from simple conceptual models, also ontological approaches have been attempted. Ferrandis et al. [32] promoted the use of foundational ontologies to avoid errors while creating and curating genomic domain models for personalized medicine. The approach of ontological clarification has been employed to support the explanation of complex domains such as human metabolic pathways [16] and the viral genome with the related events of infection, sampling, sequencing, and annotation for SARS-CoV-2 sequences [9]. Similarly, OntoRepliCov [27] showed an initial conceptual framework targeting the translation event during SARS-CoV-2 replication.

Despite the growing interest interest in conceptual models in the area of genomics and some technological efforts to gather and integrate different human variation data [12,31,54], to the best of our knowledge, the proposal presented here is the first explicit, reusable reference meta-model that targets the Variant Interpretation process.

4   A Meta-model for Variant Interpretation Guidelines

Let us begin by recalling that, as previously stated, variants can be classified according to a variety of interpretation guidelines. In the model proposed here (see Fig. 1), each GUIDELINE is defined by its *title, authors*, and its *applicability*, i.e., the specific context in which the guideline is applicable, such as for instance "Mendelian disorders" –a specific type of disorder–, or "copy number variants" –a specific type of variant. In addition, guidelines have a *URL* that points to the publication or file where they can be examined.

For the purpose of this model, we consider that the VARIANT only characteristic is an unique *identifier* (e.g., "rs556540177" for a single nucleotide variant, or "nsv3875336" for a copy number variant). This particular domain oversimplification enabled us to reduce the complexity of the model. However, an extended version of this model that includes additional information such as the position of the VARIANT on the distinct genomic sequences, as well as the reference and alternative alleles exists. A CLASSIFICATIONRESULT (e.g., "benign", "pathogenic", or "protective") is the classification obtained for a certain VARIANT using a specific GUIDELINE.

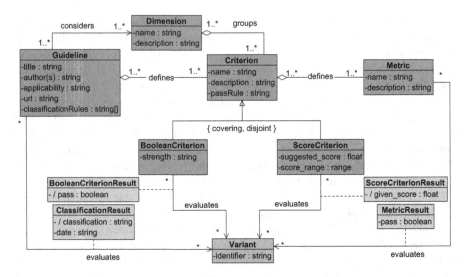

Fig. 1. Meta-model for variant interpretation guidelines. Concepts associated with the definition of clinical guidelines are depicted in green, the DNA-associated concepts (i.e., the variant that is interpreted by the clinical guideline) are depicted in red, and the concepts used to describe the results of interpreting a variant via a clinical guideline are depicted in lilac. (Color figure online)

Each GUIDELINE defines a number of criteria (i.e., a set of CRITERION) to be evaluated in order to obtain the most adequate *ClassificationResult* for a VARIANT. This classification is calculated based on the *classificationRules* defined in a GUIDELINE, which state the combination of criteria that must be met to achieve a specific *ClassificationResult*. An example of a classification rule is "pathogenic: PS1, benign: BP1", which specifies that a variant would be classified as "pathogenic" if the PS1 criterion was met, and as "benign" if the BP1 criterion was met.

A CRITERION is decomposed into more specific aspects, called metrics. Each METRIC evaluates to either a `true` or a `false` value for a particular VARIANT (i.e., representing a METRICRESULT). Similarly to GUIDELINES, each CRITERION defines a specific rule, named *passRule*, which performs logical operations over the set of METRICRESULTS to determine whether the CRITERION is met. It is worth noting here that the same METRIC can be used to calculate multiple criteria (as represented by the cardinalities between the METRIC and the CRITERION classes).

We recognize two different kinds of CRITERION: the BOOLEANCRITERION and the SCORECRITERION. The BOOLEANCRITERION returns a `true` or `false` value (i.e., BOOLEANCRITERIONRESULT) and is defined by a *strength* that represents the extent to which the criterion supports a specific classification. For instance, a "strong" value indicates that the fulfillment of the criteria provides strong support for a certain classification, whereas a "moderate" value indicates that the criteria only offers moderate support. The SCORECRITERION returns a numeric value (i.e., SCORECRITERIONRESULT) and has a float *suggested_score* (e.g., "0.25") within a *score_range* (e.g., "[0, 0.45]").

Lastly, the DIMENSION groups distinct criteria that share given aspects. For instance, some criteria focus on evaluating specific characteristics of a VARIANT position in our DNA sequence, in which case we have a DIMENSION with the *name* "Variant position", and the *description* "Criteria that evaluate aspects of the variant location in the DNA". Making this common background explicit among various criteria improves interoperability among different GUIDELINES.

4.1 Example: PM1 Criterion of the ACMG-AMP 2015 Guidelines

Here, we provide an illustration of the use of the meta-model by instantiating the PM1 criterion of the ACMG-AMP 2015 variant interpretation guidelines (see Fig. 2 for a textual description). This is one of 16 criteria that support the analysis of a variant's pathogenicity according to these guidelines. More specifically, it evaluates whether a variant is found in a region of our DNA known as a "mutational hotspot" (i.e., a DNA region that has a high frequency of pathogenic variants) and/or in a "protein domain" (i.e., a stable, independent part of a protein that can perform vital protein functions) that is critical for its correct functioning with no previously reported benign variations.

PM1 Located in a mutational hot spot and/or critical and well-established functional domain (e.g., active site of an enzyme) without benign variation

Certain protein domains are known to be critical to protein function, and all missense variants in these domains identified to date have been shown to be pathogenic. These domains must also lack benign variants. In addition, mutational hotspots in less well-characterized regions of genes are reported, in which pathogenic variants in one or several nearby residues have been observed with greater frequency. Either evidence can be considered moderate evidence of pathogenicity.

Fig. 2. The two criteria identified in the textual description of PM1 are highlighted in blue and brown frames. The four metrics identified in the textual description of PM1 are highlighted in green, pink, purple, and yellow frames. The blue-framed criterion comprises three metrics, whereas the brown-framed criterion only comprises one. (Color figure online)

During the instantiation process of the PM1 criterion, two major issues emerged. The first one arises from the actual definition of the criterion, which appears to describe two distinct criteria rather than just one. Indeed, a variant

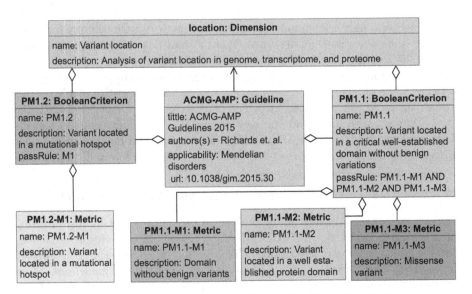

Fig. 3. The classes are depicted in the same colors used to highlight criteria and metrics in the textual description of PM1 in Fig. 2.

meets the PM1 criterion if it is discovered in a mutational hotspot, a functional domain without any known benign variations, or both of them. These scenarios provide different characteristics to be met and different requirements to be evaluated. Regardless of the fact that both hotspots and functional domains are genomic regions, they are of different types: hotspots are found in our DNA sequence, whereas domains are found in proteins. Furthermore, the absence of benign variation is only important for assessing the condition associated with protein domains. Therefore, the PM1 criterion descriptions collapse two different criteria. When they are considered separately, as promoted by our model, the evaluation of the criterion becomes clearer and simpler.

The second issue concerns the imprecise definition provided in PM1. According to this criterion, the variant must be "located in a mutational hot spot and/or critical and well-established functional domain without benign variations". However, a careful reading of the complete description of the criterion reveals that the part of PM1 regarding protein domains is only valid for missense variants (i.e., a variant that leads to an amino acid change in the protein sequence).

Figure 3 shows the resulting instantiation of the PM1 criterion. The criterion has been instantiated as two different Boolean criteria (PM1.1 and PM1.2) that evaluate to either **true** or **false**. On the one hand, if a missense variant (PM1.1-M3 metric) is located in a well-established functional domain (PM1.1-M2 metric) with no benign variants (PM1.1-M1 metric), the PM1.1 criterion evaluates to true –the *passRule* of the criterion is composed by the conjunction of these three metrics. On the other hand, if a variant is found in a DNA region known to be a mutational hotspot (PM1.2-M1 metric), the PM1.2 evaluates to true.

Here, the BOOLEANCRITERION has a much simpler *passRule*, only including the measurement of M1.

The meta-model has allowed us to unpack and make explicit the constructs underlying the ACMG-AMP PM1 criterion, which were previously hidden in the convoluted nature of its textual description. This unpacking process was supported by the part-hood relationships defined between the GUIDELINE and CRITERION classes, and between the CRITERION and METRIC classes. These part-hood relationships are made explicit via the formulas defined in the *passRule* and *ClassificationRules* attributes. A CRITERION's classification result is based on the evaluation of its metrics. Similarly, a GUIDELINE's classification result is based on the evaluation of its criteria. Our metamodel enables the decomposition of variant interpretation guidelines into more precise constructs, which can serve as a solid foundation for clinical guidelines operationalization.

5   Variant Misinterpretation Patterns

The meta-model characterizes the constructs and underlying structure of interpretation guidelines. This characterization has led us to the identification of four patterns that hinder the variant (mis)interpretation process. These patterns highlight the main inconsistencies in the interpretation processes when used by different experts; they also elucidate the disparities in the variant classification results. We have identified four different patterns: 1) the use of a single METRIC leading to different METRICRESULTS; 2) the use of a single CRITERION measured according to different METRICS; 3) the use of a GUIDELINE with diverse CRITERIA; and 4) the use of one CRITERIA with different purposes within diverse GUIDELINES. All such patterns are allowed in the meta-model and represented by several real-world examples; however, they are at the basis of situations unclear/incoherent interpretations of variants. Details and examples are provided in the next sections.

5.1   Same Metric – Different Metric Results

The lack of data sharing is a significant issue in genomics [39]. Indeed, differential access to privately stored data is one of the most common causes of discrepancies in variant interpretation [13,21]. Because of this, different experts may evaluate the same criterion's metric differently depending on the data they have access to.

Let us consider the following example. Determining whether a variant co-occurs with a pathogenic variant is frequently regarded as proof of the benignity of the variant under investigation [43]. It is common for laboratories that perform genetic testing to have their own variant repository that they do not share publicly [33]. As a result, one laboratory may have identified cases in which the variant co-occurs with a pathogenic variant while another laboratory may not hold this information [13]. Consequently, when the metric "*The variant co-occurs with a pathogenic variant(s)*" is evaluated, different metric results may be obtained, depending on the data that the laboratory uses.

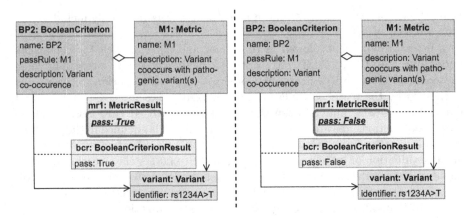

Fig. 4. Example model of pattern "Same metric – different metric result"

Different metric results will influence whether or not a particular criterion is met. A practical example of this situation is depicted in Fig. 4. The variant rs1234A>T has met the criterion that evaluates variant co-occurrence (BP2 criterion) in the first scenario because the metric *"The variant co-occurs with pathogenic variant(s)"* (metric M1) has been met. However, in the second scenario, the variant fails the BP2 criterion because the metric M1 is not met, thereby impacting also the BOOLEANCRITERIONRESULT pass value. Our meta-model has allowed us to identify that the misinterpretation of the BP2 criterion is due to different metric evaluation results.

5.2   Same Criterion – Different Metrics

Interpretation guidelines have contributed to the standardization of the variant interpretation process. However, due to the lack of specificity in these guidelines, different experts may apply the same criterion differently [22]. This indicates, according to our meta-model, that different metrics have been employed to evaluate the same guideline's criterion.

This is especially common when determining a variant's allele frequency [13]. Variant interpretation guidelines frequently recommend using the allele frequency of the variant as a benignity criterion if it is *greater than expected for that specific disorder*. Such a definition makes the frequency's cutoff entirely dependent on the knowledge and experience of the expert performing the interpretation [25]. As a result, given the criterion for evaluating allele frequency, one expert could define a metric that states, for instance, that *"the variant should have an allele frequency greater than 0.5%"*, whereas an alternative expert – with a stricter approach – could define a different metric stating that *"the variant should have an allele frequency greater than 1%"*. This difference in metrics may obviously result in different assessments of whether or not the same criterion is met.

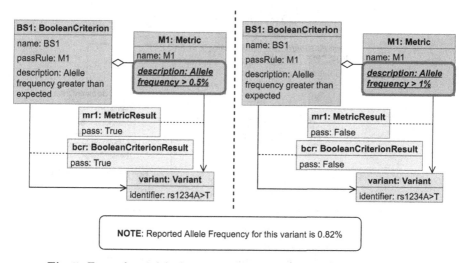

Fig. 5. Example model of pattern "Same criterion – different metrics"

Figure 5 depicts an actual instance model of this situation. When the criterion BS1 (evaluating whether *"the allele frequency of the variant is greater than expected for the disorder"*) is applied to the rs1234A>T variation, it produces different results, depending on the different definitions of the (only) metric which this criterion depends on. Again, our meta-model is able to pinpoint clearly the origin of criterion assessment differences.

5.3 Same Guideline – Different Criteria

Most common misinterpretations occur when merging results from different sources that follow different guidelines. One would expect that this could not happen *within* the context of a specific guideline, as these intend to create a well-defined framework for selecting the most appropriate interpretation for a variation. Surprisingly, differences in interpretation results are common even when using the same interpretation guideline [3,4]. This is related to the fact that laboratories that perform the "interpretation" activity may be unable (for diverse reasons–economic, time-related, or motivational) to apply all of the criteria specified in the guidelines.

This is frequently the case in functional studies. Many variant interpretation guidelines recommend using well-conducted functional studies to assess the potential impact of a variation in a gene or gene product [11,43]. This type of research, however, is extremely difficult to pursue due to the significant monetary and time investment required. As a result, only 36% of clinical experts apply this criterion during the variant interpretation process [55].

Because functional studies provide strong evidence of the pathogenicity of the variant, the choice of the expert to use this type of evidence will have a significant impact on the interpretation of the variation. This is especially important for

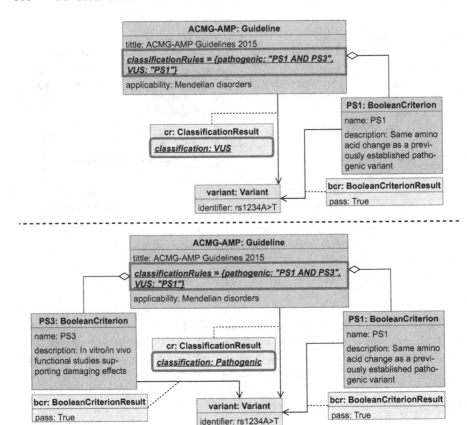

Fig. 6. Example model of pattern "Same guideline – different criteria"

variants whose significance is unclear, and a functional study can determine whether the variant should be discarded as benign or further investigated for its potential to cause disorder [5,18].

The impact that the used criteria can have on the interpretation of a variation is demonstrated practically in Fig. 6. The expert in the top scenario only considered criterion PS1, thus concluding that the variant has an Uncertain Significance (VUS) based on that information. However, the expert in the bottom scenario considered both PS1 and PS3; according to the classification rule that assigns the "pathogenic" value when both PS1 and PS3 hold, or the "VUS" value when only PS1 holds, this expert concluded that the variant should be classified as pathogenic. The additional evidence provided by functional studies (criterion PS3) was fundamental in this case. The meta-model provides a clear representation of each expert's interpretation process and pinpoints the source of inconsistencies in the interpretation of variant rs1234A>T.

5.4   Same Criterion – Different Guidelines

Different variant interpretation guidelines establish different criteria and metrics depending on their applicability. Nevertheless, there are well-established criteria that usually appear in multiple guidelines.

In clinical guidelines, each criterion is defined using two alternative approaches: Boolean-based or score-based. When a Boolean criterion is used, the criterion is either met or not. When a score criterion is used, instead, a criterion is accepted if its associated value falls within a predefined range. Consequently, even when guidelines include the same criterion, its assessment may be different depending on the approach adopted by the guideline.

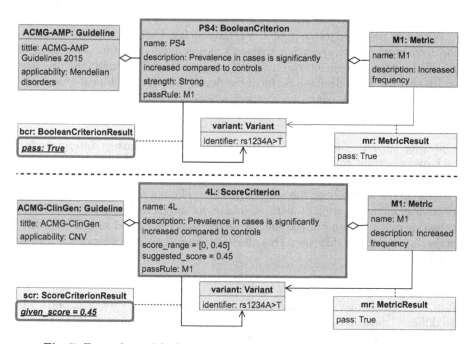

Fig. 7. Example model of pattern "Same criterion – different guidelines"

A typical case when this difference emerges involves the criterion that evaluates whether a variant is more frequent in cases than in controls. The criterion is evaluated by the ACMG-AMP 2015 guidelines as a Boolean criterion [43], and in the ACMG-ClinGen as a score criterion [44]. Figure 7 illustrates the example. In the ACMG-AMP Guideline, the criterion PS4 analyzes whether the frequency of the variant rs1234A>T is increased in affected individuals – by means of the metric M1. The M1 result evaluates as true and, consequently, the PS4 criterion results are also evaluated as true. In the ACMG-ClinGen Guideline, the equivalent criterion 4L evaluates the same metric for the same variant. In this case, the criterion result is a particular score (0.45), whose value is obtained based on the score range and the suggested score stated in the criterion definition.

Our meta-model clearly illustrates the differences between both guidelines and - in general - allows experts to identify variant interpretation differences that arise from the use of different approaches for variant interpretation.

6   Discussion

Variant interpretation is a critical step in achieving better diagnoses and treatments based on each individual's genomic information. However, the imprecise and vague nature of the variant interpretation guidelines poses difficulties in its application in a real clinical setting. We have used a conceptual modeling approach to define a meta-model that allows us to identify the structure and constructs behind interpretation guidelines.

With the proposed meta-model, we have defined and explained the common framework for representing various types of guidelines (Sect. 4); we then identified patterns of misinterpretation of variants (Sect. 5); finally, the previous results enabled us to disentangle intricate details of existing clinical guidelines, as we analyzed in the examples of the previous section. Below, we summarize the lessons learned during this process.

Unpacking variant classification results : Differences in variant interpretation can have important consequences on a patient's health. The reason behind these differences sometimes is not the use of a different guideline or criterion but a conflicting evaluation of the same criterion. Thanks to the description of a criterion as an aggregation of metrics, we are not only able to identify a different evaluation of a criterion but the specific metric that has caused such a difference. Section 5.1 illustrates this case. This allows for a precise unpacking of the variant classification results.

Disambiguating criterion definitions : Because the interpretation guidelines are often not clear enough for their unambiguous application, various experts will use different measurements to determine whether a criterion is met. As seen in Sect. 5.2, the metric definition has allowed us to identify the collection of constructs an expert uses to assess a certain criterion. This enables us to provide a standard framework for comparing various interpretations of the same criterion.

Clarifying interpretation guidelines application : A precise set of criteria are specified in the interpretation guidelines to direct the classification outcome. As Section 5.3 shows, not all experts employ all criteria, which makes it difficult to derive the precise procedure that was used. The meta-model enables a precise characterization of the particular criteria applied for variant interpretation as well as the components assessed in each criterion, enabling full traceability of the outcomes.

Making connections explicit : The 22 interpretation guidelines currently available have important differences in their applicability, the criteria considered most important to assess the role of a variant in the disorder process, or even in their approach for evaluating such criteria (boolean or score). Precisely identifying the differences and commonalities among the guidelines is key to comparing the interpretation approach followed by different experts and the possible implications for the classification results. Section 5.4 reflects how the meta-model has allowed us to make explicit connections among different interpretation guidelines.

Operationalization of guidelines : Clinical guidelines were originally defined in an abstract manner thus hampering their direct operationalization. The generated conceptual schema poses the basis for building workflows that systematically: 1) explain the complex interpretation domain (on the lines of [19]) and the related process in place (a sort of process explainability [1]); 2) highlight current differences, inconsistencies, and misinterpretations; 3) propose refinements to current criteria and metrics; and 4) derive a complete operationalization of the guidelines' application process. A conceptual model can serve as the foundation for operationalizing clinical guidelines by making them more accessible, guiding decision-making, facilitating interdisciplinary collaboration, and encouraging continuous improvement. As a result, inconsistencies in their application will be reduced.

Current limitations of the meta-model : During the development and use of the meta-model, we identified four limitations. First, there are external elements that may have an impact on classification results, but they are not represented. These elements include, for example, the fact that some variants are pathogenic only when appear in combination with other variants, or that other variants may overcome a variant's pathogenic effect. Second, variant interpretation has not been examined in the context of complex disorders in this work. In these disorders, the existence of many variants are required to cause the manifested disorder. Extra factors such as penetrance and population specificities must be considered also, but they are not included in this first version of the model. Third, the actors participating in the interpreting process are not modeled. Knowing who performed the interpretation, what annotation tool was used, or what information they relied on to evaluate each criterion helps increasing the interoperability and reproducibility of the interpretation results. Fourth, we represent the *classificationRules* as an array of strings. Although this approach works correctly, we are aware that more appropriate appropriate approaches exist. For instance, specific classes that better capture the nature of these rules.

7   Conclusion and Future Outlook

In this paper, we proposed a novel meta-model for the representation of the DNA Variant Interpretation Guidelines. Variant interpretation is a very common process in the working routine of clinicians and geneticists and it is of critical importance that it is managed in a correct way to ensure patients well-being. Unfortunately, current practice still presents many shortcomings; the presence of several guidelines with diverse criteria and metrics – possibly based on different approaches or with apparent discrepancies – is hampering the reliability of the interpretation results.

Paving the way to a complete standardization and systematization of this process, here we proposed a meta-model that aims to explain and clarify the morphology of interpretation guidelines and their internal elements. Additionally, we proposed a set of patterns in which these guidelines led to the potential misinterpretation of variants. These patterns reveal common challenges encountered when interpreting variants and each of them is associated with a practical use case where the pattern arose. Finally, we discussed lessons learned during the modeling effort and how these reflect on the presented problematic use cases.

In the future, we plan to address the meta-model's limitations identified above. First, we intend to represent the variant's genomics context to show how the existence of other variants may influence the variant's classification. Second, our model will incorporate a classification of variant groups that operate together to produce a disorder. This will facilitate the interpretation of complex disorders. Third, we will incorporate a detailed description of all the steps that precede variant interpretation as well as the actors that conducted the interpretation process. Finally, a new entity capturing the complexity and interconnections of the classification rules will be defined.

In addition, we plan to thoroughly expand the patterns catalog, proposing operational rules to avoid such incorrect situations to occur. As previously discussed, this preliminary meta-model effort will be applied to practical frameworks for two main purposes. First, we aim to explain the complex variant interpretation process, reporting differences, inconsistencies, and misinterpretations. Second, we aim to propose refinements to current criteria and metrics and completely operationalize the guidelines' application process.

Acknowledgements. This work was supported by the Valencian Innovation Agency and Innovation through the OGMIOS project (INNEST/2021/57), the Generalitat Valenciana through the CoMoDiD project (CIPROM/2021/023) and ACIF/2021/117, and the Spanish State Research Agency through the DELFOS (PDC2021-1212 43-I00,MICIN/AEI/10.13039/501 100011033) and SREC (PID 2021-123824OB-I00) projects, and co-financed with ERDF and the European Union Next Generation EU/PRTR.

References

1. Adadi, A., et al.: Peeking inside the black-box: a survey on explainable artificial intelligence (XAI). IEEE Access **6**, 52138–52160 (2018)
2. Agaoglu, N., et al.: Consistency of variant interpretations among bioinformaticians and clinical geneticists in hereditary cancer panels. Eur. J. Hum. Genet. **30**, 378–383 (2022)
3. Amendola, L.M., et al.: Performance of ACMG-AMP variant-interpretation guidelines among nine laboratories in the clinical sequencing exploratory research consortium. Am. J. Hum. Genet. **98**, 1067–1076 (2016)
4. Amendola, L.M., et al.: Variant classification concordance using the ACMG-AMP variant interpretation guidelines across nine genomic implementation research studies. Am. J. Hum. Genet. **107**(5), 932–941 (2020)

5. Anderson, C., et al.: How functional genomics can keep pace with VUS identification. Front. Cardiovasc. Med. **9** (2022)

6. Belloir, N., et al.: Characterizing fake news: a conceptual modeling-based approach. In: Ralyté, J., Chakravarthy, S., Mohania, M., Jeusfeld, M.A., Karlapalem, K. (eds.) Conceptual Modeling, ER 2022. Lecture Notes in Computer Science, vol. 13607, pp. 115–129. Springer, Cham (2022). https://doi.org/10.1007/978-3-031-17995-2_9

7. Bernasconi, A., et al.: A comprehensive approach for the conceptual modeling of genomic data. In: Ralyté, J., et al. (eds.) Conceptual Modeling. Lecture Notes in Computer Science, vol. 13607, pp. 194–208. Springer, Cham (2022). https://doi.org/10.1007/978-3-031-17995-2_14

8. Bernasconi, A., et al.: Ontological representation of fair principles: a blueprint for fairer data sources. In: Proceedings of the 35th International Conference on Advanced Information Systems Engineering (CAiSE 2023) (2023)

9. Bernasconi, A., et al.: Semantic interoperability: ontological unpacking of a viral conceptual model. BMC Bioinform. **23**(Suppl 11), 491 (2022)

10. Booch, G., et al.: The unified modeling language. Unix Rev. **14**(13), 5 (1996)

11. Brnich, S., et al.: Recommendations for application of the functional evidence PS3/BS3 criterion using the ACMG/AMP sequence variant interpretation framework. Genome Med. **12**, 3 (2019)

12. Canakoglu, A., et al.: GenoSurf: metadata driven semantic search system for integrated genomic datasets. Database **2019** (2019)

13. Furqan, A., et al.: Care in specialized centers and data sharing increase agreement in hypertrophic cardiomyopathy genetic test interpretation. Circ. Cardiovasc. Genet. **10**(5), e001700 (2017)

14. Gao, P., et al.: Challenges of providing concordant interpretation of somatic variants in non-small cell lung cancer: a multicenter study. J. Cancer **10**(8), 1814–1824 (2019)

15. García, S.A., et al.: The challenge of managing the evolution of genomics data over time: a conceptual model-based approach. BMC Bioinform. **23**(11), 472 (2022)

16. García, S.A., et al.: An ontological characterization of a conceptual model of the human genome. In: De Weerdt, J., Polyvyanyy, A. (eds.) Intelligent Information Systems, CAiSE 2022. Lecture Notes in Business Information Processing, vol. 452, pp. 27–35. Springer, Cham (2022). https://doi.org/10.1007/978-3-031-07481-3_4

17. Genetics, A.: Scheme for autosomal dominant and x-linked mendelian diseases, Ambry Genetics (2015). https://submit.ncbi.nlm.nih.gov/ft/byid/zfkfvckw/mid-7377_ambry_classification_scheme_oct_2015.pdf. Accessed 24 May 2023

18. Guidugli, L., et al.: Functional assays for analysis of variants of uncertain significance in BRCA2. Hum. Mutat. **35**(2), 151–164 (2014)

19. Guizzardi, G., Bernasconi, A., Pastor, O., Storey, V.C.: Ontological unpacking as explanation: the case of the viral conceptual model. In: Ghose, A., Horkoff, J., Silva Souza, V.E., Parsons, J., Evermann, J. (eds.) ER 2021. LNCS, vol. 13011, pp. 356–366. Springer, Cham (2021). https://doi.org/10.1007/978-3-030-89022-3_28

20. Guizzardi, R., Bravalheri, A., Guizzardi, G., Sales, T.P., Simeonidou, D.: A reference conceptual model for virtual network function online marketplaces. In: Laender, A.H.F., Pernici, B., Lim, E.-P., de Oliveira, J.P.M. (eds.) ER 2019. LNCS, vol. 11788, pp. 302–310. Springer, Cham (2019). https://doi.org/10.1007/978-3-030-33223-5_25

21. Harrison, S.M., et al.: Scaling resolution of variant classification differences in ClinVar between 41 clinical laboratories through an outlier approach. Hum. Mutat. **39**(11), 1641–1649 (2018)

22. Harrison, S.M., et al.: Clinical laboratories collaborate to resolve differences in variant interpretations submitted to ClinVar. Genet. Med. **19**(10), 1096–1104 (2017)
23. Karczewski, K.J., et al.: The mutational constraint spectrum quantified from variation in 141, 456 humans. https://doi.org/10.1101/531210
24. Kim, Y.E., et al.: Challenges and considerations in sequence variant interpretation for mendelian disorders. Ann. Lab. Med. **39**, 421 (2019)
25. Kim, Y.E., et al.: Challenges and considerations in sequence variant interpretation for mendelian disorders. Annals of Laboratory Medicine 39, 421 (09 2019)
26. Kopanos, C., et al.: VarSome: the human genomic variant search engine. Bioinformatics **35**(11), 1978–1980 (2018)
27. Laddada, W., et al.: OntoRepliCov: an ontology-based approach for modeling the SARS-CoV-2 replication process. Procedia Comput. Sci. **192**, 487–496 (2021)
28. Lebo, M.S., et al.: Data sharing as a national quality improvement program: reporting on BRCA1 and BRCA2 variant-interpretation comparisons through the Canadian open genetics repository (COGR). Genet. Med. **20**(3), 294–302 (2018)
29. Li, Q., et al.: InterVar: clinical interpretation of genetic variants by the 2015 ACMG-AMP guidelines. Am. J. Hum. Genet. **100**(2), 267–280 (2017)
30. Luo, X., et al.: ClinGen myeloid malignancy variant curation expert panel recommendations for germline RUNX1 variants. Blood Adv. **3**(20), 2962–2979 (2019)
31. MacDonald, J.R., et al.: The database of genomic variants: a curated collection of structural variation in the human genome. Nucleic Acids Res. **42**(D1), D986–D992 (2014)
32. Martínez Ferrandis, A.M., Pastor López, O., Guizzardi, G.: Applying the principles of an ontology-based approach to a conceptual schema of human genome. In: Ng, W., Storey, V.C., Trujillo, J.C. (eds.) ER 2013. LNCS, vol. 8217, pp. 471–478. Springer, Heidelberg (2013). https://doi.org/10.1007/978-3-642-41924-9_40
33. Mighton, C., et al.: Data sharing to improve concordance in variant interpretation across laboratories: results from the Canadian open genetics repository. J. Med. Genet. **59**(6), 571–578 (2022)
34. Naithani, N., et al.: Precision medicine: uses and challenges. Med. J. Armed Forces India **77**, 258–265 (2021). https://doi.org/10.1016/j.mjafi.2021.06.020
35. Nicora, G., et al.: CardioVAI: an automatic implementation of ACMG-AMP variant interpretation guidelines in the diagnosis of cardiovascular diseases. Hum. Mutat. **39**, 1835–1846 (2018)
36. Nicora, G., et al.: A machine learning approach based on ACMG/AMP guidelines for genomic variant classification and prioritization. Sci. Rep. **12**(1), 2517 (2022)
37. Niehaus, A., et al.: A survey assessing adoption of the ACMG-AMP guidelines for interpreting sequence variants and identification of areas for continued improvement. Genet. Med. **21**(8), 1699–1701 (2019)
38. Palacio, A.L., et al.: A method to identify relevant genome data: conceptual modeling for the medicine of precision. In: Trujillo, J.C., et al. (eds.) Conceptual Modeling. Lecture Notes in Computer Science, pp. 597–609. Springer, Cham (2018). https://doi.org/10.1007/978-3-030-00847-5_44
39. Powell, K.: The broken promise that undermines human genome research. Nature **590**, 198–201 (2021)
40. Ramdaney, A., et al.: Beware the laboratory report: discrepancy in variant classification on reproductive carrier screening. Genet. Med. **20**, 374–375 (2017)
41. Reis-Filho, J.S.: Next-generation sequencing. Breast Cancer Res. **11**(3), S12 (2009)

42. Reyes Román, J.F., et al.: Applying conceptual modeling to better understand the human genome. In: Comyn-Wattiau, I., et al. (eds.) Conceptual Modeling. Lecture Notes in Computer Science, pp. 404–412. Springer, Cham (2016). https://doi.org/10.1007/978-3-319-46397-1_31

43. Richards, S., et al.: Standards and guidelines for the interpretation of sequence variants: a joint consensus recommendation of the American college of medical genetics and genomics and the association for molecular pathology. Genet. Med. **17**(5), 405–423 (2015)

44. Riggs, E., et al.: Technical standards for the interpretation and reporting of constitutional copy-number variants: a joint consensus recommendation of the American college of medical genetics and genomics (ACMG) and the clinical genome resource (CLINGEN). Genet. Med. **22**, 1–13 (2019)

45. García, A., et al.: A conceptual model-based approach to improve the representation and management of omics data in precision medicine. IEEE Access **9**, 154071–154085 (2021)

46. Scott, A.D., et al.: CharGer: clinical characterization of germline variants. Bioinformatics **35**(5), 865–867 (2019)

47. Santos, L.O.B.S., et al.: Towards a conceptual model for the fair digital object framework. In: Proceedings of the 13th International Conference on Formal Ontology in Information Systems (FOIS 2023) (2023)

48. So, M.K., et al.: Reinterpretation of BRCA1 and BRCA2 variants of uncertain significance in patients with hereditary breast/ovarian cancer using the ACMG/AMP 2015 guidelines. Breast Cancer **26**, 510–519 (2019)

49. Tavtigian, S.V., et al.: Modeling the ACMG/AMP variant classification guidelines as a Bayesian classification framework. Genet. Med. **20**(9), 1054–1060 (2018)

50. Vihinen, M.: Problems in variation interpretation guidelines and in their implementation in computational tools. Mol. Genet. Genom. Med. **8**(9), e1206 (2020)

51. Weiss, A.P., et al.: Toward a comprehensive model of fake news: a new approach to examine the creation and sharing of false information. Societies **11**(3), 82 (2021)

52. Whiffin, N., et al.: Cardioclassifier: disease- and gene-specific computational decision support for clinical genome interpretation. Genet. Med. **20**(10), 1246–1254 (2018)

53. Zeggini, E., et al.: Translational genomics and precision medicine: moving from the lab to the clinic. Science **365**(6460), 1409–1413 (2019)

54. Zhang, J., et al.: The international cancer genome consortium data portal. Nat. Biotechnol. **37**(4), 367–369 (2019)

55. Zirkelbach, E., et al.: Managing variant interpretation discrepancies in hereditary cancer: clinical practice, concerns, and desired resources. J. Genet. Couns. **27**(4), 761–769 (2018)

A Conceptual Modeling Approach for Risk Assessment and Mitigation in Collision-Free UAV Routing Planning for Beyond-the-Visual-Line-of-Sight Flights

Gerrit Burmester[1]([⊠]), David Kugelmann[1], Dietrich Steinmetz[1], Hui Ma[2], and Sven Hartmann[1]

[1] Clausthal University of Technology, Clausthal-Zellerfeld, Germany
gerrit.burmester@tu-clausthal.de
[2] Victoria University of Wellington, Wellington, New Zealand

Abstract. The domain of beyond-the-visual-line-of-sight (BVLOS) flights of unmanned aerial vehicles (UAVs) has unique navigational challenges such as the reliable estimation, evaluation and mitigation of the risk of the associated flight paths. To tackle these challenges domain data from heterogeneous sources is needed. Failing to integrate this data carefully could result in inaccurate navigation decisions, poor situational awareness, and in general unsafe flight operations. In this paper we present a conceptual model that can be used to design conceptual graph databases that integrate the information of several domains to BVLOS. Furthermore, we show that our proposed conceptual graph database schema scales well for increasing sizes of stored domain and application data and permits constant query execution times for important recurring queries.

Keywords: Conceptual Modeling · Risk-based UAV Routing · BVLOS · Graph Database Model · Dynamic Data · Collision Avoidance · Multi-Criteria Optimal Flight Path · Risk Assessment · Risk Mitigation

1 Introduction

In recent years, the deployment of unmanned aerial vehicles (UAVs), also known as drones or unmanned aircraft systems (UAS), has had a remarkable surge in the public airspace [20]. This trend is likely to continue as the value of commercial drone manufacturing and related service activity in the United States is projected to rise from \$8 billion in 2017 to \$20 billion by 2026 [7]. UAVs have a wide range of applications in many emerging fields [17]. While most of these applications have been restricted to *visual-line-of-sight (VLOS)* operations in the past due to technological limitations and strict regulations, current advancements in the field make the expansion of *beyond-visual-line-of-sight (BVLOS)* operations appear

© The Author(s), under exclusive license to Springer Nature Switzerland AG 2023
J. P. A. Almeida et al. (Eds.): ER 2023, LNCS 14320, pp. 394–411, 2023.
https://doi.org/10.1007/978-3-031-47262-6_21

increasingly feasible [12,17,21]. There is a large range of operations that could benefit from autonomous BVLOS UAV operations [12]. With respect to this, autonomous path planning is an essential part of UAV operations [20,21], which has gained a lot of attention in the literature recently. In the context of BVLOS operations the mitigation of risk is generally seen as a main priority [17]. This gives rise of the *risk-based UAV path planning* problem.

Path planning can generally be interpreted as a search and optimization problem [21]. Many approaches to path planning have been proposed thus far, some of which employ graph theory-based routing algorithms (e.g., the approach given in [18]). Graph databases have shown promise with applications related to vehicle routing problems, such as taxi ridesharing [24], which would suggest that they may also be applicable to graph theory-based UAV path planning problems. Despite this, most approaches to UAV path planning do not attempt to capture domain-relevant information so that they can be used to effectively search for quality paths. To effectively use graph databases to solve UAV path planning, we need to elaborate a proper database model to capture a majority of domain-relevant information, which can be used to find good paths and mitigate risks. The needed information to setup such a system includes not only static data sets for path planning and storing relevant information, but also dynamic data to integrate rapidly changing parameters like wind speeds and pressure as well as the positions of other UAVs or other moving objects.

The aim of this paper is to propose a conceptual modeling approach for risk assessment and mitigation in UAV routing. While graph databases do not need to have a database schema we found it useful to start with designing a schema first in order to cover all the concepts that are relevant for our application and to understand their semantics. Our schema will be able to capture both static and dynamic data of UAVs and their environment. In particular we will argue that it is semantically rich and can store domain-relevant information with respect to typical risk hazards in UAV flights. Based on the schema we develop a graph database to capture domain-relevant information and use it for risk-based UAV path planning in a grid-space. A prototype of our graph database is implemented using Neo4j, a popular graph database management system, which has built-in spatial functions [1].

We will present an approach to estimate the risk of traversing any given direct leg between neighboring locations. Using this approach a risk-based UAV path planning graph is constructed and a risk-optimal flight path can be found. For that, some recurring queries are identified to retrieve the information from our proposed graph database. Lastly, an evaluation using an artificially created flight space is conducted to validate the functionality of the proposed graph database.

The major contributions of this paper are the following:

- We propose a common conceptualization for various collaborators in the field of risk mitigation for UAVs.
- We propose a conceptual graph database schema for UAV risk-based path planning for a flight space that is shared by multiple UAVs.
- We propose graph database constraints to ensure the creation of collision-free flight paths for UAV.

– We demonstrate how our proposed graph database can be supportive in assessing and mitigating important types of hazards such as ground risk under dynamic weather conditions.
– We evaluate our approach using some initial experiments to show the practicability of our approach.

Organization. This paper is organized as follows: In Sect. 2 the current literature on the domain and on graph data modeling is reviewed. Section 3 covers basic concepts and preliminaries. In Sect. 4 we present our proposed conceptual design of our graph database. In Sect. 5 an approach to estimating risk and finding points-of-impact is presented. Section 6 gives an approach for generating a path planning graph and finding efficient paths. In Sect. 7 we conduct experiments to investigate the scalability of our approach. Lastly, in Sect. 8 potential future work is discussed and concluding thoughts are given.

2 Literature Review

In this section we review the literature for UAV path planning and risk assessment and present existing work on graph database modeling.

UAV Risk Assessment and Path Planning. In recent years a great attention has been paid to risk assessment of unmanned BVLOS flights [17]. Most risk assessment models are based on data from manned flights [17]. Three common types of hazards appear throughout the literature, *ground risk*, *mid-air collisions of aircrafts*, and *obstacle hazards*.

Approaches to defining ground risk are concerned with the risk to the population on the ground in case of an unplanned descent of the UAV as a result of system failure. To compute the ground risk, typically a descent is modeled, often probabilistically, to estimate the point-of-impact in case of an unplanned descent. In [9] a probabilistic model for estimating the location of impact in case of a ballistic descent of a small unmanned aircraft is presented. A second-order drag model is used to calculate the point-of-impact based on travel direction, speed, mass, and a drag coefficient of the aircraft based on which a probability density function is presented to account for uncertainties in travel speed and drag, as well as wind. In [8] this work is built upon by introducing additional descent types and calculating risk of fatal impact as a result of population density and a sheltering factor at any given point-of-impact as well. In [17] this approach is used to generate a probabilistic ground risk map for a given unmanned aircraft system (UAS) by assuming uniformly distributed speed.

A model for calculating mid-air collision risk of UAVs is given in [13]. Here collision risk is calculated by considering their vertical, horizontal, and temporal overlap probability. [6] proposes a framework for classifying risk controls for managing the risk of mid-air collision accidents for UAVs. In [14] an air risk map is generated based on the risk of mid-air collisions and the resulting risk of fatalities in case of a collision. In [18] a UAV routing algorithm with collision avoidance is given. To detect obstacle hazards, a data-driven approach for stochastic risk assessment of UAV operations is proposed and illustrated on an artificially generated hazard map in [20].

With regard to UAV path planning, multiple factors are usually considered. Besides risk, distance/air-time is a relevant factor for path planning as fuel is limited [19]. Risk-based UAV path planning can be regarded as a multi-objective optimization problem. For example, [20] uses a multi-objective evolutionary algorithm to find a Pareto-optimal path with respect to risk and distance in the hazard map. The survey paper [10] focuses on two key aspects of the path planning domain for UAVs. Techniques and methods from the literature to generate a feasible path for autonomous UAVs are compared and their limitations highlighted. Also, the representation of environmental factors are analyzed. The aim was to identify those factors, which are essential for developing a practical path planner in future research.

Graph Database Modeling. To the best of our knowledge, there is no existing graph database model for risk-based UAV path planning in the literature. In [26] a secure flight data recording service is proposed. It uses a small graph database scheme to store and analyze flight data recordings with the aim of identifying parties at fault in the event of accidents. That paper, however, is not on path planning, but on documenting and does not address risk analysis for future planning purposes.

A a risk database is used in [16] to integrate geo-spatial data sets from heterogeneous data sources into risk layers with the goal of providing comprehensive risk models and to enable highly informed decision-making processes for UAV flights. The focus is on the integration process and uses expert knowledge to adjust their layers. Finally a 3D-risk map can be derived from the heterogeneous data sets to enable mission specific risk assessment and UAV path planning. Graph models are not investigated in that work.

A risk-based path planning framework for UAVs is presented in [21], which uses a geo-spatial SQLite/SpatiaLite database to manage terrain and risk data. In contrast to ours, [21] does not use a grid map nor calculate ground impact points, but uses a sampling-based algorithm to generate a search graph and find risk-aware paths without considering descent models for UAVs. The problem studied is different from ours and the focus is not on conceptual modeling. For one example the sampling took more than a day of preprocessing. By restricting the search space for a UAV path into corridors their approach was not able to produce solutions for certain scenarios. As only a single UAV is considered, collision avoidance for multiple UAVs is not addressed. For their problem, also query answering did not scale well due to the known limitations of relational databases for performing joins. This was an important lesson for us.

Unlike in the case the relational databases, the conceptual modeling of graph databases has not yet been extensively studied. In particular, there do not yet exist broadly accepted modeling rules for improving the efficiency of using graph databases [24]. [23] uses an conceptual modeling approach to handle an advanced routing problem in which vehicles need to be organized to platoon together and therefore safe fuel or energy. They proposed unifying structures and common conceptualization for routing, scheduling and platoon life-cycles in context of the Vehicle Platooning Problem. Furthermore, working applications are presented to identify common paths for the vehicles in the network and store all information about platoons and especially the path each vehicle takes in a solution. The conceptual design of the model showed promising features in handling the complex data of a routing problem. In [11] a conceptual framework for dynamic alternative route planning is presented. It is able to react to changes in the underlying street network and demonstrates the usefulness of conceptual modeling techniques in the logistics domain.

3   Preliminaries

Concepts relating to the Risk of UAV Flights. There are various ways of defining risks and hazards in BVLOS UAV flights. There are, however, commonalities. In general, risk is the potential for harm or loss to people, property, or critical infrastructure. Three common types of hazards appear throughout the literature: ground risk hazards, mid-air collision risk, and obstacle hazards. Ground risk is typically calculated as a function of multiple factors, including flight-independent environmental factors such as the population density in a given area, and the factor of wind, as well as flight dependent factors such as the UAV's flight speed, direction, and mass. Thus these factors should be considered for the graph database. Mid-air collision risk mainly arises as a result of tempo-spatial overlaps of multiple UAV's flight paths, which suggests that tempo-spatial overlaps should be addressed in the graph database. Since this paper is mainly motivated by navigating a UAV via a routing network, obstacle hazards should be taken into consideration as they often indicate regions where no safe flight operations are possible and affected legs should not be used.

Problem Description. A *flight-space* through which a UAV u is to navigate can be seen as a graph $FS = (L, C)$, where L is a set of nodes such that each node represents a *location* ℓ in the flight-space which can be reached by the UAV. The set of edges $C \subseteq L \times L$ represents the direct connections (also called *legs*) between the aforementioned locations. In an edge (ℓ_0, ℓ_1) the nodes ℓ_0 and ℓ_1 are called the head and the tail of the edge. A path from location ℓ_0 to ℓ_m in the flight-space is a sequence of edges $(\ell_0, \ell_1), (\ell_1, \ell_2), \ldots, (\ell_{m-1}, \ell_m)$.

A *flight* f by a UAV u has a start location ℓ_s, an end location ℓ_e, a flight speed v, and a time interval d representing the period of time in which the flight is to occur. Within the flight-space, a flight just corresponds to a path starting at location ℓ_s and ending at location ℓ_e.

Given a start location, an end location, a time interval, a UAV and a flight speed there can be many different paths in the flight-space. In practice one often faces the situation that one needs to consider multiple options and has to choose among multiple candidate paths. Very often one wants to select a flight path that is optimal with respect to risk. For that, however, it is crucial to assess the risk associated with different paths. If there are multiple UAVs that share the same flight-space then the flight paths of the different UAVs must be selected such that they do not interfere in order to prevent mid-air collisions. This task is often referred to as *risk-based UAV path planning*.

To capture the information needed for searching for optimal solutions of the risk-based UAV path planning problem, in this paper we propose a conceptual modeling approach to design a graph database, which can then be used to effectively solve the problem.

Use of Property Graphs. Property graphs are often used to represent graph databases, cf. [2,5]. A *property graph* is a tuple $(N, E, \alpha, \beta, \lambda, \nu)$ where N and E are two disjoint finite sets of objects called *nodes* and *edges*, α and β are two functions that maps each edge to its tail and head, respectively, λ is a function that maps nodes and edges to finite sets of labels, and ν is a partial function that maps properties of nodes and edges to domain values.

We use property graphs to include those entities and relationships that are relevant in the domain of interest, i.e., risk-based UAV path planning. As common in the context of graph databases we will often refer to edges in property graphs as relationships. Labels that are assigned to nodes and edges can be interpreted as types of entities and relationships, respectively. While nodes and edges can have multiple labels, in the present paper each node as well as each edge has a single label which we refer to as its type. Types may be regarded as abstract concepts that give rise to a schema for the graph database.

In the present paper, our proposed conceptual schema of our graph database is illustrated as a diagram, see Fig. 1, but can easily be presented using a more formal approach using a *PG-Schema*, i.e., a collection of node types, edge types and graph types that describe the nodes and edges that occur in a property graph, cf. [3].

4   A Graph Database for Risk-Based UAV Routing

The conceptual schema in Fig. 1 constitutes a complete tempo-spatial conceptual model of the physical environment of the flight space including multiple simultaneous interacting unmanned aerial vehicles (UAVs). This schema serves as the basis for conducting ground risk assessment during flight planning, considering factors such as population density and sheltering effect. The ground risk assessment takes into account the spatial-temporal dynamics, e.g., wind speed and wind directions in the flight space, enabling a comprehensive evaluation of potential risks associated with UAV operations.

To ensure collision-free operation of the simultaneously planned flights involving multiple UAVs, a constraint is enforced, guaranteeing the safety and avoidance of any potential collisions between multiple UAVs. Consequently, optimal flight plans are generated, striking a balance between risk, and additional factors like distance or energy consumption.

Locations and Legs. Locations and the legs between them are core concepts for navigating a UAV which will be represented in the graph database. Locations ℓ are nodes of type `Location`. Each location has properties `longitude`, `latitude` and `altitude` to capture its geographic coordinates.

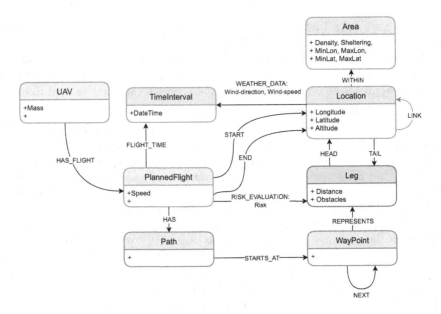

Fig. 1. The conceptual schema of our proposed graph database

Legs g are nodes of type **Leg**. Note that for the present paper, we have chosen a bipartite modeling approach where both locations and legs are represented by nodes in the graph database. The reason for modeling legs as nodes (rather than relationships) in the graph database is to allow for the modeling of further relationships between other nodes and legs which will be introduced later. For a leg g connecting a location ℓ_t with another location ℓ_h in the flight-space there will be a relationship *tail* from g to ℓ_t and a relationship *head* from g to ℓ_h in the graph database. ℓ_t and ℓ_h will also be referred to as the tail location and head location, respectively, of g. Each leg has a property `distance` to capture the distance from ℓ_t and ℓ_h. Tails *tail* and heads *head* are relationships of type TAIL and type HEAD, respectively.

Areas. To assess ground risk, ground data such as population density and the presence of shelter is an important factor [8]. Often ground data is represented as a grid map of the ground assuming the ground is a plane where each box within the grid is assigned some risk value [17].

Motivated by this idea, we have chosen the following approach. Every area a in the ground grid is represented by a node in the graph database. Areas a are of type **Area**. Each area has four properties `minlon, minlat, maxlon, maxlat` representing geographic coordinates that define four geographic points $sw = $ (`minlon, minlat`), $se = $ (`minlon, maxlat`), $nw = $ (`maxlon, minlat`), and $ne = $ (`maxlon, minlat`). These four points are taken as the corners of the rectangle (sw, se, nw, ne), which functions as a geographic bounding box defining a specific area on the ground. This is similar to the common approach for defining geographic bounding boxes [15]. The coordinates can be well chosen for each area a, so that the set A defines a seamless ground grid.

In addition, each area a has properties to capture ground data for the area which is relevant to the calculation of ground risk. For that the properties `Density` and `Sheltering` to store the area's population density and the sheltering factor, i.e., the percentage of the area which is unsheltered [8], respectively.

Query 2. An important query that should be supported by the graph database in the case of an unplanned descent of a UAV is to find the area a within whose bounding box the UAV would impact the ground. A naive approach is to, given a set of coordinates representing the point-of-impact, search all areas and test for each area a whether the impact coordinates lie within the bounding box defined by a. We will refer to this query as Query 2 as it plays an important role for risk assessment and mitigation.

An optimized approach is to first limit the perimeter in which the search is performed. If each area a can be represented by a single set of coordinates such as the longitude and latitude values in a location ℓ, one could first search all sets of coordinates representing areas a which lie within a given perimeter around the point-of-impact, and then test for each area a within the perimeter whether or not the impact coordinates lie within its bounding box (Query 2 with perimeter). This motivates our interest in the topological relationship between locations and areas. There is a relationship *within* from location ℓ to area a in the property graph, provided the point given by the longitudinal and latitudinal coordinates of ℓ lies within the bounding box defined by area a. The relationship *within* is of type `WITHIN` and has no properties.

This previous observation may suggest that areas are merely viewed as extensions of locations and thus areas and locations may be modeled as a single node in the graph. However, in order to make the graph database versatile and adaptable, it was chosen to keep these concepts distinct in the graph as they are semantically distinct.

Weather Data and Time Intervals. In order to assess flight risk, wind data is an important factor [8,9,17]. As wind is not static across time, weather forecasts are an important tool used for future flight planning [20,27]. Moreover, [13] emphasizes that tempo-spatial overlap of UAV flights are a major predictor of collision risk. This motivates the addition of a temporal dimension to the graph database, too. A time interval d can be defined as a tuple (t_1, t_2) where t_1 denotes the starting time and t_2 denotes the ending time, thus $t_1 < t_2$ must hold. Alternatively a time interval d may be represented by a single value, assuming a standardized length such as an hour. For the sake of simplicity this approach was chosen. Thus, a time interval d is represented as a node of type `TimeInterval` and with a property `DateTime`.

To represent the wind conditions in a given location ℓ and given time interval d a relationship *weatherData* from ℓ to d is used. The relationship is of type `WEATHER_DATA` and has properties `Wind-direction` and `Wind-speed`.

Query 1. In order to assess the risk of each leg with respect to a given flight speed and time interval, the legs along with their tail and head locations, and the weather data of their head locations for this time interval need to be queried from the graph database (Query 1).

Depending on the size of the region captured in the graph database, and depending on the distance between the start and end location of the flight with respect to which the risk is to be assessed, there may be reason to not query the entirety of legs in the graph but only those within a certain perimeter. Depending on the size of the perimeter there may then be a slim chance that an efficient path may not be found but this may be deemed acceptable in certain cases. One way to define such a perimeter is to find the mid point p_c between the start and end location and draw a circle in the geographic coordinate system with p_c as its center and a radius r where r is at least half the distance between the start and end location of the flight, and then to only query the legs within this perimeter (Query 1 with perimeter).

UAVs and Planned Flights. It is to be expected that a flight space is not only occupied by a single UAV at any given time. Thus, a graph database which only represents the physical environment of a flight, without storing any information with respect to other UAVs and their flights in the flight space would be insufficient for representing the real circumstances of a flight and thus for enabling interoperability between multiple actors. Hence information about UAVs and flights need to be represented in the graph database, too.

A planned flight f is represented as a node of type `PlannedFlight` in the graph database. According to the problem description, a planned flight can be identified by the time interval, the start and end locations, the UAV performing the flight and the flight speed used by the UAV. As locations and time intervals are already represented in the graph database, we now discuss how to represent the remaining factors.

UAVs are real-world entities the physical properties of which are relevant to ground risk [8]. Thus, they will be represented in the graph database. A UAV u is represented as a node of type `UAV`. A physical property that is relevant to ground risk is the UAV's mass, cf. [8]. This can be represented as a property `Mass` assigned to UAVs. A UAV typically has a range of possible flight speeds, so that the speed of any particular flight cannot simply be derived from the physical properties of the UAV, and thus needs to be represented separately. Assuming constant speed for a given flight f, flight speed can be represented in the graph database as a property `Speed` of flights.

A flight f can now be unambiguously represented in the graph database by adding the following relationships: $hasFlight$ from the UAV performing the flight to f, $start$ from f to its start location ℓ_s, end from f to its end location ℓ_e, $flightTime$ from f to the time interval `TimeInterval` during which the flight is to occur. The relationship $start$ is of type `START`, end is of type `END`, $hasFlight$ is of type `HAS_FLIGHT` and $flightTime$ is of type `FLIGHT_TIME`.

Query 3. If the risk value of a leg is assessed with respect to a given flight f, it may be useful to store it in the graph database, to avoid redundant risk calculations in the future if a optimal path is to be found for a flight the risk values already found may simply be queried from the graph database (Query 3), as well as to be able to reconstruct why a particular path was chosen.

Note that the risk value cannot be stored at the leg nodes themselves, as the risk is dependent on each particular flight. Therefore a relationship re from a given flight f to a leg g is added to the graph database to represent the risk assessment of g with respect to f. This risk value can be stored as a property risk of re. The relationship re is of type RISK_EVALUATION.

Flight Paths. When a flight path is chosen for a planned flight f, it is also useful to store this path in the graph database in order to keep track of all the flight paths in a certain time interval, and thereby to be able to assess collision risk. A flight path p can be represented as a path graph where each node corresponds to a leg g linked by an edge to the next node in the path.

However, the nodes should not be the legs themselves, as this would create confusion once a leg is part of multiple flight paths, since its successor nodes as well as its predecessor nodes could not be identified unambiguously. Therefore we represent a flight path by a sequence of waypoints wp of type WayPoint along with relationships of type NEXT where each waypoint corresponds to a leg node.

A relationship $represents$ from a waypoint wp to a leg g is used to express that wp represents g. This relationship is of type REPRESENTS. To denote the start node of a path, a node p of type Path is added to the graph database together with a relationship $pathStart$ of type PATH_START from p to the first waypoint belonging to the path. In Fig. 2 the general principle of constructing a path through the given flight-space is shown.

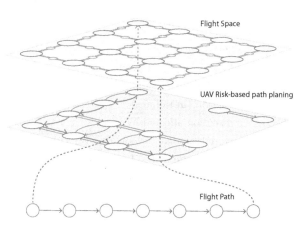

Fig. 2. Sketch of the gradual construction of an instance of our proposed conceptual graph database schema. Herein, locations are displayed as green nodes, legs as red nodes (together forming the flight space), and waypoints as blue nodes (forming a flight path). (Color figure online)

5   Risk Assessment Using Our Proposed Graph Database

In this section we describe how our graph database can be used for estimating the ground risk of each relevant leg with respect to a given flight.

Initial Assumptions. To assess the ground risk of a UAV in a given point in space, it is common to consider the risk of fatally impacting a person on the ground in case of an unplanned descent [8]. In practice, multiple descent models are used to estimate risk, usually with a probability density function to account for unknowns. While the graph database proposed above contains all the necessary entities and data to enable such a calculation, this is clearly beyond the scope of the present paper. Here we just want to illustrate how our graph database can be supportive during ground risk assessment. Thus, we make the following assumptions:

1. All required data for the risk calculation are known and static for the examined time interval.
2. For a given leg g with tail location ℓ_t and head location ℓ_h, the ground risk at the leg's head location when flying along the leg is a suitable estimate for the risk associated with the leg.
3. Given a ballistic descent model, ground risk can be approximated sufficiently well as the probability of fatality (Table 1).

Table 1. Notions related to ground risk assessment for a UAV.

Symbol	Meaning
v	UAV's flight speed
w	wind speed
v'	UAV's speed affected by wind
KE	UAV's kinetic energy at ground impact
θ	flight direction (in radians)
ψ	wind direction (in radians)
θ'	UAV's direction affected by wind
λ_1, φ_1	longitude, latitude at tail location (in radians)
λ_2, φ_2	longitude, latitude at head location (in radians)
λ_3, φ_3	longitude, latitude at ground impact (in radians)
$\Delta\lambda$	difference between longitudes at tail and head location
g	gravitational acceleration
R_e	earth radius

Ballistic Descent. A ballistic descent happens when a UAV experiences a flight-terminating failure which causes it to lose most of its lift [8]. This may happen, for example, if a wing breaks off or a motor physically separates from the body. Then the UAV's descent is solely governed by its aerodynamics, cf. [8].

Following [8], we use a simple horizontal projectile model to describe the UAV's ballistic descent, where the primary force acting on it is gravity and the acceleration of the UAV itself within the wind frame. For a horizontal projectile with a known horizontal speed v_0 and starting height h_0 the horizontal range d of the projectile, being the distance traveled until point-of-impact, is then calculated as: $d = v_0\sqrt{\frac{2h_0}{g}}$, where g represents the gravitational acceleration acting upon the projectile. The impact speed v_R of the projectile is calculated as: $v_R = \sqrt{v_0^2 + 2gh_0}$. With this the kinetic energy of the projectile can be calculated as: $KE = \frac{1}{2}mv_R^2$, where m is the mass of the projectile.

Direction and Speed and Wind. To be able to find the descending UAV's point-of-impact, first it's flight direction and speed at the moment of failure t_0 needs to be found. The UAV's flight direction θ at l_2 is calculated as the final bearing of the leg assuming a spherical earth [25] as:

$$\theta = atan2(sin \Delta\lambda \cdot \cos \varphi_2, \cos \varphi_1 \cdot \sin \varphi_2 - \sin \varphi_1 \cdot \cos \varphi_2 \cdot \cos \Delta\lambda) \qquad (1)$$

The effect of wind on the UAV's speed v' and direction θ' at l_2 is calculated by adding the polar vectors of the UAV, given by v and θ, and of wind, given by w and ψ.

Point-of-Impact. Given the UAV's longitude λ_2 and latitude φ_2 (in radians) at the time of failure t_0, the longitude λ_3 and latitude φ_3 in radians at the point-of-impact assuming a spherical earth [25] can be approximated as:

$$\varphi_3 = asin(\sin \varphi_2 \cdot \cos \frac{d}{R_e} + \cos \varphi_2 \cdot \sin \frac{d}{R_e} \cdot \cos \theta') \qquad (2)$$

$$\lambda_3 = (\lambda_2 + atan2(\sin \theta \cdot \sin \frac{d}{R_e} \cdot \cos \varphi_2, \cos \frac{d}{R_e} - \sin \varphi_2 \cdot \sin \varphi_3)), \qquad (3)$$

where R_e is the radius of the earth.

Probability of Fatality. Following [8], the probability of fatality is calculated as follows:

$$p_{fatality} = p_{event} \cdot p_{impact\,person} \cdot p_{fatal\,impact}, \qquad (4)$$

where p_{event} is the probability of a descent occurring, $p_{impact\,person}$ the probability of a person being impacted in the case of a descent, and $p_{fatal\,impact}$ the probability that an impact is fatal. Assuming the probability of a ballistic descent occurring is uniformly distributed across all legs, this factor can be neglected in assessing risk, as no other descent model is considered.

The population density PD_{impact} (as person per m^2) and shelter factor S_{impact} at the UAV's point-of-impact can be used to approximate $p_{impact\,person}$ by using the following formula (adapted from [8]):

$$p_{impact\,person} = S_{impact} \cdot PD_{impact} \qquad (5)$$

The area weight kinetic energy method for assessing $p_{fatal\,impact}$ converts the kinetic energy of an impacting object to the probability of fatality as a result of the point-of-impact [8].

Table 2. Probability of fatality and impact on a person (from [8])

Probability of fatality	Kinetic energy (J)
0.01	43
0.10	66
0.30	92
0.50	114
0.90	194

Table 2 was adapted from [4] and converts the probability of fatality of a person standing in an open area impacted by a UAV to the UAV's kinetic energy. The probability seems to grow nearly linearly with the kinetic energy. [4] describes a more elaborate model for ground collision severity which, however, is beyond the scope of the present paper. Thus a linear approximation function was derived from the data by way of the least squares method in order to approximate $p_{fatal\ impact}$. The function takes the form $f(x) = mx \cdot b$ where $m = 0.00607884$ and $b = 0.256826$. This yields the following estimation for $p_{fatal\ impact}$ in Eq. (6):

$$p_{fatal\ impact} = \begin{cases} 0 & \text{if } f(KE) < 0 \\ f(KE) & \text{if } 0 \leq f(KE) \leq 1 \\ 1 & \text{if } 1 < f(KE) \end{cases} \quad (6)$$

6   Risk Mitigation Using Our Proposed Graph Database

In the previous section we have explained how the risk of the legs in the flight-space can be evaluated for a given time interval, starting position, end location, UAV and flight speed with the support of our proposed graph database. In this section will now describe how we can further use our graph database to perform tasks related to risk-based UAV path planning.

Outline of Risk-based UAV Path Planning. To find a suitable flight path for a flight f using our graph database we can proceed as follows:

1. Retrieve the relevant information (UAV data, weather data, location data, time intervals) to compute the ground impact point for a node g of type Leg (Query 1)
2. Compute the ground impact point for the node g of type Leg
3. Determine the node of type Area for the ground impact point and return population density and sheltering data (Query 2)
4. Compute the risk value for the node g of type Leg based on results from Query 1 and 2
5. Store the risk value in a newly created relationship of type RISK_EVALUATION, connecting the node f of type PlannedFlight and the node g of type Leg

6. Repeat steps 1–5 for each node of type `Leg`
7. Retrieve a relationship of type `RISK_EVALUATION` to a node g of type `Leg`, and create a relationship of type `LINK` between the nodes of type `Location` adjacent to node g
8. Store the risk value and the energy consumption as properties of the relationship of type `LINK`
9. Repeat steps 7–8 for each relationship of type `RISK_EVALUATION` (Query 3)
10. Compute a risk-optimal flight path in the graph induced by the relationships of type `LINK`

Recall the definition of a flight-space $FS = (L, C)$ in Sect. 3. Assume we are given a start location ℓ_s, an end location ℓ_e, a time interval d, a UAV u, and a flight speed v. Let C^{Link} be the subset of C for which the risk assessment as described in Sect. 5 was possible and resulted in a finite risk value. Further let L^{Link} be the subset of L that is induced by C^{Link} and that contains ℓ_s and ℓ_e. Note that C^{Link} might be much smaller than C as many edges might be eliminated due to their associated ground risk or observed obstacle hazards. In particular, edges with obstacles that would affect the UAV will be removed here. Similarly, L^{Link} might be much smaller than L. In particular, locations that are already used by other UAVs during the given time interval, have been eliminated to to avoid collisions. The subgraph $PPG = (L^{\text{Link}}, C^{\text{Link}})$ is also called the *path planning graph* of the UAV.

In Sect. 5 we described how to compute the risk values for the edges in C^{Link}. Let c^{risk} denote the resulting function which may be regarded as a cost function. The risk of a path is defined as the sum of the risk values of all the edges in the path. A path from the start location ℓ_s to the end location ℓ_e that has minimal risk is called *risk-optimal*.

Sometimes risk is not the only criterion that is of interest, but other criteria must be taken into consideration as well. For UAVs, energy consumption is often used as a further criteria when looking for suitable flight paths for a UAV. The energy consumption for the edges in PPG can be estimated using the UAV's energy consumption function, which takes into account the distance, the wind speed and direction at the location, and parameters based on the UAV's technical specifications for flying. Let c^{energy} denote the resulting function which may be regarded as a cost function, too. Then a multi-criteria optimization approach can be used to find flights paths for the UAV that offer a good balance between risk and energy consumption.

Handling Ground Risk. The construction of the path planning graph allows to search for an optimal path in regards to ground risk. The expected risk is displayed directly as a cost on the edges in PPG. By adding the energy consumption as a cost to the edges we are able to identify multi-criteria optimal paths in respect to the balance between energy consumption and expected risk.

Handling Collision Risk. As collision risk is mainly a factor of tempo-spatial overlap of two UAVs [13], a simple approach to mitigate collision risk would be to use a deconfliction protocol which disallows multiple UAVs from flying through the same location in the same time interval. A naive way to achieve this in our proposed graph database is, when performing Query 1, to remove all legs with a head location which is already a head location of a leg within a chosen path relating to a flight in the same time interval from the result set of Query 1 (Query 1 with deconfliction).

Handling Obstacle Risk. Obstacle hazards may not affect the path of a UAV. Therefore the information on obstacles is stored as a property in the nodes of type Leg. When the obstacles associated to some leg prevent safe operation of the UAV then this will be dealt with during risk assessment and the corresponding links will not occur in the *PPG*. This ensures that the UAV safely flies around the obstacles in the selected flight path.

7   Experimental Evaluation

For the evaluation of our approach we implemented the proposed graph database using Neo4j. Based on the outline of risk-based UAV path planning given in Sect. 6, we conducted tests for different sizes of instances to compare the execution times of queries and show that they do not increase for larger instances. Further, we implemented an enhanced version of the model, which only considers nodes and edges from a geographically selected area based on the starting and ending positions of the respectively flight. This restriction enables faster query execution times and therefore a faster overall time to generate optimal paths.

An artificially generated grid network of the size 50 × 50 was the basis for the graph database. Other attributes were deducted from average values found in the literature, such as mass and speed of a UAV [8] or population density and sheltering factors [22]. In addition, we complemented missing data like wind direction and speed with randomly produced values. These haphazardly appearing attributes are not arbitrary, but are related to each other when describing geographically close points in the respectively instance. In the example, wind direction and speed are similar in neighboring locations to better simulate real-world scenarios. Note, that the scalability of the approach can be assumed to be similar when using real-world data; only the stored risk values would be different.

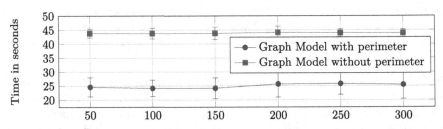

Fig. 3. Time to conduct steps 1–5 (Query 1 and Query 2) for our proposed risk mitigating for a 50 × 50 grid network with artificially generated nodes and relationships of type PlannedFlight, TimeInterval, RISK_EVALUATION, WEATHER_DATA

We generated larger instances by inserting artificial nodes of type `PlannedFlight` and their respectively relationships `RISK_EVALUATION`, as well as nodes of type `TimeInterval` and the many relationships of type `WEATHER_DATA` to each location node to be able to store a huge amount of nodes and edges into our model instance. In each test, we increased the number of nodes respectively by 50 to analyze the scaling of our approach. Please note, that this leads to a very huge number of connection, as each newly created node of the former mentioned types has a large number of edges.

All experiments were conducted on a computer with an Intel(R) Core(TM) i5-7600 CPU (3.5 GHz) with 32 GB RAM. Results of our experiments can be seen in Fig. 3. Here, the processing time for performing steps 1 to 5 is shown. The time to carry out the first 5 steps, including the time for computing risk values and generating risk-evaluation relationships for risk assessment, shows a stable behavior. Thus, query times can be assumed to be stable over different and especially larger instances of the data model.

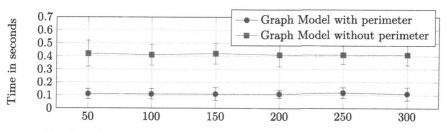

Number of respectively generated Nodes (`PlannedFlight` and `TimeInterval`)

Fig. 4. Time to conduct steps 7 and 8 (Query 3) for our proposed risk mitigating for a 50 × 50 grid network with artificially generated nodes and relationships of type `PlannedFlight`, `TimeInterval`, `RISK_EVALUATION`, `WEATHER_DATA`

In Fig. 4 the time to retrieve all information to calculate the final risk-optimal flight path (steps 7 and 8) is investigated. In both evaluations the optimized query with perimeter (which reduces the number of locations considered) was significantly faster than the query, in which all locations are considered.

8   Conclusion and Outlook

In this paper we proposed a conceptual modeling approach for risk assessment and mitigation in UAV routing. In particular, our proposed approach can describe the entities and relationships that are relevant for risk-based UAV path planning, and compose them in a conceptual graph database schema that serves as the conceptual basis of a graph database. Furthermore, we presented a new approach for estimating risk in form of ground risk based on the proposed conceptual model. By considering calculated points-of-impact for faulty UAVs we enhanced our approach for risk assessment with more details and accuracy. Due to the thorough design the creation of collision-free flight paths was ensured.

With the prototypical implementation of the proposed conceptual graph database schema we were able to demonstrate that fundamental tasks can be carried out in a fast manner and scale well for increased sizes of stored data and a complex structure of connections within the model. The execution times of those tasks were independent of the considered amount of data in the graph database.

In the future we plan to extend our experiments to include real-world data sets, larger instances and a wider range of parameters. It would also be interesting to integrate more data sets from the domain and to consider additional decent models for UAVs. Lastly, the integration of data streams to enable the real-time processing of dynamic data, such as weather, would be worthwhile in practice.

References

1. Spatial functions - Neo4j cypher manual (2021). https://neo4j.com/docs/cypher-manual/current/functions/spatial/
2. Angles, R., Arenas, M., Barceló, P., Hogan, A., Reutter, J., Vrgoč, D.: Foundations of modern query languages for graph databases. ACM Comput. Surv. **50**, 1–40 (2017)
3. Angles, R., et al.: PG-schema: schemas for property graphs. Proc. ACM Manag. Data **1**, 198:1–198:25 (2023)
4. Arterburn, D.R., Ewing, M.S., Prabhu, R., Zhu, F., Francis, D.: FAA UAS center of excellence task A4: UAS ground collision severity evaluation (2017)
5. Bonifati, A., Furniss, P., Green, A., Harmer, R., Oshurko, E., Voigt, H.: Schema validation and evolution for graph databases. In: Laender, A.H.F., Pernici, B., Lim, E.-P., de Oliveira, J.P.M. (eds.) ER 2019. LNCS, vol. 11788, pp. 448–456. Springer, Cham (2019). https://doi.org/10.1007/978-3-030-33223-5_37
6. Clothier, R.A., Williams, B.P., Fulton, N.L.: Structuring the safety case for unmanned aircraft system operations in non-segregated airspace. Saf. Sci. **79**, 213–228 (2015)
7. Cohn, P., Green, A., Langstaff, M., Roller, M.: Commercial drones are here: the future of unmanned aerial systems. McKinsey (2017)
8. la Cour-Harbo, A.: Quantifying ground impact fatality rate for small unmanned aircraft. J. Intell. Robot. Syst. **93**, 367–384 (2019)
9. la Cour-Harbo, A.: Ground impact probability distribution for small unmanned aircraft in ballistic descent. In: International Conference on Unmanned Aircraft Systems (ICUAS), pp. 1442–1451 (2020)
10. Gugan, G., Haque, A.: Path planning for autonomous drones: challenges and future directions. Drones **7**, 169 (2023)
11. Hartmann, S., Alshami, J., Ma, H., Steinmetz, D.: A conceptual framework for dynamic planning of alternative routes in road networks. In: Dobbie, G., Frank, U., Kappel, G., Liddle, S.W., Mayr, H.C. (eds.) ER 2020. LNCS, vol. 12400, pp. 539–554. Springer, Cham (2020). https://doi.org/10.1007/978-3-030-62522-1_40
12. Matalonga, S., White, S., Hartmann, J., Riordan, J.: A review of the legal, regulatory and practical aspects needed to unlock autonomous beyond visual line of sight unmanned aircraft systems operations. J. Intell. Robot. Syst. **106**, 10 (2022)

13. McFadyen, A., Martin, T., Perez, T.: Low-level collision risk modelling for unmanned aircraft integration and management. In: IEEE Aerospace Conference, pp. 1–10 (2018)
14. Milano, M., Primatesta, S., Guglieri, G.: Air risk maps for unmanned aircraft in urban environments. In: International Conference on Unmanned Aircraft Systems (ICUAS), pp. 1073–1082 (2022)
15. OpenStreetMap: Bounding box - openstreetmap wiki (2022). https://wiki.openstreetmap.org/w/index.php?title=Bounding_Box&oldid=2386165. Accessed 18 Mar 2023
16. Ortlieb, M., Konopka, J., Adolf, F.M.: Modular modelling of ground and air risks for unmanned aircraft operations over congested areas. In: AIAA/IEEE Digital Avionics Systems Conference (DASC), pp. 1–9. IEEE (2020)
17. Primatesta, S., Rizzo, A., la Cour-Harbo, A.: Ground risk map for unmanned aircraft in urban environments. J. Intell. Robot. Syst. **97**, 489–509 (2020)
18. Razzaq, S., Xydeas, C., Everett, M.E., Mahmood, A., Alquthami, T.: Three-dimensional UAV routing with deconfliction. IEEE Access **6**, 21536–21551 (2018)
19. Roberge, V., Tarbouchi, M., Labonte, G.: Comparison of parallel genetic algorithm and particle swarm optimization for real-time UAV path planning. IEEE Trans. Ind. Inf. **9**, 132–141 (2013)
20. Rubio-Hervas, J., Gupta, A., Ong, Y.S.: Data-driven risk assessment and multicriteria optimization of UAV operations. Aerosp. Sci. Technol. **77**, 510–523 (2018)
21. Schopferer, S., Benders, S.: Minimum-risk path planning for long-range and low-altitude flights of autonomous unmanned aircraft. In: AIAA Scitech Forum, pp. 137:1–137:17 (2020)
22. StatistischesBundesamt: Regionalatlas Deutschland (2023). https://regionalatlas.statistikportal.de/
23. Steinmetz, D., Hartmann, S., Ma, H.: A conceptual modelling approach for the discovery and management of platoon routes. In: Ghose, A., Horkoff, J., Silva Souza, V.E., Parsons, J., Evermann, J. (eds.) ER 2021. LNCS, vol. 13011, pp. 282–296. Springer, Cham (2021). https://doi.org/10.1007/978-3-030-89022-3_23
24. Steinmetz, D., Merz, F., Burmester, G., Ma, H., Hartmann, S.: A modeling rule for improving the performance of graph models. In: Ralyte, J., Chakravarthy, S., Mohania, M., Jeusfeld, M.A., Karlapalem, K. (eds.) Conceptual Modeling. ER 2022. LNCS, vol. 13607, pp. 336–346. Springer, Cham (2022). https://doi.org/10.1007/978-3-031-17995-2_24
25. Veness, C.: Calculate distance and bearing between two latitude/longitude points using haversine formula in Javascript. http://web.archive.org/web/20230223150117/, http://www.movable-type.co.uk/scripts/latlong.html
26. Yapp, J., Seker, R., Babiceanu, R.: Providing accountability and liability protection for UAV operations beyond visual line of sight. In: IEEE Aerospace Conference, pp. 1–8. IEEE (2018)
27. Zhang, B., Tang, L., Roemer, M.: Probabilistic weather forecasting analysis for unmanned aerial vehicle path planning. J. Guid. Control Dyn. **37**, 309–312 (2014)

QuantumShare: Towards an Ontology for Bridging the Quantum Divide

Julian Martens[1,3], Indika Kumara[1,2(✉)] [iD], Geert Monsieur[1,2],
Willem-Jan Van Den Heuvel[1,2], and Damian Andrew Tamburri[1,3]

[1] Jheronimus Academy of Data Science, Sint Janssingel 92,
5211 DA 's-Hertogenbosch, The Netherlands
[2] Tilburg University, Warandelaan 2, 5037 Tilburg, AB, The Netherlands
{i.p.k.weerasinghadewage,g.monsieur,
w.j.a.m.vdnHeuvel}@tilburguniversity.edu
[3] Eindhoven University of Technology, 5612 Eindhoven, AZ, The Netherlands
{j.p.a.martens,d.a.tamburri}@tue.nl

Abstract. As quantum computing matures, organizations must engage early with the technology and eventually adopt it in their business operations to achieve a competitive edge. At the same time, quantum computing experts (e.g., researchers and technology providers) expect extensive input and collaboration with potential adopters to explore new application areas. However, the inherently counter-intuitive and complex theoretical principles of quantum theory discourage non-expert adopters of the technology from engaging in research and development. As a result, an increasing knowledge gap emerges. This paper proposes the *QuantumShare* ontology to capture and share quantum computing knowledge to support the collaboration between quantum experts and non-expert adopters, thereby bridging the present knowledge gap. We used the NeOn methodology to create *QuantumShare* systematically. We evaluated *QuantumShare* by applying it to the usage scenarios extracted from the literature and end-users.

Keywords: Ontology · Quantum divide · Quantum computing · Knowledge sharing

1 Introduction

Quantum computing is still maturing but holds the potential to overcome the computational limitations of classical computing to enable the development of better and faster solutions for problems in domains such as optimization, simulation, and machine learning [3]. The global interest in quantum computing has shown an upward trend over the past ten years. As a result, it is now fueling the development of new technologies for science, industries, and governments [4,21].

Organizations must test and experiment with quantum technology early to gain a competitive advantage and eventually adopt it in their business operations [4]. However, many organizations still lack the workforce with the

J. P. A. Almeida et al. (Eds.): ER 2023, LNCS 14320, pp. 412–429, 2023.
https://doi.org/10.1007/978-3-031-47262-6_22

appropriate skills and knowledge in the technology for its testing and evaluation [1]. Moreover, the inherent counter-intuitive and complex theoretical principles of quantum theory (e.g., superposition, entanglement, and interference), used throughout scientific publications, make quantum theory unintelligible and enigmatic for non-experts [21]. Consequently, it might be difficult for novices to explore the risks and opportunities of quantum computing, as reading into publications on quantum theory requires a considerable understanding of theory and practice [14,21]. Hence, organizations potentially interested in adopting quantum computing technologies might be discouraged from engaging. Nevertheless, as applying quantum algorithms to new problem areas must be explored, quantum theorists/experts increasingly need extensive input and collaboration with practitioners in other fields [3,17]. In general, the barriers to effective collaboration between all relevant stakeholders of quantum technologies can create a *quantum divide*, an increasing knowledge gap between those who develop quantum technologies and those who are not [21]. The quantum divide is impeding responsible research and innovation in the technology and exploiting its full potential, while also catalyzing the monopolization of the technology [10,21].

Capturing, mapping, and sharing information about business problems and quantum solutions understandably and unambiguously can help alleviate the quantum divide [5,21]. Several studies have attempted to collect and synthesize various types of quantum computing knowledge, for example, quantum algorithm catalogs [11], use cases [3], and tools for developing and executing quantum applications [22]. However, the information represented in natural languages may not be precise and unambiguous, making searching for and integrating such information problematic. We envision a semantic-enabled framework for quantum computing knowledge sharing and problem-solving to address these limitations and provide a better solution to bridging the quantum divide. Such a framework can enable various stakeholders (e.g., quantum researchers, algorithm developers, non-expert solution seekers, and educators) to publish and discover information about problems and solutions, including problem/solution classes, candidate algorithms, implementation and execution details, and relevant publications.

Towards realizing our vision for a collaborative knowledge-sharing platform for quantum computing, this paper presents the *QuantumShare* ontology that represents and integrates relevant domain knowledge around quantum computing, from the business problems of organizations to the execution of quantum-based solutions. We systematically developed *QuantumShare* by applying the NeOn ontology engineering methodology [20]. *QuantumShare* was fully represented using OWL2 Web Ontology Language. Furthermore, we developed a knowledge-based system using *QuantumShare* on Amazon cloud services, and used it to realize different knowledge-sharing and exploration scenarios for evaluating *QuantumShare*'s capabilities to help alleviate the quantum divide.

This paper is organized as follows. Section 2 describes the *QuantumShare* ontology and its development process. Section 3 presents the implementation of the knowledge-based system and the scenario-based evaluation of *QuantumShare*. Section 4 reviews the related work, and Sect. 5 concludes the paper.

2   QuantumShare Ontology

2.1   Development of QuantumShare

To systematically develop *QuantumShare* we followed the NeOn ontology engineering methodology [20]. NeOn features nine scenarios for building ontologies. Each scenario consists of a set of ontology development activities. To develop *QuantumShare*, we applied scenario 1 (*from specification to implementation*), scenario 2 (*reusing and re-engineering non-ontological resources*), scenario 6 (*reusing, merging, and re-engineering ontological resources*), and scenario 7 (*reusing ontology design patterns*). We selected NeOn as it is a highly flexible and comprehensive methodology [19]. For example, nine scenarios cover the various ways to develop an ontology, and the detailed description of ontology-building activities (per each scenario) helps systematically carry out those activities. Figure 1 shows the workflow of our methodology. In the rest of this section, we briefly discuss each phase in the workflow.

Requirements Analysis and Specification. We derived use cases (UC) and competency questions (CQs) by studying the related literature and interviewing eight potential users of *QuantumShare*. The participants included two non-expert potential adopters, three academic quantum researchers, and three practitioners from the Dutch national quantum ecosystem[1]. Due to limited space, we put the coded transcripts of the interviews in the *QuantumShare* GitHub repository (see Sect. 3.1). The detailed description of the CQs and requirements, along with their justification (i.e., the references to the relevant literature and interview data), is also in the repository. We identified three use cases for *QuantumShare*.

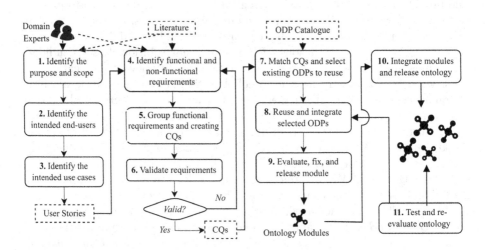

Fig. 1. Overview of the Ontology Engineering Process

---

[1] https://quantumdelta.nl/.

Table 1. Competency Questions of *QuantumShare*

Category		Competency Questions (CQs)
Business Problems	CQ1	What problem is solved with an algorithm execution?
	CQ2	How can the problem be described?
	CQ3	To what problem type belongs the problem?
	CQ4	To what complexity class belongs the problem?
	CQ5	To what application area belongs a problem?
Quantum Algorithms	CQ6	To what algorithm type belongs the algorithm?
	CQ7	How can the algorithm be described?
	CQ8	To what speedup class belongs the algorithm?
	CQ9	What is the computational model that expresses the algorithm?
	CQ10	How is the algorithm implemented?
	CQ11	What is the execution of the algorithm?
Software in Implementation	CQ12	What software is used in the implementation?
	CQ13	What software is contained in a software development kit?
	CQ14	What properties characterize the software?
	CQ15	What software is compatible with the computational resource?
	CQ16	What organization provides the software?
	CQ17	What organization developed the implementation?
Hardware in Implementation	CQ18	What is the computational resource used in the implementation?
	CQ19	What is the technology required by the computational resource?
	CQ20	What properties characterize the computational resource?
	CQ21	What organization provides the computational resource?
	CQ22	What resource platform offers the computational resource?
	CQ23	What computational model is compatible with the computational resource?
Execution of an Implementation	CQ24	What implementation was used in the execution?
	CQ25	What organization was involved in the execution?
	CQ26	What is the input of the execution?
	CQ27	What output resulted from an execution?
	CQ28	What is the classification/application area of the organization?
	CQ29	Where is an organization situated?
Publications	CQ30	What are the publications about quantum algorithms?
	CQ31	What are the publications about implementations?
	CQ32	What are the publications about executions?
	CQ33	What metadata describes a publication?

- UC1: *QuantumShare* will be used for representing the business problems and their mappings to the computational problems that can be resolved using quantum algorithms.
- UC2: *QuantumShare* will be used for describing quantum algorithms, their software implementations, and their deployment and execution contexts.
- UC3: *QuantumShare* will be used for representing the knowledge about publications related to algorithms, implementations, or particular executions.

Table 1 shows the CQs of *QuantumShare*. We grouped CQs to enable a modular development of the ontology.

Table 2. A Summary of OWL2 Representation of QuantumShare and its Modules

Module	Classes	Object Properties	Data Properties	Axioms	CQs
Parameter	3	4	2	42	–
Organization	12	6	1	132	28, 29
Problem-Execution	30	25	2	355	1, 2, 3, 4, 5, 25, 26, 27
Publication	14	8	2	77	33
Quantum Algorithm	21	7	1	80	6, 7, 8, 9
Quantum Implementation	41	22	2	357	12, 13, 14, 15, 16, 17, 18, 19, 20, 21, 22, 23
Integrated Ontology	69	40	2	647	10, 11, 24, 30, 31, 32

Modeling. QuantumShare consists of ontology modules per a group of related CQs. We used the DOLCE+DnS Ultra Lite (DUL) ontology [6] as the foundational ontology. To develop ontology modules, we reused the ontology design patterns (ODPs) from the ODP catalog[2]. We chose DUL as the upper ontology since it is lightweight and the source of our ODPs. Moreover, we can add domain-specific concepts as sub-classes of the core base concepts of DUL instead of using ontology properties. This can reduce the complexity of building a domain-specific ontology by extending a general-purpose ontology in practice [2]. We used CQs as the criteria for finding suitable ODPs. To adopt the selected patterns, as necessary, we applied the operations (*Import, Clone, Specialization, Generalization, Composition,* and *Expansion*) recommended by the literature [7,20]. Once the ontology modules were created and validated, they were integrated while performing alignment tasks as appropriate.

Evaluation. We implemented *QuantumShare* using OWL2 Web Ontology Language. To validate *QuantumShare*, we instantiated it with sample data and answered all CQs using SPARQL queries. In addition, we also reviewed *QuantumShare* with the domain experts to assess its syntax, domain cohesion, structure, functionality, and usability. Throughout the *QuantumShare* development process, we used the ontology evaluation tool OOPS (i.e., Ontology Pitfall Scanner) [18] to assess and improve the ontology continuously.

2.2   Representation of QuantumShare

QuantumShare comprises six modules: parameter, organization, quantum algorithm, implementation, problem-execution, and publication. Table 2 summarizes the OWL2 representation of the ontology modules in terms of the number of classes, axioms, object properties, data properties, and the CQs addressed. In the remainder of this section, we discuss each module in detail. Please consider that, due to limited space, we do not include all object/data properties and specializations of classes in the diagrams of the semantic models.

Parameter Module. Figure 2 shows the parameter module. The parameters are mainly used to describe a concept's properties and metadata, with

---

[2] http://ontologydesignpatterns.org/wiki/Main_Page.

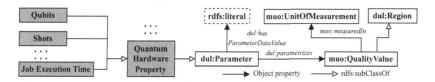

Fig. 2. Parameter Module: Key Concepts and their Relations. The shaded rectangles are concepts introduced by *QuantumShare*.

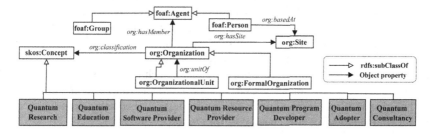

Fig. 3. Organization Module: Key Concepts and their Relations

a corresponding dimension and unit of measurement. To explicitly model the physical properties and quantities, we constructed this module by integrating parameter-related axioms of the DUL ontology with an ontology of units of measure (namely, MUO[3]). Every parameter (i.e., *dul:Parameter*) parametrizes a certain quality (i.e., *muo:QualityValue*), which is a logical dimension of the parameter (e.g., *duration* and *amount*). Furthermore, a dimension usually has units (i.e., *muo: UnitOfMeasurement*) in which it is measured (e.g., *seconds*). By representing a parameter's quality and the unit of measurement, multiple observations of a particular parameter can be accurately compared [2].

The other ontology modules in *QuantumShare* use the parameter module as necessary by specializing the class *dul:Parameter*. For example, as shown in Fig. 2, the sub-classes *Job Execution Time*, *Qubits*, and *Shots* specify the limit for the execution time of a quantum program and the maximum number of qubits (quantum bits) and shots that a quantum hardware resource supports. A qubit is a basic unit of quantum information, and a shot is a single execution of a quantum algorithm on a QPU (quantum processing unit). These sub-classes are part of the implementation ontology module.

Application Scenario. IBM Eagle quantum computer has a 127-qubit quantum processor and supports 8192 shots (i.e., the instances of *Qubits* and *Shots*).

Organization Module. This module describes an organization or part of an organization, and the classification and site that identify the organization. We created it by cloning the relevant axioms from the organization ontology of the W3C Consortium[4], which describes organizational structures and can support sharing of organizational information across various domains.

---

[3] https://databus.dbpedia.org/ontologies/elite.polito.it/ontologies--muo-vocab--owl.
[4] https://www.w3.org/TR/vocab-org/.

As shown in Fig. 3, an organization is a collection of people (*foaf:Agent* and *foaf:Person*) organized together in a specific structure to achieve a particular goal. However, some organizations are not legally identified. For example, social networks are considered informal organizations, while corporations and universities are formal (i.e., *org:FormalOrganization*). Consequently, formal organizations are considered a subclass of organizations. Moreover, an organization may consist of a set of units. For example, a research department (i.e., *org:OrganizationalUnit*) is part of a university (i.e., *org:Organization*).

We specialized the organization ontology for use in the use cases of *QuantumShare* by introducing concepts for representing different stakeholders in a quantum knowledge-sharing environment: research, education, software development (e.g., algorithms and tools), compute resource provider, technology adoption (i.e., the organizations that apply quantum technology to solve their business problems), and consultancy. Since we intended to group organizations without changing their structures, we used the property *org:classification* and a concept scheme (instead of sub-classes of *org:Organization*).

Application Scenario. The research unit (i.e., *organizational unit*) of Matthias Troyer (i.e., *person*) is part of ETH Zürich (i.e., *formal organization*). The ETH Zürich can be classified as an institute for quantum research and education (i.e., *classification* as *quantum research* and *quantum education*). The research unit is located at the "Building HIT, Wolfgang-Pauli-Str. 27, 8093 Zürich" (i.e., *site*).

Quantum Algorithm Module. This module represents quantum algorithms (see Fig. 4). We created it by partially cloning and specializing the DUL ontology. Quantum algorithms can be distinguished into *Collections* of algorithms with shared properties: speedup class (e.g., polynomial, super-polynomial, and exponential) and algorithm class (e.g., factoring, optimization, machine learning) [11]. While speedup seems instantaneous, the degrees of speedup are considered ranges and, consequently, *Collections*. We used the *comment* property of the RDF Schema to represent human-readable descriptions of algorithms. An algorithm is considered an expression of a computational model, as computational models contain mathematical rules that define how computation is performed [22]. We imported an axiom of the DUL ontology to enable information objects (i.e., *quantum algorithms*) to express other information objects (i.e., *computational models*). There are two main computation models: adiabatic (or quantum annealing) and gate-based [22]. The former model primarily focuses on solving optimization problems. The latter model represents a computation as a quantum circuit, which applies a sequence of logic gates (transformations) to a set of qubits and classical bits.

Application Scenario. Consider algorithms from the quantum algorithm zoo [11]. Shor's algorithm (i.e., *quantum algorithm*) solves the factorization problem (i.e., *algorithm class*) in polynomial time (i.e., *speedup class*). It can factor 15 into 3 and 5, using a gate-based (i.e., *computational model*) quantum computer with 7 qubits (i.e., *circuit property*).

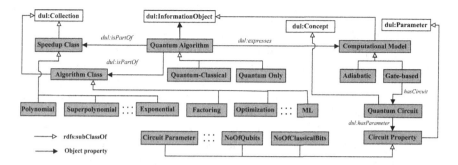

Fig. 4. Quantum Algorithm Module: Key Concepts and their Relations

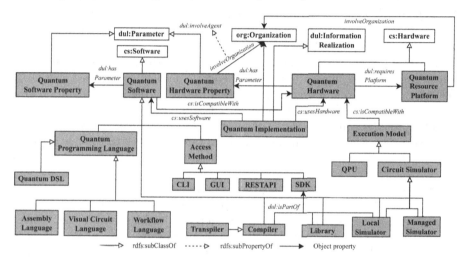

Fig. 5. Algorithm Implementation Module: Key Concepts and their Relations

Algorithm Implementation Module. This module represents the knowledge about an orchestration of software and hardware that implements a quantum algorithm (see Fig. 5). We created it by complementing the DUL ontology with the CS-CP (Computer System Content Pattern)[5], which can model computer systems by defining relationships between software and hardware used by them.

A quantum implementation uses software and hardware resources. Cloud platforms typically offer these resources. The primary hardware resource is a quantum device that can execute quantum algorithms using either quantum processing units (QPU) or quantum circuit simulators [16]. The developers can use the simulators hosted and managed by the resource providers or run the simulators locally on-premise. They can use various ways to access a cloud platform's quantum resources: command-line interfaces, graphical user interfaces, web services/APIs, or software development kits (SDKs). The programming languages for implementing quantum algorithms can be classified into four main

---

[5] http://ontologydesignpatterns.org/wiki/Submissions:Computer_System.

categories [22]: assembly languages, quantum domain-specific languages (DSLs), visual circuit design languages, and workflow languages. Typically, a quantum program is compiled and transpiled before executing it. A compiler translates a quantum algorithm written in a high-level language to a lower-level language (e.g., assembly language) that can be executed on a particular quantum resource. A transpiler can optimize a quantum circuit to match the constraints and characteristics of a given quantum resource.

The platforms and their resources can be modeled as hardware (*cs:Hardware*). Access methods, libraries, local simulators, programming languages, and compilers are considered sub-classes of software (*cs:Software*). Software is often hardware-dependent, and we use the *cs:isCompatibleWith* property to capture this dependency. Similarly, a quantum program execution model should be compatible with a quantum hardware resource. We used the parameter module to capture the properties of quantum software and hardware resources. Accordingly, software and hardware properties are sub-classes of a parameter. Compilers, libraries, local simulators, and access methods are often contained in a software development kit (SDK). Therefore, an SDK is modeled as a DUL collection. Three types of organizations are involved in the implementation of a quantum algorithm. A resource provider offers hardware resources, a software provider provides software, and a quantum algorithm implementation involves an organization that uses software and hardware resources to solve a business problem.

Application Scenario. We consider the scenarios from Larose [13]. A quantum algorithm can be implemented using ProjectQ (i.e., *quantum implementation*), a framework developed by the research group of Matthias Troyer (i.e., *implementing organization*). ProjectQ software properties are version 0.3.6, license Apache-2.0, and it operates on Mac, Windows, or Linux systems. It can be implemented using its ProjectQ quantum programming language, hosted on Python (i.e., *embedded quantum DSL*). Furthermore, ProjectQ can connect to the IBM cloud (i.e., *resource platform*) for the universal quantum computer IBMQX5, which consists of a QPU that supports 16 qubits (i.e., *hardware properties*). If so, OpenQASM (i.e., *assembly language*) will also be used. One can also use ProjectQ's C++ simulator (i.e., *local simulator*), which has 28 qubits and a gate set of 20 (i.e., *software properties*).

Problem-Execution Module. This module represents the execution of an algorithm's implementation through which an organization's problem is solved. We developed it by specializing in the TE-CP(Task-Execution Content Pattern)[6]. The TE-CP can represent the actions performed by an agent to execute tasks.

Figure 6 shows the problem-execution module. A problem is solved by executing an algorithm implementation. Thus, we model the execution as a sub-class of the action class and the problem as a sub-class of the task class (from TE-CP). In

---

[6] http://ontologydesignpatterns.org/wiki/Submissions:TaskExecution.

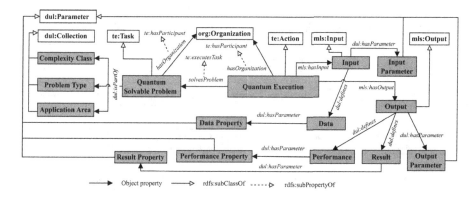

Fig. 6. Problem-Execution Module: Key Concepts and their Relations

addition, we represent the agent participating in the action as an organization. We use the *comment* property of the RDF Schema to capture problem descriptions. The problems can also be classified into groups with shared properties, such as the complexity class, problem type, and application area. We partially adopted the Algorithm-Implementation-Execution CP[7] to model the details of an execution. This CP enables us to define inputs, outputs, and configuration settings of an execution. In our model, an input defines data and configuration parameters, and an output defines results and performance metrics. We use the parameters to specify their properties, e.g., data and performance proprieties.

Application Scenario. We consider the scenarios from Harwood et al. [9]. Exxon-Mobil and IBM (i.e., *organizations*) collaboratively explored quantum solutions to routing problems (i.e., *problem type*). They aimed to solve a vehicle routing problem with time windows (i.e., *problem*) in the context of maritime shipping (i.e., *application area*). Vehicle routing problems require combinatorial optimization and thus are considered NP-hard (i.e., *complexity class*). ExxonMobil and IBM approached the problem as QUBO (Quadratic Unconstrained Binary Optimization) with an ADMM (Alternating Direction Method of Multipliers) solver (i.e., *execution*). Mathematical formulations (i.e., *input*) were composed of parameters for the routes traveled and feasible movements between customers and ports (i.e., *input parameter*). The execution uses a small dataset that contains initial inventory, storage capacity, production rate, and port fee for two supply ports and three demand ports (i.e., *data properties*). In addition, the numerical experiments in the execution provide metrics such as success probabilities, feasible solutions, the number of iterations, and the number of qubits required (i.e., *performance and result properties*).

---

[7] http://ontologydesignpatterns.org/wiki/Submissions:AlgorithmImplementationExecution.

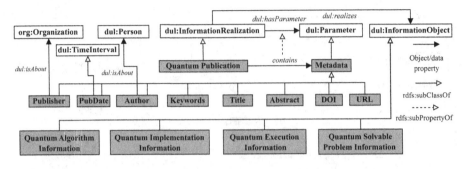

Fig. 7. Publication Module: Key Concepts and their Relations

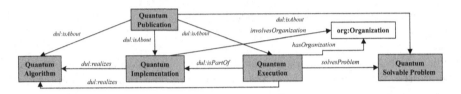

Fig. 8. Integration of Ontology Modules in *QuantumShare*

Publication Module. As shown in Fig. 7, the publication module represents the information about the research articles related to quantum computing. We model a publication as a specialization of a DUL information realization (i.e., *dul: InformationRealizaion*), as it is a written document containing the text or visual information of problems, algorithms, implementations, or executions (modeled as *dul:InformationObject*). Furthermore, publications consist of metadata, which is a specialization of a parameter. Examples of metadata are authors, titles, and links (sub-classes of metadata).

Application Scenario. Dorit Aharonov, Itai Arad, Elad Eban, and Zeph Landau (i.e., *author*) wrote a publication titled "Polynomial quantum algorithms for additive approximations of the Potts model and other points of the Tutte plane" (i.e., *title*). The publication can be found by its link "https://arxiv.org/abs/qua-ntph/0702008" (i.e., *URL*). It contains the text describing additive approximation algorithms (i.e., *quantum algorithm information*).

Integration of Ontology Modules. As shown in Fig. 8, *QuantumShare* integrates its ontology modules to support describing quantum computing use cases by modeling the information about the algorithm, implementation, and problem-solving execution of the implementation. The publications can provide information about quantum algorithms, implementations, and executions. We use the object property *dul:isAbout* to represent these relationships. Quantum implementation (i.e., *dul:InformationRealization*) and execution (i.e., *dul:Action*) enable the realization of a quantum algorithm. Thus, we use the object property *dul:realizes* to represent the relevant relationships. Finally, we model an execution as a context-dependent part of a quantum implementation, providing the problem, organization, and performance measures of a quantum implementation.

Application Scenario. The publication of Harwood et al. [9] titled "Formulating and Solving Routing Problems on Quantum Computers" (captured in the publication module) describes an application of variational algorithms, such as the variational quantum eigensolver and the quantum approximate optimization algorithm (captured in the quantum algorithm module). These algorithms were implemented by accessing IBM's quantum simulators, accessed with SDK Qiskit (captured in the quantum implementation module). Part of this implementation aimed to optimize specific mathematical formulations in the maritime shipping area (captured in the problem-execution module).

3   Implementation and Evaluation

3.1   GitHub Repository

We have fully implemented the *QuantumShare* ontology using OWL2. In Sect. 2.2, we provided a summary of the OWL-based representation of *QuantumShare*. We used SPARQL queries to implement the CQs. We also developed a knowledge-based system using *QuantumShare* on Amazon cloud services (AWS) as a proof-of-concept. The QuantumShare GitHub repository[8] includes the artifacts used by the implementation, including OWL files and Python scripts.

3.2   QuantumShare Knowledge-Based System

Figure 9 shows a high-level workflow of the *QuantumShare* system, which follows the hydration-orchestration-consumption solution architecture from AWS[9]. First, the hydration process extracts the data from their sources, preprocesses, and transforms the extracted data to match the data format the knowledgebase expects. Next, the orchestration process organizes and merges the ingested data with the existing knowledge in the system. Finally, in the consumption phase, the clients retrieve the relevant information from the knowledgebase.

We developed the ontologies using the Protégé tool, stored them in an AWS S3 bucket, and deployed them on the Amazon Neptune graph database service. We used two data sources to populate the ontology with sub-classes and instances: PlanQK GitHub repository[10] and Quantum Algorithm Zoo [11]. PlanQK repository included the data of application areas, software tools, and problem types (as JSON files). Quantum Algorithm Zoo consisted of information about 64 quantum algorithms. Furthermore, we also extracted the metadata from 541 references to these algorithms. We used Python scripts to extract the

---

[8] https://github.com/IndikaKuma/QuantumShare.

[9] https://tinyurl.com/5n6s7u6n.

[10] Platform and Ecosystem for Quantum Applications: https://github.com/PlanQK.

data and generate the triples that can be ingested into the knowledgebase. As necessary, we manually analyzed additional publications to find sample data for the quantum algorithm implementation and problem-execution-related entities. Finally, we used SPARQL queries to retrieve the knowledge stored in the Neptune server to answer CQs. Our GitHub repository includes all SPARQL queries. Figure 10 shows a SPARQL query related to CQ33. We used the Jupyter notebooks (hosted in AWS SageMaker) to execute the scripts for extracting and transforming data, loading triples into the database, and answering CQs.

Figure 11 illustrates the workflow of the *QuantumShare* system. Firstly, the hydration process classifies the content of a publication into defined entities (e.g., title and authors, problem complexity, and organizations involved). For example, it classifies "Formulation and Solving Routing Problems on Quantum Computers" as the title present in the metadata of the publication. Next, the identified knowledge is represented by leveraging the semantic relationships defined in the ontological model. For instance, the graph represents the "Vehicle Routing Problem" as part of the application area "Maritime Shipping" and complexity class "NP-Hard". Finally, the knowledge is presented to an end-user by assembling the facts resulting from a user information request.

3.3 Scenario-Based Evaluation

We implemented three knowledge-sharing and exploration scenarios using the *QuantumShare* system to evaluate its capabilities to help bridge the quantum divide. Based on the literature and interview participants' feedback, we created these hypothetical scenarios. This section only provides a summary of each scenario due to limited space. Our GitHub repository includes a detailed description of the scenarios, including SPARQL queries and the results returned.

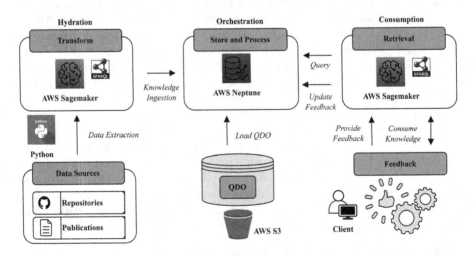

Fig. 9. An Overview of the *QuantumShare* Knowledge-based System

```
PREFIX quantumshare: <http://www.semanticweb.org/20173656/ontologies/2022/5/QuantumShare#>
PREFIX algo: <http://www.semanticweb.org/20173656/ontologies/2022/5/QuantumAlgorithm#>
PREFIX dul: <http://www.ontologydesignpatterns.org/ont/dul/DUL.owl#>
PREFIX pe: <http://www.semanticweb.org/20173656/ontologies/2022/5/ProblemExecution#>
SELECT ?ref ?value
WHERE {?execution dul:realizes algo:Quantum_Approximate_Optimization .
?ref dul:isAbout ?execution .
?ref dul:hasParameter ?metadata.
?metadata dul:hasParameterDataValue ?value}
```

Fig. 10. An SPARQL query example

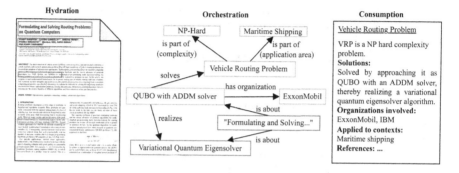

Fig. 11. Conceptual view of information flow in the *QuantumShare* System

Exploration of Quantum Algorithms by Experts. A software developer (with a good knowledge of quantum computing) connects to the *QuantumShare* system and retrieves the information about the quantum algorithms, including their speedup classes and algorithm classes (CQs 6 and 8). Alternatively, the developer may search only for a specific algorithm class, e.g., approximation and simulation algorithms (CQs 7 and 8). For example, assume that the developer found a quantum approximate optimization algorithm. Next, the developer requests all scientific publications related to this algorithm (CQs 30 and 33) to find more information about the algorithm.

Exploration of Quantum Applications by Experts and Non-expert Adopters. The developer of the approximate optimization algorithm needs an industrial use case to test it and approaches a local energy and petrochemical company. The local company is entirely unaware of quantum computing and thus requires information about another company's application of a similar algorithm. Firstly, the developer and an employee from the local company use the *QuantumShare* system to query the information about the organizations in the energy sector where a department was involved in using the quantum approximate optimization algorithms (CQs 11, 25, 28, and 29). They discover that ExxonMobil has been experimenting with this algorithm. Next, they try to find what problem ExxonMobil is solving (CQs 1, 3, 4, 5, and 11). The search results show that ExxonMobil used an optimization algorithm to solve a vehicle routing problem in the maritime shipping domain. After understanding the problem, the developer requests additional information, such as inputs and outputs of the execution of the optimization algorithm by ExxonMobi (CQs 26 and 27). The developer discovers that the input consists of constraints, e.g., the routes traveled and the order of visited locations. The output is a set of evaluation metrics defined by numerical experiments, e.g., the number of qubits and iterations. Next, the developer searches for publications that may refer to this execution (CQs 32 and 33) and locates two publications.

Exploration of Quantum Implementations by Experts and Non-expert Adopters. While reading the publications, the developer and the local company discover they lack the relevant skills and knowledge to implement the optimization algorithm. Thus, they approach a consultancy firm to create an overview of a potential implementation method. First, the dedicated consultants use the *QuantumShare* to retrieve the implementation framework used by ExxonMobil (CQ 24). They find out that ExxonMobil's execution used Qiskit. Afterward, they try identifying the quantum resources compatible with Qiskit (CQs 18, 20, and 21). The search results indicate that Qiskit uses IBMQX5, a QPU (Quantum Processing Unit). This QPU has multiple properties, such as 16 qubits, a minimum coherence time of 31 microseconds, and a single-qubit gate fidelity of 99.5%. Next, the consultant firm also searches for information on the software involved in the Qiskit implementation (CQs 12 and 14). They find information such as the Qiskit version (0.5.4), its license (Apache-2.0), supported OS (Mac, Windows, and Linux), and programming languages used.

4 Related Work

Several recent studies attempted to understand the barriers to quantum computing adoption [1,5]. Two identified barriers were the challenges of communicating quantum computing knowledge to non-experts and lacking technical expertise in most organizations. Furthermore, they emphasized including business and strategic context to knowledge on quantum technologies, supporting the adoption of this knowledge by non-experts. To this end, we developed the *QuantumShare* ontology as a set of modules to facilitate different uses of the ontology. Moreover, *QuantumShare* relates organizations to problems, quantum algorithm implementations, and executions.

Several studies have analyzed and categorized quantum computing domain knowledge. For example, Quantum Algorithm Zoo [11] maintains a catalog of quantum algorithms. The algorithm type, speedup class, and description for each algorithm are recorded. Vietz et al. [22] provided a taxonomy of quantum application development technologies along with examples, which include SDKs, programming languages, quantum cloud services, quantum circuit modelers, and quantum computing resources. In [3], 24 industrial use cases from four problem domains (i.e., optimization, simulation, machine learning, and cryptography) and four application domains (i.e., material science, engineering and design, production and logistics, post-quantum security) were presented. Compared with these and similar other works, we aimed to represent the quantum computing knowledge using semantic models to enable the reuse, semi-automated maintenance, and interoperability of the knowledge.

Regarding the semantic modeling of the quantum computing knowledge, in [12], we presented our vision for an ontology-enabled framework to support the collaborative development of service-oriented quantum applications. Martyniuk et al. [15] developed an ontology for representing the information about quantum computing algorithms and their implementations. However, they did not represent problems and organizations, and only partially considered publications and executions. Furthermore, the competency questions and the engineering methodology were also not presented. The alignment of their ontology with foundational ontologies was also not discussed. In comparison, we attempted to develop the *QuantumShare* ontology systemically following a well-accepted ontology development methodology. *QuantumShare* supports 33 competency questions, reuses the relevant ontology design patterns, and aligns with the foundational ontology DUL. Further, *QuantumShare* can represent and integrate knowledge about algorithms, implementations, executions, publications (from algorithms to executions), organizations, and problems. Such an end-to-end ontology is crucial for bridging the knowledge gap between quantum experts and non-expert adopters.

5   Conclusion and Future Work

In this paper, we presented *QuantumShare*, an ontology, which aims to represent and relate the knowledge necessary for effective collaboration between expert and non-expert stakeholders in the quantum computing domain. We discussed the ontology development process and ontology modules in *QuantumShare*. The ontology and its competency questions were realized using OWL2 and SPARQL. Furthermore, we developed a knowledge-based system using the *QuantumShare* ontology and employed it to implement three knowledge-sharing and exploration scenarios extracted from the literature and end-users (interview participants). In the future, we plan to apply our ontology and knowledge-based system in an industrial context to render the evaluation more externally valid.

We envision that there will be repositories adhering to the *QuantumShare* ontology that can be populated by experts and searched by non-experts. Our interviews of the eight potential users of the *QuantumShare* system revealed that such an environment could benefit both experts and non-experts. Hence, our future work will also focus on realizing our vision. In particular, we plan to automate the population of the *QuantumShare* knowledgebase by extracting the information from the multi-vocal literature sources using natural language processing techniques. Moreover, we plan to extend the *QuantumShare* ontology to consider hybrid (classical-quantum) computing and to support the assessment and selection of various quantum technologies (as in [8]). Finally, we aim to develop intuitive user interfaces tailored to different classes of the stakeholders of the *QuantumShare* system to make their engagement with the system effective.

References

1. Awan, U., Hannola, L., Tandon, A., Goyal, R.K., Dhir, A.: Quantum computing challenges in the software industry. A fuzzy AHP-based approach. Inf. Softw. Technol. **147**, 106896 (2022)

2. Bassiliades, N., et al.: PaaSport semantic model: an ontology for a platform-as-a-service semantically interoperable marketplace. Data Knowl. Eng. **113**, 81–115 (2018)

3. Bayerstadler, A., et al.: Industry quantum computing applications. EPJ Quantum Technol. **8**(1), 25 (2021)

4. Buchholz, S., Golden, D., Brown, C.: A business leader's guide to quantum technology (2021). https://www2.deloitte.com/us/en/insights/topics/innovation/quantum-computing-business-applications.html. Accessed May 2023

5. Coenen, C., Grinbaum, A., Grunwald, A., Milburn, C., Vermaas, P.: Quantum technologies and society: towards a different spin. NanoEthics **16**(1), 1–6 (2022)

6. Gangemi, A., Mika, P.: Understanding the semantic web through descriptions and situations. In: Meersman, R., Tari, Z., Schmidt, D.C. (eds.) OTM 2003. LNCS, vol. 2888, pp. 689–706. Springer, Heidelberg (2003). https://doi.org/10.1007/978-3-540-39964-3_44

7. Gangemi, A., Presutti, V.: Ontology design patterns. In: Staab, S., Studer, R. (eds.) Handbook on Ontologies. IHIS, pp. 221–243. Springer, Heidelberg (2009). https://doi.org/10.1007/978-3-540-92673-3_10

8. van Geene, S., Kumara, I., Monsieur, G., Heuvel, W.J.V.D., Tamburri, D.A.: Faasonto: a semantic model for enabling function-as-a-service platform selection. In: Shishkov, B. (ed.) BMSD 2023. Lecture Notes in Business Information Processing, pp. 145–162. Springer, Cham (2023). https://doi.org/10.1007/978-3-031-36757-1_9

9. Harwood, S., Gambella, C., Trenev, D., Simonetto, A., Bernal, D., Greenberg, D.: Formulating and solving routing problems on quantum computers. IEEE Trans. Quantum Eng. **2**, 1–17 (2021)

10. Holter, C.T., Inglesant, P., Srivastava, R., Jirotka, M.: Bridging the quantum divides: a chance to repair classic(al) mistakes? Quantum Sci. Technol. **7**(4), 044006 (2022)

11. Jordan, S., et al.: Quantum algorithm zoo (2011). https://quantumalgorithmzoo.org/. Accessed May 2023

12. Kumara, I., Van Den Heuvel, W.-J., Tamburri, D.A.: QSOC: quantum service-oriented computing. In: Barzen, J. (ed.) SummerSOC 2021. CCIS, vol. 1429, pp. 52–63. Springer, Cham (2021). https://doi.org/10.1007/978-3-030-87568-8_3

13. LaRose, R.: Overview and comparison of gate level quantum software platforms. Quantum **3**, 130 (2019)

14. Leymann, F., et al.: Quantum in the cloud: application potentials and research opportunities. In: Proceedings of the 10th International Conference on Cloud Computing and Services Science, pp. 9–24 (2020)

15. Martyniuk, D., Falkenthal, M., Karam, N., Paschke, A., Wild, K.: An analysis of ontological entities to represent knowledge on quantum computing algorithms and implementations. In: Qurator (2021)

16. Massoli, F.V., Vadicamo, L., Amato, G., Falchi, F.: A leap among quantum computing and quantum neural networks: a survey. ACM Comput. Surv. **55**(5), 1–37 (2022)

17. Montanaro, A.: Quantum algorithms: an overview. npj Quantum Inf. **2**(1), 15023 (2016)

18. Poveda-Villalón, M., Suárez-Figueroa, M.C., Gómez-Pérez, A.: Validating ontologies with OOPS! In: ten Teije, A., et al. (eds.) EKAW 2012. LNCS (LNAI), vol. 7603, pp. 267–281. Springer, Heidelberg (2012). https://doi.org/10.1007/978-3-642-33876-2_24
19. Ramírez-Durán, V., Berges, I., Illarramendi, A.: Extruont: an ontology for describing a type of manufacturing machine for industry 4.0 systems. Semant. Web **11**, 887–909 (2020)
20. Suárez-Figueroa, M.C., Gómez-Pérez, A., Motta, E., Gangemi, A.: Ontology Engineering in a Networked World. Springer, Heidelberg (2012). https://doi.org/10.1007/978-3-642-24794-1
21. Vermaas, P.E.: The societal impact of the emerging quantum technologies: a renewed urgency to make quantum theory understandable. Ethics Inf. Technol. **19**(4), 241–246 (2017)
22. Vietz, D., Barzen, J., Leymann, F., Wild, K.: On decision support for quantum application developers: categorization, comparison, and analysis of existing technologies. In: Paszynski, M., Kranzlmüller, D., Krzhizhanovskaya, V.V., Dongarra, J.J., Sloot, P.M.A. (eds.) ICCS 2021. LNCS, vol. 12747, pp. 127–141. Springer, Cham (2021). https://doi.org/10.1007/978-3-030-77980-1_10

Author Index

J. P. A. Almeida et al. (Eds.): ER 2023, LNCS 14320, pp. 431–432, 2023.
https://doi.org/10.1007/978-3-031-47262-6

Printed in the United States
by Baker & Taylor Publisher Services